BRIT GUIDE

ORLANDO

WALT DISNEY WORLD

2008

Simon & Susan Veness

foulsham
LONDON • NEW YORK • TORONTO • SYDNEY

foulsham

The Publishing House, Bennetts Close, Cippenham, Berkshire, SL1 5AP, England

Foulsham books can be found in all good bookshops or direct from www.foulsham.com

While every effort has been made to ensure the accuracy of all the information contained within this book, neither the author nor the publisher can be liable for any errors. In particular, since prices, times and any holiday or hotel details change on a regular basis, it is vital that each individual checks relevant information for themselves.

ISBN: 978-0-572-03381-1

Look out for the latest editions of Foulsham travel books:

A Brit's Guide to Las Vegas, Karen Marchbank with Richard Evans
A Brit's Guide to Disneyland Resort Paris, Simon and Susan Veness
A Brit's Guide to New York, Amanda Statham
Getting Married Abroad, Amanda Statham
Top 50 Ski and Snowboard Resorts in Europe, Pat Sharples and Vanessa Webb

Dedication: To Benjamin Haass, whose unique insights make research even more fun!

SPECIAL THANKS

Special thanks for this edition go to: Travel Industry Association of America, The Walt Disney Company, Alamo Rent A Car, Universal Orlando, Orlando/Orange County Convention and Visitors Bureau, Kissimmee Convention and Visitors Bureau, Daytona Beach Area Convention and Visitors Bureau, St Petersburg/Clearwater Convention and Visitors Bureau, Anheuser-Busch Parks, Mount Dora Area Chamber of Commerce, Allan Oakley at Alexander Holiday Homes, Nigel Worrall at Florida Leisure, Andy James and James Brown at Florida Dolphin Tours, Ian Davies of Accredited Florida, Nina and Pete Dew, Margie Long and Michelle Peters at Boggy Creek Airboats.

Our sincere thanks also go to all the hard-working people at Foulsham who help to bring our work to life every year.

Printed in Dubai

CONTENTS

FOREWORD

Simon says… It's a whole new year in the non-stop excitement of Central Florida, and there is more than ever before to look forward to. There are new attractions at both Disney and Universal, while SeaWorld unveils its stunning sister water park, Aquatica, in the spring, and the shopping choices just get better and better. It all goes to underline that a visit to Orlando remains as complex and demanding as ever (plus great fun!), and it is vital that visitors take the time to assess what's in store and plan accordingly. Regular readers may well notice a whole new look for this edition (our 14th) but newcomers will simply find the definitive source of inside information on this amazing part of the Sunshine State. This is how you prepare for all the entertainment in store, avoiding the pitfalls, circumventing the queues, saving money – and relishing the anticipation of the holiday of a lifetime! Combine this with our dynamic website (see below) and we are confident you will have the very best start to all that's in store in this wonderful destination.

Susan says… The pace rarely slows down in Orlando and the same held true for our work this year, both in finding new places to tell you about and in our unique online *Personalised Itinerary Planner* service, which enjoyed a banner year in 2007. While Central Florida remains our primary passion, there is much to be seen further afield, prompting us to branch out a bit this year, with greater focus on split-stay holidays to the likes of Miami, Fort Lauderdale and other unmissable destinations along both coasts. In highlighting beach escapes and the gentler pace outside the main tourist areas, we hope to point you in the right direction toward the perfect balance of all the excitement and relaxation this magnificent state has to offer. And now, on with the planning!

Simon and Susan Veness
(visit us at **www.askdaisy.net/orlando** or email **britsguide@yahoo.com**).

Introduction

Get ready for the most exciting holiday experience in the world, bar none, guaranteed! The area of central Florida we call 'Orlando' is a vast conglomeration of adventure rides, thrills, fun and fantasy that has no equal anywhere else on earth. And we are not just talking about the amazing *Walt Disney World Resort*.

First off, this is a BIG venture in every sense of the word and you must be aware of the extensive and complex nature of this tourist wonderland. Disney is the leading attraction, but there is a strong supporting cast, led by Universal Orlando and SeaWorld. There is something for all tastes and ages – young or old, families, couples or singles – but it exacts a high toll. You'll walk a lot, queue a lot and probably eat a lot. You'll have a fabulous time, but you'll end up exhausted, too. It is not so much a holiday as a military campaign!

Eight theme parks

In simple terms, there are 8 essential major theme parks, and at least one will require 2 days to make you feel it has been well and truly done. Add a day at one of the water parks, a trip to see some of the wildlife or other nature attractions, and the lure of the nearby Kennedy Space Center, and you have 12 days of pure adventure mania. Then mix in the night-time attractions of *Downtown Disney*, Universal's CityWalk and a host of dinner shows, plus some world-class shopping, and you get an idea of the awesome scope of the place. Even with 2 weeks, something has to give – just make sure you keep a grip on your patience/wallet/sanity!

So, how do you get full value from what is still, without doubt, a truly magical holiday? The basic answer is good planning. Read, reflect and prepare. At the back of this book is a handy outline guide for all that you might want to do. Be aware of the time demands of the parks and make sure you build in a quiet day or two by the pool or at one of the smaller attractions. With SO much on offer, it just isn't possible to 'do it all', so try to ensure you get full value from your choices. Also, note the vast scale of everything here. It is well spread out and it takes time even to get from park to park. But do stop to admire the clever detail and imagination of what's on offer.

Orlando

Orlando itself is a relatively small but bright young city that has become synonymous with *Walt Disney World* in its south-west corner. When Walt's dream (sadly, he died in 1966 before it was ever realised) of a vast resort opened in 1971 with the *Magic Kingdom Park*, it led to a massive tourist expansion that simply hasn't stopped. New attractions pop up all the time and it is easy to get carried away by the sheer volume on offer, which varies from terrific to tacky.

The tourist area we call 'Orlando' actually consists of 4 counties. Orange County is home to the city of Orlando, but part of *Walt Disney World* is in Osceola County to the south, with Kissimmee its main town. Seminole County, home of Orlando Sanford International Airport, is north-east of Orange County, while Lake County is immediately to the north and west, with Mount Dora its principal town. The local population numbers around 2 million, of which almost 250,000 are employed in the tourist business. And, in 2007, some 52 million people were expected to make Orlando their holiday choice, spending more than $30 billion. Britain accounts for 40% of foreign visitors, and in 2006 that was 1,010,000 of us. Orlando International Airport has seen traffic boom from 8 million passengers in 1983 to a record 34.8 million in 2006. In addition, the Metro Orlando area boasts around 113,000 hotel rooms and 4,000 places to eat. Shopaholics also have the choice of some 250 shopping centres, including 30 malls. But let's give you a quick taste of the main attractions.

Walt Disney World Resort in Florida

This is where the 'magic' really starts – and the effect is vividly real. This vast resort actually consists of 4 separate theme parks, 20 speciality hotel resorts, a camping ground, 2 water parks, a sports complex, 4 18-hole golf courses, 4 mini-golf courses and a huge shopping and entertainment district (*Downtown Disney*). It covers 47sq mls/122sq km. The likes of Alton Towers and Thorpe Park would comfortably fit into its car parks! Indeed, Alton Towers, Britain's biggest theme park, is 60 times smaller. On average, there are estimated to be 200,000 visitors at any one time. The Disney organisation does things with the most style, but the others are no slouches, and there are always new projects on the drawing board. They all maintain an extremely high level of customer service, led by Disney, where everyone who works for them is officially a Cast Member, not just staff, and they take that ethic to heart. Here's a quick rundown of what's on offer:

Magic Kingdom Park: this is the essential Disney, including the fantasy of its wonderful animated films, the adventures of the Wild West and Africa, the excitement of thrill rides like Space Mountain (a huge indoor roller-coaster), the 3-D film fun of Mickey's PhilharMagic and splendid daily parades and fireworks.

Epcot: Disney's 2-part park, with the technology-inspired Future World, plus a potted journey around the globe in World Showcase. Though more educational than adventurous, it still has some memorable rides, including Test Track, Mission: SPACE and the superb Soarin', along with excellent dining.

Disney-MGM Studios: here you can ride the movies in style, meeting Star Wars™, the Muppets and Indiana Jones; drop into the fearsome Tower of Terror or the high-speed Rock 'n' Roller Coaster Starring Aerosmith; and learn the tricks of the film trade at the likes of the epic Lights, Motors, Action!™ Extreme Stunt Show.

Disney's Animal Kingdom: billed as 'a new species of theme park', this delivers another contrasting and entertaining scenario. With realistic animal habitats, including a 100 acre/40.5ha safari savannah,

Terminator 2: 3-D at Universal

Florida

How far from Orlando to …

Bradenton	130mls/210km	Fort Myers	190mls/306km	Sarasota	140mls/225km
Clearwater Beach	110mls/176km	Jacksonville	155mls/250km	Silver Springs	80mls/129km
Cocoa Beach	40mls/64km	Key Largo	294mls/470km	St Augustine	120mls/193km
Cypress Gardens	40mls/64km	Key West	375mls/604km	St Pete Beach	105mls/169km
Daytona Beach	60mls/97km	Miami	220mls/354km	Tampa	75mls/120km
Fort Lauderdale	205mls/330km	Naples	230mls/370km	Venice	160mls/257km

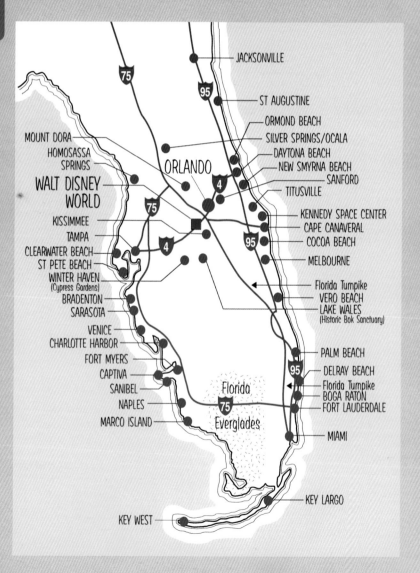

captivating shows and terrific rides, it offers a pleasant change of pace.

Disney's Typhoon Lagoon Water Park: bring your cozzie and spend a lazy day splashing down waterslides and learning to surf in the world's biggest man-made lagoon.

Disney's Blizzard Beach Water Park: the big brother of all the water parks, this has a massive spread of rides in a 'snowy' environment.

Downtown Disney: this incorporates *Pleasure Island, Marketplace* and the *West Side* with themed restaurants, a cinema multiplex, the *DisneyQuest* arcade of interactive games, Virgin Megastore and the famous Cirque du Soleil® company. *Pleasure Island* is nightclub central, with 7 different clubs.

The picture-perfect **Wedding Pavilion** offers marriage ceremonies in true fairytale style overlooking Bay Lake.

The other parks
If you think Orlando is all about Disney, be amazed at the huge range of other attractions on offer.

Universal Orlando: this is the other big resort development, with 2 theme parks, an entertainment district and 3 speciality hotels. The parks are **Universal Studios** where you Ride The Movies as you encounter Jaws, the Men In Black and ET, the Shrek 4-D show and Revenge of the Mummy ride, plus Woody Woodpecker's KidZone and the amazing Terminator 2: 3-D show; and **Islands of Adventure**, a superb blend of thrill rides, all-the-family attractions, shows and eye-catching design, with some of the world's most advanced hardware (like the Amazing Adventures of Spider-Man).

Wet 'n Wild: although on International Drive, this water park is Universal-owned and offers plenty of fun rides and slides.

SeaWorld: don't think this is just another dolphin show; SeaWorld is *the* place for creatures of the deep, with killer whales the main attraction, a bright, refreshing atmosphere (check out the Waterfront district and the amazing Blue Horizons and Believe shows) and a serious ecological approach, plus thrill rides Journey to Atlantis and Kraken and a dedicated area for rides and other activities for children. Its exclusive neighbour, **Discovery Cove**, offers the opportunity to swim with dolphins, among other things, and the stunning new water park **Aquatica** opens in spring 2008.

BRITTIP
Beware travel-agent pressure to buy more tickets than you need. You simply won't get full use out of, say, a 14-day Disney ticket and a 5-Park Orlando FlexTicket in a 2-week holiday.

Busch Gardens: the sister park to SeaWorld, here it's creatures of the land, with a good mix of rides and shows. Highlights are the SheiKra mega-coaster, the Rhino Rally ride, Myombe Reserve, a close-up look at the endangered central African highland gorillas, the Edge of Africa 'safari' experience, and amusing Pirates 4-D film show. A real family treat, plus a must for coaster fans.

Other key attractions: Kennedy Space Center, the dramatically upgraded home of space exploration, with the new Shuttle Launch Experience; **Cypress Gardens**, Florida's oldest 'theme park' reborn in 2004 with coasters and other rides, as well as wonderful gardens; **Silver Springs**, a close look at Florida nature via various boat journeys on the crystal-clear Silver River, plus various animal exhibits; **Fantasy of Flight**, an aviation museum experience that includes the world's largest private collection of vintage aircraft, plus fighter-plane simulators.

Disney tickets

Most people buy one of the multi-day passes that allow you to move between the theme parks on the same day and grant unlimited access to the transport system. Make no mistake, you cannot walk between the parks (except for a long haul between *Epcot* and *Disney-MGM Studios*), and trying to do more than one a day is hard work. The choice of tickets is bewildering, so be sure you buy ONLY what you need.

Disney's basic ticket system is called Magic Your Way and is horribly complicated for the first-timer. Happily, it also has simplified tickets for UK visitors! All multi-day passes offer savings against 1-day tickets but unused days expire unless you buy an upgrade at the parks.

Magic Your Way: If you just turn up at the ticket booths, you must choose from the Magic Your Way menu.

• Choose the number of days (1–10).

• Decide if you want *Park Hopping* (to visit more than 1 park on the same day for a $45 flat rate).

• Decide if you want the *Water Park Fun & More Option* (3–6 extra visits to the water parks, *Pleasure Island*, *DisneyQuest* and *Disney's Wide World of Sports*™ for $50).

• Decide if you want the *Non-expiration Option* (at $10–155, depending on the number of days of ticket). This option can be added *after* the initial purchase, but you still pay based on the original length of the ticket; e.g., if you buy a 7-day ticket and decide after 5 days you won't use the rest of the ticket on this visit, you can add non-expiration for $90 and save the remaining 2 days for the future. You can upgrade within the first 14 days of use.

• Per-day ticket savings increase with the more days you buy: 1 day = $67 plus tax; 10 days = $216 plus tax, or $21.60/day.

BRITTIP
Buy your theme park tickets in advance, NOT at the park gates. You will save time AND money as there is a built-in advance purchase discount.

UK tickets: The bonus of coming from the UK means there are really only 4 tickets to consider, sold in advance (2 exclusively in Britain), and all good value. They are the 5- and 7-Day Premium Ticket, and the 14- and 21-Day Ultimate Ticket (see chart on page 11). However, 1-, 2-, 3- or 4-day Disney tickets can be bought *only* in the US.

BRITTIP
To avoid the queues at the Disney park ticket booths, you can also buy tickets in advance from the Guest Services office at *Downtown Disney*.

Other tickets

When it comes to Universal Orlando, SeaWorld and Busch Gardens, the choice can be equally complicated. Again, you have **1-** and **2-Day Tickets**, but all 3 parks have introduced a variety of new tickets, plus some online specials. The **Orlando FlexTicket** remains the best value, providing 14 consecutive days' access to either both Universal parks, Wet 'n Wild and SeaWorld (4-Park FlexTicket) or those 4 plus Busch Gardens. Otherwise, you can choose from the **2-Park Unlimited Access** ticket (online only from **www.universal orlando.com** for 7 days at Universal Orlando's 2 parks; a **2-Day 2-Park Ticket** with 3rd day free; or the **3-Park Ticket**, which is both Universal parks plus Wet 'n Wild for 5 days in a 2-week period. Look out, also, for Universal periodically offering FREE child places with every 2-Day and 3-Park ticket. SeaWorld and Busch Gardens have also introduced a **2-Park Ticket**, which can vary for its length of use from 7 consecutive days to a UK-only ticket good for up to 21 days. Check

Choosing a ticket

Ticket type	Park	Allowance
1-Day Ticket	Any Disney park, Universal Orlando parks, SeaWorld or Busch Gardens	Access to 1 park ONLY for 1 day; not available in advance
5-Day Premium Ticket	*Magic Kingdom Park, Epcot, Disney-MGM Studios, Disney's Animal Kingdom Theme Park*	Access for 5 days, with multiple parks on same day; plus 4 visits to water parks, *Pleasure Island, Disney's Wide World of Sports*™ and *DisneyQuest*; valid for 14 days after first use; non-expiration option available
7-Day Premium Ticket	*Magic Kingdom Park, Epcot, Disney-MGM Studios, Disney's Animal Kingdom Theme Park*	Access for 7 days, with multiple parks on same day; plus 6 visits to water parks, *Pleasure Island* and *DisneyQuest*; valid for 14 days after first use; non-expiration option available
14-Day Ultimate Ticket	All Disney parks	Unlimited access to all Disney attractions, including water parks, *Pleasure Island, DisneyQuest* and *Wide World of Sports*™ for 14 days after first use; NO non-expiration option; available only in advance in the UK
21-Day Ultimate Ticket	All Disney parks	Unlimited access to all the attractions, including water parks, *Pleasure Island, DisneyQuest* and *Wide World of Sports*™ for 21 days after first use; NO non-expiration option; available only in advance in the UK
Annual Pass	*Magic Kingdom Park, Epcot, Disney-MGM Studios, Disney's Animal Kingdom Theme Park*; includes discounts for shops, dining and tours	Unlimited admission and free parking for 365 days after purchase date. If ordered online, you get a voucher which must be activated at a park; the 365 days start on the first day you activate the pass
Premium Annual Pass	All Disney parks; includes numerous discounts for shops, dining and tours	Unlimited admission and free parking for 365 days after purchase date; plus discounts on sports and recreation
1-Day 2-Park Ticket	Universal Studios, Islands of Adventure	Access to both Universal parks for 1 day
2-Park Unlimited Admission Ticket	Universal Studios, Islands of Adventure, CityWalk	7 consecutive days' access to both Universal parks and CityWalk clubs (Universal online exclusive only)
2-Day 2-Park Ticket with 3rd Day Free	Universal Studios, Islands of Adventure, CityWalk	Access to both Universal parks for 3 days in a 14-day period; access to CityWalk for all 14 days
3-Park Ticket	Universal Studios, Islands of Adventure, Wet 'n Wild, CityWalk	Access to both Universal parks, plus Wet 'n Wild for 5 days in a 14-day period; access to CityWalk for 14 days
Orlando FlexTicket	Universal Studios, Islands of Adventure, SeaWorld, Aquatica and Wet 'n Wild	Access to all 5 parks, with multiple parks on same day, for 14 days from first use, plus clubs of CityWalk
Orlando FlexTicket Plus	Universal Studios, Islands of Adventure, SeaWorld, Aquatica, Wet 'n Wild and Busch Gardens	Access to all 6 parks, with multiple parks on same day, for 14 days from first use, plus clubs of CityWalk
2-Park Unlimited Admission Ticket	Sea World and Busch Gardens	7 consecutive days' access to both parks

Orlando – Main Attractions and Routes

A Magic Kingdom Park
B Epcot
C Disney-MGM Studios
D Disney's Animal Kingdom Park
E Universal Orlando
F SeaWorld Adventure Park
G Busch Gardens
H Kennedy Space Center/US Astronaut Hall of Fame
I Cypress Gardens
J Historic Bok Sanctuary
K Silver Springs
L Gatorland
M Disney's Typhoon Lagoon Water Park
N Disney's Blizzard Beach Water Park
O Fantasy of Flight
P Old Town
Q Wet 'n Wild
R Discovery Cove by SeaWorld
S Holy Land Experience
T Ripley's Believe It Or Not
U Titanic – The Experience
V Orange County History Center
W Downtown Disney area
X Aquatica by SeaWorld

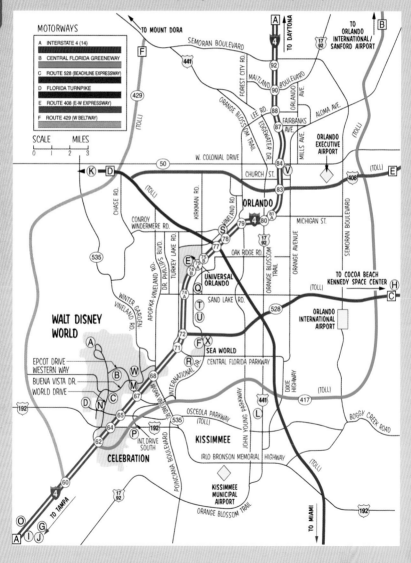

online or with the various UK ticket brokers for the latest deals.

A trip to the exclusive **Discovery Cove** includes a free **7-Day Pass** for either SeaWorld or Busch Gardens, or the option for 14 days' consecutive access to BOTH parks for an additional $30.

For CityWalk, there is also a **CityWalk Party Pass** ($11.99 plus tax) or a **Party Pass with Movie** ($15.40 plus tax), as the centre has a 20-screen cinema. You can also get **Dinner with a Movie** for $21.95 plus tax (choice of one main meal at any of 9 CityWalk restaurants).

BRITTIP

You can save money on some of the smaller attractions, dinner shows, restaurants, shops and more with the FREE **Orlando Magicard** from the Orlando Tourism Bureau at **www.orlandoinfo.com/uk** Go online and download it, order it directly, or call in to the Official Visitor Center on International Drive.

Another choice is the **Go Orlando Card**, which offers 1, 2, 3, 5 or 7 days of visits in the space of 14 days to more than 50 Florida attractions, including Kennedy Space Center, Gatorland, Cypress Gardens, airboat rides, mini-golf, dinner shows and more. $59–249 adults, $49–199 3–12s. You'd have to work hard to get full value for the 7-day card, but the 3- or 5-day ones are a good catch-all for some of the smaller attractions. It also comes with a handy guidebook to the attractions, with maps and other useful info. Look up more on **www.goorlandocard.com**

With price hikes every year, it is worth buying your tickets as soon as you book. We recommend shopping around, as many ticket outlets have periodic sales and special offers, but stick with a reputable agent and always use your credit card where possible for added security. These all come well recommended:

Attraction Tickets Direct (0845 130 3876, **www.attraction-tickets-direct.co.uk**), Britain's top direct-sell Florida ticket broker, with a sharp bookings team, has no credit card fees, free delivery in 7 days and a promise to beat any other brochure price (plus a full range of dinners, shows, tours and sports, and a keen online Florida Forum and info centre). It also offers Disney hotels, with the same price-match guarantee as their attraction tickets; **Keith Prowse Attraction Tickets** (08701 232425, **www.keithprowsetickets.co.uk**) also offers various excursions (notably to the Kennedy Space Center and Clearwater) and an array of options like Orlando Retail Therapy and Deep Sea Fishing; **Theme Park Tickets Direct** (part of Theme Park Holidays Ltd) is another well-priced Orlando specialist (on 0870 040 0210, **www.themeparkticketsdirect.com**); **Tickets 4 Fun**, an Orlando specialist of 16 years, offers all the main attractions and tours, plus its *Freedom Ticket*, which combines Disney's Ultimate Ticket with the Orlando FlexTicket for maximum flexibility, as well as villa rentals, insurance and car hire. It guarantees ticket despatch by the next working day for late bookers (0870 890 3402, **www.tickets4fun.com**).

There are numerous others, and you may well find various attractive short-term deals – BUT beware the timeshare lures and other phone scams for 'free' tickets. If something

SheiKra at Busch Gardens

sounds too good to be true, it usually IS too good to be true. Stick with one of these main brokers, who feature the right product, the right service and local knowledge.

Don't forget to plan your theme park days with the benefit of our Busy Day Guide on page 345. You simply cannot do the parks in one big chunk without ending up exhausted, especially if you hit, say, the Magic Kingdom, on one of its busy days.

The climate
The next question is when to go. Florida's weather varies from bright but cool winter days from November to February, with the odd drizzly spell, to furiously hot and humid summers punctuated by torrential tropical downpours.

The most pleasant option is to go between the two extremes, in spring or autumn. (when you also avoid the worst of the crowds). However, as most families are governed by school holidays, Easter and July–August remain the most popular months for British visitors, so we have plenty of advice on how to stay ahead of the high-season crush. If you do need to visit during summer, opt for the second half of August, as many US schools have resumed by then.

BRITTIP
The humidity levels – up to 100% – and fierce daily rainstorms in summer take a lot of visitors by surprise, so carry a lightweight, rainproof jacket or buy a cheap plastic poncho locally.

The mood
Orlando is big, brash and fun, but above all it's American and that means everything is well organised, with a tendency towards the raucous rather than the reserved. It's clean, well maintained and anxious to please: Floridians generally are an affable bunch, but they take affability to new heights in the theme parks,

where staff are almost painfully keen to make sure you 'have a nice day'.

Tipping
Close to every American's heart is the custom of tipping. With the exception of fast-food restaurant servers, just about everyone who serves in hotels, bars, restaurants, buses, taxis, airports and other public amenities will expect a tip. In bars, restaurants and taxis, the usual rate is 15% of the bill, while porters expect $1/bag and chambermaids $1/day per adult. It's important to know and remember that all service industry workers are taxed on the basis of receiving 15% in tips, whether they get it or not.

BRITTIP
Tipping guide

Bill	Suggested tip
$15	$2.25
$20	$3.00
$25	$3.75
$30	$4.50
$40	$6.00
$50	$7.50

Visa requirements
Holiday visitors to America do not need a visa providing they hold a valid *machine-readable passport* (MRP) showing they are a British citizen. Any passport issued from 26 October 2005 must also include a digital photograph (not glued or laminated). All passports issued from 26 October 2006 must include the new biometric data. Each family member must have his or her own passport that does not expire for 90 days from the time of entry. Provided your passport conforms to the above, all you do is fill in a green visa waiver form and hand it in with your passport to the US immigration official after landing.

However, British subjects, those without a machine-readable passport or those who fail to meet the photo/biometric data criteria, DO

Immigration forms

En route to the US, you will be required to fill in 2 forms – your immigration details and a customs form (these are given to you on the plane or at check-in; there are also plenty on arrival but it's better to have completed them in advance). If travelling under the visa waiver programme, you fill in a green I-94W form (both sides) with your personal details, flight number and holiday address. Every member of your group or family must fill out an immigration form. Those with a US visa need a white I-94 form (fill in the front only). Every family group must then fill out one white customs form, which asks for some of the same info but also the value of any goods that will remain in the US (put $0 unless you are bringing gifts for friends). Hand both documents with your passports to the immigration official who checks you through and takes the fingerprints and photo. The customs form will be handed back to you to present to another official when you exit the baggage hall.

BRITTIP

US immigration now requires that ALL visitors (aged 14–79) give fingerprint and photo ID on arrival. It slows things down but the process is simple – first, left index finger then right index finger on their glass panel, then stand still for the camera.

need a visa (£60), and should apply at least 2 months in advance to the US Embassy.

Some travellers may NOT be eligible to enter under the visa waiver programme and will have to apply for a special restricted visa or they may be refused entry. This applies to those who have been arrested in the past (even if it did not result in a conviction), have a criminal record (the Rehabilitation of Offenders Act does not apply to US visa law), have a serious communicable illness (and the US includes AIDS sufferers in this category), or have previously been refused admission into, been deported from, or have overstayed in the US on the visa waiver programme. Minor traffic offences that have not resulted in an arrest and/or conviction do not count.

In England, Scotland and Wales, write to the Visa Office, US Embassy, 24 Grosvenor Square, London W1A 1AE (020 7499 9000). In Northern Ireland, write to US Consulate General, Danesfort House, 223 Stranmillis Road, Belfast BT9 5GR (028 9038 6100). You can call 09042 450 100 (£1.20 per min; 8am–8pm Mon–Fri, 9am–4pm Sat) for more detailed advice, or visit **www.usembassy.org.uk**

Flight information

Airlines are now required to collect Advance Passenger Information (API) before your flight to the US, and this includes your exact holiday address for the first night. You can't state 'touring' (or similar) either to the airline or on the immigration form. Most airlines should give you the opportunity to do this in advance, either when you book or online, but make sure you have all your details at check-in. Check in advance with your tour operator or travel agent, especially for fly-drive holidays, as they should have a specific formula for this.

BRITTIP

Check with your airline in advance for the latest info on any cabin baggage restrictions, as these often change.

Mariachi Cobre at Epcot

© Disney

All **luggage** is now liable to random searches (especially in the US) and you are advised NOT to lock your suitcases or bags at check-in as security officials have the power to break into them. Using zip-lock seals that can easily be snipped open is permissable and some airlines provide them free.

Do not pack food or beverages in checked bags; pack footwear on top of other contents; put belongings in clear plastic bags to reduce chances of a screener having to handle them, and spread books out – do not stack them; don't place film in checked bags as screening equipment will damage it; leave any gifts unwrapped in case screening require them to be opened; and put scissors, tweezers, pocket-knives and other sharp items in checked bags, never your carry-on.

BRITTIP

Complete your immigration form *carefully* in block capitals. Mistakes are often sent to the back of the queue. Please be courteous with the immigration officials – they do a difficult job in demanding circumstances, and jokes about terrorism do *not* go down well.

The Wizarding World of Harry Potter

What's new

In keeping with Orlando's tradition of providing an ever-changing profile, there is always much that is new.

Walt Disney World: new attractions in 2008 include the opening of the **Toy Story Mania** ride at *Disney-MGM Studios* as well as the (overdue) arrival of a new parade, the **Block Party Bash**. The *Epcot* park has an all-new version of the **Spaceship Earth** ride and the **Gran Fiesta Tour Starring the Three Caballeros** in the Mexico pavilion (updating the river ride). Then, at *Downtown Disney*, prepare for a major new dining adventure at **T Rex: A Prehistoric Family Adventure**. There are also significant additions being made to **Disney's Contemporary Resort** and **Animal Kingdom Lodge**.

Universal Orlando: arguably the biggest splash will be here as, at the Universal Studios park, spring 2008 sees the debut of **The Simpsons Ride** with a whole new state-of-the-art simulator journey through the crazy world of TV Springfield family. Then, at their **Islands of Adventure** park, you will notice a lot of work to prepare for their biggest development in almost 10 years with **The Wizarding World of Harry Potter** – a complete land dedicated to JK Rowling's young wizard. This 'theme park within a theme park' will add new rides, shops, restaurants and completely original theming, including Hogwarts Castle and Hogsmeade Village. However, it will not open until late 2009. NB: Despite some claims in the UK media, this is NOT a separate theme park but only a new 'island' at IoA.

SeaWorld: talking of splashes, here's the debut of Orlando's first major water park since Disney's Blizzard Beach opened in 1995. **Aquatica** (March 2008) will be a magnificent 59 acre/24ha spread of rides and slides with a colourful tropical animals-and-more style. This is on top of new children's rides and a **Sesame Street** show at SeaWorld itself in 2007.

Busch Gardens: at Tampa, the sister park now has a floorless (eek!) version of its massive **SheiKra** coaster, while 2008 will see an exciting new makeover to its Congo area, including the **Jungle Village** playground for kids and additional animal exhibits, notably its wonderful white tigers.

Elsewhere: the unique **Ron Jon Surf Park** should finally be open at the Festival Bay Mall on International Drive, while **Wet 'n Wild** water park has added the dizzying Brain Wash attraction. For shopping addicts, **Prime Outlets** is due to complete a fabulous $250m renovation in April 2008, which adds a whole new world of retail opportunity, while **The Pointe Orlando** has finished its huge renovation, with a wealth of shops and restaurants. Down in Kissimmee, **The Loop West** shopping centre is under construction, due to open in early 2008.

Accommodation: a host of new options includes the beautiful **Blue Heron Resort** and **Rapallo Resort** in Lake Buena Vista, the stunning **Aqua** and **Blue Rose** condo-resorts on International Drive, the **Point Orlando Resort** and the **Village of Imagine**, also on I-Drive, plus the luxury condo-hotel of **The Mona Lisa at Celebration** in the town of Celebration and the Mediterranean-inspired **Tuscana** condos at Champions Gate. And there's even more in the offing – Disney is now partnering with the **Four Seasons** hotel group to build a luxury resort and holiday home community at the back of *Walt Disney World*, as well as a new shopping-dining-hotel district at its new western gateway, all of which will begin to open from 2010.

There are also likely to be other new attractions that beat our deadline, so please be sure to check our website regularly for the latest info and updates. Just log on to **www.ask daisy.net/orlando** and we'll have live, first-hand accounts of all that's new – and more besides!

Central Florida festivals

Here are some major – and unusual – annual events worth keeping an eye out for in 2008.

Blue Spring Manatee Festival: 26–27 Jan (**www.themanateefestival.com**). Beautiful Blue Spring State Park is home to the wonderful manatee, and special celebrations are staged around their seasonal migrations, with craft shows, park tours and interpretive programmes. This park in Orange City is worth seeing at any time of year (off exit 118 on I-4).

33rd Annual Arts Festival: 2–3 Feb (**www.mountdora.com**). The charming town of Mount Dora, north-west of Orlando, hosts 17 festivals each year, of which this is one of the best – a nationally ranked fiesta with artists from all over the world (take Florida Turnpike, the Western Beltway 429 and Highway 441 to Mount Dora).

Florida State Fair: 7–18 Feb (**www.floridastatefair.com**). This 104-year-old fair just outside Tampa (right on I-4) draws big crowds to its mix of fairground rides, arts, crafts, livestock and live entertainment, and offers a variety of contests and competitions.

Bob Marley – a Tribute to Freedom

Silver Spurs Rodeo: 15–17 Feb, 4–6 Oct (TBC) (**www.silverspurs_rodeo.com**). A twice-yearly celebration of an original American sport at Osceola Heritage Park in Kissimmee, it features top-quality events, plus associated crafts and activities (just off the eastern end of Highway 192).

Florida Strawberry Festival: 28 Feb–9 Mar (**www.flstrawberry festival.com**). One of the most unusual and fun events, a country fair in Plant City based on the local produce but with concerts, shows, exhibitions and parades, plus activities for kids (off exit 19 on I-4).

Daytona Beach Bike Week: 29 Feb–9 Mar (**www.officialbikeweek.com**). A lively celebration of all things 2-wheeled and mechanical, with races at Daytona Speedway, concerts, parades and street festivals.

Sidewalk Arts Festival: 15–17 Mar (**www.wpsaf.org**). Winter Park hosts one of America's most prestigious arts festivals, with arts, food, music and children's events (exit 87 on I-4).

Antique Boat Festival: 27–30 Mar (**www.mountdora.com**). A unique fiesta of boats, antiques and more in the second of Mount Dora's major festivals. Almost like a 3-day street party, it is well worth sampling.

Fun 'n Sun: 16–22 Apr (**www.sun-n-fun.org**). Annual aviation spectacular in Lakeland, with museums, vintage planes, aerobatics and more; one of America's biggest (off exit 27 on I-4).

Zellwood Corn Festival: 24–25 May (**www.zellwoodcornfestival.com**). Another offbeat but fun offering, with the festival featuring corn-eating contests, carnival rides, live entertainment, games, arts and crafts (25mls/40km north-west of Orlando on Highway 441; follow directions for Mount Dora).

Independence Day: 4 July. A huge US national holiday, but watch out for big annual special events at Lake Eola (downtown Orlando), Lakefront Park (Kissimmee), Mount Dora, Celebration and Winter Park, plus most of the theme parks.

Mount Dora Craft Fair: 26–27 Oct (**www.mountdora.com**). Some of the best national crafters line up for this annual competition featuring a huge range of arts and crafts.

Great Outdoor Festival: 26–27 Oct (TBC) (**www.floridakiss.com**). At the end of Kissimmee's annual 8-week Anglers' Challenge (a huge local fishing festival), try this celebration of family fun, races, live music and outdoor recreation exhibits at the Osceola Heritage Park.

Plan your visit

The next few chapters will tell you all you need to know to plan the ideal holiday. Make a rough itinerary and then fine tune it with this book and online at **www.askdaisy.net/orlando**. You can also take advantage of our unique *Personalised Itinerary Planner* (see page 49). Now read on and enjoy…

Winter Park Christmas Parade

© Disney

2 Planning and Practicalities

or How to *Almost* Do It All and Live to Tell the Tale

There is one simple rule once you have decided Orlando is the place for you. Sit down and PLAN what you want to do very carefully. This is not a place where you can 'make it up as you go along'. Frustration and exhaustion lie in wait for all those who do not have a sound plan of campaign!

First, work out WHEN you want to go, then decide WHERE in this vast area is best for you. Next, consider WHAT sort of holiday you're looking for, WHO you want to trust to arrange your holiday, and crucially – HOW MUCH you want to try to do.

When to go

If you want to avoid the worst of the crowds, the best periods are October–December (but not the week of Thanksgiving in November or 20 December to New Year); early January to mid-March (avoiding President's Day in February); and the week after Easter to the end of May.

Orlando gets seriously busy at Easter; from Memorial Day (the last Monday in May, the official start of the summer season) to mid-August (plus the Labor Day weekend, the first Monday in September and the last holiday of summer); and over the Christmas period. It peaks at the *week of Easter* itself; the big *Fourth of July* national holiday; and (massively so) from just before *Christmas to 2 January*. At these times, it is not unknown for some of the parks to close to new arrivals by mid-morning.

The best combination of good weather and smaller crowds are in April (avoiding Easter) and October. However, few attractions are affected by rain (roller-coasters and water rides close only if lightning threatens) and you'll be one jump ahead if you have waterproofs as the crowds noticeably thin out if it rains. All the parks sell cheap plastic ponchos (even cheaper at Wal-Mart or other

The Brit's Guide research team

PLANNING AND PRACTICALITIES

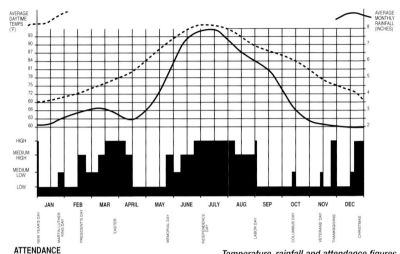

AVERAGE DAYTIME TEMPS (°F)

AVERAGE MONTHLY RAINFALL (INCHES)

HIGH
MEDIUM HIGH
MEDIUM LOW
LOW

JAN | FEB | MAR | APRIL | MAY | JUNE | JULY | AUG | SEP | OCT | NOV | DEC

NEW YEAR'S DAY | MARTIN LUTHER KING DAY | PRESIDENT'S DAY | EASTER | MEMORIAL DAY | INDEPENDENCE DAY | LABOR DAY | COLUMBUS DAY | VETERANS DAY | THANKSGIVING | CHRISTMAS

ATTENDANCE

Temperature, rainfall and attendance figures

supermarkets). In the colder months, take a few warm layers for early morning queues then, when it heats up, leave them in the park lockers. When it gets too hot, take advantage of the air-conditioned attractions and restaurants (and drink LOTS of water).

Where to stay

The choice of where to stay is equally important. Inevitably, there is a huge choice of locations and prices. As a guide, 4 main areas make up the great Orlando tourist conglomeration.

Walt Disney World Resort in Florida: some of the most sophisticated, convenient and fun places to stay are Disney's own hotels. The same imagination that created the theme parks has been at work on the likes of *Disney's Polynesian Resort* and *Disney's Animal Kingdom Lodge*. They all feature free transport to the parks, your own resort ID card (so you can charge meals and souvenirs to your room, and have purchases delivered to the hotel), free parking and the BIG bonus of **Extra Magic Hours**. This allows Disney resort guests entry to one theme park each day, either a full hour before the official opening time or 3 hours after closing, meaning you

can do many of the main attractions with only a fraction of the crowds (though the evening magic hours can still be busy). Many resorts also have great kids' clubs and babysitting services. The drawback here is, with the exception of *Disney's All-Star* and *Pop Century Resorts*, their hotels are among the most expensive, especially to eat in, and are a fair way from Universal and other attractions. They make a good 1-week base, though.

Lake Buena Vista: around the eastern fringes of *Walt Disney World Resort* and along Interstate 4 (I-4), this features some upmarket hotels. It is also handy for all the Disney fun, with most hotels offering free transport to the parks, plus there is excellent dining and shopping. Still a bit pricey, but its proximity to I-4 makes it convenient for much of Orlando.

BRITTIP

Beware the holiday homes (and some hotels) that insist they are just 'minutes from Disney World'. This is often a gross exaggeration, and you may be 30 minutes or more from the parks. Try to get the exact address of the property and then do a location check on **www.mapquest.com**

International Drive: the ribbon development known as I-Drive lies midway between Disney and downtown Orlando and is therefore an excellent central location. Running parallel to I-4, it is about 20 minutes' drive from Disney, closer to Universal and SeaWorld. It is also a well-developed tourist area in its own right, with great shops, restaurants and attractions like Wet 'n Wild, Ripley's Believe It Or Not, WonderWorks and SkyVenture. The downside is it gets heavily congested in peak periods, especially the evenings. But it does represent good value and is one of the few areas with extensive pavements, making it easy to explore on foot. A sub-district off I-Drive is the Universal area of Kirkman Road and Major Boulevard.

Kissimmee: budget holiday-makers can be found in their greatest numbers along the tourist sprawl of Highway 192 (the Irlo Bronson Memorial Highway), an almost unbroken 20ml/32km strip of hotels, motels, restaurants and shops. It offers some of the best economy accommodation and is handy for Disney attractions, though it is further from Universal and downtown Orlando. A car is most advisable here, though the now-completed BeautiVacation project, which has provided much of 192 with pavements, landscaping, bus shelters,

benches and water fountains, has made it much better for getting around on foot or by bus. **Highway 27** is often referred to as 'Kissimmee' but is actually either in Lake County (on the northern stretch) or Polk County (to the south). This is prime holiday home territory, with numerous community developments along its 13ml/21km extent (and counting!).

> **BRITTIP**
>
> The junction of I-4 and Highway 408 in downtown Orlando will remain an ongoing major roadwork project until mid-2009 and can cause some nasty snarl-ups. The Beachline Expressway (Highway 528) is also likely to be a problem until early 2009, with major construction between the airport and the Florida Turnpike.

Split holidays

Florida has so much to offer that many people opt to split their holiday by having a week or two in Orlando and a week elsewhere, such as the Gulf Coast, Miami or Florida Keys. The Atlantic coast has some great beaches only an hour's drive to the east, the magnificent Florida Everglades are some 3–4 hours to the south, and there are more wonderful beaches and pleasant coast roads to the west. There's great shopping

Caladesi Island

almost everywhere, while Florida boasts some stunning golf courses and there are plenty of opportunities to play or watch tennis, baseball and basketball, or go fishing, boating or canoeing. The main tour companies offer a huge variety of packages, with some popular cruise-and-stay options. If you can afford the time (and expense), the best option is to have 2 weeks in Orlando then a week relaxing on one of Florida's fabulous beaches. A 2-week, half-and-half split is a regular choice, but can make your time in Orlando rather hectic, unless your additional week is somewhere like Cocoa Beach (near the Kennedy Space Center), which gives you the chance for day trips back to Orlando. Some companies offer a worthwhile 10/4-day Orlando/coast split, which is a better idea for 2 weeks. Fly-drives offer the greatest flexibility, but there is a lot to tempt you in 2 weeks and you may find it better to book a 2-centre stay that includes a car and accommodation so you can still travel but avoid too much packing and unpacking (see also Chapter 9, the Twin Centre Option).

Travel companies

There is serious competition for your hard-earned holiday money but the travel companies work hard to keep Florida costs down, whether you fly-drive, book your own flights or take a package. Shop around to get the best value but make sure the company you book with has some kind of bonding – either with ABTA in the case of travel agents or ATOL for flights – in case anything should go wrong. At the last count, there were more than 60 tour operators offering holidays to Florida. They divide roughly into the Big Boys, the Specialists, and the Online Agents.

The big boys

Travel City Direct: the UK's largest direct-sell Florida operator, with more than 170,000 customers a year. It is part of the XL Leisure Group, which provides its own in-house airline, plus sister companies Kosmar, Freedom Flights and Aspire Holidays. It offers a wide range of holidays at ultra-competitive prices (because you book direct), including fly-drives, 1- and 2-centre holidays, private pool villas

John's Pass Village at Clearwater

and Caribbean cruise-and-stay holidays (notably with the fun Carnival Cruises). Its valuable *Freetime Check-In* service (at its Welcome Lounge at Lake Buena Vista Factory Stores) allows guests to make the most of their last day by checking in luggage early on the final morning – and reduces the time needed at the airport. Most flights year-round are with TCD's own airline (from Gatwick or Manchester), while others depart from Cardiff and Glasgow (and other regional airports using other charter airlines), with some of the most generous leg-room in economy for a charter, plus free drinks, meals and headsets. Their Sunshine First service has seats with a 50in/127cm pitch that recline almost flat, upgraded menus and individual video screens, a 88lb/40kg luggage allowance, and priority boarding and check-in.

More: call 0871 911 2576 or visit **www.travelcitydirect.com** *Airlines:* Travel City Direct, plus XL Airways, BA, Virgin, US Airways, American Airlines, Continental Airlines and charters. *Airports:* Orlando Sanford International (Travel City Direct, XL Airways and charters), Orlando International (BA, US Airways, Virgin, American and Continental).

Virgin Holidays: the UK's biggest scheduled tour operator to Florida, Virgin offers the most extensive programme to the Sunshine State, with a vast variety of combinations – more than 180 properties to choose from, including Miami, Daytona Beach, the Keys, New York, Boston, Mexico and the Caribbean, plus some tempting cruises with Disney, Royal Caribbean and Carnival. With Virgin's non-stop scheduled service to Orlando (up to 14 times a week from Gatwick and 8 a week from Manchester, plus a new peak season service from Glasgow and daily from Heathrow to Miami), it offers award-winning in-flight entertainment, free drinks, kids' packs, meals and games. It has a wide choice of accommodation (including most Disney resorts and a value

section) and is popular for fly-drives, flying into Orlando and out of Miami, and vice versa. Virgin also has a valuable *Downtown Disney* check-in service for return flights, allowing guests to check in on the morning of departure, freeing up the rest of the day to enjoy at leisure.

More: call 0870 220 2788 or visit **www.virginholidays.co.uk** *Airline:* Virgin Atlantic. *Airports:* Orlando International, Miami, Fort Myers.

Airtours: another leading tour operator, Airtours flies from 8 UK airports with good in-flight entertainment, and seat-back TVs (on selected flights). It offers an excellent PremiAir Gold upgrade (extra leg-room and baggage allowance, free bar, pre-selected menu, late UK check-in) and has some novel 10- and 11-night packages (from Manchester and Gatwick only) for a more flexible choice, plus a wide range of car-hire options and upgrades. There are some good 2-centre combos, including a week at a Disney resort or the Gulf Coast and a week on I-Drive. Airtours also has an extensive range of Florida fly-drives for great flexibility and a time-saving new off-airport check-in. MyTravel's upmarket **Tradewinds** brand (0870 609 1340) also offers fully tailor-made holidays to Florida.

More: call 0870 900 8639 or visit **www.airtours.co.uk** *Airline:* MyTravel. *Airport:* Orlando Sanford International.

Hard Rock Hotel

First Choice: a comprehensive programme from 6 UK airports (Gatwick, Manchester, Nottingham East Midlands, Glasgow and Bristol) using the revamped and quality-conscious First Choice Airways long-haul flights, with seat-back entertainment, more leg-room, wider seats and all meals included, plus premium cabin upgrades (Star Class Premier, with a 92cm/36in pitch and leather seats, a 9in TV screen, 30 channels to choose from and a choice of meals). Other First Choice brands selling Florida are: **First Choice Villas** for a solely villa-based holiday; **First Choice Premier** for a selection of 5-star hotels; **Eclipse Direct**, a direct-sell operator with a standard accommodation range (0870 501 0203, www.eclipsedirect.co.uk); and **Sunstart**, the budget operator, featuring mainly 2- and 3-star hotels (0870 243 0636).

More: call 0870 750 0001 or visit **www.first choice.co.uk/florida** *Airline:* First Choice Airways. *Airport:* Orlando Sanford International.

Thomson: another of the large, mass-market operators, Thomson has scaled back its winter Florida programme, but still offers 7 departure airports (including Birmingham, Cardiff, Newcastle, Glasgow and Belfast), with good in-flight entertainment and attractive kids' packs.

More: call 0870 165 0079 or book online at **www.thomson.co.uk** *Airline:* Thomsonfly and other charters. *Airport:* Orlando Sanford International.

British Airways Holidays: another company to benefit from its own direct, scheduled air service, it offers great flexibility with almost any duration and combination possible, from budget to luxury 5-star accommodation, plus 45 hotels with 'free night' bonuses. Beach add-ons, 2 centres – both coasts and the Florida Keys – and an extensive selection of great-value private homes and condos are all on offer, plus an

© Disney

The Tree of Life at Disney's Animal Kingdom

increased range of pre-bookable tours and excursions. BAH also flies to Miami and Tampa, opening up plenty of fly-drive and multi-centre possibilities.

More: call 0870 243 3407 or visit **www.baholidays.com** *Airline:* British Airways. *Airport:* Orlando Sanford International.

Thomas Cook: another company to have scaled back its winter programme, it still mainly uses its Thomas Cook charter airline (from Birmingham, Cardiff, Gatwick, Glasgow, Manchester and Newcastle), with one of the best punctuality records of all the charter airlines and excellent in-flight service. It has good wedding packages and tempting twin-centre options, including the Bahamas, Jamaica, Miami and cruises.

More: call 0870 111 111 or visit **www.thomascook.com** *Airlines:* Thomas Cook, Thomsonfly, Monarch. *Airport:* Orlando Sanford International.

Cosmos: with a long history in Florida, Cosmos focuses on the key resort areas in Orlando and the Gulf Coast (Clearwater, St Pete Beach and Naples). With a full range of hotels (including Disney and Universal), suites and villas, it offers 7-, 14- and 21-night holidays on a package, fly-drive and flight-only basis (though not winter 2007), and is particularly well priced for car hire.

More: call 0870 443 5275 or visit **www.cosmos.co.uk** *Airline:* Monarch. *Airport:* Orlando Sanford International.

The specialists

Thomas Cook Signature: now here's an operation to compete with the Virgins of this world – a more quality-conscious and selective offering using only scheduled flights (though still with competitive prices). It tends to suit repeat visitors especially, ticketing info and material are first class, and there is a strong tailor-made element to the range of choice. The holiday home selection is particularly good.

More: call 0870 443 4481 or visit **www.tcsignature.com** *Airlines:* Virgin Atlantic, BA, American Airlines, Continental, United. *Airports:* Orlando International, Miami, Tampa.

Funway Holidays: the sister company of America's largest tour operator and a leading specialist in holidays to the US, Funway offers a tailor-made service to match Orlando with any option, providing total flexibility from no fewer than 18 UK airports. Its Orlando private homes are a big feature but it also serves up an array of hotels throughout Florida. It also features a 'Boutique Collection' of hotels, all with added style.

More: call 0870 990 3333 or visit **www.funway holidays.co.uk** *Airlines:* various scheduled, including Virgin Atlantic, BA and Continental. *Airport:* Orlando International.

Style Holidays: one of the UK's top Florida specialists, Style offers a huge selection of villas with private pools, self-catering apartments and a wide range of hotels, as well as fly-drive options. All properties are in named, well-described locations and can be booked either as a package with a hire car or on accommodation-only basis.

More: call 0870 442 3661 or visit **www.styleholidays.co.uk** *Airlines:* various charters. *Airport:* Orlando Sanford International.

Jetsave: this Florida specialist puts the accent on flexibility, with a wide choice on flights with scheduled airlines. You have the full selection of hotels, apartments and an exhaustive choice of holiday homes, with simple, accurate star ratings given for each property.

More: call 0870 161 3402 or visit **www.jetsave.co.uk** *Airline:* Virgin Atlantic. *Airport:* Orlando International.

Continental Airlines Vacations: an attractive new brand in 2007 with flights to 11 destinations in Florida from 7 UK airports, offering daily scheduled services for great flexibility of holiday choice. Its Glasgow and Edinburgh routes are particularly popular, while it also features a huge range of multi-centre options, including a New York stopover.

More: call 0870 942 4040 or visit **www.covacations.co.uk** *Airline:* Continental Airlines. *Airport:* Orlando International.

Other specialists worth checking out include **Jetlife** (0870 787 7877, **www.jetlife.co.uk**); the high-quality style of **Kuoni** (01306 747002, **www.kuoni.co.uk**); **Transolar Holidays**, also good for attraction ticket offers (0151 630 3737, **www.transolar holidays.com**); **USAirtours**, tailor-made US itineraries, many with villas in Orlando (0800 0350 149, **www.usair tours.co.uk**); and **Premier Holidays**, more tailor-made choice and seasonal specials (0870 043 5950, **www.premierholidays.co.uk**).

Boggy Creek airboat ride

The online agents

The growth of online travel agents has been huge in recent years, and you will often find the best deals in this group, whether for packages, flights only or just accommodation. Some are familiar names that have grown online, others are internet-only. The main ones are:

Expedia: one of the biggest companies worldwide, with simple, easy-to-use booking, e-mail updates and a useful Deals section. Visit **www.expedia.co.uk** or call 0871 226 0808; **LastMinute:** a company set up online purely to offer late deals has now become a major mainstream agent, with the full range of holidays, flights, hotels, etc. Visit **www.last minute.com** or call 0871 222 5969; **eBookers:** originally the travel agent arm of Flightbookers (now part of the international Travelport travel conglomerate, including the Orbitz and CheapTickets agencies in the US), this is another big company with a good reputation for flights, hotels, insurance and more. Visit **www.ebookers.com** or call 0870 223 5000. **Travel Supermarket:** a service that instantly searches multiple online travel sites, and gives you the best price match it can find. Plus it also has Fare Alert and Bargain Hunters features, weekly e-mails and various travel forums. Visit **www.travel supermarket.com**.

Similar sites are **Kelkoo** (**www.kelkoo. co.uk**), **Kayak** (**www.kayak.co.uk**), **Travel Jungle** (**www.traveljungle.co.uk**) and **Sidestep** (**http://uk.sidestep.com**), though their package holiday choice tends to be limited. Also, the highly rated **Attraction Tickets Direct** is now selling Disney hotels (with a Price Match Guarantee), so you can book accommodation and tickets at the same time (020 7359 4544, **www.attraction-tickets-direct.co.uk/ hotels/**). Other useful online agents include **Trailfinders**, the UK's largest independent travel firm (0845 058 5858, **www.trailfinders.com**), **Travelbag** (0800 082 5000, **www.travelbag.co.uk**), and **Opodo** (0871 277 0090, **www.opodo.co.uk**).

For flight only, try **Flight Centre** (0870 499 0040, **www.flight centre.co.uk**), **Airline Network** (0871 700 1777, **www.airline-network.co.uk**) and **Dial A Flight** (0870 333 4488, **www.diala flight.com**). For flight price comparison services, **Sky Scanner** (**www.sky scanner.net**) and **Cheap Flights** (**www.cheapflights.co.uk**) are also worth a visit.

Disney Cruise Line

Apart from the charter airlines, there is only a handful of choices for *direct* flights to Orlando, notably **Virgin Atlantic**, **British Airways** and **Aer Lingus** (from Dublin), but you can often save money on indirect flights. Choose from **Delta** (from Gatwick via New York, Atlanta or Cincinnati; Manchester via New York or Atlanta; or Edinburgh via Atlanta); **American Airlines** (from Gatwick via Raleigh-Durham or Dallas; Heathrow via New York, Boston, Miami or Chicago; or Manchester via Boston, Miami, New York and Chicago); **Continental** (from Gatwick, Manchester, Birmingham, Bristol, Belfast, Dublin, Glasgow and Edinburgh via Houston or New York); **Northwest** (from Gatwick via Detroit or Minneapolis); **United** (from Heathrow via Washington or Chicago); **US Airways** (from Gatwick via Charlotte or Philadelphia; Manchester or Glasgow via Philadelphia); and **Flybmi** (from Manchester via Chicago). The obvious drawback is the extra journey time, and you may arrive in Orlando late in the evening after the connecting flight. However, it does give you the chance to break the journey, and places like Detroit and Atlanta can often process international passengers quicker than Orlando, meaning less hassle when you arrive in Florida. **Icelandair** (from Heathrow, Glasgow and Manchester; 0870 787 4020, **www.icelandair.co.uk**) became the first *scheduled* airline to operate transatlantic to Orlando Sanford International Airport in March 2006. All flights go via Reykjavik in Iceland and, for passengers embarking at Glasgow, this is a great stopover option as they are invited to take a complimentary dip in the Blue Lagoon geothermal spa, or go whale-watching in summer. Also worth a look is Scotland's low-cost specialist **Flyglobespan**, which began direct flights from Glasgow to Orlando Sanford in June 2006 and added Belfast in 2007 (as well as offering some package holidays and

an online discount; 08712 710 415, **www.flyglobespan.com**).

Finally, for those looking to book flights themselves but wanting help with Disney accommodation, meal reservations, etc., try the excellent **Dreams Unlimited Travel**. Visit **www.dreamsunlimitedtravel.com** for the essential information on this free service that can save time, money and hassle. Other Orlando hotels (with some serious discounts) also feature, plus a discount ticket agency.

What to see when

Once you arrive, the temptation is to head for the nearest theme park, then the next, and so on. Hold on! If there is such a thing as theme park indigestion, that's the best recipe for it. Some days at the parks are busier than others, while it is inadvisable to attempt 2 of the main parks on successive days at peak times. So here's what you can do.

With the aid of the Holiday Planner on pages 344–5 (or the *Brit's Guide* Personalised Itinerary Planner – see page 49), make a note of all the attractions you want to see over the length of your stay. The most sensible strategy is to plan around the 8 'must-see' parks – *Magic Kingdom Park, Epcot, Disney-MGM Studios, Disney's Animal Kingdom Theme Park*, Universal Studios, Islands of Adventure, SeaWorld and Busch Gardens. If you have only a week, drop Busch Gardens and concentrate on Disney, Universal Studios and

Kissimmee Old Town

© Disney

SeaWorld. Space travel fans would be foolish not to include the Kennedy Space Center, but it would probably bore young children.

As a basic rule, the *Magic Kingdom Park* is the biggest hit with children, and families often find it requires 2 days. The same can be said for *Epcot*, but there are fewer rides to amuse the younger ones. Only the most fleet of foot with the benefit of relatively low crowds would be able to negotiate *Epcot* in a day. The *Animal Kingdom Park* is also a little short on attractions for the youngest visitors, but it still requires nearly a whole day. *Disney-MGM Studios* is usually possible to do in a day (not forgetting the evening Fantasmic! show), while SeaWorld occasionally needs rather longer and Universal Studios can be a 2-day park at its busiest. Islands of Adventure will almost certainly keep everyone, except possibly under-5s, busy all day, too. Busch Gardens, extremely popular with British families, is another full-day affair, especially as it is a 75-minute drive away in Tampa to the south-west. However, an early start to the Kennedy Space Center (an hour's drive to the east) will mean you can be back relaxing in your swimming pool by teatime.

All the attractions are described in detail in Chapters 5–8, so it's best to try to get an idea of the time requirements before you pick up your pencil.

Historic Bok Sanctuary

Smaller attractions

Of the other, smaller-scale attractions, the nature park of Silver Springs is a full day out as it also involves a near 2-hour drive to get there, and the revamped Cypress Gardens will certainly keep you occupied all day, but everything else can be fitted around your Big 8 itinerary. The water parks make for a relaxing ½-day, as does the quieter Historic Bok Sanctuary. Gatorland is a unique look at some of Florida's oldest inhabitants and is a good combination with Boggy Creek Airboats. Aviation fans must not miss a trip to Fantasy of Flight (further down I-4) for a novel experience. Then there are the likes of Ripley's Believe It Or Not museum and the WonderWorks house of fun, both of which offer several hours of entertainment, the high-thrills of Sky Venture (an indoor 'sky-diving' vertical wind tunnel) and the more old-fashioned lure of go-karts and other fairground-type rides at Fun Spot, Magical Midway and Old Town. Many also stay open after the major theme parks have closed.

Disney also offers *DisneyQuest*, an imaginative interactive 'arcade' that guarantees several hours of fun (especially for older children) in its *Downtown Disney* area, while each main area is also well served by creatively designed mini-golf courses for that extra hour or two.

Evenings

The evening entertainment harbours a similarly wide choice of extravagant fun-seeking. By far the best, and worth at least one evening each, are *Downtown Disney's Pleasure Island* and *Universal's CityWalk*. Both will keep you busy until the early hours. Dinner shows provide a lot of fun; 2-hour cabarets based on themes like medieval knights, pirates, Arabian Nights and murder mysteries that all include a hearty meal. Rounding it up is the huge variety of nightclubs and bars, many offering live music.

Our must-do experiences

Soarin' and IllumiNations show (*Epcot*)

Cirque du Soleil (*Downtown Disney*)

The Amazing Adventures of Spider-man and The Hulk rides (Islands of Adventure)

Boggy Creek Airboats (Kissimmee)

Expedition Everest and Festival of The Lion King (*Animal Kingdom*)

Wishes fireworks and Pirates of the Caribbean ride (*Magic Kingdom*)

Fantasmic! show and Star Tours ride (*Disney-MGM Studios*)

Orlando Premium Outlets (shopping)

Believe and Blue Horizons shows (SeaWorld)

KaTonga show and SheiKra coaster (Busch Gardens)

Shrek 4-D (Universal Studios)

Shuttle Launch Experience (Kennedy Space Center)

A Disney character meal

A day at a water park

Shopping

Shopping in Orlando is world class (see Chapter 12). Your battle plan should include at least a day to visit the spectacular malls and discount outlets and speciality centres, like the excellent Orlando Premium Outlets or Prime Outlets and Festival Bay on International Drive.

What to do when

There are several general guidelines for avoiding the worst of the tourist hordes, even in high season. The vast majority of fun-seekers in town are American, who tend to arrive at weekends and head for the main theme parks first. That means Monday is generally a bad time to visit the *Magic Kingdom Park*, as is Sunday, while Tuesday is usually also humming at *Epcot*. The opening of Expedition Everest has definitely boosted the attendance at *Disney's Animal Kingdom*, too, so try to avoid

that on Monday, Wednesday and Saturday. Disney's *Extra Magic Hours* programme, which allows its hotel guests entry to 1 park a day either an hour early or 3 hours after regular closing time, also creates a greater build-up of crowds, so, if you are NOT staying at a Disney hotel, you need to avoid these EMH days. For much of the year, they follow a regular weekly pattern, as follows (where you should avoid the parks on that day, unless you are a Disney hotel guest): *Magic Kingdom*, Tue and Thurs in peak season, Thurs only off peak; *Epcot*, Sun in peak, Tue off peak; *Disney-MGM Studios*, Mon and Fri in peak, Sat off peak; *Animal Kingdom*, Wed and Sat in peak, Mon off peak. However, the EMH days *can* change from month to month, and we are able to reflect this on our **website** by regularly updating the essential Busy Day Guide (see page 345), which shows at a glance the busiest and quietest days at each Orlando park. The *Animal Kingdom* is also the hardest to get round when it's crowded, while Epcot handles the crowds best of all. *Disney's Blizzard Beach* and *Typhoon Lagoon* water parks hit high tide at the weekend, and Thurs and Fri in summer.

BRITTIP

In the first edition of the *Brit's Guide* in 1995, a typical burger-and-chips park meal cost around $5.65. Now it's more likely to be $9–$10.

At Universal Orlando, the picture is different as there are no early entry days, and the busiest days are usually the weekends when locals visit. This often means Monday is quietest at both Universal and Islands of Adventure, getting busier through the week, with the former being slightly more crowded. If *Walt Disney World* is humming in the early part of the week, that makes it a good time to visit SeaWorld, Busch Gardens, Silver Springs or the Kennedy Space Center.

Avoid Wet 'n Wild at the weekends when the locals come out to play. We expect SeaWorld's new Aquatica water park to be very busy all week when it first opens in spring 2007 and then just hectic Friday to Sunday after the initial novelty wears off.

Ensuring you get the most out of your days at the main parks is another art form, and there are several practical policies to pursue. The official opening times seldom vary from 9am but arriving early is highly advisable. Apart from being near the head of the queues (and you will encounter some SERIOUS queues, or lines as the Americans call them), the parks sometimes open earlier than scheduled if the crowds build up before the official hour. So, you can be a step ahead of the masses by arriving at least 30 minutes before opening time, or an hour early during the main holiday periods. Apart from anything else, you will be better placed to park in the huge car parks and catch the tram to the main gates (anything up to half a mile away).

© Disney

Meeting the Disney Characters

BRITTIP

If your hotel is not far away, take a mid-afternoon break from the park and return for a siesta or a swim. Your car park ticket is valid all day, and the evening is often the best time to be in the parks.

Once you've put yourself in pole position, don't waste time on the shops, scenery and other frippery that will lure the unprepared first-timer. Instead, head straight for some of the main rides and get a few big-time thrills under your belt before the main hordes arrive. You will quickly work out where the most popular attractions are as the majority of early birds will flock to them. Use Chapters 5 and 6 to help plan your park strategies.

You can also benefit from doing the opposite of what the masses do after the initial rush has subsided. Try not

to have all your meals in the parks, too. Eating here is becoming a touch expensive and it can be $10/person for even a basic counter-service meal. Instead, eating as much as you can at a good buffet breakfast somewhere like Ponderosa or Golden Corral means you can skimp on lunch and save $$$s!

Pace yourself

Another word of warning: Disney's parks, notably the *Magic Kingdom*, stay open late for the main holidays, until midnight at times, and that can be a l-o-n-g day for children. It's vital to pace yourself, especially if you have been among the first through the gates. There are plenty of options to take time off for a drink or a sit-down somewhere air-conditioned, and you can benefit from the American propensity to take mealtimes seriously by *avoiding* lunchtime (noon–1.30pm) and dinnertime (5.30–7pm). So, after you've had a couple of hours of park going, it pays

BRITTIP

The water IS safe to drink in the US but it may not taste great as it's heavily fluoridated. Bottled water is cheap at supermarkets – and you'll save big time on buying it in the parks.

Top things to do for FREE!

While Orlando has a magnificent array of paid-for attractions, there are still many things you can do that don't cost a cent.

Disney's Boardwalk Resort: free nightly entertainment includes jugglers, comedy skits and live music. Time your visit to coincide with the 9pm IllumiNations fireworks extravaganza at nearby *Epcot*.

Florida Eco-Safaris: out in the Florida countryside is this wonderful nature preserve (see page 250). As well as its highly recommended paid-for tours, horse-lovers will want to know this is home to a rare horse-training operation that is happy to let visitors watch (and learn!) for free. Dean van Camp and Sandra Wise are the equine educators, and it is a fascinating study (**www.floridaeco-safaris.com**).

Fort Christmas Historical Park: 20mls/32km east of Orlando in the town of Christmas is this replica of an 1837 US Army fort from the Seminole Indian Wars, with exhibits, video presentations and restored homes, and special events at some weekends; 10am–5pm Tue–Sat, 1–5pm Sun (**www.nbbd.com/godo/FortChristmas**).

Lake Eola Park: take a walk on the mild side in the heart of downtown Orlando. The kids can play or feed the swans, and there is live entertainment in summer at the recently revamped Walt Disney Amphitheater (see Parks & Recreation at **www.cityoforlando.net**).

Lake Tibet-Butler Preserve: just 5 minutes from Disney but light years from the theme park hustle-bustle (CR 535, Winter Garden-Vineland Road) is this local nature preserve, with quiet trails, lake overlook and interpretive centre. Open 9am–dusk daily (not public holidays), it is on the Great Florida Birding Trail and is a minor gem of native wildlife, including armadillos, gopher tortoises and occasional deer (**http://myfwc.com/viewing/sites/site-c07.html**).

Lakeridge Winery and Vineyards: join a free wine-tasting tour and you'll know why Lakeridge (in nearby Clermont) has won more than 300 awards. Be sure to designate a driver as sample sizes are generous! 10am–5pm Mon–Sat, 11am–5pm Sun (**www.lakeridgewinery.com**).

Leu Gardens: just north of downtown Orlando, this sanctuary of peace and quiet, with wildlife, nature trails and the 1880s' Leu House Museum is free every Mon 9am–noon (**www.leugardens.org**).

Morse Museum of American Art: this superb little museum in tranquil Winter Park, dedicated to American paintings, ceramics and representative arts from the 19th and 20th centuries, is open 4–8pm every Fri Sep–May (see **www.morsemuseum.org** and page 241).

Old Town, Kissimmee: the biggest vintage car parade in the US every Saturday, with cars on display from 1pm and the parade at 8.30pm, a Friday Night Cruise (classic cars from 1978 to 1985) at 9pm and Bike Nites every Thurs at 6pm, with up to 700 motorbikes each week, plus live music nightly (**www.old-town.com**).

Peabody Duck March: turn up at 11am or 5pm at the Peabody Hotel to see the resident mallards get the red carpet treatment as they either arrive or leave their lobby fountain 'home' (**www.peabodyorlando.com**).

Pianoman Bob Jackson: Disney's Port Orleans Riverside Resort hosts some excellent free entertainment with Pianoman Bob on Wed–Sun evenings, who gets everyone doing the Chicken Dance and singing along with old favourites in a family-friendly atmosphere.

Sanford Museum: some quaint history is well presented through the personal collections of city founder Henry S Sanford (11am–4pm Tue–Fri). Combine a visit with a walking tour, including the new Riverwalk (**www.ci.sanford.fl.us/cf03.html**).

to take an early lunch (before noon), plunge back into it all for another 3 hours or so, have another snack mid-afternoon and then return to the main rides as the parks quieten down a little in late afternoon.

Comfort and clothing

You may feel jet-lagged for the first day or two after your arrival, but this can be reduced by avoiding alcohol and coffee on the plane and drinking plenty of water.

BRITTIP

Don't be tempted to pack a lot of smart or formal clothing – you really won't need it in hot, informal Florida.

The most important part of your holiday wardrobe is your footwear – you will spend a lot of time on your feet, even at off-peak periods. The smallest of the parks is 'only' 100 acres/40ha, but that is irrelevant in relation to the amount of time you spend queuing. This is *not* the time to break in new sandals or trainers! Comfortable, well-worn shoes or trainers are essential (many people rate Crocs shoes as ideal park

footwear). Otherwise, you need dress only as the climate dictates. T-shirts and shorts are appropriate in all the parks and nearly all restaurants will accept casual dress. However, swimwear is not acceptable away from pool areas.

If, after a long day, you feel the need for a change of clothes or a sweater for the evening, take advantage of the handy lockers (unlimited use all day, even if you change parks). All the parks are also well equipped with pushchairs (or 'strollers') for hire, and baby services are located at regular intervals. It is *vital* to use high-factor sun creams at all times, even during the winter when the sun may not feel strong but can still burn. Nothing is guaranteed to ruin your holiday like severe sunburn. Orlando has a sub-tropical climate and you need to use higher factor creams than you would in the Mediterranean. Use sun block on sensitive areas like nose and ears, and splash on the after-sun lotion liberally at the end of the day. You also need waterproof sun cream for swimming. Skincare products are widely available and usually inexpensive (at the likes of Wal-Mart, Kmart and Target).

Celebration

© Disney

Disney's Port Orleans Resort

Wear a hat during the day, and avoid alcohol, coffee and fizzy drinks until the evening as they are dehydrating and make you liable to heatstroke. You must increase your fluid intake *significantly* during the summer, but stick to still soft drinks such as Gatorade, an energy squash, and lots of water.

BRITTIP
One of the best ways to keep cool in the Florida sun is to visit a supermarket and buy a simple mist spray fan (about $7.99), which you carry with you and just refill with water.

Want to see more?
If, like us, you want to make the most of every holiday opportunity, you could also travel a little further afield in America with the help of its efficient low-cost airline system. Orlando is an excellent base from which to explore city destinations like New York, Chicago, Boston, Dallas, Washington, Baltimore and Memphis, and great states like Georgia, South Carolina, Virginia and Pennsylvania, plus the Caribbean and Mexico, all of which are only 2 hours' flight away, or go even further to glittering Las Vegas, Los Angeles, San Francisco or San Diego. With the benefit of cheap hotel deals (check out **www.hotels.com** and **www.orbitz.com**), you can seriously spread your wings (ahem) by using the likes of **AirTran Airways**, Florida's leading low-cost carrier which is based at Orlando International Airport and also flies from 8 other Florida airports, including Tampa, Miami, Palm Beach and Fort Myers. Skip ahead to page 339 for more info on how to extend your holiday. Repeat visitors may like to consider this, and it represents only a small additional investment after going all the way to Florida (look up **www.air tran.com** for its timetable and fares).

BRITTIP
If you fear the onset of blisters, buy some moleskin footpads from the nearest supermarket.

Medical aid
Should you require medical treatment, whether for sunburn or other first aid, consult your tour company's information about local hospitals and surgeries. In the event of a medical or other **emergency**, dial 911 as you would 999 in Britain. It cannot be over-stressed that you should take out comprehensive travel and health insurance (see pages 35–6) for any trip to America, as there is NO National Health Service and ANY form of medical treatment is expensive and must be paid for. Keep all the receipts and put in a claim on your return home.

Busch Gardens Africa

BRITTIP

The summer is mosquito time and a spray-on or roll-on insect repellent is highly advisable. Brands to look for locally are Cutter, Repel and Off!

Emergency outpatient departments can be found with **Centra Care** at Florida Hospital Medical Center in 15 Central Florida locations and can provide hotel in-room services (407 200 2300) and free transport (407 239 6463). Open from 8am daily, Centra Care centres can be found at: 12500 S Apopka-Vineland Road near the Crossroads shopping centre and *Downtown Disney* at Lake Buena Vista (until midnight on weekdays, 8pm Sat, Sun; 407 934 2273); 7848 West Irlo Bronson Memorial Highway (192), in Formosa Gardens Village (until 8pm Mon–Fri, 5pm Sat, Sun; 407 397 7032); 6001 Vineland Road, near Universal Studios (7am–7pm Mon–Fri, 8am–6pm Sat, Sun; 407 351 6682); on Sand Lake Road, between John Young Parkway and Orange Blossom Trail (8am–8pm Mon–Fri, 9am–5pm Sat, Sun; 407 851 6478); and 4320 West Vine Street, near Medieval Times (until 8pm Mon–Fri, 5pm Sat, Sun; 407 390 1888). Look up more on **www.centracare.org**

Sand Lake Hospital on 9400 Turkey Lake Road has an emergency outpatient department (407 351 8500). The **East Coast Medical Network** (407 648 5252, **www.the medicalconcierge.com**) also makes hotel 'house calls' 24 hours a day. House Med Inc operates **MediClinic**, a walk-in facility on 2901 Parkway Boulevard, Kissimmee (open daily 9am–9pm; 407 396 1195).

BRITTIP

If you take regular prescription drugs, check with your doctor or pharmacist to see if they have a different name in the US. Many do (for example, adrenaline is known as epinephrine) and it is worth finding out and carrying the drug with both names in case of an emergency. The US name for paracetamol is acetaminophen.

The two largest chemists ('drug stores' in the US) are **Walgreens** (**www.walgreens.com**) and **CVS** (**www.cvs.com**), and the Walgreens at 12100 S Apopka-Vineland Road (near *Downtown Disney*), 5935 W Irlo Bronson Memorial Highway (Highway 192 in Kissimmee), 6201, 8050, 8959 and 12650 International Drive (among others) are open 24 hours a day.

Toon Lagoon at Universal

American-speak

Many words and phrases have a different meaning across the Atlantic. For instance, when Americans say the first floor, they mean the ground floor, the second floor is really the first, and so on. (NB: NEVER ask for a packet of fags; 'fag' is a crude, slang term for a homosexual.) Here are a few everyday words to help you:

American	English	American	English
Appetiser	Starter	Fender	Car bumper
Band aid	Plaster	Freeway	Motorway
Bathroom	Private toilet	Fries	Chips
Biscuit	Savoury scone	Gas	Petrol
Broiled	Grilled	Graham cracker	Digestive biscuit
Cellphone	Mobile phone	Hood	Car bonnet
Check	Bill	Intersection	Junction
Chips	Crisps	Nickel	5 cents
Collect call	Reverse charge phone call	No standing	No parking OR stopping
Cookie	Biscuit	'Pound sign'	The # on a phone keypad
Cot/rollaway	Fold-up bed		
Crib	Cot	Purse	Handbag
Diaper	Nappy	Quarter	25 cents
Dime	10 cents	Ramp	Slip road
Divided highway	Dual carriageway	Restroom	Public toilet
Eggplant	Aubergine	Seltzer	Soda water
Eggs 'over easy'	Eggs fried both sides but soft	Shrimp	King prawn
		Soda	Fizzy drink
Eggs 'sunny side up'	Eggs fried on just one side (soft)	Stroller	Pushchair
		Trunk	Car boot
Entree	Main course	Turn-out	Lay-by
Facecloth/washcloth	Flannel	Yield	Give way
Faucet	Tap	Zucchini	Courgette

Travel insurance

Having said you shouldn't travel without insurance, you shouldn't pay too much for it either. Your travel agent may imply that you need to buy its policy (which can be expensive, and you should be free to buy elsewhere). In all cases make sure you are covered in the USA for: **medical cover** of at least £2m; **personal liability** up to £2m (though this won't cover driving abroad; you would still need Supplementary Liability Insurance with your car hire firm);

cancellation or **curtailment** cover up to £5,000; **personal property cover** up to £1,500 (but check on expensive items, as most policies limit single articles to £250); **cash and document** cover, including your passport and tickets; and finally that the policy gives you a 24-hour **emergency helpline**. If you want to go horse riding, check your policy includes **dangerous sports cover**. Shop around at reputable dealers like **American Express** (0800 028 7573, **www.americanexpress.com/uk**), **AA**

© Disney

Rock 'n' Roller Coaster starring Aerosmith

(0800 085 7240, **www.theaa.com**),
Direct Travel (0845 605 2700,
www.direct-travel.co.uk), **Club Direct**
(0800 083 2466, **www.clubdirect.com**),
Columbus (0870 033 9988,
www.columbusdirect.com), **Norwich
Union** (0808 101 6705, **www.norwich
union.com**), **Egg** (08451 222 888,
www.egg.com), **Thomas Cook** (0870
750 5711, **www.thomascook.com**) and
Worldwide Travel Insurance (0870
112 8100, **www.worldwideinsure.com**).
MoneySupermarket.com also
compares many different travel
insurers at **www.moneysuper
market.com/insurance**

Florida with children

We are often asked what we think is
the right age to take children to
Orlando, and there is no set answer.
Some toddlers take to it instantly,
while some 6- or even 7-year-olds are
overwhelmed. Quite often, the best
attractions for young children are the
hotel swimming pool or the tram ride
to a park's front gates! Some love the
Disney characters instantly, while
others find them frightening. There is

no predicting how they will react, but
at 4½, Simon's oldest boy loved just
about every second of his first
experience (apart from the fireworks –
see page 38) and still talks about it. A
3-year-old may not remember much,
but WOULD have fun and provide
you with some great memories,
photos and videos. Here are some top
tips for travelling with youngsters:

The flight: try to look calm (even if
you don't feel it) and relaxed. Small
children soon pick up on any
anxieties and make them worse. Pack
a bag with plenty of little bits for them
(comics, sweets, colouring books,
small surprise toys, etc.) and keep
vital 'extras' like Calpol (in sachets, if

BRITTIP

Look out for several tour operators
– and some ticket brokers – offering
a *Kids Eat Free* card for Orlando. This
was a new programme in 2007 for
children aged 11 and under that could
save you $200 or more in meals. Look
up more details at **www.kidseatfree
card.com**

Hurricane alert?

Florida was hit by an unprecedented 4 hurricanes in 2004, 3 of which affected Orlando, with a lot of resultant publicity and worry. But the simple fact is this was the worst weather in more than a century and big storms are rare in central Florida. The hurricane 'season' is Jun–Nov, with Aug–Sep the most storm-prone. However, even the extremes of 2004 caused no significant damage to the theme parks and the biggest inconvenience for tourists was losing electricity for a few days. In the unlikely event of a major storm, switch your TV to the Weather Channel and local news station WESH 2 and follow their advice.

possible), a change of clothes, a small first-aid kit (plasters, antiseptic cream, baby wipes), sunglasses, a hat and sunscreen in your hand luggage.

BRITTIP

Pushchairs (strollers) are essential, even if your children are a year or two out of them. The walking wears kids out quickly and a pushchair can save a lot of discomfort. You can take your own, hire them at the parks or, better still, buy one at a local supermarket for as little as $15.

Once you're there: take things slowly and let your children dictate the pace to a large extent. In hot, humid summer, only the most placid children (and few under 5s, in our experience) will happily queue for an hour or more at a ride, so use Disney's FastPass system (see page 108) judiciously. The heat, in particular, can result in grizzly kids in no time, so take breaks for drinks and splash zones or head for attractions with air-conditioning. Remember to carry your small first-aid kit. Baby wipes always come in handy, and it is a good idea to take spare clothes, which you can leave in the lockers at all the main parks. Going back to the hotel for an afternoon snooze is a good idea – you

will also dodge the worst of the heat and crowds.

In the sun: carry sun cream and sun block at all times and use it frequently, in queues, on buses, etc. A children's after-sun lotion is also advisable. And make sure they drink a lot of water or non-fizzy drinks. Tiredness and irritability are often the result of mild dehydration.

Dining out: look for 'kids eat free' deals in many places, as they can apply to children up to 12, and take advantage of the many buffet options (see Chapter 11, Dining Out) to fill up the family or for picky eaters. Many restaurants do Meals To Go if you want a quiet meal in your own accommodation without the worry of the kids playing up. And try to let your children get used to the characters and the size of them before you go to one of the many fab Disney character meals.

Discovery Cove

✠ BRITTIP

Avoid making phone calls from your hotel room – they're hugely expensive. It's cheaper to buy a local phonecard and use a normal payphone. British tri-band mobiles are also costly to use in the US. To call home from the US, dial 011 44, then drop the first 0 from the UK area code.

Having fun: let your children do some of the decision-making and be prepared to go with the flow if they find something unexpected they like (the many squirt fountains and splash zones in the parks are an example – bring swimsuits and/or a change of clothes!). The Orlando rule of 'You Can't Do It All' applies especially with children. And beware the evening fireworks as they are loud and youngsters can get distressed (Simon's 4-year-old had to be taken out of *Epcot* in a hurry). The resort hotels around the *Magic Kingdom* offer safe ways to view the fireworks – at a distance.

All the parks have **baby centers** for nursing mothers and can provide baby food and nappies on request (check the park map for the locations). The centres can even provide spare children's underpants for those little accidents. All Disney's hotel gift shops stock baby food and nappies. Expectant mothers are strongly advised not to ride some of the more dynamic attractions and coasters, and there will be clear warnings on park maps and at the rides. Basically, the rides to avoid are: *Magic Kingdom*: Space Mountain, Splash Mountain; *Epcot*: Test Track, Body Wars, Mission: SPACE; *Disney-MGM Studios*: Tower of Terror, Rock 'n' Roll Coaster Starring Aerosmith, Star Tours; *Disney's Animal Kingdom*: Dinosaur!, Primeval Whirl, Kali River Rapids, Expedition Everest; *Universal Studios Florida*: The Simpsons, Men In Black – Alien Attack, Revenge of the Mummy, Earthquake, Jimmy Neutron ride (unless you use the static seats); *Islands of Adventure*: Incredible Hulk Coaster, Dr Doom's Fearfall, Popeye

Dueling Dragons at Islands of Adventure

Top 10 romantic restaurants

1 Tchoup Chop, Universal's Royal Pacific Resort

2 California Grill, *Disney's Contemporary Resort*

3 Todd English's bluezoo, *Walt Disney World Dolphin Resort*

4 Zen, Omni Orlando Resort at Champion's Gate

5 Jiko, *Disney's Animal Kingdom Lodge*

6 The Boheme, Grand Bohemian Hotel

7 Manuel's on the 28th, Bank of America building, downtown Orlando

8 Old Hickory Steakhouse, Gaylord Palms Resort

9 Cola Bella, Rosen Shingle Creek Resort

10 Jardins du Castillon, Park Avenue, Winter Park

and Bluto's Bilge-Rat Barges, Dudley Do-Right's Ripsaw Falls, Jurassic Park River Adventure, Dueling Dragons; *SeaWorld*: Wild Arctic (avoid simulator ride), Journey to Atlantis, Kraken; *Busch Gardens*: SheiKra, Gwazi, Kumba, Montu, The Scorpion, Congo River Rapids, Stanley Falls Log Flume, Tanganyika Tidal Wave, The Phoenix, Sandstorm, Cheetah Chase.

Babysitting is available through many Disney resorts and some of the bigger hotels elsewhere, while **Kids Night Out** is a service providing parents with a chance to have an evening out on their own. They offer in-room sitters or helpers during your stay at a rate of $14/hour for the first child, $16.50 for 2, $19 for 3 and $21.50 for 4, with an additional $2/hour after 9pm (children 2 years and older only). There is a 4-hour minimum and reservations are required on 1800 696 8105 or 407 828 0920.

Travellers with disabilities

The parks pay close attention to the needs of visitors with disabilities and Florida in general is extremely disabled-friendly (though Americans tend to use the word 'handicapped' as we use 'disabled'). Though there are few rides that cannot cater for them, wheelchair availability and access is almost always good. For hearing-impaired guests, there are assistive listening devices and reflective captioning at attractions where a commentary is part of the show. Braille guidebooks are available, plus rest areas for guide dogs. Disney hotels all have disabled-accessible rooms – call 407 939 7807 or visit **www.disneyworld.com** – and Disney publishes a *Guidebook for Disabled Guests* (as does Universal), available in all 4 main parks (and online). Life-jackets are always on hand at the water parks, and there are special tape cassettes for blind guests. If you require help while queuing or have children with special needs, call in at any Disney guest relations office to ask what provisions are available. Walt Disney World also has a Disabled Guests Special Requests Line on 407 939 7807 and can produce a Guest Assistance Card (GAC) tailored to your specific needs. It *doesn't* provide front-of-the-line access (which many people believe) but it can make the waiting more comfortable. Universal, SeaWorld and Busch Gardens provide similar assistance through their Guest Services offices.

Please note, the rules for disabled drivers using their blue UK disabled parking permits in Florida have changed. To use any of the plentiful designated parking areas at all the parks – and elsewhere – drivers need to obtain a **Temporary Disabled Parking Permit**, which costs $15 locally. You can either go to a local tax collection office, with your UK blue badge and a form of ID, when you arrive (but bear in mind that most open 8.30am–5pm Mon–Fri only), or apply at least 4 weeks in advance by mail. You need to send a photocopy of your Blue Badge (both sides), a copy of your passport ID page, and a money order for $15 (or your credit card details, for which there is a $2 surcharge) to: Tag Department, Osceola County Tax Collector, 2501 E. Irlo Bronson Memorial Highway, Kissimee, Florida 34744, USA. For more info, call 407 742 4000 or fax 407 742 3995 (Mon–Fri 8am–4.30pm). For a list of tax collection offices in Orange County (for the Orlando area), call 407 836 4145 (**www.octaxcol.com**, and click on Office Locations), or in Osceola County (for Kissimmee), call 407 742 4000 (**www.osceolatax collector.com**). The temporary permits are valid for 6 months throughout Florida.

✚ BRITTIP

A new project by a local builder should see a vacation home community that is completely disabled-friendly completed in 2008. **Monticelli** is just off Highway 27 near Haines City, about 25 minutes from *Walt Disney World* (see also page 103).

Local company **Suntastic Tours** can help travellers with both physical and mental disabilities in many different areas, including travel, arranging tours of the parks and many other accessibility issues. Call it on 1877 226 6750 or look up **www.suntastic tours.com**. For other local assistance, **Walker Medical & Mobility Products** (407 518 6000, **www.walkermobility.com**) specialises in 3-wheeled electric scooters and wheelchair rentals, with free delivery and pick-up even from holiday villas. **Rainbow Wheels**, with

© Disney
There's no age limit to having fun

three locations in central Florida (407 977 3799, **www.rainbowwheels.com**), hires out full-size or mini vans equipped for wheelchair users. The discussion forums on **www.wdw info.com** also include a board that is geared to visitors with disabilities.

Orlando for grown-ups

You don't need to have kids in tow to enjoy Orlando. There is so much clever detail and imagination, it is usually the grown-ups who get the most out of the experience. In fact, as many couples and single people visit the parks as families.

Certainly, when you look at the entertainment on offer at *Pleasure Island* and CityWalk, the downtown district and the great range of bars and fine restaurants, with a good number of romantic offerings, it is easy to see the attraction for those of 21 and over. As well as Florida being a key honeymoon destination, its friendly, social atmosphere provides an ideal place for singles, while couples without children can also take advantage of the late opening hours at the parks and clubs like Jellyrolls and Atlantic City Dance Hall at *Disney's Boardwalk Resort*.

Orlando for seniors

The more mature traveller can also benefit from a healthy dose of the Sunshine State. And, if our parents (all into their senior years) are any guide, they will have just as much fun, within slightly different parameters.

Two-way radio rentals

Two-way radios have taken on a popular new role in Orlando, in terms of both safety and convenience. Many families buy these 'walkie-talkies' to keep in touch around the parks and it is common to see them in use in preference to mobile phones. You can pick them up locally for as little as $35 in stores like Wal-Mart, Best Buy, Circuit City, Radio Shack, Office Depot and Staples. However, they cannot be used back home as they use the same frequency as the UK emergency services.

For the older person, staying in a Disney hotel is highly recommended as it removes the stress of driving. The extra cost is offset, Simon's parents feel, by the beauty and convenience of their surroundings. In the parks they still find plenty to do, even if they aren't keen on most of the thrill rides (though just watching can be entertainment enough!). *Epcot* and *Disney's Animal Kingdom* both have much to engage the older visitor, while the shows of *Disney-MGM Studios* make that a popular choice, too, and the *Magic Kingdom Park*, while 'probably the noisiest of all the parks', still represents an essential experience.

The *Downtown Disney* area can feel a bit frenetic for the senior crowd, but the *Boardwalk Resort* is popular and the whole of the *Epcot* resort area offers much in the way of fine dining and relaxation. In fact, this is often a prime area for seniors, notably the quieter *Disney's Yacht and Beach Club Resorts*, and the superb Swan-Dolphin complex.

Simon's parents highlight the following for their age group: Jim Henson's Muppet Vision 3-D and Fantasmic! at *Disney-MGM* Studios; Kilimanjaro Safaris, the Maharajah Jungle Trek and Festival Of The Lion King at *Disney's Animal Kingdom Theme Park*; Spaceship Earth, Soarin', Universe of Energy, Test Track and IllumiNations at *Epcot* (plus the wonderful gardens and architecture); The Haunted Mansion, Jungle Cruise, Pirates Of The Caribbean and the monorail ride to the *Magic Kingdom*; watching the children at the many parades and character greetings; dinner at the California Grill in *Disney's Contemporary Resort*; shopping at Orlando Premium Outlets; most of Universal Studios, but less of Islands of Adventure (though they were wowed – as most are – by the Amazing Adventures of Spider-Man).

In terms of the weather, March was just about ideal for them, but they wouldn't be keen to visit in the summer. Seniors can also take advantage of many discounts and special deals for their age group at the attractions as well as at many restaurants and hotels. The official Visitor Center on I-Drive (see page 50) publishes a brochure of all the deals (**www.orlandoinfo.com**).

Downtown Disney

© Disney

Scenic lake tour, Mount Dora

Repeat visitors

Repeat visitors create a large part of the Orlando market and are always on the lookout for something new after they have done all the main parks. To that end, our Off the Beaten Track chapter is largely designed with them in mind. Listed here are 10 things worth doing once you have Been There and Done That:

1 Behind the scenes tours at the Disney parks

2 Dolphin watch cruise from Dolphin Landings at St Pete Beach

3 A weekend visit to *Disney's Wilderness Preserve* in Poinciana, Kissimmee

4 The scenic boat ride and Morse Museum in Winter Park

5 Historic Bok Sanctuary in Lake Wales

BRITTIP

If you have a fridge in your hotel, put drink cartons in the freezer overnight and they will be cool for much of the next day in your back-pack. Better still, buy a cheap coolbag, freeze it with some water bottles in, and leave it in the car – great after a day in the parks.

6 Lunch or dinner (and a visit to the soup cannery!) at the eclectic Chalet Suzanne – also Lake Wales

7 Boggy Creek Airboats and Wildlife Safari Ride

8 The amazing SkyVenture on I-Drive

9 Merritt Island National Wildlife Refuge at Titusville

10 A visit to Mount Dora, north-west of Orlando

Measurements

American clothes sizes are smaller than ours, hence a US size 12 dress is a UK size 14, or an American jacket sized 42 is really a 44. Shoes are the opposite: a US 10 should fit a British size 9 foot. Their measuring system is also still imperial, not metric.

You've got mail

Sending postcards and letters home is easy but the American postal system can be hard to understand. You won't find postboxes in many locations and some post offices don't seem to know the fees for postage to the UK. So here's what you need to know – all the parks DO have postboxes and you can get stamp books from most stamp machines and City Hall at the *Magic Kingdom*; a standard postcard costs 81c; a birthday or other greetings-type card in an envelope requires an 90c stamp; standard postage within the US is 41c; the main post office for the Disney area is at **10450 Turkey Lake Road** (just north of the junction with Palm Parkway and Central Florida Parkway; 8am–7pm Mon–Fri, 9am–5pm Sat); in Kissimmee, try **2600 Michigan Avenue** (8am–6.30pm Mon–Fri, 9am–4pm Sat) or **1415 W Oak Street** (8.30am–5pm Mon–Fri, 9am–2pm Sat). You will also find a full-service post office inside the **Mall at Millenia**, off the lower level of the Grand Court.

Wedding bells

Florida is an increasingly popular choice for couples looking to tie the knot (some 20,000 couples a year at the last count). Its almost guaranteed sunshine, lush landscape and natural beauties make it a huge hit as a wedding backdrop. Orlando also has some terrific services, wedding co-ordinators and scenic venues like Cypress Grove Park, Magnolia Acres, Southport Park, Winter Park, the Leu Gardens and the many resort hotels and even golf courses. More unusual ones include getting married in a hot-air balloon or a helicopter, on the beach or a luxury yacht, in the pit-lane of the Richard Petty Driving Experience at *Walt Disney World* or even at 145mph/233kph around the speedway itself!

Walt Disney World's Wedding Pavilion offers true fairytale romance, with the backdrop of Cinderella Castle. You can opt for traditional elegance in this Victorian setting with up to 260 guests or the full Disney experience, arriving in Cinderella's coach with Mickey and Minnie as guests. Disney's wedding planners can tailor-make the occasion for you (407 828 3400) but at a price – rates start at $3,000/couple for the basic ceremony and can easily top $20,000. All the main tour operators feature

wedding options and co-ordinated services, and offer a variety of ceremonies. Prices vary from around £300/couple (for a basic civil ceremony) to more than £2,000.

To obtain a marriage licence you can visit one of the local courthouses, which include the Osceola County Courthouse, Courthouse Square, Suite 2000, Kissimmee (just off Bryan Street in downtown Kissimmee) 8am–4pm Mon–Fri (407 343 3500); the Orange County Courthouse, 425 North Orange Avenue (downtown Orlando) 7.30am–4pm Mon–Fri (407 836 2067); Clermont Courthouse, 1206 Bowman Street, Clermont (in Sunnyside Plaza) 8.30am–4.30pm (closed for lunch 12–1pm; 352 394 2018). All courthouses are closed on US bank holidays. Both parties must be present to apply for the marriage licence, which costs $93.50 (in cash, travellers' cheques or by credit card) and is valid for 60 days, while a ceremony (equivalent to a British register office) can be performed at the same time by the clerk for an extra $20 (times vary according to courthouse). Passports and birth certificates are requested, and if you have been married before you should bring your decree absolute.

Cinderella Wedding at Walt Disney World Resort

© Disney

After acquiring a licence, a couple can get married anywhere in Florida. Neither witnesses nor blood tests are necessary and there are no residence qualifications. It is also possible to obtain a licence *before* arriving in Florida; visit **www.floridamarriage licencebypost.com** for more info.

Of even greater significance is an internet business dedicated to organising weddings for couples from the UK. Run by Briton Lorraine Ellis, who has specialised in Orlando marriages for many years, **Get Married In Florida** (407 226 3383, **www.getmarriedinflorida.com**) offers the complete service for the perfect wedding – as we can personally vouch for! We can also add our recommendation for caterers **Levan's** (**www.levans.com**) and the amazing **www.andreacheesecake.com** Another wedding specialist is harpist **Christine MacPhail**, who can provide an elegant touch to the occasion (407 239 1330; **www.orlandoharpist.com**). For photographer recommendations, try **Abba Photography** (407 672 1121, **www.abbaphotography.com**) or **Broadway Fotographics** (by Bill Otten, 407 339 5542, **www.broadway foto.com**).

If you would prefer to get married in a church or another place of worship, contact the **Center of Light Church & Spiritual Center** on East Robinson Street (407 228 0101), the **First Baptist Church** on John Young Parkway (407 425 2555), **St Nicholas Catholic Church** on Sand Lake Road (407 351 0133) or **Trinity Lutheran Church** on East Livingston Street downtown (407 422 5704, **www.trinitydowntown.org**). Another church worth noting for general worship (Sun 8.30 and 11am and Thur 7.30pm) is the **Community Presbyterian Church** in the town of Celebration (near Kissimmee) at 511 Celebration Avenue (407 566 1633 or **www.commpres.com**).

Disney special occasions

Birthday badges: free badges can be found at City Hall in the *Magic Kingdom Park* and Guest Services at *Epcot, Disney-MGM Studios* and *Disney's Animal Kingdom Theme Park*. Cast Members like to make a fuss over children (and adults!) wearing a birthday badge.

Birthday cakes: contact room service at your resort or Guest Services at one of the parks. All Disney restaurants can offer cakes (from $8.99). Be sure

Downtown Disney West Side

TriceraTop Spin at Disney's Animal Kingdom

© Disney

to tell the Cast Member at check-in (or when you make your reservation) as well as hostesses and/or servers in restaurants if someone in your group has a birthday. While not guaranteed, Disney staff often go out of their way to make the day special. If characters know it's a birthday when they sign a child's autograph book, they may add a special birthday wish in it.

Birthday cruise: the IllumiNations Birthday Cruise (to *Epcot*) provides cake, drinks, streamers and balloons for a 90-minute tour from *Disney's Yacht and Beach Club Resort* marina for $275.

Birthday parties: *Disney's Beach Club, Boardwalk* and *Animal Kingdom Lodge* resorts all arrange themed birthday parties with various lunch options at their kids' clubs for ages 4 and up. A 2-hour party for up to 12 guests is $200; 3 hours is $300. Parties are 11am–1 or 2pm. *Winter-Summerland Miniature Golf* hosts 2-hour birthday parties for 10 or more, including pizza, soda, cake and a round of mini-golf at $15.95 a head, plus tax. Call 407 939 7529 (at least a week in advance) for either. *DisneyQuest* has Birthday Tickets at $33/adult ($27 for 3–9s), which include admission, a meal coupon, one $5 Prize Play card and 20% off merchandise at the Emporium (good for day of the event only).

Safety first

While crime is not a serious issue in central Florida, this is still big-city America so don't leave your common sense at home.

International Drive has its own dedicated police unit (a division of the Orlando City Police), with several dozen officers patrolling purely this long tourist corridor, arranging crime prevention seminars with local hotels and generally ensuring I-Drive takes good care of its visitors. You will often see these police out on mountain bikes, and they are a polite, helpful bunch should you need assistance. Tourism is such a vital part of the economy, the authorities have a highly safety-conscious attitude. However, it would be foolish to ignore the usual safety guidelines when travelling abroad.

BRITTIP

Don't want to take your mobile with you for fear of high charges? Hire a phone for your holidays from **Adam Phones** and take advantage of its special local rates for the US. Call 0800 123 000 or visit **www.adam phones.com**

Emergencies

General: for police, fire department or ambulance, dial 911 (9-911 from your hotel room). It is a good idea to make sure your children are aware of this number, while for smaller-scale crises (mislaid tickets or passports, rescheduled flights, etc.) your holiday company should have an emergency contact number in the hotel reception. If you are travelling independently and run into passport or other problems that need the assistance of the **British Consulate** in Orlando, its office is at Sun Bank Towers, 200 South Orange Avenue, with walk-in visitors' hours 9.30am–noon and 2–4pm, or call 407 426 7855

(9.30am–4pm). **Phonecards,** which you need to make a call from a local payphone – and are much cheaper than using your hotel room phone – are available from most 7–Eleven stores or from your tour rep.

Hotel security

While in your hotel, always use door peepholes and security chains when someone knocks at the door. DON'T open the door to strangers without asking for identification, and check with the hotel desk if you are still not sure. It is stating the obvious, but keep doors and windows locked at all times and always use deadlocks and security chains. Always take your cash, credit cards, valuables and car keys when you go out (or put them in the room safe), and don't leave the door open at any time, even if you are just popping down the corridor to the ice machine.

Most hotels now have electronic card-locks (which cannot be duplicated) for extra security and can offer deposit boxes in addition to the standard in-room mini-safes. Don't

Dinosaur World

BRITTIP

If your room has already been cleaned before you go out for the day, hang the 'Do Not Disturb' sign on the door. Always keep your valuables out of sight, whether in the hotel or the car.

be afraid to ask reception staff for safety advice for the surrounding areas or if you are travelling somewhere you are not sure about.

Safety is a major issue for the Central Florida Hotel/Motel Association and hotel staff are usually well briefed to be helpful. A bumbag (Americans say 'fanny pack'!) is a better bet than a shoulder bag or handbag.

And try not to look too obviously like a tourist! The map over the steering wheel is a giveaway, but other no-nos are wearing lots of jewellery and carrying lots of camera equipment. The biggest giveaway is leaving a camera or camcorder on view in the car (and the heat may ruin them). Finally, and this is VERY strong police advice, in the unlikely event of being confronted by an assailant, DO NOT resist or 'have a go', as this can often make a bad situation worse.

Money matters

It is useful to know dollar travellers' cheques can be used as cash and can be readily replaced if lost or stolen, so it is not necessary (as well as not advisable) to carry large amounts of cash around. However, sterling travellers' cheques can be cashed only in major banks – most outlets will not accept them. You will need to carry ID with you in many cases, though, even for credit card purchases (the new UK driving licence card is useful for this).

BRITTIP

For your journey to the US, use a business address rather than your home address on all your luggage. It is less conspicuous and safer should any item be stolen or misplaced.

Now you can order our special **Park Touring Plans** separately and build your own itinerary. We have designed these special touring plans especially for those who like to work things out themselves (or who might be too late to order our *Personalised Itinerary Planner*). Each park plan can be bought separately, so you just need to decide which parks you are likely to visit, then go to our online bookstore at **www.askdaisy.net/orlando**. Simply select which park plans you want, add them to your shopping basket and check out. There are 3 different categories of plan: for parents with pre-school children; for parents with older children; and for those without children. The plans all run to 3 pages for each park and should add significantly to your enjoyment, as well as helping to ensure you get the best out of your holiday and avoid the worst of the queues.

The **Secrets of the Parks** is another new product that we have been working on for some time, and which has been Susan's particular hobby-horse. It's a series of e-books looking at little-known and hidden facets of the 4 Disney parks and the Universal Orlando duo. Guaranteed to be an asset to the repeat visitor, they provide a wealth of detail on a number of often-overlooked features; highlight fascinating facts behind the attractions; reveal some of the clever interactive elements that many people miss; and tell the story of the parks in a unique, user-friendly way from an independent standpoint. Buy all 6 and you have the equivalent of a full book's worth of extra reading and insight into the best theme parks in the world. Log on to **www.askdaisy.net/orlando** and check out our bookstore for more details. Want to learn more about Simon and Susan's work? Visit **www.venesstravelmedia.com**

BRITTIP

Want the best exchange rate for your holiday cash? Check out **www.comparetravelmoney.co.uk** for the best deals on a day-by-day basis.

Having a credit card is almost essential as they are accepted everywhere and provide extra buying security. In some cases, notably car hire, you can't operate without your flexible friend. Visa, Mastercard and American Express are all widely accepted. It is worth separating the larger notes from the smaller ones in your wallet to avoid flashing all your money in view. Losing £200 of travellers' cheques shouldn't ruin your holiday – but losing $300 in cash might. All of the theme parks have cash dispensers (or ATM machines, as they are known in the US) at which you can use your credit card to withdraw cash. Some UK banks (notably Nationwide and Chase Bank) have no currency conversion charges for using their credit card in the US.

Take note: all Orlando prices, both in this book and on every price tag you see, do not include the 6–7% Florida Sales Tax. There is also a 4–5% Resort Tax on hotel rooms.

Car safety

Car crime has led to some lurid headlines in the past, especially in the Miami area in the mid-1990s. Once again, it pays to make basic safety checks before you set off. The first thing is to familiarise yourself with the car's controls BEFORE driving off – which button is the air-conditioning, which control operates the indicators, where the windscreen wiper switch is, and so on.

Also, try to memorise your route in advance, even if it is only a case of knowing the road numbers. Most hire firms now give good directions to all the hotels, so check them before you set off. Make sure the petrol tank is well filled and never let it get near empty. Running out of 'gas' in an unfamiliar area holds obvious

Orlando Fire Museum

Twister at Universal

hazards. If you stray off your pre-determined route, stick to well-lit areas and ask for directions only from official businesses like hotels and petrol stations or the police.

BRITTIP

American banknotes are all the same size and predominantly green, with just the occasional splash of colour in the newer notes. The only real difference is the picture of the president and the denomination in each corner.

You will find THREE kinds of police locally. The **State** police (in khaki uniforms) drive beige-and-black cars with circular blue badges with 'State Trooper' and 'FHP' (Florida Highway Patrol) on and are mainly found on the motorways. Each **County** then has its own police force, which drives white vehicles with gold stars marked 'Orange County Sheriff', or 'Osceola County Sheriff', and similar (both Orange and Osceola County deputies have green uniforms). Bigger cities also have **City** police, and Orlando's drive white cars with blue and yellow stripes and have dark blue uniforms. Learn more at **www.fhp.state.fl.us**, **www.ocso.com**, **www.osceola.org** and **www.cityoforlando.net/police**

Always try to park close to your destination where there are plenty of

lights and DO NOT get out if there are suspicious characters around. Always keep windows closed (and air-conditioning on), and don't hesitate to lock the doors from the inside if you feel threatened (larger cars have doors that lock automatically as you drive off). Don't forget to lock up when you leave the car. Not all rental cars have central locking, so check. It is comforting to know Orlando does not have any no-go areas in the main tourist parts. The nearest is the portion of the Orange Blossom Trail south of downtown Orlando. This hosts a selection of strip clubs and 'adult bars' that can be downright seedy at night.

For more information on safety, contact the Community Affairs office of Orange County Police (407 836 3720) or the International Drive police team office (407 351 9368).

Mini-golf at Daytona Beach

Let us plan your holiday ...

... with our unique *Personalised Itinerary Planner*

In conjunction with the *Brit's Guide* website – **www.askdaisy.net/orlando** – our *Personalised Itinerary Planner* (PIP) will help you get the very most out of your time in central Florida. *This is a service no other agency can offer.* We will design an itinerary tailored to your individual plans for the parks and attractions of central Florida. In your planner (which usually runs to 30-plus pages for a 2-week itinerary), we will indicate the best days to visit the parks to avoid the crowds, all the main show and parade times, any rides that may be closed for refurbishment and provide a detailed touring plan for each park, a shopping guide, updates on new rides, etc., as well as up-to-the-minute advice right from the source of the fun, plus a host of additional Brit Tips and Brit Picks (our special favourites) that we can't fit into this book.

All you have to do is visit the *Brit's Guide* website and click on the **Itinerary Planner** link. Fill out the online form with your travel dates, hotel and family details, the tickets you have bought (or are buying) and what you would like to fit into your visit. Submit the form, along with your payment, and you will receive an acknowledgement of your requirements. A few days before you go, you will receive, by email, your *Personalised Itinerary Planner*, which will consist of:

1   An official *Brit's Guide* welcome from Simon and Susan Veness.

2   A full day-by-day plan for the length of your holiday.

3   A touring strategy for ALL 8 main parks, the water parks and shopping centres, avoiding the crowds and taking advantage of the latest developments.

4   An alternative plan in case of bad weather.

5   All the main parade and fireworks times with your daily plans.

6   A note of any rides/shows that are closed during your visit.

7   A special selection of Brit Tips and local advice specifically for you.

8   Our Brit Picks – a guide to a range of personal favourites from restaurants to shops – that we feel may appeal to you most.

9   The ultimate insider knowledge, as both Simon and Susan are based in the heart of the Orlando magic and are fully up to date on all developments.

10 Our special bonus – an exclusive Platinum VIP Passport for Orlando Premium Outlets (not available to the general public), providing extra savings at select upmarket stores at this fabulous shopping venue (in addition to its free VIP Coupon Book we offer to all readers – see inside Back Cover).

All in all, it adds up to the most comprehensive package of specialised holiday information anywhere, and it represents the secret to the most fun, in the most hassle-free way, in the most exciting place on earth. What more could you ask for? Just check us out on **www.askdaisy.net/orlando** and we'll do the rest for you.

Please note: There is a minimum order period, so do check the website and make sure you apply for your PIP in good time before your holiday (usually at least 2 weeks). We are not a travel agency or ticket service and you MUST know your ticket requirements in advance.

Know before you go

You can contact these organisations for advance information. **Visit Florida** (online at **www.visitflorida.com/uk**) has an information line (0870 770 1177) on which you can order a copy of its free Vacation Guide. The **Orlando Tourism Bureau** in London has a 24-hour information line (0800 018 6760) where you can request its free holiday planning pack, or **www.orlando info.com/uk/** and request (or download) its free (and valuable) **Orlando Magicard** (see page 13). You

BRITTIP

You'll find masses of info on all things Orlando on the fun-packed discussion forums at **www.wdw info.com** and **www.attraction-tickets-direct.co.uk**, to which we also contribute. They also have features, theme park info, restaurant advice, news, weather, facts and tips.

can also visit the **Kissimmee Convention & Visitors Bureau** at **www.floridakiss.com**

It's worth checking Orlando's ONLY official **Visitor Center** (daily 8am–7pm) at 8723 International Drive (407 363 5872) for discounted attraction tickets, free brochures and accommodation advice, free information pamphlets and maps. The **Kissimmee Visitor Center** (8am–5pm Mon–Fri) is at 1925 E Irlo Bronson Memorial Highway, or Highway 192 (407 847 5000 or toll-free in the US on 1800 333 5477) and also

offers free maps, discount coupons and brochures.

The official sites aren't bad, though Disney's can be hard work: **www.disneyworld.co.uk** (for opening hours, rides, parades, etc. and bookings). Then see **www.universal orlando.com**, **www.seaworld.com** and **www.buschgardens.com**. The local newspaper's online service (**www.orlandosentinel.com**) is packed with info (especially for shopping, dining and nightlife), while the free Orlando Weekly is also worth checking (**www.orlandoweekly.com**).

Among the many other useful websites are **www.thedibb.co.uk** ('Disney with a British accent'), the well-designed **www.wdisneyw.co.uk** (with more pages for UK visitors), **www.allearsnet.com** (notably the Disney dining section), and **www.orlandorocks.com** (for all theme park addicts). Now, on to the next step of the holiday, your transport…

Orlando Convention & Visitor Bureau Center on International Drive

© OCVB

3

Driving and Car Hire

For the majority, the introduction to Orlando proper comes immediately after clearing the airport via the potentially bewildering road system in a newly acquired, automatic, left-hand-drive hire car. Yet driving here is a lot easier and more enjoyable than in the UK. Anyone familiar with the M25 should find Florida FAR less stressful.

Before you get to your hire car, though, you need to be aware of your arrival details at either Orlando International Airport or Orlando Sanford International Airport.

🇬🇧 **BRITTIP**

Make sure you fill out your Immigration form accurately. The official will send you to the back of the queue if there are errors or crossings out. For country of residence put 'UK', and you must give a valid US address for your first night's accommodation.

Orlando International Airport

This is one of the most modern and enjoyable airports in the world, but it can be bewildering for newcomers. All flights arrive at one of 4 satellite terminals and you then take a shuttle tram (like a mini monorail) to the main terminal. If you are an **international arrival** with British Airways or Virgin Atlantic, you arrive at the satellite for Gates 60–99, where you first need to go through Immigration and Customs.

There are individual queues for each of the Immigration kiosks, and you just need to get in any of the lines marked 'Visitors' and wait for the official to call you forward (the lines on the right tend to move a bit quicker as they are next to the US Citizens lanes, which are often not too busy). Once through Immigration, you need to collect your baggage from the carousel and go through the Customs check. But then you have to deposit your checked luggage on *another* conveyor belt to take it to the main terminal while you go upstairs to the shuttle with your hand luggage only (an odd system, which the airport is trying to avoid in future). Once in the main terminal, you are on Level 3 and you follow signs down to Baggage Claim B on Level 2. You need to allow about an hour from arrival to reaching the car hire desks in the main terminal.

For anyone arriving on a US **domestic flight** (i.e. from another US gateway), you arrive at the satellite terminal and proceed *straight* to the main terminal on the shuttle to collect your baggage on Level 2 (either A or B side, depending on arrival gate).

Once at the main baggage claim, porters can help you to Level 1 (for $1/bag tip) for all car hire, shuttles and buses. Trolleys need $3 in change (or a credit card) to operate – they are not free as at UK airports. Kerbside pick-up is just outside the doors on Level 2. If a driver is meeting you, he will wait on Level 2, either at the bottom of the escalators or by your baggage reclaim. Several tour operators have help desks here, too.

The public bus system, Lynx (see page 54), operates ONLY from the A side of Level 1, in spaces 38–41. Links 11, 41 and 51 depart every ½ hour (less frequently on Sundays and bank holidays) for Orlando city centre (about 45 minutes away), while Link 42 serves International Drive (about a 60-minute journey). Fares are $1.50.

BRITTIP

Visit www.orlandoairports.net for a photo preview of the arrival process at Orlando International Airport and other handy info.

If you are arriving late, consider staying at the **Hyatt Regency** hotel inside the airport or the recently revamped **Orlando Airport Marriott** nearby (see Chapter 4), rather than driving off tired. You will feel far more ready to drive the next day (and the car hire queues will be shorter).

The hire companies with check-in desks right at the airport are Dollar, National, L & M, Budget, Avis, and of course Brit's Guide partners **Alamo**, and all offer a full service (NB: Alamo used to be off-airport but is now well established inside the airport for maximum convenience. Look out also for its clever new automated self-service kiosks, as these are gradually being introduced to their busier locations and can save even more queuing time.) A phone desk on Level 1 connects to another 17 companies at off-airport depots, including Hertz, E-Z, Thrifty and Enterprise. Off-airport firms have a free shuttle on

Level 1 to take you to their depots, but obviously this takes much longer. Hertz and Avis are the biggest US companies, but Dollar and Alamo are tops for tourist business. Dollar is used for packages with Thomson, Airtours, Virgin, Style Holidays, Travel City and First Choice: Alamo is the main client for Funway, Jetsave, Kuoni, BA Holidays and Thomas Cook.

BRITTIP

If you are hiring a car from one of the on-airport companies, save time by sending the driver to complete the paperwork BEFORE collecting your luggage on Level 2.

After completing your paperwork with the on-site companies, you walk out of Level 1, across the road to the multi-storey car park and collect your car. It's that simple. When you drive out of the airport, DON'T look for signs to 'Orlando'. The main tourist areas are south and west of the city proper, so follow the respective signs for your accommodation. For International Drive (or I-Drive), take the North Exit and the Beachline Expressway (Route 528) west until it crosses I-Drive just north of SeaWorld. Most hotels on I-Drive are to the north, so keep right at the exit.

BRITTIP

The Martin Andersen Beachline (formerly Beeline) Expressway (528) and Greeneway (417) are both toll roads, so make sure you have some US currency before leaving the airport. Toll booths hate to change notes above $20, while some auto-tolls take ONLY coins.

For Kissimmee, Disney and villas in Clermont/Davenport, take the South Exit for 3mls/5km and pick up the Central Florida Greeneway (Highway 417) west. For most Disney resorts, take exit 6 and follow the signs; for *Animal Kingdom* resorts, use exit 3 and take Osceola Parkway west. For eastern Kissimmee, come off Highway 417 at exit 11, the Orange

Blossom Trail (Highway 17/92), and go south. For west Kissimmee and Clermont/Davenport (Highway 27), take exit 2, turn right on Celebration Avenue and left on to Highway 192, which runs west all the way to Highway 27.

Orlando Sanford International Airport

Arriving at Sanford (in Seminole County) couldn't be easier. The list of airlines visiting this easy-to-use airport is growing all the time but currently includes Travel City Direct, XL Airways, MyTravel, Thomsonfly, First Choice, Monarch, Thomas Cook Airlines, Flyglobespan and Icelandair. It generally takes only 30–40 minutes from arrival to leaving the baggage hall, but there may be delays in peak season when several planes arrive at once as its handling capacity is limited. It's only a short walk from the plane to the immigration hall (where the queuing has just 2 lines that feed through to the kiosks), you then collect your baggage, pass through Customs and walk straight out to car hire, shuttle or taxi pick-up.

BRITTIP

Don't want to drive? Consider a multi-centre stay within Orlando itself, staying first at, say, I-Drive or Universal Orlando and then a Disney resort, to get the best of free or cheap transport options.

You will find the tour operator welcome desks and Dollar car hire offices immediately in front of you, while our *Brit's Guide* **Alamo** partners have a large, new welcome centre that you reach via a covered walkway and boardwalk behind this, and its British-dedicated operation is pretty smooth. National, Avis, Enterprise, Thrifty and Hertz are also on-airport (turn sharp right out of Customs then take the first door on the right), while there are another 4 that can be called from off-airport depots. Look up more on **www.orlandosanfordairport.com**

It may be 35mls/56km to the north and involve more driving (and taxis and shuttles are more expensive – a town car service would be around $100 one-way to I-Drive and a taxi $80), but you usually save time by your quicker exit. There is just one main road out, on to Lake Mary Boulevard, and you then take the Seminole Expressway (Highway 417, which becomes Central Florida Greeneway in Orange County) south. The slip road on to this toll motorway is just under the flyover on your LEFT, and you need $4.50 to reach Disney or Kissimmee or $3.75 for I-Drive (via the Beachline Expressway). You can avoid the tolls by staying on Lake Mary Blvd for 6mls/10km until you get to I-4, but you are likely to hit heavy traffic through the city centre. The Expressway/Greeneway is an excellent, easy-driving introduction to Orlando, even if it does cost a few dollars. For radio traffic news and reports, tune to 1680AM (WLAA) or 580AM (WDBO). If you have a tri-band mobile phone, dial 511 for traffic info on I-4.

ORLANDO WITHOUT A CAR

Although being mobile is advisable, it is possible to survive without a car. However, few attractions are within walking distance of hotels, and taxis can be expensive. You also need to plan with greater precision to allow for extra travelling time (and with children, taking buses can be tiring). For non-drivers, your best base is either *Walt Disney World* itself (free transport throughout, but harder to get to the rest of Orlando) or

The I-Ride trolley bus

International Drive for its location, 'walkability' and the great I-Ride Trolley. Many hotels have free shuttles to some of the parks or a cheap, regular mini-bus service. There are basically 4 main options: public transport; shuttle services; town cars and limousines; and taxis.

Public transport

The reliable, cheap, but slightly plodding **Lynx bus system** (407 841 5969, **www.golynx.com**) covers much of Orlando. Its online system map shows all its routes (or 'links') and the main attractions. Worth noting are **Link 42** from Orlando International Airport to I-Drive; **Links 56** and **304** to Disney from Kissimmee (the Osceola Square Mall all the way along Highway 192, via Old Town and Celebration to Disney's Transportation & Ticket Center (T&TC) by the *Magic Kingdom*) and the I-Drive area (Oak Ridge Road to *Downtown Disney*, via Sand Lake Drive and Vineland Road); **Link 18** from Kissimmee to downtown Orlando (from Osceola Square Mall, east on Highway 192 and north on Boggy Creek Road, Buenaventura Boulevard and Orange Avenue); **Link 55**, which covers Kissimmee's Highway 192 from Osceola Square Mall west to Four Corners/Summer Bay Resort; **Link 38**, I-Drive to downtown Orlando (from the Convention Center via The Mercado, Wet 'n Wild, Kirkman Road and I-4); and **Links 50** (from the T&TC via SeaWorld and I-4) and **300** (from *Downtown Disney* via I-4), from Disney to downtown Orlando.

Lynx fares are $1.50 a ride (transfers are free) or $12 for a weekly pass (children 6 and under go free with a full-fare passenger). The service is every 30 minutes in the main areas, every 15 minutes 6–9am and 3.30–6.30pm, but you must have the right change. Lynx bus stops are marked by pink paw-print signs and all buses are wheelchair accessible. There can be long queues for buses out of Disney at closing time, so you

could take Disney transport to *Downtown Disney*, then get a taxi back to your hotel (about $25 to I-Drive).

The I-Drive area also has the great-value **I-Ride Trolley**, which operates 2 routes along a 14ml/23km stretch of this tourist corridor. The *Main Line* has 85 stops and runs from Universal Orlando resort area (Windhover Drive and Major Boulevard) in the north, via Prime Outlets shopping centre at the top of I-Drive, to SeaWorld via Westwood Boulevard and Sea Harbor Drive, and south to Orlando Premium Outlets. The *Green Line* basically covers Universal Boulevard, with 22 stops from SeaWorld north to the junction of I-Drive and Kirkman Road. Running every day, 8am–10.30pm at roughly 20-minute intervals (30 minutes on the Green Line), it costs $1/trip (25c for seniors) – please have the right change – or you can buy Unlimited Ride passes for 1, 3, 5, 7 or 14 days at $3, $5, $7, $9, $16. If you need to transfer between routes, ask for a transfer coupon when you board (transfers are free with Unlimited Ride passes). Kids 12 and under go free with an adult, and all trolleys have hydraulic lifts for wheelchairs. Passes are sold at more than 100 locations in the I-Drive area, including the Official Visitor Center and most hotel desks (407 248 9590 or US freephone 1866 243 7483, **www.iridetrolley.com**).

Another regular service worth noting is from SeaWorld to Busch Gardens in Tampa, with 6 departure points, daily 8.15–9.30am. Called the **Busch Shuttle Express**, it costs $10/person

BRITTIP

Cheapest way to get from I-Drive to Disney? Take the $1.50 Lynx bus Link 50 from SeaWorld – 6600 Sea Harbor Drive – to the Transportation & Ticket Center next to the *Magic Kingdom Park*. All Disney transport then operates from here. You can use the I-Ride Trolley to get to SeaWorld.

Mears town car

but is FREE if you have bought Busch tickets in advance (included in the 5-Park FlexTicket). For more details, see page 11 or call locally on 1800 221 1339 toll-free.

Shuttle services

An alternative to public transport is the raft of well-organised firms offering set-fee shuttles to the attractions that pick up at hotels. There are more than a dozen, offering everything from Hummer limos to buses. **Mears** (407 423 5566, **www.mearstransportation.com**) has the most comprehensive service, with a 1,000-vehicle fleet from limousines to town cars and coaches. Typical round-trip shuttle fares would be: airport to *Walt Disney World*, round-trip $31 adults, $23 under 12s, under 4s free ($19 and $15 one way); airport to I-Drive, $27 and $20 ($17 and $13 one way); airport to Highway 192 in Kissimmee $43 and $34 ($25 and $21 one way); *Walt Disney World* to Universal Orlando, $16 round trip; I-Drive to *Walt Disney World*, $16; I-Drive or *Walt Disney World* to Kennedy Space Center, $30. You can book a Mears shuttle on arrival at one of its desks in the luggage halls, but be aware it can be a longish journey if it has a full van making several hotel drop-offs before yours.

Several shopping malls also have their own shuttle service. **Lake Buena Vista Factory Stores** collects guests free each day from 49 hotels in the Orlando and Kissimmee areas (check your hotel for details, call 407 363 1093 or visit **www.lbvfs.com**); Orlando

Premium Outlets (407 390 0000) provides a free shuttle from the Lake Buena Vista area and for $10 a round trip from Kissimmee hotels; and the **Florida Mall** has a free shuttle twice daily from hotels on I-Drive and in Lake Buena Vista (check with your hotel concierge or call 407 851 6255).

Excursion services are also offered by *Brit's Guide* partners **Florida Dolphin Tours** (407 352 5151, **www.florida dolphintours.com**) and **Gator Tours** (see pages 255–6).

> **BRITTIP**
>
> A 'town car' is an American term for a deluxe saloon, such as a Cadillac or Lincoln.

Town cars and limousines

When it comes to limousine and town car services, look no further than *Brit's Guide* partner **Skyy Limousines**. Not only is it a dynamic, British-run company, all our readers qualify for a special *12½% discount* by using the coupon with sister company Florida Dolphin Tours (see inside back cover). Just call on 407 352 4644 and ask for the *Brit's Guide* discount. Skyy has some of the latest and smartest cars (including the Hummer limo; see **www.floridadolphintours.com/skyy**), personable staff and offers transport throughout central Florida. It covers airport and cruise transfers, special occasions, a night on the town and all-day services, and can also provide tailor-made journeys. Sister company **Florida Dolpin Tours** offers several meal-and-limo combinations (great for the entire family), featuring dinner with the Disney characters followed by a drive around town and a visit to the *Downtown Disney* area – a real holiday highlight. **Skyy's Town Car** service also specialises in airport transfers, trips to the beach, concerts and personalised excursions, and rates are always competitive.

Quick Transportation (407 354 2456 or 1888 784 2522, **www.quicktrans portation.com**) is also a good bet for airport transfers and tailor-made transport packages. Town cars cope with a family of 4, while luxury vans cater for larger parties and all offer a ½-hour grocery stop, if required, for an extra $20. Luxury van rates (for up to 7) one-way from the airport range from $49.75 to the I-Drive area up to $76.50 for the farthest parts of *Walt Disney World*. Up to 11 can use a van for a small additional fee per person. Larger parties may need a luggage trailer for $20 extra each way. Town car rates are $82.50 from the airport to anywhere in Greater Orlando and $164 for a round trip, while stretch limos are $139.50 and $278 (all prices subject to a fuel surcharge). It serves all the parks and attractions and offers online quotes for all services.

Taxis

For groups of 4 or 5, taxis can be a more cost-effective option than the shuttles. Orlando International Airport to I-Drive would be $30–35 (plus tip), making it around $7 each for 5; $43–55 for Kissimmee; $55 to *Magic Kingdom* resorts and $50 for the *Epcot* resort area; $10 from I-Drive to Universal Orlando; and $25 from I-Drive to *Downtown Disney*. You will find plenty of taxis waiting in ranks at the parks, hotels and shopping centres, but they don't cruise around looking for fares, so it is usually best to book one in advance. You also need to ensure you choose a reliable, fully insured company (Orlando has what are known as 'gypsy' cab drivers, who appear to be with reputable firms but often do not have full passenger insurance). Check the name and

International Drive by night

© OCVB

phone number of the cab company is clearly displayed on the side, the driver's ID and insurance are visible and their rates are shown on the window or inside the car. 'Gypsy' drivers look for fares in the airport baggage hall, which is strictly illegal – all legitimate taxis should be in the rank on Level 1.

The **Mears** group (407 422 2222) has 3 firms that work (via a computer system) through it – Checker Cabs, Yellow Cabs and City Cabs – all of which are reliable. Mears is the main taxi company for Orlando Sanford International Airport, and you can pre-book its cabs for around $78 to I-Drive, $93 to Lake Buena Vista and $98 to Disney hotels. Most taxis are metered but it is also acceptable to ask what the fare is in advance. Other reputable firms include **Ace Metro/ Luxury Cab** (407 855 1111), **Star Taxis** (407 857 9999) and **Diamond Cab Co** (407 523 3333). Several hotels have town cars at their ranks, and these will not have meters, so you can either ask the fare or call one of the companies listed above yourself.

BRITTIP
Your first call for car hire should be to *Brit's Guide* partners Alamo. See inside the front cover for our special readers' offer.

THE CAR

Ultimately, having a car is the key to being in charge of your holiday and, on a weekly basis, it tends to work out quite reasonable, too. Weekly rental rates can be as low as $100 for the smallest car, an **Economy** (or sub-compact), usually a Fiesta-sized hatchback; next up is the **Compact**, a small family saloon like a Ford Focus; the **Midsize** (or Intermediate) is a more spacious 4-door, 5-seater; and the **Fullsize** would be a larger-style executive car. You can go up the scale further, with **Premium**, **Luxury** and **Convertible**, plus the **Minivan** (a Ford

Galaxy or Renault Espace type). The car models, will, of course, all be mainly American – Chevrolet, Dodge, Pontiac, Buick, Chrysler, Ford, Mercury and Lincoln.

🇬🇧 BRITTIP

Double check you have your driving licence BEFORE you leave home (both parts of it with the new photo-card type). Without it you will simply NOT be given a hire car.

But beware the low starting rates. There are a number of essential insurances, taxes and surcharges, and these can take the weekly rate up to $300 or more. However, all the big rental companies now offer all-inclusive rates, which can work out significantly cheaper if booked in advance in the UK, and you also benefit from easier processing at the Orlando end, making the whole business quicker.

🇬🇧 BRITTIP

The boot (trunk) size of American cars tends to be slightly smaller than the British equivalent. And you will not get 7 adults PLUS all their luggage in a 7-seat people carrier ('van')!

For other car rental companies, you can try **Dollar** (0808 234 7524), **Avis** (0870 60 60 100), **Budget** (0880 181181), **Thrifty** (01494 751 600), **Hertz** (0870 844 8844), **National** (0870 400 4581) or **Suncars** (0870 500 5566). The scale of the car-hire operation is huge, with as many as 1,000 visitors arriving at a time. Most British holiday companies offer 'free car hire', but that does not mean it won't cost you anything. It is only the rental cost that is free and you must still pay the insurance, taxes and other extras BEFORE you drive away (which makes the all-inclusive packages more attractive).

Having a credit card is essential, and there are two main kinds of insurance, the most important being the Loss or Collision Damage Waiver (LDW or CDW). This costs $23–25 a day and covers you for any damage to your hire car. You can do without it, but the hire company will insist on a deposit in the order of $1,500 on your credit card (and you are liable for ANY damage). You will also be offered Supplemental Liability Insurance (SLI) or Extended Protection at around $13 a day. Not an essential, but it does cover you against being sued by any litigation-happy American you may happen to bump into.

Relatively new and again optional is the Underinsured Motorists Protection (in case somebody with only minimal cover runs into you) at around $6 a day. Drivers must be at least 21, and those under 25 have to pay an extra $25 a day. Other rental costs include local and Florida state taxes, which can add $20 a week to your final bill, and the Airport User Fee at $6–7 a day. Then there's fuel, though this is still much cheaper than in the UK.

🇬🇧 BRITTIP

Be firm with the car hire company check-in clerk; some can push you into having extras, like car upgrades, that you don't need.

For those on a budget, you can cut costs by taking travel insurance through specialists like **Extrasure** (01242 518300, **www.extrasure**

Sunshine Skyway Bridge at St Pete's

© OCVB

online.co.uk), whose Americasure policy offers both LDW and SLI at around £14 a day. You may still need to leave a credit card imprint with the hire firm, but it should accept these policies (but check in advance).

BRITTIP
Ask to return the tank full yourself, as this saves on the hire company's (expensive) fill-up option.

Most people soon find driving in America is a pleasure, mainly because nearly all hire cars are automatics and rarely more than a year old. And, because speed limits are lower (and rigidly enforced), you won't often be rushed into taking the wrong turn. Keep your foot on the brake when you are stationary as automatics tend to creep forward, and always put the automatic gear lever in 'P' (for Park) after switching off.

BRITTIP
With an automatic, you won't be able to take the keys out of the ignition unless you put the gear lever in the 'Park' position first.

Controls

All cars have air-conditioning, which is essential for most of the year. Turn on the fan with the A/C button or it won't work! Don't worry if a small pool of liquid forms under the car – it's condensation off the A/C unit. Power steering is also universal and larger cars have cruise control, which lets you set the desired speed and take your foot off the accelerator. There will be 2 buttons on the steering wheel, one to switch on cruise control, the other to set the desired speed. To cancel cruise control, either press the first button again or simply touch the brake.

The handbrake may also be different. Some cars have an extra foot pedal to the left of the brake, and you need to push this to engage the handbrake. To

release it, you pull the tab just above it, if there is one, or give a second push on the pedal. The car probably won't start unless the gear lever is in 'P'. To put the car in 'D' for Drive, depress the main brake pedal. D1 and D2 are extra gears for steep hills (none in Florida!). Not all cars have central locking, so make sure you lock ALL the doors before leaving it.

Getting around

Your car-hire company should provide you with a basic map of Orlando, plus directions to your hotel. Insist they give you these, as all the hire companies make a big point of this in their literature. Try to familiarise yourself with the main roads in advance and learn to navigate by the road numbers (as it's mainly those that are given on the signposts) and the exit numbers of the main roads.

BRITTIP
Be organised – get your directions in advance off the internet at sites like www.mapquest.com or use Google Earth to source maps, directions and even check out the lie of the land in advance. Download it free from its website at http://earth.google.com

The system of signposting and road-naming can be confusing. For instance, you cannot fail to find the main attractions, but retracing your way back out can be tricky because park exits are often some distance from the entrance.

It is vital to learn the main road numbers (and directions, either east–west or north–south) around the attractions so you know where you are heading, and whether you want I-4 east/west or 192 as you exit *Epcot* or *Disney-MGM Studios*.

Exits off motorways can be on EITHER side of the carriageway, not just on the right, but you can overtake in ANY lane on multi-lane highways, not only the outside ones. Therefore, you can sit in the middle lane until you see your exit. You don't get much advance notice of turn-offs, though.

Orlando has yet to come up with a comprehensive tourist map of its streets, and the maps supplied by the car-rental companies tend to be simplified. It helps that none of the main attractions is off the beaten track, but the support of a front-seat navigator can be useful. Around town, road names are displayed at every junction, hung underneath the traffic lights but suspended ABOVE the road. This road name is NOT the road you are on, but the one that you are CROSSING. Once again there is no advance notice of each junction as it appears and the road names can be difficult to read as you approach them, especially at night, so keep your speed down if you think you are close to your turn-off, to get in the correct lane. If you do miss a turning, most roads are on a grid system, so it is usually easy to work your way back.

Occasionally you will meet a crossroads where no right of way is obvious. This is a 4-way stop, and the priority goes in order of arrival. So, when it's your turn, you just indicate and pull out slowly (America doesn't have many roundabouts, so this is the closest you may get to one).

BRITTIP

Disney is notoriously poor at sign-posting to help find your way out. Get a copy of its Transportation Guide/ Map from Guest Services.

Tolls and traffic lights

For the toll roads, have some change handy in amounts from 25c to $2. They all give change (in the GREEN lanes), but you will get through much quicker if you have the correct money (in the BLUE lanes). On minor exits of Osceola Parkway and the Greeneway, there are auto-toll machines only, so keep some loose change in the car.

As well as the obvious difference of driving on the 'wrong' side of the road, there are several differences in procedure. The most frequent British errors occur at traffic lights (which are hung above the road, not on posts). At a red light it is still possible to turn RIGHT, providing there is no traffic coming from the left and no pedestrians crossing, unless otherwise specified (signs will occasionally indicate 'No turn on red'). Turning left at the lights, you have the right of way with a green ARROW, but you have to give way to traffic from the other direction on a SOLID green.

The majority of accidents involving overseas visitors take place on left turns, so take extra care here. There is also no amber light from red to green, but there IS from green to red. A flashing amber light at a junction means proceed but watch for traffic joining the carriageway, while a flashing red light indicates it is okay to turn if the carriageway is clear.

BRITTIP

The Osceola Parkway toll road that runs parallel to Highway 192 is a much easier route into *Walt Disney World* from eastern Kissimmee and costs only $1.50. Use Sherberth Road for Disney access from west 192 or the new Western Beltway (Highway 429).

Restrictions

Speed limits are always well marked with black numbering on white signs and the police are pretty hot on speeding, with steep on-the-spot fines. Limits vary from 55–70mph/88–113kph on the Interstates (where there is also a 40mph/64kph minimum speed limit) to just 15–20mph/24–32kph in built-up areas.

Seat belts are compulsory for all front-seat passengers, while **child seats** must be used for under 4s and can be hired from the car companies at $10–15 a day (better still, bring your own or buy one locally for $70–80). Children aged 4 or 5 must use a seat belt, in the front or back, or have a child seat fitted.

It is illegal to park within 10ft/3m of a fire hydrant or a lowered kerb, and never park in front of a yellow-painted kerb – they are stopping points for emergency vehicles and you will be towed away. Never park ON a kerb, either. Park bonnet first – reverse parking is frowned upon because number plates are only on the rear of cars and police then can't see them. If you park parallel to the kerb, you must face the direction of traffic.

Flashing orange lights over the road indicate a school zone and school buses must not be overtaken in *either* direction when they are unloading and have their hazard lights on. U-turns are forbidden in built-up areas and where there is a solid line down the middle of the road. You must pull to the side of the road to allow emergency vehicles to pass when they have lights and/or sirens going. Also, on multi-lane highways in Florida, the recent Move Over law means you must pull out into an adjacent lane if you see a police car on the hard shoulder, or slow down if you can't move over. And you must put on your lights in the rain.

Biketoberfest Races, Daytona Beach

BRITTIP

On the Greeneway (417) heading south, just after exit 34, it appears to split into two where it meets Highway 408. Stay in the RIGHT lane to stay southbound.

Finally, DON'T drink and drive. Florida has strict laws, with penalties of up to 6 months in prison for first-time offenders. The blood-alcohol limit is lower than in Britain, so it is safer not to drink at all if you are driving. It is also illegal to carry open containers of alcohol in the car.

Bonus for AA members: your membership is recognised by the equivalent AAA in the US and you also benefit from a number of special offers. Take your AA card and, where you see the AAA 'Show & Save' signs in hotels, shops and restaurants, just produce it to enjoy the same money-saving benefits as the locals. Visit **www.aaasouth.com** and click on 'Savings' for the full low-down (use the zip code 32819 when prompted).

Accidents

In the unlikely event of an accident, no matter how minor, you must contact the police before the cars can be moved (except on the busy I-4). Car-hire firms will insist on a full police report for the insurance. If you break down, there should be an emergency number for the hire company in its literature or, if you are on a main highway, raise the bonnet and wait for one of the frequent police patrol cars to stop (or dial *FHP on your mobile). Always carry your driving licence (*both* parts with the new card type) and hire agreement forms in case you are stopped by the police.

Key routes

The main route through Orlando is **Interstate 4** (or I-4), a 4-, 6- or 8-lane motorway linking the coasts. Interstates are always indicated on blue shield-shaped signs. For most of its length, I-4 travels east–west but, around Orlando, it swings north–south, though directions are still given east (for north) or west (for south). All main motorways are prefixed I, the even numbers generally going east–west and odd numbers north–south. Federal Highways are the next grade down, numbered with black numerals on white shields, while state roads are known as Routeways and are prefixed SR (black numbers on white circular or rectangular signs). All the attractions of *Walt Disney World*, plus those of SeaWorld and Universal Orlando are well signposted from I-4. Historic Bok Sanctuary and Cypress Gardens are a 45-minute drive from central Orlando west (south) on I-4 and Highway 27, while Busch Gardens is 75–90 minutes down I-4 to Tampa. I-4 undergoes regular roadworks – and you can check the latest up-dates on the website **www.trans4mation.com**.

All American motorways now have their junctions numbered in mileage terms, which makes it easy to calculate journey distances. I-4 starts at exit 1 down in Tampa and goes all the way to exit 132 at Daytona. In Orlando, the main junctions run from exit 55, at Highway 27, to exit 83 (downtown Orlando) and exit 101, for the Seminole Expressway (417) and Sanford Airport.

International Drive (or I-Drive) is the second key local roadway, linking a 14½ml/24km ribbon of hotels, shops, restaurants and attractions like Wet 'n Wild, The Pointe Orlando and Festival Bay (I-Drive South, from Highway 192 in Kissimmee north to Route 535, is NOT the main stretch and the 2 sections are linked by a short stretch of Route 535 and World Center Drive). From I-4, take exits 71, 72, 74A or 75A going east (north), or 75B, 74A or 72 going west (south). To the north, I-Drive runs into Oak Ridge Road and the South Orange Blossom Trail,

which leads to downtown Orlando (junctions 82C-84 off I-4). I-Drive is also bisected by Sand Lake Road and runs into World Center Drive (536), to the south, also convenient for Disney.

I-Drive is a major tourist centre and makes an excellent base, especially around the Sand Lake Road junction, as it is fully pedestrian-friendly. It's a 20-minute drive to Disney and 10 minutes from Universal. However, at peak travel times, it's best to avoid the stretch from the Convention Center north, so use Universal Boulevard instead.

The other main tourist area is the city of **Kissimmee**, south of Orlando and south-east of Disney. Its features are grouped along a 20ml/32km stretch of the Irlo Bronson Memorial Highway (192), which intersects I-4 at junction 64B, and is only 10 minutes from *Walt Disney World*, 20 from SeaWorld and 25 from Universal. The downtown area of Kissimmee is off Main Street, Broadway and Emmett Street and is ideal for walking. A handy visual along Highway 192 is the Marker Series from Formosa Gardens (number 4) to just past Medieval Times (number 15). These highly visible signs are good locators for hotels, restaurants and attractions, and much of this stretch is also now walkable (although few places are

International Drive

close together). The unique Disney-inspired town of **Celebration** is also here (just south of *Walt Disney World*). At the west end of **Highway 192**, you find **Highway 27**, which runs north to Clermont and south to Davenport (and Haines City). Highway 27 is now a major area of holiday home developments which are, generally, quite convenient for *Walt Disney World*. However, many home owners here claim they are only '5 minutes from Disney', which is extremely misleading. It is usually a good 15 minutes from Highway 27 to the edge of Disney property. There is not much else here, though developers are starting to add shops and restaurants (notably several Publix supermarkets and a Wal-Mart).

The newest roadway, the (toll) **Western Beltway** (429) was completed late in 2006. This provides a western 'by-pass' to Disney, avoiding the often-crowded I-4 and links with the Florida Turnpike and Apopka (north of Orlando). More importantly, it offers a new western gateway to *Walt Disney World*, which is handy for the Davenport/Clermont areas. Check out the useful maps on **www.expresswayauthority.com**

Fuel

Nearly all American petrol ('gas'), stations are self-service and most require you to pay before filling up. However, the pumps usually allow you to pay by credit card without having to visit the cashier's office (some stations have switched to

Highway 192 in Kissimmee

© OCVB

asking for a local zip code with a credit card swipe, and this means you DO need to go inside). Always use unleaded fuel and, to activate the petrol pump, you may need first to lift the lever underneath the pump nozzle. RaceTrac and Hess petrol stations are often the cheapest. The two Hess stations in *Walt Disney World* are, surprisingly, among the cheapest in the area, while the Wal-Mart on SR535 (Vineland Road) is also a cheap option. Petrol stations in Lake Buena Vista just outside Disney are outrageously expensive!

Local maps

The best of the free maps is the bright orange *Welcome Guide Map* (also full of discount coupons), available in the main tourist areas, and the pull-out map inside the *Kissimmee-St Cloud Visitors' Guide* (from the Official Visitor Center on East Highway 192, call 407 847 5000). You can also download some useful maps from **www.floridakiss.com** (under Travel Tools). AA members are also well catered for (see page 60). However, by far the best and most up-to-date map of the area is actually a British production, created by Disney fan (and cartographer) Steve Munns. **Orlando Maps** is his wonderful creation, and it was fully updated in 2007 at a price of £6.50 (including postage). It is magnificently detailed for the I-4 corridor, Highway 192 and *Walt Disney World*, with special sections on I-Drive and villa locations. All the main attractions, hotels and even many restaurants are clearly indicated and there is accompanying text and photographs to bring the whole thing to life. The website even provides regular updates to important landmarks and other insider tips. In our opinion it is the perfect companion to the *Brit's Guide* and you won't go wrong with it. Just visit **www.orlandomaps.co.uk** (online orders only).

Now, let's go on to the next vital step, your holiday accommodation…

Accommodation

or Making Sense of American Hotels, Motels and Condos

To list all the accommodation in this area would fill a book much larger than this. Metro Orlando has the second highest concentration of hotels in the world (after Las Vegas) and more are being built all the time – with 115,000 rooms and counting. Therefore what follows is a general guide to the bigger, better and budget types.

HOTELS

American hotels, particularly in the tourist areas, tend towards the motel type. The service and facilities are fine but are not necessarily all located in one main building. Your room may be in one of several blocks sited round the pool, restaurant or other amenities. Room size rarely alters, even from 2- to 4-star hotels; their amenities and services are the basis of their star ratings. A standard room usually has 2 double beds and will accommodate a family of 4 (couples should ask for a king room, with an extra-size bed). All hotels should offer non-smoking rooms.

The other feature of motel-type accommodation is often the lack of a restaurant, because American hotels operate almost exclusively on a room-only basis – meals are usually extra – so you may have to drive to the nearest restaurant (of which there are many – see Chapter 11) just for breakfast. Check the dining facilities before you book.

Most hotels are big, clean, efficient and great value. You'll find plenty of soft-drink and ice machines, with ice buckets in all the rooms (but it's much cheaper to buy drinks from a supermarket). All accommodation will be air-conditioned and, when it is really hot, you have to live with the drone of the A/C unit at night. If you need a more spacious room, look for one of the many suite hotels, which provide sitting rooms and mini-kitchens, as well as 1, 2 or even 3 bedrooms.

Note that the most expensive place from which to make a phone call is your hotel room. Most hotels add a 45–70% surcharge to every call (Disney resorts even add a

Disney's Boardwalk Resort

© Disney

connection fee), while you can also be charged for a call even if no one answers, if it rings 5 or more times. Buy a phonecard instead (see pages 38 and 46). Remember, too, hotel prices (in this book and in Orlando) are always per *room* (not per person). They will be cheaper out of the main holiday periods but can vary from month to month, with special deals at times.

Always ask for rates if you book yourself and check if any special rates apply during your visit (don't be afraid to ask for their 'best rate' at off-peak times, which can be lower than published rates). There may be an additional charge ($5–15/person) for more than 2 adults sharing the same room, plus there is a per night state tax and a resort fee that can add $10–20 to the rate.

⚜ BRITTIP

Buy soft drinks at the supermarket, and a polystyrene cooler for about $4 that you can fill from your hotel ice machine to keep drinks cold.

If you've just arrived and still need accommodation, visit one of the official Visitor Centers: International Drive just south of The Mercado (on the corner of Austrian Court, daily 8am–7pm; 407 363 5872); or on east Highway 192 in Kissimmee (8am–5pm; 407 847 5000), where they have brochures and info on all the latest

Disney's All-Star Movie Resort

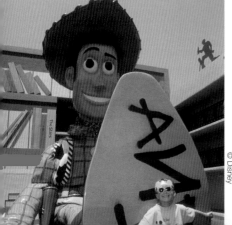

© Disney

Suite things

Suites hotels, virtually unknown in the UK, provide a combination of hotel and apartment, with extra value for large families or groups. Typically, a suites room gives you a living room and kitchenette, including microwave, coffee-maker, fridge, cutlery and crockery, while many offer a complimentary continental breakfast (or better). All have pools and grocery stores or snack bars and several have restaurants. They vary only in the number of bedrooms and can usually sleep 6–10 people.

deals. If you're keen on auction websites like **www.priceline.co.uk**, you may land a bargain. Other useful agencies are **Expedia** (0871 226 0808, **www.expedia.co.uk**), **Hotel Anywhere** (01444 410 555, **www.hotelany where.co.uk**), the multi-search facility **Travel Supermarket** (**www.travel supermarket.com**), and, in the US, **Hotels.com** (1800 246 8357, **www.hotels.com**) and **Orbitz** (1888 656 4546 in the US or 001 312 416 0018 from the UK, **www.orbitz.com**).

There is no widely accepted star rating, so (with the exception of Disney's resorts), we group hotels into 4 ranges: Budget, Standard, Superior and Deluxe, where the rough price groups per night will be:

Budget	=	up to $50
Standard	=	$51–99
Superior	=	$100–160
Deluxe	=	$161 plus

Our price guide is only a rough reckoner as rates can vary from month to month. The main factor to bear in mind is the extra facilities involved. Hence, a Deluxe grading will include the highest level of facilities and service, while a Budget grade will be a basic motel-type. A key factor in price, though, is your location – the closer to Disney and the other parks, the higher the price, so you can save money if you don't mind a longer drive to your accommodation.

Kidsuites = happy families!

Orlando has pioneered a new type of family accommodation in recent years, and these are worth seeking out if you have kids who enjoy bunk beds. Basically, a kidsuite is a separate area within the hotel room that gives kids their own 'bedroom' (with bunks), usually also with their own TV and games console.

Disney hotels

Our review of Orlando's hotels starts with *Walt Disney World Resort*. Conveniently sited on the doorstep of the main attractions – and linked by an excellent free transport system of monorail, buses and boats – Disney's hotels, holiday homes and campsites are all magnificently appointed and maintained. It also groups them into 4 types: Value (equal to our Standard category), Moderate (our Superior), Deluxe (the same) and Home Away From Home (with a strong element of self-catering – *Wilderness Lodge Villas, Old Key West, Boardwalk Villas, Saratoga Springs Resort & Spa* and *Fort Wilderness* cabins). They range from the Deluxe *Grand Floridian Resort & Spa* to the Value but still fun style of the *Pop Century Resort* – and Disney's imagination and attention to detail here are as good as at the theme parks. There are some 28,000 rooms, while *Fort Wilderness Resort & Campground* has 1,190 sites.

Grand accommodation comes at a price, though. A regular room at the Grand Floridian can cost $500 a night in high season (suites can top $2,000) and even the Moderate Caribbean Beach Resort can top $150 a night. Dining at resort hotels is not cheap either, and you'll find few fast-food outlets on site.

Staying with the Mouse is one of the great thrills, for the style, service and extras. The19 resorts offer a superb array of facilities, and children especially love being a part of Disney

full-time. The benefits are: **Resort ID card**: every guest receives a card with which to charge almost all your food, gifts and services while on site to your room account. **Package delivery**: in conjunction with your ID card, you can have park purchases sent back to your hotel gift shop. **Free parking**: with your ID card, there is no charge for your car at any of the parks. **Free transport**: forget the car and use the monorail-bus-boat network. **Refillable mugs**: all Disney resorts sell collectable drinking mugs, which are well worth buying (about $13 each) as you can then help yourself to refills at their self-service cafés. **Dining priority**: many Disney restaurants hold tables for resort guests, while you can book 180 days in advance plus the length of your stay (i.e. 194 days if you are going for 2 weeks). Call 407 939 3463 or dial *88 on any Disney phone or press the Dining button on your resort phone (non-Disney hotel guests can book restaurants only 180 days in advance). **Priority golf**: the best tee times are reserved for resort guests and can be booked 90 days in advance on 407 939 4653. **Children's services**: all resorts have in-room or group babysitting (subject to availability, so book in advance on 407 827 5444) and 8 of the 9 Deluxe resorts have supervised activity centres and dinner clubs (around $11/child per hour), usually open until midnight. **Mickey on call**: what better way to wake up than with an alarm call from the Mouse himself? **Extra Magic Hours**: this is the BIG bonus, the chance to get into one of

Disney's Beach Club Resort

© Disney

the parks each day either an hour early or for 3 hours after regular park closing, and enjoy many rides with reduced crowds.

Value resorts

Disney's All-Star Resorts: these were Disney's first foray into the more modestly priced market in 1994. Here you can stay in one of the 5 **Sports**-themed blocks (surfing, basketball, tennis, baseball and American football) centred around a massive food court, 2 swimming pools, a games arcade and shops; the **Music**-themed version (Jazz, Rock, Broadway, Calypso and Country); or the **Movies** complex (*Mighty Ducks, 101 Dalmatians, Fantasia, Love Bug* and *Toy Story*). The latter is possibly the most imaginative, with its Fantasia pool and kids' play areas, and the most popular blocks are Toy Story and 101 Dalmatians (both non-smoking). All 3 centres, which total 5,760 rooms, have pool bars, shops, laundry facilities, video games rooms and a pizza delivery service. Bright and compact (if a little tight for families of 4 with older children), they are well designed for families who want to enjoy all the Disney conveniences but without the full price tag. Close to Disney's *Animal Kingdom* is a large **McDonald's**, if the resort's food courts don't appeal. Transport to all the parks (and *Downtown Disney*) is provided by a highly efficient bus service. New in 2006 was a radical revamp of the *All Star Music Resort* to convert nearly 400 single rooms into 192 impressive **2-room suites** sleeping up to 6. Each suite has 2 bathrooms, a well-stocked kitchenette, lounge and private master bedroom, making the accommodation choice here much more flexible.

✠ BRITTIP

To make a reservation at any *Walt Disney World Resort*, call 407 934 7639. For further information, visit **www.disneyworld.co.uk**.

Disney's Pop Century Resort is in a similar vein, themed round the decades of the 20th century. There are 10 blocks with giant icons – such as yo-yos, Rubik's cubes and juke-boxes – and a riot of period sayings and visual gags. The first half of the resort (the **Classic Years**, 1950s–90s) opened in December 2003 and features a huge 10-pin bowling lane incorporating one of the 3 pools (the others are shaped like a computer and a flower), a huge table football set-up and open-air Twister mats. Blocks are grouped around a main building housing a spacious check-in area (with large-screen TV showing Disney films, of course), a large and imaginative food court, a lounge (with quick-breakfast bar), a Disney store and games arcade. The 177 acre/72ha complex also features a central lake and lots of bright, lively landscaping. The second half of the resort remains half-built and unused, but there is a strong feeling it will be converted in 2008 to the kind of 2-room suites being retro-fitted to the *All Star Music Resort*. It all adds significantly to Disney's budget-orientated offerings and has a well-organised bus service to the parks. The drawbacks? Long queues to check in for much of the afternoon and a rather hectic feel, even late in the evening. You need to request a hairdryer from reception and rooms are, again, rather small.

Moderate resorts

Going up a level, **Disney's Caribbean Beach Resort** opened in 1988 and has 2,112 rooms spread over 5 Caribbean 'islands' (with an inter-island bus service). Rooms are still relatively plain but comfortably sleep 4, and the food court, main restaurant **Shutters**, and outdoor activities (with a lakeside recreation area with themed waterfalls, slides and games arcade) are a big hit with children. The 6 counter-service outlets in the food court at **Old Port Royale Town Center** (the hub of this pretty resort) can get busy in the morning, and the Trinidad South and Barbados 'islands' are a fair walk from the centre. But it is an action-packed resort with some imaginative touches, like Parrot Cay Island Playground with its tropical birds and play area. Transport to the parks is solely by bus.

Disney's Port Orleans Resort opened in 1991 and is a 2-part complex (formerly Port Orleans and Dixie Landings) split into the 2,048-room Riverside – with a steamboat reception area, a great cotton mill-style food court, a full-service Cajun-themed restaurant and an old-fashioned general store (gift shop) – and the 1,008-room French Quarter, which has the **Sassagoula Floatworks and Food Factory** court, 2 bars, a games room and shopping arcade. The Riverside includes **Ol' Man Island**, a magnificent 3½ acre/1.5ha playground with swimming pool, kids' area and a fishing hole, while the French Quarter has Doubloon Lagoon, with Mardi Gras dragon slide, alligator fountains and a play area. The eye-catching landscaping and design vary from rustic Bayou backwoods to turn-of-the-century New Orleans. Transport for both sections is by bus to the parks and bus or boat to *Downtown Disney*.

BRITTIP

Disney resort restaurants CAN (and should) be visited even if you are not staying there. Book in advance at any of the parks from any Disney phone (dial *88) or call 407 WDW DINE.

Disney's Coronado Springs Resort is possibly the best value of this trio as it is newer (built in 1997) and has slightly more facilities for its 1,921 rooms spread over 125 acres/50ha: 4 pools (including the massive Lost City of Cibola), 2 games arcades, a boating marina, bike rentals, restaurant, food court and convenience store, lounge bar, gift shop, beauty salon and health club, business centre and 2 guest

launderettes. Constructed on a scenic Mexican/Spanish theme in 3 'villages' (Casitas, Ranchos and Cabanas), Coronado is an often-overlooked treasure. Check out the **Maya Grill** and its New Latino cuisine. Coronado is also only 5 minutes from *Disney's Animal Kingdom* and is well served by the bus network.

Deluxe resorts

More than anything, Disney specialises in high-quality hotels with all manner of special design features, amenities and splendid restaurants. All 9 Deluxe resorts offer a Concierge level, which adds an exclusive, personalised service, and a private lounge with meals and snacks. The first 2 (refurbished several times since) opened with the *Magic Kingdom Park* in 1971. Situated on the monorail, right next to the park, the 15-storey **Disney's Contemporary Resort** has 1,008 remodelled rooms, a cavernous foyer, 5 shops, 4 restaurants, 2 lounges, a real sandy beach, a marina, 2 pools (1 with waterslide), 6 tennis courts, a video games centre and health club – and fabulous views, especially from the superb, hotel-top **California Grill** (one of the most romantic settings in Orlando; try to get a reservation to coincide with the park's fireworks).

Don't miss **Chef Mickey's** here for a breakfast or dinner buffet with your favourite characters, while the

Disney's Port Orleans Resort

© Disney

monorail runs right through the hotel – fascinating for kids. Rooms are some of Disney's largest and were all completely renovated in 2005–06, adding elegant new decor, dark-wood furniture and ultra-comfy duvets. Within walking distance of the *Magic Kingdom Park*, transport to the other parks is by bus.

Disney's Polynesian Resort, the other 1971 original, is a South Seas tropical fantasy with modern sophistication and comfort. Beautiful beaches, lush vegetation and architecture are home to 853 rooms built in wooden long-house style, all with balconies and superb views. Also on the monorail line opposite the Magic Kingdom, it boasts a lovely 3-storey atrium, with 75 varieties of tropical plants, parrots and a waterfall. The Polynesian's large rooms, like those of the Contemporary Resort, have been extensively refurbished recently to revive the Pacific isles theme, with custom-made furniture, tapestries and warm, earth colours. The resort offers excellent eating: **'Ohana** is an entertaining and stylish dinner venue that also offers lively character breakfasts, while the **Kona Café** is slightly less formal but still with an extensive menu, and **Captain Cook's Snack Company** offers more basic counter-service fare. Then there are canoe rentals, a beautiful pool area with waterslide, a games room, shops and children's playground. **The Neverland Club** caters for 4–12s (4pm–midnight). Catch the monorail or a boat to the *Magic Kingdom*, and buses to the other parks. The Poly is also home to the nightly *Spirit of Aloha* dinner show (see page 289), which is open to non-resort guests and makes a great evening among the torch-lit paths and gardens. The

Resort's beach area is also a great location from which to view the nightly *Magic Kingdom* fireworks.

Next to open, in 1988, was **Disney's Grand Floridian Resort & Spa**, a true 5-star hotel built like an elaborate Victorian mansion, with 867 rooms, an impressive domed foyer and staff in period costume. Again on the monorail, one stop from the *Magic Kingdom*, the rooms and facilities are truly luxurious – hence the mega prices, though it is worth a look even if you are not staying. Its 6 restaurants include the top-of-the-range **Victoria and Albert's** (where the set 6-course dinner with wine costs $165), the chic seafood-based **Narcoossee's** (one of our favourites), with its excellent view over Seven Seas Lagoon (for the nightly Electrical Water Pageant), and Mediterranean-styled **Citricos**. You will also find 4 bars and impressive sporting and relaxation facilities, notably the fabulous Spa and Salon. There's a wonderful second pool area, complete with zero-depth entry and waterslide. **The Mouseketeer Club** caters for 4–12s (4.30pm–midnight) and the **1900 Park Fare** restaurant is hugely popular for character breakfasts and dinners, plus the children's **Wonderland Tea Party** with Alice and friends, 1.30–2.30pm Mon–Fri, $28.17/child (not for grown-ups!).

For young princesses, the Garden View Lounge hosts **My Disney Girl's Perfectly Princess Tea Party** (10.30am–noon daily except Tues and Wed), featuring Princess Aurora from *Sleeping Beauty* and with storytelling, singalongs and a princess parade, plus a princess doll and gifts for each child (3–11). The cost for 1 adult and child is a whopping $225 ($150 each additional child), plus $75 for an additional adult, but reservations are still advisable on 407 WDW DINE. The Garden View Lounge also serves a variety of traditional **Afternoon Teas** 2–4.30pm daily, $8.50–24.50 a head. Transport to the *Magic Kingdom* is by boat and monorail; by bus to the other parks.

BRITTIP

Dine in superb South Seas style at 'Ohana's but don't ask for salt – unless you want to spark an amazing reaction…!

BRITTIP

Watch out for the free nightly Electrical Water Pageant on Bay Lake and Seven Seas Lagoon (see page 290), which you can see from all the *Magic Kingdom* resorts.

The refined, almost intimate, **Disney's Yacht** and **Beach Club Resorts** added more quality when they opened in 1990 with 630 and 583 nautical-themed rooms respectively. Set around Crescent Lake next to the *Epcot* park, they help to form one massive resort area that is a delight to walk around at any time but especially at night. For dinner, the **Yachtsman Steakhouse** offers friendly, polished and elegant dining at the Yacht Club, while the sister hotel features **Cape May Café** for lovely character breakfasts and a nightly New England-style clambake buffet. **Beaches & Cream** can also be found here, a classic 1950s-style diner for burgers, shakes and sundaes. Both resorts are set along a white-sand beach like a tropical island paradise and share water fun at **Stormalong Bay**, a superb 2½ acre/1ha recreation area with waterslides and a sandy lagoon. You can go boating or catch a water-shuttle to *Epcot*; other park transport is by bus. The **Sand Castle Club** here caters for 4–12s (4.30pm–midnight).

The unmistakable **Walt Disney World Swan** and **Dolphin** hotels also went up on Crescent Lake in 1990 and, while not actually owned by Disney, they conform to the same high standards. They have some of the most extensive facilities of all the resorts, a wonderful location, fabulous restaurants and a night-time view second to none, while they are usually slightly cheaper than the main Disney Deluxe resorts. They are within walking distance of *Epcot* and *Disney-MGM Studios*, *Disney's Boardwalk Resort* and the *Fantasia Gardens* Miniature Golf Courses, but also have a boat service to both parks (and bus to the others). The 'entertainment architecture' style is extensive and fun, with the Swan featuring a 45ft/14m statue on top, as well as 758 large rooms (including 55 suites), while the Dolphin (1,509 rooms, 136 suites) is crowned by 2 even bigger statues. Both were extensively refurbished in 2003–4 with a luxury look by the original architect, Michael Graves. They now feature the popular Westin Heavenly Bed and unlimited access to high-speed in-room internet. The Dolphin also boasts the brand new Balinese-inspired Mandara Spa, tea garden and Meru Temple. This resort boasts 17 restaurants, 4 tennis courts, 5 pools (one an amazing grotto pool with hidden alcoves and waterslide), a kids' pool and white-sand beach, 2 health clubs, bike and paddle boat rentals, a great range of shops, video arcade and the **Camp Dolphin** centre for 4–12s (6pm–11pm, $10/hour).

Even for non-guests, **Shula's Steak House** and celebrity chef Todd English's **bluezoo** (both Dolphin) are worth seeking out (with seafood-themed bluezoo one of our top-recommended restaurants, see page 319). New in 2007 was Il Mulino Trattoria, New York's top Italian restaurant. **Fresh**, the Dolphin's Mediterranean-style market, serves breakfast and lunch, featuring all made-to-order menu items and both à la carte and tableside dining. At the Swan, the **Garden Grove Café** is set indoors in a tropical gazebo, with à la

Disney's Grand Floridian Resort & Spa

© Disney

carte or buffet breakfasts – including character breakfasts on Saturdays and Sundays. The restaurant is transformed in the evening with à la carte menus, themed buffets and Disney characters every weeknight. **Picabu Buffeteria** (formerly Tubbi's) in the Dolphin is open 24 hours. With its ideal location close to the 2 parks and the BoardWalk district, this is very nearly the perfect resort (407 934 3000, **www.swandolphin.com**).

Disney's Wilderness Lodge opened in 1994 and is one of the most picturesque resorts, as well as being a great romantic destination. It is a detailed re-creation of a National Park lodge, from the stream running through the massive wooden balcony-lined atrium into the gardens, past the swimming pool (with hot and cold spas) to a geyser that erupts each hour. Offering authentic backwoods charm with true luxury, the resort is connected to the *Magic Kingdom Park* by boat and bus only (and buses to the other parks). Rooms are all spacious with some lovely furniture, while the Courtyard View rooms are the best of the regular rooms (though at a slight premium). Deluxe rooms sleep up to 6 and the suites (at up to $815 a night) are truly sumptuous. It also has 2 restaurants: the brilliant **Artist's Point** (lunch and dinner) and the **Whispering Canyon Café** (lively breakfast and huge all-you-can-eat buffets) – plus a snack bar and pool bar. **The Cubs' Den** is for

Disney's Wilderness Lodge

© Disney

BRITTIP

If you visit no other Disney resort, you should definitely try *The Boardwalk*, preferably in the evening.

4–12s (4.30pm–midnight). The **Villas at Wilderness Lodge** is a recent Home Away From Home development of 136 studios and 1- and 2-bedroom villas. Facilities include living areas, kitchens, private balconies and whirlpool baths. There is a quiet pool area, spa and health club.

Completing the Crescent Lake resorts next to *Epcot* in 1996 was the 45 acre/18ha **Disney's BoardWalk Inn and Villas Resort**, one of the most extravagant on-site hotels and a key ingredient in this entertainment 'district'. It features a 372-room hotel, 520 villas, 4 themed restaurants, a TV sports club and 2 nightclubs, plus an array of shops, sports facilities and a huge, free-form swimming pool with a 200ft/60m waterslide, all on a semi-circular boardwalk around the lake. The effect is stunning, and the in-room attention to detail excellent. Highlights are the summer cottage-style villas, tapas-style restaurant **Spoodles** (breakfast and dinner) and the **Big River Grille Brewing Company** (lunch and dinner) for a great range of beers from its own micro-brewery. Top of the lot is the expensive but superb seafood of the **Flying Fish Café** (dinner only). You can try the **Boardwalk Bakery** for a snack, while Spoodles has a quick-service window for takeaways. It is a delightful place to visit for a meal, the nightlife (especially **Jellyrolls** piano bar and **ESPN Club**) or just to wander along the boardwalk. Transport is by boat to *Epcot* and *Disney-MGM Studios* and by a bus service to the other parks.

Disney's Animal Kingdom Lodge opened in 2001, a stunning private game lodge on the edge of a 33 acre/13ha animal-filled savannah, which many rooms overlook. The

Lodge re-build

The top two floors of the *Animal Kingdom Lodge* are being converted into Disney Vacation Club rooms for 2008 (with the main building being renamed Jambo House), and a whole new wing of Vacation Club accommodations (Kidani Village) is under construction for 2009, with a new feature restaurant, pool and kids' play area, plus extended animal savannahs.

pervasive African theme is almost overwhelming, and the effect of opening your curtains to a vista of giraffes and zebras is immense. This wonderful creativity comes before you consider the amenities of this 1,293-room resort: 2 restaurants, café, bar, elaborately themed 'watering-hole' main pool (with waterslide) and kids' pool, massage and fitness centre, large gift shop, children's play area and an awesome 4-storey atrium. The main restaurant, **Jiko**, is spectacular, but there is also the buffet-style **Boma**, a 'marketplace' restaurant featuring African dishes from a wood-burning grill and rotisserie for breakfast and dinner. The lavishness and detail are superb, right down to the guides who can tell guests about the 200 animals and their habitats, the African folklore stories around the outdoor firepit and the chance for children to become junior safari researchers while Mum and Dad do some wine-tasting (the hotel boasts the largest collection of South African wines in America).

BRITTIP

Jiko at *Disney's Animal Kingdom Lodge* offers an imaginative, New World cuisine menu, attentive service and authentic ambience, and is a wonderfully romantic choice.

Rooms range from standard doubles to 1- and 2-bedroom suites, some of which have bunk beds. **Simba's Cubhouse** is for 4–12s (4.30pm–midnight), and all transport is by bus (with the *Animal Kingdom* barely 5 minutes away).

Home from home resorts

Possibly the best value of all the Disney properties can be found at **Disney's Fort Wilderness Resort & Campground**, which opened with all the initial development in 1971. Situated on Bay Lake, almost opposite the *Magic Kingdom*, it offers impressive camping facilities and chalet-style homes that can house up to 6 in a 750 acre/304ha spread of Florida countryside. Two 'trading posts' supply fresh groceries and there are 2 bars and cafés plus a range of on-site activities, including 2 swimming pools, the thrice-nightly *Hoop-Dee-Doo Musical Revue*, Mickey's Backyard Barbecue (a character buffet dinner), campfire programme, open-air films, sports, games and a prime position from which to view the nightly Electrical Water Pageant. You can rent bikes or boats or take horse rides around the country trails, while the Tri-Circle D ranch has a small petting zoo. The **Trails End** restaurant (sit-down and takeaway) offers a great value buffet breakfast, lunch and dinner, while **Crockett's Tavern** serves pizza and appetisers (dinner only). Buses and boats link the resort with other areas (and the short boat ride to the *Magic Kingdom* is a great start to the day).

If you need a lunch or afternoon break from the *Magic Kingdom*, hop on the boat to *Disney's Fort Wilderness Resort* and try the family-friendly Trail's End Buffet – only $11.99 for adults and $7.99 for 3–9s.

Disney's Old Key West Resort (Disney's first Vacation Club resort in 1992) is primarily a 5-star holiday ownership scheme (one of 6 such 'timeshare' properties), but the 1-, 2- or 3-bed studios in a Key West setting can also be rented nightly when not in use by members. Facilities include 4 pools, tennis courts, games room,

Walt Disney World and Lake Buena Vista Accommodation

1 Disney's Contemporary Resort
2 Disney's Polynesian Resort
3 Disney's Wilderness Lodge
4 Disney's Grand Floridian Resort & Spa
5 Walt Disney World Swan
6 Walt Disney World Dolphin
7 Disney's Caribbean Beach Resort
8 Disney's Yacht Club Resort
9 Disney's Beach Club Resort
10 Disney's Boardwalk Inn & Villa Resort
11 Disney's All-Star Resorts
12 Disney's Port Orleans Resort (French Quarter)
13 Disney's Port Orleans Resort (Riverside)
14 Disney's Coronado Springs Resort
15 Disney's Saratoga Springs Resort & Spa
16 Disney's Old Key West Resort
17 Disney's Fort Wilderness Resort & Campground
18 Disney's Animal Kingdom Lodge
19 Disney's Pop Century Resort
20 Hilton at Walt Disney World
21 Grosvenor Resort
22 Buena Vista Palace Resort & Spa
23 Doubletree Guest Suites Resort
24 Best Western at Lake Buena Vista
25 Hotel Royal Plaza
26 Holiday Inn in the Walt Disney World Resort
27 Hyatt Regency Grand Cypress
28 Orlando World Center Marriott
29 Embassy Suites Resort Lake Buena Vista
30 Extended Stay America Deluxe
31 Holiday Inn Express Lake Buena Vista
32 Staybridge Suites by Holiday Inn
33 Sheraton Vistana Resort
34 Sheraton Safari Resort
35 Holiday Inn Sunspree Resort
36 Marriott Village
37 Orlando Vista Hotel
38 Nickelodeon Family Suites
39 Lake Buena Vista Resort Village & Spa
40 Perri House Bed & Breakfast
41 Blue Heron Beach Resort
42 Country Inn & Suites
43 World Quest Resort

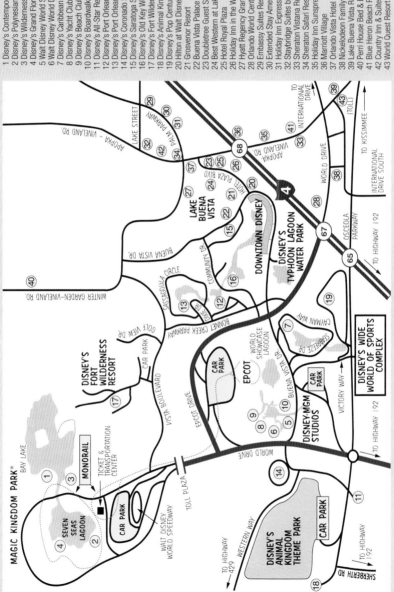

shops and fitness centre, plus the lovely **Olivia's** restaurant. Transport to all parks is by Disney's bus service.

Disney's Saratoga Springs Resort & Spa is the newest member of the Disney Vacation Club line-up, a 65 acre/26ha apartment complex opposite *Downtown Disney* with some wonderful views over the lake and right next to the beautiful Lake Buena Vista Golf Course. With the third phase completed in 2007, it now has 828 units, from standard 2-bed hotel-style studio rooms to huge 2-storey, 3-bed apartments sleeping 12. The first phase opened in May 2004 and the theme is the 1880s' New York resort of the same name, with a peaceful, gracious look and a great array of facilities, from the free-form, zero-depth entry main pool (with waterslide and squirt-fountains), a smaller quiet pool, the health-conscious dining room (the **Artist's Palette**, offering breakfast, lunch and dinner, plus groceries), a large video arcade, tennis courts and a wonderful full-service spa and gym. This is spacious, elegant accommodation for large groups. The standard 1-bed apartment can sleep 4; the 2-bed version sleeps 8 and there's a 3-bed, 3-bath villa for 12. All but the hotel-style studios have a kitchen (with dishwasher and microwave), washer-dryer, whirlpool bath and DVD player, with TVs in the living room and each bedroom. The resort includes a guest services desk, room service, babysitting and childminding services plus a water launch to the shops and entertainment at

Downtown Disney. Rates for the 3-bed villas top $1,000 a night, but the 1-bed units are more modestly priced and, although it is a Vacation Club property, some rooms are available to the general public. Transport to all parks is by bus.

Disney Hotel Plaza

In addition to the official hotels, there are another 7 'guest' hotels on Disney property at the **Disney Hotel Plaza** on the doorstep of *Downtown Disney* (where we now revert to our ratings of Budget, Standard, Superior and Deluxe). There's a free bus service to the attractions, guaranteed admission to the parks (even on their busiest days), and you can make reservations for shows and restaurants before the general public, but they tend to be more expensive than similar hotels outside Disney property (though the convenience of being able to walk to *Downtown Disney* and the Crossroads shopping plaza is worth a lot).

The 18-storey, tropically themed **Best Western Lake Buena Vista** has 325 rooms (all with high-speed internet access) with views over the Marketplace, in-room coffee-makers and hairdryers, while the huge top-floor suites are magnificent. Garden-themed **Traders Island Grill** is pleasant for breakfast or dinner, plus there is a Pizza Hut Express and the deli-style **Parakeet Internet Cafe**, as well as a large pool, video arcade

Best Western Lake Buena Vista

and small gym, with a Garden Gazebo for special occasions, including weddings (407 828 2424; Standard). Going more upmarket, the **Grosvenor Resort** has 626 rooms, great service and colonial decor, plus 2 pools, a large hot tub and a children's pool and playground. There is a Disney character breakfast 3 days a week at **Baskervilles**, plus a sports bar, poolside bar and grill and a 24-hour café, **Crumpets**. There is also the fun **MurderWatch** dinner theatre here on Saturdays. Extra facilities include tennis, basketball, volleyball and a state-of-the-art fitness centre (407 828 4444; Superior). The recently renovated **Hotel Royal Plaza** has a pleasant aspect, boasting 372 ultra-spacious and well-equipped rooms and 22 suites (in 5 categories accommodating up to 5) that feature their plush new Royal Beds. There is a full-service diner-restaurant (the **Giraffe Café**, featuring an excellent breakfast buffet; free for under-11s), lounge bar, deli-style café, landscaped pool area and pool bar, 4 tennis courts, a health club and fitness centre and Disney gift shop. Standard rooms include a sitting area and balcony (407 828 2828; Superior). If you want extra space with your accommodation, the contemporary

Doubletree Guest Suites offers 229 family suites with every convenience, from in-room safe to biscuits, high-speed internet access, wet bar, 2 TVs, fridge and microwave. There are excellent kids' facilities, with their own check-in area, pool, playground and video arcade, and a casual restaurant, lounge and bar, **Streamers**, plus a large main pool (albeit right next to noisy I-4), an exercise room and tennis court (407 934 1000; Superior).

Arguably the outstanding property here is the **Buena Vista Palace** (formerly the Wyndham Palace Resort; 407 827 2727; Superior), an elegant, 27-storey cluster offering 1,012 beautifully furnished rooms and suites (in 8 categories, many with a view of *Epcot*'s Spaceship Earth). It boasts a European-style spa, 3 heated pools, tennis court, jogging track, basketball and sand volleyball court and no fewer than 5 restaurants. Its Australian-styled **Outback Restaurant** (not part of the Outback Steakhouse chain) is a beautiful venue for a high-quality meal. The chic **Watercress Café** is a great venue for its buffet breakfast and lunch, or a Sunday breakfast with Disney characters (reservations not needed).

Nickelodeon Family Suites

Top of the list (for service, mod cons and price) is the 10-storey, 814-room **Hilton**. With 2 excellent pools, 7 restaurants and lounges and a superb health club, it fully deserves its high rating. It is also the only 'outside' hotel to enjoy Disney's *Extra Magic Hours* feature, while there is a babysitting service and a Disney character breakfast on Sundays. The recently renovated rooms offer all mod cons, including high-speed wireless internet. The dining choices feature the outstanding **Benihana** restaurant for sushi, sashimi, chicken and great steaks; **Covington Mill** for a casual breakfast and lunch; **Andiamo Italian Bistro**; the 24-hour **Mainstreet Market** deli; a pool bar and grill; and a coffee/wine bar (407 827 4000; Deluxe). For more info on hotels in this area, go to **www.downtowndisney hotels.com**

The **Holiday Inn in the Walt Disney World Resort** (formerly the Courtyard by Marriott), with 323 rooms in a 14-storey tower and 6-storey annex completes the line-up in this area, but it is currently closed for major renovations and no re-opening date was available as we went to press.

Beyond Disney

Once you move outside the confines of *Walt Disney World*, your hotel choice becomes more diverse. The Budget and Standard types are the most common, and the area you stay in also has an effect on the price: the further you go from Disney on Kissimmee's Highway 192, the cheaper the hotel/motel, while parts of International Drive are more expensive than others (generally, north of Sand Lake Road is cheaper). Facilities vary little and what you see is usually what you get. All the big hotel chains can be found here, with rates as low as $30/room off-peak (but remember the tax and resort fee). Some also have rooms with a kitchenette (what they call an 'efficiency'). Be prepared to shop around, especially along Highway 192, where many hotels advertise their rates on their billboards. And feel free to ask to see a room before you book (some of the motels can be pretty ordinary at best). So, looking at things from the price perspective, here is a guide to the main selections.

Budget hotels

Chain hotels can be found at their most numerous in this category and you will find few frills from what is an identikit bunch. All will have pools but only a handful have restaurants and none will have bars or lounges (although quite a few provide a free continental breakfast). Conversely, many of the hotels offer fridges and microwaves that help to add real value. At the bargain basement end are **Motel 6** (1800 466 8356, **www.motel6.com**) and **Red Roof Inn** (1800 733 7663, **www.redroof.com**), the latter of which has several newly renovated properies in Orlando. The **Super 8 Motel** chain varies a lot, with its newer motels (notably on American Way, near Universal Orlando) being good value, but others looking old and tired (1800 800 8000, **www.super8.com**). Among the most consistent are **EconoLodge**, with a free continental breakfast (1877 424 6423, **www.econolodge.com**), **Microtel Inn & Suites**, which tend to have much newer properties (1800 771 7171, **www.microtelinn.com**), and **Travelodge**, also on American Way (1800 578 7878, **www.travelodge.com**).

BRITTIP

Hotels designated Maingate East or Maingate West should be close to Disney's main entrance on Highway 192, though it is wise to check.

The **Days Inn** chain varies widely, from tatty older properties to smart relatively recent ones, and with free continental breakfast (1800 329 7466, **www.daysinn.com**); sister brand the **Days Suites** is distinctly smarter. The **Rodeway Inn** chain (in the Choice Hotels group, like Econolodge) has slipped from Standard to more Budget territory in recent years (1877 424 6423, **www.choicehotels.com**). **Knights Inn** (1800 843 5644, **www.knightsinn.com**) is a smart choice in this area, and **Masters Inn** is another to offer free continental breakfast to add value (1800 633 3434, **www.mastersinn.com**). The **Howard Johnson** chain tends to have older properties here, many with a 'kids eat free' option, but their rooms are often more spacious (1800 446 4656, **www.hojo.com**).

There are also dozens of smaller, independent outfits that offer special rates from time to time (especially a battery of cheap and cheerful motels along Highway 192 in Kissimmee).

Standard hotels

At first glance there may not seem much difference here, as some of these are still firmly in motel-style territory. They should have generally smarter facilities but not all will have their own restaurant. **Ramada** hotels represent good value at this level as some have complimentary breakfast

Our budget recommendations

In this range, the ones we rate among the best include the **Magic Castle Inn & Suites Maingate** in Kissimmee (good range of amenities – free continental breakfast, free Disney transport, in-room fridge, microwave, safe, kids' playground and guest laundry; 1800 446 5669, **www.magicorlando.com**); The **Inn at Summer Bay** at the Clermont end of Highway 192 (the budget part of the big Summer Bay complex, just across the Highway, but still benefiting from the many facilities; 863 420 8282 **www.summer bayresort.com/inn.html**); and **Knights Inn Maingate**, also in Kissimmee (reliable, cheap option in a great location, with free Disney transport, daily breakfast and fridges in all the rooms; 407 859 5410, **www.knightsinn.com**).

(1800 272 6232, **www.ramada.com**) and **Quality Inns** are also a sound, popular choice, with a great reputation for value, while some of their hotels boast an exercise room (1877 424 6423, **www.choicehotels.com**).

The **Comfort Inn** chain is equally identikit (not surprisingly as part of the big Choice Hotels worldwide group), but offers a valuable free breakfast, while sister brand **Comfort Suites** have some smart, newer properties. The **Clarion Inn** (and Suites) is another notable Choice brand, and often includes restaurants, though properties vary considerably in age. Its **Sleep Inn** brand is aimed more at business travellers but tends to have a choice of newer properties, and free breakfasts (1877 424 6423, **www.choicehotels.com**).

AmeriHost Inns have some newer motels here, too, also with a free breakfast bonus (1800 434 5800, **www.amerihostinn.com**). For pure no-frills, clean and consistent chains with more space than many in this category (and kitchens in most hotels), look for **Extended Stay America**, which also has **Extended Stay Deluxe** properties (formerly the Sierra Suites). Sister brand **StudioPLUS** offers extra facilities (1800 804 3724, **www.extendedstay america.com**).

Fairfield Inns are the budget version of the impressive Marriott chain and usually have smart, new hotels, many with gyms and most offering free breakfast (0800 221 222 in the UK, **www.marriott.com**). **Hampton Inns** (and Suites) are also above average in this category, with a free breakfast bar and tea/coffee in the lobby 24 hours a day (1800 426 7866, **www.hampton inn.com**), while **AmeriSuites** (the Hyatt chain's budget brand) is another good name, with large, well-fitted rooms and free hot breakfast (1877 877 8886, **www.amerisuites.com**).

Kissimmee Accommodation

1 Country Inn & Suites at Calypso Cay
2 Buena Vista Suites
3 Caribe Royale Resort
4 Radisson Resort Orlando-Celebration
5 Radisson Worldgate Resort
6 Summer Bay Resort
7 Omni Orlando Resort at Champions Gate
8 Magic Castle Inn & Suites Maingate
9 Seralago Inn Hotel & Suites Maingate East
10 Holiday Inn Maingate West
11 Orlando Sun Resort
12 Best Western Lakeside
13 Celebration Hotel
14 Gaylord Palms Resort
15 Comfort Suites Maingate
16 Tropical Palms Fun Resort
17 Nickelodeon Family Suites by Holiday Inn
18 Orange Lake Resort
19 Villages at Mango Kay
20 Liki Tiki Village
21 Wonderland Inn
22 Comfort Suites Maingate East
23 Meridian Palms Hotel
24 Reunion Resort
25 Palms Hotel by Lexington
26 La Quinta Inn & Suites Orlando Maingate
27 Quality Suites Maingate East
28 Holiday Inn Hotel Maingate East
29 Mystic Dunes Resort & Golf Club
30 Windsor Palms Resort
31 Mona Lisa at Celebration
32 San Marco Resort
33 Tuscana Resort
34 World Quest Resort
35 Village at Town Center
36 Regency Suites
37 Floridays Resort Orlando
38 Regal Oaks Resort

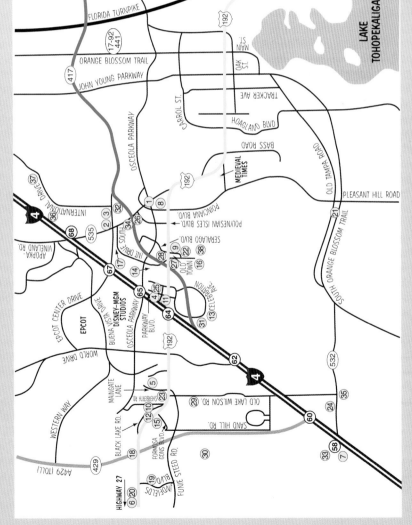

BRITTIP

Not all hotels provide hairdryers, though they can often be ordered from the desk. For your own, you will need a US plug adaptor (with 2 flat pins). Their voltage is 110–120 AC (ours is 220) so appliances will be sluggish.

Moving to the upper end of this category you find the **Best Western** group, all with good facilities, family-orientated but large (0800 393 130 from the UK, **www.bestwestern.com**) and the smart **La Quinta Inn** (and Suites), which has some notable new hotels in Orlando (1800 642 4271, **www.lq.com**). The **Holiday Inn** chain varies a bit but provides some great value (and well-equipped) hotels in the Standard/Superior range. Kids eat free (with their parents) at all properties and many include some sophisticated pools and extra facilities like games rooms (0800 405 060 from the UK, **www.holidayinn.com**). Possibly the best overall value here, though, is provided by the **Radisson** group, which has some excellently priced hotels in the area. All have above-average amenities and services and are most well situated for the parks (0800 374 411, **www.radisson.com**).

There is also a handful of notable individual properties in this category. Look out in particular for the **Seralago Inn Hotel** and **Suites Maingate East** (formerly a Holiday

Doubletree Castle Hotel on I-Drive

Inn), which also boasts deluxe suites, 2-room suites and kidsuites, plus great kids' facilities (including free films in their own cinema), making it an outstanding family resort. Its proximity to Old Town is also handy, while under-13s eat breakfast and dinner free (1800 411 3457, **www.seralagohotel.com**). The reliable 2-bed studios of **Enclave Suites** (on Carrier Drive, just off I-Drive) are excellent value as 'kids eat free' with parents, there's free breakfast and a good array of facilities – though in places the resort could do with some updating (1800 457 0077, **www.enclave suites.com**). Similarly, the rebuilt **Palms Hotel & Villas** right on Parkway Boulevard off Highway 192 in Kissimmee (close to I-4) features spacious 2-room suites (with fully equipped kitchens), large pool, sports court, free shuttle to the Disney parks and free continental breakfast but no restaurant (407 396 2229, **www.thepalmshotelandvillas.com**).

BRITTIP

It is usual to tip hotel chambermaids by leaving $1/adult each day before your room is made up.

Superior hotels

This is a category where there are far fewer of each brand, so we highlight a few worthy individuals as well as the chain details. All properties will provide a good pool (often with extra facilities like a waterslide, kids' pool and/or playground), at least 1 restaurant, bar and café, and extra in-room amenities, such as tea/coffee-makers. The **Doubletree chain** offers smart, modern properties with fewer frills than most but more spacious rooms (1800 222 8733, **www.doubletree.com**), while **Homewood Suites** (both are part of the Hilton chain) provide extra room for larger families in 1- and 2-bed suites with full kitchens, a free hot breakfast daily and a more upmarket feel with mid-range pricing (1800 222 4663,

Our standard recommendations

Standout properties in this range include the **Radisson Resort Orlando-Celebration** in Kissimmee (on Parkway Boulevard, close to the Highway 192 junction with I-4), in 20 tropical acres/8ha and with 3 landscaped swimming pools, a state-of-the-art fitness centre, comfortable rooms and great dining choices, all in a great location (407 396 7000, **www.radisson.com/kissimmeefl**); **La Quinta Inn I-Drive North** (formerly the Red Horse Inn, near Wet 'n Wild), is a fun choice, with a striking south-western design and large, comfy rooms, all refurbished recently, plus a generous free continental breakfast and an oasis-themed pool area; there is no restaurant but the neighbouring Sheraton Studio City is only a short walk away and a Denny's diner is next door (407 351 4100, **www.lq.com**); **Holiday Inn and Suites Maingate East** (formerly a Travelodge) in Kissimmee (between Markers 8 and 9), which underwent a complete rebuild in 2007 to refurbish its 446 rooms (including kidsuites) in 2 high-rise towers; there's an oversized pool, kids' pool, waterslides, gym, children's theatre, food court and lobby lounge, plus a 'kids eat free' programme (1800 337 1128, **www.orlandofunspots.com**); and the **Meridian Palms**, also in Kissimmee at Maingate West just off Highway 192, a completely refurbished ex-Hampton Inn which now has a smart, contemporary look (more like a Superior class hotel), ultra-comfy rooms, a great location close to Disney, free shuttle to the main theme parks, free buffet breakfast and a relaxing pool area; there is no restaurant but there is plenty of choice nearby (1800 391 7909, **www.meridianpalmsorlando.com**).

www.homewoodsuites.com). The **Doubletree Hotel Universal Orlando** is a twin-tower complex with a smart resort feel, with 742 spacious, smartly furnished rooms (plus 23 suites, all with high-speed wireless internet access), a large pool, kids' playground, pool bar, arcade, fitness centre, 2 new bars, full-service restaurant, sports bar and grill, a deli and a Starbucks. It also offers a free shuttle to Universal (across the road), SeaWorld and Wet 'n Wild (407 351 1000, **www.doubletreeorlando.com**).

Other good, spacious hotels (often at below-average prices) are the **Springhill Suites** and **Residence Inn** chains, both part of the Marriott group (along with the more upmarket **Courtyard** hotels). Residence Inns tend to be newer and feature free breakfast and exercise rooms but both brands have microwave, fridge and tea/coffee-making facilities (1888 236 2427 in the US, 0800 221 222 in the UK, **www.marriott.com**). The **Marriott Village** complex in Lake Buena Vista features a Fairfield Inn, Courtyard and Springhill Suites (**www.marriotvillage.com**), with 24-hour gated security, free *Walt Disney World* transport and great facilities.

A relative newcomer but highly worthwhile is the **Baymont Inn & Suites** group, which boasts several properties in the area (1866 999 1111, **www.baymontinns.com**), while the **Country Inn & Suites** are almost identical, newer hotels with spacious rooms and a pleasant country-house style lobby, serving an extensive free breakfast (1888 201 1746, **www.country inns.com**). The property on Universal Boulevard is possibly the best, with 170 standard rooms with in-room safe, coffee-maker, hairdryer and iron/ironing board, while the 48 king suites include microwave and fridge.

Meridian Palms family room

Sheraton Studio City

It is 1ml/1.6km from Universal Orlando and half that from Wet 'n Wild, yet much quieter than many I-Drive hotels (407 313 4200).

If you want a slightly more upmarket touch, the **Staybridge Suites** (1800 225 1237, **www.staybridge.com**) and **Hawthorn Suites** (1800 527 1133, **www.hawthorn.com**) feature spacious 1- and 2-bed suites that will sleep up to 6 and fully fitted kitchens, plus a hearty free breakfast and free local phone calls. However, to our mind the best suites here are the **Embassy Suites** properties, with smart interior courtyards, good restaurants and relaxing pool areas (1800 362 2779, **http://embassysuites1.hilton.com**).

Sheraton hotels are well represented in Orlando and boast a smart, revamped look in recent years (as part of the Starwood group). Several are themed and feature extra facilities and good dining (1888 625 5144, **www.starwoodhotels.com**). A novel choice is the African-themed **Sheraton Safari Hotel** in Lake Buena Vista, which offers a waterslide, heated pool and kids' pool, free transport to Disney parks and 'kids eat free' with parents. Its rooms are large and well equipped, and there's a

good selection of restaurants and shops nearby (407 239 0444, **www.sheratonsafari.com**). **Marriott** is another well-represented group here, with some of the smartest hotels in this category. They often provide extra facilities and more landscaped grounds, with a choice of restaurants and some of the largest standard rooms. Recent improvements include stylish and user-friendly features, like their signature Revive beds for a guaranteed good night's sleep. The **Orlando Airport Marriott** has recently undergone major renovation to its public rooms and guest rooms and is a great choice for either your first night (especially if you are arriving late) or the final day, letting you relax around the tropical indoor/outdoor pool area and indulge in some fine dining at its excellent steakhouse, Porterhouse (1800 380 6751, **www.marriott.com**).

The Hilton chain is notable here for its **Hilton Garden Inn** brand, with a number of attractive, modern hotels (1877 7829 444, **www.hilton gardeninn.com**), and also its **Grand Vacation Club** holiday ownership resorts, which are available on an individual rental basis at times. They

Nickelodeon fantasy

Not so much a hotel as a theme park in resort form, **Nickelodeon Family Suites by Holiday Inn** (almost opposite Orlando World Center Marriott, on I-Drive South) provides a wonderfully striking and kid-friendly holiday choice. Characters from the Nickelodeon TV station adorn strategic points and there is plenty of live interaction (notably at breakfast). A huge range of daily activities includes scavenger hunts, arcade tournaments, pirate fun and much more, including films and Studio Nick stage shows in its mini-theatre. There is also an evening programme and babysitting to allow parents some free time! Suites come complete with bunk or twin beds, a TV and video console system. The water features have been enhanced to form 2 huge play areas, complete with all manner of sprays, showers, pools, slides and flumes, and there are poolside games, a video arcade, mini-golf and a large shopping arcade. The suites feature 1, 2 and 3 bedrooms, a living room and bathroom, microwave and fridge (and full kitchen with some). The **Nicktoons Café** offers buffet dining (plus à la carte in the evening), with 'kids eat free' at all times. Plus there is a food court, pool bar and grill, along with the **Nick@Nite Lounge**. It all adds up to a striking (if rather raucous) holiday base in an excellent location conveniently close to Disney (1866 462 6425; **www.nickhotel.com**).

feature superb facilities and wonderfully spacious accommodation (studios and 1-, 2- and 3-bed villas). Its 2 properties on I-Drive, by SeaWorld and Orlando Premium Outlets, are especially eye-catching (1800 230 7068, **www.hilton grandvacations.com**).

The **Hyatt** group is also rare in tourist territory, but one prime example is the **Hyatt Regency** at Orlando International Airport, especially if you arrive late and could benefit from a first-night rest. It has 2 excellent restaurants and a smart pool deck, plus a fitness room, lounge and business centre. Rooms are superbly spacious, particularly the corner rooms, and many feature internal balconies overlooking the 6-storey airport atrium. Surprisingly, there is no noticeable aircraft noise and none of the bustle you would expect of an airport hotel. Staying there gives the distinct advantage of collecting your hire car in the morning rather than straight after a long flight (407 825 1234, **http://orlandoairport.hyatt.com**).

Crowne Plaza Hotels have made a mark for themselves in recent years with some fabulous new properties (**www.ichotelsgroup.com**). They feature great pool areas, whirlpools, good-quality restaurants, fitness centres

and ultra-comfortable rooms. The **Crowne Plaza Orlando Universal** is a fine example, with 398 rooms and suites in 2 distinct, stylish blocks and a spectacular circular atrium. Two restaurants, a cocktail lounge, guest laundry and fitness centre, plus a huge heated pool, add up to top quality and value in an ideal location on Universal Boulevard's junction with Sand Lake Road (407 355 0550, **www.cporlando.com**). The **Crowne Plaza Resort** (on I-Drive south of SeaWorld) is equally smart but in a quieter location, and with a pleasant Key West styling (notably in its **Pineapple Grille Restaurant & Lounge**, with its Florida cuisine). Just 5mls/8km from Disney, it is ideal for anyone wanting a rest from the usual holiday hustle-bustle. It also benefits from a new multi-million dollar pool complex (this hotel is owned by the Superior Homes Group, which has plans for a 700-unit condo project at the resort; 407 239 1222, **www.crowne plazaorlando.com**). One last group is the **Rosen Hotels & Resorts** of Florida. Four of its hotels are budget-minded properties on I-Drive (including the highly Brit-popular Quality Inn Plaza and Quality Inn International), but it also has the **Rosen Plaza Hotel,** a distinctive 800-room property with excellent resort facilities – including

2 restaurants, a pizza shop, deli, fitness centre and nightclub – and spacious, recently redecorated accommodation (1800 627 8258, **www.rosenplaza.com**).

When it comes to other notable individuals in the Superior category, there are only a few non-chain properties hereabouts.

The **Wyndham Orlando Resort** in the heart of I-Drive offers a formidable line-up of facilities (3 pools, a full-service restaurant and bar, a deli and ice-cream shop, 2 pool bars, a pool restaurant, tennis courts, a kids' club and game arcade, and a health club) in beautifully landscaped grounds but without the high price tag you would expect. The resort covers 42 acres/ 17ha and takes some getting around, but it is one of the best all-round hotels for the money (407 351 2420; **www.wyndham.com**). Also of note is the recently refurbished and fun-styled **Orlando Vista Hotel** (formerly the Doubletree Club) on Apopka-Vineland Road in Lake Buena Vista, which includes kidsuites. The location at the entrance to *Downtown Disney*, pleasant bar and café, large pool deck, kidsuites and spacious, airy rooms make this a bargain (1800 521 3297, **www.orlandovistahotel.com**).

Other suites worthy of note include the well-appointed **Buena Vista Suites** (1800 537 7737, **www.bv suites.com**) and the stylish **Caribe Royale Resort** (1800 823 8300, **www.cariberoyale.com**), both on World Center Drive just off the lower end of I-Drive. The former is the more basic type, with spacious 2-room suites, a full free breakfast, heated pool, whirlpool, tennis courts, gift shop, mini-market and the **Vista Bistro**. The Caribe Royale is the 5-star version, with a choice of 1-bed suites and 2-bed villas, a super pool area with waterslide, tennis courts, 2 fitness rooms and one of the best free breakfast buffets in town. Its **Venetian Room** is a real treat for lovers of fine continental cuisine, and there are 4 other cafés and lounges.

Deluxe hotels

When it comes to the finest hotels, it is very much a question of individuals. There is only a handful of genuinely deluxe properties in this area, and they are all highly distinctive, with an excellent range of facilities, outstanding service and, usually, at least one 5-star restaurant. We have already detailed Disney's luxury offerings, so we'll start here with Universal's counterparts.

Orlando Vista Hotel

Our superior recommendations

The 21-storey **Sheraton Studio City Hotel** is an I-Drive icon near Universal Orlando and features a 1950s' film theme throughout. Facilities include a heated outdoor pool and paddling pool, games room, mini-golf, fitness room and free shuttle to Universal, Wet 'n Wild and SeaWorld. All 301 well-appointed rooms have coffee makers and Nintendo games, plus superb views over the surrounding area (ask for a Universal view if possible). The **Starlight Grille** restaurant is a minor gem, with a fun ambience for breakfast, lunch or dinner, and an imaginative dinner menu, while you can also grab a drink at **Oscar's Lounge** and enjoy being a 'movie star' (407 351 2100, **www.sheratonstudiocity.com**). The recently remodelled **International Plaza Resort and Spa** condo-hotel (formerly the Sheraton World Resort), just off the main I-Drive area, is another fine choice. Set in 28 acres/11ha, the resort offers 3 pools, 2 kiddie pools, a playground and mini-golf and well-furnished rooms and extra-large suites. Its dining options are fairly standard, but the tropical grounds give it a more upmarket ambiance (407 352 1100, **www.internationalplazaresortandspa.com**). The **Embassy Suites Hotel International Drive South** consistently gets good reader feedback. It is exceedingly smart, with excellent service and spacious rooms (either standard 2-room suites sleeping 4 or double-doubles for 6) providing 2 TVs, coffee maker, fridge and microwave. There's a great outdoor pool deck, kids' splash pool and indoor pool, plus a sauna, steam room and gym. The **Sedona Café** and **Hurricane's Lounge** give it a real edge in dining options and it also offers a free Disney shuttle service and transport to the other parks (407 352 1400, **www.embassysuitesorlando.com**). Finally, the spectacular 24-storey **Rosen Center Hotel** is a real star property (opposite The Pointe Orlando) and one of the largest hotels in the area. It caters mainly for the convention trade (it is next door to the massive Convention Center), but also offers excellent facilities with 1,334 rooms and 80 suites. It has a huge swimming grotto, tennis courts, exercise centre, 2 top-quality restaurants (the excellent seafood-orientated **Everglades** and casual all-day choice **Café Gauguin**, plus a handy 24-hour deli), and 2 smart bars. The overall style is distinctly luxurious, yet the prices aren't (1800 204 7234, **www.rosencenter.com**).

Universal Orlando

When Universal decided to build its own hotels, it teamed up with the Loews group and consequently ended up with 3 of the best. They also come with a rare privilege – *Universal Express*, front-of-line access to the main attractions of both parks.

The 53 acre/21ha, 1,000-room **Royal Pacific Resort** has an exotic South Seas feel, transporting you back to a 1930s' hotel in the tropics, and you really feel as if you have stepped into another world as you cross the bamboo bridge into the elegant lobby, faced by the splendid Orchid Garden courtyard. Extensive use of rich, dark woods, cool stone floors and masses of greenery (58,000 plants and 2,500 trees) give the place an opulent, colonial feel, while the rooms and facilities are equally impressive. Standard rooms feature hand-carved

Balinese furniture, among many refined touches, and there is also a Club level, with separate lounge and extended facilities, and some superlative suites. **Islands Dining Room** offers breakfast, lunch and dinner in a setting of oriental simplicity (children have their own buffet area with TV screen), while fine dining is taken to a new dimension by

Royal Pacific Resort

a magnificent restaurant run by top American chef Emeril Lagasse called **Tchoup Chop** (possibly the best in Orlando, see page 320). There is a pool snack bar and luau garden area, with the **Wantilan Luau** buffet on Saturdays (and Fridays in summer – $49.50 adults, $29 under-13s), featuring a Polynesian feast and dinner show. The huge free-form pool is ideal for kids, with zero-depth entry at one end and a boat-shaped interactive play area of squirting fountains. Add a health club (with jacuzzi, sauna and gym), kids' club (with computer games, TVs and organised activities), video arcade and 2 shops and you have superb value, even at this end of the scale.

All Universal resort guests benefit from a number of exclusive privileges: resort ID card (for buying food, merchandise and other items throughout Universal Orlando); free water taxi transport; priority seating at most restaurants (show your room key card); package delivery to your room; the chance to buy a special Length of Stay pass (for unlimited parks access while you are at the resort); and, most importantly, Universal Express no-wait access to all the rides all day just by showing your room key card. For all Universal hotels, call 1888 273 1311 or go to **www.universalorlando.com**

The **Hard Rock Hotel** is possibly the coolest hotel in Orlando. This icon of rock chic is themed as a former rock star's home, with 650 rooms and suites in California mission style. High ceilings, wooden beams, marble floors and eclectic artwork give an eye-catching style, with a rock-star theme to most public areas, music memorabilia, black-suited foyer staff and fairly constant music. The 14 acre/6ha site includes 3 bars (including the ultra-cool Velvet Bar), 2 restaurants (the full-service **The Kitchen** and the 5-star, dinner-only **Palm Restaurant**), plus a take-away café, fitness centre, gift shop, kids' club (for 4–14s) and games room. The lido area that is the hotel's focus is terrific, with a large, free-form pool and 240ft/73m waterslide, two jacuzzis, a beach and volleyball court, shuffleboard and life-size chess and draughts. The pool even has an underwater sound system! The rooms (including 14 kidsuites) are big, beautifully furnished in the hotel's chic style and superbly comfortable.

The **Portofino Bay Hotel** is the jewel in Universal's crown, a splendid re-creation of the famous Italian port and a stunning resort with every facility. The elaborate porticos, genuine *trompe l'oeil* painting, harbourside piazza and faithful ornamentation of the waterfront make it one of the most memorable settings in Florida. The 750 rooms are impeccably appointed, with lashings of Italian style. Standard rooms are true luxury, with huge beds, spacious bathrooms, mini-bar and coffee facilities, ironing board and hair-dryer, while the exclusive Villa rooms feature butler service and private pool. There are 18 kidsuites with separate themed rooms that include TV, CD player and Sony Playstation. The resort facilities are equally breathtaking – a Roman aqueduct-style pool with waterslide (and poolside films on Saturday evenings), an enclosed kids' play area and wading pool, a separate quiet pool, jacuzzis, the beautiful **Mandara Spa** and fitness centre, business centre, gift shops and video games room.

Portofino Bay Hotel

ACCOMMODATION

The largest Marriott on earth!

A firm *Brit's Guide* Deluxe favourite over the years that never seems to lose its lustre is **Orlando World Center Marriott**, a hugely impressive landmark on Disney's outskirts, set in 200 landscaped acres/810ha and surrounded by a beautiful golf course. With 2,000 spacious rooms (most of them boasting fabulous views up to 28 storeys high), 10 restaurants and 6 pools (holding a million gallons of water), it is a monumental prospect, set among landscaped tropical foliage and with fabulous facilities, including a Bill Madonna Golf Academy, tennis courts, volleyball, basketball, spa and state-of-the-art gym. Among the highlights are the **Mikado Japanese Steakhouse**, **Ristorante Tuscany** and **Champions Sports Bar**, while there are also excellent children's amenities and programmes – plus the whizziest glass-fronted lifts in Orlando! It does get busy with convention business, but the picturesque main pool area offers true relaxation bliss (407 239 4200, **www.marriottworldcenter.com**).

There is also the Campo Portofino activity centre for kids aged 4–14 (5–11.30pm, $12 hour/child, $12/meal). The Portofino also has 8 restaurants and lounges, including the 5-star (and very romantic) **Bice Ristorante**, the boisterous **Trattoria del Porto** (with family-themed dinner entertainment Thurs and Sat, and character dinners 6.30–9.30pm on Fridays), **Mama Della's**, an authentic Italian family dining experience (watch out for Mama herself!), an aromatic deli, a pizzeria and gelateria. It is only a short boat ride from Universal, but it feels light years away in terms of its tranquil ambience.

BRITTIP

For some wonderful gift shopping, check out Portofino Bay's Galleria Portofino where you'll find magnificent art and jewellery.

International Drive Area

Stepping back outside Universal, the superb **Renaissance Orlando Resort** (788 rooms on Sea Harbor Drive, behind SeaWorld) is highly notable for its style, service and genuine hospitality. It boasts a massive 10-storey atrium lobby and some equally enormous rooms and suites, an extensive (recently remodelled) pool area with bar and grill, tennis courts, fitness centre with sauna and steam room, plus kids' play areas and activities. There is a choice of bars and shops, and all rooms have recently been renovated to a high standard as part of a $31million makeover in 2007, which added extra bathroom amenities, flat-screen TVs and the Marriott company's signature Revive bedding. The new dining line-up includes the **Mist Sushi Lobby Bar**, the **Boardwalk Sports Bar**, the upscale but casual **Tradewinds** for breakfast, lunch and dinner, **The Deli** and a **Starbucks** cafe. The hotel offers some great packages in conjunction with SeaWorld, which is a 2-minute walk across the car park, and their rates are often found to be the best in the Deluxe category (1800 327 6677, **www.marriott.com**).

The 230 acre/93ha **Rosen Shingle Creek Hotel** opened in September 2006 and ranks firmly among the grandest. In the middle of the award-winning Shingle Creek Golf Club (with its acclaimed Brad Brewer Golf Academy), just to the east of I-Drive

Gingerbread House at Disney's Grand Floridian

© Disney

International Drive Accommodation

1 Peabody Orlando
2 Wyndham Orlando Resort
3 Renaissance Orlando Resort
4 Sheraton Studio City
5 La Quinta Inn
7 Holiday Inn Express
8 Quality Inn International
9 Quality Inn Plaza
10 Embassy Suites Jamaica Court
11 Howard Johnson Plaza
12 Howard Johnson Inn
13 Rosen Plaza Hotel
14 Crowne Plaza Orlando Universal
15 Enclave Suites

16 Parc Corniche
17 Wynfield Inn
18 Staybridge Suites by Holiday Inn
19 Comfort Suites
20 The Doubletree Castle
21 Rosen Center Hotel
22 Hawthorn Suites
23 Holiday Inn & Suites at Universal
24 Best Western Plaza
25 Embassy Suites I-Drive South
26 Doubletree Hotel at Universal Orlando
27 Portofino Bay Hotel
28 Hard Rock Hotel
29 Amerisuites Convention Center

30 International Plaza Resort & Spa
31 Extended Stay America Deluxe
32 Homewood Suites
33 Country Inn & Suites
34 Royal Pacific Resort
35 Grande Lakes Orlando
36 Holiday Inn Convention Center
37 Shingle Creek Resort & Golf Club
38 Hilton Grand Vacations Club at
   SeaWorld
39 Best Western Movieland
40 The Point Orlando Resort
41 The Blue Rose Resort
42 The Village of Imagine

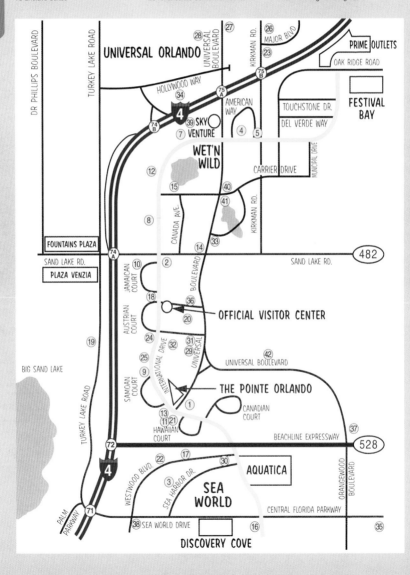

behind the new Convention Center, it boasts 1,500 rooms and suites, all with immaculate furnishings and comfort, as well as a full-service spa and state of the art fitness centre. Rooms vary from standard doubles to presidential suites, but all with fabulous flat-screen TVs, wireless internet access, fridges and first-class toiletries. Amenities include 5 restaurants, 4 bars, a lounge, coffee house, deli and ice-creamery, plus 3 outdoor pools, tennis courts, basketball, volleyball and nature trails. There is also a neat kids club, The Swamp, for 4–14s (Thurs 5–11pm, Fri–Sat 5pm–midnight; $12/hour first child, $8/hour each additional child). The whole resort is built in a 1900s' Spanish revival style, and it provides immaculate, 5-star service (especially at the concierge level). Look out in particular for **A Land Remembered**, its upscale steakhouse (named after a famous Florida novel) in the golf Club House, and **Cala Bella**, a spectacular fine-dining Italian restaurant, with truly out-of-this-world desserts from its renowned pastry chef (407 996 9939, **www.shinglecreekresort.com**).

BRITTIP

Don't miss the 1.5ml/2.4km nature trail at the Rosen Shingle Creek Hotel, out among the native cypress trees, creeks and lush natural vegetation, where you might spot some of the local wildlife.

Equally classy, if more conventional, is the **Peabody Orlando** on International Drive, a luxurious, 891-room tower block, with an Olympic-size pool, health club, 4 tennis courts and some superb restaurants, notably the gourmet **Dux** (jacket advisable), classy Italian **Capriccio**, and the amazing **B-Line Diner** (see page 314). Service is superb and the style is a cut above normal tourist fare – just check out the Royal Duck Palace! Larger-than-average rooms and huge suites add to the quality, but conference business can make it a bit hectic (407 352 4000, **www.peabodyorlando.com**).

BRITTIP

Don't miss Peabody's twice-daily red-carpet Duck March at 11am and 5pm, when its trademark ducks take up residence in the lobby fountain.

Further afield

Beyond I-Drive and the parks is a further selection of high-quality offerings, including the new golfing paradise of the **Omni Orlando Resort at Champions Gate**. With 730 rooms and suites, and overlooking a superb golf set-up with 2 Greg Norman-designed courses, this is an imposing hotel with impressive facilities, including the world HQ of the renowned David Leadbetter golf academy, main swimming pool and activity pool (including a 'lazy river' feature, fountains and waterslide), 4 restaurants (notably the superb Asian cuisine of **Zen** and the chic **David's Club** bar-restaurant), coffee bar, deli, 3 lounge bars, state-of-the-art health club and full service spa. Just 10 minutes south of Disney and right off I-4, this is well situated yet slightly off the beaten track for those looking for something different (especially golfers). Set in 1,200 landscaped acres/486ha and with a magnificent vista as you walk in the front doors, it

Mandara Spa at the Portofino Bay Hotel

© OCVB

© OCVB

Bössendorfer Lounge at the Grand Bohemian

suits both business traveller and leisure-seeker alike. New in 2006 were 59 stunning 2- and 3-bed **villas**, affording a more private stay, with full kitchen facilities and an amazing array of specialised services in addition to opulent furnishings (407 390 6664, **www.omnihotels.com** and **www.championsgategolf.com**).

At the other end of the scale is the **Celebration Hotel** in the Disney-inspired town of Celebration. Just off Highway 192, the Central Florida Greeneway and I-4, this unique hotel offers a refreshing small-town America style. It has an elegant lounge and 2 reception desks, and you are a long way from the usual tourist hurly-burly. With just 115 rooms in its 1920s' wood-frame design, the Celebration has a classy ambience and a wealth of high-quality touches, notably in the ultra-comfy rooms. These come in a choice of an attic-like Retreat, Traditional (with either a king or 2 queen-size beds), Studio or a 2-room suite and they are all beautifully furnished. Lovely artwork, courteous staff and a good array of facilities – pool, jacuzzi and fitness centre, plus the superb **Plantation Room Restaurant** (excellent buffet breakfasts and a range of 'new Florida' dishes) – mark this hotel out as a real

gem. In addition, it is within a short stroll of the town's shops, restaurants and lakeside walks. It is also ideal for a romantic stay (407 566 6000, **www.celebrationhotel.com**).

Sister property **The Grand Bohemian Hotel** (formerly the Westin Grand Bohemian) has added a touch of class to the downtown scene. It features an early 20th-century Austrian theme, with the accent on fine art, fine dining and good service. Its 14 storeys make it a major landmark and it boasts the wonderful **Boheme** restaurant and über-stylish **Bösendorfer Lounge** – with great live entertainment nightly – plus a 14th-floor concierge suite, heated pool, spa, fitness centre, Gallery of Fine Art and Starbucks lounge. The rooms are superbly appointed: all are equipped with high-speed internet access, mini-bars, CD players and interactive TVs, plus there are 36 superb suites. Every room features the ultra-comfy Sumptuous Bed (407 313 9000, **www.grandbohemianhotel.com**).

One of the most dramatic hotels is the 1,406-room **Gaylord Palms Resort** on the junction of I-Drive South and Osceola Parkway (ideal for Disney). A cross between a convention centre and a vast turn-of-the-century Florida mansion, it features 4½ acres/2ha of indoor gardens, fountains and 'landscaped' waters under a glass dome. Three intricately themed indoor areas bear witness to great creativity, and the resort offers every creature comfort, with an array of restaurants and bars, full-service spa, children's centre and 10 shops. Its wonderfully imaginative outdoor Recreation Park has 2 full-size pools (1 family-orientated, with octopus waterslide and kids' splash area; the other a sophisticated adults-only area), bocce court (a type of boules), volleyball, croquet lawn and a realistic 9-hole putting challenge. The standard rooms are some of the smartest and most spacious in the area, while the suites are enormous. There is even a hotel-within-a-hotel, as the central Emerald Tower offers an even more upmarket room choice and concierge facilities.

One area is landscaped like the Everglades, with native plants, trees and animals; another copies the old-world charm of St Augustine – with replica Spanish fort; and the third reproduces the offbeat style of Key West, with a mock-up marina and sailboat (and a fun-themed daily Sunset Celebration with live entertainment). To walk into the resort's marbled lobby and cavernous interior at night is like entering a future world. The elaborate settings add to the resort's signature fine dining, with the choice of **Old Hickory Steakhouse** (naturally aged Black Angus beef a speciality), **Sunset Sam's** (for fine seafood) and the Spanish buffet-style **Villa de Flora** (with 6 show kitchens). The Canyon Ranch Spa Club is one of the region's largest, with a state-of-the-art spa, fitness facilities and beauty salon. There are an amazing 13 shops, plus the **Java Coast** coffee shop, **Auggie's Jammin' Piano Bar**, **H2O Sports Bar and Grille** and the **Candlelight Lounge**. The hotel stages regular special events and it is also a great venue for weddings (407 586 0000, **www.gaylordhotels.com**).

BRITTIP

The Gaylord Palms features the stunning Christmas celebration ICE!, a wonderland of ice sculptures, snow scenery and ice slides. Early Nov–2 Jan, tickets $19.95 for adults, $15.95 for over-55s and $9.95 for 4–12s.

The area's first genuine Deluxe resort is also still one of the best. The **Hyatt Regency Grand Cypress** (which opened in 1984) is a mature 1,500 acre/608ha resort with a unique mix of facilities, including the only 9-hole pitch-and-putt golf course in town, 27 holes of regular golf (designed by Jack Nicklaus), a golf academy, boating lake and even an equestrian centre. The elegant lobby is just the start of a wonderfully luxurious adventure, almost on the doorstep of Disney and yet blissfully self contained (on Winter Garden-Vineland Road, just around the corner from the Crossroads Plaza at Lake Buena Vista). The 750 rooms and generous suites are all beautifully furnished, but it is the amenities once you step outside the room that are so memorable. The huge free-form swimming pool, complete with jacuzzis, waterfalls and slide, the white sand beach, health club and the magnificent array of restaurants make for a sumptuous stay. **Cascades** is the ideal venue for a casually elegant lunch, **Hemingways** is its Key West-styled dinner spot and **La Coquina** is the specialist gourmet restaurant,

Hemingways

© OCVB

with a novel Chef's Table inside the kitchen 3 evenings a week and a sensational Sunday Brunch. There is also a sports bar and grill, 3 lounge bars, pool bar, a deli-style café and a general store. Once among its richly landscaped grounds, you could easily be light years away from the theme park hustle-bustle (407 239 1234, http://grandcypress.hyatt.com).

Finally, the luxury element is taken to the full at the 500 acre/200ha **Grande Lakes Orlando**, a combination of a 584-room, 5-star Ritz-Carlton Hotel, a 1,000-room JW Marriott Hotel, 40,000sq ft/3,700sq m health spa, an 18-hole Greg Norman-designed golf course, tennis centre and a range of shops and 11 restaurants, including the outstanding **Norman's**, featuring the 'new world' cuisine of celebrity chef Norman Van Aken. Located on the edge of a forestry preserve, it feels secluded and remote – quite a feat in this area. It is slightly off the beaten tourist track – at the junction of John Young and Central Florida Parkway – yet only 2mls/3km from SeaWorld, 7mls/11km from Universal Orlando and 10mls/16km from Disney and Orlando International Airport.

The **Ritz-Carlton** is the first of the company's properties in central Florida, and the scale and detail are wonderful: lush gardens, abundant lakes and streams, Venetian-inspired architecture and a wealth of genuine antiques. It has a large, sloped-entry pool, kids' pool, 3 floodlit tennis courts, a signature shop and 5 restaurants, plus a separate children's check-in and the excellent Ritz Kids Club (for 5–12s), while all the restaurants offer child menus. The rooms are gorgeous – beautifully furnished, with high-quality products

Ritz-Carlton Orlando

in the marbled bathrooms – and feature plasma-screen TVs, radio/CD, mini-bar, hair-dryer, slippers and robes, and all have balconies. There are 66 spacious suites and 92 Club rooms on the top 2 floors, with concierge and butler service, food and drink presentations in the Club Lounge, and Bvlgari amenities. Two kidsuites feature a separate bedroom and bathroom, with toys, games, TV and video games for guaranteed child appeal.

The **JW Marriott** is the new flagship hotel for the Marriott group, with Spanish-Moorish design, a formal Italian restaurant, French brasserie, Starbucks coffee lounge and a pool bar and grill. It also has a unique 'lazy river' mini water park (providing the largest pool deck in Florida), plus a children's zero-depth entry pool, splash fountain and a separate kids' check-in. And, while the Marriott is more convention-orientated, it is still well geared for families with all the facilities, a variety of shops and the option to use the Ritz Kids programme and dining options next door. Rooms are plush and ultra-comfortable, 70% have balconies and there are 64 suites. The golf course is immaculate, and every foursome is assigned a free caddie (virtually unknown for a public course in

BRITTIP

Head for the Ritz-Carlton's lobby lounge for afternoon tea or drinks in style with a magnificent view, especially at sunset.

Florida). The beautiful citrus-tinged Health Spa is the best in the region, with a huge fitness centre and aerobics studio, lap pool (all free to guests at both hotels), lovely spa-cuisine restaurant and a huge array of massages and therapies. The pricing is suitably upscale, but it is a rare holiday treat (407 206 2400/2300, **www.grandelakes.com**).

Condo-hotels

Orlando is currently experiencing a major hotel boom and there is much new development in the offing. Much of it is of the **condo-hotel** variety – think of a cross between a villa and a hotel and you are most of the way there! Instead of a villa, people buy hotel 'rooms' in these big developments (which look, to all intents and purposes, like regular resorts), which they then own – unlike timeshare, where you just 'own' a time period for a resort. All the rooms are identically furnished, unlike villas, but also include kitchens and separate bedrooms and are then rented out by a management company on behalf of the owners. For guests, they are booked as you would for any hotel. Some are owned and run by hotel groups like Starwood and Four Seasons, while others are just managed by hotel specialists to ensure the facilities are maintained to the necessary standards. They are usually built in tower blocks around communal facilities with a Club

House and guest check-in, and include pools (often with elaborate water features and play areas), restaurants, fitness centres and even luxury spas. They will be more expensive than a typical hotel room, but they do provide more style and amenities. In some instances, you can still buy condo units in the various properties as well as enquire about staying there on a hotel basis. All of the following are due for completion between 2007 and 2009.

The **Bella Casa Resort**, a 200-room condo-hotel on International Drive, in elaborate Italianate style (407 260 6464, **www.bellacasaresort.com**); **Mona Lisa at Celebration**, a luxury 5-storey, 240-unit condo-hotel in Celebration with a rooftop sundeck and up-scale restaurant, (407 566 0444; **www.mona lisaatcelebration.com**); **San Marco Resort** at Lake Buena Vista (on Lake Bryan), boasting 1-, 2- and 3-bed condos in two 16-storey towers, with a large pool, lazy river feature and waterslides, plus a signature restaurant (**www.sanmarcoresort.com**); **WorldQuest Resort**, 612 2- and 3-bed condos being built in 18 5-storey buildings at the top end of I-Drive South, with a signature pool area and

Orlando World Center Marriott

restaurant (**www.worldquestresort.com**); **The Point Orlando Resort** condo-hotel on I-Drive features some smart 1- and 2-bed units in four 12-storey buildings around extensive resort facilities, including clubhouse, pool, sauna, shop and bistro restaurant (**www.thepointorlando.com**); **Blue Heron Beach Resort** (though the nearest 'seaside' is an hour away!) on SR-535 features 140 1-, 2- and 3-bed condos with 6,000sq ft/557sq m pool, kids pool, video game room, fitness centre and wetlands walk right on Lake Bryan in Lake Buena Vista, with the first phase (of 4) open in June 2007 (407 387 2910, **www.blueheronbeach resort.com**); **Tuscana** at Champions Gate has 2- and 3-bedroom condos, each with 2 full baths, balcony, fully equipped kitchen, washer and dryer. The $2 million clubhouse boasts a Café and Tiki Bar, pool, kiddie pool, cabanas, exercise facilities and a 35-seat movie theatre (1877 448 8722, **www.tuscana.net**); **Village at Town Center**, an all-suite condo-hotel conversion, on Lake Wilson Road in Davenport just off exit 58 of I-4, with 1-, 2- and 3-bedrooms, plus fitness centre, pool and tennis court (863 424 7606, **www.villagetowncenter.com**).

Clubhouse at Tuscana

Disney's Boardwalk Inn

There are even grander condo-hotel projects in store, including **The Blue Rose**, a sensational 39-storey tower complex on Universal Boulevard, featuring 1,545 rooms, a theatre, 6 restaurants and other entertainment, with the first phase due in late 2008 (**www.thebluerose.com**); and the extensive **Village of Imagine**, a 30 acre/12ha resort of 1,000 homes, and condo-hotel units, also on Universal Boulevard (**www.villageofimagine.com**).

B & B choice

Bed-and-breakfast in Orlando is offered in a more upscale, almost boutique style than we know it in the UK. The 11-room **Wonderland Inn** in Kissimmee is a restored Historic Registry property off the beaten track but only 10 minutes from the Highway 192 area. Each of its rooms has a delightful, individual touch, and several are designed for singles as well as doubles, and there's also 1 honeymoon suite. The staff are wonderfully attentive and even the lovely gardens have an old-fashioned charm. It also offers 5-course Wine Down Dinners, each course being paired with its own wine (1877 847 2477, **www.wonderlandinn.com**).

The pretty Lake Eola district downtown has two fine B&Bs. **The Veranda** has 12 individual, cottage-style rooms, ranging from Queen

Fort Wilderness cabin

© Disney

Studio and King Suites to a lovely honeymoon suite in landscaped gardens with a private courtyard, pool and spa area. Breakfast consists of fresh pastries, seasonal fruits, juices, tea and coffee, and it's a quiet spot, though an easy walk to some good restaurants and shops (407 489 0321, **www.theverandabandb.com**). The nearby **Eo Inn and Urban Spa** is a genuine boutique hotel and spa (with a huge range of treatments), featuring 17 deluxe rooms. The lush grounds, rooftop terrace and lake vistas provide a refreshing alternative to the usual hotel experience (407 481 8485, **www.eoinn.com**).

One final choice is the lovely **Perri House B&B**, beautifully tucked away in a quiet location yet only 5 minutes from Disney property. With a genuine country-house charm and semi-rural setting (on a voluntary bird sanctuary), its 8 rooms and Villa de Perri, which has a full kitchen and sleeps up to 6, are a true delight and the whole property is a real one-off in this rare location (on Winter Garden-Apopka-Vineland Road). It makes a wonderfully romantic little hideaway as all rooms have king 4-poster or queen canopy beds and some sweet individual touches. There is also a pool and jacuzzi, plus a hearty continental breakfast buffet (407 876 4830, **www.perrihouse.com**).

RESORTS AND HOLIDAY HOMES

This is in many ways the biggest area of accommodation in Orlando, especially for UK visitors. There has been a huge development of holiday homes in the last 15 years, and it shows no sign of stopping. The homes boom has been mirrored by timeshare-style resort development, and the two have even merged into one in some cases. Generally speaking, vacation homes and resorts provide a valuable way for large families and groups to stay together and cut costs by self-catering. The homes (or 'villas'), whether individual houses, collections of houses, resorts or condominiums (apartment blocks), often have access to other communal facilities like large pools and recreation areas, and are always equipped with microwaves, TVs and washer-dryers. For these, a hire car is usually essential, but the savings can be significant.

Holiday resorts

This accommodation type combines the best of hotels, suites and villas, though some of the resort-style, purpose-built complexes double as timeshare resorts (or vacation ownership) and the new condo-hotel type. Resorts also have the advantage of a greater variety of facilities. They include the extensive **Orange Lake Resort**, 4½mls/7km west of Maingate on Highway 192 (407 239 0000,

Orange Lake Resort

Universal's Hard Rock Hotel

www.orangelake.com), with a mixture of 2-bed, 2-bath villas and suites, golf, water sports and cinema (plus an amazing new 12 acre/4.8ha water park, **River Island**, complete with lazy river, 2 zero-depth entry pools, mini-golf, spas and waterfalls), and the **Villages at Mango Key** on Lindfields Boulevard, 4mls/6.4km west of Maingate (863 424 4070, www.mangokey.com), has smart, new 2- and 3-bed townhouses with pool, jacuzzi, tennis and volleyball.

Liki Tiki Village on the western fringe of Highway 192 is a timeshare set-up that often has good-value apartments to rent on a weekly basis. Its newest blocks offer huge 2-bed apartments, with well-equipped kitchens (all with coffee and ice makers), while the 64 acre/26ha complex boasts 2 pools, a mini water park, tennis courts, paddle boats, bikes, pool-bar and grill and free continental breakfast Mon–Fri when timeshare presentations are held – but you don't have to attend the timeshare hard-sell (407 239 5000, www.islandone.com). Another extensive operation is the **Sheraton Vistana Resort**, just off the lower end of I-Drive in Lake Buena Vista, where facilities include fitness centres with steam and sauna rooms, 7 pools and

13 tennis courts, basketball, volleyball and shuffleboard, games rooms, bike rental and mini-golf to back up its luxurious 1- and 2-bed villas sleeping 4–8 (407 239 3100, **www.starwood vo.com**). Similarly, **Sheraton Vistana Villages**, further up I-Drive, is a beautiful resort with a good range of facilities but rather less hustle-bustle (407 238 5000).

The **Windsor Palms Resort** (just off West Highway 192 in Kissimmee) is also popular, offering private 3-, 4-, 5- and 6-bed pool homes and 2- and 3-bed condos with a clubhouse and gym, tennis courts, an Olympic-sized pool, a kiddie pool and spa, basketball, billiard room, playground and a 50-seat cinema showing recent films (1800 503 1127, **www.windsor palmsresort.com**). The **Mystic Dunes Resort and Golf Club** (formerly the Wyndham Palms Resort), tucked away in a quiet corner of Kissimmee, is primarily a holiday ownership property but it also offers hotel rentals, often at terrific rates. It is a truly luxurious resort with just about every facility you could think of, plus an impressive array of beautiful 1-, 2- and 3-bed villas that sleep up to 12 (407 226 9501, **www.mystic-dunes-resort.com**).

The wonderful **Bahama Bay Resort**, on Lake Davenport in Davenport (at the west end of Highway 192, then south on Highway 27, or enter off of Westside Blvd), opened in 2003 and is spread over 70 acres/28ha, with 498 condos (of 2 and 3 bedrooms, all with balconies) in 38 buildings, 2 and 3 storeys high. The resort-style community is woven with tropical landscaping that includes water features, a recreation centre and clubhouse, restaurant and snack bar, internet café, fitness centre, sauna and spa (the fabulous **Eleuthera Spa & Salon**), tennis, basketball and volleyball, 4 heated pools and kiddie pools. You can fish in the lake, which has a sandy beach, plus there is a video arcade and small cinema. A regular shuttle goes to and from the theme parks for a small charge. The 4 types of condo offer 2-bed, 2-bath (sleeping 6, with a sofa-bed in the lounge) and 3-bed, 2-bath (sleeping 8, again with sofa-bed), with fitted kitchen, laundry room/washer-dryer, living room and dining area. The Grand Bahama 3-bed condo has 1,739sq ft/162sq m of space and is one of the most elegant (0870 160 9632 in the UK, 1866 830 1617 in the US or visit **www.bahamabay.com**).

The **Summer Bay Resort** (also on West Highway 192) is a mixture of Budget motel (The Inn at Summer Bay), Standard hotel (Holiday Inn Express), some 3-bed vacation homes and new 1-, 2- and 3-bed villas and condos. The 700 rooms spread over 64 acres/26ha are all smart, while the facilities include outdoor heated pools and kiddie pools, an elaborate children's water-play area, mini-golf, clubhouse with volleyball, tennis, basketball, shuffleboard and fitness room, video arcade, gift shop and snack bar. The lake provides jet-skis, paddle boats, water-skiing and more, plus daily kids' activities and organised sports. Even those in The Inn and Holiday Inn (which has its own pool deck and breakfast area) benefit from the clubhouse facilities, while there is a Denny's diner and Publix supermarket next door. It represents good value in this area and wonderful accommodation in the condos, and is still only 15 minutes from Disney (1800 654 6102, **www. summerbayresort.com**).

One of the newest and smartest of the area's condo-hotels is **Floridays Resort Orlando**, extremely well situated in a quieter part of I-Drive but close to Orlando Premium Outlets

Floridays Resort

and with a free shuttle service to the parks. The full site (Phase I) consists of 6 condo blocks (each with 72 rooms), 2 pools (including the elaborate main zero-depth entry pool and water-play area), a pool bar and grill, fitness centre, stylish Welcome Center, dinosaur-themed toddlers' playroom, and games room. There's also a Starbucks and a Marketplace for groceries, toiletries and sundries. With concierge services, a business centre and meeting facilities, it is also highly versatile. The water-jet play area will probably keep kids amused for hours without having to set foot outside the resort! The 2- and 3-bed grand suites are beautifully furnished and will easily sleep 6–10, and have either a balcony or patio. Living rooms include large-screen plasma TVs, high-speed internet, games console and stereos, while each bedroom has a TV, too. And, if you don't feel like cooking, you can take advantage of the delivery service from the Marketplace. All rooms are wheelchair-accessible and some are specifically adapted for the disabled with roll-in showers (407 238 7700, **www.floridaysresortorlando.com**).

The **Lake Buena Vista Resort Village & Spa** opened in 2006 with the first of what will eventually be 14 blocks of stylish 2-, 3- and 4-bed condos, right next to Lake Buena Vista Factory Stores on Highway 535. The first phase included 2 blocks, one of the

pools, a fitness centre, games room, convenience store and gift shop, plus an ice-cream/smoothie shop and a specialist pub-restaurant. The rooms themselves (all with full kitchens, jacuzzi tubs, digital TVs and internet) are comfortable and stylish, with the 4-bed condos incredibly spacious. The completed village (late 2008) will feature 4 pools, jacuzzis, children's play areas, tennis courts, clubhouse and full-service signature spa, plus more restaurants and shops (407 597 0214, **www.lbvorlandoresort.com**).

The final option is arguably the grandest, **Reunion Resort & Club**, of keen interest to golfers and all who appreciate the 5-star touch. On Highway 532 in Kissimmee, just off exit 58 of I-4 south of Disney, this fledgling 'community' will have 6,000 units when complete in 2012, but it already boasts a mind-boggling line-up, with condos, townhouses and luxury homes set around 3 superb golf courses (designed by Arnold Palmer, Tom Watson and Jack Nicklaus). The current line-up is deluxe in every way: 1-, 2- and 3-bed immaculately furnished **condo villas** (many with stunning views overlooking the golf courses and all with free high-speed internet access); a range of **private homes**, from modest 3-beds to mansion-style 8-beds (costing upwards of $1.8m), but all available for rent (and some for sale); a stylish golf **clubhouse** with excellent bar and restaurant; a full-service **spa**, with a superb array of beauty and health treatments; the scenic **Seven Eagles pool**, complete with **Pavilion Bar & Grille**, jacuzzis, fitness room and children's activity centre; 5 floodlit **tennis courts** with professional instruction; an amazing **water park**, consisting of lazy river, slides, pools, waterfalls and interactive kids' area; and miles of **biking and hiking trails**. Its first high-rise condo, the **Reunion Grande**, opened in 2007, with 82 ultra-luxurious 1- and 2-bed suites, magnificent fine-dining chophouse

Reunion Resort

Rental Accommodation

1 Cumbrian Lakes
2 Eagle Pointe
3 Indian Pointe
4 Country Creek
5 Bass Lake Estates
6 Lake Berkley Reserve
7 Four Winds Estates
8 Montego Bay
9 Chatham Park
10 Hamilton's Reserve
11 Indian Wells
12 Buena Ventura Lakes
13 Hunters Creek
14 Oak Island
15 Formosa Gardens
16 Indian Creek
17 Rolling Hills
18 Windsor Palms
19 Indian Ridge
20 Lindfields
21 Sunset Lakes
22 Emerald Isle
23 Polo Park
24 Polo Park East
25 Davenport Lakes
26 Bass Lake
27 Lake Davenport Estates
28 Magnolia Glen/ Tuscan Hills
29 Bahama Bay Resort

30 Wellington Reserve
31 Highlands Reserve
32 Westridge
33 Hampton Lakes
34 Florida Pines
35 Calabay Parc
36 Tuscan Ridge
37 Santa Cruz
38 Lorna Del Sol
39 Lorna Vista
40 West Haven
41 Happy Trails
42 Omni Orlando Resort at Champions Gate
43 Reunion Resort
44 Bentley Oaks
45 Bridgewater Crossing
46 Sunridge Woods
47 Ashley Manor
48 Pinewood Country Estates
49 Thousand Oaks
50 Sandy Ridge
51 Terrace Ridge
52 Regal Palms Resort
53 Woodridge/Clear Creek
54 High Grove
55 Sunrise Lakes
56 Eagle Ridge
57 Orange Tree
58 Greater Groves
59 Weston Hills

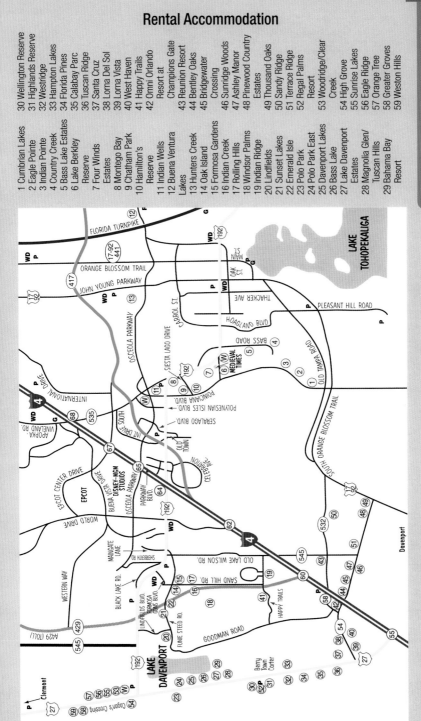

Forte, (with its understated elegance and fresh, inspired menu), state-of-the-art fitness facility and, uniquely for central Florida, a rooftop pool and the chic **Eleven** bar, serving up tapas, signature cocktails and panoramic views of the surrounding area. It all comes with personal concierge service and even private in-room dining that marks this out as one of Florida's most upmarket resorts. The water park is due to expand with the construction of the surrounding **Reunion Square** in 2008, while another massive condo-hotel will feature some of the resort's most exclusive 1-, 2- and 3-bed units, as well as associated shops, restaurants, cafés, bars and boutiques. Much is still to be finished, but all the golf courses are working, and the clubhouse also benefits from the supervision of outstanding executive chef Shawn Kane, who has made a name for himself with Disney and others. Only those staying here or members can play on the courses, but the scale and imagination of the resort make it quite awesome. There is even an activity programme for children. Kids Crew (8am–5pm Sun–Fri, 8am–11pm Sat), at $10/hour per child and $6 for lunch (1888 418 9611, **www.reunionresort.com**). Reunion is also home every April to the annual **LPGA Ginn Clubs & Resorts Open**, one of the newest and biggest women's golf tournaments. Reunion Resort guests can improve their own technique at state-of-the-art facility

Lakeside Inn, Mount Dora

Annika's Academy of Golf and Fitness, created under the careful supervision of Annika Sorenstam, one of the world's premier women golfers. Classes are led by her long-time coach, Henri Reis.

Holiday homes

Holiday homes (or 'villas') to rent are big business in central Florida and now account for a huge slice of the British market as they are ideal for repeat visitors, large groups and those who like their privacy and own facilities. They tend to be grouped in newly built estates and several are gated communities for added security. Nearly all offer a private pool and the largest can sleep up to 16. Some are classed as 'executive' homes, and this usually means more facilities (DVD, games rooms, barbecues, etc.) rather than any increase in size. If you're booking independently, there are several key questions to ask:

Do you need to go to an office some way away to pick up the keys or is there a combination-lockbox at the house? Is there a local contact if anything goes wrong (most owners do not live in Florida) and is the property maintained by an on-the-spot company? Does it offer a security bonding for your booking, and is it a member of a reputable organisation like the Better Business Bureau of Central Florida? In winter, is the pool heated, and what is the charge for heating? Finally, is it as close to Disney as it says – some homes can be down in Polk County, 30–40 minutes' drive away. One final warning – once you have sampled pool-at-home life, you may never go back to a hotel!

There are thousands of homes on offer these days, spread right across Kissimmee and out in both Polk and Lake Counties to the west and south-west of Disney. Some are brand new and still suffer from ongoing construction, others are now well

Superior resorts

As a half-way house between the pure resorts and vacation homes, British-founded company the Superior Group LLC has pioneered a mix of attractive resorts offering some of the best features of both. While Superior owns and manages a number of straightforward homes (notably in the lovely Highlands Reserve community on Highway 27), as well as the Crowne Plaza Hotel on I-Drive, its **Regal Palms Resort** next door to Highlands Reserve offers a pleasing mix of 3- and 4-bed townhouses and 4-, 5- and 6-bed private pool homes, all set around a beautiful resort facility that includes a mini water park (with lazy river and waterslides), pools, jacuzzis and extensive sunbathing terraces. It also features a pub that shows live UK sports, a business centre, gym and gift shop/grocery store, plus an indulgent Spa & Health Club (**www.regalpalmsorlando.com**, 863 424 6141). New in 2008 will be **Oakmont Resort & Spa**, a grand development of 3- to 6-bed pool villas in a series of 'villages' just off Highway 27 in Davenport. Set around their own clubhouse, they will benefit from extensive resort facilities, which include a large tropical pool complex, with waterslide, lazy river, pools, children's play area and sun terraces, plus a full-service spa. **Regal Lakes**, just off Highway 192 south of Disney's *Animal Kingdom*, will add an equally extensive layout of designer 2-, 3- and 4-bed townhouses in a Mediterreanean setting. Once again, it follows the formula of offering a central clubhouse with extensive pool and resort facilities. Finally, Superior will open **Regal Oaks** in 2009. Next to Old Town in Kissimmee, this will be a mix of luxury townhouses, varying from 3-bed, 2-bath units to grand 4-bed, 3-bath homes. Again, guests will have the benefit of the elaborate clubhouse, water features, restaurant and other facilities. It all adds up to terrific value. For info on all Superior resorts, visit **www.superiorus.com**

established and mature (Highlands Reserve is a good example), while others may be in need of repairs. You can rent either direct from the owners (on sites like **www.vrbo.com** and **www.lastminutevillas.net**) or from a property management company, which will look after multiple villas. Ironically, there is also a move to 'townhomes,' which are a more British style of terraced houses (so developers can fit in more!); for a 'detached' house, ask for a 'single family home'.

The bottom line is you must do your homework and shop around as you would for any significant purchase, and check with organisations like **Central Florida Property Managers**

Association and the **Guild of Florida Owners** (**www.floridaowners.org**), the latter of which is geared towards regular inspections of existing villas, aimed at identifying a gold standard of accommodation in this area (as well as some resorts and hotels). It provides an official GFO seal of approval for owners to use on their websites, while its website also offers impartial advice to present and potential owners. Its regular magazine, *The Guild*, is also worth picking up.

Last minute villas offer a range of properties

Check them out!

The Central Florida Property Managers Association has a new website designed to promote villa rentals and make booking easier. Look it up at **www.vacationwith confidence.com**. There is also another general website that sets out the advantages at **www.discovervacationhomes.com**

Lake Eola Park Fountain

The following companies all pass the *Brit's Guide* credibility test:

Family-owned **Alexander Holiday Homes**, in Kissimmee, manages 260 properties, from standard condo-villas to luxury executive homes sleeping up to 10, all with pools and immaculately furnished, within 15–20 minutes of Disney. This company was the first of its kind in Orlando and still offers a highly personable, efficient service. It was only the third management company in Florida to earn a lofty AAA (American Automobile Association) rating and definitely gets our approval. It also shows prices in UK and US currency and even offers an airport meet-and-greet service to ensure you get to your home. Its website is full of useful area info, as well as providing photo tours of all its homes (1800 621 7888 in the US, 0871 711 5371 in the UK, **www.floridasunshine.com**).

Premier Vacation Homes offers a good range of spacious properties with 2–6 bedrooms, sleeping up to 14, in secure residential communities within a 15-minute drive of Disney. All are privately owned and have been purchased and furnished as holiday homes, with screened pools, 2 TVs, fully equipped kitchens (including dishwasher, washer-dryer, microwave

and coffee maker), at least 1 king or queen bed, and free local phone calls. Maid service can be added for a fee. The **Luxury** homes (2–4 beds) are the standard accommodation, while **Executive** homes (3–6 beds) are bigger, with an extra TV, VCR and barbecue (407 396 2401 or 0500 892 634 in the UK, **www.premier-vacation-homes.com**).

Another company we know well and can recommend is British-owned **Florida Leisure Vacation Homes**, which pays great attention to detail. With almost 100 homes (2–7 beds) in the Kissimmee area (most just a few years old), it prides itself on a personal touch and offers some of the biggest and newest properties, as well as a fully automated online booking system. Many are in the Executive range, with the fullest array of amenities in addition to their private, screened pools, and often in a secure, gated community. All homes have lockboxes, which means you don't need to visit the management office to check in. You can see all their homes online (in extended photo and video) plus lots of local info, especially for restaurants and golf, while its new testimonial sections provide first-hand visitor feedback. Its handy office is on Highway 192 in Kissimmee, at the junction with Apopka-Vineland Road, SR 535 (407 870 1600; **www.floridaleisure.com**).

An alternative, UK-based company is **Sun Villas Florida Direct**, launched in September 2001 by a former managing director of Lunn Poly to provide a bespoke holiday offering villa accommodation, flights, attraction tickets and car hire. It has a variety of properties from Orlando

BRITTIP

You'll find Marmite, Ribena, McVities etc., at the Publix supermarkets on Highway 192, or the 24-hour Goodings stores at Crossroads and on I-Drive.

ACCOMMODATION

VIP example

A good example of the kind of homes on offer are provided by typical UK owners Nina and Pete Dew, who have 3 Orlando properties on the website **www.floridavipvacation homes.com**. Set in 2 new communities – Sandy Ridge and Terrace Ridge – just to the south of Disney (but still barely 15 minutes' drive away), they are representative of the more upmarket, executive-style homes.

down to Sarasota and Naples, and maintains consistently high standards (01926 336 611, **www.sunvillas floridadirect.com**). **Advantage Vacation Homes** has also been in the villa rental business for many years now and looks after its customers well. None of its 2–6 bed homes (the majority are on West Highway 192 and Highway 27 in Clermont and Davenport) is more than 6 years old, while many are 2–3 years at most. It also manages an increasing portfolio of condos (in the Bahama Bay and Sun Lake resorts). It offers 24-hour management, with courteous and efficient staff, at its office just off west Highway 192 (plus an attraction ticket service), open 9am–10pm daily. Its holiday homes are rated Silver, Gold or Platinum, with the difference in quality measured in the extras rather than size or facilities (larger-screen or plasma TVs, tiled floors rather than carpeting and perhaps a jacuzzi). Its newest properties on Highway 27 usually have communal playgrounds and tennis courts (1800 527 2262, **www.advantagevacationhomes.com**).

For a luxury touch, **Loyalty Homes** promises all its homes are no more than 4mls/6.5km from Disney, with digital door locks (i.e. no key collection required) and many with games rooms (407 397 7475, **www.loyaltyusa.com**).

Florida Choice Vacation Homes provides townhouses (3–4 beds with communal pools and recreation facilities), standard and executive

homes (3–7 bed private properties) in Orlando and Naples, some with heated pools and with free local phone calls. There is optional maid service and cot and highchair rentals (407 397 3013, **www.floridachoice.com**). **Villa Direct** is another major Orlando specialist, and one of the biggest, with some 600 properties in the area and a good user-friendly website, plus an excellent range of guest services, including arrival groceries and even mobility equipment rental. Its office is handily located on Highway 192, just 2 mls from Disney, and its range of properties is extensive (1877 259 9908, **www.villadirect.com**).

Finally, another local British specialist is the **FRO Group**, which is actively involved in creating a villa community of homes that are purpose-designed for people with disabilities. It already features a select range of new homes in some of the smartest local developments, like Formosa Garden Estates and Emerald Island Resorts, and a rare twin-centre option with some lovely beachfront villas on the Gulf Coast at Indian Shores (near St Pete Beach). Its concierge service offers the chance to arrange many other services in advance (like dining), while its website features a Last Minute Deals section, which is a great way to save money. It is also extremely pro-active at helping out smaller management

There are more than 100 golf courses in Orlando

© OCVB

companies under the company umbrella, and is building an advice centre for people looking to expand their businesses or simply relocate to sunny Florida under the heading 'A Passage to Florida' (1866 394 2583; **www.fro-group.com**).

BUYING A HOLIDAY HOME

The quality of life, the favourable 26-year high exchange rate, emerging 'buyer's market' and fabulous weather are all compelling reasons to consider acquiring your own vacation home, for holidays, investment, a winter retreat or as a retirement home. But, apart from the fact that it's easy to be starry-eyed on holiday, there are companies willing to exploit naive tourists and investors alike, so be sure to do your homework, especially to understand the terminology of US property buying.

If you have looked in the window of a realtor (a US estate agent), you will know the big price difference compared with the UK. New homes are still popular, but the quality can vary, so you need to find a proven builder. **Meritage Homes** (formerly Greater Homes; 407 869 0300, **www.meritagehomesflorida.com**) has an

unimpeachable reputation and gets full *Brit's Guide* approval. It is a family-run company that has been building here since 1965 and has sold more than 3,000 homes to British owners. It's a reliable and quality-conscious firm and its website carries essential info for anyone considering buying here (including mortgage terminologies). Its latest vacation homes developments, **Lucaya Village** and **Aviana**, are both resort-style communities with many amenities necessary for a holiday. **Lexington Green** is another collaboration development that is currently offering sites within Providence, a golf and country club community.

All the above are zoned for short-term rentals, plus they are 10–25 minutes from Orlando International Airport and the popular attractions in the area. The highest recommendation we can offer is that when we bought a Greater Home in 2004 we could not have been more satisfied with our purchase, the ease with which it was conducted and the after-sales care. Other builders worth considering are **Beazer Homes** and **KB Homes**, both rated above average for build quality. More useful home-buying info can be

Omni Orlando Resort at Champions Gate

Disabled-friendly villas

While a handful of vacation homes have been converted to assist those with disabilities, they are hard to track down and rarely as user-friendly as they could be. But the FRO Group has teamed up with Monticelli Signature Homes and some of the top names in home design for the disabled to pioneer a first-of-its-kind development in Davenport that will start to become available in 2008. **Monticelli at Tower Lake** will be a community of 59 homes all incorporating the very latest accessible design features that go above and beyond the usual ADA guidelines. Easy-access entryways, fully wheelchair-accessible rooms, including unique kitchens and bathrooms, and all pools with an individual lift are some of the basic requirements, and there are sure to be more clever details in the finished product. Check out the latest at **www.fro-group.com**.

found from **Alexander Holiday Homes (www.floridasunshine.com)** and **Florida Leisure (www.florida leisure.com)**, a registered realtor that publishes a free *Home Buying Guide* from its website. UK magazines *International Homes* (**www.international-homes.com**), *Homes Overseas* (**www.homesoverseas.co.uk**), and *Overseas Property TV Magazine* (**www.mripropertyoverseas.com**) all have big Florida sections and are worth picking up. Make sure you cast an eye over all the new deals being offered for **condos** and **condo-hotels**, as these can be especially good value.

Owning a piece of the magic is tempting, but you must get all the facts first, then look for a company that specialises in assisting British buyers. Many firms primarily offer vacation-style properties, and several deal mainly with the British. Consider investigating one of the firms that allows you to fund your mortgage in sterling, through a UK bank, rather than the dollar equivalent. If you live in the UK and are paid in sterling, a US dollar mortgage can be costly and inconvenient. For instance, US mortgage companies often 'sell' new mortgages to another lender after closing a loan, making it hard to track. Repayment of a dollar mortgage with sterling is also subject to fluctuating exchange rates.

In this instance, a company we have come to know well through our contacts with the British–American Chamber of Commerce, and which we have been happy to recommend for many years, is the **British Homes Group Florida (www.britishhomes group.com)**. When we first met its team, it had just completed a market test in Orlando of a new British currency mortgage designed specifically for UK residents buying investment properties in Florida. The test was a great success and British currency mortgages are now available to UK buyers for properties anywhere in the Sunshine State.

BRITTIP

Good legal advice for house-buying, business and (especially) immigration matters is *essential*. Contact Orlando firm **LaVigne, Coton & Associates** (407 316 9988, **www.lavignelaw.us**) for the best advice on all these matters.

This revolutionary programme, called *British Mortgages Abroad*, was developed in collaboration with Abbey National and is now offered by the British subsidiary of GE through the British Homes Group. It allows Brits to purchase buy-to-let villas and second homes using the Florida property (rather than the buyer's UK home) as security for a pound-denominated mortgage, thus avoiding monthly payment currency exchange risks. **British Home Loans Florida**, the BHG's fully licensed Florida mortgage brokerage company,

The Waterfront at SeaWorld

also offers a broad selection of US dollar mortgages for UK buyers preferring to keep their Florida transactions in US currency, plus a new multi-currency mortgage from Lloyds TSB that, once set up, allows borrowers to switch the currency of their mortgage without the usual closing cost fees. British Home Sales Florida, the group's estate agency, can help search for the ideal property anywhere in the state and, with online access to more than 20,000 properties in Central Florida, there is definitely a lot to choose from. Add in the BHG's useful Florida Advisory Panel, free Florida rental booking and listing services, and a Florida Blog for the latest local info, and it is easy to see why it has become one of the best resources for British investors in Florida. It has a UK freephone number (0800 096 5989) and provides a starting point for your property search, an evaluation of a proposed purchase, or an assessment of your existing mortgage position, all free and without obligation (see inside back cover for current promotion). Call (in Florida) 407 396 9914, email **info@britishhomesgroup.com** or visit its offices at 2960 Vineland Rd, Kissimmee, above the Edwin Watts Golf Shop at the junction of Routes 535 and 192.

But, whoever you go with, ensure they can refer you to experts in UK and US taxation, immigration, hazard insurance, structural warranties and other issues essential for hassle-free ownership in Florida. Property in Orlando has increased in value over the last 10 years, but there is never any guarantee, and rates fluctuate.

Bob's buying tips

Bob Mandell, Division President of Meritage Homes, offers these essential tips for anyone looking to buy a holiday home:

1 Get references from UK owners and check management company references.

2 Try to stay in the community on holiday before you buy.

3 Make sure the home meets all requirements for short-term rentals, such as emergency exit lighting, smoke detectors in all bedrooms and a keyed, locked owners' closet.

4 Ensure the builder offers a warranty.

5 Walk through the community and talk to people there.

6 Ensure the property allows you to let it on a short-term basis.

7 Make sure you have all the proper US fees, registrations and taxes.

5 The Theme Parks: Disney's Fab Four

or Spending the Day with Mickey Mouse and Co

By now you should be prepared to deal with the main business of any visit to Orlando: Walt Disney World Resort in Florida and the other main theme parks of Universal Orlando, SeaWorld and Busch Gardens.

If you have only a week, this is where you should concentrate your attention but even then you may decide Busch Gardens is a bridge too far. If you have less than a week, you should focus on seeing as much of *Walt Disney World* as possible. There is SO much packed into every park and the main tourist areas, even 2 weeks is scarcely enough to give first-timers more than just an outline of central Florida.

Buying your tickets in advance is highly advisable, but work out your requirements first – you wouldn't get full use out of, say, a 7-Day Premium ticket AND a 5-Park Orlando FlexTicket in just a 2-week holiday. There are so many ticket outlets these days, you need to check what measure of security they offer (ABTA bonding, etc.) and what they do in case of lost or stolen tickets during shipping. Try to use your credit card for all purchases – there is built-in additional security (for our list of recommended ticket outlets, see page 13). You will also find **discount coupons** in tourist publications

distributed in Orlando for many of the smaller attractions (or from the Guest Services desk at your hotel – it's often worth asking), while the **tour operators'** welcome meetings usually have special offers and tickets for the latest excursions.

BRITTIP

Offers of 'free' Disney tickets usually mean timeshare firms, who also claim to have 'official' visitor centres. I-Drive has the only genuine Official Visitor Center.

The **Official Visitor Center** is at 8723 International Drive in the Gala Center on the corner of Austrian Row (407 363 5872, **www.orlandoinfo.com/uk**, see map on page 86) is also worth checking out for discounts. Equally, the Universal Attractions booths at

Mickey's PhilharMagic

© Disney

several shopping malls have great deals (3 days for the price of 2, 2-for-1 drinks etc.) on many attractions. Yes, it IS possible to bag free tickets by attending timeshare presentations, but they can easily take half a day of your precious holiday. Other sites worth visiting for discounts etc. are the *Orlando Sentinel's* info-based **www.go2orlando.com** and **www.orlando savings.com**

Ratings

We judge all the rides and shows on a unique rating system that splits them into **thrill rides** and **scenic rides**. Thrill rides earn T ratings out of 5 (hence a TTTTT is as exciting as they get) and scenic rides get A ratings out of 5 (an AA ride is likely to be over-cute and missable). Obviously, it is a matter of opinion to a certain extent, but you can be sure, a T or A ride is not worth your time, a TT or AA is worth seeing only if there is no queue, a TTT or AAA should be seen if you have time, but you won't miss much if you don't, a TTTT or AAAA ride is a big-time attraction that should be high on your list of things to do, and finally a TTTTT or AAAAA attraction should not be missed! The latter will have the longest queues, so you should plan

Guests at the Magic Kingdom

BRITTIP

If you DO want to check out timeshare options, look first at Disney Vacation Club for the guaranteed way to secure memorable holidays. A tour (for which you will be picked up) will take around 3 hours, but you will be given some Disney FastPasses in return to save time back at the parks. Call 407 566 3300, 1800 500 3990 or visit **http://dvc.disney.go.com/dvc/index**

your visit around them. Some rides have height restrictions and are not advisable for people with back, neck or heart problems or for expectant mothers. Where this is the case we say, for example, 'Restrictions: 3ft 6in/106cm'. Height restrictions (strictly enforced) are based on the average 5-year-old being 3ft 6in/106cm tall, those aged 6 being 3ft 9in/114cm and 9s being 4ft 4in/132cm.

BRITTIP

Smoking is not permitted in the parks, apart from in a handful of designated areas. Check park maps for their exact locations. All restaurants are strictly non-smoking.

© Disney

Character dining

Having a meal with Mickey and Co (or Winnie the Pooh, Cinderella or Mary Poppins) is one of the great Disney experiences – even if you don't have children! It is also often the best way to meet your favourite characters without long, hot waits. All reservations can be arranged up to 90 days in advance by phoning 407 WDW DINE (939 3463), calling at any Guest Services desk in a hotel, or by touching *88 on a Disney resort phone.

Some meals are difficult to get. Breakfast at **Cinderella's Royal Table** at the *Magic Kingdom* sells out 180 days in advance, within the first few minutes. **Chef Mickey's** and the **Princess Storybook** meals also go quickly. If you cannot book in advance, try calling the day you'd like to dine or, as a last resort, show up to see if there have been any cancellations. You must check in at the podium 5 minutes prior to your time and you will be given the next available table. Some characters don't enter the restaurant so, if they are in the lobby, you'll want to meet them before you are seated. Dining is all-you-can-eat, served buffet, pre-plated or family-style.

Inside the restaurant, characters circulate among the tables giving attention to each group (particularly when children are holding the camera!). Character interaction is top-notch, especially if you dine off-hours when the restaurant is quieter. Be sure to bring your autograph book, a fat pen or marker (easier for the characters to hold) and plenty of film or an extra digital card for your camera. Some characters are huge, and children may be put off by them. If you aren't sure how they'll react, see how they are with the characters in the park before going along to a character meal. Price range: breakfast $18.99–31.99 for adults, $10.99–21.99 for children; lunch $20.99–33.99 and $11.99–22.99; dinner $27.99–39.99 and $12.99–24.99.

The meals

Magic Kingdom: **Crystal Palace** for breakfast, lunch or dinner with Winnie the Pooh, Tigger, Eeyore and Piglet – especially good for smaller children; **Cinderella's Royal Table** for the fixed-price, fixed-menu Once Upon A Breakfast, with Cinderella and her Princess Friends; Fairytale Lunch with Cinderella and Friends; fixed-price dinner hosted by the Fairy Godmother (no other characters). Payment in full on your credit card is required to book, $10 per person may be charged for no-shows (photo package included in price, additional photos available for a fee); **Liberty Tree Tavern** for dinner with Chip 'n' Dale, Meeko, Minnie and Pluto.

Epcot: **Garden Grill** for lunch or dinner with Farmer Mickey, Pluto, Chip 'n' Dale; **Princess Storybook Dining** for breakfast, lunch and dinner; an alternative to Cinderella's, with some of Belle, Jasmine, Snow White, Pocahontas, Mulan, Sleeping Beauty and Mary Poppins but NOT Cinderella. Credit card needed to book, $10 per person charged for no-shows.

Disney-MGM Studios: **Hollywood & Vine** for breakfast or lunch with the *Playhouse Disney* Pals, including JoJo and Goliath from JoJo's Circus and June and Leo from Little Einsteins.

Disney's Animal Kingdom: **Donald's Breakfastasaurus** for breakfast with Donald, Goofy, Pluto and sometimes Mickey.

Disney Resorts: **Chef Mickey's** for *Contemporary Resort*; breakfast or dinner with Mickey, Minnie, Goofy, Pluto, Chip 'n' Dale – peak times book up quickly; **1900 Park Fare** for *Grand Floridian Resort and Spa*; breakfast with Alice and her Wonderland Friends; dinner with Cinderella, Perla, Suzy, Fairy Godmother and, sometimes, Prince Charming – again, book early; **Wonderland Tea Party** for *Grand Floridian Resort and Spa*; 1.30–2.30pm Mon–Fri, 3–10s only, $28.17, lunch, activities and storytelling with Alice and friends. $10 no show; **'Ohana** for *Polynesian Resort*; breakfast with Lilo, Stitch, Pluto and Mickey; **Cape May Café** for *Beach Club Resort*; breakfast with Goofy, Chip 'n' Dale and Pluto; **Mickey's Backyard Barbecue** for *Fort Wilderness*; $44.99 and $26.99, games, storytelling, live entertainment, music and dancing with Mickey and Co; unlimited beer, wine, iced tea and lemonade – seasonal; **Walt Disney World Swan** for Garden Grove Café; Sat breakfast with Goofy and Pluto. Gulliver's Grill; 6pm dinner with Timon and Rafiki Mon–Fri, Goofy and Pluto Sat and Sun.

© Disney

Liberty Belle Riverboat

Disney's FastPass

One essential aid to queuing is **Disney's FastPass Service**. Most of the main attractions have this wonderful service that allows you to roam while you wait for an allotted time to ride. How it works: insert your main park entrance ticket into the FastPass (FP) machine (to the side of the attraction's entrance) and you get another ticket giving you a period of time in which to return for your ride with only a minimal wait (NB: you need a FP ticket for every person who wants to ride, not just 1 per group). You can hold only 1 FP ticket per 2-hour period, though once you've used it you can get another. If you start by going to one of the FP rides, collecting your ticket and returning later, you can by-pass a lot of standing in queues. You can also get another FP as soon as your 'window' opens: if your time slot for Space Mountain in *Magic Kingdom Park* is 10–11am, you could get another FP for, say, Buzz Lightyear's Space Ranger Spin at 10.01

BRITTIP

Purchase a lanyard for your park tickets if you plan to use FastPass often. This keeps your tickets together and easily accessible.

and then go and ride Space Mountain! Many people still miss out on this, but it is FREE (FastPass rides are indicated by FP in descriptions).

With young ones

All Disney's parks offer pushchair ('stroller') hire, and you can save $2 per day by purchasing a multi-day rental at your first park. Children of ALL ages seem to get a big thrill from collecting autographs from the various Disney characters, and most shops sell handy **autograph books**.

Pal Mickey

If you want the ultimate theme park friend to help you queue, offer tips, play games and help find the characters, just ask Mickey – Pal Mickey, that is. This is a high-tech 10½in/27cm tall cuddly toy that talks to you around the parks (using wireless communication) as a kind of tour guide, with hints (e.g. in *Disney-MGM Studios*: 'Fantasmic! will be starting in about an hour'), insider info (on Main Street USA: 'See the names written on those second-storey windows? Those folks helped Walt build his *Magic Kingdom*!') and interactive games while you queue (which still work when you get home).

Disney's Year of a Million Dreams

If you visit in October–December 2007 you will still find *Disney's Year of a Million Dreams* going on. All visitors to Walt Disney World stand a chance of receiving special random 'Dreams' from Cast Members, such as special parties and one-off events, private character greetings, being the Grand Marshall at parades, a FastPass for all the main attractions and even the chance of the ultimate Disney fantasy – a night in Cinderella's Castle! This 15-month celebration is designed to make a host of Disney dreams come true on a daily basis. All you need to do is turn up.

Sounds fun? Wait for the price – Pal Mickey costs a whopping $65.

PhotoPass

This unique and worthwhile scheme is available in all Disney's theme parks and (occasionally) in *Downtown Disney*. Disney photographers take photos of guests throughout Walt Disney World and, instead of receiving a paper claim ticket, you receive a *Disney PhotoPass* that links together all your vacation pics into one online account for easy online viewing. There is no charge for obtaining a *PhotoPass* or for viewing or sharing photos online (though there is if you want to download and print them), while each photo can be enhanced with Disney characters and special borders. Guests typically have

30 days after their photos were taken to decide if they want their photos (visit **www.disneyphotopass.com**), or you can view them at one of 3 *PhotoPass* shops – at the *Magic Kingdom*, the *Epcot* park or *Disney's Grand Floridian Resort*. Collect as many photos as you want (up to 300!) and have them all burned on to one CD for a bargain $124.95.

Cast Members

Disney Cast Members or CMs (they are never referred to as 'staff' as they all play a 'role' in the entertainment) are renowned for their helpful and cheerful style and are always willing to assist, offer advice or just stop and chat. Interaction with CMs often provides some of the best memories of a visit. So, if you've had exceptional service or a CM has gone out of their way to help you, let Disney know as it values such feedback (and CMs get credit for it, too). Call in at Guest Relations on your way out (or City Hall at the *Magic Kingdom Park*) and record your vote of thanks.

Child swap

Where families have small children, but Mum and Dad both want to try a ride with height restrictions, you DON'T have to queue twice. When you reach the entrance to the queue, tell the operator you want to do a child swap. This means Mum can ride while Dad looks after junior in a quiet area and, on her return, Dad can have his go. You may also be given a child swap ticket while you wait.

Primeval Whirl at Disney's Animal Kingdom

© Disney

Magic Kingdom Park

The starting point for any visit has to be the *Magic Kingdom*, the park that best embodies the genuine enchantment Disney bestows on its visitors. It's the original development that sparked the tourist boom in Orlando back in 1971. In comparative terms, the Magic Kingdom is similar to the *Disneyland Park* at *Disneyland Resort Paris®* and *Disneyland California*. Outside those, it has no equal as a captivating day out for all the family. However, although superficially some rides are the same as those in Paris or Los Angeles, there are key differences, notably on Pirates of the Caribbean, Big Thunder Mountain Railroad and the Haunted Mansion. And Space Mountain is a completely different ride from the one in Paris.

And even if a couple of attractions are closed for refurbishment, you won't be short of things to do!

We will now attempt to steer you through a typical day at the park, with a guide to the main rides, shows and places to eat, how to park, how to avoid the worst of the crowds and how much you should expect to pay. *The Magic Kingdom* takes up just 107 acres/43ha of Disney's near 31,000 acres/12,555ha but attracts almost as many visitors as the rest put together. It has 7 separate 'lands', like slices of a large cake, centred on Florida's most famous landmark, Cinderella Castle. More than 40 attractions are packed into the park, not to mention numerous shops and restaurants (though the eating opportunities are less impressive than in *Epcot* and

Magic Kingdom Park at a glance

Location	Off World Drive, Walt Disney World
Size	107 acres/43ha in 7 'lands'
Hours	9am–7pm off peak; 9am–10pm President's Day (see page 19), spring school holidays; 9am–midnight high season (Easter, summer holidays, Thanksgiving and Christmas)
Admission	Under-3s free; 3–9 $60 (1-Day base ticket), $272 (5-Day Premium), $276 (7-Day Premium); adult (10+) $71, $310, $314. Prices do not include tax.
Parking	$10
Lockers	Next to stroller and wheelchair hire $7 ($2 deposit refunded)
Pushchairs	$10 and $18 (Stroller Shop to right of main entrance); length of stay price varies
Wheelchairs	$10 or $40 ($5 deposit refunded) (Main Ticket Centre)
Top Attractions	Splash Mountain, Space Mountain, Mickey's PhilharMagic, Big Thunder Mountain Railroad, Pirates of the Caribbean, most rides in Fantasyland
Don't Miss	Disney Dreams Come True Parade, SpectroMagic Parade (certain nights) and Wishes fireworks (most nights)

Hidden Costs	Meals	Burger, chips and coke $8.98
		3-course dinner $40 (Cinderella's Table)
		Kids' meal $3.99–7.49
	T-shirts	$20–32
	Souvenirs	$1–37,500
	Sundries	Face painting $8–15, or silhouettes $8, with oval frame $15.95

© Disney

Smiles are guaranteed!

Disney-MGM Studios). It's easy to get overwhelmed by it all, especially as it gets so busy (even the fast-food restaurants have big queues in high season), so study the notes and plan your visit around what most takes your fancy.

Location

The *Magic Kingdom Park* is situated at the innermost end of the vacation kingdom, with its entrance Toll Plaza ¾ of the way along World Drive, the main entrance off Highway 192. World Drive runs north–south through *Walt Disney World*, while the Interstate 4 (I-4) entrance, *Epcot* Drive, runs east–west. Unless you are staying at a Disney resort, you have to pay the $10 parking fee at the Toll Plaza and that brings you to the massive car park.

The majority arrive 9.30–11.30am, so the car parks are busiest then, which

BRITTIP

For the smoothest entry by road from Highway 192, take Seralago Boulevard opposite the Seralago Hotel & Suites next to Old Town, turn left on to a non-toll stretch of Osceola Parkway and follow the signs to your chosen park. On West 192, turn off on Sherberth Road, go north to the first traffic lights and turn right, then pick up the Disney signs.

is another good reason to get here EARLY. If you can't make it by 9am during peak periods, you might want to wait until after 1pm, or even later when the park is open as late as midnight. Remember to note exactly what area you parked in and the row number, e.g. Mickey, Row 30, otherwise you'll be struggling because many hire cars look the same!

BRITTIP

An easy way to remember where you parked is to take a picture of the Section and Row number on your digital camera or your phone. Then simply delete it when you get back to your car.

A motorised tram takes you from the car park to the Transportation and Ticket Center at the heart of the operation. Unless you already have your ticket (which will save you valuable time), you have to queue up at the ticket booths. From here, the monorail or a ferryboat will bring you to the doorstep of the *Magic Kingdom* itself. The monorail (straight ahead) is quicker if there isn't a queue, otherwise bear left and take a slower ferryboat. If you are staying at a Disney hotel, the resort buses deliver you almost to the park's front door (or the monorail or boat will if you are staying at one of the *Magic Kingdom* resorts).

ADVENTURELAND

1 Swiss Family Treehouse
2 Jungle Cruise
3 Magic Carpets of Aladdin
4 The Enchanted Tiki Room (under new management)
5 Pirates of the Caribbean

FRONTIERLAND

6 Splash Mountain
7 Big Thunder Mountain Railroad
8 Country Bear Jamboree
9 Raft to Tom Sawyer Island

LIBERTY SQUARE

10 Liberty Tree Tavern
11 Liberty Square Riverboat
12 The Haunted Mansion
13 The Hall of Presidents

FANTASYLAND

14 'It's a Small World'
15 Cinderella's Golden Carrousel
16 Mad Tea Party
17 The Many Adventures of Winnie The Pooh
18 Snow White's Scary Adventures
19 Dumbo The Flying Elephant
20 Mickey's PhilharMagic
21 Peter Pan's Flight
22 Castle Forecourt Stage
23 Cinderella's Royal Table
24 Ariel's Grotto
25 Fairytale Garden (Storytime with Belle)
26 Pooh's Playful Spot

MICKEY'S TOONTOWN FAIR

27 Mickey's Country House
28 Minnie's Country House
29 Toontown Hall of Fame
30 The Barnstormer at Goofy's Wiseacre Farm
31 Donald's Boat

TOMORROWLAND

32 Space Mountain
33 Tomorrowland Indy Speedway
34 Tomorrowland Transit Authority
35 Walt Disney's Carousel of Progress
36 Astro Orbiter
37 Stitch's Great Escape!
38 Buzz Lightyear's Space Ranger Spin
39 Monsters Inc. Laugh Floor
40 Galaxy Palace Theater

TRANSPORT

41 Walt Disney World Railroad
42 Boat Dock
43 Monorail Station
44 Bus Station

MAGIC KINGDOM PARK

Find the characters

Can't find Mickey and Co? This is often one of the main laments of those who come in unprepared. Check in at City Hall and they can tell you where the characters can be found. In fact, City Hall is your best friend for a variety of queries, from the location of baby facilities to meal bookings (but there are NO baby facilities at City Hall). Character meet-and-greets are also shown on all park maps with a Mickey's glove icon.

Finally, the *Magic Kingdom* is the only 'dry' park – that is, there's absolutely no alcohol on sale.

Main Street USA

Right, we've finally reached the park itself… but not quite. Hopefully you've arrived early and are among the leading hordes aiming to swarm through the main entrance. The published opening time may say 9am, but the gates can open up to 45 minutes earlier.

BRITTIP

Save paying up to 3 times more for your drinks by bringing your own bottled water in a backpack to all the parks and using the many drinking fountains dotted about for refills.

You will find yourself in **Main Street USA**, the first of the 7 'lands'. At opening time, there is an informal Welcome Parade, with costumed singers and dancers, and the Character Train then arrives at Main Street Station to bring a variety of characters for a friendly meet-and-greet in Town Square (get those autograph books ready!). A family is then chosen at random to sprinkle some 'pixie dust' to open the park officially for the day. Immediately on your right is **Exposition Hall**, a photographic centre featuring archive film material, interactive games, a mini cinema showing Disney classics and some cartoon photo

opportunities. On your left is **City Hall**, where you can pick up a park map and daily schedule (if you haven't been given them at the Toll Plaza) and make bookings for the restaurants (highly advisable at peak periods). You can also find out where the characters will appear and when. Ahead of you is **Town Square**, where you can take a 1-way ride on a horse-drawn bus or fire engine and visit the **Car Barn** mini museum. The Street itself houses the park's best shopping (check out the massive Emporium), plus the **Walt Disney World Railroad** (AAA), a Western-themed steam train that circles the park and is one of the better attractions when the queues are long elsewhere (though Town Square station is also the busiest).

BRITTIP

For the best chance of being chosen to march in the Main Street Family Fun Day Parade, be in the Castle Forecourt area at least 15 minutes before the parade.

For dining, the Italian-style **Tony's Town Square Restaurant** serves lunch and dinner, **The Plaza Restaurant** offers salads and sandwiches (lunch and dinner), and **The Crystal Palace** (breakfast, lunch

Main Street USA

© Disney

and dinner) is buffet-style food with Winnie the Pooh, Tigger and Co. Quick bites can be bought from **Casey's Corner** (hot dogs, chips and soft drinks), **Main Street Bakery** (coffee and pastries), **Main Street Cinema** and **Main Street Confectionary** (chocolate and sweets) and the **Plaza Ice Cream Parlor**. Disney characters also appear periodically outside Exposition Hall.

Look out for the **Guest Information Board** at the top of Main Street (on the left) that gives waiting times for all the attractions. The Baby Center (for nursing mothers) is also at the top of Main Street, to the left next to the Crystal Palace, along with the park's First Aid station. Unless you are a late arrival, give Main Street no more than a passing glance and head for the end of the street to the real entrance to the park. This is where you await the official opening hour for the famous 'Rope drop', and you should adopt 1 of 3 tactics here, each aimed at doing some of the most popular rides before the queues become substantial (waiting times of an hour-plus for Splash Mountain are not unknown).

One: if you fancy the 5-star, log-flume ride Splash Mountain, keep left in front of the Crystal Palace with the majority of the crowd, who will head for the same place. **Two**: if you have young children who can't wait to have a ride on Cinderella's Golden Carrousel or the other Fantasyland rides, stay in the middle and pass around the Castle. **Three**: if the thrills of the indoor roller-coaster Space

Mountain appeal first, move to the right by The Plaza Restaurant and you'll get straight into Tomorrowland. Now you'll be in pole position for the initial rush (and it *will* be a rush; take care if you're here with small children).

The **Main Street Family Fun Day Parade** generally runs three times daily, from Main Street USA to Town Square. Disney characters lend a hand in making this decidedly American parade a real flag-waving, Yankee Doodle dandy!

Adventureland

If you head to the left (effectively going clockwise around the park – always a good idea), you will enter Adventureland. If you're going to Splash Mountain first, you'll pass the Swiss Family Treehouse on your left and bear right through an archway (with toilets on your right) into Frontierland, where you turn left and Splash Mountain is straight in front of you. Stopping in Adventureland, however, these are the attractions:

Swiss Family Treehouse: this imitation Banyan tree is a clever replica of the treehouse from Disney's 1960 film *Swiss Family Robinson*. It's a walk-through attraction where the queues (rarely long) move steadily if not quickly, providing a fascinating glimpse of the ultimate treehouse, complete with kitchen, rope bridges and running water! AA.

Jungle Cruise: it's not so much the scenic, geographically suspect boat ride (where the Nile suddenly becomes the Amazon) that is so amusing here as the patter of your boat's captain, who spins a non-stop yarn about your adventure that features wild animals, tropical plants, hidden temples and sudden waterfalls. Great detail but long queues, so visit either early morning (opens at 10am) or late afternoon (evening queues are shortest, but you'll miss some of the detail in the dark). AAAA (FP).

The Jungle Cruise

© Disney

When you are faced by more than one queue for an attraction, head for the left-hand one. Almost invariably this moves slightly quicker.

Pirates of the Caribbean: one of Disney's most impressive attractions that involves its pioneering work in audio-animatronics, life-size figures that move, talk and, in this instance, lay siege to a Caribbean island! Your 8-minute underground boat ride takes you through a typical pirate adventure and into the world of Captain Jack Sparrow and his nemesis Captain Barbossa as they search for buried treasure. It's terrific family fun (though a bit spooky for very young children, with one small drop in the dark) and the 2006 addition of the *Pirates of the Caribbean* film characters, and some new special effects, means this is again highly popular. Queues are longest from midday to mid-afternoon. AAAAA.

The Enchanted Tiki Room (under new management): a bird-laden, audio-animatronics show features Iago (from *Aladdin*) and Zazu (from *The Lion King*) leading a colourful 16-minute revue that will especially appeal to younger children. Queues are rare (and it is air-conditioned if you need to cool down!). AAA.

Magic Carpets of Aladdin: here, in an Agrabah-themed area styled after the animated film, this ride spins you up, down and around as you try to dodge the spitting camel! Your 'flying carpet' tilts as well as levitates, but it is basically simple stuff geared for younger children (and virtually identical to the Magic Carpets of Agrabah in the *Walt Disney Studios in Disneyland® Resort Paris*). TT (TTTT under 5s).

Shrunken Ned's Junior Jungle Boats: this costs an extra $2 (!!) for kids to try their hand at steering rather tame toy boats. T.

Young swashbucklers should look for **Captain Jack Sparrow's Pirate Tutorial** near Pirates of the Caribbean, with shows running up to 7 times daily. Captain Jack and his sidekick Mack invite youngsters to join them in sword fights and treasure hunting, ending with the Pirate Oath as children become honorary buccaneers.

Disney characters also turn up near Pirates of the Caribbean and Magic Carpets rides. The area's best shopping is in the **Pirates Bazaar**. For food, you have **Aloha Isle** (yoghurt and ice cream), **Sunshine Tree Terrace** (fruit, snacks, yoghurt, tea and coffee), and the more substantial tacos, empanadas and taco salads of **El Pirata y el Perico Restaurante**.

Magic Carpets of Aladdin

© Disney

Frontierland

Passing through Adventureland brings you to the target for many of the early birds. This Western-themed area is one of the busiest and is best avoided from late morning to late afternoon.

Splash Mountain: based on the 1946 classic Disney cartoon *Song of the South*, this is a watery journey into the world of Brer Rabbit, Brer Fox and Brer Bear. The first part is all jolly cartoon scenery and fun with the main characters and a couple of minor swoops in your 8-passenger log boat. The conclusion, a 5-storey plummet at 45 degrees into a mist-shrouded pool, seems like you are falling off the edge of the world! A huge adrenalin rush, but busy almost all day (try it first thing or during one of the parades to avoid the longest queues). You'll also get VERY wet! Restrictions: 3ft 4in/101cm. TTTTT (FP).

Big Thunder Mountain Railroad: when Disney does a roller-coaster you can be sure it will be one of the classiest, and here it is – a runaway mine train that swoops, tilts and plunges through a mock abandoned mine filled with clever scenery. You should ride at least twice to appreciate all the detail, but again queues are heavy, so go first thing (after Splash Mountain) or late in the day. Restrictions: 3ft 4in/101cm. TTTT (FP).

Country Bear Jamboree: now here's a novelty, a 16-minute musical revue presented by audio-animatronic bears! It's great family fun with plenty of novel touches (watch for the talking moose-head). Again, you'll need to beat the crowds by going early morning (opens 10am) or early evening. AAA.

Frontierland Shootin' Arcade: this is the only other attraction in the park to cost extra ($1), as you shoot the animated targets. TT.

Woody's Cowboy Camp: rounds up a posse of youngsters 6 times daily on

© Disney

Big Thunder Mountain Railroad

the Frontierland street just outside Country Bear Jamboree. Sam the Singin' Cowboy leads the hoedown while Woody, Jesse and Bullseye kick up their heels for some rootin'-tootin' interactive fun. AA, or AAAA for under-6s.

Tom Sawyer Island: take a raft over to an overgrown playground of mysterious caves, grottos and mazes, rope bridges and Fort Sam Clemens, where you can fire air guns at passing boats (opens 10am). A good get-away in the early afternoon when the crowds are at their biggest, while **Aunt Polly's Dockside Inn** is a refuge within a refuge for snacks and soft drinks. TT.

Frontierland shops sell cowboy hats, guns and badges as well as Native American and Mexican handicrafts. For food, try **Pecos Bill Café** (salads, sandwiches and burgers), **Frontierland Fries** (McDonald's fries and drinks) or the **Turkey Leg Cart** (massive, smoke-grilled turkey legs). For shopping, try the nicely themed **Briar Patch** and the **Prairie Outpost** for interesting gifts.

Liberty Square

Continuing the clockwise tour brings you next to a homage to post-independence America. A lot of the historical content will go over the heads of British visitors, but it still has some great attractions.

Liberty Square Riverboat: cruise America's 'rivers' on an authentic paddle steamer, be menaced by Native Americans and thrill to the stories of How the West Was Won (opens 10am). This is also a good ride to take at the busiest times of the day, especially early afternoon. AAA.

The Haunted Mansion: a clever delve into the world of ghost train rides that is neither too scary for kids nor too twee for adults. Not so much a thrill ride as a scenic adventure. Watch out for the fun touch at the end when your car picks up an extra 'passenger'. Longish queues for much of the day, however, so try to visit late on. AAAA, or TTTT for under-6s.

The Hall of Presidents: this is the attraction that is likely to mean least to us, a 2-part show that is first a film about the history of the Constitution and then an audio-animatronic parade of all 43 American presidents (opens 10am). Technically it's impressive, but dull for youngsters, though it is another air-conditioned haven. AAA.

Shopping here includes **Ye Olde Christmas Shoppe** and **The Yankee Trader**, while eating options are the full-service **Liberty Tree Tavern** (hearty soups, steaks and traditional dishes like meatloaf and pot roast, plus dinner with Mickey and Co), **Columbia Harbor House** (counter-service fried chicken or fish and some excellent soups, salads and sandwiches, notably for vegetarians)

BRITTIP

Get more value for your money at the parks by ordering sodas 'without ice' to get a full cup.

and **Sleepy Hollow** (a picnic area serving snacks, fresh fruit and drinks).

Fantasyland

Leaving Liberty Square, you walk past Cinderella Castle and come into the park's spiritual heart, the area with which young children are most enchanted. The attractions are designed with kids in mind, but some of the shops are quite sophisticated.

'It's a Small World': this recently revamped attraction could almost be Disney's theme ride, a family boat trip through the different continents, each represented by hundreds of dancing, singing audio-animatronic dolls in delightful set-piece pageants. If it sounds twee, it actually creates a surprisingly striking effect, accompanied by an annoyingly catchy theme song that young children adore. Crowds peak in early afternoon. AAAA.

Cinderella's Golden Carrousel: the centrepiece of Fantasyland shouldn't need any more explanation other than it is a vintage carousel ride that kids adore. Long queues during the main part of the day, though. T, or TTT for under-5s.

Mad Tea Party: again, the kids will insist you take them in these spinning, oversized tea cups that have their own 'steering wheel' to add to the whirling effect. Actually, they're just a heavily disguised fairground ride. Again, go early or expect crowds. Characters from Alice in Wonderland also visit from time to time. TT, or TTTT for under-5s.

The Many Adventures of Winnie the Pooh: building on the timeless popularity of Pooh, Piglet and Co, this family ride offers a musical jaunt through Hundred Acre Wood with some clever special effects (get ready to 'bounce' with Tigger!) and another original soundtrack. AAA, or AAAAA for under-5s (FP). In front of the ride is **Pooh's Playful Spot**, a themed Hundred Acre Wood play area with slides, climbs and the ever-popular pop-jet fountains (guaranteed to get youngsters good and wet!), plus character appearances from Pooh, Tigger and Eeyore.

Snow White's Scary Adventures: this lively indoor ride tells the cartoon story of Snow White with a few ghost train effects that may scare small children. Good fun, though, for parents and kids. Again, you need to go early or late (or during the main parade) to beat the queues. TTT, or TTTTT for under-5s.

Dumbo the Flying Elephant: parents hate it but kids love it and all want to do this 2-minute ride on the back of a flying elephant that swoops in best Dumbo style (even if the ears don't flap). Ride early here or expect a long queue. TT, or TTTT for under-5s.

Mickey's PhilharMagic: this dramatic and utterly fun 10-minute 3-D film show has a host of in-theatre special effects as Donald tries to conduct the Enchanted Orchestra – to comic effect. Set in the PhilharMagic Concert Hall, it features a 150ft/46m wide screen to immerse guests in the 3-D world of *Beauty and the Beast*, *The Little Mermaid*, *The Lion King*, *Peter Pan* and *Aladdin*, with the hapless Donald surviving a string of

adventures before Mickey brings him back to earth. The lavishness of the theatre, the artistry of the new animation, the interweaving of the special effects (you can even smell the food!) and the all-round family entertainment add up to one of Disney's most enjoyable attractions. There is no scare factor here (though the sudden plunge into darkness at one point and the noise of the 'orchestra' can spook young children), while you'll be enchanted when Tinkerbell seems to fly right out of the screen in front of you. AAAAA (FP).

Peter Pan's Flight: don't be fooled by the long queues; this is a rather tame ride, though still a big hit with kids. Its novel effect of flying with Peter Pan quickly wears off, but there's a lot of clever detail as your sailing ship journeys over London to Neverland. AA, or AAAAA for under-6s (FP).

Dream Along With Mickey: Set on the Castle Forecourt Stage, this is a superb show for character interaction, a 20-minute fantasy featuring Donald, Mickey, Minnie, Goofy and various Princesses and their Princes. Peter Pan and Wendy join the battle against the evil Maleficent and Captain Hook to help Donald remember the power of believing in your dreams. AAA.

it's a small world

© Disney

Mad Tea Party

Mickey's Toontown Fair

In the top corner of Fantasyland (just past the Mad Tea Party) is the shrub-lined entrance to **Mickey's Toontown Fair** (opens 10am). It is easy to miss, but it does have a station on the railroad. Its primary appeal is to young children as they can meet their favourite characters. Exceptionally kid-friendly and well landscaped, it features a huge merchandising area, the **County Bounty** – wallets beware! There is also the **Toon Park** playground to give youngsters the chance to let off some steam.

Mickey's Country House: here is a walk-through opportunity to see Mickey at home and have your picture taken with him in the Judge's Tent. AAA (plus TTTTT for the photo opportunity!).

Minnie's Country House: this is a chance to view Minnie's home and unique memorabilia, all designed in a country and western style. AAA.

Toontown Hall of Fame: 3 'rooms' of classic Disney characters for photo meet-and-greets with Minnie, Daisy and Pluto; Chip 'n' Dale and Goofy; and the Storybook Princesses (including Snow White, Cinderella and Aurora). TTTTT (for kids!).

The Barnstormer at Goofy's Wiseacre Farm: a mini roller-coaster just for the young 'uns, its masterful design features a swoop right through the barn itself (though it is a pretty short ride after the slow-moving queue). TTT, or TTTTT for 4–8s. Restrictions: 3ft/91cm.

Donald's Boat: parents beware, youngsters get seriously wet here! If you've seen the pavement fountains at *Epcot*, prepare for more watery delights as this boat-themed playground spouts off in all sorts of wonderful ways. Ideally, bring a change of clothes or swimsuit for the kids. It's also a great place to revitalise tired or irritable children. AAAA for under 10s.

Ariel's Grotto, behind Dumbo, offers the chance to meet The Little Mermaid (which draws a queue at peak periods), while periodically in the **Fairytale Garden**, on the corner of the Castle facing Tomorrowland, you can listen to *Storytime with Belle*.

Eating opportunities are at **The Pinocchio Village Haus** (pizza and Italian fare), the **Enchanted Grove** (ice drinks and juices), **Scuttle's Landing** and **Mrs Potts' Cupboard** (for ice creams and sundaes). **Cinderella's Royal Table** is a fine setting for the hugely popular character breakfast and lunch (dinner is also served, but with the Fairy Godmother rather than Cinderella and Co). The majestic hall, waitresses in costume and well-presented food – salads, seafood, roast beef, prime rib and chicken – provide a memorable experience. It's distinctly pricey, though ($108 for a family of 4 for breakfast, $114 for lunch). Shop at **Tinkerbell's Treasures**, the excellent **Sir Mickey's**, **Fantasy Faire** and **Pooh's Thotful Shop**. New in 2007 was the **Bibbidi Bobbidi Boutique**, in Cinderella's Castle, following on from the success of this 'little princesses salon' in *Downtown Disney*. Young girls can choose from three makeover packages ($35–245), and three different hairstyles – the Disney Diva, Pop Princess or Fairytale Princess. The salon is open 8am–7pm and children must be 3 or older.

© Disney

Space Mountain

Check out the **Toontown Farmers Market** for fruit, snacks and drinks.

Tomorrowland

The last of the 7 lands, this has a cartoon-like space-age appearance that is guaranteed to appeal to youngsters, while it also boasts some original shops.

Space Mountain: this is one of the 3 most popular attractions in the park, and its reputation is deserved. It is a fast, tight-turning roller-coaster completely in the dark save for occasional flashes as you whiz through the galaxy. Don't do this on a full stomach! The only way to beat the crowds is to go either first thing, late in the day or during one of the parades (or, of course, get a FastPass). Restrictions: 3ft 8in/111cm. TTTTT (FP). Children are also likely to gravitate to the **Tomorrowland Arcade** as you exit the ride.

Tomorrowland Indy Speedway: despite the long queues, this is a rather tame ride on supposed race tracks that just putt-putts along on rails with little real steering required (children must be 4ft 4in/132cm to drive alone). T, or TTTT for under-6s.

Astro Orbiter: a jazzed-up version of Dumbo in Fantasyland, this ride is a bit faster and higher and features rockets. Large, slow-moving queues are another reason to give this a miss unless you have young children. TT, or TTTT for under-10s.

Walt Disney's Carousel of Progress: this will surprise, entertain and amuse. It is a 100-year journey through 20th-century technology with audio-animatronics and a revolving theatre that reveals different stages in that development. Its 22-minute duration is rarely threatened by crowds (open only at peak periods). AAA.

Tomorrowland Transit Authority: a neat 'future transport system', this offers an elevated view of the area, including a glimpse inside Space Mountain, in electro-magnetic cars. Queues are usually short. AAA, or TTT for under-8s.

Stitch's Great Escape!: this 15-minute experience has replaced the former Alien Encounter and receives mixed reviews – some like it for the audio-animatronic prequel to Disney's *Lilo & Stitch*, with visitors being recruited into the madcap Galactic Federation prison service (where things go hilariously wrong as a new prisoner – Stitch – arrives and proceeds to cause havoc), while others find it rather puzzling. Young children can also be scared by the complete darkness at times. There are 2 pre-show areas before recruits are ushered into the sit-down chamber (with shoulder restraints) where Stitch is let loose to bounce, dribble and even belch over the unsuspecting audience. Restrictions: 3ft 2in/101cm. AA (FP).

Buzz Lightyear's Space Ranger Spin: kids will not want to miss this chance to join the great *Toy Story* character in his battle against the evil Emperor Zurg. Ride into action against the robot army and shoot them with laser cannons! A sure-fire family winner, especially as you get to keep score. TTT, or TTTTT for under-8s (FP).

The Laugh Floor Comedy Club: this innovative and amusing show is based on the hit Pixar film *Monsters Inc.* With 'live' animation, special effects and high-tech voice links, guests can meet and dare to match wits with the likes of Mike, Sulley and Roz and be entertained by their clever patter and amusing antics. Billy Boil opens the show, introducing various comedians (including a two-headed jokester named Sam-n-Ella), with the main objective of capturing the audience's laughter (the most powerful source of fuel in Monstropolis). Guest interaction is an integral part of the show. Keep an eye on the screen – you may become a main feature! The show changes slightly so visit more than once. AAA.

The Galaxy Palace Theater hosts live musical productions, featuring Disney characters and high school bands, at various times of the day. For food, **Cosmic Ray's Starlight Café** has burgers, chicken, pasta, soups and salads, **The Plaza Pavilion** does pizza, subs and salads, **Auntie Gravity's** (ouch!) **Galactic Goodies** serves ice cream and juices, the **Lunching Pad**

(double ouch!) offers smoked turkey legs, snacks and drinks. The **Tomorrowland Terrace Noodle Station** offers a healthier line-up of Asian stir-fry, soup and vegetarian dishes. Shopping highlights include **Mickey's Star Traders** and **Merchant of Venus.**

> **BRITTIP**
>
> To watch a parade, sit on the left side of Main Street USA (facing the Castle) to stay in the shade if it's hot. People start staking out the best spots an HOUR in advance.

Having come full circle, you are now back at Main Street USA and it's best to return here in early afternoon to avoid the crowds and have a closer look at the impressive array of shops.

The afternoon highlight, though, is the **Disney Dreams Come True Parade**, a typically enchanting multi-float presentation featuring all the favourite characters. With clever theming, lively music and non-stop (and hard-working!) dancing, the parade halts at regular intervals to reveal some eye-catching special effects. Mickey, Minnie and a host of Disney Princesses all make an appearance, plus some of the classic villains, and it is sure to captivate viewers both young and old (though it is especially popular with children). At Easter and Christmas, the daily parade takes on extra seasonal charm with appearances by the Easter Bunny and Father Christmas. AAAAA.

Buzz Lightyear's Space Ranger Spin

© Disney

There's more

If you think the park looks good during the day, prepare to be amazed at how wonderful it appears at night – some of the lighting effects are astounding. When the park is open into the evenings (during the main holiday periods and weekends), you can see the **SpectroMagic Parade** (when there are 2 a night, the second is less crowded), which is a mind-boggling light and sound festival full of glitter and razzamatazz, with the Disney characters at the centre of a multitude of sparkling lights and fibre-optic effects. It is difficult to do it justice in words, so just make sure you see it. AAAA.

Firework finale

Most nights at the Magic Kingdom finish with the stunning **Wishes** fireworks show over the Castle. With a clever soundtrack narrated by Jiminy Cricket and featuring memorable moments from an array of Disney classics, it is magnificently

choreographed and culminates in a sequence of pyrotechnic explosions (many designed especially for this show), which truly dazzle the eyes and mind. Starting with an appearance by Tinkerbell (from the Castle's top turret), it continues for 12 minutes of typical Disney emotional heart-tugging and is the perfect pixie-dust farewell to a memorable day at this park. AAAAA.

Prefer not to fight the crowds for a fabulous view of Wishes? Book one of 3 speciality **Wishes Cruises** to view the fireworks from Seven Seas Lagoon. The Basic Cruise holds up to 8 guests onboard a 21ft pontoon boat and costs $225 (includes water, soft drinks and snacks). The Premium Cruise holds up to 10 guests on a 25ft pontoon boat at a cost of $275, including water, soft drinks, snacks and an audio feed to the Wishes music. Splash out for the Celebration Cruise, which adds special occasion decorations to the Basic Cruise for a total of $250 and the Premium Cruise for $300.

Wishes fireworks show

© Disney

MAGIC KINGDOM PARK with children

Here is a rough guide to the attractions that appeal to different age groups. Obviously, children vary in their likes and dislikes but, as a general rule, you can be fairly sure the following will have most appeal to the ages concerned (height restrictions have been taken into account):

Under-5s

Buzz Lightyear's Space Ranger Spin, Cinderella's Golden Carrousel, Country Bear Jamboree, Donald's Boat, Dream Along With Mickey, Dumbo the Flying Elephant, The Enchanted Tiki Room (under new management), 'It's a Small World', Jungle Cruise, Liberty Square Riverboat, Main Street Vehicles, Many Adventures of Winnie the Pooh, Mickey's Country House, Mickey's PhilharMagic, Monsters Inc. Laugh Floor, Peter Pan's Flight, Pooh's Playful Spot, Tomorrowland Indy Speedway (with a parent), Tomorrowland Transit Authority, Walt Disney World Railroad.

5–8s

Astro Orbiter, The Barnstormer at Goofy's Wiseacre Farm, Big Thunder Mountain Railroad, Buzz Lightyear's Space Ranger Spin, Country Bear Jamboree, Donald's Boat, Dream Along With Mickey, The Enchanted Tiki Room (under new management), Haunted Mansion, Jungle Cruise, Liberty Square Riverboat, Mad Tea Party, Magic Carpets of Aladdin, Many Adventures of Winnie the Pooh, Mickey's Country House, Mickey's PhilharMagic, Monsters Inc. Laugh Floor, Pirates of the Caribbean, Snow White's Scary Adventures, Space Mountain (with parental discretion), Splash Mountain, Stitch's Great Escape!, Swiss Family Treehouse, Tom Sawyer Island, Tomorrowland Indy Speedway (with parent), Tomorrowland Transit Authority, Walt Disney World Railroad, Walt Disney's Carousel of Progress.

9–12s

Astro Orbiter, The Barnstormer at Goofy's Wiseacre Farm, Big Thunder Mountain Railroad, Buzz Lightyear's Space Ranger Spin, Country Bear Jamboree, The Haunted Mansion, Mad Tea Party, Mickey's PhilharMagic, Monsters Inc. Laugh Floor, Pirates of the Caribbean, Space Mountain, Splash Mountain, Stitch's Great Escape!, Tomorrowland Indy Speedway (without parent).

Over-12s

Astro Orbiter, Big Thunder Mountain Railroad, Buzz Lightyear's Space Ranger Spin, Haunted Mansion, Mad Tea Party, Mickey's PhilharMagic, Pirates of the Caribbean, Space Mountain, Splash Mountain, Stitch's Great Escape!.

The monorail IS quicker than the ferry when you leave the park, but you will need to be patient at peak times – it can take up to an hour to get back to your car. Also, if the crowds get too heavy during the day, you CAN escape by leaving in the early afternoon (get a hand-stamp for re-admission and keep your car park ticket, which is valid all day) and returning to your hotel for a few hours' rest or a dip in the pool. Alternatively, catch a boat to one of the Disney resorts for an hour or so – *Disney's Fort Wilderness* is especially fun for young children and boasts the great value **Trails End Buffet** for lunch or dinner.

Cinderella Castle

© Disney

Fireworks at the Magic Kingdom

© Disney

Halloween and Christmas

Two additional annual events in the *Magic Kingdom Park* are **Mickey's Not So Scary Halloween Party** (selected dates in Oct) and **Mickey's Very Merry Christmas Party** (late Nov and Dec), which provide a separate, party-style ticketed event from 7pm to midnight, with most of the rides open and extra themed fun and games. The Halloween event sees many visitors dress up for the typical American trick-or-treat fun, and on the way there are plenty of treats and sweets for youngsters. With special music, storytelling, parades and fireworks (and some wonderful lighting effects), plus a free family photo, tickets go on sale about 6 months in advance and sell out quickly. The Christmas party sees 'snow' on Main Street and an array of magnificent festive decorations and theming. There is free hot chocolate and cookies, plus a family photo, as well as a parade and more fireworks. The whole atmosphere is truly enchanting, though occasionally the evening is prone to some unfriendly Florida weather.

Halloween party tickets are $48.94/adult and $42.55/child on the day (or $41.49 and $35.10 in advance); the Christmas party is $51.07 and $42.62

(or $43.62 and $36.16 in advance). Book in advance on 407 934 7639.

Disney's Pirate and Princess Party was tested in 2007 and hopefully will continue into 2008. It is a fun family event after regular park closing (advance purchase $41.49 adults, $35.10 3–9s or $48.94/$42.55 at the gate), with activities such as Swashbuckling Training, plenty of character meet-n-greets, a special parade and fireworks and the chance to fill your treasure bag with goodies at various 'treasure spots'.

Finally, one of the park's little-known secrets is the **Keys to the Kingdom**, a 4–5-hour guided tour of many backstage areas, including the service tunnel under the park, and entertainment production buildings. It's an extra $60 (including lunch; not available for under-16s) but is a superb journey into the park's creation. Call 407 939 8687 for more information. **Disney's Family Magic Tour** is a 2-hour guided adventure that takes you on a search for clues throughout the park at $27/person, or you can experience **Disney's The Magic Behind Our Steam Trains** tour ($40/person; no under-10s) as you join the crew that prepares the park's trains each day.

Epcot

Epcot actually stands for 'Experimental Prototype Community of Tomorrow' but it might be more accurate to say Every Person Comes Out Tired. For this is a BIG park, with a lot to see and do, and much leg-work required for its 300 acre/122ha extent. Actually, it is not so much a vision of the future as a look at the world of today, with a strong educational and environmental message. At almost 3 times the size of the *Magic Kingdom Park*, it is more likely to require a 2-day visit (though under-5s might find it less entertaining) and your feet in particular will notice the difference!

Location

Epcot is situated off Epcot Drive and the parking fee is again $10 as you drive into its main entrance (there is a separate entrance for guests at the *Epcot* resort hotels, called International Gateway). It opened in October 1982 and its giant car park is big enough for 9,000 vehicles, so a tram takes you from your car to the main entrance (though if you are staying at a Disney hotel you can catch the monorail, boat or bus service to the gates). And don't forget to note where you are parked (e.g. Create, row 78). Once you have your ticket, you pass through the turnstiles

Epcot at a glance

Location	Off Epcot Drive, *Walt Disney World*
Size	300 acres/122ha in Future World and World Showcase
Hours	9am–7pm Future World (except Test Track, Mission: SPACE, Soarin'™, 9am–9pm), 11am–9pm (World Showcase)
Admission	Under-3s free; 3–9 $60 (1-Day base ticket), $272 (5-Day Premium), $276 (7-Day Premium); adult (10+) $71, $310, $314. Prices do not include tax.
Parking	$10
Lockers	Through the main entrance to the right hand side and at International Gateway $7 ($2 refund)
Pushchairs	$10 and $18 to the left after the main entrance and at International Gateway; length of stay price varies
Wheelchairs	$10 or $40 ($5 deposit refunded), with pushchairs
Top Attractions	Mission: SPACE, Test Track, Spaceship Earth, Soarin'™, 'Honey, I Shrunk the Audience', Maelstrom, Universe of Energy, American Adventure
Don't Miss	IllumiNations: Reflections of Earth, Disney Character Connection (inside, behind Fountain View Bakery), live entertainment (including Off Kilter in Canada, JAMMitors in Innoventions plaza and Miyuki in Japan), and dinner at any of the World Showcase pavilions
Hidden Costs	**Meals** Burger, chips and coke $8.98 / 3-course dinner $37.97 (Coral Reef, Canada) / Kids' meal $3.99–7.49 **T-shirts** $20–30 **Souvenirs** $1–3,700 **Sundries** *Epcot* 'Passport' $9.95

Future World

1 Universe of Energy
2 Wonders of Life (seasonal only)
3 Mission: SPACE
4 Test Track
5 Odyssey Center
6 Imagination! (including Honey, I Shrunk the Audience)
7 The Land (including Soarin'™)
8 The Seas with Nemo and Friends
9 Spaceship Earth
10 Innoventions West
11 Innoventions East

World Showcase

12 Mexico
13 Norway
14 China
15 Germany
16 Italy
17 The American Adventure
18 Japan
19 Morocco
20 France
21 International Gateway (to Epcot resort hotels)
22 United Kingdom
23 Canada
24 Friendship Boats to Italy and Morocco
25 America Gardens Theater
26 Showcase Plaza
27 Monorail Station
K Kidcot Fun Stops

EPCOT

and wait in the immediate entrance plaza for Rope Drop, which is signalled by Mickey and Co arriving to greet guests.

Epcot is divided into 2 distinct parts arranged in a figure of 8 and there are 2 tactics to help you avoid the worst of the crowds. The first or lower half of the '8' consists of **Future World**, with 7 different pavilions arranged around Spaceship Earth (which dominates the *Epcot* skyline) and Innoventions. The second part, or top of the '8', is **World Showcase**, a potted journey around the world via 11 internationally presented pavilions that feature a taste of each country's culture, history, entertainment, shopping and cuisine.

Once through the entrance plaza, you should aim to get the 3 big-time rides – Test Track, Mission: Space and Soarin'™ – under your belt first, then move into World Showcase for its 11am opening time. Continue around World Showcase until 4 or 5pm, then return to Future World to catch up on the other attractions there, as the majority of the crowds will have moved on (apart from at the three main rides). As a general tactic, head first for the magnificent new **Soarin'**™, then go across to the other side of Future World and grab a FastPass for **Test Track**. While you wait for your ride time, you can queue up for **Mission: SPACE** and perhaps even take in **Universe of Energy**. Alternatively, if the rides don't appeal quite so much as a visit to such diverse cultures as Japan and Morocco, spend your first couple of hours in the Innoventions centres (busy from mid-morning), then head into World Showcase at 11am and you'll be ahead of the crowds for several hours. The other thing you should do early on is book lunch or dinner at one of the many fine restaurants around World Showcase (Mexico, Canada and Japan are all highly recommended). The best reservations go fast, but check in at Guest Relations (on the left of the Innoventions plaza) for advice and to make bookings.

Future World

Here is what you will find in the first part of your *Epcot* adventure:

Universe of Energy: there is just the one attraction here but it is a stunner. **Ellen's Energy Adventure** is a 35-minute show-and-ride with comedienne Ellen DeGeneres and Bill Nye the Science Guy exploring the creation of fuels from the age of dinosaurs to their modern-day usages. The film elements convince you that you are in a conventional theatre, but then your seats rearrange themselves into 96-person solar-powered cars and you are off on a journey through the prehistoric era, with some realistic dinosaurs! Queues are steady but not overwhelming from mid-morning. AAAAA.

Mission: SPACE: this is more high-tech Disney imagination at work, a journey into the future to join the International Space Training Center. The space-age building alone prepares you for a major adventure as you enter through Planetary Plaza, with its giant replica planets (check out the model showing the Moon landings). At the main entrance you have a choice of 4 queues – FastPass Collection, Stand-by (the main

Soarin'™

© Disney

queue), Single Riders and FastPass Return, and the clever organisation keeps queues to a minimum. As you enter the training facility, there are some superb models and graphics (like the giant revolving Gravity Wheel) to look at while you queue to reach Team Despatch. Here, the 4 ready rooms form you into teams of 4 for the ride itself, and you will be either Navigator, Engineer, Pilot or Commander, each with different functions to perform. You will also have the choice to do either the full, dynamic version of the ride or a new, toned-down alternative that avoids the 'spinning' effect (though it lacks the excitement).

BRITTIP

If the thrills of Mission: SPACE and Test Track appeal to you most, head here FIRST when you arrive, grab a FastPass for Test Track, then ride the other. Mission: Space draws only half the queues of Test Track.

Once briefed (by actor Gary Sinise), you enter the Preparation Room to learn your mission – a flight to Mars. And then it is quickly into the ride vehicle – capsules that close down tightly with outer doors, shoulder restraints and screens that move forward to just 18in/46cm from your face (this is NOT the ride for you if you suffer from claustrophobia). The sense of realism, with the control consoles, individual speakers and the

Epcot monorail

© Disney

countdown is magnificent. For those on the full version of the ride, the blast-off feels VERY real as you experience some of the genuine forces of a rocket launch (thanks to their huge centrifugal machine, which is part-ride and part-simulator).

Each member of the team has to perform their duties on cue (Sinise will prompt you if you forget) and you experience a simulated sling-shot flight around the Moon and on to Mars, where the landing is an adventure in itself. It is a truly original, aggressive ride, but you should heed the advice to keep your head still and look straight into the screen or you WILL feel sick (unless you are on the tamer version, where the capsules just tilt and turn). We think the full-on experience is much too intense for young children, and there is no backing out once you blast off (parents could try it first to check it out), while it is definitely not for expectant mothers. Restrictions: 3ft 8in/112cm. TTTTT+ (FP).

BRITTIP

Even if you don't ride Mission: Space, you (and your children) should check out the post-ride area of games and fun. Just enter through the Cargo Bay gift shop to the left of the pavilion.

As you exit the ride, there is an elaborate post-show with more activities. **Space Base** is an excellent play area for children who can't ride (and those who just like to explore, climb, slide and crawl); **Space Race** is a great game for 2 teams of 60 players to propel their rocket back to Earth via a series of on-screen challenges; **Expedition Mars** is a computer game to rescue stranded astronauts; and **Postcards from Space** offers you the chance to send a space video email to friends and family. There is then the inevitable (and well-stocked) gift shop to negotiate on the way out. All in all, it is a mind-boggling

EPCOT

© Disney

Test Track

experience, and a real taste of space exploration without even leaving the building!

Test Track: this is another big production, a 5½-minute whirl along Disney's longest and fastest track. It starts with an elaborate queue line that demonstrates General Motors' safety techniques and quality control, and prepares riders for a taste of the vehicle testing to come. The way the cars whiz around the outside of the building (at up to 65mph/104kph) provides a glimpse of what's in store. The reality is pretty good, too, as you are taken on a tour of a GM proving ground, including a hill climb test, suspension test (hold on to those fillings!), brake test, environment chamber, barrier test (beware the crash test dummies!) and the steeply banked, high-speed finale.

Once you regain your breath, there is a post-show area with a multimedia film, an animated presentation featuring future GM products and technological innovations, and the chance to view the latest GM models. Along with a smart gift store and ride photo opportunity, it makes for an extremely involved exhibit. A **Kidcot** stop also adds some creative fun for youngsters. The downside is its HUGE queues, topping 2 hours at times, while the available FP service often runs out by midday. Head straight here when it opens or come back in the evening to keep your queuing to bearable levels. If you are on your

own, save time by using the Singles Queue. Restrictions: 3ft 4in/101cm. TTTT, or TTT for teens (FP).

The Odyssey Center next door offers baby-care and first-aid facilities, telephones and restrooms.

Wonders of Life: this pavilion is the poor relation of the Future World line-up and spent much of 2007 closed. We were assured it was to re-open in peak periods, but there is reason to believe it will eventually close for good. If open, it offers **Body Wars**, a hectic simulator ride through the human body (quite a violent adventure, too, not recommended for people who suffer from motion sickness, those with neck or back injuries, or pregnant women). Restrictions: 3ft 4in/101cm. TTT; **Cranium Command**, a hilarious theatre show set in the brain of a 12-year-old boy, showing how he negotiates a typical day. It is both audio-animatronic and film-based (see how many famous TV and film stars you can name in the cast). AAA; and **The Making of Me**, a sensitive film on the creation of human life, which therefore requires parental discretion for children as it has its explicit moments, though not without humour. AA.

BRITTIP

Innoventions East and West are good places in which to spend time if you need to cool down, or if it's raining.

Imagination!: The 2-part attraction here starts with **Journey into Imagination with Figment**, a quirky ride into experiments with imagination, in the company of Eric Idle (as Dr Nigel Channing of the Imagination Institute) and the cartoon dragon, Figment. The sight laboratory sees Figment having fun with a vision chart, the sound lab is a symphony of imaginative melodies and Figment's house is a truly topsy-turvy world (and watch out for the skunk in the smell lab!). It is gentle fun and rarely draws a crowd. AAA. (Fans of the original Dreamfinder may leave slightly bemused, but Figment is prominent once again, while the ride's theme song, 'One Little Spark', has been reinstated.)

You exit into **Image Works – The Kodak 'What If' Labs**, an interactive playground of sights and sounds, which will probably amuse children more than adults (though you may be tempted to buy various cartoon images and select-your-own CDs).

Come out of the building and turn right for the fabulous 3-D experience of '**Honey, I Shrunk The Audience**', as Rick Moranis reprises his hapless inventor character Wayne Szalinski. A neat 8-minute pre-show is the perfect prelude to the fun and games in store. If you have seen Jim Henson's Muppet*Vision 3-D at *Disney-MGM Studios* you'll have an idea of what to expect. Special effects and moving seats add to the feeling that you have shrunk in size. And beware the sneezing dog! AAAAA (FP).

Outside, kids are always fascinated by the **Jellyfish** and **Serpentine Fountains** that send water squirting from pond to pond, and there is always one who tries to stand in the way and catch one of the streams of water. Have your cameras and camcorders ready!

The Land: this pavilion combines three elements to make a highly entertaining but educational experience on food production and nutrition – plus the spectacular new Soarin'™ ride, which is a pure thrill and a huge draw. **Living with the Land** is an informative 14-minute boat ride well worth the usually long queue. A journey through various types of food production may sound dull, but it is informative and enjoyable, with plenty to make children of all ages sit up and take notice through the 3 ecological communities, especially the greenhouse finale. AAAA (FP).

Having ridden the ride, you can also take the **Behind the Seeds** guided tour through the greenhouse complex and learn even more about Disney's horticultural projects. It takes an hour ($14 adults, $10 3–9s). **The Circle of Life** is a 15-minute live-action/animated story, featuring characters from the film *The Lion King*, that explains environmental concerns and is easily digestible for kids. Queues are not a problem here. AAA. **Soarin'**™ is *Epcot*'s latest and greatest, a hugely imaginative 'flight simulator' that offers an equally exhilarating ride for young and old. A copy of the Soarin' Over California simulator ride in *Disney's California Adventure* in Los Angeles, it features a

'Honey, I Shrunk the Audience'

breathtaking swoop over the notable landmarks of California, complete with 'aromavision' (smell those orange groves!). An elaborate queuing area is arranged like an airport departure lounge, with the passengers embarking on rows of seats that are then hoisted into the air over a giant screen. The feeling is somewhat akin to taking a hang-glider ride as the special film, sounds and scents become all-encompassing. Feet dangling, you soar over the Golden Gate Bridge, sweep through a redwood forest and glide above Napa Valley with the wind in your hair. The finale includes a close encounter with a certain Disney theme park in LA! The ride's realism, magnificent music and superb technology ensure a 5-star experience – but also some serious queues. The lines move slowly and FastPasses often run out before 11am, so visit early and use FastPass for a second ride. Restrictions: 3ft 4in/101cm. AAAAA (FP).

The **Sunshine Season Food Fair** offers the chance to eat some of Disney's home-grown produce, and provides healthy alternatives to the usual fast-food fare, while the **Garden Grill** restaurant is a slowly revolving platform that offers more traditional food, including roast meats, pasta, seafood and a vegetarian selection, all in the company of Mickey, Goofy, Pluto and Chip 'n' Dale.

The Seas with Nemo and Friends: this pavilion does for the oceans what The Land does for terra firma. It has also been dramatically revamped to introduce the undersea world of Nemo and Co, from the Pixar film *Finding Nemo*. You start with the pavilion's new signature ride, **The Seas With Nemo and Friends**, which takes riders in 'clamobiles' on an underwater journey to meet the Pixar characters (which are brilliantly interwoven into the huge aquarium – to all intents and purposes swimming with the real fish!). Nemo has gone missing (again), hence the ride becomes a quest to reunite him with teacher Mr Ray and the rest of the fishy class in a rousing musical finale. AAAA. You then exit into the main part of this 2-level development, which offers 6 modules presenting stories of undersea exploration and marine life, including a research centre that provides a close encounter with the endangered manatee. Plenty of interactive elements and educational touch-screens are on offer, plus additional fish tanks displaying Caribbean reef fish, jellyfish and the curious cuttlefish, while there is also an excellent demonstration of a diving chamber. Crowds are steady throughout the day, but queues rarely get too long – with one exception. **Turtle Talk With Crush** is a splendidly interactive and original meet-and-greet with the cartoon surfer dude turtle and his fishy friend Dory from *Finding Nemo*. Crush is literally the star of the show as he swims up and engages children in the audience with some genuinely fun banter (with help from Dory). AAAA. Next door, **Bruce's Shark World** is an elaborate photo opportunity with some more of the *Finding Nemo* characters. AA.

The pavilion also includes the highly recommended **Coral Reef Restaurant** that serves magnificent seafood, as well as providing diners with a grandstand view of the massive aquarium. Dinner for 2 will be around $80, which isn't cheap, but the food is first class.

The Seas with Nemo and Friends

© Disney

Spaceship Earth: spiralling up 18 storeys, this attraction has been extensively revamped (in 2007) to become a time-travel story into various ancient technologies, notably communication. From cave paintings to the internet (with a superb depiction of Michelangelo's Sistine Chapel along the way, the gentle ride unfolds in highly imaginative historical stages, culminating in an interactive finale that invites riders to 'predict' the future. Sponsor Siemens (the electronics giant) has added a post-show area of interactive demonstrations (including predictive surgery and a driving challenge), which makes for an entertaining diversion after the 15-minute ride. Queues are heavy all morning but almost non-existent late in the day. AAAA.

Innoventions West and East: these 2 centres of hands-on exhibits and computer games – subtitled **The Road to Tomorrow** – include a glimpse of Disney's latest investigations into virtual reality entertainment and other demonstrations of current and future technologies, especially the internet and computers, by the likes of IBM, Underwriters Laboratories and Society of Plastics Industry, Inc. Both sides are routed like a journey into the future and will reward enquiring minds in areas like **Test the Limits Lab** and **Tom Morrow 2/0's Playground**. In Innoventions West, the kids will gravitate to the free **Video Games of Tomorrow** selection presented by Disney Interactive and may take a bit of moving on! Also worth waiting for are the 20-minute **Ultimate Home Theater Experience**, presented by Lutron, and the **Thinkplace**, presented by IBM and featuring a demonstration of voice recognition technology. More interactive stuff is presented by the **Rockin' Robots** exhibit presented by Kuka, which gives guests a chance to direct robotic arms as they play percussive instruments.

In Innoventions East, you can send a video email to friends in the **Internet**

© Disney

Spaceship Earth

Zone, check out **The Underwriters Lab**, which offers an interactive area with various testing stations and Video D-Mail, and take the 15-minute walk through the **House of Innoventions**, full of smart gadgets and new technologies. You must also take a look at the latest form of transport here – the wonderful 2-wheeled Segway Human Transporter (which you can also pay to ride – see page 136) and try the new **Fantastic Plastics** (create your own robot to take home!).

Live entertainment is provided periodically in the Innoventions plaza, where imaginative acts include the unique **JAMMitors** percussion group. The majestic fountains are also choreographed to an hourly music performance. Food outlets include the self-service **Electric Umbrella Restaurant** for lunch and dinner (sandwiches, pizza, burgers and salads) and the **Fountain View Espresso and Bakery** for tea, coffee and pastries. Look out also for **Club Cool** presented by Coca-Cola®, where you can check out the latest Coke-inspired products. You'll also find the huge gift shop **Mouse Gear** in Innoventions East, featuring stacks of quality *Epcot* and Disney souvenirs (and don't forget to look up at the wacky ceiling architecture!).

World Showcase

If you found Future World staggering, prepare to be amazed by the equally imaginative pavilions around the World Showcase Lagoon. Each features a glimpse of a different country in dramatic settings. Several have rides or films to showcase their main tourist features, while in nearly every case the restaurants offer some of Orlando's best international fare.

Mexico: starting at the bottom left of the circular tour of the lagoon and moving clockwise, your first encounter is the spectacular pyramid that houses Mexico. Here you will find the amusing boat ride **Gran Fiesta Tour Starring The Three Caballeros**, a 9-minute journey through the people and history of the country with Donald Duck, Panchito and José Carioca as your guides. Queues here tend to be surprisingly long from late morning to mid-afternoon. AAA. The rest of the pavilion comprises shops and cafés. The **San Angel Inn** is a romantic restaurant offering typical (and tasty) Mexican fare while the new **Tequila Bar** has tempting cocktails! Outside, the counter-service **Cantina de San Angel** (tacos, chilli and burgers) is due to undergo a renovation in 2008 to add more seating with a lagoon view, and a new menu. As in all World Showcase pavilions, there is live entertainment and music like **Mariachi Cobre**.

BRITTIP

The Cantina de San Angel is a great spot from which to watch the nightly IllumiNations pyrotechnics show, but you will need to arrive at least an hour early.

Norway: next up is Norway, which has the best ride in World Showcase, the Viking-themed **Maelstrom**. This 10-minute longboat journey through the country's history and scenery features a short waterfall drop and a North Sea storm. It attracts longish queues during the afternoon, so the best tactic is to go soon after World Showcase's 11am opening. TTT (FP). There are periodical Norwegian-themed exhibits in the reconstructed **Stave Church** and twice-daily guided tours (sign up at the Tourism desk). The pavilion also contains a clever reproduction of Oslo's Akershus Fortress. The **Akershus Royal**

Banquet Hall offers the Princess Storybook dining for breakfast, lunch and dinner, complete with a host of Disney Princesses, and the **Kringla Bakeri Og Kafé** serves sandwiches, pastries and drinks.

China: the spectacular landscapes of China are well served by the pavilion's main attraction, the stunning **Reflections of China**, a 360-degree film in the circular Temple of Heaven. Here you are surrounded by the sights and sounds of one of the world's most enigmatic countries in a special cinematic production, the technology of which alone will leave you breathless. Queues build up to ½ hour during the main part of the day (but the waiting area is fully air-conditioned). AAAA. Two restaurants, the **Nine Dragons** (full service, due for a major upgrade in 2008) and the counter-service **Lotus Blossom Café** (recently renovated and with a tasty new menu, including Beijing barbecue chicken and a delicious sliced beef sandwich) offer tastes of the Orient, while **Yong Feng Shangdian Dept Store** is a warehouse of Chinese gifts and artefacts. Don't miss the periodic shows of Oriental music and acrobatics (like the stunning **Dragon Legend Acrobats**) on the plaza in front of the temple.

The **Outpost** between China and Germany features hut-style shops and snacks, with entertainment from Africa and the Caribbean.

Germany: this provides more in the way of shopping and eating than entertainment, though you still find strolling players and a magnificent re-creation of a Bavarian **Biergarten**, with lively Oktoberfest shows featuring the resident brass band at regular intervals. It also offers hearty portions of German sausage,

BRITTIP

The lunch and dinner menus at many of the World Showcase restaurants are similar, so choose the lunch version – it's cheaper!

sauerkraut and rotisserie chicken. The **Sommerfest** is fast food German-style (bratwurst and strudel). This pavilion has more shops than any others in *Epcot* and includes chocolates, wines, porcelain, crystal, toys and cuckoo clocks. An elaborate outdoor model railway is popular with children.

Italy: similarly, Italy has pretty, authentic architecture (including a superb reproduction of St Mark's Square in Venice), live music and comedy shops, 3 tempting gift shops (including wine, chocolates, Armani collectables, fine crystal, porcelain and Venetian masks) and full-service restaurant **Tutto Italia**. However, this is only a temporary cover for a new, upscale themed restaurant offering regional specialities which began construction in late 2007. The provisional opening date is October 2008 and it replaces L'Originale Alfredo di Roma Ristorante. Watch out, too, for **Sergio**, a madcap juggler who loves to involve his audience.

America: at the top of the lagoon and dominating World Showcase is **The American Adventure**, not so much a pavilion as a celebration of the country's history and Constitution. A colonial fife and drum band and the wonderful a cappella group Voices Of Liberty add authentic sounds to the 18th-century setting, overlooked by a faithful reproduction of Philadelphia's

Italy pavilion

© Disney

Liberty Hall. Inside you have the spectacular American Adventure show, a magnificent film and audio-animatronic production lasting ½ hour, which details the country's struggles and triumphs, its presidents, statesmen and heroes. It's a glossy, patriotic display, featuring some outstanding technology and, while some of it will leave foreign visitors fairly cold, it is difficult not to be impressed. Avoid at midday because of the queues. AAAA. If you have time, check out the **American Heritage Gallery** and its special exhibition, (throughout 2008) *National Treasures*.

Outside, antiques and handcarts provide touches of nostalgia, along with the **Heritage Manor Gifts** store, while **Liberty Inn** offers fast-food lunch and dinner. The **America Gardens Theater**, facing the lagoon, presents Disney fun and concerts from worldwide artists from time to time (particularly during the International Flower and Garden and Food and Wine Festivals).

Japan: next up on the clockwise tour, you will be introduced to typical Japanese gardens and architecture, including the breathtaking Chi Nien Tien, a round half-scale reproduction of a temple, some magnificent art exhibits (notably the Bijutsu-kan Gallery), musical shows and dazzling live entertainment (especially child-friendly **Miyuki**, a lovely lady who spins amazing candy creations out of toffee sugar). Great food is also a highlight, and the revamped restaurant line-up consists of the wonderful fine dining **Teppan Edo** (formerly the Teppanyaki Rooms, and still with their traditional chefs at each table) and **Tokyo Dining**, a new venue featuring typical cuisine and ingredients, showcasing sushi and innovative presentation. **Yakitori House** is their fast-food equivalent, with great soups, teriyaki and tempura dishes. Periodic music presentations feature the vibrant **Matsuriza** drummers.

Morocco pavilion

BRITTIP

The Tangierine Café in Morocco is a peaceful haven in which to enjoy a quiet, healthy lunch, especially if you are vegetarian, while there is also a tempting coffee and pastry counter.

Morocco: as you would expect, this is a real shopping experience, with bazaars, alleyways and stalls selling a well-priced array of carpets, leather goods, clothing, brass ornaments, pottery and antiques (seek out that Magic Lamp!). All of the building materials were faithfully imported for the pavilion, which was hand-built to give Morocco a greater degree of authenticity, even by World Showcase's high standards. You'll be unable to keep your eyes off the clever detail around the winding alleyways and gardens, which can be enjoyed on daily (free) 45-minute walking tours.

The **Gallery of Arts and History** offers more historical and cultural insight into the country, while the **Fez House** depicts the style of a typical Moroccan home. **Restaurant Marrakesh** provides a full Moroccan dining experience, complete with traditional musicians and a belly dancer. It's rather pricey ($40.95/person for the Taste of Morocco Marrakesh Royal Feast) but the atmosphere is lively and entertaining. However, better value can be had at **Tangierine Café**, with a healthy array of Morrocan foods (hummus, tabbouleh, couscous, roast lamb, lentil salad and Moroccan breads) at more down-to-earth prices, and with vegetarian options ($7.95–13.95). Watch out, too, for some familiar characters from Disney's film *Aladdin* and a new live musical show, MoRockin' with a variety of Arabic rhythms served up in fun style.

France: France is predictably overlooked by a replica Eiffel Tower, but the smart streets, buildings and the sheer cleanliness is a long way from modern-day Paris! This is pre-World War I France, with official buskers and comedy street theatre acts adding to the rather dreamy atmosphere (look out for **Le Serveur Amusant** for some eye-catching antics). Don't miss **Impressions de France**, another big-film production that serves up all the grandest sights of the country, accompanied by the music of Offenbach, Debussy, Saint-Saëns and Satie. Crowds get quite heavy from late morning. AAAA. This is also the pavilion for a gastronomic experience provided by 3 restaurants, of which **Chefs de France** and **Bistro de Paris** are major discoveries. The former is an award-winning, full-service (and expensive) establishment featuring top-quality cuisine created by French chefs on a daily basis, while the latter, upstairs, offers more intimate bistro dining, still with an individual touch (and, if anything, slightly more expensive) and plenty of style (starters $9–19, main courses $28–36, Bistro 4 Course Tasting Menu $70, with wine parings $105). The Bistro books only 30 days in advance. Alternatively, the **Boulangerie Patisserie** is a sidewalk café offering more affordable and more modest fare (and wonderful pastries, as you'd expect). Shopping is also suitably chic, with a patisserie, wine shop and Guerlain perfumery.

United Kingdom: the least inspiring of all the pavilions, and certainly with little to entertain those who have ever visited a pub or shopped for Royal Doulton or Burberry goods, it is partly offset by some good street entertainers and the excellent Beatles tribute band, the **British Invasion**, but that really is the sum total here. **The Rose and Crown Pub** is antiseptically authentic, but you can get better elsewhere at these prices (ploughman's $13.99, cottage pie $15.99, fish and chips $16.99, and a pint of Bass, Harp Lager or Guinness for a whopping $8). There is also a take-away **Harry Ramsden's** fish and chippie. Other shops are the Tea Caddy, the Magic of Wales, the Queen's Table, Crown and Crest (perfumes and heraldry) and the Toy Soldier (traditional games and Disney toys); look for a Mary Poppins and Friends meet-and-greet.

Canada: completing the World Showcase circle, the main features here are **Victoria Gardens**, based on the world-famous Butchart Gardens on Vancouver Island, some spectacular Rocky Mountain scenery, a replica French gothic mansion, the Hôtel de Canada, and another stunning 360-degree film, **O Canada!** As with China and France, this showcases the country's sights and scenery in a terrific, 17-minute advert for the Canadian Tourist Board. It's at its busiest from late morning to late afternoon. AAA. Resident band **Off Kilter** are also one of the most entertaining acts we've seen anywhere. Want to hear rock 'n' roll bagpipes? This is the group for you! **Le**

Cellier Steakhouse is a modestly priced dining room offering great steaks, prime rib, seafood, chicken and several vegetarian dishes for lunch and dinner.

Around World Showcase are 11 **Kidcot Fun Stop** activity centres, at which children can play games and collect a special *Epcot* Passport to get stamped at each pavilion. Kids will also want to pick up **Goofy's Epcot Guide** at the main entrance, which asks them to answer various questions around World Showcase and solve Goofy's dilemma. You will also find characters in various pavilions, usually in keeping with their country of origin (Aladdin in Morocco, Belle and the Beast in France). Ask any Cast Member for times and locations.

For those who enjoy new technology, World Showcase offers the **Around the World at Epcot** tour (at 7.45, 8.30, 9 and 9.30 each morning) on the innovative 2-wheeled **Segway Human Transporter**. It costs a hefty $85/person extra but the 2-hour tour includes full instruction and plenty of travel time on these amazing contraptions, which can go up to 12.5mph/20kph. It's open to only 10 guests at 9am each day (minimum age 16), or you can try the **Simply Segway** tour, a simplified 1-hour experience, mainly indoors (at $35/person, daily except Tues). It's advisable to book in advance on 407 939 8687.

Planning your visit

If you plan a 2-day visit, it makes sense to spend the first day in World Showcase, arriving by 11am and going straight there while the majority stay in Future World, booking your evening meal around 5.30pm, then lingering around the lagoon for the evening entertainment. For your second visit, try arriving in mid-afternoon and then doing Future World in a more leisurely fashion. Queues at most of the pavilions are almost non-existent for rides like

EPCOT with children

Here is our rough guide to the attractions that appeal to different age groups in this park:

Under-5s
Circle of Life, Gran Fiesta Tour Starring The Three Caballeros, Journey into Imagination with Figment, Kidcot stops, Living with the Land, The Seas with Nemo and Friends, Soarin'™ (if tall enough), Spaceship Earth, Turtle Talk with Crush, Universe of Energy.

5–8s
All the above, plus The American Adventure, Body Wars, Cranium Command, 'Honey, I Shrunk The Audience' (with parental discretion), Image Works, Innoventions, JAMMitors, Maelstrom (Norway), Miyuki the Candy Lady, Test Track.

9–12s
All the above, plus Dragon Legend Acrobats, Impressions de France, Matsuriza Drummers, Mission: SPACE, O Canada!, Sergio, Le Serveur Amusant, Wonders of China.

Over-12s
All the above, plus Bijutsu-kan Gallery, British Invasion (UK), Land of Many Faces (China), Off Kilter (Canada).

Universe of Energy, Spaceship Earth and Journey into Imagination, though Test Track, Soarin'™ and Mission: Space stay busy all day. You CAN do *Epcot* in a day – if you arrive early, put in some speedy legwork and give some of the detail a miss. But, of all the parks, it is a shame to hurry this one. In the shops (almost 70 in all), try to save your browsing for the times when the rides are busiest.

IllumiNations: Reflections of Earth

The day's big finale and an absolute show-stopper, this firework and special-effects extravaganza is awesome even by Disney standards. British composer Gavin Greenaway provided the original music for a 15-minute performance of vivid brilliance. Some 2,800 firework shells are launched as a celestial backdrop to a series of fire-and-water effects on the World Showcase Lagoon. The central icon is a 28ft/9m video globe of Earth that opens in a spectacular climax of choreographed pyrotechnics. Truly magnificent. However, people start staking out the best lagoon-side spots up to 2 HOURS in advance. The ultimate way to view

IllumiNations is by private boat on one of 3 **speciality cruises** from *Disney's Boardwalk* or *Yacht and Beach Club Resorts* (for non-residents, too). The price range is $250–275 per boat (holding 4–10 guests) and can be used for special celebrations. The Basic cruise costs $250 and the pontoon boat holds a maximum of 10. It includes water, soft drinks and snacks. The Celebration cruise costs $275 and adds a suitable range of occasion decorations. The classic motorboat *Breathless* costs $250 (up to 7 adults). Call 407 939 7529 up to 90 days in advance to book. Be aware that cruises launch regardless of whether fireworks are taking place.

International Food and Wine Festival

© Disney

© Disney

The main aquarium at The Seas With Nemo and Friends

Behind the scenes

Epcot also has some special behind-the-scenes tours (not for under-16s). **Dolphins in Depth** ($150, including refreshments, souvenir photo and T-shirt) is a 3-hour dip into the backstage and research areas of The Seas with Nemo and Friends pavilion, including a chance to meet the resident dolphins (13–17s must be accompanied by an adult). **Undiscovered Future World** is a 4½-hour journey into the creation of *Epcot*, Walt's vision for the resort and backstage areas like IllumiNations ($49). **Dive Quest** ($140/person, 10 and over) is a 3-hour experience, with a 30-minute dive into the Living Seas aquarium, plus a behind-the-scenes look at the facility at 4.30 or 5.30pm every day, and you need to have scuba certification (T-shirt and certificate for all participants; theme park admission not required). The new **Aqua Seas Tour** ($100/person, 8 and over; under-18s must be accompanied by an adult; inclusive of T-shirt and group photo; again, theme park admission is not required for this tour) is similar to Dive Quest but without the scuba diving element

(daily at 12.30pm). The most comprehensive tour, **Backstage Magic** ($199, 16 and over), goes behind the scenes of *Epcot*, *Magic Kingdom Park* and *Disney-MGM Studios* on a 7-hour foray into little-seen aspects, such as the backstage areas of *Disney-MGM Studios* and the tunnels below the *Magic Kingdom*. Book these tours on 407 WDW TOUR (407 939 8687).

Annual festivals

There are 2 other annual *Epcot* events to watch out for. The **International Flower and Garden Festival** literally puts the whole park in full bloom with an amazing series of set-pieces, seminars and mini-exhibitions from mid-Apr to early June. All the exhibits and lectures are free and they add a beautiful aspect to an already scenic park. The **Food and Wine Festival** runs for 45 days from 1 Oct and showcases national and regional cuisines, wines and beers, with the chance to attend grand Winemakers' Dinners and Tasting Events, or just sample the inexpensive offerings of more than 20 food booths dotted around World Showcase.

Disney-MGM Studios

Welcome to a journey into the world of film and TV, an epic voyage of discovery, creation – and fun. Here you will learn plenty of tricks of the trade; movie-making secrets and behind-the-scenes glimpses that have been cleverly turned into rides, shows and other attractions with guaranteed entertainment appeal.

Rather bigger than the *Magic Kingdom* at 154 acres/62ha but substantially smaller than *Epcot*, *Disney-MGM Studios* is a different experience yet again with its rather chaotic combination of attractions, street entertainment, film sets and smart gift shops. Like the *Magic Kingdom*, the food on offer may not win awards, but some of the restaurants (notably the Sci-Fi Dine-in Theater and '50s Prime Time Café)

have imaginative settings. The park also has rather more to occupy smaller children than *Epcot*, but you can still easily see all of it in a day unless the crowds are heavy.

Location

The entrance arrangements will be fairly familiar if you have already visited the other parks. *Disney-MGM Studios* is located on Buena Vista Drive (which runs between World Drive and *Epcot* Drive) and parking is $10. Remember to make a note of where you park before you catch the tram to the main gates, where you must wait for the official opening time. If the queues build up quickly, the gates will open early, so be ready for a running start. Once through the gates, you are into Hollywood

Disney-MGM Studios at a glance

Location	Off Buena Vista Drive or World Drive, Walt Disney World		
Size	154 acres/62ha		
Hours	9am–7pm off peak; 9am–10pm high season (Easter, summer holidays, Thanksgiving and Christmas)		
Admission	Under-3s free; 3–9 $60 (1-Day base ticket), $272 (5-Day Premium), $276 (7-Day Premium); adult (10+) $71, $310, $314. Prices do not include tax.		
Parking	$10		
Lockers	Next to Oscar's Super Service, to right of main entrance $7 ($2 refundable)		
Pushchairs	$10 and $18 from Oscar's Super Service		
Wheelchairs	$10 or $40 ($5 deposit refunded), with pushchairs		
Top Attractions	Twilight Zone™ Tower of Terror, Rock 'n' Roller Coaster Starring Aerosmith, Star Tours, The Great Movie Ride, Voyage of the Little Mermaid, Jim Henson's Muppet*Vision 3-D, Lights, Motors, Action!™ Extreme Stunt Show		
Don't Miss	Disney Stars and Motor Cars Parade/Block Party Bash, Indiana Jones™ Epic Stunt Spectacular!, Fantasmic!		
Hidden Costs	Meals	Burger, chips and coke $8.98 3-course lunch $32.27 (Hollywood Brown Derby) Kids' meal $3.99	
	T-shirts	$12–38	
	Souvenirs	$1–6,500	
	Sundries	Rock 'n' Roller Coaster Starring Aerosmith ride photo $16.95; poster-size $29.95	

1 Parade Route … Disney Stars and Motor Cars Parade/Block Party Bash
2 Sorcerer Mickey
3 The Great Movie Ride
4 ABC Sound Studio 'Soundds Dangerous' starring Drew Carey
5 Indiana Jones Epic Stunt Spectacular
6 Star Tours
7 Jim Henson's Muppet*Vision 3-D
8 Honey, I Shrunk the Kids Movie Set Adventure
9 Catastrophe Canyon on Disney-MGM Studios Backlot Tour
10 Disney-MGM Studios Backlot Tour
11 Meet Mickey Mouse
12 Toy Story Mania (spring 2008)
13 Walt Disney: One Man's Dream
14 Voyage of the Little Mermaid
15 The Magic of Disney Animation
16 Playhouse Disney – Live on Stage!
17 Rock 'n' Roller Coaster Starring Aerosmith
18 The Twilight Zone™ Tower of Terror
19 Beauty and the Beast – Live on Stage
20 Fantasmic!
21 Guest Information Board
22 Toy Story Pizza Planet
23 Lights, Motors, Action!™ Extreme Stunt Show
24 Al's Toy Barn
25 '50s Prime Time Café
26 Hollywood and Vine
27 Hollywood Brown Derby
28 Mama Melrose's
29 Sunset Ranch Market
30 Sci-Fi Dine-in Theater Restaurant
31 Journey into Narnia

DISNEY-MGM STUDIOS

© Disney

Catastrophe Canyon

Boulevard, a street of mainly gift shops, and you have to decide which of the main attractions to head for first, as these are the ones where the queues will be heaviest nearly all day. Try to ignore the lure of the shops as it is better to browse in the early afternoon when the attractions are at their busiest.

Incidentally, if you thought Disney had elevated queuing to an art form in their other parks, wait until you see how cleverly arranged they are here. Just when you think you have got to the ride itself, there is another twist to the queue you hadn't seen or an extra element to the ride that holds you up. The latter are holding pens, which are an ingenious way of making it seem you are being entertained instead of queuing. Look out for them in particular at the Great Movie Ride, Twilight Zone™ Tower of Terror and Jim Henson's Muppet*Vision 3-D.

An up-to-the-minute check on queue times at all the attractions is kept on a **Guest Information Board** on Hollywood Boulevard, just past its junction with Sunset Boulevard, where you can also book for the restaurants. The **Baby Center** here is located just inside the main gates on the left, next to Guest Relations, along with **First Aid**. *Disney-MGM Studios* is laid out in a rather more confusing fashion than its counterparts, which

have neatly packaged 'lands', so you will need to consult your map often to make sure you're going in the right direction.

The main attractions

The opening-gate crowds will all surge in one of 3 directions, which will give you a pretty good idea of where you want to go. By far the biggest attraction here is the **Twilight Zone™ Tower of Terror**, a magnificent haunted hotel ride that culminates in a 13-storey drop in a lift, where queues hit 2 hours at peak periods. So, if the Tower appeals to you, do it first! Head straight up Hollywood Boulevard then turn right into Sunset Boulevard where you'll see it at the end, looming ominously over the park. It's a FastPass (FP) ride (see page 108), as is the **Rock 'n' Roller Coaster Starring Aerosmith**, at the end of Sunset Boulevard on the left, which is another huge draw, so you can get a FastPass for one and ride the other.

Star Tours, the great *Star Wars*™ simulator ride, and **Voyage of the Little Mermaid** are also serious queue-builders and FP attractions. If you are not up for the really big thrills, grab a FP for Mermaid (straight up Hollywood Boulevard, past Sunset, turn right into Animation Courtyard), then head for Star Tours (back across the main square past the Indiana

Jones™ show). After Star Tours and Little Mermaid, another gentler experience (and also worth doing early on) is the highly amusing **Muppet*Vision 3-D** show, which is also a major draw through the main part of the day. It has the benefit of being air-conditioned, too, for when you need a rest. The park's most recent attraction, **Lights, Motors, Action!™ Extreme Stunt Show**, plays 3–5 times a day and has proved to be hugely popular, so it's a good idea to take a FastPass here.

> ### BRITTIP
> People begin queuing for the Lights, Motors, Action!™ Extreme Stunt Show a good half-hour before seating, and the midday shows are always full. Go for the first performance, or wait until later.

Here's a full rundown of the attractions, in a clockwise direction:

The Great Movie Ride: this faces you (behind the hat icon) as you walk in along Hollywood Boulevard and is a good place to start if the crowds are not too serious. An all-star audio-animatronics cast re-creates a number of box office smashes, including Jimmy Cagney's *Public Enemy*, Julie Andrews in *Mary Poppins*, Gene Kelly in *Singin' in the Rain* and many more masterful set-pieces as you undertake your conducted tour. Small children may

The Twilight Zone™ Tower of Terror

© Disney

> ### BRITTIP
> If you have young children, be aware there is some (loud) mock gunfire in the Lights, Motors, Action!™ Extreme Stunt Show, which can upset sensitive ears, while the motorbike scene includes a rider catching fire, which can be frightening for them, too.

find the menace of *The Alien* too strong, but otherwise the ride has universal appeal and features some clever live twists (there are 2 variations on this ride, a cowboy and a gangster version – ask a Cast Member if there's one you specially want to do). AAAA.

High School Musical Pep Rally: learn the latest cheers and dance moves with the cheerleaders and basketball players from East High in this energetic, interactive show, filled with Wildcat fever. Fans of the movie will recognise their favourite Disney TV characters, but others may find the show rather puzzling. Showing 6 times daily, the 25-minute show can be found near the Sorcerer's Hat.

ABC Sound Studio 'Sounds Dangerous' Starring Drew Carey: a sound FX special that features American comedian Drew Carey in an instalment of a spoof undercover police show *Sounds Dangerous*. Most of the 12-minute show is in the dark – which upsets some children – and is centred on your special headphones as Carey's stakeout goes wildly wrong. Clever and amusing – if a bit tame for older children – you exit into the Sound Works Studio to try out some well-known sound effects. AAA.

Indiana Jones™ Epic Stunt Spectacular: consult your park map for the various times that this rip-roaring stunt cavalcade hits the stage. A specially made movie set creates 3 different backdrops for Indiana Jones'™ stunt people to put on a dazzling array of clever stunts, scenes and special effects from the Harrison Ford films. Audience participation is an element and there are some amusing sub-plots. Queues for the 30-minute show begin to form up to ½ hour beforehand, but the auditorium holds more than 2,000 so everyone usually manages to get in. TTTT (FP).

Star Tours: anyone remotely interested in the *Star Wars*™ films will enjoy just queuing for one of our favourites, a breathtaking 7-minute spin in a Star Speeder. The elaborate walk-in area is full of *Star Wars*™ gadgets and gizmos that make the long wait (sometimes up to an hour) pass quickly. From arguing robots C-3PO and R-2D2 to your robotic pilot, everything has a brilliant sense of space travel, and the ride doesn't disappoint! Restrictions: 3ft 4in/ 101cm, no children under 3. TTTT (plus AAAAA) (FP).

Jim Henson's Muppet*Vision 3-D: the 3-D is crossed out here and 4-D substituted in its place, so be warned that strange things will be happening! A wonderful 10-minute holding-pen pre-show takes you into the Muppet Theater for a 20-minute experience with all of the Muppets, 3-D special effects and more – when Fozzie Bear points his squirty flower at you,

prepare to get wet! It's a gem, and the kids love it. Queues build up through the main parts of the day, but Disney's queuing expertise makes them seem shorter. AAAAA (FP).

Honey, I Shrunk the Kids Movie Set Adventure: this adventure playground gives youngsters the chance to tackle massive blades of grass that turn out to be slides, crawl through caves, investigate giant mushrooms and more. However, some may turn round and say 'Yeah. A big ant. So what?' and head back for the rides. There can be long queues here, too, so arrive early if the kids demand it (and bring plenty of film). TT, or TTTT for under-9s.

Lights, Motors, Action!™ **Extreme Stunt Show:** a direct import from the *Walt Disney Studios* in Paris, this is a truly amazing live action stunt spectacular, featuring cars, motorbikes, jet-skis and stuntmen of all kinds. It is one of the most remarkable shows you will see anywhere, full of genuine high-risk stunts that will leave you shaking your head in amazement. Seating starts 30 minutes prior to a show, and there is some amusing pre-show chat before the serious stuff starts. The set is

Lights, Motors, Action!™ *Extreme Stunt Show*

© Disney

Toy Story Mania

based on a typical Mediterranean village and is magnificently crafted. Once the preliminaries are completed, you are treated to a 40-minute extravaganza of daredevil stunts, with a Car Ballet sequence, a Motorbike Chase and a Grand Finale that features some surprise pyrotechnics to complete an awesome presentation (keep your eyes on the windows below the video screen at the end). Each scene – featuring a secret-agent goody and various baddies – is explained by a movie director and the results of each shoot are played back on screen to show how each effect was created. All the cars were specially created for the show by Vauxhall, and there are some extra tricks in between the main scenes. The whole thing was designed by Frenchman Rémy Julienne, the doyen of film car stunt sequences, who has worked on James Bond films *Goldeneye* and *Licence to Kill* and other action-packed epics such as *The Rock*, *Gone in 60 Seconds* and *Enemy of the State*.

Finally, the exit can be quite a scrum as 5,000 people have to leave together, and it can take 15 minutes to clear the auditorium, hence if you can sit towards the front, you will be

out rather quicker. The fact that it involves so much genuine, live co-ordination makes for a truly thrilling experience and you may well want to see it more than once, which is another reason to see it early on. TTTTT. Look out for **Lightning McQueen** and **Mater the Tow Truck** – two of the principal characters of the 2006 Pixar blockbuster *Cars* – waiting to greet guests in the plaza outside.

The Disney-MGM Studios Backlot Tour: before you board the special trams for a look at the off-limits part of the studios in this 35-minute walk-and-ride tour, you are treated to some special effects (involving an amusing water tank with a mock Pearl Harbor attack). The tram takes you round the production backlot and then to **Catastrophe Canyon** for a demonstration of special effects that try to both drown you and blow you up! AAA (plus TTTT). You exit into the **American Film Institute** showcase of costumes and props from recent films.

BRITTIP

Don't queue for the Backlot Tour when Lights, Motors, Action! Has just ended – it will be far too crowded.

Toy Story Mania: this replaces the old Who Wants To Be A Millionaire attraction in early summer 2008, with an innovative dark ride featuring the cast of the Pixar film *Toy Story* in a fun ride-and-shoot combination that promises to be a completely new Disney experience. If you can imagine the Buzz Lightyear Space Ranger Spin ride from the *Magic Kingdom* park, then add in some of the elements of Universal's two top rides, Men In Black: Alien Attack and The Amazing Adventure of Spider-Man, you will have some idea of what Disney's Imagineers are working on. There will be different skill levels and different challenges with every ride.

Right opposite all this development, you can still look for the **Meet Mickey Mouse** character greet, plus characters from **JoJo's Circus** nearby.

Walt Disney: One Man's Dream: this interactive show-and-tell exhibit chronicles Walt himself and his lifetime of accomplishments. From archive school records to a model of the Nautilus from *20,000 Leagues under the Sea*, the story of the man behind the Mouse comes to vivid life. The homage ends with a preview of Disney's future developments, plus a 10-minute film encapsulating everything Walt achieved and dreamed about. AAAA.

Journey into Narnia: originally a temporary exhibit for Christmas 2005, this encounter with the snowy world of *The Lion, The Witch and the Wardrobe* was a surprise hit with guests. Entering through the wardrobe doors, you meet the White Witch and learn the (abbreviated) story of Narnia with the help of a film show. You then exit through a series of maquettes and props. Lightweight stuff, but sure to interest the many fans of this enchanting film. AA.

Voyage of the Little Mermaid: a 17-minute live performance that is primarily for children who have seen the Disney cartoon. It brings together a creative mix of actors, animation and puppetry to re-create the film's highlights. Parents will still enjoy the clever special effects, but queues tend to be long, so go early or late. Those in the first few rows may also get a little wet. AAA, or AAAAA for under-9s (FP).

BRITTIP

Try to sit at least half-way back in the Mermaid Theatre, especially if you are with young children, as the stage front is a bit high.

The Magic of Disney Animation: an amusing and entertaining 30-minute show-and-tour through the making of cartoons. It starts with a special theatrical performance by Mushu, the Eddie Murphy-voiced dragon from the animated film *Mulan*. From there you exit into a hands-on area of interactive fun (especially for children); Ink & Paint is a colouring challenge, at Sound Stage you can try a voice-over, and You're a Character will tell you what Disney character you most resemble. From there, you have the choice of joining the Animation Academy for a tutored class in cartoon art, or exiting via the Animation Gallery, which has some fabulous gifts. Queues are rarely serious, so it's a good one for the afternoon. AAAA.

Journey into Narnia

© Disney

Playhouse Disney – Live on Stage!: straight out of several popular kids' TV series comes this 20-minute live show with pre-school favourites *Bear in the Big Blue House, JoJo's Circus, Rolie Polie Olie* and *The Little Einsteins*. Much of this can be seen in the UK only on cable or satellite TV, but it is colourful and entertaining. AAA, or AAAAA for under-5s.

Rock 'n' Roller Coaster Starring Aerosmith: Disney's first big-thrill inverted coaster is a sure-fire draw for the high-energy ride addicts, with a magnificent indoor setting and nerve-jangling ride. It features a clever 3-D film show starring rock group Aerosmith in their recording studio. That preamble leads to the real fun, set to specially recorded tracks from the band itself and with outrageous speaker systems, as riders climb aboard Cadillac cars for this memorable whiz through a mock Los Angeles setting (watch out for a close encounter with the Hollywood sign!). The high-speed launch and inversions ensure an up-to-the-minute roller-coaster experience. Go first thing or expect serious queues. Restrictions: 4ft/124cm. TTTTT (FP).

The Twilight Zone™ Tower of Terror: the second-tallest landmark in *Walt Disney World Resort in Florida* (at 199ft/60m; only the new Expedition Everest at *Disney's Animal Kingdom* is

Playhouse Disney – Live on Stage!

© Disney

higher) invites you to experience another dimension in this mysterious Hollywood Tower Hotel that time forgot. The exterior is intriguing, the interior is fascinating, the ride is scintillating and the queues are huge! Just when you think you are through to the ride, there is another queue, so spend your time inspecting the superb detail. The ride was also revamped in 2003 to add a new, random element to the drop sequence and other special effects, while lap bars have been replaced with seat-belts for a more hair-raising experience! Restrictions: 3ft 4in/ 101cm. TTTTT (FP).

Beauty and the Beast – Live on Stage: an enchanting live performance of the highlights of this Disney classic will entertain the whole family for 20 minutes in the nearby Theater of the Stars. Check the schedule for show times (and try to catch the a capella singing group Four for a Dollar who perform before each show). AAA.

> ## BRITTIP
>
> Beat the crowds by booking a Fantasmic! dinner package when you enter the park (or on 407 939 3463). Just reserve an early dinner at the Hollywood Brown Derby, Mama Melrose's or Hollywood and Vine, ask for the Fantasmic! package and you get VIP seating later for the show.

Fantasmic!: this special-effects spectacular is simply not to be missed. Staged every night in a 6,900-seat amphitheatre, it features the dreams of Mr M Mouse, portrayed as the sorcerer's apprentice, through films such as *Pocahontas, The Lion King* and *Snow White*, but hijacked by various Disney villains, leading to a tumultuous battle with Our Hero emerging triumphant. Dancing waters, shooting comets, animated fountains, swirling stars and balls of fire combine in a breathtaking presentation – but beware of the giant, fire-breathing dragon! The

© Disney

Hollywood Brown Derby

25-minute show begins seating up to 90 minutes in advance and it is advisable to head there at least 30 minutes before (watch out for the splash zones!). AAAAA.

Daily parade

In keeping with the park's movie-star style, the daily parade in 2007 was **Disney Stars and Motor Cars**, with the theme of a Hollywood film première of the '30s and '40s and a series of genuine vintage cars and clever replicas being used to mount a riotous cavalcade of Disney showbiz favourites. It featured 15 crazily customised cars – including a 1929 Cadillac – providing the likes of **Aladdin**, **Mary Poppins**, **Mulan**, the **Muppets** and **Monsters Inc** with a chance to show off in larger-than-life fashion. The lead car also features any special guests at the Studios that day – or a visiting family. AAAA.

Due to take over the parade duties in 2008, we believe, is the **Block Party Bash**, direct from *Disney's California Adventure* park in Anaheim. This high-energy cavalcade features 60 singers, dancers, gymnasts and Pixar movie characters – from *The Incredibles*, *Toy Story*, *Bug's Life* and *Monsters Inc* – in a street party that stops periodically to interact with guests. With lively music, vibrant costumes and some remarkable aerial acrobatics, it is guaranteed to captivate and amaze.

Disney characters are out and about along Mickey Avenue, as are performing actors and actresses in Hollywood Boulevard. You can catch the *Toy Story* characters by **Al's Toy Barn**, The Incredibles at the Magic of Disney Animation and the Power Rangers at the bottom of Streets of America at regular intervals.

And, for that something-different factor, watch out for the classic live rock 'n' roll performances of **Mulch, Sweat and Shears**, either on Streets of America or by Rock 'n' Roller Coaster.

Places to eat

While the choice of food may not be wide, there is plenty of it and at reasonable prices. **The Hollywood Brown Derby** offers a full-service restaurant in fine Hollywood style (reservations necessary – special Early Evening Value meals 4–6pm), while **Mama Melrose's Ristorante Italiano** is a wonderful table-service Italian option (one of our favourites).

BRITTIP

We always recommend the Sci-Fi Dine-In Theater Restaurant or '50s Prime Time Café for a main meal with a difference.

The **Sci-Fi Dine-In Theater Restaurant** is a big hit with kids as you dine in a mock drive-in cinema, with cars as tables, waitresses on roller skates and a big film screen showing old black-and-white science-fiction clips. The **'50s Prime Time Café** is another hilarious experience as you sit in mock stage sets from American TV sitcoms and eat meals 'just like Mom used to make' (the waiters all claim to be your aunt, uncle or cousin and warn you to take your elbows off the table! Good fun). Reservations necessary. The fast-food eateries consist of the **ABC Commissary** (fish and chips, burgers, sandwiches and stir-fries), **Backlot Express** (excellent burgers and hot dogs), **Rosie's All-American Café** (chicken, burgers and salads) and **Toy Story Pizza Planet** (pizza, salads and drinks). More healthy fare can be found at the **Studio Catering Co. Flatbread Grill** (wraps, salads and chicken stew). A good buffet dinner is also available at **Hollywood & Vine Cafeteria of the Stars** ($23.99 adults, $11.99 3–9s) in addition to the **character breakfast** and **lunch** with the Playhouse Disney Pals.

Shopping

There are 21 gift and speciality shops around the Studios – 6 of them along Hollywood Boulevard – worth checking out in the early afternoon. **Sid Caheunga's One-of-a-Kind** (just to the left of the main gates as you enter) stocks rare movie and TV items, including many celebrity autographs. Try the **Legends of Hollywood** (on Sunset Boulevard) for some different souvenirs and **AFI Showcase Shop** (in the Backlot), which has a selection of MGM logo products and movie-related gifts. **Keystone Clothiers** (at the top of Hollywood Boulevard) offers some of the best apparel.

Studios at Christmas

At Christmas (in fact, from late Nov to 3 Jan), one of the most amazing spectacles anywhere is the **Osborne Family Lights**, which are switched on every evening in the Streets of America area. The display of 5 million twinkling, themed fairy lights draws a huge crowd all evening (try to go during a Fantasmic! performance to avoid the worst of the throngs) and is simply stunning.

Mickey's Very Merry Christmas Parade

DISNEY-MGM STUDIOS with children

Here is our general guide to the rides that appeal to the different age groups in this park (and it is, possibly, the best spread of all):

Under-5s

Beauty and the Beast – Live on Stage, Disney Stars and Motor Cars parade/Block Party Bash, Fantasmic!, Honey I Shrunk the Kids Movie Set Adventure, The Magic of Disney Animation, Playhouse Disney – Live On Stage!, Voyage of the Little Mermaid.

5–8s

Beauty and the Beast – Live On Stage, Disney-MGM Studios Backlot Tour, Disney Stars and Motor Cars parade/Block Party Bash, Fantasmic!, Honey I Shrunk the Kids Movie Set Adventure, Indiana Jones™ Epic Stunt Spectacular, Jim Henson's Muppet*Vision 3-D, Journey Into Narnia, Lights, Motors, Action!™ Extreme Stunt Show, The Magic of Disney Animation, 'Sounds Dangerous' Starring Drew Carey, Toy Story Mania, Voyage of the Little Mermaid.

9–12s

Beauty and the Beast – Live on Stage, Disney-MGM Studios Backlot Tour, Fantasmic!, The Great Movie Ride, Indiana Jones™ Epic Stunt Spectacular, Jim Henson's Muppet*Vision 3-D, Journey into Narnia, The Magic of Disney Animation, Lights, Motors, Action!™ Extreme Stunt Show, Rock 'n' Roller Coaster Starring Aerosmith, 'Sounds Dangerous' Starring Drew Carey, Star Tours, Twilight Zone™ Tower of Terror, Toy Story Mania.

Over-12s

Disney-MGM Studios Backlot Tour, Fantasmic!, The Great Movie Ride, Indiana Jones™ Epic Stunt Spectacular, Jim Henson's Muppet*Vision 3-D, Lights, Motors, Action!™ Extreme Stunt Show, The Magic of Disney Animation, Rock 'n' Roller Coaster Starring Aerosmith, Star Tours, Twilight Zone™ Tower of Terror, Walt Disney: One Man's Dream, Who Wants to Be a Millionaire – Play It!

Skywalker and Co

Star Wars™ film fans will want to make a beeline for the Studios during weekends in late May and early June when the park becomes a playground for characters, film stars, photo-opportunities, competitions and other memorabilia based on anything to do with Luke Skywalker and Co. There is no additional fee to rub shoulders with (and get autographs from) various *Star Wars*™ personalities, and the Studios take on an extra (space) dimension each weekend. Don't miss the **Jedi Training Academy**, which is now part of the park's main daily show attractions. On a stage in front of the Star Tours ride, a Jedi Master takes on Darth Vader and Darth Maul – and some youngsters get the chance to wield a light saber! TTT.

Jedi Training Academy

© Disney

Disney's Animal Kingdom Theme Park

Disney's newest and smartest theme park opened in 1998 representing a completely different experience. With an emphasis on conservation and nature, it largely eschews the non-stop thrills and attractions of the other parks and instead offers a change of pace, a more relaxing motif, as well as Disney's usual seamless entertainment style – plus 3 excellent thrill rides.

The attractions are relatively few, just 6 out-and-out rides, plus 2 scenic journeys, 2 nature trails, 5 shows (including the hilarious 3-D film *It's Tough To Be A Bug!* and the full-blown theatre of *Festival Of The Lion King*), an elaborate adventure playground, conservation station and petting zoo, and a Disney character greeting area. It's a far cry from the hustle-bustle of the *Magic Kingdom*, and its serious environmental message aims to create a greater understanding of many of the world's ecological problems.

It is outrageously scenic, notably with the 145ft/44m Tree of Life, the Kilimanjaro Safaris and the Asian village of Serka Zong (home to the mountainous new Expedition: Everest™ ride), but it won't overwhelm you with Disney's usual grand fantasy. Rather, it is a chance to explore and experience; to learn and appreciate; and to soak up the gentler ambience of nature at its finest. It is not a zoo in the conventional sense, but it is home to 200-plus species of birds and animals (in some wonderfully naturalistic settings). It carries a strong environmental message and children in particular may pick up the essential conservation undertones of things like Kilimanjaro Safaris and Maharajah Jungle Trek. However, the

Disney's Animal Kingdom Theme Park at a glance

Location	Directly off Osceola Parkway, also via World Drive and Buena Vista Drive		
Size	500 acres/203ha divided into 6 'lands'		
Hours	9am–5 or 6pm off peak; 8am–7pm in high season		
Admission	Under-3s free; 3–9 $60 (1-Day base ticket), $272 (5-Day Premium), $276 (7-Day Premium); adult (10+) $71, $310, $314. Prices do not include tax.		
Parking	$10		
Lockers	Either side of Entrance Plaza $7 ($2 refundable)		
Pushchairs	$10 and $18 at Garden Gate Gifts, through entrance on right		
Wheelchairs	$10 or $40 ($5 refund), with pushchairs		
Top Attractions	DINOSAUR!, Kilimanjaro Safaris, It's Tough To Be A Bug!, Kali River Rapids, Festival Of The Lion King, Finding Nemo – The Musical, Expedition: Everest™		
Don't Miss	Pangani Forest Exploration Trail, Maharajah Jungle Trek, Rafiki's Planet Watch, Mickey's Jamming Jungle Parade, dining at Rainforest Café		
Hidden Costs	Meals	Burger, chips and coke $8.98 3-course meal at Rainforest Café $34.97 Kids' meal $3.99	
	T-shirts	$20–45	
	Souvenirs	$1–20,000	
	Sundries	Caricature drawings $15, $20, $28	

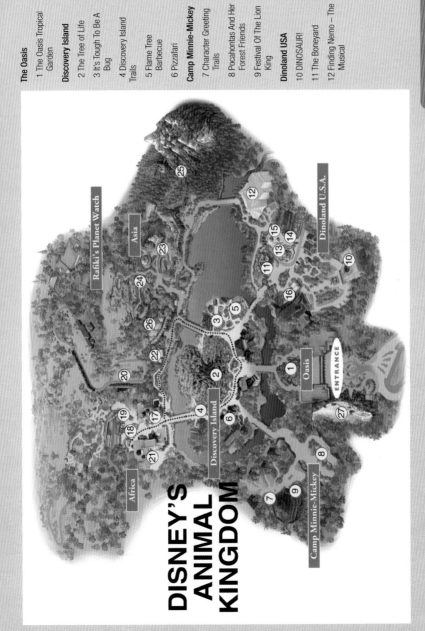

The Oasis

1 The Oasis Tropical Garden

Discovery Island

2 The Tree of Life
3 It's Tough To Be A Bug
4 Discovery Island Trails
5 Flame Tree Barbecue
6 Pizzafari

Camp Minnie-Mickey

7 Character Greeting Trails
8 Pocahontas And Her Forest Friends
9 Festival Of The Lion King

Dinoland USA

10 DINOSAUR!
11 The Boneyard
12 Finding Nemo – The Musical

13 Chester And Hester's Dino-Rama!
14 TriceraTOP Spin
15 Primeval Whirl
16 Restaurantosaurus

Africa

17 Harambe
18 Kilimanjaro Safaris
19 Pangani Forest Exploration
20 Rafiki's Planet Watch
21 Tusker House Restaurant

Asia

22 Flights Of Wonder
23 Kali River Rapids
24 Maharajah Jungle Trek
25 Expedition: Everest™
26 Yak 'n Yeti Restaurant
27 Rainforest Café

DISNEY'S ANIMAL KINGDOM

Rafiki's Planet Watch

Asia

Dinoland U.S.A.

Discovery Island

Oasis

ENTRANCE

Africa

Camp Minnie-Mickey

park does get crowded, the walkways can be congested and there are also fewer places to cool down. It is definitely a good idea to be here on time and use FastPass (FP) to minimise queuing.

Getting there

If you are staying in the Kissimmee area, *Disney's Animal Kingdom Park* is the easiest of the parks to find. Just get on the (toll) Osceola Parkway and follow it all the way to the toll booths, where parking is $10. Alternatively, coming down I-4, take exit 65 on to Osceola Parkway. From West Highway 192, come in on Sherberth Road and turn right at the first traffic lights. If you arrive early (which is advisable), you can walk to the Entrance Plaza. Otherwise, the usual tram system will take you in, so make a note of the row you park in (e.g. Unicorn, 67). The Plaza is overlooked by the mountainous **Rainforest Café**, with its 65ft/20m waterfall, which is a must for breakfast, an early lunch or dinner (busy 12.30–3.30pm). With Orlando so hot in the summer months, you need to be at the park as early as possible to see the animals before they take cover in the shade.

BRITTIP

An early start is especially advised for Kilimanjaro Safaris. You will see far more animals in the first few cooler hours of the day than during the hotter afternoon.

For the early birds, here is your best plan of campaign. Once through the gates, animal lovers should head first for Kilimanjaro Safaris, through the Oasis, Discovery Island and Africa. After the Safari, go straight to Pangani Forest Exploration Trail and you will have experienced 2 of the park's best animal encounters. Alternatively, thrill-seekers should walk straight through Discovery Island for Asia, where the Expedition: Everest™ ride is the big draw. With that one safely under your belt before the serious crowds arrive, head to Kilimanjaro Safari in Africa or the nearby Kali River Rapids raft ride, followed by the scenic Maharajah Jungle Trek. The best combination for the first arrivals is to get a FastPass (FP) for Expedition: Everest™ then ride Kilimanjaro Safaris, and, once you have done that (and depending on your FP time), either do your Everest

Finding Nemo – the Musical

© Disney

© Disney

It's Tough to Be a Bug

ride or go straight to Kali River Rapids. Check your show schedule for Festival Of The Lion King and try to catch one of the first 2 performances, as the later ones draw sizeable queues. The wait time board at the entrance to Discovery Island is also helpful. Right; those are your main tactics – here is the full rundown.

The Oasis

The Oasis Tropical Garden is a gentle, walk-through introduction to the park, a rocky, tree-covered area featuring several animal habitats, studded with streams, waterfalls and lush plant life. Here you will meet miniature deer, macaws, parrots, iguanas, sloths and tree kangaroos in a wonderfully understated environment that leads you across a stone bridge to the main open park area. This is a good place to visit in early afternoon when many of the rides are busy. AAA.

Discovery Island

This colourful village is the park hub, themed as a tropical artists' colony, with animal-inspired artwork, 4 main shops and 2 eateries. Here you will also find various character meet-and-greets, plus the fun **Beatniks** percussion group and the South American sounds of **Inkas Wazi**.

The Tree of Life: this arboreal edifice is the park centrepiece, an awesome creation that seems to have a different perspective from wherever you view it. The trunk and roots are covered in 325 carvings representing the Circle of Life, from the dolphin to the lion. Trails lead round the tree, interspersed with habitats for flamingos, otters, ring-tailed lemurs, macaws, axis deer, cranes, storks, ducks and tortoises. The tree canopy spreads 160ft/49m, the trunk is 50ft/15m wide and the roots spread out 170ft/52m in diameter. It has 103,000 leaves (all attached by hand) on more than 8,000 branches! AAAA.

It's Tough To Be A Bug!: winding down among the Tree's roots brings you 'underground' to a 430-seat theatre and another example of Disney's artistry in 3-D films and special effects. This hysterically funny 10-minute show, in the company of Flick from the Pixar film *A Bug's Life*, is a homage to 80% of the animal world, featuring grasshoppers, beetles, spiders, stink bugs and termites (beware the 'acid' spray!) as well as a number of tricks I couldn't possibly reveal. Sit towards the back in the middle of a row (allow a good number of people in first as the rows are filled up from the far side) to get the best of the 3-D effects. Queues build up from midday, but they do move quite steadily. Don't miss the 'forthcoming attractions' posters in the foyer for some truly excruciating bug puns on famous films. AAAAA (FP).

BRITTIP

The dark, special effects and mock creepy-crawlies in It's Tough To Be A Bug! can be quite scary. Use caution with young children here.

Shopping is at its best here, with a huge range of merchandise, souvenirs and gifts (notably in **Disney Outfitters** and **Island Mercantile**), while both counter-service restaurants, **Pizzafari** and **Flame Tree Barbecue**, are good choices. Indeed, provided it is not too hot, the Flame Tree is a relaxing and picturesque option, set among some pretty gardens, pools and fountains right on the bank of Discovery River.

Camp Minnie-Mickey

A woodland retreat featuring gently winding paths and more of Disney's clever scenery – the benches, lighting and the gurgling stream, with Donald Duck and his nephews hiking down the side, that develops into a series of kid-friendly squirt fountains.

Character Greeting Trails: 4 trails lead to a series of jungle encounters with Disney characters such as Mickey and Minnie (naturally), Winnie the Pooh and Tigger, Chip 'n' Dale, Baloo and King Louie, Timon and Rafiki. AAAAA (for kids).

Pocahontas And Her Forest Friends: based on characters from the Disney film *Pocahontas*, this 15-minute show sees various animals – raccoons, rabbits, cranes, a skunk, armadillo and porcupine – interacting with the central actress and Mother Willow in the question of 'Who can save the forest?'. However, it doesn't seem to do much for small children, there's not much shade in summer and it is standing room only once the 350 seats have been filled. AAA.

Festival Of The Lion King: not to be missed, this high-powered 40-minute production brings the hit film to life in spectacular fashion with giant moving stages, huge animated figures, singers, dancers, acrobats and stilt-walkers. All the well-known songs are given an airing in a coruscation of colour and sound, and it serves to underline the quality Disney brings to live shows. Queuing begins 30 minutes in advance for the 1,000-seat theatre, so try to take in one of the earlier shows. AAAAA.

DinoLand USA

Somewhat at odds with the natural theming of the rest of the park, DinoLand USA is a full-scale palaeontology exercise, with this mock town taken over by a university fossil dig. Energetically tongue-in-cheek (the students who work in the area have the motto 'Been there, dug that', while you enter under a mock brachiosaurus skeleton, the 'Oldengate Bridge' – groan!), it still features some glimpses into dinosaur research and artefacts.

Kilimanjaro Safaris

© Disney

The Boneyard at Animal Kingdom

DINOSAUR!: renamed after Disney's big animated film (it was initially called Countdown to Extinction), the original fast, jerky ride has been toned down a little for a more family-friendly experience (though the dinosaur menace is too scary for many young children). It is a wonderfully realistic journey back to the end of the Cretaceous period and the giant meteor that put paid to dinosaur life. You enter the high-tech Dino Institute ('a discovery center and research lab dedicated to uncovering the mysteries of the past') for a multimedia show of dino history that leads to a briefing room for your 'mission' 65 million years in the past. However, one of the Institute's scientists hijacks your journey to capture a dinosaur, and you go careering back to a prehistoric jungle in your 12-passenger Time Rover. The threat of a carnotaurus (quite frightening for some children; try to sit them on the inside of the car) and the impending doom of the meteor add up to a breathtaking whiz through a stunning environment. You will need to ride at least twice to appreciate all the detail, but queues build up quickly, so go either first thing or late in the day. Restrictions: 3ft 4in/101cm. TTTT plus AAAA (FP).

The Boneyard: a hugely imaginative adventure playground, it offers kids the chance to slip, slide and climb through the 'fossilised' remains of triceratops and brontosaurs, explore caves, dig for bones and splash through a mini-waterfall. The amusing signage will be wasted on most kids, but it is ideal for parents to let their young 'uns loose for up to an hour (though not just after the neighbouring Finding Nemo show has finished). TTTT (kids only).

Finding Nemo – The Musical: opened in 2006 (after replacing the old Tarzan Rocks show in the rebuilt Theater in the Wild), this all-new production is a first for Disney entertainment, taking a non-musical animated feature and turning it into a fully fledged all-singing extravaganza. The show combines colourful puppets, dancers, acrobats and animated backdrops with innovative lighting, sound and special effects. The basic idea remains faithful to the story of Nemo, his dad Marlin and friends Dory and Crush and features larger-than-life puppetry, plus rod, bunraku and shadow puppets, all designed by Michael Curry, who created the award-winning Broadway version of Disney's *The Lion King* show. It is a spectacular combination of music and grand staging, and performs several times a day. AAAA.

BRITTIP

Finding Nemo – The Musical is a popular addition to the park and we recommend catching an early show if you possibly can.

Chester & Hester's Dino-Rama!: this mini-land of rides, fairground games and stalls adds a rather garish element to DinoLand USA. Its main icon is a towering Concretosaurus (!), and it is designed to have a quirky, tongue-in-cheek style reminiscent of 1950s' American roadside attractions. The top rides are: **TriceraTOP Spin**: another version of the Dumbo/Aladdin rides in the *Magic Kingdom Park*, a flying, twirling, spinning top bounces you up and down with a surprise at the top. AA, or TTTT for under-5s. **Primeval Whirl**: coaster fans will definitely get a laugh out of

© Disney

Primeval Whirl at Animal Kingdom

this wacky offering that sends its riders through a maze of curves, hills and (quite sharp) drops that make it seem much faster than it actually is. It is basically a fairground lampoon of the DINOSAUR! ride, a mock journey 'way back in time', with plenty of cartoon frippery. Extra fun is provided by the fact that the cars spin, which gives an unpredictable element to each 3-minute ride (plunging through the jaws of a skeleton dino at one point!). The queuing area is a riot of visual gags, but the ride itself is not recommended for anyone with back or neck problems. Restrictions: 4ft/122cm. TTTT (FP).

The **Fossil Fun Games** are 6 fairground-type stalls, each costing a rather hefty $2–6, designed to tempt you into trying to win a large cuddly dinosaur, all with the larger-than-life Dino-Rama trademark. Dining options include the (you've guessed it!) **Restaurantosaurus**, counter-service burgers and hot dogs and a snack bar. Shopping is centred on the huge **Chester and Hester's Dino-Rama! – Dinosaur Treasures**, the 'Fossiliferous Gift Store' with groan-inducing slogans like Merchandise of Extinction, Prehistoric Prices and Last Stop for 65 Million Years!

Africa

The largest land in the park, it recreates magnificently the forests, grasslands and rocky homelands of equatorial Africa's most fascinating residents in a richly landscaped setting that is part rundown port town and part savannah. There's hardly a glimpse of the outside world, which seems thousands of miles away.

Harambe: a reconstruction of a Kenyan port village, with white coral walls and thatched roofs, is the start point for your adventure. The Arab-influenced Swahili culture is depicted in the native tribal costumes and architecture. Here you'll find 2 more shops, including the **Mombasa Marketplace/Ziwani Traders**, where you can suit up safari style, and the all-new buffet offerings at **Tusker House Restaurant** (with character meal, *Donald's Safari Breakfast*, and non-character buffets at lunch and dinner – reservations advised), plus 4 snack and drink bars, notably **Kusafiri Coffee Shop**. The splendid **Mor Thiam** drummers, **Tam Tam's of Congo** and **Karuka Acrobats** also perform here on selected days.

Kilimanjaro Safaris: the queuing area alone earns high marks for

Walt Disney World at Christmas

If you can visit from the end of November to the week before Christmas, you will get the benefit of all the added decorations and atmosphere and none of the overwhelming crowds (which pack Walt Disney World from around 20 December to 2 January). Each of the parks takes on a festive character, with the addition of artistic artificial snow, Christmas lights and a huge, magnificently decorated fir tree.

Disney-MGM Studios also features the eye-popping **Osborne Family Lights** while, at the *Magic Kingdom Park*, Main Street USA is transformed into a Christmas extravaganza, dominated by a 60ft/18m tree. The unmissable **Mickey's Very Merry Xmas Parade** replaces the main 3pm parade in December and is a positive delight for its lively music and eye-catching costumes. Another seasonal extra is the colourful **'Twas The Night Before Xmas** show at the Galaxy Palace Theater.

Epcot is the jewel in the Christmas crown, though, with 2 outstanding features. At 6pm, the daily **Christmas tree lighting ceremony** is quite breathtaking as the rest of the park lights go out and then the World Showcase bridge and the tree itself are illuminated in dramatic stages to some grand musical accompaniment. The nightly **Candlelight Processional** also draws a crowd, with a guest narrator telling the story of Christmas to the backdrop of a large choir and elaborate candle parade. It is tasteful, dramatic and eye-catching, but you should arrive early as people start queuing almost 3 HOURS in advance. However, you can get a reserved seat if you buy the **Candlelight Processional Dinner Package** ($30.99–45.99, plus tax, depending on which World Showcase restaurant you select, and $12.99 for 3–11s), by calling well in advance on 407 939 3463 (credit card details required).

authenticity, preparing you for the sights and sounds of the 110 acre/45ha savannah beyond. You board a 32-passenger truck, with your driver/guide relaying information about the flora and fauna on view and a bush pilot overhead relaying facts and figures on the wildlife, including the dangers threatening them in the real world. Hundreds of animals are spread out in various habitats, with no fences in sight (the ditches and barriers are all well concealed) as you splash through fords and cross rickety bridges, and you should get good close-ups of lions, rhinos, elephants, giraffes, antelope, zebras, hippos, baboons and ostriches.

Once again, the authentic nature of all you see (okay, some of the tyre 'ruts' and termite mounds are concrete and the baobab trees are fake) is quite awesome, with the

BRITTIP

The best (i.e. the most jolting) ride with the Kilimanjaro Safaris is at the back of the truck, though there's much less to see from midday to late afternoon when many of the animals take a siesta.

spread of the vegetation and the landscaping, and the only drawback is the lack of any photo stops along the way (the ride is pretty bumpy). The animals also roam over a wide area and can disappear from view. Not recommended for expectant mothers or anyone with back or neck problems. AAAAA (FP).

Pangani Forest Exploration Trail: as you leave the Safari, you turn into an overgrown nature trail that showcases gorillas, hippos, meerkats and rare tropical birds. You wander the trail at your own pace and visit several research stations to learn more about the animals on display, including the underwater view of the hippos (check out the size of a hippo skull and those teeth!) and the savannah overlook, where giraffes and antelope graze and the amusing meerkats frolic. The walk-through aviary gives you the chance to meet the carmine bee-eater, pygmy goose, African green pigeon, ibis and brimstone canary, among others, but the real centrepiece is the silverback gorilla habitat, in fact 2 of them. The family group is often just inches away from the plate-glass window, while the bachelor group further along can prove more elusive. Again, the natural aspect of the trail is breathtaking and it provides a host of photo opportunities. It is best to visit early on to see the animals at their most active (and because it quickly becomes quite crowded). AAAAA.

Rafiki's Planet Watch: the little train journey here, with its peek into some of the backstage areas, is just the preamble to the park's interactive and educational exhibits. The 3-part journey starts with **Habitat Habit!**, where you can see cotton-top tamarins and learn how conservation begins in your own back garden. **Conservation Station** is next up with a series of exhibits, shows and information stations about the environment and threats to its ecology, which are aimed primarily at children. Look out for *Sounds of the Rain Forest*, the story of endangered species, at the Mermaid Tales Theater and the Eco-Heroes (who can be quizzed on-screen) trying to redress the balance, then take a self-guided tour of the park's backstage areas such as the veterinary treatment centre, the hatchery and neonatal care. You can easily spend an hour absorbing the information here, along with Disney's Wildlife Conservation Fund. Plus, youngsters can meet Rafiki and some of his animal chums.

Kali River Rapids

© Disney

The **Affection Section**, a petting zoo of lambs, goats, donkeys, sheep and guinea pigs, completes the Planet Watch line-up. AAA.

Asia

The final 'land' of the park is elaborately themed as the gateway to the imaginary south-east Asian city of Anandapur, with temples, ruined forts, landscape and wildlife.

Flights of Wonder: another wildlife show, this portrays the talents and traits of a host of birds, built into a production of mildly amusing proportions. A trainer showcases the ability of a number of birds, including hawks and macaws, before being interrupted by a bumbling tour guide – Guano Joe (groan) – who needs to be set straight on various conservation issues. This is the cue for some fun frolics with our feathered friends (watch out for singing parrot Gaucho), as an assortment of vultures, eagles and toucans join in. The Caravan Stage is not air-conditioned, though, and is fiendishly hot in summer. AAA.

Kali River Rapids: part thrill-ride, part scenic journey, this bouncy raft ride will get you pretty wet (not great for early morning in winter). It starts out in tropical forest territory before launching into a scene of logging devastation, warning of the dangers of clear-cut burning. Your raft then plunges down a waterfall (and one unlucky soul – usually the one with his or her back to the drop – gets seriously damp) before you finish more sedately. Queues can be long through the main part of the day, so make use of FastPass here. You may also want to experience the ride twice to appreciate all the clever detail. Restrictions: 3ft 6in/106cm (a few rafts have adult-and-child seats allowing smaller children to ride). TTT (plus AAAA) (FP).

Maharajah Jungle Trek: Asia's version of the Pangani Forest Trail is another picturesque walk past decaying

DISNEY'S ANIMAL KINGDOM PARK with children

Here is our general guide to the rides that appeal to the different age groups in this park:

Under-5s

Affection Section, The Boneyard, Character Greetings Trails, Discovery Island Trails, Festival Of The Lion King, Finding Nemo – The Musical, Kilimanjaro Safaris, Maharajah Jungle Trek, Pangani Forest Exploration Trail, TriceraTOP Spin.

5–8s

All the above, plus Conservation Station, DINOSAUR! (with parental discretion), Flights Of Wonder, Habitat Habit!, It's Tough To Be A Bug, Kali River Rapids, Pocahontas And Her Forest Friends, Primeval Whirl.

9–12s

All the above, plus Expedition: Everest™.

Over-12s

DINOSAUR!, Expedition: Everest™, Festival Of The Lion King, Flights Of Wonder, It's Tough To Be A Bug!, Kali River Rapids, Kilimanjaro Safaris, Maharajah Jungle Trek, Pangani Forest Exploration Trail, Primeval Whirl.

temple ruins and various animal encounters. Playful gibbons, tapirs, Komodo dragons and a bat enclosure (including the flying fox bat, the world's largest variety) lead up to the main viewing area, the 5 acre/2ha Tiger Range, which includes a pool and fountains and is a popular playground early in the day for these magnificent big cats. An antelope enclosure and walk-through aviary complete this breathtaking trek (which rarely draws very heavy crowds). AAAAA.

Expedition: Everest™: a major new attraction, this wonderfully clever roller-coaster takes you deep into the Himalayas for an encounter with the mythical Yeti. The queuing area alone will convince you of its authentic location (try to do the main queue at least once rather than FastPass to appreciate all the fine detail) as it delivers you to an old abandoned tea plantation railway station. Here you undertake the ride to the foothills of Mount Everest, but you must first brave the perils of the Forbidden Mountain – lair of the Yeti – to get there. Will the beast be in evidence? You bet! The ride becomes a typically fast-paced coaster whiz (though with

no inversions), both forwards AND backwards, as you attempt to escape the creature's domain. The final encounter with a massive audi-animatronic Yeti is truly jaw-dropping and underlines the splendidly creative nature of this massive ride. It has proved to be a fabulous new attraction, with plenty of twists and turns, but it draws a crowd all day, so make it one of the first things you do. You can also take advantage of a Single Rider queue here (to the right of the FastPass entrance) if you don't mind the possibility of your group

Expedition Everest

© Disney

BRITTIP

Although Expedition: Everest™ is a FastPass ride, its popularity means that FastPasses often run out, so don't leave it too late to visit here.

being split up. Restrictions: 3ft 8in/115cm. TTTTT (FP). The fab new **Yak and Yeti** restaurant was due to open here in late 2007, with tempting Asian-fusion cuisine, a full-service bar, fast-food option and beer garden.

Returning to the front entrance gives you the chance to sample or just visit (and shop at) the **Rainforest Café**, the second on Disney property. If you haven't seen the one at *Downtown Disney* Marketplace, you should definitely call in to witness the amazing jungle interior with its audio-animatronic animals, waterfalls, thunderstorms and aquariums. A 3-course meal will set you back about $35 (kids' meals at $7.99), but the setting alone is worth it and the food is above average. Try breakfast or an early dinner here to avoid the crowds.

Jammin' Jungle Parade

The daily highlight is **Mickey's Jammin' Jungle Parade**. The Imagineers have created a series of fanciful 'Expedition Rovers' that give Disney characters the chance to celebrate the animals that live here. The parade is enhanced by puppets, stilt-walkers and mobile sculptures, plus live percussionists as it snakes down a narrow path from Harambe, around Discovery Island and back. Set to memorable music, it sounds as well as looks good, while 25 park guests are chosen to take part every day, travelling on the back of rickshaws that follow each character jeep. AAAAA.

Finally, for a behind-the-scenes look at the park, **Backstage Safari** is a wonderful 3-hour journey into the handling and care of all the animals ($65, no under-16s), while **Wild By Design** offers a 3-hour tour of the park's art, history and architecture and how it was all created ($58, no under-14s). Book on 407 939 8687.

But don't stop here. There's plenty more theme park fun in store …

Mickey's Jammin' Jungle Parade

6

Five More of the Best

or Expanding Orlando's Universe

It is time to leave the wonderful world of Disney now, and venture out into the rest of central Florida's great attractions. And, believe us, there is still a terrific amount in store.

For a start, they don't come much more ambitious than **Universal Orlando**. The area that used to consist of just the one theme park, Universal Studios, is now a fully fledged resort in its own right. A second park, Islands of Adventure, opened in 1999, hot on the heels of the CityWalk entertainment district. The first resort hotel, Portofino Bay, opened in 1999, followed by the Hard Rock Hotel in 2000, and the Royal Pacific Resort in 2002.

A waterway network connects the hotels to the CityWalk hub, while the multi-storey car parks, for more than 20,000 vehicles, have done away with the need for any other transport system as it is easy to move between parks. The Orlando FlexTicket tie-up with SeaWorld and Busch Gardens, plus the Busch purchase of the Wet 'n Wild water park, has also proved a success – not to mention great value. The addition of Islands of Adventure certainly makes this a multi-day resort and there are periodic special deals for multi-day tickets – in summer 2007, UK ticket retailers were offering a 2-Day/2-Park ticket with an extra day free and a 3-Park Ticket (with Wet 'n Wild) with a 5-day duration. Sadly, Universal has eliminated its *free* Universal Express system, now offering only the paid-for **Universal Express Plus**, a day pass that provides one-time access to the top rides with minimal queuing – for an extra $15–40 ($25–50 for both parks) per person, depending on time of year. A limited number go on sale an hour after park opening and sell fast, but they can also be bought in advance online at **www.universal orlando.com** (for a specific day) or in the parks themselves for another day. It DOES save time but, at quieter times of the year, it can be an unnecessary expense. Universal hotel guests benefit from Express ride priority ALL DAY by producing their room key. In addition, many rides have **Single Rider** queues, which save time if you want to go on one by yourself or don't mind splitting up your group. Once again, any height or health restrictions are noted in the ride description.

The Blue Man Group

The **Universal Meal Deal** ticket, which can be bought online, at either park's front gate or at any of the 6 participating restaurants (3 in each park) may be a money saver for those with a hungry brood to feed. You exchange your ticket for a Meal Deal wristband the first time you dine and you can 'eat all day for one low price'. Just show your wristband each time you pass through the counter-service queue, returning as many times as you like, all day. Each time you can claim 1 main course and 1 dessert (but drinks are extra – unless you also buy their Meal Deal Sipper Cup for an extra $8.99 a day). The 1-Day/1-Park Meal Deal ticket is $19.99/adult ($9.99 under-10s); the 1-Day/2-Park ticket is $24.99 ($12.99 under-10s) and includes 1 dinner entrée at select CityWalk restaurants. We reckon if you have 2 full meals and 1 snack during the course of the day, you will save money.

Blue Man Group joined the Universal line-up in 2007, bringing its unique brand of humour to the Orlando nightlife scene (see page 287).

Universal Studios Florida®

Universal opened its first Florida park in June 1990 (its original Los Angeles site has been open to the public since before World War II) and quickly became a serious competitor to Disney. For the visitor, it means a consistently high standard and good value (though the choice can be bewildering!). If you have been to the LA Studios, this one is quite different. The obvious question here is do you need to do *Disney-MGM Studios* as well as Universal? We say YES! Universal is a different animal to Disney, with a more in-your-face style that appeals to teens. Younger children are also well catered for in Woody Woodpecker's KidZone.

Universal Studios

Universal parks in high season can need more than a full day. Strategies are the same as at Disney: arrive EARLY (up to 30 minutes before the official opening), do the big rides first, avoid main meal times and step out for an afternoon break (try shopping, dining or visiting the cinemas at CityWalk) if it gets too crowded.

Location

Universal Studios Florida® is sub-divided into 6 main areas, set around a huge, man-made lagoon, but there are no great distinguishing features, so you'll need your map. The main resort entrance is just off Interstate 4 (I-4 eastbound take exit 75A; westbound take exit 74B) or via Universal Boulevard from International Drive by Wet 'n Wild. Parking in its massive multi-storey car park costs $11 and there is quite a walk (with moving walkways) to the front gates (there is also preferred parking, closer to the parks, for $16 and valet parking for $18).

Once through, your best bet is to turn right on to Rodeo Drive, along Hollywood Boulevard and Sunset Boulevard and into World Expo for Men in Black – Alien Attack. From there, head across the bridge to Jaws,

Universal Studios Florida® at a glance

Location	Off exits 75A and 74B from I-4; Universal Boulevard and Kirkman Road
Size	110 acres/45ha in 7 themed areas
Hours	9am–6pm off peak; 9am–10pm high season (Washington's birthday, Easter, summer holidays, Thanksgiving, Christmas)
Admission	Under 3s free; 3–9 $56 (1-Day Ticket), $95 (2-Park Unlimited Ticket), $160.95 (Orlando FlexTicket), $199.95 (Orlando FlexTicket Plus); adult (10+) $67, $95, $194, $239.95. Prices do not include tax.
Parking	$11 (preferred parking $16; valet parking $18)
Lockers	Immediately to left in Front Lot $8
Pushchairs	$11 and $17 (kiddie, with steering wheel), $14 and $19 (double, with steering wheel), next to locker hire
Wheelchairs	$12 and $40 (with photo ID as deposit), with pushchairs
Top Attractions	Revenge of the Mummy, Men in Black, Jaws, ET Adventure, Shrek 4-D, The Simpsons (spring 2008), Terminator 2: 3-D
Don't Miss	Universal 360: A Cinesphere Spectacular (peak season only), Curious George Playground (for kids), The Blues Brothers
Hidden Costs	**Meals** Burger, chips and coke $8.38 3-course dinner $24.97 (Lombard's) Kids' meal $4.99 ($6.75–6.95 in Lombard's Seafood Grill) **T-shirts** $18.95–25.95 **Souvenirs** 95c–$285 **Sundries** Caricature drawings $15–36

then go back along the Embarcadero for Earthquake and into New York for Revenge of the Mummy. This will get most of the main rides under your belt before the crowds build up, and you can then take it a bit easier by seeing some of the shows. Alternatively, try to be among the early birds flocking to the Shrek 4-D film show in Production Central and Revenge of the Mummy in New York to avoid the queues that build up here, then visit the likes of Terminator 2 and Men in Black. The opening of the fab new Simpsons ride (see pages 168–9) in spring 2008 is likely to make this the hottest new ride in town, so consider making this your main target (along with Men in Black) if the appeal of Bart and Co. is a strong one for you. Here's a full blow-by-blow guide to the Studios. For CityWalk, see Chapter 10. Watch out for the helpful mobile electronic **Wait Times** boards placed around both parks, too.

Production Central

Coming straight through the gates brings you immediately into the administrative centre, with a couple of large gift stores (have a look at these in mid-afternoon) plus **Studio Sweets**. Call at **Guest Services** here for guides for disabled visitors, TDD and assisted listening devices, and to make restaurant bookings, which can also be made at a kiosk to the right after the turnstiles, next to the Beverly Hills Boulangerie. **First aid** is available here (and on Canal Street between New York and San Francisco), while there are facilities for nursing mothers at **Family Services** by the bank through the gates on the right. In addition, Universal Studios hosts **Total Non**

Production Central

1 Guest Services
2 Shrek 4-D
3 Jimmy Neutron's Nicktoon Blast
4 Donkey's Photo Finish
5 Monsters Café

New York

6 Twister
7 Revenge Of The Mummy
8 The Blues Brothers
9 Alley Climb
10 Finnegan's Bar and Grill
11 Louie's Italian Restaurant

San Francisco/Amity

12 Earthquake – The Big One
13 Jaws
14 Beetlejuice's Graveyard Revue
15 Central Lagoon
16 Lombard's Seafood Grille
17 Fear Factor Live

World Expo

18 The Simpsons Ride (spring 2008)
19 Men In Black – Alien Attack

Woody Woodpecker's Zidzone

20 Animal Actors On Location!
21 Fievel's Playland
22 A Day In The Park With Barney
23 ET Adventure
24 Woody Woodpecker's Nuthouse Coaster
25 Curious George Goes To Town

Hollywood

26 Universal's Horror Make-Up Show
27 Terminator 2: 3-D Battle Across Time
28 Lucy: A Tribute
29 The Lucy And Ricky Show
30 Mel's Drive-In
31 Café La Bamba

UNIVERSAL STUDIOS FLORIDA

BLUE MAN GROUP

UNIVERSAL STUDIOS FLORIDA®

Stop Action Wrestling (Apr–July), with tickets available on a first-come, first-served basis. Coming to the top of the Plaza of the Stars brings you to the business end of the park.

Shrek 4-D: this adds a whole new dimension to the genre of 3-D films as the original cast of the Oscar-winning *Shrek* movies (Mike Myers, Eddie Murphy, Cameron Diaz and John Lithgow) return for a 13-minute prequel to *Shrek 2*. The evil but vertically challenged Lord Farquaad is back in ghost form to welcome visitors to his dungeons and reveal his plan to ruin the honeymoon of Shrek and Princess Fiona. The amusing 7-minute pre-show leads into the 500-seat main theatre, where you don your Ogre Vision 3-D glasses and prepare to enter a new world. The film is funny enough as Shrek and Donkey have to rescue the Princess, but the addition of a host of special effects (watch out for the spiders!) and moving seats mean this is almost a ride as much as a show, and the effect is both startling and hugely entertaining. State-of-the-art digital projection and audio systems, lighting effects, fog and smoke (plus a hilarious finale featuring an out-of-control Tinkerbell) ensure a real laugh-fest. It is a major draw, so try to go first thing or expect waits well in excess of an hour. AAAAA+.

Jimmy Neutron's Nicktoon Blast: anyone not familiar with the cartoon antics of Jimmy Neutron (Boy Genius) and other members of the Nicktoon stable (Rugrats, the Fairly Odd Parents and SpongeBob SquarePants) might be left bemused by this rather noisy simulator ride experience. It revolves around Jimmy tangling with the evil (but hapless) Emperor Ooblar and battling to save the world with the help of his zany inventions and cartoon friends. It is a big hit with under 10s and the ride is quite dynamic. It quickly draws a queue as it is one of the first you encounter through the gates. There is no height restriction as long as a child can sit unaided, but it is not recommended for anyone with heart, neck or back problems (though there are stationary seats). TTT.

The main eating outlet here is the magnificently themed **Monsters Café**, specialising in salads, pasta, ribs, pizza and chicken. The counter-service area is done up like Frankenstein's lab, with the dining areas subdivided into Swamp, Space,

Shrek 4-D

Crypt and Mansion Dining, all to the accompaniment of old black-and-white horror film clips. Shopping includes **On Location** (film, sundries, apparel, 2-way radio rentals), **Nickstuff** (Toon merchandise with Jimmy Neutron, SpongeBob SquarePants and Dora the Explorer), **Universal Studios Store** (Universal souvenirs) and **It's A Wrap** (discounted items).

New York

From Production Central, you head on to New York and some great scene-setting in the architecture and detail of the buildings and streets. It's far too clean to be authentic, but the façades are first class.

Twister: this experience, based on the hit film, brings audiences 'up close and personal' with the awesome destructive forces of a tornado. The 5-storey terror will shatter everything in its path (okay, so it's pretty tame compared with the real thing), building to a shattering climax of destruction (watch for the flying cow!). The noise is stunning, but can be a bit much for young children (parental discretion advised for under-13s). The pre-show area is almost a work of art but, unless you do it early, save this for late in the day. TTT.

Revenge of the Mummy

Revenge of the Mummy: this awesome recent offering in Orlando's roller-coaster catalogue is a high-tech, high-thrill, high-fun journey into the world of the highly successful *Mummy* film series (replacing the old King Kong attraction). It features an indoor spin into Ancient Egypt, fusing new coaster technology with space-age robotics and special effects. It starts out as a dark ride (a slow journey through the shadowy, curse-ridden interior of Hamunaptra, The City of the Dead) but soon evolves into something far more dynamic – with a breathtaking launch.

BRITTIP

For the best ride experience on Revenge of the Mummy, try to get a back row seat. You are not allowed to carry anything on the ride – loose items must be left in the lockers provided.

The basic premise of the film studio becoming a fully fledged archaeological discovery is a good one, and the transition from dark ride to coaster is ingenious, with a host of special effects and eye-popping audio-animatronics as you brave the realm of *The Mummy*. The high-speed whiz into the dark (backwards to start with) does not involve any inversions but is still a thrill with its tight turns and sudden dips, while there are several clever twists we won't reveal (the front row may get slightly damp!). It is a superb, immersive experience and, with the elaborately themed queuing area, adds a real 5-star attraction to the park. However, it is probably too dark and threatening for under-8s. Be sure to preview your ride photos ($18–21) just before you enter the gift shop. Restrictions: 4ft/122cm. TTTT½.

The Blues Brothers: fans of the film will not want to miss this live show as Jake and Elwood Blues (or pretty good doubles anyway) put on a stormin' performance on New York's Delancey Street 4 or 5 times a day. They cruise

Jaws

up in their Bluesmobile and go through a series of the film's hits before heading off into the sunset, stopping only to sign a few autographs. Terrific stuff! AAAA.

Anyone feeling energetic can try the **Alley Climb** (rock wall) on 5th Avenue for $5. For dining, you have 2 main restaurants. **Finnegan's Bar and Grill** offers shepherd's pie, fish and chips, corned beef and cabbage, along with more traditional New York fare like prime rib, burgers, fries and a good range of beers, plus Irish-tinged entertainment and Happy Hour 4–7pm ($3.25 Bud and Bud Light; $2.95 drinks), while **Louie's Italian Restaurant** (and **Starbucks**) has counter-service pizza and pasta, ice-cream and tiramisu. For shops, you have **Sahara Traders** for Mummy souvenirs, as well as jewellery and toys, **Rosie's Irish Shop** for all things Irish and **Aftermath** for Twister souvenirs. New York also boasts the inevitable noisy amusement arcade.

San Francisco/Amity

Crossing Canal Street brings you right across America to San Francisco/Amity and two more serious queues.

Earthquake – The Big One: this 3-part adventure gets busy from mid-morning until late afternoon. Go behind the scenes first to 2 stage sets where some of the special effects of the Charlton Heston film are explained and audience volunteers show how blue-screen filming is done (with a clip from *U-571*). Then you enter the Bay Area Rapid Transit underground and arrive in the middle of a full-scale earthquake that shakes you to your boots. Tremble as the walls and ceilings collapse, trains collide, cars fall in on you and fire erupts all around, followed by a seeming tidal wave of water. It's not for the faint-hearted (or small children), while those who have bad backs or necks or are pregnant should not ride. Restrictions: 4ft/122cm (unless accompanied by an adult, with parental discretion). TTTT.

Jaws: the technical wizardry alone will amaze you here, and queues of an hour are common as you head out into the waters of this mini 'Amity'. This is no ordinary ride, and its 6-minute duration will seem a lot longer as your hapless boat guide steers you through an ever more spectacular series of stunts, explosions and menace from the Great White. We defy you not to be impressed – and just a little scared! A 2007 refurbishment left no doubt that Jaws is now a 'wet ride' (cue the chum barrel!), and those sitting on the right-hand side can expect to get just a bit damp! TTTT.

Beetlejuice's Graveyard Revue: *Disney-MGM Studios* has *Beauty and the Beast* and *The Little Mermaid*, Universal goes for *Dracula, Frankenstein, The Wolfman* and *Frankenstein's Bride* in this 20-minute 'shock 'n' roll' extravaganza, compered by Beetlejuice himself. Updated in 2006 with new music, costuming and a surprise new ending, it eschews the twee prettiness of Disney's attractions yet still comes up with a fun family show with lots of laughs, as the graveyard characters perform specially adapted rock and pop anthems (like Dancing in the Dark and Jump) with a mock-horror theme in a great setting. AAAA.

Fear Factor Live: in this live action version of the popular American reality TV programme, audience volunteers are asked to take part in a series of hair-raising (and stomach-churning!) challenges, with a head-to-head competition to find the biggest daredevil. Auditions take place 70 minutes before each show, and the audience is then invited in to see the chosen few battle it out, with clips from the TV show interspersed with live action. Some of the stunts are distinctly off-colour (anyone for a maggot milkshake?) and may not be good viewing for young children (or anyone of a weak disposition!), but it is a very well-staged production. TTT.

San Francisco also has the park's best dining choices, with **Lombard's Seafood Grill** the highlight (reservations accepted). Great

The Simpsons

seafood, pasta and sandwiches are accompanied by a good view over the Central Lagoon, and there's a separate pastry shop for desserts and coffee. **Richter's Burger Co** offers a few interesting burger variations (far superior to Mel's Drive-In in Hollywood). For a quick snack, **Midway Grill** provides Nathan's hot dogs and fries. For shopping, try **Quint's Surf Shack** (men's and women's clothing), **OakleyT** (sunglasses and accessories) and the **San Francisco Candy Factory**. An added attraction is a boardwalk of fairground games (which cost $2–5 to play), including a Guess Your Weight stall that usually attracts a good crowd for the fun patter of the person in charge.

World Expo

Crossing the bridge from Amity brings you to a rather nondescript area, but home to the park's newest 5-star thrill attraction.

The Simpsons: this takes over the former Back To The Future building in spring 2008, bringing Springfield to life in a 'Simpson's mini-zone' themed as Krustyland amusement park. Brainchild of the irascible Krusty the Clown, this bizarre funfair is the setting for a hectic, breathtaking ride in the company of Homer, Bart, Lisa, Marge and Maggie. A wicked sound system combines with state-of-the-art motion simulator technology in a frantic race through outlandish attractions (watch out for the Tooth Chipper!) with the Simpsons by your side. Prepare to be amazed by the technical wizardry Universal is about to unleash as it introduces the next generation of ride experience in this blockbuster mega-attraction. Height restriction is expected to be 3ft 4in/ 101cm. TTTT (expected).

Men in Black – Alien Attack: this combination thrill/dark ride takes up where the hit films, starring Will Smith, left off. Visitors are secretly introduced to the MIB Institute in an

© The Simpsons ™ Twentieth Century Fox Film Corporation

inventive mock-futuristic setting and enrolled as trainees for a battle around the streets of New York with a horde of escaped aliens. Your 6-person car is equipped with laser zappers for an interactive shoot-out that is like a real-life arcade game,

BRITTIP

For a big score in Men in Black, when you meet the Big Bug – push the big red button!

and the aliens can also shoot back and send your car spinning. The finale features a close encounter with a 30ft/9m bug that is all mouth. Will you survive? Only your collective shooting skills can save the day, and there are numerous ride variations according to your accuracy. Will Smith and Rip Torn are your on-screen hosts, and Will returns at the end to reveal whether your score makes you Galaxy Defenders, Cosmically Average or Bug Bait! Fast, frantic and a bit confusing, this will have you coming back for more until you can top 250,000 (Defender status). Restrictions: 3ft 6in/106cm. TTTT. *NB: Simon's best score, 265,550; reader James Home (aged 10) 301,425!*

BRITTIP

Along the lagoon in the World Expo/KidZone area is Central Park, a quiet spot where you can stop to take a break from the theme park whirl for a while.

The International Food and Film Festival here is a food court-style indoor diner offering burgers, sandwiches, meatball subs and salads (in air-conditioned comfort). For gifts, there is **MIB Gear** (clothes, jewellery, toys, sunglasses, towels).

Woody Woodpecker's KidZone

Animal Actors on Location!: this show features an amusing mix of video, animal performances and audience interaction. Several children are invited to take part and present a series of unlikely feats and stunts featuring a range of fairly tame wildlife, from a racoon to a snake, and on to cats and dogs. Many have been rescued from animal shelters and gone on to feature in films before finding a home at Universal. The big theatre also provides an escape from the afternoon crowds. AAAA.

Fievel's Playland: strictly for kids (and to give parents a break), this playground, based on the enlarged world of the cartoon mouse, offers them the chance to bounce under a 1,000-gallon hat, crawl through a giant boot, climb a 30ft/9m spider's web and shoot the rapids (a 200ft/61m waterslide) in Fievel's sardine can. TTTT (young 'uns only!).

A Day in the Park with Barney: again strictly for the younger set (ages 2–5), the purple dinosaur from the kids' TV show is brought to super-dee-duper life on stage in a large arena that

Men in Black – Alien Attack

features a pre-show before the 15-minute main event, plus an interactive post-show area. Parents will cringe but the youngsters love it. NB: check out the amazing loos! AA, or AAAAA for under-5s.

ET Adventure: this is as glorious as scenic rides come, with a picturesque queuing area like the pine woods from the film and then a spectacular leap on the trademark flying bicycles to save ET's home planet. Steven Spielberg (Universal's creative consultant) has added some special effects and characters, and you have an individual ET greeting at the end. The masses often overlook this corner of the park, hence it is worth saving for later in the day. There is a height restriction of 4ft/122cm to ride alone, but smaller children can ride with parents. AAAAA.

Woody Woodpecker's Nuthouse Coaster: anchoring the excellent under-10s adventure land is this child-sized but still quite racy roller-coaster. The brilliant red 800ft/244m track reaches only 28ft/8m high and 22mph/35kph, but it seems the real deal to youngsters. However, there is still a height restriction of 3ft/91cm. TTTT (juniors only).

Curious George Goes To Town: kids of all ages just love this amazing adventure playground and huge range of activities – and plenty of ways to get wet (bring swimsuits or a change of clothing here). It combines toddler play, water-based play stations and a hands-on interactive ball area, and is a real bonus for harassed parents. The town theme includes buildings to climb, pumps and hoses to spray water, a ball factory in which to shoot, dump and blast thousands of foam balls and – the tour de force – two 500 gallon/ 2,275 litre buckets of water that regularly dump their contents on the street below. TTTTT (under 12s).

Curious George himself roams the KidZone from time to time, while other characters make regular appearances. For snacks, **Kidzone Pizza Company** offers pizza, chicken fingers and other delights. Shop at the **Cartoon Store**, **Barney Store** or **ET's Toy Closet and Photo Spot**.

Hollywood

Finally, your circular tour of Universal brings you back towards the main entrance via Hollywood (where else?).

Universal's Horror Make-Up Show: (not recommended for under-12s) this demonstrates some of the often amusing ways in which films have attempted to terrorise us, with clips from modern additions to the genre like *Van Helsing*. It's a 20-minute show, queues are rarely long and the special effects secrets are well worth discovering. AAA.

Woody Woodpecker's Kidzone

UNIVERSAL STUDIOS with children

Our guide to the rides that generally appeal to the different age groups:

Under-5s
Animal Actors On Location!, Curious George Goes To Town, A Day In The Park With Barney, ET Adventure, Fievel's Playland.

5–8s
Animal Actors On Location!, Curious George Goes To Town, ET Adventure, Fievel's Playland, Jimmy Neutron's Nicktoon Blast, Men In Black, Shrek 4-D, Woody Woodpecker's Nuthouse Coaster, as well as Earthquake – The Big One (with parental discretion).

9–12s
Animal Actors On Location!, Beetlejuice's Graveyard Revue, Curious George Goes To Town, Earthquake – The Big One, ET Adventure, Fear Factor Live!, Jaws, Jimmy Neutron's Nicktoon Blast, Men In Black – Alien Attack, Revenge Of The Mummy, Shrek 4-D, The Simpsons, Terminator 2: 3-D Battle Across Time, Twister, Universal 360: A Cinesphere Spectacular, Woody Woodpecker's Nuthouse Coaster.

Over-12s
Beetlejuice's Graveyard Revue, The Blues Brothers, Earthquake – The Big One, ET Adventure, Fear Factor Live, Jaws, Jimmy Neutron's Nicktoon Blast, Men In Black – Alien Attack, Revenge Of The Mummy, Shrek 4-D, The Simpsons, Terminator 2: 3-D Battle Across Time, Twister, Universal 360: A Cinesphere Spectacular, Universal's Horror Make-Up Show.

Terminator 2: 3-D Battle Across Time: another first-of-its-kind attraction, this is hard to describe. Part film, part show, part experience but all action, it cost $60m to produce and is sure to leave its audience in awe. The 'wow!' factor works overtime as you go through a 10-minute pre-show representing a trip to the Cyberdyne Systems from the *Terminator* films and then into a 700-seat theatre for a 'presentation' on its latest robot creations. Needless to say, nothing runs to plan and the audience is subjected to a huge array of (loud) special effects, including indoor pyrotechnics, real actors interacting with the screen and the audience and a climactic 3-D film finale that takes the *Terminator* story a step further. The original cast, including Arnold Schwarzenegger and director James Cameron, all collaborated on the 12-minute movie (which, at $24m, is some of the most expensive frame-for-frame film ever made) and the overall effect is quite dazzling. However, you need to arrive early or expect queues in excess of an

BRITTIP

Universal's trademark Halloween Horror Nights programme (see page 182) is now shared between the Studios and Islands of Adventure. Check **www.universalorlando.com** for updates.

hour all day (parental discretion for under-12s). TTTTT.

Lucy: A Tribute: the last attraction (or first, depending on which way you go round) will mean little to all but devoted fans of the late Lucille Ball and her 1960s' TV comedy *The Lucy Show*. Classic shows, home movies, costumes and scripts are all paraded, but youngsters will find it tedious. AA. Also look for the new **The Lucy And Ricky Show** on Hollywood Boulevard. Lucy, Ricky and a 7-piece band have guests dancing in the streets to a hot Cuban beat. AAA.

If you haven't eaten by now, there are 4 contrasting but highly enjoyable eateries. **Mel's Drive-In**, a re-creation from the film *American Graffiti*, serves all manner of burgers and hot dogs (though Richter's has better burgers), while **Café La Bamba** offers rotisserie chicken, ribs, salad and burgers, plus Margaritas and beer (Happy Hour 3–5pm). **Schwab's Pharmacy** provides sandwiches, old-fashioned milkshakes, sundaes and ice-cream, and the **Beverly Hills Boulangerie** does baked breakfast treats, pastries, Cheesecake Factory items, juices and coffee. Shop for Terminator gifts and clothing in **Cyber Image**, movie memorabilia in **Silver Screen Collectibles**, and Hollywood legends' jewellery in **Studio Styles**. Budding magicians won't want to miss the small **Theater Magic** shop, with merchandise and magic shows several times daily.

Street entertainment

Watch out for a variety of characters that appear around the park at various intervals. **The KidZone Character Bus** arrives along Hollywood Boulevard and at the KidZone Plaza, while doubles for the likes of Marilyn Monroe, Lucille Ball, Scooby Doo and Shaggy, Elena and Zorro also roam at regular intervals.

Other Universal characters appear for autographs and photo sessions, notably **Spongebob SquarePants** (inside the Nickstuff Store), and the **Star Toons** (by Fievel's Playland). **Shrek**, **Fiona** and **Donkey** can be found on 8th Avenue in Production Central (just round the corner from Shrek 4-D) for Donkey's Photo Finish and are well worth catching for the amusing patter (mimicking the Eddie Murphy character).

Special programmes

Universal Studios features some brilliant extra seasonal entertainment for **Mardi Gras**, with a hectic, bead-throwing parade, plus music, street entertainment and authentic New Orleans food each Saturday at 6pm from mid-Feb to late May. The evening culminates in a live concert with well-known acts (Donna Summer, Huey Lewis and the News and The Doobie Brothers to name 3 in 2007), but it does draw HUGE crowds. Universal also throws a major party for **4 July**, when the park presents a stunning fireworks spectacular.

Finally, **Universal 360: A Cinesphere Spectacular** brings down the curtain each evening during peak season and special events with a blaze of fireworks and four gigantic 'cinespheres' that allow for cinema projection. The overall effect places guests in the middle of their favourite films, with an all-new musical score (on 300 outdoor speakers), lasers and other pyrotechnics, using the spheres as video screens. It's a stunning performance, so check your park map to see if it's showing during your visit.

Universal 360

Islands of Adventure

In May 1999, Universal's creative consultant Steven Spielberg officially opened the $1b Islands of Adventure (or IoA, as the park is known) with the words: 'These are not just theme park rides, these are entertainment achievements beyond anything I have ever seen anywhere else in the world.' And that's only the beginning. Here is the most complete and thrilling theme park on offer. Complete, because the park offers a genuinely rounded and consistent concept, carried through to the full extent of its designers' aims. And thrilling because it contains more T-rides per square metre than almost all the others combined. The addition (in late 2009) of the Wizarding World of Harry Potter (see page 16) will add even more appeal to this hugely imaginative park.

It has a full range of attractions, from the real adrenaline overloads to pure family entertainment. The shopping and eating opportunities are above average and it even sounds good – with some 40 pieces of original music, you can buy the CD of the theme park! Okay, so they are not really islands (the 6 themed 'lands' form a chain around the central lagoon), but that's the only illusion. And you get a lot for your money here, unless you have extremely timid children or under-5s, in which case the Magic Kingdom is still your best bet. However, Seuss Landing will keep them amused for several hours, while Camp Jurassic is a clever adventure playground for the 5–12s. The rest of the park, with its seven 5-star thrill rides and other standout attractions, is primarily geared to kids of 8-plus,

Islands of Adventure at a glance

Location	Off exits 75A and 74B from I-4; Universal Boulevard and Kirkman Road
Size	110 acres/45ha in 6 'islands'
Hours	9am–7pm off peak; 9am–10pm high season (Washington's birthday, Easter, summer holidays, Thanksgiving, Christmas)
Admission	Under-3s free; 3–9 $56 (1-Day Ticket), $95 (2-Park Unlimited Ticket), $160.95 (Orlando FlexTicket), $199.95 (Orlando FlexTicket Plus); adult (10+) $67, $95, $194.95, $239.95. Prices do not include tax.
Parking	$11, preferred parking $16, valet parking $18
Lockers	Immediately to left through main gates $8
Pushchairs	$11 and $17; next to locker hire. Kiddie, with steering wheel $14; Double $19.
Wheelchairs	$12 and $40 (with photo ID as deposit); with pushchairs
Top Attractions	Amazing Adventures Of Spider-Man, Dueling Dragons, Incredible Hulk Coaster, Jurassic Park River Adventure, Dudley Do-Right's Ripsaw Falls, Cat In The Hat
Don't Miss	Eighth Voyage Of Sindbad, Jurassic Park Discovery Centre, If I Ran The Zoo playground (for toddlers), dining at Mythos
Hidden Costs	**Meals** Burger, chips and coke $9.88 3-course lunch $29.94 (Confisco Grille) Kids' meal $4.99–6.99 ($4.99 at Meal Deal spots) **T-shirts** $18.95–25.95 **Souvenirs** 95c–$1,600 **Sundries** Jurassic Park River Adventure ride photos: $21.25; $24.99 with frame

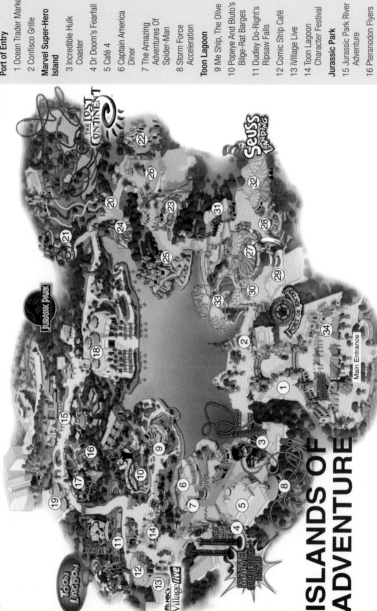

ISLANDS OF ADVENTURE

their parents and especially teenagers. There are 5 elements that look truly alarming (2 of which produce moments of supreme terror), but don't be put off – they all deliver immense fun as well as terrific spectator value! If any one ride sums up IoA, it is the Amazing Adventures of Spider-Man, the world's first moving 3-D simulator ride. Its technological wizardry is sure to leave you in awe, and it is not unknown for people to applaud at the end.

Private nursing facilities, an open area for feeding and resting (with high-chairs) and nappy-changing stations, can be found at the **Family Service Facility** at Guest Services (to the right inside the main gates), while ALL restrooms throughout the park are equipped with **nappy-changing** facilities. **First aid** is provided in Sindbad's Village in the Lost Continent, just across from Oasis Coolers and in Port of Entry.

Port of Entry

You arrive for IoA as you do for Universal Studios, in the big multi-storey car parks off I-4 and Universal Boulevard and either walk or ride the moving walkways into CityWalk, where you continue through to the entrance plaza (head for the 130ft/

40m high Pharos Lighthouse). As with Universal Studios, you can purchase the **Universal Express Plus** pass for $15–50 (depending on time of year) at the Marvel Alterniverse Store, Toon Extra or Jurassic Outfitters. Once through the gates, the lockers, pushchair and wheelchair hire are all on your left as the **Port of Entry** opens up before you. This elaborate village consists of shops and eateries, so push straight on until you hit the main lagoon. Later in the day, return to check out the retail experience at places like the **IoA Trading Company** and **Ocean Trader Market**. Enjoy a snack from **Cinnabon** (cinnamon rolls and pastries) or the **Croissant Moon Bakery** (excellent coffee, croissants and sandwiches), or chill out with a soft drink or ice-cream from **Arctic Express**. Alternatively, sit down for lunch or dinner (steak, pasta, fish, pizza, burgers and salads) at **Confisco Grille** and grab a beverage at the **Backwater Bar** (Happy Hour 3–5pm). There is also a **Character Breakfast** at Confisco Grille (9–10.30am Thurs–Sun) with various Universal characters like Spider-Man and the Cat In The Hat ($15.95 adults, $9.95 children; 407 224 4012 for reservations).

Above all, take in the wonderful architecture, which borrows from

The Incredible Hulk Coaster

Middle East, Far East and African themes and uses bric-a-brac from all over the world. At the end of the street, you are faced with 3 choices and this is where you need a plan of campaign. There are 5 attractions where the queues build up quickly and remain that way. If you are here for the big thrill rides, turn left into Marvel Super-Hero Island and head straight to Spider-Man, then do Dr Doom's Fearfall and the Incredible Hulk Coaster. Alternatively, dinosaur fans should head straight around the lagoon to Jurassic Park, where you should be able to do the River Adventure before the majority arrives. Once you are nice and wet, you might as well go to Toon Lagoon for Ripsaw Falls and the Bilge-Rat Barges. Or, if you have younger children, turn right into the multi-coloured world of Seuss Landing and enjoy the Cat In The Hat and the new High In The Sky Seuss Trolley Train Ride prior to the main crowd build-up.

Marvel Super-Hero Island

Going clockwise, you arrive first in the elaborate comic-book pages of the super-heroes. As with all the islands, the experience is total immersion. The amazing façades of this world surround you with an utterly credible alternative reality that is one of the park's triumphs – and that's before you have even tried the rides.

Islands of Adventure

The Incredible Hulk Coaster: roller-coasters don't come much more dramatic than this giant green edifice that soars over the lagoon, blasting 0–40mph/64kph in 2 seconds, and reaching a top speed of 65mph/105kph. It looks awesome, sounds stunning and rides like a demon as you enter the gamma-ray world of Dr David Banner, aka the Incredible Hulk, and zoom into a weightless inversion 100ft/30m up!

BRITTIP

At the Hulk Coaster, keep left where the queue splits up and you will be in line for the front car for an even more extreme Hulk experience.

Just watching is mind-boggling, and the after-effects are distinctly brain-scrambling! You will need to deposit ANY loose articles (cameras, sunglasses, coins etc.) in the lockers at the front of the building as the ride is guaranteed to shake anything out of your pockets. Crowds build up rapidly but the queues move quite quickly. Restrictions: 4ft 6in/137cm. TTTTT+.

Dr Doom's Fearfall: stand by for one of those 2 moments of supreme terror we mentioned. This is where, oh hapless visitor, you wander into the lair of the evil Dr Doom – arch-enemy of the Fantastic Four – and his sinister cohorts. His latest creation is the Fearfall, a device for sucking every iota of fear out of his victims, and YOU are about to test it. Sixteen riders at a time are strapped into chairs at the bottom of a 200ft/60m tower, the dry ice rolls, and whoooosh! Up you go at breakneck speed, only to plummet back seemingly even faster, with an amazing split second in between when you feel suspended in mid air. Summon up the courage to do this and we promise an astonishing (if brief!) experience. Queues are substantial during the main part of the day. Restrictions: 4ft 4in/132cm, and we reckon this is way too scary for under-10s. TTTTT+.

The Amazing Adventures of Spiderman

You exit Fearfall into the inevitable high-energy video arcade, or you may prefer to calm your nerves with a meal at the Italian buffeteria **Café 4** (pizza, spaghetti, sandwiches and salads) or a burger at the **Captain America Diner**. For shopping, each ride has its own character merchandise, while the **Comic Book Shop** and **Marvel Alterniverse Shop** sell other whacky souvenirs.

The Amazing Adventures of Spider-Man: just queuing is a novel experience as your visit to the *Daily Bugle*, home of ace reporter Peter Parker (or Spider-Man to his enemies), turns into a reporting assignment in one of the 'Scoop' vehicles. Prepare for an audio-visual extravaganza as the combination of 3-D and motion simulator takes you into a battle between Spidey and arch-villains like Dr Octopus with his anti-gravity gun, culminating in a 400ft/122m sensory drop off a skyscraper as the contest literally hots up. There are numerous jaw-dropping special effects and you will need to ride at least twice to appreciate it all. Ride early on or leave it until late in the day – queues often top an hour. Restrictions: 3ft 4in/101cm. TTTTT+.

Storm Force Accelatron: this ride, aimed primarily at youngsters, puts you in the middle of a whirling,

twirling battle between X-Men super-heroine Storm and arch-nemesis Magneto, with a range of special effects. It's basically an updated spinning-cup ride, but with some neat twists (there is a 3-way rotation where the cars look set to collide with each other at any moment). TTT, or TTTTT for under-12s.

You can also meet the **Marvel Super-Heroes** for autographs here several times a day.

Toon Lagoon

The thrills continue here with a watery theme and more comic-book elements as the (American) newspaper cartoon characters take a bow. Children will love to play with the fountains, squirt pools and overflowing fire hydrants, plus a purpose-built playland **Me Ship, The Olive**, a 3-storey boat full of interactive fun and games, including slides, bells and water cannons (perfect for squirting at the riders on the Bilge-Rat Barges below), in best Popeye style. TTTT (youngsters only).

Popeye And Bluto's Bilge-Rat Barges: every park seems to have a variation on the white-water raft ride, but none is as outrageously themed and downright wet as this. Fast, bouncy and unpredictable, it has water coming at you from every direction, a couple of sizeable drops and a whirl through the Octoplus Grotto that adds to the fun. If you don't want to get wet, don't ride, because there is no escaping the deluge here. This is also one of the top 5 for long queues, but it's definitely worth the wait. Restrictions: 4ft/122cm. TTTTT.

Dudley Do-Right's Ripsaw Falls: Universal's designers have again

BRITTIP

A change of clothes is often advisable after the Barges, unless it's so hot you need to cool down in a hurry. Bring along a waterproof bag for your valuables.

Comic Strip Café

taken an existing ride concept and given it a new spin, as this becomes the first flume ride to send its passengers through the water surface and out the other side at high speed. You join guileless mountie Dudley Do-Right in a bid to save girlfriend Nell from the evil Snidely Whiplash. The action builds to an explosive showdown at the top of a 75ft/27m precipice that drops you through the roof of a ramshackle dynamite shack and into the lagoon below. Just awesome – as are the queues from mid-morning to late afternoon. Wet? You bet! Restrictions: 3ft 8in/111cm. TTTTT. You can also try the Water Blasters (for 25c) on the bridge overlooking the final drop to get riders even wetter!

Toon Lagoon's Amphitheatre is also home to a live TV show Mon–Fri at noon. NBC's **iVillage Live** is an interactive chat and lifestyle programme (with prizes!), involving the audience and an online element at **www.ivillagelive.com** Tickets need to be requested at least a day in advance by calling 1866 448 5360 or emailing **ivillagelivetickets@nbcuni.com** (no under-10s).

Comic Strip Lane is the place to meet characters like Beetle Bailey, Hagar the Horrible, Krazy Kat and Blondie (some of whom will mean little to a British audience). There is the usual array of character shops, like **Gasoline Alley** and **Toon Extra**, while you can grab a humongous sandwich at **Blondie's: Home of the Dagwood**, a trademark hamburger or hot dog at **Wimpy's**, sample the **Comic Strip Café** food court (Mexican, Chinese, American and Italian) or grab something colder at **Cathy's Ice Cream**. Watch out for a big Toon Lagoon **character meet-and-greet** in the Main Street area, where you can have fun with the likes of Popeye, Olive Oyl, Bluto and Dudley Do-Right. The Tip Board next to Watsamotta U is a handy source for up-to-date attraction wait times.

Jurassic Park

Leaving the comic-book lands behind, you travel back to the Cretaceous age and the credible make-believe dinosaur film world. Again, the immersive experience is first class and the lavish scenery will have you looking over your shoulder for stray dinos.

Jurassic Park River Adventure: the mood change from scenic splendour to hidden menace is startling as your journey into this magnificent waterborne realm brings you up close and personal with the most realistic dinosaurs created to date. Inevitably, your passage is diverted from the safe to the hazardous, and the danger increases as the 16-person raft climbs into the heights of the main building – with raptors loose everywhere. You are aware of something large lurking in the shadows – will you fall prey to the T-Rex, or will your boat take the 85ft/26m plunge to safety (with a good soaking for all)? Queues usually move quite briskly at this ride. Restrictions: 3ft 6in/106cm. TTTTT.

The more adventurous can then try the **Rock Climbing Wall** (just outside River Adventure) for an extra $7. There is also a Tip Board across from the ride's entrance.

Pteranodon Flyers: the slow-moving queues are a major turn-off, especially for a fairly average ride, which glides gently over much of Jurassic Park (though at heights of almost 30ft/9m at one point). It is designed mainly for kids, though, and the height range of 3–4ft 8in/91–142cm) requires anyone OVER the upper limit (usually 11 or older) to be accompanied by a child of the right height. TT, or TTTT for under-9s.

Camp Jurassic: more excellent kids' fare here with the mountainous jungle giving way to an 'active' volcano for youngsters to explore, climb and slide down. Squirt guns and spitter dinosaurs add to the fun. TTTT (children first, but parents are allowed to explore).

Discovery Center: this indoor centre offers various interactive opportunities, including creating a dinosaur through DNA sequencing, mixing your own DNA with a dino via a computer touchscreen, seeing through the eyes of various large reptiles and even handling 'dino eggs', plus other fun hands-on exhibits. Being air-conditioned, this is a good place to visit in the hotter part of the day (open 11am–5pm). AAA. Best of the shopping is in the Discovery Center itself, while you can eat at the **Burger Digs** (some huge burger platters), visit the **Pizza Predattoria** or the **Watering Hole** (Happy Hour 3–5), or go for the rotisserie chicken at the rustic **Thunder Falls Terrace** (counter service), which boasts a great view of the River Adventure.

The Lost Continent

This land will be heavily rebuilt in the next 18 months to allow for the new Harry Potter 'island', but it will still offer some great attractions.

Dueling Dragons: there is no disguising the intense nature of this magnificent double coaster, with its 100ft/30m drop, multiple loops, twists and 3 near-miss encounters. There is a lot more, too, as the queuing area is a real mind-boggler – 1,060yd/969m, most of it along a dark, winding path through the ancient castle that is the domain of the dragons, Fire and Ice. You are given their story while you wait, and Merlin arrives in time to cast a spell to ensure you survive. You choose which dragon to ride (the tracks differ slightly), and you can join an additional queue for the front seats. Unlike the Hulk, this is a suspended coaster, so your legs dangle free, and the initial drop is like going into free-fall (Supreme Terror moment No. 2!). Coaster aficionados reckon the best ride is in the back of the Ice (Blue) dragon, but both offer an awesome experience. Restrictions:

Dueling Dragons

4ft 6in/137cm, and you will need to leave all loose items in the lockers to the left of the entrance. TTTTT+.

The Flying Unicorn: this junior-sized coaster is aimed primarily at youngsters and features a wizard's workshop, hidden in an enchanted wood, which is the gateway to a magical journey inspired by the Unicorn. There are no big drops, but it delivers a surprisingly fast-paced whirl. TTTTT (for 6–12s).

The Eighth Voyage of Sindbad: this stunt and special effects show is another marvel, as much for its elaborate staging as its performance. Mythical adventurer Sindbad and sidekick Kabob (a name that's the cue for a truly awful pun) tackle evil witch Miseria in a bid to rescue Princess Amoura, and the action springs up in surprising places. There are several loud bangs that could scare young children, but otherwise it's good family fun. At peak times arrive 20 minutes before showtime, but everyone usually gets in. There is also a great post-show feature where the cast reappears for photos and autographs. TTT/AAAA.

Poseidon's Fury: a walk-through show that puts its audience at the heart of the action as it journeys in the company of a hapless young archaeologist (who ignores the various warnings) beneath the sea to the lost temple of Poseidon. The route passes through an amazing water

Poseidon's Fury

vortex and your expedition takes a wrong turn, awakening an ancient demon. Again, there is an element of suspense, but the special effects showdown between Poseidon and the demon is amazing. Queuing is tedious, but at least you are inside in summer. TTT.

For an extra few dollars, try the **Pitch and Skill Games**, or shop at **The Coin Mint** (coins forged and struck before your eyes), or visit **Historic Families-Heraldry** (explore the history of your family name and coat of arms in a medieval armoury), **The Pearl Factory** (pick an oyster), and **The Dragon's Keep** (dragon apparel, games and toys). **Star Souls – Psychic Readers** is also fun for a bit of mystic manipulation. **The Fire-Eater's Grill** (sausages, chips and drinks) and **Frozen Desert** (sundaes and sodas) provide the snacks, while you mustn't miss the magnificent **Enchanted Oak Tavern** (inside a vast, sculpted oak tree) and **Alchemy Bar** for counter-service hickory-smoked chicken, ribs and salads (Happy Hour 3–5pm). The elaborate **Mythos Restaurant** provides the best dining in IoA, though. Not only is the food first class (seafood, salads, grills, pizza and pasta), but the setting (inside a dormant volcano with streams, fountains and clever lighting) is an attraction in its own right.

Finally, watch out for **The Mystic Fountain** in Sindbad's Village. It has the ability to strike up a conversation – and soak you when you least expect it!

Seuss Landing

There is not a straight line to be seen in this vivid 3-D working of the books of Dr Seuss. The characters may not mean much to those unfamiliar with the children's stories, but everyone can relate to the fun here (though queues build up quickly). There is so much clever detail, from squirt ponds to beach scenes, it can be easy to miss something, so take your time.

ISLANDS OF ADVENTURE with children

Our guide to the rides that generally appeal to the different age groups:

Under-5s
Caro-Seuss-el, The Cat In The Hat, Eighth Voyage Of Sindbad, High In The Sky Seuss Trolley Train Ride, If I Ran The Zoo, Jurassic Park Discovery Center, Me Ship, The Olive, One Fish, Two Fish, Red Fish, Blue Fish.

5–8s
All the above, plus Amazing Adventures Of Spider-Man, Camp Jurassic, Flying Unicorn, Jurassic Park River Adventure (with parental discretion), Pteranodon Flyers, Storm Force Accelatron.

9–12s
Amazing Adventures Of Spider-Man, Camp Jurassic, The Cat in the Hat, Dr Doom's Fearfall, Dudley Do-Right's Ripsaw Falls, Dueling Dragons, Eighth Voyage Of Sindbad, Flying Unicorn, Incredible Hulk Coaster, Jurassic Park Discovery Center, Jurassic Park River Adventure, Popeye And Bluto's Bilge-Rat Barges, Pteranodon Flyers, Storm Force Accelatron.

Over-12s
Amazing Adventures Of Spider-Man, Dr Doom's Fearfall, Dudley Do-Right's Ripsaw Falls, Dueling Dragons, Eighth Voyage Of Sindbad, Incredible Hulk Coaster, Jurassic Park Discovery Center, Jurassic Park River Adventure, Popeye and Bluto's Bilge-Rat Barges, Storm Force Accelatron.

Caro-Seuss-el: this intricate carousel ride on some of the Seuss characters – like cowfish, elephant-birds and dog-a-lopes – has rider-activated features that are a big hit with youngsters. AAA, or AAAA for under-5s.

One Fish, Two Fish, Red Fish, Blue Fish: a fairground ride with a twist as you pilot these Seussian fish up and down according to the rhyme that plays while you ride. Get it wrong and you get squirted! More fun for the younger kids. TTT, or TTTTT for under-5s.

The Cat in the Hat: prepare for a ride with a difference as you board these crazy 6-passenger coaches to meet the world's most adventurous cat and his friends, Thing One and Thing Two. You literally go for a spin through this storybook world, and it may be a bit much for very young children. The slow-moving queues are a bit of a drag, so try to get here early or leave it until later in the day. AAAA/TTT.

If I Ran the Zoo: interactive playgrounds don't get any better for the pre-school brigade than with these 19 different Seuss character scenarios, some of which can get the kids quite wet. Hugely imaginative and great fun to watch. TTTTT (under-5s only).

The High in the Sky Seuss Trolley Train Ride: new in 2006 was this fun family adventure high above Seuss Landing. Originally meant to be part of the park opening, it took 7 years to redevelop and bring to life but it has terrific appeal to youngsters. Board your special trolley car and journey into the world of the Sneetches, visiting the Inking and Stamping Room, the Star Wash Room and a circuit inside the wonderful Circus McGurkus Café Stoo-pendous. It is

High in the Sky

slow-paced, scenic and eye-catching, but it does draw slow-moving queues, so head here early on if your children are the requisite age (2–8). AAAA.

If you have been captivated by the land, you can buy the book at **Dr Seuss' All The Books You Can Read Store**, or visit the **Mulberry Street Store** for all the characters. **Snookers and Snookers Sweet Candy Cookers** is a super sweet shop, while snacks and drinks can be had at **Hop On Pop Ice Cream Shop** and **Moose Juice Goose Juice**. The **Circus McGurkus Café Stoo-pendous** is a mind-boggling cafeteria for fried chicken, lasagne, pizza and spaghetti, all with clowns and pipe organs.

Finally, the park debuted a new water show on the central lagoon in summer 2007, and we expect this to return in peak season in 2008. The 20-minute **HydroAction Ski Show** is performed up to 5 times a day and features some daredevil stunts from wakeboarders, jet-skis and amazing 'sky skiers', all with a vibrant musical backing. Perfect for teen tearaways!

Halloween Horror Nights

Universal's massively popular Halloween celebration throughout Oct each year. The Horror Nights have become a real trademark and add a wonderfully bloodthirsty touch. The parks are transformed by some highly imaginative re-creations and set-pieces from various horror movies, with a parade and shows that include live (terrifyingly so, in some cases) character interaction. All the horror genres are well represented, and the Scare Houses feature some superb 'scare actors' and special effects. The rides are also all open (anyone for The Hulk and Dueling Dragons in the dark?!), adding more novelty to the park experience, but this over-the-top (and occasionally downright grisly) extravaganza is definitely not for kids (especially as alcohol is freely available). It goes down a treat with adults with the right sense of humour, though, and begins every evening at 7.30pm. It is a separate event costing around $65/person and it is highly advisable to book in advance on **www.universal orlando.com** or through Attraction Tickets Direct. There is even a Frequent Fear Pass for multiple visits on selected evenings (but not weekends, when crowds are heaviest).

And that, folks, is the full low-down on arguably the world's best theme park. Miss it at your peril.

Halloween Horror

SeaWorld Adventure Park

SeaWorld is firmly established with British visitors as one of the most popular parks for its more peaceful and naturalistic aspect, the change of pace it offers and the general lack of substantial queues. Like Disney's *Epcot* park, it is large enough to handle big crowds well (though it still gets busy in peak season). It is a big hit with families in particular, but also has some dramatic rides and imaginative attractions. An extensive development programme by owners Anheuser-Busch has given it the big-park treatment in recent years, with an impressive 12 acre/5ha entrance plaza and rebranding as an Adventure Park, and it now demands at least a full day's attention. The opening, in 2000, of a separate sister park Discovery Cove (see pages 194–7), an exotic tropical 'island' with dolphin,

stingray and snorkelling adventures, added still more. Then in 2006 a **1-week ticket** for the price of a 1-day one was introduced, and it continued in 2007, so watch out for it through UK ticket sources. SeaWorld has raised the bar for its entertainment offerings in recent years, too. It debuted the fabulous *Blue Horizons* show in 2005, and 2006 saw the even more ambitious – and brilliantly staged – *Believe* in Shamu Stadium. Together with a rash of new kiddie rides, a new Shamu Rocks show (peak season only) and the introduction of a host of Sesame Street characters, it means this remains a wonderfully fresh and invigorating place to visit.

Happily, this is a park where you can still proceed at a relatively leisurely pace, see what you want without too

SeaWorld Adventure Park at a glance

Location	7007 SeaWorld Drive, off Central Florida Parkway (Junctions 71 and 72 off I-4)
Size	More than 200 acres/81ha, incorporating 25 attractions
Hours	9am–6pm off peak; 9am–10pm high season (Easter, summer holidays, Thanksgiving, Christmas)
Admission	Under-3s free; 3–9 $53.95 (1-Day Ticket), $160.95 (Orlando FlexTicket), $199.95 (Orlando FlexTicket Plus), $85 (SeaWorld/Busch Gardens Combo ticket); adult (10+) $64.95, $194.95, $239.95, $85
Parking	$10, $15 preferred parking
Lockers	By main entrance $1.50 (also by Shamu's Emporium)
Pushchairs	$9.39 and $16.90 (to right of Guest Services inside park)
Wheelchairs	$10 and $35; with pushchairs
Top Attractions	Shamu Stadium, Shark Encounter, Journey To Atlantis, Kraken, Wild Arctic, Blue Horizons
Don't Miss	Mistify At The Waterfront (high season), Manatee Rescue, behind-the-scenes tours, Odyssea show, Believe, dining at Sharks Underwater Grill
Hidden Costs	**Meals** Burger, chips and coke $10.28 3-course lunch (Sharks Underwater Grill) $38; Kids' meal $5.99 ($7–10 at Sharks Underwater Grill) **T-shirts** $18–24 **Souvenirs** 99c–$9,299 **Sundries** Caricatures $14.95–24.95

1 Information
2 Wild Arctic
3 Shamu Stadium
4 Backstage at Believe
5 Shamu Underwater Viewing
6 Blue Horizons
7 Atlantis Bayside Stadium
8 The Waterfront
9 Seaport Theater
10 Seafire Inn/ Mahaiki Luau
11 Sky Tower
12 Nautilus Theater – Odyssea
13 Clydesdale Hamlet
14 Anheuser-Busch Hospitality Center
15 Manatee Rescue
16 Pacific Point Preserve
17 Sea Lion and Otter Stadium
18 Extreme Zone
19 Shamu's Happy Harbor
20 Shark Encounter
21 Sharks Underwater Grill
22 Penguin Encounter
23 Key West at SeaWorld
24 Stingray Lagoon
25 Turtle Point
26 Dolphin Cove
27 Journey To Atlantis
28 Kraken
29 Dolphin Nursery
30 Mistify
31 Mango Jo's Café
32 Mama's Kitchen
33 Voyager's Restaurant
34 The Spice Mill

SEA WORLD

Main Entrance

much jostling and yet feel you have been well entertained (even if the restaurants do get crowded at mealtimes). SeaWorld is also a good starting point if this is your first Orlando visit as it gives you the hang of negotiating the vast areas, navigating by the various maps and learning to plan around the showtimes. This park has a strong educational and environmental message, plus three 1-hour, behind-the-scenes tours (book up as soon as you enter or online), which provide a great insight into SeaWorld's marine conservation, rescue and research programme, as well as its entertainment resources.

The Polar Expedition provides a close-up of the penguin and polar bear environments; **Saving a Species** showcases the park's animal rescue and rehabilitation programme, with a chance to hand-feed exotic birds in the free-flight aviary ($1 of the tour fee also goes to the Anheuser-Busch Conservation Fund); and **Predators!** offers a backstage view of Shark Encounter and Shamu Stadium. You pay an extra $18 ($12 3–9s) for these tours, but they are worth it and, if you take one early on, it will increase your appreciation of the park. There are also discounts and special offers by booking online at **www.seaworld.com**, where you can print your own tickets and save waiting in a queue.

Five additional programmes provide other unique insights and experiences. The 7-hour **Adventure Express Tour** offers visitors their own tour guide, with back-door access to the rides, reserved seating at shows and animal feeding opportunities (an extra $95 for adults, $80 for 3–9s; book up first thing at the Guided Tours counter, online or call 1800 406 2244); The **Marine Mammal Keeper Experience** accommodates 2 visitors daily (aged 13 or above) to find out about the care necessary to rehabilitate injured manatees, plus bottle-feed some of them, meet the

seals and walruses and prepare meals for the beluga whales. It starts at 6.30am and lasts around 8 hours for $399/person (including lunch at the Shark Encounter, T-shirt, special book, souvenir photo and 7-day SeaWorld pass); **Sharks Deep Dive** is a totally captivating experience, a chance to suit up and dive in a specially constructed cage into the huge shark aquarium, and spend ½ hour up close and personal with these amazing creatures. The 2-hour programme includes an educational induction into the world of sharks, what they are and what makes them tick (with important pointers like never wear jewellery in the sea – sharks are attracted by the glitter, mistaking it for the reflection off fish scales). Then you are equipped for the dive with wetsuit (the water IS chilly), gloves, dive belt and a special underwater helmet that also allows communication (no scuba gear needed) in the reinforced steel cage that glides slowly from one end of the 125ft/38m long tank to the other and back. Getting a fish-eye view of these creatures is an astounding experience, and you won't tire of the underwater panorama (which includes waving to people in the shark tunnel!). It is an eye-opening and addictive programme, but the best part is you get to wear a really cool wetsuit with 'Scubapro' on the front! It costs $150 (including a great souvenir T-shirt and shark book;

Shamu Express

participants must be 10 and over); the 1-hour **Dolphin Nursery Close-Up Tour** provides an educational glimpse into bottlenose dolphin characteristics, reproduction and calf-rearing. Animal Care Specialists hosts up to 10 guests backstage (age 10 and over only, $40/person) for a poolside interactive experience, with various elements dependent upon imminent births, the weather and veterinary needs. Finally, the **Beluga Interactive Program** (for ages 13 and over) is unique: a chance to meet some of the park's biggest (but most benign) denizens in their own environment. Swimming isn't necessary but guests must be comfortable in the water. Touching, feeding and using hand signals are all part of the programme, which is highly informative and utterly captivating. It costs $179/person (including a book on whales; no expectant mothers) and runs every day, rain or shine. All tours can be booked online at **www.seaworld.com**

Location

SeaWorld is located off Central Florida Parkway, between I-4 (exit 71 going east or 72 heading west) and I-Drive, and parking is $10 ($15 if you choose Shamu's preferred parking, which gets you close to the main entrance). It is still best to arrive a bit before the official opening time so you're in a good position to book one of the backstage tours or dash to one of the few attractions that draws a crowd, like Journey to Atlantis.

The park covers more than 200 acres/ 81ha, with 6 shows (7 with the nightly **Makahiki Luau** dinner show at the Seafire Inn, $45.95 adults, $29.95 3–9s; nightly, times vary, call 407 351 3600 or book online), 3 major rides, 10 large-scale continuous viewing attractions and 7 smaller ones, plus the eye-catching **Waterfront area**, relaxing gardens, a kids' play area (with rides) and a smart range of shops, which are a noticeable feature of Anheuser-Busch parks). Its hire

The Flying Fiddler

pushchairs are also the most amusing, being shaped like baby dolphins. Be warned, though: the size of the park requires a lot of to-ing and fro-ing to catch the various shows, which can be wearing. Keep a close grip on your map and entertainment schedule and try to establish a programme to allow regular breaks at the quieter spots.

For something different, you can sign up for the free 35-minute Anheuser-Busch Beer School at the Hospitality Center for a glimpse into beer-making (and tasting!). The **Brewmasters Club** teaches guests how to pair Anheuser-Busch beers with various foods, to enjoy each to the full. Samples of beer (American lager to robust stout), chocolate, fruits and cheeses are free to small groups (reservations necessary; visit the Information Counter at the front of the park or the host stand in the Hospitality Center) beginning at 11.30am daily (ages 21 and over only, with valid photo ID). There is also **Backstage at Believe**, a VIP experience 'backstage' with the killer whales and their trainers. A terrific all-you-can-eat dinner buffet on a covered terrace alongside the main pool gives you the chance to ask the trainers questions and watch some of their sessions (you may also get a little wet!). It is offered every day (times vary) but it is highly advisable to book in advance. We hesitate to recommend this as a must-see attraction at $37 for adults and $19 for children, but it is a great experience for both. New in 2007 was the **Parents Dine, Kids Party**; adults enjoy dinner at the luxurious Sharks Underwater Grill while children feast on pizza, dessert and drinks and take part in Predator-themed activities ($44 adults, $25 5–11s). For advanced booking for any of the above, call 1800 327 2424 or visit **www.sea world.com**

The main attractions

Wild Arctic: this interactive ride-and-view experience provides a realistic environment that is both educational and thrilling. It's an exciting simulator jet helicopter journey into the white wilderness arriving at a clever research base, Base Station Wild Arctic, where the passengers are disgorged into a frozen wonderland to meet polar bears, beluga whales and walruses. This one is not to be missed (but avoid just after Believe when the hordes descend). Restrictions: 3ft 6in/106cm. TTTT/AAAAA. Those who don't want to ride can walk through to the Base Station.

Shamu Stadium: SeaWorld has long outgrown its tag as just the place to see killer whales, but the new Believe show is still one of its most amazing sights. Watch the killer whales and their trainers pull off some spectacular stunts, all set within the story of a young boy's dream of interacting with these creatures of the deep. The basic message of needing to believe in your dreams is a touch schmaltzy, but there is no doubting the brilliant choreography as animals and trainers put on a seamless display – apparently without any commands. Some dramatic staging and an original music score by the Prague National Symphony Orchestra are combined with high-tech video screens that slide and rotate in eye-catching fashion to create a truly majestic extravaganza that is way beyond the usual animal shows. And, if you think it looks good during the day, return in the evening (in high season) for an even more dramatic

presentation under the lights, with the video screens coming into their own. As it is the signature new element of the park, the Shamu Stadium is extremely popular, hence you should try to take in one of the early shows. You should also arrive at least 15 minutes early as there is a fun pre-show video. In the summer months the new **Shamu Rocks** show at night adds a more high-energy, free-form version of the main show. AAAAA+. All guests can then enjoy the **Underwater Viewing** area backstage.

> **BRITTIP**
>
> The first 14 rows at Shamu Stadium get VERY wet (watch out for your cameras) – when a killer whale leaps into the air in front of you, it displaces a LOT of water on landing!

Sea Lion and Otter Stadium: the venue for a wonderful show, *Clyde and Seamore Take Pirate Island*, it features the resident sea lions who, with their pals the otter and walrus (plus a couple of humans as the fall guys), put on a hilarious 25-minute performance of watery stunts and gags. Arrive early for some first-class audience mickey-taking from the resident pirate mime. In high season, there is a second evening show, *Clyde and Seamore Present Sea Lions Tonight*, which serves up a parody of other SeaWorld shows. AAAA.

Xtreme Zone next door has a Trampoline Jump and Rock Climbing Wall, for an extra fee (reservations required).

Believe!

Blue Horizons: this wonderful show serves up another big helping of dramatic animal behaviour in best Broadway production style. Replacing the Key West Dolphin Fest, it features dolphins, false killer whales and exotic birds (including an Andean condor), but a lot more besides as the general (and rather abstract) theme of a girl's dream about maritime wildlife is brought to life. The elaborate set design is the first eye-catching element, with a 40ft/12m sea-meets-sky backdrop that also conceals the setting for a host of additional performers, from high divers to bungee jumpers and trapeze-like aerialists. There is no obvious interaction between trainers and animals as the show moves from one scene to the next, both above and below the water, but there is plenty to admire as the stage is filled with graceful and quite daring action. The complex staging and vivid costuming (all created by Broadway designers) is also underpinned by a stirring original score by the Seattle Symphony Orchestra and it all adds up to a magnificent 25 minutes that often draws a huge ovation. AAAAA.

Elmo and the Bookaneers: Sesame Street favourites Elmo, Bert, Ernie, Rosita and their pirate pals take over the Bayside Stadium in a 25-minute song and dance fest, encouraging youngsters to realise the 'treasure' to be found in reading. Jet-skis trailing colourful kites add a bright element of interest to the show, which is geared firmly at preschool kids. Under-6s won't want to miss the post-show character meet-and-greet. AA, or AAAA (depending on age).

BRITTIP

The weather may occasionally mean some outdoor entertainment is cancelled, but don't let that stop you enjoying yourself. Cheap, plastic ponchos will appear in the shops at the first sign of rain!

The Waterfront: not so much an attraction as a 5 acre/2ha village at the heart of SeaWorld, offering fine dining, smart shops, several shows and street entertainment. This area forms an arc around part of the central lake, is themed like an eclectic harbour and offers 3 excellent eateries: the **Seafire Inn** for gourmet steak burgers, salads and coconut-fried shrimp; **Voyagers** for wood-fired pizzas, pasta and sandwiches, plus a low-carb option. Not cheap, but quite delicious and our favourite, **The Spice Mill** is a cafeteria-style restaurant offering succulent and spicy variations on soups, sandwiches, grilled chicken and jambalaya. There

Blue Horizons

Believe!

are also 3 snack bars: **Café de Mar** for pastries, coffees and soft drinks; **Smugglers Feast** for smoked turkey legs; and **Freezas** for frozen yoghurt and other drinks. Plus there are 4 interlinked boutique-style shops with some stylish souvenirs (check out **Allura's Treasure Trove** and **Under The Sun**) and some amusing street performers. Keep a particular eye out for the amazing percussive pots-and-pans rhythms of the **Groove Chefs**.

BRITTIP

Grab an evening meal at The Spice Mill, then head out on to its open-air terrace for one of the best seats in the house to experience the Mistify nightly finale.

The unique **The Oyster's Secret** shop features resident pearl divers who can be viewed underwater as they collect the pearl-bearing oysters on request, to be incorporated into jewellery pieces by the shop's artisans. **The Tower** is the centrepiece of the Waterfront, with a 400ft/122m landmark offering (at an extra $3) slowly rotating rides for a bird's-eye view of the park. Here you will find the **SandBar**, a water's edge cocktail bar, with musicians performing from time to time, serving snacks and speciality drinks. It's the perfect place to watch the sun go down. Kids can play in the area's 2 **squirt fountains** (remember the swimming costumes!) and the whole scene is characterised by lovely landscaping and clever ocean sound effects. AAAA.

Pets Ahoy!: just inside the Waterfront is the air-conditioned haven (during the hottest part of the day) of the Seaport Theater, which hosts this cute 25-minute giggle featuring the unlikely talents of a menagerie of dogs, cats, birds, rats, pot-bellied pigs and others, the majority of which have come from local animal rescue shelters. AAA.

Odyssea: fans of the old Cirque de la Mer show in the Nautilus Theater will be sad to know it has gone – but happily it has been replaced by the even smarter and more captivating Odyssea. It's a 30-minute fantasy featuring some mind-boggling acrobatic feats, engaging live music, clever lighting and a host of in-theatre special effects. The show tells the spectacular, if stylised, story of a seaman who falls into the ocean and descends through various levels to the sea bed, encountering an assortment of creatures along the way. Think of a watery version of Cirque du Soleil® and you are not far wrong. This is a great place to be when it's hot or raining! AAAAA.

The Nautilus Theater is also home to various weekend events throughout the year, notably **Jack Hanna's Animal Adventure**, the **Bud and BBQ Country Music Festival,** and the **Viva La Musica** Latin weekends.

Clydesdale Hamlet: these massive stables are home to the Anheuser-Busch trademark Clydesdale dray horses. They make a great photo opportunity when fully harnessed and there is a life-size statue outside, which creates a good backdrop. The Hitching Barn shows how the horses are prepared for the twice-daily parade, including washing, grooming and braiding. AA.

Anheuser-Busch Hospitality Center: adjoining Clydesdale Hamlet, here you can sample the company's most famous product, the world's number 1 bottled beer, Budweiser, and its cousins (seek out the new Bare Knuckle Stout!). Sadly, it's only 3 small samples per visitor 21 or over (with valid photo ID) but you can enjoy them outside on the terrace, which provides a pleasant break from all the hustle and bustle. AA. You'll also find the **Beer School** and **The Brewmasters Club** here, while **The Hospitality Deli** restaurant is an attractive proposition, serving freshly carved turkey and beef, German sausage, sauerkraut, freshly baked breads and delicious desserts.

Manatee Rescue: here is an exhibit to tug at your heartstrings as you learn the plight of this endangered species of Florida's waterways. Watch these lazy-looking creatures (half-walrus, half-cow?) lounge in their man-made lagoon, then walk down the ramp to the circular theatre where a 5-minute film with 3-D effects reveals the dangers facing the harmless manatee. Then pass into the underwater viewing section, with hands-on TV screens offering more information. It's a magnificent exhibit and should invoke a strong sense of animal conservation. It is also right behind Blue Horizons, so DON'T go just after a show. AAA ½.

Pacific Point Preserve: this carefully re-created rocky coast habitat shows the park's seals and sea lions at their most natural. A hidden wave machine adds the perfect touch, while park attendants provide informative talks at regular intervals. You can also buy small packs of smelt to throw to these ever-hungry mammals. AAA.

Shamu's Happy Harbor

Shamu's Happy Harbor: 4 acres/1.6ha of brilliantly designed adventure playground and rides await youngsters of all ages here. Activities include a 4-storey net climb, 2 tented ball rooms to wade through, a giant trampoline tent and a splashy water maze (great on a hot day). The signature junior-sized coaster **Shamu Express** offers mild thrills over more than 800ft/245m of track. The **Jazzy Jellies** is a jellyfish-themed samba tower ride that lifts and spins, while **Swishy Fishes** features oversized seats that spin round a giant waterspout. **Flying Fiddler** (a 20ft/6.1m tower ride on a giant crab), **Ocean Commotion** (a rocking tug ride) and **Sea Carousel** (a traditional carousel featuring 56 sea creatures) completed the line-up in 2007. The area gets busy from midday, but the kids seem to love it at any time. Next door is the **Shamu Splash Attack** (water-balloon catapults), the inevitable video arcade and funfair games for a few extra dollars. TTTT.

Shark Encounter: the world's largest collection of dangerous sea creatures can be found here, brought dramatically to life by the walk-through tubes that surround you with more than 50 prowling sharks (including sand tigers, black tips, nurse sharks and sand bars), sawfish, tropical fish and gigantic groupers. It's an eerie experience (and perhaps too intense for young children), but brilliantly presented and, again, highly informative. You can also watch the intrepid souls in the Sharks Deep Dive cage as it traverses the aquarium (see page 185). Queues build up here at peak times, though. AAAA or TTTT.

Once you have ridden the moving walkway, head for the best restaurant in the park for another close-up at the **Sharks Underwater Grill**. Not only do you have an amazing backdrop for your meal in a clever, subterranean environment (check out the incredible bar, which is a mini-

🇬🇧 BRITTIP

If the main adult portions look too big at the Sharks Underwater Grill – and they are pretty hefty – you can order from the Young Adults menu for smaller portions of 4 regular dishes. Check out the kids' dessert menu, too.

aquarium), but the upscale restaurant features an appetising 'Floribbean'-style menu, blending local and spicy Caribbean fare. The emphasis is on seafood – and wonderful creations with scallops, jumbo shrimp (king prawns), grouper and sea bass – plus pasta, filet mignon, chicken and pork, and desserts to die for. Some refreshing (non-alcoholic) cocktails and menus for under-10s and teens complete the picture; it's a real treat on a hot day. Open from 11am to park closing, it's very busy at lunch but quieter in late afternoon, so we advise booking (at the restaurant itself) as soon as you arrive. A 3-course meal costs around $38.

Penguin Encounter: always a hit with families (and one of the more crowded exhibits), the ever-comical penguins are brilliantly presented in this chilly showpiece. You have the choice of going close and using the moving walkway along the display or standing back and watching from a non-moving position. Both afford fascinating views of the 17 different species both above and below the water. Feeding time is highly popular, so arrive early if you want a prime spot. There is also a question-and-answer session at 2pm every day – the winner gets to pet a penguin. AAAA.

Key West at SeaWorld: a whole collection of exhibits are grouped together here under the clever Key West theme. Stingray Lagoon, where you can feed and touch fully grown rays, includes a nursery for newborn rays, while the park's rescued and rehabilitated sea turtles can be seen at Turtle Point. The centrepiece, the 2.1 acre/0.8ha Dolphin Cove, is a more spectacular, naturalistic development and offers the chance to get close enough to feed this community of frisky Atlantic bottlenose dolphins. There is also an excellent underwater viewing area, and park photographers patrol here ready to snap you at play with the dolphins; two 6 x 8 photos will set you back $19.99; two 4 x 6s are $16.99; frames are an additional $7, $10 or $15.

🇬🇧 BRITTIP

If you drop your fish on the ground when feeding the dolphins, seals or sea lions you are asked to throw it away, for the animal's health and safety.

The whole area is designed in the tropical flavour of America's southernmost city, Key West, with beach huts, lifeguard chairs, dune buggies, themed shops and other eclectic elements, but it also underlines the environmental message of conservation through interactive graphics and video displays adjacent to the animal habitats, and children of all ages will find it a fun, educational experience. The selection of shops is above average, too. AAAA.

Journey to Atlantis: unique in Orlando, this terrific water-coaster gave SeaWorld its first 5-star thrill attraction in 1998. The combination of extra elements here ultimately makes it a one-off, with some illusory

Journey to Atlantis

Kraken

special effects giving way to a high-speed water ride that becomes a runaway roller-coaster. The discovery of Atlantis in your 8-passenger 'fishing boat' starts gently through the lost city. But evil spirit Allura takes over and riders plunge into a dash through Atlantis, dodging gushing fountains and water cannons, with hundreds of dazzling holographic and laser-generated illusions, before the heart-stopping 60ft/18m drop, which is merely the entry to the roller-coaster finale back in the candle-filled catacombs. An amazing creation. Be ready to get soaked in the course of the ride, which is great in summer but not so clever first thing on a winter morning. Restrictions: 3ft 6in/106cm. TTTTT. Riders exit into the **Sea Aquarium Gallery**, a combination gift shop and huge aquarium full of sharks, stingrays and tropical fish (don't forget to look upwards).

Kraken: this member of the coaster family is one of Florida's most breathtaking. Based on the mythical sea monster, Kraken is an innovative pedestal ride (you are effectively sitting in a chair without a floor – pretty exposed!) that plunges an initial 144ft/44m, hits 65mph/105kph, dives underground 3 times, adds 7 inversions (including a vertical loop, a diving loop, a zero-gravity roll and a cobra roll) and a flat spin before riders escape the beast's lair. The ride from the front row, especially down an opening drop at an angle best described as ludicrous, is positively blood-curdling, and sitting in the rear is thrilling, too. Restrictions: 4ft 6in/137cm. TTTTT+.

SeaWorld specials

For extra fun, there is live entertainment daily around the Key West attractions. Throughout the summer high season, when the park is open until 10pm, there are often other live elements, leading up to the big **Mistify** finale on the Waterfront lagoon. This is a neat mix of pyrotechnics and special effects, invoking giant sea creatures with stunning laser images. The show dazzles with towering fountains (up to 100ft/30m high), mist sprays,

SEAWORLD with children

The following gives a general idea of the appeal of SeaWorld's attractions to the different age groups:

Under-5s
Believe, Blue Horizons, Clyde And Seamore Take Pirate Island, Clydesdale Hamlet, Elmo And The Bookaneers, Manatee Rescue, Odyssea, Pacific Point Preserve, Penguin Encounter, Pets Ahoy!, Shamu's Happy Harbor, Waterfront entertainment, Wild Arctic (without the ride).

5–8s
All the above, plus Mistify, Shark Encounter, Wild Arctic (with the ride).

9–12s
All the above, plus Journey to Atlantis and Kraken.

Over-12s
Believe, Blue Horizons, Clyde And Seamore Take Pirate Island, Journey To Atlantis, Kraken, Mistify, Odyssea, Shark Encounter, Wild Arctic.

flames, unique fireworks (including some that burn under water) and an epic soundtrack. By far the largest and most spectacular evening show SeaWorld has yet produced, it doesn't quite rival Disney pyrotechnics, but it should not be missed.

As well as all the main set-pieces, several smaller ones can be equally rewarding for their more personal touch. The **Dolphin Nursery** provides close encounters with the park's younger dolphins, and there are the **Flamingo**, **Pelican** and **Spoonbill Exhibits**. The flamingo **pedal-boats**, which rent for $6/½ hour (for 2 people) in one corner of the lagoon, are also fun. Look out, too, for the best photo opportunity of the day as a big, cuddly Shamu will greet the kids just inside the main entrance.

You can choose to eat at a further 9 venues, with the best of the bunch being **The Hospitality Deli** (in the Anheuser-Busch Hospitality Center, see pages 189–90), **Mama's Kitchen**, (sandwiches, salads, chilli, chicken fingers), **Smoky Creek Grill** (a Texas-style barbecue) and **Mango Joe's Café** (delicious grilled fajitas, speciality salads and sandwiches). As in the other main parks, try to eat before midday or after 2.30pm for a crowd-free lunch, and before 5.30pm if you want a leisurely dinner (or better still,

book Sharks Underwater Grill or Dine With Shamu). Your wallet will also be in peril in any of the 24 shops and photo kiosks. Make sure you visit at least **Shamu's Emporium** (for a full range of cuddly toys), **Manatee Cove** (more cuddlies), **Friends of the Wild** (dedicated to animal lovers) and **The Label Stable** for Anheuser-Busch gifts and merchandise (some of it extremely smart). Your purchases can be forwarded to Package Pick-up in Shamu's Emporium to collect on your way out, provided you give them at least an hour.

Finally, non-drivers will probably want to make a note of the special daily bus service from SeaWorld (and other points on I-Drive) direct to sister park **Busch Gardens** (see page 200), which you can book at Guest Relations.

Sharks Underwater Grill

Discovery Cove

Fancy a day in your own tropical paradise, with the chance to swim with dolphins, encounter sharks, snorkel in a coral reef and dive through a waterfall into a tropical aviary? Well, Discovery Cove is all that and more. The only drawback is the price. This mini theme park comes at a premium because it is restricted to just 1,000 guests a day, creating an exclusive experience that is reflected in the admission fee. The flat rate entrance fee is $259 ($279 in peak season) and the only reduction is $100 off for those not wishing to do the Dolphin Swim and for 3–5s; under-3s are free.

The **Trainer for a Day** programme adds an exciting opportunity to go behind the scenes into the training, feeding and welfare of the park's animals. You get to work with the experts as they interact with dolphins, birds, sharks, stingrays and tropical fish. The programme includes a behavioural training class, the chance to experience a double-foot push (ride on the front of two dolphins), souvenir shirt, dolphin book and waterproof camera, and participants must be at least 6 and in good health. You need to book well in advance on 020 8668 4218 or **www.discovery cove.com**. The cost? A healthy $479 ($458 non-peak seasons), including the entrance fee.

The **Dolphin Lover's Sleepover** is your chance to spend the night (from 7pm) at Discovery Cove in a tent on the beach next to the dolphin lagoon – with stories and snacks – and then be among the first to enjoy a full day in the park when you wake up. It is designed for families (but not under-6s) as it features arts, crafts and other child-friendly activities, and also provides breakfast, lunch and dinner. It costs $449/person and runs only on select Saturdays in warmer months (1800 406 2244 or book online).

So, just what do you get for your money at Discovery Cove? Well, as you would expect, it is a supremely personal park. You check in at the beautiful entrance lobby as you would for a hotel rather than a theme park, and you have a guide to take you in and get you set for the day. All your basic requirements – towel, mask, snorkel, wet-jacket, lockers, beach umbrellas, food and drink – are included, and the level of service is excellent. A valuable week's pass for SeaWorld or Busch Gardens is also included (valid for 7 consecutive days before or after your Discovery Cove visit; or you can upgrade to 14 consecutive days at both for $30). Continental breakfast, snacks and beverages (including Anheuser-Busch products) as well as lunch at the buffet-style **Laguna Grill** are all included. But the gift shop and photographic prices reflect the entrance fee – expensive.

Discovery Cove

Ray Lagoon

Location

Situated on Central Florida Parkway, almost opposite the SeaWorld entrance (open year-round 9.30am–5.30pm; parking free), the whole 30 acre/12ha park is magnificently landscaped, with lovely thatched buildings, palm trees, lush vegetation, white-sand beaches, gurgling streams – even hammocks. The overall effect is of being transported to a tropical paradise.

The usual tourist hurly-burly is left far behind. The 5-star resort feel is enhanced by a high staff-to-guest ratio (the lifeguards seem to outnumber guests at times) and there are no queues (though the restaurant may get busy at lunch), while the highlight Dolphin Encounter is world class. Visitors with disabilities are well catered for, with special wheelchairs that can move across the sand and into shallow water, and an area of the Dolphin Lagoon to allow those who can't enter the water still to be able to touch the dolphins. The essence of a day here involves close encounters with all the animals – though not too close because of the sharks! The ultimate feeling is total relaxation, a holiday from your holiday.

The main attractions

Coral Reef: a huge rocky pool, filled with several thousand tropical fish, offers the most amazing man-made snorkelling experience you'll find. The water teems with silverjacks, angelfish and yellowtail snapper and, even if the 'coral' is hand-painted concrete, it is a clever environment. Some of the larger stingrays inhabiting the bottom of the reef are fascinating to watch. Swimmers also come within inches of sharks and barracuda – all safely behind a Plexiglass partition – which adds another novel element. If you stay reasonably still in the water, many of the tropical fish will crowd around to inspect their latest pool-mate! AAAA.

Ray Lagoon: another carefully sculpted pool provides the opportunity to paddle among several dozen southern and cownose rays – harmless, but with a hint of menace to the fascination. AAAA.

Tropical River: this 800yd/732m circuit of gently flowing bath-warm water is a variation on the lazy river feature of many of the water parks, though with a far more naturalistic aspect and none of the inner tubes. It is primarily designed for snorkellers and features rocky lagoons, caves, a beach section, a tropical forest segment, sunken ruins and an underwater viewing window into the Coral Reef. The lack of fish makes it seem a bit bland after the Tropical Reef and Ray Lagoon, but it is as much about relaxing as having fun. It is up to 8ft/2.4m deep at points, so non-swimmers are advised to use a flotation vest. AAA.

Aviary: this recently enhanced 3-part adventure is both an area in its own right and a 40yd/37m section of the Tropical River. You can walk in off the beach or swim in through one of the 2 impressive waterfalls that guard each end, which is a beautifully scenic touch and fun for snorkellers. Some 200 tropical birds (plus tiny Muntjac deer) fill the main enclosure and, if you stand still, they are likely to use you as a perch. An expansion in 2002 effectively doubled the size of the aviary by adding a small-bird sanctuary – full of finches, honeycreepers and hummingbirds – and a large-bird enclosure, featuring toucans and the red-legged seriema. Guides will introduce you to specific birds (which you can hand-feed) and tell you about their habits, habitats and conservation issues. AAAAA.

Dolphin Swim: the headline attraction at Discovery Cove is the encounter with the park's Atlantic bottlenose dolphin community. A 20-minute orientation programme in one of the 4 thatched beach cabañas, with a film and instruction from two of the animal trainers, sets you up for this thrilling experience. Groups of 6–8 go into the lagoon with careful supervision from the trainers and, starting off standing in the waist-deep (slightly chilly) water as one of the dolphins comes to you, you gradually become more adventurous until you are swimming with them. Timid swimmers are catered for and there are flotation vests for those who need them. The lagoon is up to 12ft/3.6m deep so there is a real feeling of being in the dolphins' environment. You will learn how trainers use hand signals and positive reinforcement to communicate with them, and get the chance to stroke, feed and even kiss your dolphin. The encounter concludes dramatically as you are towed ashore by one of these awesome animals, which can weigh up to 600lb/272kg, though the activities vary according to the dolphins' attention span. You spend around 30 minutes in the water and it is totally unforgettable. Under-6s are not allowed into the lagoon. TTTTT+.

Truly, Discovery Cove is an attraction with huge style and appeal – not to mention the stuff of which cherished memories are made – but it will take a BIG bite out of your holiday budget. A

Dolphin Swim

Twilight Discovery programme

family of 4, with children old enough to do the Dolphin Swim, could pay $1,796 (including tax) for the day in peak season. Even with a free 7-day SeaWorld pass included, it is a massive outlay. The charge for ages 3–5 is also pretty steep, in our opinion. Your sundries add up, too. An 8 x 10 photo is $24.99. Then there are various photo packages at $29.99, $62.99 and $99.99, while the video of your experience (which includes 30 minutes of highlights of the whole park) costs $59.99 ($69.99 for a DVD). A CD with 5 images is $100, 11 images is $150 and 22 images is $200. There are 3 digital packages too: an interaction DVD with 5 images on CD for $150; the DVD with 11 images for $200; and the DVD with 22 images for $250. Poster-size photos (24 x 36) are available for $49.99.

The weather can get distinctly cool in the winter months, but the water is always heated (apart from the dolphin lagoon, which remains at 72°F/22°C) and full wetsuits are also available to keep out the chill. The attention to detail is superb and guest satisfaction ratings are extremely high (it is hugely popular with British visitors – up to 40% of the daily attendance at times). However, if any element falls below expectations, it is worth bringing it to the attention of a manager as they are always keen to rectify any oversights. An alternative to the full day's activity is the summer **Twilight Discovery** programme – the

chance to visit the park, be wined and dined in style, swim in the Coral Reef and pools and enjoy a shallow-water dolphin encounter. The emphasis is on a refined tropical party experience for just 150 guests a night (3–9pm Tues–Fri in summer). The exclusive feel is enhanced by a festive welcome reception, tropical drinks, snacks and beverages (including Anheuser-Busch products), a truly superb buffet, dinner at Laguna Grill and live Caribbean-style music, desserts on the beach and the special dolphin interaction. It includes a 7-day pass to either SeaWorld or Busch Gardens (or a 14-day combination pass for an additional $30). The cost is still a hefty $259 (or $159 without the dolphin encounter) but it's another unique opportunity and a seriously different ambience.

Special occasions

For that special birthday or anniversary or for somewhere completely different to propose marriage, Discovery Cove has a range of options that involve dolphin interaction and private beach cabañas. The **Platinum Ring** (an extra $474.95/couple) includes sharing your special moment with a dolphin, who delivers a specialised message buoy, a private cabana, a bottle of champagne with souvenir champagne chiller and 2 crystal flutes, a dozen roses, assorted chocolates, safe and secret storage of the engagement ring and a video of the occasion. The **Golden Ring Package** ($224.95/couple) and **Sweetheart Package** ($149.95) are scaled-down versions of the same. The **Birthday Package** ($74.95) includes dolphin activity, cake, photo and souvenir buoy, plus a T-shirt, and a **Premium** version ($174.95) adds a disposable underwater camera and a video of the occasion. For more details, visit **www.discoverycove.com**. You can book online – preferably at least 3 months in advance – or call 407 370 1280 in the US.

Busch Gardens

When is a zoo not a zoo? When it is also a theme park like the 335 acre/136ha Busch Gardens in Tampa. The second big Anheuser-Busch park in the area started life as a mini-menagerie for the wildlife collection of the brewery-owning Busch family (Budweiser). In 1959, it opened a small, tropical-themed hospitality centre next to the brewery and now it is a major, multi-faceted family attraction, the biggest on Florida's west coast and a little more than an hour from Orlando. It is rated among the top 4 zoos in America, with more than 2,700 animals representing over 320 species of mammals, birds, reptiles, amphibians and spiders. But that's just the start. It boasts a safari-like section of Africa spread over 65 acres/26ha of grassy veldt, with

special tours to hand-feed some of the animals. Interspersed among the animals are more than 20 bona fide theme park rides, including the mind-numbing roller-coasters **Kumba**, **SheiKra**, **Montu** and **Gwazi**, with guaranteed fun for coaster addicts, plus plenty of scaled-down rides for younger children. Then there are the animal shows, comedians, musicians, strolling players and *KaTonga*, a family show extravaganza that takes place in the impressive Moroccan Palace Theater.

The overall theme is Africa, hence the park is divided into areas like Nairobi and Congo, and dining and shopping are equal to most of the other theme parks. It doesn't quite have the pizzazz of *Epcot* or Universal, and the staff are a bit more laid back, but it

Busch Gardens at a glance

Location	Busch Blvd, Tampa; 75–90 minutes' drive from Orlando		
Size	335 acres/136ha in 11 themed areas		
Hours	9 or 10am–6 or 7pm off peak; 9am–8pm Easter, Thanksgiving, Christmas; 9 or 9.30am–10.30pm summer		
Admission	Under-3s free; 3–9 $47.95 (1-Day Ticket), $85 (Busch/SeaWorld Combo ticket), $199.95 (Orlando FlexTicket Plus, including Universal Studios, SeaWorld and Wet 'n Wild); adults (10+) $61.95 ($51.95 online Advance Purchase), $85, $239.95		
Parking	$9		
Lockers	In Morocco, Congo, Egypt and Stanleyville $5		
Pushchairs	$10 and $15		
Wheelchairs	$10 and $35, with pushchairs		
Top Attractions	Congo River Rapids, Gwazi, Kumba, Montu, Pirates 4-D, Rhino Rally, SheiKra, Tanganyika Tidal Wave		
Don't Miss	Edge of Africa, Animal Keeper talks, Ka Tonga, Myombe Reserve, Mystic Sheikhs band		
Hidden Costs	Meals	Burger, chips and Pepsi $8.88 3-course meal $17–23.75; family-style diner $12.95 and $6.95 (Crown Colony House) Kids' meal $6.45	
	T-shirts	$13–26	
	Souvenirs	95c–$695	
	Sundries	Ride photos $12.99 ($17.99 with frame)	

Morocco
1 Zagora Café
2 Marrakesh Theater
3 Moroccan Palace Theater
4 Gwazi
5 Myombe Reserve

Egypt
6 Crown Colony House Restaurant
7 Edge of Africa
8 Clydesdale Hamlet
9 Show Jumping Hall of Fame
10 Skyride Station
11 Montu
12 Tut's Tomb

Nairobi
13 Curiosity Caverns
14 Elephant Habitat
15 Rhino Rally

Timbuktu
16 Scorpion
17 Cheetah Chase
18 Phoenix
19 Carousel Caravan
20 Sandstorm
21 Kiddie Rides
22 Timbuktu Theater: Pirates 3D

23 Desert Grill
24 Sultan's Arcade

Congo
25 Kumba
26 Congo River Rapids
27 Jungle Village (Summer 2008)
28 Ubanga-Banga Bumper Cars
29 White Tiger Habitat (Summer 2008)

Stanleyville
30 Stanley Falls Log Flume
31 Tanganyika Tidal Wave
32 SheiKra
33 Stanleyville Theater
34 Skyride Station
35 Zambia Smokehouse

Bird Gardens
36 Bird Show Theater
37 Lory Landing
38 Aviary
39 Hospitality House
40 Land of the Dragons
41 Gwazi Pavilion
42 Train Stations

has guaranteed, 5-star family appeal, especially with its selection of rides just for kids, and it is a big hit with British visitors. In a way, it is like the big brother of Chessington World of Adventures in Surrey, though on a much grander scale (and in a better climate). Busch Gardens is the only park to offer 1-Day Tickets with a **rain guarantee**, which means if you get rained out on your visit, you can return FREE within 7 days. Look for self-serve ticket machines to the right of the park entrance to save time waiting for an attended booth.

Location

Busch Gardens is the hardest place to locate on the sketchy local maps and the signposting is not as sharp as it could be but, from Orlando, the directions are pretty simple. Head west on I-4 for almost an hour (it is 55 miles/88km from I-4's junction with Highway 192) until you hit the intersecting motorway I-75. Take I-75 north for 3½ miles/5.5km until you see the exit for Fowler Avenue (Highway 582). Continue west on Fowler for another 3½ miles/5.5km, then just past the University of South Florida on your right, turn LEFT into McKinley Drive. A mile/1.6km down McKinley Drive, Busch Gardens' car park is on your left, where it costs $9 to park.

Those without a car can use the daily **Busch Gardens Shuttle Express** bus service, which makes several round trips a day from Orlando at $10 a time

Rhino Rally

(free if you have a 5-Park FlexTicket). You board at SeaWorld, Goodings Shopping Plaza (I-Drive), Orlando Premium Outlets, Universal Studios, Ramada Maingate West, Best Western Lakeside or Old Town in Kissimmee and pick-up times range from 8.30 to 9.40am, returning at 6 or 7pm. Book at the **Guest Services** window at SeaWorld or call 1800 221 1339.

You may think you'll have left the crowds behind in Orlando but, unfortunately, in high season you'd be wrong. It is still advisable to be here in time for opening, if only to be first in line to ride the amazing Rhino Rally or the dazzling roller-coasters, which all draw major queues (especially SheiKra). The Congo River Rapids, Stanley Falls Log Flume ride and Tanganyika Tidal Wave (all opportunities to get wet!) are also prime rides. New in 2007 was 'floorless' **SheiKra**, making an already spectacular ride even more jaw-dropping as the floor has, literally, dropped out from beneath you. If you thought it was intimidating (and hugely thrilling!) before, wait until you see it with nothing between you and the track but air. The queues do take longer to build up here, though, so for the first few hours at least you can enjoy a relatively crowd-free experience.

On your left through the main gates is the **Tours Centre** window, and you should go there straight away (or book in advance on 813 984 4043 or email **bgt.viptours@buschgardens.com**) if you'd like to do the wonderful Serengeti Safari or one of its other Adventure Tours (see pages 207–8). Busch Gardens is divided into 11 main sections, with the major rides all a bit of a hike from the main entrance. Check the back of your park map for times and locations of various organised animal encounters throughout the park – then watch out for passing flamingos as they take the first of their twice-daily promenades through the main courtyard!

Rhino Rally, which opened in summer 2001, is one of the prime attractions, so you should head here first (especially as the animals are more evident early in the day). Bear right through Morocco, turn left into Nairobi, pass the train station, and the Rally entrance is opposite the elephant habitat. Coaster fans flock in serious numbers to **SheiKra**, the world's highest and fastest dive coaster, and queues can hit 3 HOURS by mid-afternoon so, if you are tempted by this first, bear left through Morocco past the Zagora Café, through the Bird Gardens and up into Stanleyville. **Gwazi**, the fabulous wooden double-coaster, is another to draw a crowd relatively quickly, and you could do this en route. Then continue through Stanleyville to Congo for **Kumba**, and retrace your steps to do **Congo River Rapids** and the other 2 water rides. Alternatively, turn right through the main entrance and visit Egypt for **Montu**. Here is the full park layout.

Morocco

Coming through the main gates brings you first into Morocco, home of all the main guest services and a lot of the best shops. *Epcot*'s Moroccan pavilion sets the scene rather better, but the architecture is still impressive and this version won't overstretch your wallet quite as much as Disney's does! For a quick meal, try the **Zagora Café**, especially at breakfast, when the marching, dancing, 8-piece brass band **Mystic Sheikhs** swings by to entertain the early crowds. Alternatively, the enticing **Sultan's Sweets** serves coffee and pastries. Watch out, too, for the strolling **Men of Note**, a 4-piece a cappella group, and costumed characters such as TJ the Tiger and Hilda Hippo.

Turning the corner brings you to the first animal encounter, the Alligator pen. Morocco is also home to 2 of the park's biggest shows. The Marrakesh Theater offers the **Mirage Canteen** song and dance show, with live piano music, singers and dancers all in an amusing pastiche of a 1940's dance hall musical review, evoking the Golden Age of Hollywood. AAA.

KaTonga: is a lavish Broadway-style spectacle, featuring an 18-strong cast of singers, dancers, acrobats and puppeteers. Subtitled *Musical Tales from the Jungle*, this 35-minute theatrical extravaganza celebrates African animal folklore with an ingenious mix of live actor presentation and the award-winning larger-than-life puppets of Michael Curry (who helped create Disney's *The Lion King* show in London and New York). With 57 costumes, 45 puppets and a troupe of stunning Chinese acrobats, it makes for a truly eye-catching performance, up to 5 times a day, that is way above usual theme park standards. It is also air-conditioned, a welcome relief in

Congo River Rapids

summer. Arrive a little early as the Moroccan Palace Theater doors close right on showtime. AAAAA.

Gwazi: this is Busch's second largest roller-coaster, a massive 'duelling' wooden creation in the classic mould (i.e. no going upside-down). The 2 sets of cars, the Gwazi Lion and Gwazi Tiger, each top 50mph/80kph and generate a G-force of up to 3.5 as they career around nearly 7,000ft/2,134m of track with 6 fly-by encounters. You get to choose your ride in the intricately themed 8 acre/3ha village plaza and then you are off up the 90ft/27m lift for a breathtaking 2½ minutes. The shake, rattle 'n' roll effect of a classic coaster is cleverly re-created and the Lion and Tiger rides are slightly different, so you need to do both. Even if you don't like roller-coasters, you have to try this one. Restrictions: 4ft/122cm. TTTTT.

Children can also try here the **bungee trampoline** and **rock climbing wall** ($5 each or $7 for both), while **Gwazi Gliders** is a gentle 'hang-gliding' ride for the preschool crowd.

Nairobi

Nairobi is home to the awesome **Myombe Reserve**, one of the largest and most realistic habitats for the threatened highland gorillas and chimpanzees of Central Africa. This 3 acre/1.2ha walk-through has a superb tropical setting where the temperature is kept artificially high and convincing with the aid of lush forest landscaping and hidden water mist sprays. Take your time, especially as there are good, seated vantage points, and be patient to catch these magnificent creatures on their daily routine. It is also highly informative, with attendants usually on hand to answer any questions. AAAAA.

Rhino Rally: this wonderfully dramatic and scenic ride starts out as an off-road jeep safari and changes into an innovative raft adventure as your 17-passenger vehicle gets caught in a flash flood. The 8-minute whirl

Montu

through the wilds of Africa includes encounters with elephants, rhinos, crocodiles, antelope and more, as the off-road part of the ride is just about as real as they can make it. Your driver adds to the fun with some amusing spiel about the rally and your Land-Rover built vehicle, but it soon becomes clear that your navigator (the front seat passenger) has led you into a blind gully. An unused pontoon bridge is your only way out, but fate has a unique twist in store, which opens the way to part 2 of the ride and the thrilling raging river section that is unlike any attraction we've experienced to date. Check this out (but you must get here early to beat the queues). Height restriction is just 3ft 3in/99cm. TTTT/AAAAA.

The **Serengeti Plain** is a 49 acre/20ha spread of African savannah that is home to buffalo, antelope, zebras, giraffes, wildebeest, ostriches, hippos, rhinos and many exotic birds, and can be viewed for much of the journey on the **Serengeti Express Railway**, a full-size, open-car steam train that chugs slowly from its main station in Nairobi to Egypt and all the way round to Congo, Stanleyville and back. It's a good ride to take during the main part of the day when the queues are building up at the thrill rides. AAA.

Edge of Africa: a 15 acre/6ha safari experience that guarantees a close-up encounter almost as good as the real thing. The walk-through attraction puts you in an authentic setting of natural wilds and native villages (right down to the imported plants and even the smells), from which you can view giraffes, lions, baboons, meerkats, crocodiles, hyenas, vultures and even get an underwater view of a hippopotamus habitat. Look out for the abandoned jeep – you can sit in the front cab while the lions are lounging in the back! Wandering 'safari guides' and naturalists offer informal talks, and the attention to detail is superb. AAAAA.

BRITTIP

Edge of Africa offers some fantastic photo opportunities but, in the hot months, come here early in the day as many animals seek refuge from the heat later.

Back at **Myombe Gifts** you can buy cuddly baby gorilla toys and get a snack or soft drink at the **Kenya Kanteen**. This is also the place to see the Asian elephants (check the advertised times for the **Elephant Wash**) and visit the **Nairobi Field Station**, an animal nursery and care centre that houses all manner of rehabilitating and hand-reared creatures. Continuing round the nursery brings you to the **Reptile House** and **Tortoise Habitat**. The **Curiosity Caverns**, just to the left of the nursery, are easy to miss but are a must if you want to catch a glimpse of some nocturnal and rarely seen creatures very much at home in a cave-like setting.

Timbuktu

Passing through Nairobi brings you to the more ride-dominated area of the park, starting with Timbuktu. Here in a North African desert setting you will find many of the elements of a typical funfair, with a couple of brain-scrambling rides and two good shows.

Scorpion: a 50mph/80kph roller-coaster, this features a 62ft/19m drop and a 360-degree loop that is guaranteed to dial D for Dizzy for a while! The ride lasts just 120 seconds, but seems longer. Queues build here from late morning, and you must be at least 3ft 6in/106cm to ride. TTTT.

Edge of Africa

Cheetah Chase: this family-orientated 'Crazy Mouse' style coaster is surprisingly energetic, rising as it does some 46ft/14m and adding some tight turns and swift drops. Top speed is only 22mph/35kph, which won't excite Kumba fans, but it certainly seems faster and will thrill the younger lot. TTT, or TTTTT for under-10s.

Other rides include **The Phoenix**, a positively evil invention that involves sitting in a gigantic, boat-shaped swing that eventually performs a 360-degree rotation in dramatic, slow-motion style. Don't eat just before this one! Restrictions: 4ft/122cm. TTTT. **Sandstorm** is a fairly routine whirligig contraption that spins and levitates at high speed (hold on to your stomach). Restrictions: 3ft 6in/106cm. TTT. A series of scaled-down **Kiddie Rides** are usually a hit with the under-10s (and give mum and dad a break as well). The **Carousel Caravan** offers the opportunity to ride a genuine Mary Poppins-type carousel (TT), while there is the inevitable **Electronic Arcade** and a **Games Area** of side shows and stalls that require a few extra dollars, or buy the new **Games Pass** (it can be loaded and reloaded in the Games area) and simply swipe your card each time you play.

Desert Grill is a themed buffet-diner (serving great sandwiches, salads, pasta and kids' meals in souvenir buckets) that also offers live musical entertainment in air-conditioned comfort. AAAA.

Kumba

Pirates 4-D: the final element and a thoroughly fun 3-D film romp that will appeal especially to children of all ages. The story centres on a band of hapless pirates lead by a swaggering, incompetent captain (Leslie Nielsen) and his equally blundering first mate (Eric Idle). Treasure and mutiny cue a riot of 3-D visuals plus many clever (and hilarious) special effects – think water, and lots of it! The film lasts 15 minutes, with full surround-sound, and it draws a good crowd through the main part of the day, so go early or leave it until later when you need to cool down. AAAA.

Congo

As you cross into the Congo area, watch out for the start of a major revamp here, with a complete rebuild of the white tiger habitat to include some all-new animal enclosures. This will eventually be another of Busch Gardens' dramatic animal habitats, with a look similar to Edge of Africa.

You're into serious ride territory here, with the unmistakable giant turquoise structure of **Kumba** looming over the area. First of all, it's one of the largest and fastest roller-coasters in the south-east United States and, at 60mph/97kph, it features 3 unique elements: a diving loop that plunges the riders a full 110ft/33m; a camelback, with a 360-degree spiral that induces a weightless feeling for 3 seconds; and a 108ft/33m vertical loop. For good measure, it also dives underground! It looks terrifying close up but is absolutely exhilarating, even for non-coaster fans. Restrictions: 4ft 6in/137cm. TTTTT.

Congo River Rapids: these look pretty tame after **Kumba**, but don't be fooled. The giant rubber rafts will bounce you down some of the most convincing rapids outside of the Rockies, and you will end up with a fair soaking for good measure. Restrictions: 3ft 6in/106cm. TTTT.

Ubanga-Banga Bumper Cars: they are just that, typical fairground dodgems (restriction: 3ft 6in/106cm; TT), and you won't miss anything if you pass them by. **Jungle Village** will be the new feature here (late summer 2008), a mixture of elaborate children's play area, white tiger and orang utan habitats, and innovative zip-line ride, plus additional shops and a restaurant.

Stanleyville

You pass over Claw Island, home to the park's spectacular rare white **Bengal tigers**, to get to Stanleyville, which seems to merge into one area from the Congo. Here there are more watery rides, with the popular **Stanley Falls Log Flume** ride (almost identical to the ones at Chessington, Legoland, Thorpe Park and Alton Towers), which guarantees a good soaking at the final drop (restrictions: 3ft 10in/116cm; TTT) and the distinctly cleverer **Tanganyika Tidal Wave**, which takes you on a scenic ride along 'uncharted' African waters before tipping you down a 2-stage drop that really does land with tidal-wave force. Restrictions: 4ft/122cm. TTTT.

> ### BRITTIP
> Don't stand on the bridge by Tanganyika Tidal Wave or by the SheiKra splashdown unless you want to get seriously wet!

SheiKra: the park's outstanding big-thrill attraction is the giant steel structure of this monstrous coaster. A world first at 200ft/62m tall and hitting 70mph/112kph, this is the ride to put Alton Towers' fearsome Oblivion in the shade. Higher, longer and faster, it features an initial drop at an angle as near vertical as makes no difference (with a delicious moment of stop-go balance as you teeter on the edge!), a second drop of 138ft/42m into an underground tunnel, an Immelman loop (an exhilarating rolling manoeuvre) and a

water splashdown over ½ ml/1km of smooth-as-silk track. And if all that sounds thrilling, add to it the fact that there is nothing between your seat and the track but air. SheiKra has gone completely floorless! The whole ride lasts 3 minutes and is almost as much fun (or terror, depending on your point of view) to watch as to ride. It also draws crowds like nothing else in the park, so get here early or expect to queue for up to 2 hours. You can also buy your ride video for $19.99 or a 6 x 9 photo for $12.99. Restrictions: 4ft 6in/137cm. TTTTT+.

Stanleyville Theater: a good place to put your feet up as you watch the resident entertainers turn on the style. This varies seasonally and is slated to include an animal encounter show in 2007. AAA½.

For a hearty meal (and a great view of SheiKra), visit the **Zambia Smokehouse**, where its wood-smoked ribs platter is a delight among a heavily BBQ-orientated menu (also with salads, sandwiches and kids' meals).

Bird Gardens

Your route around the park now brings you to the **Bird** Gardens, the most peaceful area and the original starting point of the park in 1959. Here it is possible to unwind from the usual theme park hurly-burly. The exhibits and shows are all family-orientated, too, with the 25-minute *Wild Wings of Africa* presented in the **Bird Show Theater** (AAA) and the **Hospitality Patio**, where the resident band plays a mix of musical favourites, past and present. **Lory Landing** is a desert island-themed walk-through aviary featuring lorikeets, hornbills, parrots and more, with the chance to become a human perch and feed the friendly lorikeets (or have your ear nibbled!). A cup of nectar costs $3, but is a great opportunity for a memorable photo. Take a slow walk round to appreciate the lush, tropical foliage and special

Serengeti Safari

displays such as the walk-through **Aviary**, **Flamingo Island** and **Eagle Canyon**. AAA.

Parents will want to know about **Land of the Dragons**. This large, wonderfully clever area of activities, entertainment, rides and attractions is devoted purely to the young ones. It features a 3-storey treehouse complete with towers and maze-like stairways, a rope climb, ball crawl and outdoor **Dragon's Tale Theater**, which presents the 15-minute show *Friends Forever* – with the resident cuddly dragon, a knight and a beautiful princess teaching a gentle message of friendship. It's all good, family-friendly, well-supervised stuff, and some of the kiddie rides are superbly inventive, as well as offering plenty of opportunity to get wet. TTTTT (youngsters only).

A free taste of Anheuser-Busch products is on offer in **Hospitality House**, where you can also enrol for **Beer School**, a 40-minute lesson in the process of beer-making. It offers a fascinating glimpse into the brewery world, and is excellently explained, with the bonus of some tasting! You will also receive a Brewery Master certificate. AAA (21s and over only). Also here is the new **Brewmasters Club**, a 30-minute experience sampling 7 Anheuser-Busch products

and their ideal chocolate, cheese and fruit pairings. Reservations are required (ages 21 and up only with valid photo ID; registration located just inside the admission turnstiles). Youngsters may utilise the children's area, with colouring books, free soda, water and crackers available.

Another novelty is the eye-catching **Xcursions** environmentally themed gift shop. Its live frog and gecko displays, Animal Fun Facts and Conservation info on interactive touch-screens make it worth visiting whether or not you have money to spend (but all proceeds contribute to the Busch Gardens Conservation Fund).

Egypt

The final area of Busch Gardens is somewhat tucked away, so it is best visited either first thing or late in the day. This area sits in the park's bottom right corner and much of it is carefully re-created pharaoh country, dominated by the roller-coaster Montu, named after an ancient Egyptian warrior god. Here, you can take the **Skyride** cable car (AAA) on a one-way trip to Congo (providing a great look at Rhino Rally). The **Clydesdale Hamlet** is also here, but, if you've seen the massive dray horses and their stables at SeaWorld, the set-

Serengeti Safari

up is pretty similar (AA). Next door is the **Showjumping Hall Of Fame**, which really appeals only to fans of this activity. AA.

The **Crown Colony Restaurant and Hospitality Center** is a large Victorian-style building overlooking the Serengeti Plain. It offers counter-service salads, sandwiches and pizzas downstairs or a full-service restaurant upstairs, with magnificent views of the animals roaming the plain. For a memorable meal (11.30am until an hour before park closing), head here for lunch (they don't take bookings) or, better still, come back for dinner in the early evening and see the animals come down to the waterhole.

Entering the distinctly Egyptian-themed section, you cannot fail to see the area's main attraction. **Montu**, a truly breathtaking creation, is one of the world's tallest and longest inverted coasters, covering nearly 4,000ft/1,219m of track at speeds topping 60mph/97kph and peaking with a G-force of 3.85! Like Kumba, it looks terrifying, but in reality is an absolute 5-star thrill as it leaves your legs dangling and twists and dives (underground at 2 points) for almost 3 minutes of brain-scrambling fun. Restrictions: 4ft 6in/137cm. TTTTT.

You can travel back in time on a tour of **Tut's Tomb**, as it was when discovered by archaeologist Howard Carter, with clever lighting, audio and even aroma effects. AAA. Youngsters can also make their own excavations in a neat **Sand Pit** (with some little

treasures to be found!), while the high-quality shopping at **Golden Scarab** offers hand-blown glass items and authentic cartouche paintings.

You should finally return to Morocco for a spot of shopping in the area's enticing bazaars. Middle Eastern brass, pottery and carpets will all tempt you into opening your wallet yet again at **Casablanca Outfitters**, **Genie's Bottle** and **Marrakesh Market**, while there is a full range of Anheuser-Busch products and gift ideas at the **Label Stable** and **Emporium**, if you haven't already fallen prey to the array of shops and cuddly-toy outlets around the park.

In addition...

The **Serengeti Safari** tour is a 30-minute excursion (5 times a day, taking 20 people at a time) aboard flat-bed trucks that take you to meet the Serengeti Plain's giraffes, zebras, ostriches and rhinos close up and learn more about the park's environmental efforts. You book at the Tour Office just inside the main entrance, or at the kiosk in front of Casablanca Outfitters, for an extra $33.99, and places tend to fill up quickly (children must be at least 5 to take part, and 5–15s must be accompanied by an adult).

The **Guided Adventure Tours** take 15 at a time on a VIP park trek (lasting 4–5 hours), with your own guide, reserved seating at KaTonga, front-of-line access for a number of rides (including Gwazi and Rhino Rally), counter-service lunch at Crown Colony and an up-close encounter with many of the animals and their staff, including the Serengeti Safari. A tour costs $94.99 ($84.99 for children). The **Thrill Seekers Tours** are similar but substitute more rides – including the water rides – for the animal encounters ($74.99 adults, $64.99 3–9s). The 2-hour **Animal Adventures Tour** is a personal animal experience for 7–10 people a day. The next best thing to being a park zookeeper, it provides close encounters with the Clydesdales, black rhinos, hippos, giraffes and elephants, plus involvement in animal behavioural sessions. It costs an extra $119.99/person (no under-5s).

The **Saving A Species** truck tour is a 45-minute meet-and-greet with the park's animal specialists, learning about their work and important conservation issues, including how Busch Gardens is involved in various wildlife projects worldwide. $2 of the $44.99 fee goes to the World Wildlife Fund (no under-5s).

The 45-minute **Sundowner Safari** begins at the Crown Colony Brewmasters Club, with samplings of Anheuser-Busch beers before heading out on the Serengeti Plain to hand-feed giraffes, meet the African wildlife and enjoy more premium lager as you tour. $39.99/person, 21 and over only with valid photo ID. The **Keeper for a Day** programme is an exclusive behind-the-scenes tour where you become the zookeeper. Join the animal keepers as they feed, train and care for giraffes and antelope, moving on to assist the Avian team as it works with the Serengeti's feathered inhabitants. The tour lasts 6½ hours and costs $350/person, 13 and over. Tour includes park admission.

Finally, the **Elite Adventure Tour** offers a personal, exclusive park tour, with front-of-line access to all rides, feeding a giraffe on the Serengeti Safari tour, reserved seating at shows, free bottled water throughout and lunch at the Crown Colony Restaurant – all for an extra $199.99/person (5 and over). Once

again, all tours can be booked ahead on 813 984 4043 or online at **www.buschgardens.com** You will also find a series of small-scale **animal encounters** throughout the park as the staff bring out the likes of the Asian python and the resident armadillos to meet guests.

Busch Gardens is open until 10pm for the **Summer Nights** programme (May–Aug), which features festive food and drink, live entertainment, music (including veteran rock bands like Guess Who and Grand Funk Railroad at the new Gwazi Park arena area) and DJs. There is also a huge fireworks spectacular 2–4 July. Busch Gardens' other extra programme is its annual **Howl-O-Scream** extravaganza at Halloween (late Sept–Oct). It is a separately ticketed event (c. $60/person) offering a 'new spin on horror' with various grisly goings-on and themed haunted houses, as well as the chance to ride all the big coasters at night (7.30pm–1 or 2 am). It features some imaginative shows along with all the mock-horror effects but is not advised for young children. See more at **www.howl-o-scream.com**

For a full family day out, you can also combine Busch Gardens with the next-door water park **Adventure Island** (on McKinley Drive), which is particularly welcome when it hots up (provided you plaster on the sun cream). The 25 acres/10ha of watery fun, in a Key West theme, offer a full range of slides and rides, such as the **Wahoo Run** adventure ride, a 210ft/64m plunge on the body slide **Gulf Scream** and the spiralling **Calypso Coaster**. Adventure Island is open mid-Feb to late Oct (weekends only Feb–Mar, Sep–Oct) 10am–5pm (later in high season). Tickets are $35.95 (adults) and $33.95 (3–9s), while a Busch Gardens–Adventure Island combo ticket is $65.95 and $75.95

Well, that's the lowdown on all the main theme parks, but there is still more to discover…

Katonga

7

The Other Attractions

If you think you can 'do' Orlando just by sticking to the main theme parks, think again! There is still a LOT more to discover, starting with the new-look Kennedy Space Center, which we rate as an essential place to visit these days. It will easily demand a day of your attention after its huge upgrade in 2007.

Then there are Silver Springs, Historic Bok Sanctuary and Cypress Gardens, all of which offer a taste of the more natural Florida, while Gatorland provides another great-value experience with its alligators, crocs and shows. Then you have fun venues like WonderWorks, Orlando Science Center and Ripley's Believe It Or Not. For more individual attractions, you have the unique aviation experience of Fantasy of Flight, the amazing 'sky-dive' experience of SkyVenture, plus a magnificent array of water parks. The choice is yours, but it is an immense selection. Let's start with One Giant Leap for Mankind.

Kennedy Space Center

Welcome to the past, present and future of NASA's space programme, and one of the most enjoyable, fun and downright fascinating places in Florida. The KSC has undergone huge redevelopment in recent years, culminating in 2007 with the opening of the stunning **Shuttle Launch Experience** as part of a complete overhaul of the main Visitor Complex.

This has really put the KSC among the front rank of local attractions and there is even more now to justify an all-day visit. There are 5 continually running shows (including 2 splendid IMAX films and a live theatre presentation for kids), 6 static showcases, a new children's play area, an art gallery, the captivating Astronaut Encounter and moving Astronaut Memorial, and a bus tour of the Space Center, which add up to great value. Plus there are 2 guided tours, while the **Astronaut Training Experience** and **Family Astronaut Experience** (with overnight stay) provide outstanding extras.

You enter through the futuristic ticket plaza and can spend several hours just wandering around the exhibits and presentations of the Visitor Complex itself. But, with the huge draw of its latest attraction, you should head here first and save your meandering for later on.

Kennedy Space Center

Orlando's Other Attractions

A   Winter Park
B   Downtown Orlando
C   Boggy Creek Airboat Rides
D   Port Canaveral
E   Leu Gardens
F   Warbird Adventures
G   Green Meadows Petting Farm
H   Sanford-Rivership Romance
I   Reptile World Serpentarium
J   Osceola County Pioneer Museum
K   Disney's Wilderness Preserve
L   Orlando Watersports Complex
M   Nick Faldo Golf Institute
N   Kissimmee Scenic Lake Tours

O   Richard Petty Driving Experience
P   Black Hammock Fish Camp
Q   Buena Vista Watersports
R   Dolly Parton's Dixie Stampede
S   Grand Cypress Equestrian Center
T   Horse World Riding Stables
U   Sleuth's Mystery Dinner Shows
V   Amway Arena
W   Citrus Bowl Stadium
X   Osceola County Stadium/
    Silver Spurs Arena
Y   Central Florida Zoo
Z   Sak Comedy Lab
A1 Pirates Dinner Adventure

B1 Arabian Nights
C1 Florida Eco-Safaris
D1 Disney's Fantasia Gardens Mini-golf
E1 Disney's Winter-Summerland
    Mini-golf
F1 Lake Eola
G1 Medieval Times
H1 Mickey's Backyard Barbecue/
    Hoop-Dee-Doo Musical Revue
J1 Terror in Orlando
K1 Mount Dora
L1 Dinosaur World

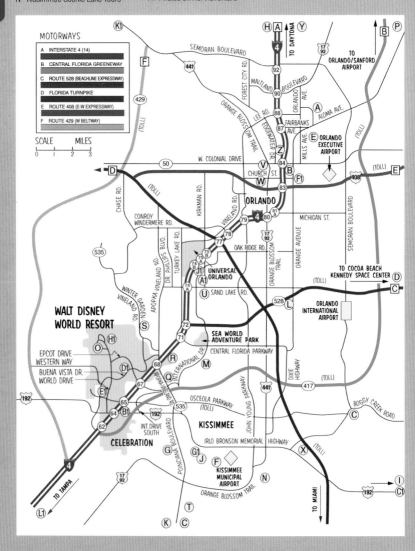

Kennedy Space Center at a glance

Location	Off State Road 405 in Titusville
Size	Visitor Complex 70 acres/28.3ha
Hours	9am–dusk (5 or 6pm) year-round; not Christmas Day or launch days
Admission	Under-3s free; 3–11 $28; adult (12+) $38. Prices do not include tax but include admission to Astronaut Hall of Fame.
Parking	Free
Lockers	No
Pushchairs	Available on a complimentary basis (with photo ID as deposit) inside the Information Center
Wheelchairs	Available on a complimentary basis (with photo ID as deposit) inside the Information Center
Top Attractions	Shuttle Launch Experience; IMAX films; Astronaut Encounter; KSC Bus Tours
Don't Miss	Apollo-Saturn V Center on Bus Tours; Astronaut Memorial; Rocket Garden; Space Shuttle Plaza
Hidden Costs	**Meals** Burger, chips and coke $8.50 3-course lunch $22.99 (MILA's Restaurant) Kids' meal $4.99 **T-shirts** $12.99–19.99 **Souvenirs** 95c–$9,000! **Sundries** Lunch with an Astronaut $15.99 children, $22.99 adults

Shuttle Launch Experience: this is the BIG one in every sense, a dramatic presentation into a real-life shuttle launch – with you on board! You enter the huge building along a life-like gantry and there is then a clever pre-show, with atmospheric lighting, dry ice (for launch 'smoke') and some clever sound and vibration effects to provide the feel of a launch. Then you enter the high-tech 'ready room' to prepare for your own blast-off into space. There are four 'capsules' of 44 passengers each, designed to look like crew cabins in the cargo hold of the Shuttle, and, once aboard you go through the full launch procedure as the vehicle moves into a near-vertical position for take-off. On the command 'Go for engine start' the fun really begins as you are at the heart of an awesome 5-minute simulation that provides all the features of a realistic launch, with the use of massive vibration generators, sound effects, cabin and seat movements and screen visuals. You get a real taste of the G-forces involved, the Rocket Booster and External Tank separations, and a moment of 'weightlessness' as you enter the earth's orbit. Finally, the cargo hold doors open above you to provide a truly awe-inspiring view. To make sure you don't get your breath back for a while, you exit the Shuttle to 'walk' back to earth via a spiral walkway surrounded by the stars and more satellite views of the planet.

Don't miss the plaques to mark every Shuttle flight – and the special

BRITTIP

All of the Shuttle Launch Experience is fully wheelchair-accessible, and there is a seat outside for potential riders to test their comfort level. For anyone wary of the full ride experience, there is a customised by-pass room where you can experience the attraction without the motion.

memorials to the tragic Challenger and Columbia missions. Even the Gift Shop is a cut above average! TTT and AAAAA.

Bus tours: the KSC's signature air-conditioned coaches depart every 15 minutes from 10am and are fully narrated throughout to provide the full overview of the Space Center. They make 3 important stops in addition to driving around much of the working areas (including the massive Vehicle Assembly Building). The first stop is the **LC39 Observation Gantry**, just 1ml/1.6km from shuttle launch pad 39A, a combination 4-storey observation deck and exhibition centre. The exhibits consist of a 10-minute launch preparation film, models and videos of a countdown and touch-screen info on the shuttle programme. Next is the **International Space Station Center**, where you can discover the full story of this amazing project and the contributions it is already making, as well as see new components being put together. A brief film tells the story of the ISSC to date, and you can walk through some full-scale replicas of the modules to feel how it is to live and work in space. Finally, you stop at the **Apollo/Saturn V Center**, one of the KSC's great exhibits, where you can easily spend 90 minutes. It highlights the Apollo missions and first moon landing with 2 impressive theatrical presentations on the risks and triumphs, a full-size 363ft/111m Saturn V rocket and a hands-on

Astronaut Training Experience

gallery that brings space exploration into sharp focus. Allow 2–3 hours to do the tour justice, but be aware that the last bus leaves the Visitor Center at 2.20 or 2.50pm, depending on time of year. AAAAA.

IMAX films: back at the Visitor Complex are the IMAX cinemas – 55ft/17m screens that give the impression of sitting on top of the action. New in 2006 was the 40-minute film **Magnificent Desolation: Walking on the Moon**, featuring rare NASA footage and narrated by Tom Hanks, that takes the audience to the lunar surface to walk alongside the astronauts. **Space Station 3-D** (narrated by Tom Cruise) is a breathtaking slice of science fact, living with the crew of the International Space Station and affording a heart-stopping look at the construction process (no extra charge for either film). AAAA.

Astronaut Encounter: this engaging feature is a daily talk and Q&A session, along with personal observations and anecdotes from various veterans of the Mercury, Gemini and Apollo programmes, plus several Space Shuttle astronauts. It is an insightful and engrossing programme, up to 3 times a day at the Universe Theater. AAAA.

Robot Scouts: this walk-through display-and-show is done in the company of Starquester 2000, your 'robot host', who explains the history of NASA's unmanned space probes in a surprising and amusing style. AAA.

Quest for Life: another film – this time narrated by *Deep Space Nine* star Avery Brooks – this provides an illuminating view of science fact rather than science fiction in the Universe Theater (alternating with the live Astronaut Encounter). AAA.

Shuttle Explorer: this exhibit allows you to inspect a full-scale replica Space Shuttle, while the recently renovated **Launch Status Center** displays shuttle and rocket history

Lunch with an astronaut

For another fully engrossing feature at the Kennedy Space Center, book its special Lunch With An Astronaut, where a small group gets to dine with the star of the daily Astronaut Encounter. The featured person gives their own special briefing, adding extra insight into their space missions, plus answers individual questions, gives autographs and poses for photos. It is $22.99 for adults and $15.99 for children at 12.15pm daily, and tickets may be bought online or by calling 321 449 4400. It's a highly worthwhile opportunity and one we strongly recommend. The buffet-style lunch is pretty good, too!

boards and rocket scale models, plus live mission briefings of upcoming launches. Free tours are available several times a day. AA.

Early Space Exploration: a clever and coherent walk-through trip into the space programme's recent past, including the *Hall of Discovery*, the *Mercury Mission Control Room* – the original consoles from America's first manned space flights – and the *Hall of History*. AAA.

Exploration in the New Millennium: this futuristic exhibit provides more appeal for youngsters, with a fun educational element from the spaceship-like *Exploring Gallery*, the *Mars Rock* exhibit and various interactive panels. AAA.

Mad Mission To Mars 2025: children in the 7–14 age range should enjoy this lively show, a mix of education and pure fun theatricals with special effects, audience participation and even its own hip-hop song, *The Newton Rap*. AAA (children only).

Other important exhibits are **Nature and Technology** (which showcases the unique balance the Center maintains with the local environment), the **Center for Space Education** (an interactive learning and teacher resource centre), the **Space Walk of Honor**, and **NASA Art Gallery** (space exhibits and artwork).

Youngsters have their own playground, the **Children's Play Dome**, which has also been upgraded recently with an exciting new range of climbing/crawling/sliding elements.

Finally, head out to see some of the hardware of space flight in the completely revamped **Rocket Garden**, which has a kids' splash fountain and an Apollo space capsule gantry, to give you the feel of that last earthbound walk before the astronauts boarded the Saturn V rocket. Free guided tours are given twice a day. Don't forget to stop at the **Astronaut Memorial**, a sombre but moving tribute to the men and women who have died in the cause of the space programme. AAA.

When you need to stop for a bite to eat, you have the choice of **MILA's Restaurant**, a full-service retro-style diner full of space race décor and with a good variety of home-cooked food, or **Orbit Food Court**, a cafeteria serving the usual range of burgers, sandwiches, pizzas and salads. You will also find the **Moon Rock Café** at the Apollo/Saturn V Center on the bus tour. There are 4 snack kiosks around the Visitor Complex, including **Space Dots** ('the ice cream of the future'), and **New Frontier**, for drinks and sandwiches, near the Universe Theater entrance. The Visitor Complex has an excellent **Space Shop** (the world's largest store for space memorabilia and gifts – enter at your peril!), the smaller **Space Shop II** by the main exit and **The Right Stuff Shop** at the Apollo/Saturn V Center.

Additional programmes

If you want to learn more about NASA past and present, **Cape Canaveral: Then and Now** is a 2-hour-plus guided journey (11.30am and 12.50pm daily) into the early days of space exploration around the older part of the facility. Highlights include the Air Force Space and Missile Museum, Mercury launch sites and

Memorial, original astronaut training facility and several active launch pads, all of which are otherwise off-limits. Photo ID is required for all visitors on this tour. The 90-minute **NASA Up Close** guided tour (10am and 1.50pm daily) in the company of a space programme expert takes visitors along the astronaut's launch-day routine, including a look at both launch pads, the landing facility, VAB and the gigantic crawler transports, as well as the International Space Station Center. Both tours cost $59 for adults, $43 for 3–11s, inclusive of KSC admission. Book online or call 321 449 4400.

Away from the main attractions, you also have the choice of the thrilling **Astronaut Training Experience (ATX)**, a full-day programme into the training required for a Shuttle mission. You progress through a sequence of simulated and hands-on preparations, with the input of various NASA veterans. The training provides a range of activities, from the multi-axis trainer and one-sixth gravity chair, to operating a full-scale Shuttle mock-up and taking the helm in Mission Control. There is an exclusive Space Center tour, with stops at the Launch Pads, International Space Station Center and NASA's Press Site. The ATX is limited to a few participants each day and you have to be at least 14 (under-18s must be accompanied by a parent). Hard-wearing clothes and athletic shoes are advised, and 'recruits' should be free of neck and back injuries. It costs $225/person (including lunch and ATX gear), but it guarantees a memorable day for 'space cadets'.

BRITTIP

Reader Les Watson advises: 'Head to Port Canaveral, and there is a recreation area called Jetty Park. It has a wooden jetty about 100yd/91m long, brilliant for watching Shuttle launches. What an experience.'

The **Family Astronaut Training Experience** is a chance for children as young as 8 to participate in a 2-day course (with an overnight stay at a nearby hotel) together with a parent. The days are spent riding realistic simulators, building and launching rockets, getting to meet some of NASA's astronauts and touring the Space Center in a unique way designed around the Family Training Experience. Finally, families will train and work together on a realistic shuttle mission to the International Space Station in the full-scale orbiter mock-up and Mission Control. The Family ATX includes hotel lodging, a 12-month pass for the Space Center, a special logo item, breakfast, dinner and lunch. It costs $675 for an adult and one child ($275 for an additional child or adult staying in the same room), and you must book in advance on 321 449 4400 or online (see below).

Getting there: take the Beachline Expressway out of Orlando (Route 528, and a toll road, see map on page 210) for about 45 minutes, bear left on SR 407 (don't follow the signs to Cape Canaveral or Cocoa Beach at this point) and turn right at the T-junction on to SR 405. The Visitor Complex is located 9mls/14km along on the right. The tours and IMAX presentations start at 10am (**www.KennedySpaceCenter.com**).

Astronaut Hall of Fame

While the Space Center tells you primarily about the machinery of putting men and women in space, the Astronaut Hall of Fame (on SR 405, just before the main entrance to the KSC) gives you the lowdown on the people involved, with fascinating memorabilia, exhibits and engaging explanations. A chronological approach divides it into 5 sections. The **Entry Experience** introduces the visions of space flight, with an 8-minute video of the astronauts as modern explorers, and leads into **Race to the Moon**, the stories of the *Mercury*, *Gemini* and *Apollo* missions

Shuttle launches

Despite the magnificent presentations at the Kennedy Space Center, the greatest thrill of all is still watching an actual Shuttle launch. You can call 321 449 4400 for information and Launch Transportation Tickets to a viewing area just 6mls/10km from the launch pad (or buy online via the Center's website). Adult tickets cost $50 ($40 for children), including admission to the Visitor Complex. There is also viewing from the Visitor Complex and nearby Astronaut Hall of Fame ($38 and $28, including KSC admission, or $17 and $13 without). But, in the event of a launch cancellation, there are NO refunds and tickets cannot be transferred to another mission. The traffic in the area is usually horrendous, too, taking anything up to 3 hours to drive from Orlando. Alternative viewing sites are available along Highway 1 in Titusville and Highway A1A through Cape Canaveral and Cocoa Beach. Call 1877 893 6272 for launch status. To be on hand to witness a shuttle launch is certainly an awe-inspiring experience.

(where you can see how incredibly *small* the first space capsules were). The **New Frontier** opens the way for Skylab and Shuttle missions, next to **Astronaut Hall of Fame**, the museum's heart and soul. The **Astronaut Adventure** room features a G-force simulator and space-walk 'chairs', moon exploration, interactive computers (try to 'land' a Space Shuttle) and Mars Mission experience.

Admission: included with Kennedy Space Center, or $17 adults, $13 3–11s on its own. Open 9am–6 or 7pm (depending on season). If you enjoyed

the KSC, try to spend a couple of hours here (it is busiest during the last few hours of the day). AAA ½.

Cypress Gardens Adventure Park

Florida's original theme park in Winter Haven (dating back to 1936) reopened in 2004 after an 18-month closure for a dramatic family-friendly makeover. The new owners (who also run the Wild Adventures Park in Georgia) have invested heavily in new rides and shows, plus a mini water park, and it now makes for a full day out (about 45 minutes south of Kissimmee).

You enter into the **Jubilee Junction** area, a mini-village of 18 shops, restaurants and cafés, plus a gazebo where you can relax, enjoy a drink and listen to some live music periodically. The shops are an eclectic bunch and include Christmas-themed **Kringles**, **Myrtle's Candle Co**, **Jubilee Mercantile** and butterfly-themed **Longwings Emporium**. The main dining choices are the down-home **Aunt Julie's Country Kitchen**, the barbecue flavours of **Backwater Bill's**, the food court choice of **Jubilee Market** and the snacks and drinks of **Gator Bites**. This is a good place to revisit when it's hot to take in **Cypress Gardens on Ice**, a vibrant ice dance show with 'A Tribute to Broadway'.

From there, you can wander the revamped **Nature's Way**, a natural animal exhibit featuring more than 150 mammals, reptiles and birds (including Tarzan, a 75-year-old alligator that once starred with

Astronaut Hall of Fame

Johnny Weissmuller in the *Tarzan* movies, a rare albino wallaby, Sheba, a female jaguar, an aviary and a petting zoo) plus 6 'Swamp Critters' educational shows daily (2 reptile, 2 birds of prey, and 2 mammal shows). **Treasure of Cypress Cove** is the area's fun-themed kids' show, full of nautical slapstick and pirate high jinks. Then you can take the **Sunshine Sky Adventure**, a massive circular arm that rises 150ft/46m for a bird's-eye view of the park. The **Cypress Cove Ferry Line** also runs from the Boardwalk on Nature's Way lakeside to the south end of the park (Fri–Sun only).

The main **Garden** section, with some of the park's original development, has been carefully brought back to life, and now looks as smart as it did in its heyday. Split into 2 areas, you have the Topiary Trail (watch out for the *The Living Garden* statue here!) and Snively Plantation, with 4 more traditional garden settings, including herb, vegetable and rose, plus the ultra family-friendly **Wings of Wonder** butterfly house. With the addition of a sparkling waterfall, the monumental topiary figures and some superb flower arrangements, this is a wonderfully eye-catching but peaceful vista, with Lake Eloise adding a sparkling backdrop. Here you will also find **Cypress Gardens Water Ski Show**, the park's long-standing tradition of spectacular water-ski stunts (including barefoot kite-flying and the traditional pyramid), several times daily.

The boat dock here (the other end of the Cypress Cove Ferry) also offers peaceful 1-hour tours of Lake Eloise on the paddle-wheel **Cypress Belle** (12.15, 2.15 and 4.15pm Mon–Thurs; 12.15 and 1.45pm Fri–Sun; $6/person; buy tickets at Cypress Landing), or stay after park closing for the wonderful **Dinner Cruise** ($29.95/adult, $21.95 children; Fri, Sun at 4pm, Sat at 4 and 6.30pm; book on the day or in advance on 863 324

© OCVB

Cypress Gardens Adventure Park

2111). The original **Botanical Gardens** feature a host of exotic plants and trees (including a massive banyan tree) and reward the casual wanderer with a myriad different paths and trails, all with a secluded feel. Boat tours of the Gardens were due to restart late in 2007, while there are free guided tours twice a day (noon and 2pm Mon–Fri) starting at the entrance to the Botanical Gardens opposite the ski stadium.

What makes this even more remarkable is that right next door is the all-new rides area of the park (41 in all), split into 2 sections (entered either via the Adventure Arcade games section or from Jubilee Junction). **Bugsville** is the new area dedicated to younger children, with 13 scaled-down rides, a huge vertical climb-and-play structure, and the Bugsville Adventure show. Also here are 3 of the biggest rides in the park, ideal for older children: classic steel coaster **Okeechobee Rampage**, the wooden coaster thrills of the **Triple Hurricane** (in memory of the storm season of 2004!), and the new **Starliner**, a vintage large-scale wooden coaster, rebuilt after being salvaged from the now defunct Miracle Strip Amusement Park in Panama Beach. Then there are 2 serious water rides, the family (spinning!) raft ride of **Storm Surge** and the single-rider **Wave Runner**, with 2 separate tubes to slide down. You will also find the **Citrus Line Railroad**, which circles both areas, and the **Grove Snacks** and **Adventure Grill** counter service cafes.

Adventure Grove is the funfair-style section, with more traditional rides like the big wheel, bumper cars, carousel, pirate ship and tilt-a-whirl. But it also boasts the unusual (and hugely enjoyable) **Disk'O**, a spinning, whirling platform, the upside-down thrills of the **Inverter**, the **Thunderbolt**, a 120ft/36.6m tower-fall ride, and **Swamp Thing**, a fast-turning suspended coaster similar to Chessington World of Adventures' Vampire. A sixth coaster, **Galaxy Spin** (of the Crazy Mouse type), completes the lineup. There is also **Sandra Dee's Diner** (for burgers, shakes and fries) and **Big Daddy's Pizza** back in the Adventure Arcade area. In truth, none of the rides would rate a TTTTT, but they do represent great fun for the 3–14 age group (and Simon's boys, then aged 6 and 8, happily spent a whole afternoon here). Stop for a show with the **Farmyard Frolics** team and (weekends only) **Road Kill Café**, where Farmer Dan and Billy Bob are looking for a few good waiters. See if you survive their 'interview' by playing Pizza Pass, Brain Freeze and Grease Fire.

Finally, at the furthest end of the park is the new 9 acre/4ha **Splash Island** water park, complete with **Paradise River**, a 1,000ft/33m lazy river feature and beach area. It boasts a 20,000sq ft/1,856sq m wave pool called **Kowabunga Bay** (inner tubes available to hire), 5 water speed slides (**Tonga Tubes**, a 40ft/12m tall twin flume complex, and **VooDoo Plunge**, a choice of 3 highly contrasting body slides; restrictions: 4ft/1.2m for all 5), and an amazing interactive children's water adventure area called **Polynesian Adventure**, with a tiki-inspired wet-play structure. All included in the one admission price (see below).

In addition, Cypress Gardens plays host to a variety of concerts each month (included with admission), from rock to jazz and country and western. Check out its website for the line-up on **www.cypressgardens.com** Christmas, 4 July and Halloween see extra fun added to the park's live entertainment, with a special **Old-Fashioned Christmas** theme for the festive season featuring dazzling lights and animated displays. There are also the **Blooms and Blossoms** festival Feb–Apr, **Taste of The South** each spring featuring traditional Southern-style menus and music around the park, and **Celebrate America** in late June and July, featuring lasers and fireworks over the lake. It is an impressive programme from this lovingly restored park.

Getting there: from Orlando, go west on I-4 to exit 55 for Highway 27 (Haines City) and south for 20mls/32km. Turn right on to SR 540 (look for signs to Cypress Gardens) and the park is 4mls/7km along SR 540, on the left. It costs $10 to park. **Admission:** 10am–6, 7, 8, 9, 10 or 11pm (depending on the season); $44.95 adults, $39.95 seniors (55-plus) and 3–9s. Ask at Guest Services for Second Day Free offer (within 6 days of your first visit). AAAA/TTT.

Triple Hurricane

Historic Bok Sanctuary

For those wishing to experience the genuine peace, tranquillity and floral ambience of Florida, there is no better recommendation than this national monument and natural garden centre at Lake Wales, 50mls/80km to the south-west of Orlando (continue past the Cypress Gardens turn-off on Highway 27). With one of the most extraordinary attractions in the state – a majestic 205ft/62.5m pink-and-grey marble carillon tower – set in 250 acres/101ha of unique parkland, this is a feast for the eyes and soul. Called the Singing Tower, the 1920s-built carillon is the centrepiece of the park and recitals are given every day at 1 and 3pm. A carillon is a series of cast bronze bells played by a keyboard or clavier. There are only around 500 in the world, and Bok Sanctuary's version consists of 60 bells (crafted in Loughborough, England) ranging from 16lb/7.2kg to nearly 12 tonnes. The park has its own resident player, or carilloneur, and his daily recitals are an undoubted highlight. The tower is also a real work of art, consisting of a neo-Gothic and art deco mix crafted from coquina stone and marble, with some stunning sculptural elements at various stages. It is wonderfully photogenic and, on a cloudless day, the combination of sight and sound is utterly captivating.

Around the tower is a wide moat, a long pond and a series of semi-formal gardens. At the highest point on

Historic Bok Sanctuary

© OCVB

Florida's peninsular (all of 298ft/90m above sea level), the view is both uncluttered and inspiring, and retains an inherent peace and solitude that persuaded the founder, the philanthropist Edward W Bok, to grant the estate to the local people almost 75 years ago. The gardens themselves provide a wildlife observatory (the Window by the Pond, where you can see up to 126 species of birds, plus reptiles, butterflies, local squirrels, turtles, rabbits and armadillos, as well as the endangered gopher tortoise), nature trails, an endangered plant exhibit, butterfly and woodland gardens, and pine forests. The acres of ferns, palms, oaks and pines create a surprisingly lush backdrop for the seasonal bursts of beautiful azaleas, camellias, magnolias and other flowering shrubs. There is even a new children's play area, plus brass rubbing and art classes.

The award-winning **Education and Visitor Center** (9am–5pm) illustrates the story of Edward W Bok (don't miss the orientation film about him and his impact on American society), his vision for the gardens, the carillon and tower architecture (with a close-up of the bells themselves), the landscape design and the ecology of Florida. The **Carillon Café** adds a pleasant opportunity for a light lunch and snacks (in the open air when it's not too hot – and there's often a pleasant breeze here), while the **Tower & Garden Gift Shop** offers some unique gift and souvenir items.

For an additional fee ($5 adults, $3 5–12s; Mon–Sat at 11am, 12.30pm, 2pm and 3.30pm, Sun at 1.30pm and 3.30pm), you can tour the **Pinewood Estate**, one of the finest examples of Mediterranean revival architecture in Florida. The 20-room mansion was built as a winter retreat for a Pennsylvania steel tycoon in the early 1930s, and has been lovingly maintained to show a slice of period opulence. With this genuine sanctuary being slightly off the beaten track yet an easy drive from Orlando (around 45–50 minutes), it makes a thoroughly worthwhile day out along with some of the other attractions of Lake Wales.

Getting there: Historic Bok Sanctuary is located off US Highway 27 on Burns Avenue. Take I-4 west to exit 55, then go south on US 27 for 25mls/40km, turn left on Mountain Lake Cutoff Road (2 traffic lights past Eagle Ridge Mall) and follow the signs.

Admission: $10 adults, $3 5–12s (under-5s free), apart from occasional specially ticketed events (mainly carillon festivals and recitals). Open 8am–6pm daily (last entry 5pm). Historic Bok Sanctuary is also an attractive wedding venue (863 676 1408, **www.boktower.org**). AAA½.

High on the list of Lake Wales' other must-see places is **Chalet Suzanne**, a wonderfully eclectic yet classy country inn and restaurant, quietly famous throughout Florida. This family-run (since 1931) delight is a 100 acre/40.5ha estate featuring 30 individual and quite charming guest rooms, a tropical sunken wedding garden, swimming pool and private lake, plus – wait for it – a soup cannery (which sent its produce to the moon)! In fact, the Chalet is such a sought-after hideaway, it has its own airstrip. Upgrades in 2006 included a new gift shop (inside the main reception), renovations to the car park, pool patio and several outbuildings, and the completion of repairs to the gardens (after the hurricanes of 2004). Its other claim to fame is its restaurant, voted one of Florida's Top 20 for more than 30 years, and a truly amazing venue. Made up of various cast-off buildings (a wing of stable here, a chicken house there) lovingly restored and melded together, the dining rooms are built on no fewer than 14 levels.

Eclectic is something of an understatement. The food is another highlight – gourmet cuisine but with a semi-set menu that barely changes year by year. Specialities include broiled grapefruit, baked sugar-cured ham, Chicken Suzanne, and its own Romaine Soup – such a favourite of Apollo 15 pilot James Irwin, he persuaded NASA to take it on the mission with them, hence it became known as Moon Soup! The set lunch is $29–39 a head ($14 under-12s), while dinner varies from $59 to $79 ($19 under-12s), depending on your main course selection (which includes filet mignon, lobster and crab thermidor). But, even if you don't stop to eat or stay in one of its remarkable Swiss-style cottage rooms ($169–229/night, plus tax), it is well worth a visit to experience the unique charm, learn the story of the Hinshaw family – and have a tour of that one-off soup cannery! Apart from anything else, a gift pack here is one of the most original souvenirs you can bring back from Florida. Call 1800 433 6011 to book (always essential) or visit **www.chaletsuzanne.com**

Getting there: Chalet Suzanne can be found just outside Lake Wales, off Highway 27 on Chalet Suzanne Road. AAA.

Head into the quaint town of **Lake Wales** and you will discover Spook Hill (where cars mysteriously roll uphill!), Grove House Visitor Center (home of Florida's natural fruit juice products – as fresh as it gets) and the quaint Museum and Cultural Center (set in a restored 1928 Atlantic Coast Line railroad station), as well as the world's sky-diving capital (from Lake Wales airport – every kind of parachuting known to man). For more info, call Lake Wales Chamber of Commerce on 863 676 3445 or visit **www.lakewaleschamber.com**

Chalet Suzanne

Silver Springs

Continuing the theme of natural attractions, we have Silver Springs, just under 2 hours' drive to the north of Orlando. This peaceful 350 acre/ 142ha nature park surrounds the headwaters of the crystal-clear Silver River. Glass-bottomed boats take you to watch the world's largest artesian springs, along with plenty of wildlife.

BRITTIP

Silver Springs and Wild Waters are both busy at the weekends, but you shouldn't encounter many queues here on weekdays, especially in summer.

Expect to have some close encounters with alligators, turtles, raccoons and lots of waterfowl, while the park also contains a collection of more exotic animals such as bears, panthers and giraffes. Five animal shows, an alligator and crocodile encounter, one of the world's largest bear exhibits, a new petting zoo, a kids' adventure playground, a tower ride and a white alligator exhibit complete the attractions. To ruin a few more illusions of the film industry, this was also the setting for the '30s and '40s *Tarzan* films starring Johnny Weissmuller (very far from Africa!).

The park's main attraction (dating back to 1878) is the **Glass-bottomed Boat Ride**, a 20-minute tour that goes down well with all the family and gives a first-class view of the 7 different springs and a host of water life. Similarly, the **Lost River Voyage** is another 20-minute boat trip down one of the unspoilt stretches of the Silver River, with a visit to the park's animal hospital. The third boat trip, the new **Fort King River Cruise**, takes you back to pioneer Florida, the Seminole wars and a reconstruction of Fort King. With sightings of native wildlife, an archaeological dig, movie set and Florida Cracker Farm, it is another gentle 20-minute historical perspective, with some storytelling from the boat captain as a bonus.

The **Wilderness Trail** (revamped in 2006/07) features a tram ride towed behind a Wrangler Jeep into a mock wilderness area populated by assorted local wildlife (including gators!). Then there are the 4 **Ross Allen Island Animal Shows**, each one lasting 15 minutes and featuring an entertaining – and occasionally hair-raising – look at the worlds of reptiles, birds (including amusing parrots, macaws and cockatoos) and non-venomous snakes. As you exit the animal shows, take time to wander **Big Gator Lagoon** and the **Crocodile Encounter** in a cypress swamp habitat, viewed from a raised boardwalk. See the largest American crocodile in captivity, the 16ft/5m, 2,000lb/900kg Sobek, as well as a collection of alligators, turtles and Galapagos tortoises (with gator feeding daily at 2.30pm). The **Florida Natives** attraction features a collection of snakes, turtles, spiders, otters and other local denizens. Here you will also find the **Non-venomous Snakes** and the **Reptiles Of The World** shows, which dispel various myths about these creatures. The **Botanical Gardens** then provide a peaceful haven in which to sit and watch the world go by. Other large-scale exhibits are the **World Of Bears**, an educational presentation including conservation information in a 2 acre/ 0.8ha spread devoted to bears of all kinds, from grizzly to spectacled and black bears, and the **Panther Prowl**, with a unique look at the endangered Florida panther and Western cougar. Both have educational presentations several times daily.

Birds Of Prey is a 30-minute show in the Silver River Showcase arena, highlighting the strengths, beauty and conservation issues of the park's collection of hawks, eagles, owls, falcons and vultures in a dramatic free-flight demonstration, while **Birds of the Rainforest** showcases the park's comical macaws and cockatoos.

Children are not forgotten, either. **The Kids Ahoy!** playland, with its centrepiece riverboat featuring slides, rides, air bounce, ball crawl, 3-D net maze, carousel, bumper boats and games, a **Carousel** and the new **Kritter Korral** (with sheep, rabbits, donkeys, llamas, pot-bellied pigs, ponies, turkeys and goats) are all big draws for the little 'uns. Older children will gravitate to the **Lighthouse Ride**, a combined carousel and gondola lift rising almost 100ft/30m above the park (and magnificently lit at night).

The Springside Mall provides an array of shops and eateries (not quite as slick as Orlando's parks), with the **Deli** offering some pleasant sandwich choices and the **Springside Café** also above average, while **Swampy's Emporium** and the **Silver Bells Holiday Store** are the best of the shopping. Silver Springs also offers a regular Concert Series at the Twin Oaks Mansion stage (included with admission) through the spring and autumn, with artists like the Spinners, Bobby Vinton and well-known country and western acts. Other special events include 4 July celebrations, themed weekends (Italian, Caribbean, Oktoberfest and Native American Festivals) Sep–Nov, and its annual Christmas **Festival of Lights** (late Nov–30 Dec, dusk–8.30pm), which features more than a million twinkling lights throughout the park, dozens of neon displays, local choirs, strolling carollers, musical stage shows, a lighted boat parade, a Holiday Buffet with all the trimmings, and, of course, Santa.

In all, you would probably want at least half a day here, with the possibility of a couple of hours in the neighbouring 9 acre/4ha water park of **Wild Waters**, which offers slides such as the Twin Twister, a pair of 60ft/18m high flumes, the free-fall Thunderbolt, the twin-tunnelled Tornado, the 220ft/67m Silver Bullet and the helter-skelter Osceola's Revenge, as well as a 400ft/122m tube ride on the turbo-charged Hurricane, a huge wave pool, and various kid-sized fun in Cool Kids Cove and Tad Pool for tots.

Getting there: Silver Springs is on SR 40 in Ocala, 72mls/116km north of Orlando. Take the Florida Turnpike (it's a toll road, see map on page 8) until it turns into I-75 and, 28mls/45km further north, go east on SR 40. Another 10mls/16km brings you to the park, just past Wild Waters on your right. **Admission:** $33.99 adults, $30.99 seniors (55+), $24.99 3–10s (under-3s free); a joint Wild Waters ticket is $36.99 and $27.99; parking $7. 10am–5pm daily (to 8.30pm for Festival of Lights season; 352 236 2121, **www.silversprings.com**). AAAA.

Gatorland

For another taste of 'real' Florida wildlife, this is as authentic as it gets and is popular with children of all ages. When the wildlife consists of several thousand menacing alligators and crocodiles in various natural habitats and 5 fascinating shows, you know you're in for a different experience. 'The Alligator Capital of the World' was founded in 1949 and is still family-owned, hence it possesses a home-spun charm and naturalism that few of its big-money competitors can match. The entrance and gift shop suffered a terrible fire in Nov 2006, but there is a temporary entry at the far end of the park until the renovations are completed in summer 2008.

Silver Springs Fort King River Cruise

BRITTIP

If you have an evening flight home from Orlando International airport, Gatorland is handy to visit on your final day. Conveniently located about 20 minutes' drive from the airport, it is the ideal place to soak up half a day.

Start by taking the 15-minute **Gatorland Express** railway around the park to get an idea of its 110 acre/45ha expanse. This costs an extra $2 but is good for multiple rides, is fully narrated (usually in amusing style) and is especially fun for kids. You also get a good look at the native animal habitat, which features whitetail deer, wild turkey and quail.

Wander the natural beauty of the 2,000ft/610m **Swamp Walk**, as well as the **Alligator Breeding Marsh Walkway,** where a 3-storey observation tower gives a close-up view of these reptiles. Do they hang around the walkway in the hope that someone might 'drop in' for lunch?

BRITTIP

If you are at Gatorland first thing in the morning, take the Swamp Walk straight away. There will be far more wildlife activity then and the peaceful ambience is quite invigorating.

Breeding pens, baby alligator nurseries and rearing ponds are also situated throughout the park to provide an idea of the growth cycle of the gator and enhance the overall feeling that it is the visitor behind bars here, not the animals. Many of the small-scale attractions have been designed with kids in mind and there is plenty to keep everyone amused. **Allie's Barnyard** is a petting zoo, while you can feed some friendly lorikeets at the **Very Merry Aviary**, and view the pink inhabitants of **Flamingo Lagoon**. Other animals to see include bats, iguanas, turtles, turkey vultures, tortoises, snakes, emus, a Florida bear and deer. However, the gators and crocs are the main attraction and it is the shows that are the real draw (though you will never find yourself on the end of a queue here). The 800-seat **Wrestling Stadium** sets the scene for some real cracker-style feats (a 'cracker' is the local term for a Florida cowboy) as Gatorland's resident 'wranglers' catch themselves a medium-sized gator and proceed to point out the animal's features, with the aid of some daredevil stunts that will have you questioning their sanity.

The **Gator Jumparoo** is another eye-opening spectacle as some of the park's biggest creatures use their tails to 'jump' out of the water and be hand-fed tasty morsels, like whole chickens! **Jungle Crocs of the World** features some of the deadliest animals of Egypt, Australia and Cuba, with authentic lairs and brilliant presentation, while the show element has its scare-raising moments as the knowledgeable guides enter the pens to tell you all about the inhabitants. The **Upclose Animal Encounters** is another amusing showcase of various creatures, from the expected snakes to less obvious cockroaches and scorpions. Great photo opportunities for brave children here!

New in 2007 was **Gator Gully**, a superb little water park area featuring numerous ways for kids to cool down, get wet and generally have lots of watery fun. The half-acre park features five different elements, including a giant jalopy with water jets for spokes and a fountain radiator, an old shack that 'explodes' with water, and giant gators with squirt guns. There is a neighbouring dry play area and chairs and tables for parents to sit back and watch their offspring expend some energy, perhaps with a drink from one of the kiosks. There is also a new **Animal Show** here, featuring some of the park's friendlier inhabitants of the furry and feathered variety, including

Gatorland

torchlight and learn more about the feeding habits of these amazing creatures – a real family treat. Bug spray is included (8.15pm summer, 6.30pm autumn and winter; $19 adults, $17 under-13s; reservations are required).

Getting there: Gatorland is on the South Orange Blossom Trail, 2mls/3km south of the Central Florida Greeneway and 3mls/5km north of Highway 192 (see map page 12). **Admission**: $22.95 adults, $14.95 3–12s (book online for a $2.50 saving). 9am–5pm (6pm summer), parking free (407 855 5496, **www.gatorland. com**). AAAA.

Fantasy Of Flight
Another wonderful and fresh alternative on the central Florida scene is this aviation attraction, which offers a 5-part adventure featuring the world's largest private collection of vintage aircraft. Even those not usually interested in aviation or the glamour of the golden age of flying should find Fantasy Of Flight fascinating.

You start by entering the **History Of Flight**, a series of expertly re-created 'immersion experiences' into memorable moments in aviation history. The entrance alone is eye-opening – along the fuselage of a DC-3 Dakota as if for a parachute drop, stepping out into a moonlit night. Then you visit set-pieces that include a dogfight over the trenches in World War I and a bomber mission with a Flying Fortress in World War II. The latter includes a walk-through of an actual B-17 as it prepares for its bombing run! Audio-visual effects and film clips enhance the experience and give everything an awe-inspiring feeling of authenticity. You exit into the **Vintage Aircraft** displays in 2 huge hangars, with the exhibits ranging from a replica *Spirit of St Louis* to a Ford Tri-Motor, an Mk-XVI Spitfire and the world's only fully working Short Sunderland flying boat. One aircraft is selected from the

a ferret called Sandy and a de-scented skunk (!), plus interruptions from one of Gator Gully's 'residents'.

Overall, Gatorland is an experience you're unlikely to get anywhere else, though encounters with these living dinosaurs may not be everyone's cup of tea. In addition, you can dine on smoked gator ribs and deep-fried gator nuggets (as well as burgers and hot dogs) at **Pearl's Smokehouse**, with excellent kids' meals at $4.99. The park is also home to hundreds of herons and egrets, providing a fascinating close-up of the nests during Mar–Aug. Gatorland is actually central Florida's largest wading-bird sanctuary and it adds an extra aspect to this user-friendly park.

Two additional programmes if you really want to get to know your gators are the exclusive **Trainer for a Day**, with the chance to work behind the scenes at the park 8am–10am, finding out what it takes to handle such dangerous animals, behavioural training and novice gator wrangling ($100 for 12s and over, includes park admission). A unique and eye-opening feature (especially if you have children) is the **Night Shine Tour**. It takes guests back into the Breeding Marsh after dark for a 1-hour tour with one of the park's senior gator experts, with torches and gator food to lure the local denizens. You can then marvel at how gator eyes shine like red beacons in the collection of more than 40 vintage planes each day as the **Aircraft Of The Day**, with a pilot holding a question-and-answer session about that plane before going on to perform an aerial demonstration over Fantasy Of Flight.

A recent addition is **Fun With Flight – For The Kid In All Of Us!**, a hands-on interactive area where guests can test their paper aeroplane-making skills in The Fly Zone, learn about the principles of lift with Bernoulli's Ball and soar though virtual-skies in **Hang In There**, a virtual-reality hang-glider and balloon simulator.

A variety of **guided tours** is given each day, with a tram tour of the restricted areas (including the Maintenance Hangar and Wood Shop, where specialists restore and rebuild wooden aircraft), a walking tour of the Backlot, and a visit to the Restoration Shop, highlighting in detail what it takes to restore and maintain these magnificent machines. Finally, **Fightertown** features 8 realistic fighter simulators that take you on a World War II aerial battle. You get a pre-flight briefing on how to handle your 'plane' (a Vought Corsair), and then climb into the enclosed cockpit to do battle with the Japanese Air Force. It's difficult, absorbing, fun and totally addictive. The whole experience is crafted in 1930s' art deco style and includes a full-service

Waldo Wright's Flying Service

diner (the excellent **Compass Rose**; 11am–3pm) and an original gift shop. There is strong Brit appeal, too, with the exhibits of both World Wars. Then there is Fantasy Of Flight's 3-hour **balloon ride** for $170 (up to 4 passengers; seasonal operations and reservations required).

Fantasy Of Flight is the brainchild of American entrepreneur and aviation whiz Kermit Weeks, and we have yet to encounter an attraction put together with more genuine affection. In fact, it is as much a work of art as a tourist attraction, and the masses have yet to discover it.

Getting there: just 20 minutes west of *Walt Disney World* on I-4 at exit 44 (Polk City), turn first right then left on SR 559 for ½ml/800m to the entrance on the left. **Admission**: $26.95 adults, $24.95 seniors (60+), $13.95 6–12s (under-6s free); 10am–5pm (closed Thanksgiving and Christmas Day), parking free (863 984 3500, **www.fantasyofflight.com**). AAAA.

Waldo Wright's Flying Service

Flying daily from the Fantasy of Flight airfield is this wonderfully authentic **biplane experience**. If you ever fancied yourself as a silk-scarf and leather-jacket-wearing flying ace, this is definitely the place for you (even if you don't, try it anyway – it's terrific fun). There are 2 distinct rides: in an open-cockpit 1929 **New Standard D-25** biplane (where the front seats can hold up to 4) for $59.95/person; or the more daring, hands-on, 2-seater 1942 **Boeing Stearman PT-17** biplane trainer, where your pilot takes you up and then lets YOU take the controls! The 30-minute experience costs $199. Both rides are fairly gentle (and just a little thrilling) as you get a slow, bird's-eye view of this pretty part of central Florida. And the way the planes seem able to turn on a wingtip gives you a deep respect for the pilots of these wonderful machines (863 873 1339, **www.waldowrights.com**).

INTERNATIONAL DRIVE

The 14½ mile/23km tourist corridor of I-Drive (see maps pages 86, 210 and 323) continues to be a fast-developing source of hotels, restaurants, shopping and, more importantly, fun. There are more than 33,000 hotel rooms, 150 restaurants and 500-plus shops, as well as 16 attractions, including 6 mini-golf courses. The **I-Ride** trolley brings it all together in transport terms and website **www.InternationalDriveOrlando.com** highlights all the options. The Official Visitors Guide has an I-Ride map and valuable money-off coupons, which you can download to get you started. There is also a hotel booking facility. Here's a look at the area's top attractions (see also Chapter 10 Orlando By Night and Chapter 12 Shopping to get the complete picture). NB: the old Brit favourite of **The Mercado** is awaiting demolition for a proposed new hotel/shopping development, but there was no timetable for this as we went to press.

BRITTIP

Ripley's, Titanic, WonderWorks and SkyVenture are all handy retreats to keep in mind for a rainy day.

Ripley's Believe It Or Not

You can't miss this particular attraction as its extraordinary tilted appearance makes it seem as though it were designed by an architect with an aversion to the horizontal. However, once inside you soon get back on the level and, for an hour or 2, you can wander through this quirky museum dedicated to the weird and wonderful.

Robert L Ripley was an eccentric explorer and collector (a real-life Indiana Jones) who for 40 years travelled the world in his bid to assemble a collection of the greatest oddities known to man. The Orlando branch of this chain features 8,900sq ft/830sq m of displays, including authentic artefacts, interactive exhibits, video presentations, illusions and music. The elaborate re-creation of an Egyptian tomb showcases a mummy and 3 rare mummified animals, while the Primitive Gallery contains artefacts from tribal societies around the world (some quite gruesome). Human and Animal Oddities, Big and Little galleries, Illusions and Dinosaurs have all received some recent updates and extra interactive elements. The collection of miniatures includes the world's smallest violin and a single grain of rice hand-painted with a tropical sunset. Larger-scale exhibits include a portion of the Berlin Wall, a two-thirds-scale 1907 Rolls-Royce built out of matchsticks and a novel version of the Mona Lisa textured from toast! **Admission**: $18.95 adults, $11.95 4–12s; daily 9am–1am (last ticket sold at midnight; 407 363 4418, **www.ripleysorlando.com**). AAA.

Titanic – The Experience

Next door to Ripley's, go back in time at the world's premier Titanic attraction. Here you can stroll through full-scale re-creations of the tragic ship's most famous rooms, including her Grand Staircase and First Class Parlour Suite. Actors in period costume portray characters like Captain Smith and Molly Brown, sharing stories of passengers and crew on a 1-hour journey aboard the most famous liner in history. The 17-room attraction also showcases an extensive Underwater Room, displaying an 8ft/2.5m replica of Titanic as she appears on the bottom of the Atlantic today, a moving Memorial Wall to the 1,523 souls who perished on that fateful night in 1912, and more than 200 artefacts and historical treasures, including memorabilia from James Cameron's blockbuster movie *Titanic*. **Admission**: $19.95 adults, $12.95 4–12s (under-4s free); daily 9am–9pm (407 248 1166, **www.titanictheexperience.com**). AAAA.

Terror in Orlando

While the fabulous Skull Kingdom closed down at the end of 2006, a new haunted house attraction arrived nearby to take its place (at 7316 International Drive, near the junction with Carrier Drive, next to Wild Jack's Steakhouse). Terror In Orlando offers a double-dose of scream-inducing frights with two contrasting maze-type attractions to explore, full of grisly goings-on, scare-riffic special effects and lurking actors who appear when you least expect them! Appearances are very deceptive here, as the narrow shop-front façade gives way to many interior secrets. *Mayhem Manor* is the full, scripted, hair-raising experience, a chance to wander the 'laboratory' of the mad Dr Morpheus Mayhem and find out what drove all his visitors insane! It's a 20-minute no-holds-barred screamfest, full of unexpected twists and turns over 2,000sq ft/186sq m of wonderfully clever mock horror, with small groups of no more than 10 taking it in turns to brave the mad Doctor's lair. *Funhouse 3-D* is a toned down version, an all-new 15-minute exercise in the weird and wacky, complete with 3-D glasses; less intense than *Manor* and more likely to appeal to a broader audience. If members of your group are not up to the former, they may well prefer to try the *Funhouse*. There is a small gift shop to peruse while you wait, and parental discretion is certainly advised.

Admission: single maze $12 adults, $10 children (12 and under), both mazes $17 and $15; noon–10pm Sun–Thur, midnight Fri, Sat, extended hours in peak season and at Halloween (407 351 4164, **www.terrorinorlando.com**). TTTT.

Fun Spot Action Park

Here's another choice for full-scale, family-sized fun, just off I-Drive on Del Verde Way (look for the 100ft/31m big wheel past the junction with Kirkman Road). The main focus is the go-karts, with 4 challenging tracks, including the max thrills of the 1,600ft/488m *Quad Helix*, the 1,000ft/305m *Conquest*, with its triple level corkscrew, the fiendish 800ft/244m *Thrasher* and the multi-level *Commander*. Then there are also bumper cars and boats, 4 daring fairground-type rides (including the jaw-dropping **Scrambler** and **Paratrooper**), an impressive 2-storey video arcade (one of the largest in Florida), 7 Kid Spot rides and a Cadet track for the little ones. This 4.7 acre/2ha park promises several hours of fun! The Oasis Snack Bar serves hot dogs, pizza, nachos, popcorn and ice-cream and the arcade games include some of the very latest. Passes are geared around children's height (above and below 4ft 4in/1.32m), with younger children getting free run of all the rides (and as a passenger on the 2-seater go-karts with an adult) and older children (and grown-ups!) having unlimited access to all the rides, go-karts and games.

Admission: Rider's Pass (2ft–4ft 4in/61cm–1.32m) $19.95, Driver's Pass (over 4ft 4in/1.32m) $29.95, seniors (55+) $14.95, Spectactor's Pass $4.95 (includes free play in upstairs arcade); 10am–11pm Sun–Thur, 10am–midnight Fri, Sat (407 363 3867, **www.fun-spot.com**). TTTT.

Outta Control Magic Show at WonderWorks

© OCVB

Magical Midway

In a similar vein, **Magical Midway** back on I-Drive (just north of Sand Lake Road) offers more go-karts, games and thrill rides (including the **Space Blast Tower**: 0–180ft/55m in 3 seconds!). New in 2006 was the amazing **StarFlyer**, a 230ft/70m tower with chair swings that lift and rotate up the full height for a dizzying view of the surrounding area as well as a stomach-churning thrill. The 2 elevated kart tracks, the double uphill corkscrew of *The Avalanche* and the sharply banked *Alpine Jump* are its signature rides (you must be at least 12 and 4ft 8in/147cm tall to drive, at least 16 to drive a passenger, and at least 5 and 3ft/91cm to be a passenger). *Fast Track*, a flat concrete track with a 25-degree bank turn (riders must be 12 and 4ft 8in/147cm to drive; single cars only) finishes the line-up. And then there are bumper cars, bumper boats, 4 more fairground-type rides and a large arcade, plus a pizza parlour and ice-cream counter.

Admission: free, then $27.95 for All Day Armband (includes unlimited go-karts and midway rides, 1 StarFlyer ride); $22.95 3-hour Armband (unlimited go-karts and midway rides for 3 hours, 1 StarFlyer ride); $15.95 Midway Armband (unlimited rides all day, 1 StarFlyer ride but not go-karts, plus 10 tokens for arcade games); individual ride tickets are $6 (go-karts), $5 (Space Blast) and $3 (other rides); must be 4ft/121cm for Space Shot, Tornado and Bumper Cars, and 3ft 6in/106cm for Bumper Boats, Kiddie Track. Open 10am–midnight daily (407 370 5353, **www.magical midway.com**). TTTT.

WonderWorks

This interactive entertainment centre is I-Drive's most unmistakable landmark, a 3-storey chamber of family fun with a host of novel elements. You bet it's unmistakable! How many upside-down buildings do you know? That's right, all the 82ft/25m edifice is constructed from the roof up! The basic premise (working on the theory that every attraction must have a story behind it) is that WonderWorks is a secret research facility into unexplained phenomena that was uprooted by a tornado experiment and dumped in topsy-turvy fashion in the heart of this busy tourist district (yeah, right!). Well, you have to give them full marks for imagination and, with the 2006 addition of high-tech virtual reality interactive exhibits, there's still a lot here, especially for the 6–12s.

WonderWorks

⚑ **BRITTIP**

WonderWorks, Fun Spot and
Magical Midway are open until
midnight in high season, long after most
theme parks are shut, so you can have a
day at the park, then let the kids loose
here for a while to tire them out!

You enter through an 'inversion
tunnel' that orientates you the same
way round as the building (look out of
the window to check!) and then
progress to various chambers of
entertaining and mildly educational
hands-on experiences that demand
several hours to explore fully. Without
ever using the words 'science' or
'museum', WonderWorks steers you
through various 'labs' of interactive
activities, including **natural disasters**
(earthquakes, hurricanes, famous
disasters and the new Global VR, a
virtual reality trek into the Desert
War); **physical challenges** (virtual
basketball and soccer, virtual 'swim
with the sharks,' Bed of Nails and the
chance to make an impression of your
entire body in 40,000 plastic nails at
Wonderwall!); **illusions** (with a
computer ageing process and 'elastic
surgery', ethnicity changer and a
'couple's morph' that combines two
faces to see what the resulting
children would look like!); and the
newest addition, **The Control Room**,
where you will find *Jet Fighters*
(virtual reality F18 fighter jet), *Shuttle
Landers* (your chance to pilot the
Discovery Space Shuttle), a Mercury
capsule mock-up, an astronaut
spacesuit and *Wonder Coaster* (a pair
of enclosed 'pods' that let you design
and ride your own coaster). Plus there
is the **WonderWorks Gift Shop** and
Café. A **Lazer Tag** game on the top
floor adds even more appeal for
youngsters. If you have already seen
DisneyQuest, WonderWorks may seem
tame, while it isn't as educational as
the Orlando Science Center, but it
also offers a fun dinner-show option,
The Outta Control Magic Comedy

Dinner Show (see page 293), with a
good value combination ticket.

Admission: $19.95 adults, $14.95
seniors (55+) and 4–11s; $4.95 for
Lazer Tag; $21.95 and $14.95 for The
Outta Control Dinner Show; $37.95
and $27.95 for WonderWorks/dinner
show combo; $22.95 and $17.95 for
WonderWorks/Lazer Tag combo; and
$38.95 and $28.95 for all 3; 9am–
midnight (407 351 8800, **www.wonder
worksonline.com**). AAA/TTT.

SkyVenture

At the junction with I-Drive and
Kirkman Road is this unmistakable
blue and yellow funnel that houses
one of the most fun 'rides' in town.
SkyVenture is billed as a 'freefall
skydiving adventure' but it is much
more than that – it is a fun, addictive,
difficult but exhilarating 'flying'
experience, with the bonus of being a
great spectator sport! The basic
premise is its huge vertical wind
tunnel, which gives you the feeling of
a freefall parachute jump, without the
hassle of having to go up in a plane,
find the nerve to jump out, wrestle
with a parachute and possibly hit the
ground too hard. The standard 1-hour
programme provides a briefing of the
hows and whys of skydiving, with a
fully qualified instructor to put you at
ease and get you suitably inspired.
Then you are provided with all the
equipment, including helmet, pads,
goggles, earplugs and flight suit, your
group of 8–12 returns to the flight
deck and you get two 1-minute
'flights' with your instructor helping
you all the way. Just watching makes
it seem all too easy but, as soon as
you hit the tunnel yourself, you
discover how fiendishly tough it is to
just 'hang' in this 125mph/200kph
column of air. However, before long it
becomes an immensely fun and
absorbing experience and it's almost
guaranteed to make you want to try
again. There is no fee for non-
participating members of your group
to watch from the observation deck,

Ron Jon's Surf Shop

and you can also turn up to see for yourself at any time (you might even see sky-dive groups practising at this popular venue).

Admission: standard flight, which includes a special certificate, is $44.95/person; add a DVD and photo CD of your flight for $25. There are discount coupons and gift certificates on its website, and you can get $8 off a second flight within 30 days with your original ticket. You can even book a Family Package for up to 5 flyers at $229.95 or a Sports Package (which doubles your actual flight time and adds a T-shirt) for $99.95. 2–11.30pm Mon–Fri, noon–11.30pm Sat, Sun (407 903 1150, **www.skyventure orlando.com**; reservations recommended). TTTT.

Ron Jon's Surf Park

Due to open (finally, after a long delay with its testing phase) in 2008 at the back of the Festival Bay mall at the top of I-Drive is this challenging and unique series of 'wave pools' that invite you to learn to surf, or improve your skills if you are already an accomplished surfer or bodyboarder. Allied with the famous Ron Jon's stores, both here and at Cocoa Beach, the outdoor $10m, 100,000sq ft/9,300sq m facility includes a Surf Shop, Ron Jon Restaurant and spectator seating that should be quite spectacular. The main Pro Pool will feature 4–8ft/1.2–2.5m waves, with ride length 180–300ft/55–90m, the Training Pool will produce waves of

up to 5ft/1.7m and there will also be lessons for novices in the 3ft/1m waves of the Bodyboard Pool. It will have a Surf School and regular demonstrations featuring some top surfing talent, so it should be well worth visiting. Prices will vary from $19.95 for the Bodyboard Pool at off-peak times (non-holiday weekdays) to $59.95 for 1 session in the Pro Pool at peak times (weekends and holidays). Call 1866 596 7873 or look up more on **www.ronjonsurfpark.com** (reservations strongly recommended).

Helicopter rides

These are another local staple, and you can go for any one of 7 tours with **Air Florida Helicopters** at 8990 International Drive (just north of the big Convention Center). A minimum of 2 people is required, and then it is just a question of whether you want the local 8-mile tour, a trip over Universal and SeaWorld, the chance to see Disney from the air or a mega 30-mile grand journey that includes flying over Windermere and the homes of the rich and famous (like Tiger Woods). Prices vary from $25 for the short flight to $355 for the longest ($20–$325 for children). There's no need to book; you just turn up and go, and they fly 10am–6pm Thurs–Sun, 10am–7pm Fri, Sat (407 354 1400, **www.airfloridahelicopters.com**).

And don't forget all the welter of mini-golf outlets up and down International Drive (see page 260).

The Holy Land Experience

Not so much a conventional attraction but right in the heart of the tourist mainstream (just outside the main I-Drive corridor) is this 15 acre/6ha 'living Biblical museum', which aims to re-create in detail the city of Jerusalem and its religious significance from 1450 BC to AD 66. Its intent is also to provide an explanation and celebration of the Christian faith.

BRITTIP

Arrive at The Holy Land Experience in time for park opening Mon–Fri and you can take part in a free 30-minute guided tour in the company of one of its Biblical Archaeologists, beginning in the Jerusalem Street Market.

All the staff are in period costume, the architecture and landscaping are impressive and the background music in both the indoor and outdoor areas is all original and suitably atmospheric (perhaps not surprising when some of the designers who worked on Universal's Islands of Adventure were also involved here). From the **Jerusalem Street Market** entrance to the **Dead Sea Qumran Caves**, **Calvary's Garden Tomb** and on to the impressive **The Great Temple** (destroyed by the Romans in AD 70), everything is portrayed in literal Biblical terms and with no little style by its presenters. **Theater of Life** shows a 25-minute film, *Seed of Promise*, which 'communicates God's master plan for redeeming mankind', while the **Wilderness Tabernacle** is a theatrical portrayal of the ancient biblical ritual, featuring the Holy Ark with lasers and pyrotechnics. The **Shofar Auditorium** houses a huge model of **Jerusalem,** which took more than a year to build and is explained in great detail several times a day in

The Holy Land Experience

the form of a guided tour. Recently opened is the **Scriptorium** centre for Biblical antiquities, another themed environment showcasing various rare artefacts in a 55-minute narrated tour that walks you through 4,500 years of history in fascinating fashion. At the end, **A Day In The Life Of A Monk** provides a look at those who transcribed the Bible during the Middle Ages.

BRITTIP

Reader Peter Crumpler suggests: 'The Holy Land is an unusual cross between a theme park and an educational tour, but I'd say British Christians would find it fascinating – both for learning more about the Bible and for seeing their livelier American cousins in action.'

Live performances include musical dramas *Moses* and *Praise Through The Ages*, dramatic vignette *The Ministry of Jesus*, and *Centurion*, another highly theatrical musical, showcasing the park's high-quality performers (look out also for *The Word Became Flesh*, a superb monologue). There is also a small kids' zone called **KidVenture**, with a rock-climbing wall, a lively 20-minute skit of *David & Goliath*, a misting station, books and games. There are 3 eateries, the **Oasis Palms Café** (featuring Goliath Burgers, Jaffa Hot Dogs and more healthy Middle Eastern fare), the **Royal Portico** for turkey legs and ice-creams and **Simeon's Corner** for hot dogs, snacks and drinks. There are also 3 major gift shops. All in all, it is a really unusual 'attraction' (though they don't call it that), a lively and literal celebration of the Christian faith, and, while it sits rather awkwardly among the main tourist fare, it is very likely to grab the interest of some.

Getting there: The Holy Land Experience can be found off exit 78 of I-4, at the junction of Conroy and Vineland Roads (just north of Universal Orlando).

Admission: $35 adults, $30 seniors (55+), $23 6-12s (save $5 if you book in advance online), parking $5; 10am–5pm Mon–Sat (closed Sundays, Thanksgiving and Christmas Day; 407 872 2272 or 1866 872 4659, www.holylandexperience.com). AAA.

Old Town, Kissimmee

In the heart of tourist Highway 192 in Kissimmee is the shopping and entertainment attraction of Old Town. The shopping element is covered in Chapter 12, but there are also many associated attractions here that are worth noting. Old Town itself features 18 out-and-out rides, from the standard and rather tame bumper cars, **Family Fun Track** go-karts ($6 single rider; $8 adult with a child) and 60ft/18m **Ferris Wheel** to the **Windstorm** roller-coaster, **Turbo Force** (a crazy version of the big wheel), the **Bull** ($10 adults, $5 children), and the immense **Old Town Human Slingshot** – a 365ft/110m bungee catapult! New in 2006 was the **Super Shot**, a free-fall-style ride of over 140ft/43m. There is a **Kids' Town** area of junior rides, plus a **Laser Tag** game, and tickets are sold separately for most rides ($1 each), but if you plan to do several, go for the Valuepak at $20 for 22 tickets or $30 for 35. There is also an All You Can Ride Wristband at $20 (children under 3ft 6in/1m) and $25 (adults), and a Ride All Day Wristband on Sundays noon–6pm for only $15. There are separate fees for Slingshot ($25; ride video

$15), bumper cars ($5), Laser Tag ($5), go-karts ($6) and Turbo Force ($10). You will also find the 2-storey **Grimm Haunted House** ($10 adults, $6.75 children), the **Hollywood Wax Museum** and the **Tower of London Experience**, a novel and well-constructed attraction with both a waxworks and a fairly grisly torture chamber replica (probably too graphic for young children). $5/person (under 5s free) or $15 for a family of 5 (2 adults, 3 children). The Old Town rides are open noon–11pm (later at peak periods; 407 396 4888, www.old-town.com). TTTT.

Right next door to Old Town is another area of rides and fun owned by Fun Spot of International Drive. The signature ride is the amazing **SkyCoaster**, a 300ft/90m tower that sends up to 3 riders at a time on a free-fall plunge that turns into a giant swing – at 85mph/136kph! A single rider flight costs $40 ($65 for 2 flights) while it is $70 for 2 riders and $90 for 3 (3pm–midnight Mon–Fri, noon–midnight Sat, Sun). Its partner ride is speed demon **G-Force**, an air-powered dual dragster car race that blasts riders 0–110mph/176kph in just 2 seconds and hits a top speed of 120mph/192kph. The ride lasts for a grand total of 11 seconds and the intense thrill costs $30 for the driver and $10 for the passenger (4pm–midnight Mon–Fri, noon–midnight Sat, Sun). Check its website at www.skycoaster.cc for coupon offers.

Old Town, Kissimmee

Another adjacent attraction is **Full Speed Race & Golf** (in the same building as the handy Brit-friendly Oasis Smokehouse Grill restaurant), which features 6 full-motion NASCAR race simulators, a racing-themed 18-hole blacklit mini golf course and a well-stocked shop. 2–11pm Mon–Fri, noon–midnight Sat, Sun; $15 for the first race, $7 for a second ($5 as a passenger), $25 for a race-golf combo (plus a free T-shirt), $50 for race-golf all day (plus free T-shirt or beverage), $10 for just golf ($8 under-13s) and $5 for a second game (407 397 7455, **www.fullspeed.cc**).

DOWNTOWN ORLANDO

The last couple of years have seen a significant move towards regenerating Orlando's city centre – the downtown area – with new offices, apartments, shops and restaurants. This has also enhanced some tourist attractions.

Orlando Science Center

Because this is Orlando, there is no such thing as a simple museum or science centre. Everything must be all-singing, all-dancing just to compete. Hence, the Orlando Science Center is more than a mere museum and far more fun than the average science centre. Here you are given a series of hands-on experiences and habitats that entertain as well as inform, and school-age children in particular will benefit greatly from it.

The Science Center has 9 main components, plus an inviting café, a night sky observatory and a giant screen cinema. **Natureworks** is an immersion-style exhibit creating a number of typical Florida habitats (with several shows like the *Circle Of Life Game* and a series of hands-on field stations). **Science City** introduces fun ways to understand and use science (including some mind-bending puzzles and challenges, notably in the Power Station), while **Dr Dare's Laboratory**

Orlando Science Center

is a new hands-on centre, with a computer guide for various experiments. **Touch The Sky** explores the science and maths behind aviation with flight simulators, interactive displays and vintage aircraft. The **Cosmic Tourist** offers a trip around our solar system with an amusing travel theme. **BodyZone** provides some fascinating insights into the human body, with an interactive element called **Measure Me**, which explores size, strength, flexibility, agility and sensory abilities, and a new 3-D film. The **Healthy Living** exhibition shows how bad habits like smoking affect a healthy body. Next door, **TechWorks** is a 4-part adventure into light, imaginary landscapes, showbiz science and a micro-world of microscopic investigation.

For those a bit too young for the educational element, **KidsTown** has plenty of junior-sized fun and games for under-8s. You'll be amazed at how much they learn in the course of having fun. **DinoDigs**: **Mysteries Unearthed** was a gift from the Walt Disney Company of their former Dinosaur Jubilee exhibit in *Disney's Animal Kingdom*. It's been re-created in the OSC as a palaeontological excavation site, complete with 8 full dinosaur skeleton replicas and some genuine fossils. The **Darden Adventure Theater** features science-themed comedy shows and demos, such as Cool Science (freezing fun with liquid nitrogen) and the audience participation of Science Spectrum.

BRITTIP

Visit the Crosby Observatory on the top of the Science Center to gaze through the region's largest publicly accessible refractor telescope. The Observatory is open Fri and Sat nights.

In addition, the centre has 2 separate programmes in the **Dr Phillips CineDome**, a 310-seat cinema that practically surrounds its audience with large-format films and digital planetarium shows (virtual tour of the universe, anyone?). It also boasts a 28,000-watt digital sound system that makes the experience unforgettable.

Getting there: the Science Center is on Princeton Street in downtown Orlando, just off exit 85 of I-4 (go east on Princeton, the Center is on your left but the multi-storey car park is on the RIGHT, see map on page 210). **Admission**: $14.95 adults, $13.95 seniors (55+), $9.95 3–11s ($9.95, $8.95 and $4.95 after 4pm Fri, Sat); parking $3.50 9am–5pm Mon–Thurs, 9am–9pm Fri, Sat, noon–5pm Sun (closed Easter Sunday, Thanksgiving, Christmas Eve and Christmas Day) **www.osc.org** AAA.

Orange County History Center

This relatively recent addition offers an imaginative journey into central Florida history, from the wildlife and Native Americans to today's tourist issues and the space programme. Again, the accent is on the interactive, with hands-on exhibits and audio-visual presentations, and it is very much a journey through time, starting outside in renovated Heritage Square, complete with cypress trees and fountains. The History Center itself is in the former 1927 Orange County Courthouse, with the foyer converted into a dome featuring more than 150 icons unique to central Florida (see how many you can identify before and after your tour).

The 4-storey adventure starts at the top with the **Orientation Theater**'s 14-minute multimedia presentation as you sit in rocking chairs on the 'front porch'. Then you visit the Natural Environment and First Peoples exhibits (12,000 years ago), before First Contact brings in the European element. Jump into the 1800s and visit a Seminole settlement, a Pioneer Cracker home (the first true 'cowboys'), hear tales of the old ranching days, the Seminole wars and learn about the citrus industry. The early 20th century brings the story of Transportation, Tourism, Aviation and the great land boom, Selling Central Florida. Witness how the region fared during the Second World War and then dramatically altered with the development of the Space Programme and the arrival of a certain Walter Elias Disney in The Day We Changed. From there, you move on to the beautifully restored Courtroom B for some more real-life Orlando history.

BRITTIP

Combine a visit to the History Center with lunch at the wonderfully eclectic Globe restaurant on the corner of Heritage Square nearby.

Finally, you reach the newest permanent exhibit, **Orlando Remembered** – a journey from the 19th century to the edge of the 21st. This tells the story beyond the theme parks and is an inclusive history of Orlando's people, uncovering secrets of the past, including significant artefacts from the collection of the Historical Society of Central Florida. An exhibit on African American history, featuring the achievements and tragedies of central Florida's African American community rounds things off, while a visit to the **Historium** gift shop completes your visit. Special large-scale exhibits scheduled for 2008 include *Kids Stuff – Great Toys From Our Childhood* (18 Jan–13 Apr) and *National Geographic*

Greatest Portraits (21 Nov 2008–18 Jan 2009).

Getting there: the History Center can be found off Central Boulevard and Magnolia Avenue downtown (exit 82C off I-4, Anderson Street, left on to Magnolia, right on to Central Boulevard, see map on page 210). Park at the Public Library multi-storey car park on Central Boulevard (History Center admission includes 2 hours' free parking if you show your ticket). **Admission**: $10 adults, $6.50 seniors (60+), $3.50 3–12s; 10am–5pm Mon–Sat, noon–5pm Sun (407 836 8500, **www.thehistorycenter.org**). AAA.

A subsidiary of the History Center is the 1926 **Orlando Fire Museum**, at 814 Rollins Avenue in Loch Haven Park. This pays homage to the professional and volunteer firemen who have served the local community, with artefacts – from helmets, lanterns and other fire-fighting apparatus to original newspaper stories about historic city fires – dating back to 1885. 9am–2pm Thur–Sat, free admission and car parking (407 898 3138 or see the History Center website above).

Staying downtown, the free **Lymmo** bus service connects the central stretch along Magnolia Avenue, from South Street to the **TD Waterhouse Center** (formerly the Orlando Arena) for sports and concerts on Amelia Street, the **Downtown Arts District and Arts Market** (on Wall Street, off Orange Avenue, every Sat 11am–9pm Oct–Apr), seasonal concerts and firework shows, plus new shops and restaurants around **Lake Eola**. The Lake itself is a beautiful area to wander around, with a park, children's play area and an extremely peaceful ambience. Children can feed the birds and fish or take a swan paddleboat ride, plus there are regular free open-air events such as concerts and storytelling.

The **Cultural Corridor** links the Downtown Arts District (which includes the Bob Carr Performing Arts Center and the Centroplex) with the Loch Haven area (where you find the Orlando Museum of Art, Mennello Museum of American Folk Art, Orlando Philharmonic Orchestra and the Orlando-UCF Shakespeare Festival), via the **Dr Phillips Performing Arts Center**, which is home of the Orlando Opera and Orlando Ballet. The 33-year-old **Orlando Ballet** is central Florida's only full-time ballet company, with national and international dancers, plus a Family Series that accommodates children. Performances in 2007 included Spartacus and Swan Lake (407 426 1733/1739, **www.orlandoballet.org**).

The Sunday **Eola Market** (formerly the Farmers Market, 9am–2pm) is another downtown focal point (at Lake Eola) with vendors now including local artisans such as glassblowers and dressmakers, as well as wonderful fresh produce. The **Thornton Park** area is currently the most happening part of Orlando, with the new Thornton Park Central (at the junction of Summerlin Avenue and Central Boulevard, just south-east of Lake Eola) offering a mix of unique boutiques and trendy restaurants. For more information, visit **www.downtown orlando.com** (click on Things To Do, and then the Downtown Historic Walking Tour link to download a neat self-guided tour of the city's more historic buildings).

Orange County History Center

© OCVB

THE WATER PARKS

Florida specialises in elaborate water parks, and Orlando boasts the very best. Predictably, Disney has the 2 most elaborate ones, but the opening of SeaWorld's Aquatica park in spring 2008 should provide real competition, while Universal-owned Wet 'n Wild is also adept at providing hours of watery fun. They adopt a variety of styles that owe much to the flair of the theme park creators, and are truly imaginative for both the rides and the imagery around them. All require at least half a day of splashing, sliding and riding to get full value from their rather high prices. Lockers are provided for valuables and you can hire towels.

Disney's Typhoon Lagoon Water Park

When *Typhoon Lagoon* opened in 1989, it was the biggest and finest of Florida's water parks. And, although it has since been superceded, in high season it is still the busiest, so be prepared for more queues. *You should definitely arrive ½ hour early if possible as entry often begins before the official opening hour.* The park's 56 acres/ 23ha are spread out around the 2½ acre/1ha lagoon fringed with palm trees and white-sand beaches. It is extravagantly landscaped and the walk up Mount Mayday, for instance, provides a terrific overview as well as adding scenic touches such as rope bridges and tropical flowers. Sun loungers, chairs, picnic tables and even hammocks are provided to add to the comfort and convenience of restful areas like Getaway Glen. However, you need to arrive early to bag a decent spot.

BRITTIP
While water parks provide a great way of cooling down, it is easy to pick up a 5-star case of sunburn. So don't forget the high-factor waterproof sun cream.

The park is overlooked by Mount Mayday, on top of which is perched the luckless *Miss Tilly*, a shrimp boat that legend has it landed here during the typhoon that gave the park its name. Watch for the water fountains that shoot from *Miss Tilly's* funnel at regular intervals, accompanied by the ship's hooter, which signal another round of 6ft/1.8m waves in the **Surf Pool** (you can hire inner-tubes to bob around on or just try body-surfing). Circling the lagoon is **Castaway Creek**, a 3ft/1m deep, lazy flowing river that offers the chance to float happily along on rubber tyres.

BRITTIP
Want to learn to surf? Typhoon Lagoon now offers Surfing School 2 hours before park opening every day. Call 407 939 7529 in advance to book at $140/person.

The series of slides and rides are all clustered around Mount Mayday and vary from the breathtaking body slides of **Humunga Kowabunga**, which drop you 214ft/65m at up to 30mph/48kph down some pretty steep inclines (make sure your swimming costume is securely fastened!) to Ketchakiddee Creek, which offers a selection of slides and pools for all youngsters under 4ft/122cm. In between, you have the 3 **Storm Slides**, body-slides that twist and turn through caves, tunnels and waterfalls, **Mayday Falls**, a wild 460ft/140m single-rider inner-tube flume down a series of banked drops, **Keelhaul Falls**, a more sedate tube ride that takes slightly longer, and **Gangplank Falls**, a family ride inside rafts that take up to 4 people down 300ft/90m of mock rapids. The imaginative (but chilly) **Shark Reef** is an upturned wreck and coral reef, which you can snorkel around among 4,000 tropical fish and a number of real, but harmless, nurse sharks. Those who aren't brave enough to dive in can still get a close-up through the underwater portholes of the sunken ship. The Reef is closed during the coldest months. Substantial queues build up here from late morning, so do this early.

The newest area is **Crush 'n' Gusher**, a fabulous trio of 'water-coaster' tube rides, plus a large heated pool with zero-depth entry (great for toddlers). It also has an extensive sandy beach, which makes it a great place to bag a spot in the sun. The 3 different slides feature tubes for 2 or 3 riders at a time that whoosh you down AND up several inclines before dropping you into the pool with a significant splash. This is also busy from midday on. There are health and 4ft/122cm height restrictions on Humunga Kowabunga and Crush 'n' Gusher (not suitable for anyone with a bad back or neck, or expectant mothers). Keeping out of the sun can also be a problem as there's not much shade, but a quick plunge into Castaway Creek usually prevents overheating.

BRITTIP

'Buy a disposable waterproof camera to tie around your wrist when you visit the water parks. We bought one cheap at Wal-Mart and have some lovely photos from *Typhoon Lagoon*,' says reader Judith Bingham.

For snacks and meals, **Lowtide Lou's** and **Let's Go Slurpin'** both offer a bite to eat and drinks, while **Typhoon Tilly's** and **Leaning Palms** serve a decent mix of burgers, sandwiches, salads and ice-cream. Avoid main mealtimes here if you want to eat in relative comfort. You can bring your own picnic (unlike the main theme parks), which you can eat in special scenic areas (but no alcohol or glass containers). You CAN'T bring your own snorkels, inner-tubes or rafts, but snorkels are provided at Shark Reef and you can hire inner-tubes for the lagoon. If you have forgotten a sunhat or bucket and spade for the kids, or even your swimsuit, they are all available at **Singapore Sal's**.

© Disney

Disney's Blizzard Beach

To avoid the worst of the summer crowds (when the park's 7,200 capacity is often reached), Monday morning is the best time to visit (steer clear of weekends at all costs), and, on other days, arrive either 30 minutes before opening or in mid-afternoon, when many decide to dodge the daily rainstorm. Early evening is also extremely pleasant when the park lights up.

BRITTIP

As the busiest of the water parks, Typhoon Lagoon can hit capacity quite early in the day in summer. Call 407 824 4321 in advance to check on the crowds.

Getting there: on Buena Vista Drive, ½ mile/800m from *Downtown Disney* (see map on page 72). **Admission**: $39 adults, $33 3–9s (under-3s free); included with Premium and Ultimate tickets; parking free; daily 9am (10am off-season)–dusk. TTTT/AAAAA.

Disney's Blizzard Beach Water Park

Ever imagined a skiing resort in the middle of Florida? Well, Disney has, and this is the wonderful result. This water park opened in 1995 and is still the largest, with all 66 acres arranged as if it were in the Rocky Mountains rather than the subtropics! That means snow-effect scenery, Christmas trees and waterslides cunningly converted to look like skiing pistes and toboggan runs. Main features are **Mount Gushmore**, a 90ft/27m mountain down which all the main slides run, including the world's tallest free-fall speed slide, the terrifying 120ft/37m **Summit Plummet**, which rockets you down a 'ski jump' at up to 60mph/97kph, **Tike's Peak**, a kiddie-sized version of the park's slides and a mock snow-beach, and **Ski-Patrol Training Camp**, a series of slides and challenges for pre-teens. **Melt-Away Bay** is a 1 acre/0.4ha pool fed by 'melting snow' (actually blissfully warm), and **Cross Country Creek** is a lazy-flowing ½ mile/800m river round the whole park that also floats guests through a chilly 'ice cave' (look out for the ice-water waterfalls!).

A ski chair-lift operates to the top of Mount Gushmore, providing a magnificent view of the park and surrounding areas. Don't miss the outstanding rides here – **Teamboat Springs**, a wild, family inner-tube adventure and arguably the best of all the water rides; **Runoff Rapids**, a choice of three tube plunges; the **Snow Stormers**, a daring head-first 'toboggan' run; and **Toboggan Racers**, which gives you the chance to speed down the 'slopes' against 7 other head-first daredevils. All 4 provide good-sized thrills without overdoing the scare factor. The **Downhill Double Dipper** is 2 side-by-side slides that send you down 230ft/70m tubes in a race timed on a big clock at the bottom, with a real jolt half-way down! For those not quite up to the immense Summit Plummet, the wonderfully named **Slush Gusher** is a slightly less terrifying body slide. There is a 'village' area with a **Beach Haus** shop and **Lottawatta Lodge** fast-food restaurant (pizzas, burgers, salads and sandwiches), offering diners a grandstand view of Mount Gushmore and Melt-Away Bay beach. Snacks are also available at **Avalunch** (ouch!), the **Warming Hut**, **Polar Pub** and **Frostbite Freddie's Frozen Refreshments**.

Getting there: just north of *Disney's All-Star Resorts* off Buena Vista Drive (see map on page 72). **Admission**: $39 adults, £33 3–9s (under-3s free); included with Premium and Ultimate tickets; parking free; daily 9am (10am off-season)–dusk. TTTTT/ AAAAA.

Adjacent to *Disney's Blizzard Beach* are the amazing **Winter Summerland Miniature Golf Courses** (where Santa's elves hang out!), with 2 wonderfully elaborate courses that provide children with a great diversion. Watch out for a riot of visual gags, as well as some tricky mini-golf.

Wet 'n Wild

If Disney scores highest for scenic content, Wet 'n Wild, the world's first water park in 1977, goes full tilt for thrills and spills of the highest quality, with its 2 newest rides also being highly sophisticated. This park is certainly going to test your swimsuit material to the limit!

Wet 'n Wild is one of the best-attended water parks in the country, and its location in the heart of I-Drive makes it a major draw. Consequently, you will encounter some crowds here, though the 15 slides and rides, **Lazy River** attraction, elaborate kids' park (with mini versions of many of the slides), **Surf Lagoon**, restaurant and picnic areas manage to absorb a lot of punters before queues develop. Waits of more than ½ hour at peak times are rare, but it is busy at weekends and throughout July.

Kids' Park Lazy River

🇬🇧 BRITTIP

The Kids Park at Wet 'n Wild was built especially for those under 4ft/122cm tall – right down to having the only junior wave pool in the world.

You are almost spoilt for choice of main rides, from the highly popular group inner-tube rides of the **Surge** and **Bubba Tub**, to the more demanding **The Flyer**, **The Blast** and **Mach 5** (head-first on a mat-slide) on to the high-thrill factor of the 2-person **Black Hole** (like *Magic Kingdom*'s Space Mountain, but in water!). For body-slides, try the high-energy plunge of **The Storm** and the sheer terror of **Der Stuka** and **Bomb Bay**. The latter duo are definitely not for the faint-hearted. Basically, they are 276ft/23m body-slides with drops as near vertical as makes no difference. Der Stuka is the straightforward slide, while the Bomb Bay adds the extra terror of being allowed to free-fall on to the top of the slide. For some reason, only a minority of the park's visitors pluck up the courage to try it! There are 4ft/122cm height restrictions on Bomb Bay and Der Stuka, while older kids can enjoy the huge, inflatable **Bubble Up**, which bounces them into 3ft/1m of water.

Our favourites? We like the thrilling toboggan-like **Flyer**, which takes 4 passengers in 8ft/2m in-line tubes down more than 450ft/137m of banked curves and straights, and **The**

Brain Wash

Blast, with its 1- or 2-passenger tubes that surprise you with sudden twists and turns, explosive pipe bursts and drenching waterspouts, leading to a final waterfall plunge. And don't miss **The Storm**, a pair of identical circular slides billed as 'body coasters' – the enclosed tubes (complete with storm sound and light effects) send the rider plunging into a circular bowl, around which they spin at high speed before landing in the splash-pool below.

New in 2005 was **Disco H2O**, a superbly themed family raft ride that plunges down an enclosed tube into a wildly swirling 'disco bowl' (featuring lights and a mirror ball!) before spitting you out through a waterfall. It is all accompanied by 1970s-style music and commentary to add to the fun. This draws big queues from midday to late afternoon, though. Its latest attraction (May 2007) is **Brain Wash**, a 65ft/20m funnel ride that sends riders on 2-, 3- or 4-person tubes down a long, enclosed flume into a huge swirling funnel that washes the tube wildly back and forth before setting it up for the final splashdown.

For those under 4ft/122cm, the recently renovated **Kids Park** has a full range of junior-sized slides, plus a new sandcastle structure with 2 semicircular waterslides and a giant bucket that fills and tips up at regular intervals. Uniquely, the children can use tubes, beach chairs and tables designed specifically for their height.

The neighbouring lake is also part of the fun (though not in chilly winter and spring), adding the options for cable-operated **Knee Ski**, **Wake-Boarding** and (for a nominal fee) the **Wild One** (large inner-tubes tied behind a speedboat). Alternatively, take a breather in the slow-flowing Lazy River as you float past palms and waterfalls, or abandon the water altogether for one of several picnic areas (though they can be crowded). The energetic can play beach volleyball. Lockers, showers and tube and towel rentals are all available; if you bring your own floating equipment, you must have it checked by the lifeguards. For food, **Bubba's Bar-B-Q** serves chicken, ribs, fries and drinks, the **Surf Grill** features burgers, hot dogs, chicken and sandwiches and another 7 snack bars offer similar fast-food fare, including a pizza bar. You can also bring your own picnic, but not alcohol or glass containers.

Getting there: Wet 'n Wild is ½ml/ 800m north of I-Drive's junction with Sand Lake Road at the intersection with Universal Boulevard (see map on page 12), and just off exit 75A and 74B of I-4. **Admission**: $36.95 adults, $30.95 3-9s (under-3s free) (included with Orlando FlexTickets). Tube rentals are $4 ($2 deposit), towels $2 and lockers $5 ($2 deposit), or $9 for all 3 ($4 deposit); parking $8; open all-year-round (with heated pools in the cooler months) from 9am in peak periods (10am at other times) until variously 5, 6, 7, 9 or 11pm (**www.wetn wildorlando.com**). TTTTT/AAA.

Aquatica by SeaWorld

Orlando's newest and arguably most eye-catching water park is due to open in March 2008, and we are expecting great things from what we have seen of the plans and the construction through 2007. Aquatica will be a 59-acre mix of lively, colourful theming, lush landscaping, innovative rides, crystal-blue rivers, iconic architecture (inspired by the Maori culture of New Zealand), animal encounters and unique features (like personal food and beverage service to your sun-lounger!). It is designed to have a fun,

South Seas feel, especially with its dolphins, tropical fish and other creatures, and it should appeal to the widest possible audience.

The basic line-up alone is mouth-watering: 36 waterslides, 6 rivers and lagoons, more than 80,000sq ft/ 7,432sq m of beach area and numerous small animal features (including kookaburras, anteaters and iguanas) in walk-around interaction opportunities, in addition to the big-scale aquatic encounters. Then, when you explore the detail, it *really* starts to look amazing.

The park's signature attraction will be the **Commerson's Dolphin Slides**, a body-slide that plunges riders down 300ft/91.5m of clear tubes and *through* a lagoon of playful, black-and-white Commerson's dolphins. That is followed by not 1 but 2 **Wave Pools**, side-by-side lagoons that operate independently or together to create 9 different wave patterns, from crashing 5ft/1.5m waves to gently rolling surf, with 860,000 gallons of water! The pools will front the huge, wide sandy **Beach**, which will be dotted by personal cabanas (for hire) and with beachside waiter service. The **Lazy River** is a gentle circuit of much of the park, with the highlight coming as you drift through a 10,000-gallon grotto filled with thousands of colourful fish and a spectacular underwater view of the dolphins. The **Adventure River** is a more dynamic experience, zipping along 1,500ft/

An artist's impression of the new Aquatica

457m of rapids and past geysers and waterfalls with a brisk current. The more adventurous will want to try the **Eight-Lane Racer**, which sends riders down a 300ft/91.5m slide, in and out of tunnels and around a 360-degree turn to the finish line, and the **Triple Drop Ride,** offering a hair-raising raft journey down a 6-storey, 250ft/76m-long tube, with a moment of 'weightlessness' down each of those 3 drops! More brain-scrambling action is the feature of the **Bowl Ride**, twin tubes that send body-sliders spinning into a pair of giant bowls before splashing them through a tunnel and into the pool below.

More family-orientated adventures are provided by the **Family Raft Ride**, with a 600ft/183m splash down 6 storeys of rafting fun, and the **Double Raft Ride**, with guests teaming up on double inner-tubes and taking a dipping, swirling adventure down AND up 4 50ft/15m slides, with highly banked curves, tunnels and water curtains. There is then a humongous **Family Play Area** – the world's largest interactive water playground – with an elaborate 60ft/18m 'rain fortress' offering kids the chance to zoom around on family slides, blast water cannons, splash in a 15,000sq ft/1,393sq m pool and generally enjoy a host of watery special effects. Even toddlers have their own area, with a separate **kiddie pool** featuring specially built rafts and pint-size tubes for little 'uns so they can still slide with mum and dad.

On top of all that, there will be 2 full-service restaurants, snack bars, kiosks and the usual Anheuser-Busch hospitality, all with a high-quality feel and eager-to-please style. The entire park is also designed to limit wait times and provide easy access to the rides, attractions and restaurants. When you add in the immense amount of landscaping – more than 2,500 tree types, including monkey puzzle trees from Chile and silk oaks from Australia, 3.1million pounds of sugary sand, rock formations and grottoes of rich tropical flowers – the high level of personal service (borrowing from its Discovery Cove park) and the unique elements provided by the various animals – from macaws to porcupines – you have a truly unique and captivating set-up. Personally, we can't wait for it to open and we count on being among the first in line!

Getting there: Aquatica is across the road from SeaWorld on International Drive, exit 71 or 72 off I-4. **Admission**: advance pricing $45 adults, $36 3-9s; included on Orlando FlexTicket (with Universal, SeaWorld and Wet 'n Wild) and new 3-Park Adventure Ticket (with SeaWorld and Busch Gardens); hours to be confirmed (407 351 3600, **www.aquaticabyseaworld.com)** TTTTT/AAAAA (expected).

So that sums up the large-scale attractions on offer, but now let's explore some alternatives to the mass-market experience…

An artist's impression of the Dolphin Slide

8 Off the Beaten Track

or When You're All Theme-Parked Out

Orlando's main attractions are undoubtedly a lot of fun, but they can also be extremely tiring and you may well need a break from all the hectic theme park activity. Or you may be visiting again and looking for a different experience. If either is the case, this chapter is for you.

Hopefully, you will already have noted the relatively tranquil offerings of Silver Springs and Historic Bok Sanctuary in the previous chapter but, to enhance your view of the area further, the following are all guaranteed to take you off the beaten tourist track. This chapter could easily be subtitled 'A Taste of the Real Florida', as it introduces the towns of Winter Park, Disney-inspired Celebration and Mount Dora, plus the natural delights of Osceola and Seminole counties, the local state parks, day-trips, eco-tours and sports.

Winter Park

Foremost among the 'secret' hideaways is this elegant northern suburb of Orlando, little more than 20 minutes' drive from the hurly-burly of I-Drive yet a world away from the relentless commercialism. It offers museums and art galleries, fabulous shopping, numerous restaurants, pleasant walking tours, a delightful 50-minute boat ride around the lakes and, above all, a chance to slow down.

The central area is **Park Avenue**, a classy street of restaurants, fine

shops, 2 museums and a wonderfully shaded park. At one end of the avenue is Rollins College, a small but highly respected arts education centre that houses the recently beautifully refurbished **Cornell Fine Arts Museum**, with the oldest collection of paintings, sculpture and decorative arts in Florida (10am–5pm Tues–Sat, 1pm–5pm Sun, closed Mon and main holidays; admission $5) and the **Annie Russell Theater** (**www.Rollins.edu**).

The **Morse Museum of American Art** is a must for admirers of American art pottery, American and European glass, furniture and other decorative arts of the late 19th and early 20th centuries, as it includes one of the world's foremost collections of works by Louis Comfort Tiffany. The dazzling chapel restoration from the 1893 Chicago World Expo is now on display in its original form for the first time since the late 19th century and is worth the entrance fee alone (as are its special Christmas exhibitions and periodic family programmes). The museum is open 9.30am–4pm Tue–Thurs, Sat; 9:30am–8pm Fri (Sept–May); 9:30am–4pm (June–Aug), 1–4pm Sun; admission $3, under-12s free, plus free admission 4–8pm every Fri Sep–May (**www.morsemuseum.org**).

The **Albin Polasek Museum and Sculpture Gardens** is worth a look for culture buffs and for the serene setting devoted to this Czech-American artist. It is also a superb setting for a wedding. 10am–4pm

Tues–Sat, 1–4pm Sun (closed July and Aug); $5 adults, $4 seniors, under-12s free (**www.polasek.org**).

The **Scenic Boat Tour** (started in 1938) is located at the east end of Morse Avenue and offers a charming, narrated 12ml/19km tour of this beautiful area. It takes you around the lakes and canals, giving a fascinating glimpse of some stunning houses, boat houses and lakeside gardens (property prices in the area start at around $1m and several top $5m!). Tours run 10am–4pm daily and cost $10 for adults and $5 for children 2–11, and it is one of the most relaxing hours you can spend in Orlando (**www.scenicboattours.com**).

You can take the **Park Avenue Walking Tour**, with free maps provided by the Chamber of Commerce on New York Avenue, while the shops of Park Avenue are a cut above most. And, while you may find the prices equally distinctive, just browsing is an enjoyable experience with the charm of the area highlighted by the friendliness hereabouts. For shops both unique and fun, look out for **Park Promenade Jewelers**, **Ten Thousand Villages** (international arts and crafts), **Bebe's** (children's clothes) and **The Doggie Door** (for pets). Also look for **Vino!**, **Olive This Relish That** (a wonderful gourmet food store with Mediterranean specialities), **Jacobson's** (clothing) and **Nicole Miller** for women, plus **Peterbrooke Chocolatier**. Regular pavement craft fairs and art festivals add splashes of colour to an already inviting scenario, plus live jazz in Central Park once a month on Sundays in summer.

Leu Gardens

© OCVB

In addition to **Park Plaza Gardens**, which specialises in Continental cuisine by local celebrity chef Justin Plank, you can sample French, Italian and Thai cuisines, among others. **Rocco's Italian Grill** is an exceptional authentic Italian choice, created by well-known restaurateurs Rocco Potami and Enrico Esposito, while **310 Park South** offers the epitome of elegant, European café culture. New choice **Beluga** – 'Seafood, Martinis, Music' – is getting rave reviews for its fresh fish and fine steaks. You can also try the pavement bistro of **Briarpatch**, the 5-star French fare of **Jardins du Castillon** (wonderfully romantic) or the Italian style of **Pannullo's**. Street parking usually allows 3 hours free, but the SunTrust Building on the corner of Comstock and Park Avenue is a better option. Keep an eye out for the **Sidewalk Art Festival** in March and **Autumn Art Festival** in October, while the **Sunday Eola Market** (9am–2pm) is equally colourful (**www.winterpark.org** and **www.parkave-winterpark.com**).

Another Winter Park highlight is **Kraft Azalea Gardens** on Alabama Drive (off Palmer Avenue at the north end of Park Avenue), 11 acres/5ha of shaded lakeside walkways, gardens and hundreds of magnificent azaleas. The main focal point, the mock Grecian temple, is a beautiful setting for weddings. To get to Winter Park, take exit 87 from I-4, Fairbanks Avenue. Turn right on to Fairbanks and head east for 2mls/3km and turn left where it intersects with Park Avenue. Midway between Winter Park and downtown Orlando is another botanical gem, **Leu Gardens**, a 50 acre/20ha retreat featuring formal gardens, peaceful walks and a boardwalk overlooking Lake Rowena. **The Leu House Museum** is open 10am–4pm (closed in July) with tours every 30 minutes (last tour 3.30pm). The gardens are open daily 9am–5pm (8pm in summer); $5 adults, $1 under-13s (free 9am–12 noon Mon). It is on the corner of Forest and

Blue Heron Cruises, Mount Dora

Nebraska Avenues, via Mills Avenue and Princeton Street from exit 85 on I-4 (**www.leugardens.org**).

Mount Dora

Another of Florida's hidden gems is this charming town just 30mls/48km north-west of Orlando on beautiful Lake Dora. A day here is a real breath of fresh air, and you can enjoy its unique mix of pleasant antique shops, speciality boutiques, restaurants, bars, inns and boat tours. Aficionados of lawn bowls will find a thriving club here, too! Mount Dora is also renowned as a festival city, with 17 main annual galas. Visit **www.mountdora.com** to see if there is one during your visit (**4 July** and **Christmas** celebrations are especially notable, while the **Antique Boat Show & Heritage Festival** each March is one of Florida's finest).

Start by taking the **Mount Dora Trolley** from the Lakeside Inn, a 1-hour narrated trundle around the streets ($10.75 adults, $8.75 2–13s), giving you a good feel for one of the 'Top 100 Great Towns of America', and a former key stop on the now-defunct Florida railroad. Then take a stroll round the compact centre, which is full of quaint shops, cafés and bars. Antique hunters are spoiled for choice but should definitely check out the unique **Pak Ratz** and extensive **Village Antique Mall**, with more than 80 individual vendors. **Uncle Al's Time Capsule** is a must for all fans of movie and celebrity

memorabilia (especially autograph hunters as owner Al Wittnebert features regular celebrity signings), while other unique stores include a **Walk In The Woods** (for clothing and Crocs shoes), **The Clockmaker Shoppe** and **Li'l Guys and Dolls**. The town even boasts its own winery, the **Ridgeback Winery**, which offers onsite tastings of its handcrafted fruit wines.

Your stroll should also take in **Royellou Museum** (the former town jail), named after the resident postmaster's children – Roy, Ella and Louis! – which displays more (free) local history, while classic car fans should visit the **Museum of Speed**, a constantly changing homage to high-powered American sports cars of yesteryear (plus other memorabilia like vintage juke boxes and Coca-Cola® machines), in a 6,000sq ft/600sq m showroom. Look out especially for the 1966 Shelby-Mustang GT-350 (1 of only 11 built). Mon–Fri 10am–5pm; $9/person (no under-14s); 352 385 1945, **www.classicdreamcars.com**

Then, when you need a leisurely lunch, **Palm Tree Grille**, **The Gables** (with its Victorian garden setting), the charming **Goblin Market** and **5th Avenue Café** are all good choices among several dozen eateries. For great pastries and cheesecake, call in at **Sunshine Mountain Bakery,** while **Mount Dora Coffee House** is the place to stop for coffee and the **Windsor Rose** is a genuine English tearoom. For something a bit stronger, **Maggie's Attic** is a fabulous wine bar (and an equally good gift shop) and there are several notable pubs – try **Al E Gator's** (!), **Retro Winery and Bistro** or the unusual Icelandic flavour of **The Frosty Mug**. All the above also offer dinner, but our choice – especially if you can get here before the sun goes down – is **Pisces Rising**, a beautiful Key-West-themed restaurant, with fresh, stylish decor, a charming outside Tiki-bar, another even more authentic interior bar – and a grandstand view of sunsets over Lake Dora. The food is excellent, too, with fresh Florida seafood and great steaks, plus an impressive wine list (352 385 2669, **www.piscesrisingdining.com**).

Another Mount Dora feature is its fine selection of B&B inns (a more upmarket, boutique choice than the UK). With more than a dozen to choose from, the award-winning **Magnolia Inn** is worth a look (347 East 3rd Avenue), along with the **Grandview Bed & Breakfast** (442 East 3rd Avenue). The **Heron Cay Lakeview B&B** (495 Old Highway 441) is another good choice, but you certainly shouldn't leave without visiting the **Lakeside Inn**. On the National Register of Historic Places, this 123-year-old hotel embodies the South's genteel charm and rewards a stroll of its grounds and public rooms. A favourite retreat of former US President Calvin Coolidge in the 1930s, it retains an air of refined quality, notably in the distinctive **Tremain's Lounge** and distinguished **Beauclaire Dining Room** (great Sunday Brunch). If nothing else, you should stop at the lovely coffee lounge, **La Cremerie Inc**, for a drink, pastry or ice-cream (352 383 4101, **www.lakeside-inn.com**).

To explore this area of mid-Florida further, **Premier Boat Tours** operates from the Lakeside Inn on the *Captain Doolittle* for a fascinating 1½–2 hour narrated tour of the lakes and the wonderfully scenic Dora Canal, lined by dense cypress trees and said by one of America's greatest writers, to be 'the most beautiful mile of water in the world'. As well as the inevitable gators, you may see raccoons, turtles, otters, birds of prey, waterfowl and other nesting birds along this unique waterway. Narrated 2-hour tours go twice daily at 10am and 2pm Mon–Fri, and 11am and 2pm Sat, Sun; $20 adults, children reduced prices; Sunset Tours $10/person Fri–Sat.

Pontoon boats, jet-skis, canoes and bikes are available for rental by the hour or full day (call 352 434 8040). Premier also operates some lovely lunch cruises and adventure outings with **Blue Heron Cruises** and **Heritage Lake Tours** from the neighbouring town of Tavares; $15 adults, children reduced prices for 90-minute fully narrated wildlife cruises at 10am, 1pm and 3pm Mon–Fri (1pm and 3pm Sun). For details, call 352 343 5608 or visit **www.florida-secrets.com/lake_county_tours.htm**

The **Inland Lakes Railway** is another way to explore this area. Choose from the 75-minute Herbie Express from Mount Dora to Tavares, Wed–Sun (1pm and 3pm, plus 11am Sat; $12 adults, $8 3–12s); the Magnolia Sun Lunch Train, a 1¾ hours journey from nearby Eustis to Tavares, every Sat at 12.45 with a set lunch ($32/person; reservations required); and the fine Southern Heritage Dinner Train every Sat at 5.15pm, a 2½-hour round trip from Eustis with dinner in a vintage 1948 dining car ($55; 352 589 4300, **www.inlandlakesrailway.com**).

Getting there: Mount Dora is on US Highway 441 north-east of Orlando. Take the (toll) Florida Turnpike to exit 267A for the (toll) Western Beltway (429), and the Beltway north to its junction with 441, from where Mount Dora is 10mls/16km further north. For more information, call the excellent **Mount Dora Chamber of Commerce** on 352 383 2165 or visit **www.mountdora.com**. And you should definitely call in at its visitor centre at 341 Alexander Street.

Celebration

In 1994, the Walt Disney Company set out to create a 'new urban' neighbourhood, a model community with strong traditional values and a friendly, welcoming spirit. The result was Celebration, where picture-perfect Victorian homes mingle with smart, well-kept townhouses surrounding a charming array of

A Brit of all right!

When owners Mark and Penny made the move to Celebration, they brought with them an innate knowledge of what people look for in a tea room and how to make guests feel like family from the moment they walk through the door. They also brought a wealth of memorabilia that **Sherlock's** proudly displays on the walls. Best of all, their dedication to doing things the proper way shows, down to the smallest touches. Sherlock's even blends its own teas, so you know you're getting impeccable quality and full, satisfying flavour. Be sure to inquire about the Royal Butler line of wines, selected by Paul Burrell (former butler to Diana, Princess of Wales) or try a 'conversational beer' (ask about your selection and the staff will strike up a knowledgeable conversation). And don't miss the Afternoon Champagne Tea!

shopping, dining and entertainment. Today, Celebration is a fully self-sufficient, bustling town with a hospital, schools, cinema and the distinctive Celebration Hotel at the centre of it all. Located just a few minutes away from Disney's southern border, Celebration is easily found off Highway 192. Enter at the landmark water tower via Celebration Ave, then follow signposting to **Celebration Hotel** (see page 88), which takes you to the centre of town.

BRITTIP

Don't stop at the first set of shops and services you come to off Highway 192. Keep going until you find Market Street and the centre-piece lake that lets you know you have found the proper downtown area.

Once in the downtown area itself you are spoiled for choice when it comes to shopping and dining. Market Street shops are open 10am–9pm Mon–Sat, noon–6pm Sun, with delightful boutique shopping at the likes of **Market Street Gallery** (featuring Disney collectables, Swarovski crystal,

Lladro, and other fine gifts), **Hopskotch** (classic women's clothing, shoes and accessories), **Downeast – An Orvis® Shop** (Orvis clothing, housewares and fly fishing equipment!), **Jerard International** (gifts from around the world, pet items and home accessories) and **Lollipop Cottage** (children's clothing and gifts). Besides having a wonderfully whimsical name, **Soft As A Grape** is the place to find casual wear for the whole family, while the old-timey **Village Mercantile** carries collections such as Tommy Bahama, Oakley, Roxy and Quicksilver. Other speciality shops include **Bloom Street Trading Co** (gifts, books and magazines), **Jewel Box** for jewellery, and **Day Dreams, Collectable Dolls & Bears**.

Stop in at **Main Street Café**, a funky 50s-style diner serving down-home American favourites such as meat loaf, turkey dinners and hearty sandwiches, or visit **Herman's Ice Cream Shoppe** for soups, sandwiches and salads. We dare you to resist its home-made ice-cream creations! Zagat award-winning **Café D'Antonio** offers authentic Italian cuisine in a sleek, family-friendly atmosphere (407 566 2233; **www.antonios online.com**), or seek out Spanish-Cuban **Columbia**, whose unique combinations of authentic ingredients serve to create some mouthwatering dishes (407 566 1505, **www.columbiarestaurant.com**). **Celebration Town Tavern** has a casual ambiance, specialising in New England seafood dishes; **Seito Japanese Restaurant** is the place to go for contemporary sushi and fusion dishes and **Boston Garden** serves up 'flown in fresh' seafood and lobster.

But the main *Brit's Guide* thumbs-up goes to **Sherlock's of Celebration** for its warm, welcoming atmosphere, intimate patio area and fabulous selection of pastries, beers, wines and traditional afternoon tea served without pretence – no chintz and ruffles here, just a comforting cup of tea in its proper vessel and a light lunch done right. Stop by for a meal (soup, salads, quiche, ploughman's lunch; you can even get Heinz beans on toast!), a pint of the finest imported brews (Italian, British, Irish and Belgian; 22 to choose from), premium Illy coffee and a fresh scone, or browse the extensive selection of 80 bottled wines available for purchase. Look for the familiar red phone box outside, then enjoy a comforting sense of home in the heart of Celebration (8am–9pm Mon–Thur, 8am–10pm Fri, 9am–10pm Sat, 9am–9pm Sun; on Bloom Street just off of Front Street). Also at new locations near Orlando Premium Outlets and at Cagan Crossings on Highway 27, near the Super Wal-Mart (407 566 1866, **www.sherlocksgroup.com**).

Think it would be fun to scoot around in one of the many smart non-emission vehicles you see parked around town? Hire one for the day at **Wheelz of Celebration** on Front Street. More traditionally minded? Wheelz also has bicycles for hire (407 566 0009, **www.wheelzofcelebration. com**). There are also miles of bike and walking paths to take advantage of here, with the pretty lakefront setting, children's play area and periodic festivals. **4 July** is a huge event, with picnics, street entertainment and face-painting plus Disney-inspired fireworks over the lake (parking is laid on at the entrance to Celebration, with a park-and-ride bus for visitors), while the **Christmas** period sees festive events and nightly snow on Market Street (**www.celebrationfl.com**).

Sherlock's

OSCEOLA COUNTY
The Kissimmee area is home to much more than just hotels, motels and Mickey Mouse. You'll find some of the most scenic and nature-orientated attractions in Central Florida here – you just need to know where to look!

Airboat rides
The thrill of airboat rides can be experienced on many of Florida's lakes, rivers and marshes. An airboat is totally different to any boat ride you will have had – it is more like flying at ground level. As much a thrill as a scenic adventure, it has the bonus of exploring areas otherwise inaccessible to boats. Airboats simply skim over and through the marshes, to give you an alternative, close-up and highly personal view. Travelling at up to 50mph/80kph means it can be loud (hence you will be provided with headphones) and sunglasses are also a good idea to keep stray flies out of your eyes. However, it is NOT the trip for you if you are spooked by crickets, dragonflies and similar insects that occasionally land in the boat! In summer months, a good insect repellent is essential.

Several operations offer airboat rides in the area, from 'you-drive' boats that do barely 5mph/8kph to much bigger ones, but for the most quality-conscious (and downright friendly) operation, our tip goes to **Boggy Creek Airboat Rides**. Its airboats can be found at its main site on Lake Toho at peaceful **Southport Park** (all the way down Poinciana Boulevard, off Highway 192 between Markers 10 and 11, and across Pleasant Hill Road into Southport Road – about a 35-minute drive) and at a secondary location on East Lake Toho. For the latter, you either take exit 17 off Central Florida Greeneway (417) and go 3mls/5km south on Boggy Creek Road, then right into **East Lake Fish Camp**, or take Osceola Parkway east until it hits Boggy Creek Road. Go left and then turn right at the Boggy Creek

T-junction, then right into East Lake Fish Camp after about 2mls/3km.

BRITTIP

Look out for discount coupons in tourist literature offering up to $3 off airboat rides.

East Lake Fish Camp is itself a little gem, offering a variety of boating and angling opportunities (407 348 2040, **www.eastlakefishcamp.net**) as well as the wonderfully authentic rural Florida charm of the **restaurant and gift shop** (8am–9pm daily). If you are heading for a morning airboat ride, consider arriving early for a huge all-day breakfast at the fish camp first, where the more adventurous will want to try the local delicacies – catfish, frogs' legs and gator tail. For another great slice of local eating, the Friday 'home-style' buffet and Saturday night seafood buffet are fabulous value at $10.95 and $12.95 each on an all-you-can-eat basis. Boggy Creek's **half-hour ride** features the most modern 18-passenger airboats in Florida, skimming over the local wetlands for a close-up of the majestic cypress trees and wildlife including eagles, ospreys, snakes and turtles, as well as the seemingly ever-present gators. The Southport Park site tends to be quieter, with more wildlife – especially in the spring – but involves a longer drive than to East Lake Fish Camp.

BRITTIP

The best time for an airboat ride is first thing on a weekday morning when the wildlife is not hiding from the weekend boaters.

You don't need to book, just turn up, as boats go every ½ hour (9am–5.30pm daily); $21.95 adults, $15.95 3–12s). Don't forget the sunscreen as you can really burn on the water (just look at the unusual red colour Boggy Creek captain Chad has acquired over

the years!). It also does a 1-hour **Night Tour** ($34.95 adults, $29.95 3–12s, Mar–Oct only) for a completely different and exhilarating experience (gator eyes glow red in the dark!), but you must book up to 2 weeks in advance. Finally, it offers a 45-minute private tour in its 6-passenger boat ($45/person), which provides an even more personal view of this amazing area. Boggy Creek Airboats make a worthwhile and enjoyable ½-day adventure by the time you stop on its covered picnic terrace for a drink or ice-cream. Call 407 344 9550 or visit **www.bcairboats.com** for more info (and a money-off coupon).

Scenic Lake Tours

Also in Kissimmee, **Scenic Lake Tours** offers a more sedate view of the local flora and fauna. Under the expert guidance of a local captain, you will head out on to Lake Tohopekaliga for a 1-hour circuit in its 24ft/7.5m pontoon boat, taking in Makinson Island and the Shingle Creek waterway (with soft drinks, water and snacks included). Your guide will point out all the wildlife, from gators and turtles to ospreys and eagles, and you will gain a valuable insight into the local ecosystems. Once again, it is an opportunity to step back in time in the real Florida, not the tourist version. Scenic Tours leaves the Toho Marina dock (on Lakeshore Boulevard every day. Take Ruby Avenue off Broadway in downtown Kissimmee. 10am, midday, 2pm and 4pm Mon–Fri, 9am, 11am, 1pm and 3pm Sat, Sun. $25 adults, $15 6–12s, 5 and under free. There is also a special sunset cruise on request (1800 244 9105, **www.fishing chartersinc.com**). Alternatively, try its fishing excursions on Lake Toho, some of the surrounding lakes or even inshore in the Fort Myers-Sanibel Island area. Fishing is from $250 for 2 anglers for 4 hours to $450 for a full day (8 hours), and saltwater inshore fishing is $275–475.

Balloon trips

Florida is one of the most popular areas for ballooning and, if you are up early enough in the morning, you will often see several, especially in Osceola County. It's a majestic experience; the utterly smooth way in which you lift off into the early morning sky is breathtaking in itself, but the peace and quiet of the ride, not to mention the stunning views from 2,000ft/600m above ground, are quite awesome. It's not a cheap experience, but it is equally appealing to all but the youngest children or those with vertigo or a fear of heights. It's also a highly personalised ride, taking up to 6 people. Some baskets take up to 12, but it's a squeeze!

BRITTIP

Dresses are not advisable for balloon trips and hard-wearing shoes for the set-up and landing areas are essential.

Orlando Balloon Rides is the main operator in central Florida, and, while it may be a new name (as of 2007), it has more than 20 years' experience of flying and working in the area. The company was created from the merger of two of Orlando's most well-established and respected companies, Orange Blossom Balloons and Blue Water Balloons. Still under British ownership (led by Ian and Fiona Swift), it flies daily (weather permitting), meeting up in the restaurant at **Best Western Lakeside** on Highway 192 (by Marker 4) at 6am – the best winds for flying are nearly always early in the morning – and then transferring to the take-off site. This is where you can help the crew set up one of the balloons (for 4, 8, 10 or 12 passengers in compartmentalised baskets), one of which is also disabled-accessible. All the balloons are brand new and specifically designed for passenger comfort and safety.

The friendly team sets you up for a leisurely but exciting experience, and you are soon up, up and away in awe-inspiring style, floating serenely up into the sky or sinking down to skim the surface of one of the many lakes (disturbing the occasional gator or deer). After about an hour, you come back to earth for a traditional champagne landing ceremony and return to the Best Western for a full breakfast and your special balloonist's certificate. The full experience lasts 3–4 hours and costs $175/person (inclusive of tax). Children 10 and under fly free with their parents (additional children $95). Hotel pick-up is also available at $10/person round trip, or you can pay $20 to be part of the chase crew and just enjoy the champagne landing and breakfast. Call 407 894 5040 for reservations (flights book up well ahead) or visit **www.orangeblossom balloons.com**

Orlando Balloon Rides

© OCVB

One other operator worth noting is **Thompson Aire**, with local pilot Jeff Thompson, a ballooning veteran with more than 30 years' experience. He also flies every day (weather permitting), meeting at the Black Angus Steakhouse on Highway 192 (by Marker 5), and returning there for a hearty breakfast. Fares are $185 ($105 for children 10–15; one child under 10 can fly free with a paying adult; discounts for 4 or more adults travelling together. Call 407 421 9322 or visit **www.thompsonaire.com**. It can also arrange hotel pick-ups for $15/person.

Warbird Adventures

Anyone even slightly interested in World War II aviation should certainly consider a trip to Warbird Adventures. *This is the best ride in town, bar none – guaranteed*. Not only do you get to fly in one of its 3 1945 T-6 Harvard fighter-trainers, but also, after a period of getting used to the front seat of this vintage 2-seater… you get to fly it! And you don't just handle the controls; your instructor will get you doing all manner of aerobatics. This is simply the most exhilarating ride we have ever tried, enhanced by in-flight video and wingtip camera to record every moment. It is the only place we know of where you can walk in off the street and, 20 minutes later, be flying a warplane with no previous experience. Roller-coasters? They're for wimps! Mind you, this is not cheap – a 15-minute flight costs $190, a 30-minute trip is $320 and an hour $590. Aerobatics (on 30- or 60-minute flights only) cost $35, while the region 1 DVD video is $50 and the stills $25. Nevertheless, this is a memory to last a lifetime, and just the thought of it is still thrilling. Maximum weight is 18 stone/115kg and minimum height is 4ft/122cm. It also operates a 1966 Bell 47-G M*A*S*H helicopter for flights and instruction ($120–390). Call 407 870 7366 or visit **www.warbird adventures.com**. You can find Warbird Adventures just off Hoagland Boulevard, ½ mile/1 km south of Highway 192 on the left.

Green Meadows Petting Farm

From one extreme to another, here is guaranteed fun for kids aged 2 to about 11 and their parents. It's the ultimate hands-on experience as, on the 2-hour guided tour, kids get to milk a cow, pet a pig, cuddle a chick or duckling, feed goats and sheep, meet a buffalo, chickens, peacocks and donkeys and learn what makes a farm tick. There are pony rides and a play area for the young ones, tractor-drawn hay rides, and the Green Meadows Express train tour. Don't forget your cameras!

✠ BRITTIP

Reader Lynda Letchford says: 'My 2-year-old really enjoyed Green Meadows. When you are in the pens with the animals, they nibble your toes and you step in all sorts so wear enclosed shoes! Also, take some hand wipes for extra hygiene.'

The shaded areas, free-roaming animals and peaceful aspect all contribute to another pleasant change of pace, especially as Green Meadows is barely 10 minutes from the tourist hurly-burly of Highway 192 (south on Poinciana Boulevard). 9.30am–4pm daily (last tour 4pm); $19 ($16 for seniors, under-2s free); allow 3–4 hours for your visit. Drinks, snacks and gifts are available, but it is also the ideal place to bring a picnic (407 846 0770, **www.greenmeadows farm.com**).

Osceola County Pioneer Museum

Only just off the beaten track in Kissimmee, but a delightful discovery, is this small-scale homage to 19th-century Florida life, with a preserved 'cracker' (cowboy) homestead portraying how the original settlers lived in the 1890s. The fascinating little museum traces the history of Osceola County, and includes a cattle camp, nature walk, school house, country store and information centre with library. New in 2006 was an 1890 citrus-packing operation from nearby Narcoossee, which was originally started by a family from the UK! But the real bonus is the volunteers who take you round, providing a fascinating view of life here more than 100 years ago. Situated on N Bass Road (turn off Highway 192 by the Wal-Mart Supercenter next to Medieval Times between markers 14 and 15). 10am–4pm Thur–Sat, noon–4pm Sun; $2 adults, $1 children (under-5s free; 407 396 8644).

Reptile World Serpentarium

Another throwback to an earlier time in Florida (albeit only BD – Before Disney) is this wonderfully kitsch roadside halt in St Cloud. Florida is actually home to a wide variety of snakes, both venomous and non-venomous, and all of them can be seen here. In all, there are more than 60 species of worldwide reptile featured in the clean, indoor exhibits (including the Australian Taipan – rated the world's deadliest snake), but the main feature is the twice-daily (at noon and 3pm) 'milking' of venom from some of the more hazardous residents – cobras and vipers – for snake research. Snakes are their stock-in-trade, but you will also meet turtles, gators and iguanas. Out on the eastern stretch of Highway 192, just past St Cloud, it's open 9am–5.30pm Tue–Sun (closed Sept); $5.70 adult, $4.70 6–17s, $3.70 3–5s (407 892 6905).

BRITTIP

If you are brave enough to volunteer during the venom show, you won't actually be asked to help in this genuinely dangerous activity, but you will get the chance to stroke a boa.

Eco-tourism

Genuine eco-tourism is still in its infancy, in general terms, in central Florida, but there are some exceptions worth knowing about. **Florida Eco-Safaris** at Forever Florida is, for our money, one of the most outstanding non-theme-park attractions. It is both a 4,700-acre/1,900ha wilderness preserve and a working ranch. As well as a close-up of Florida's flora and fauna and its conservation issues, you get a taste of the original cracker-style life ('crackers' were the original cowboys, pre-dating their Western counterparts by 50 years), which is a fascinating slice of history. Eco-safaris, horseback safaris, nature walks and, for the kids, pony rides and a petting zoo, are the highlights, as well as the magnificent **Cypress Restaurant** and **Visitor Center**, which offers an essential 30-minute orientation programme into the conservancy's creation.

Beginning as a dream of gifted young biologist and ecologist Allen Broussard, Forever Florida was completed after his death (from complications of Hodgkin's disease) by his parents, Dr William and Margaret Broussard. They continue to give their time and energy to developing the wilderness as a non-profit-making memorial to their son. The education element here alone is awesome, and tours feature a strong conservation message in this tranquil, untouched corner of Florida. The 2-hour **Guided Eco-Safaris** is its stock-in-trade, a tranquil trundle in a large-wheeled, open-sided buggy round much of the woods, swamp and prairie that make up the Crescent J Ranch and Conservancy. Your tour guide gives the low-down on the fascinating history and environmental issues of the countryside, as well as some real insights into local life long before the tourists arrived. A boardwalk along Bull Creek affords the chance to get up close with a typical cypress 'dome' and breathe the amazingly pure air it gives out. You are likely to encounter alligators (at a safe distance), turtles, whitetail deer, armadillos and a host of bird life – including bald eagles and wild turkeys – as well as the native cracker, cattle and horses (which make a great story in their own right) and leave with a good understanding of the real Florida. Eco-Safaris cost $24.95 ($19.95 6–12s) and depart daily at 10am and 1pm. **Horseback Safaris** are another feature of Forever Florida (for ages 12 and over; 10 and 11 only with proven riding experience), with the chance to enjoy its Western trail rides for 1, 2 or 3 hours with a native cracker guide, who offers his own observations on the local flora and fauna. Horseback Safaris cost $37.50, $57 or $73 (reservations needed 24 hours in advance on 1888 854 3837).

BRITTIP

For Florida Eco-Safaris' Horse Safaris, wearing long trousers and closed-toed shoes is essential. An early morning ride here was one of the most enjoyable hours we've spent in Florida.

If you want to go further into cowboy country, the **Rawhide Round-up** is a full half-day experience with cattle on the Crescent J Ranch, including lunch ($89), while the **Horse Safaris** can also be extended to 2 and 3 days ($199 and $299), staying in bunk-house-style accommodation. The ranch **riding school** (which is working to bring back the genuine Florida Cracker breed of horse) is also adjacent to the Visitor Center, where you can see some amazing horse-training feats at first hand under the tutelage of experts Dean van Camp and Sandra Wise. They are happy to demonstrate and explain their work (for free!), while they also offer roping and cow-working skills classes (for experienced riders only; call for prices). Forever Florida is a good 80-minute drive out of Orlando, 40mls/64km east on Highway 192, through St Cloud as far as Holopaw, then

7½mls/12km south on Highway 441, but is well worth the journey to experience the charm and tranquillity on offer. Call 1866 854 3837 or visit **www.floridaeco-safaris.com**.

BRITTIP

The Kissimmee Convention and Visitors Bureau (see page 50) publishes an excellent Nature and Heritage Guide (**www.floridakiss.com**).

On an equally authentic scale is **Disney's Wilderness Preserve**, run by the Nature Conservancy (the world's leading private international conservancy group) in Poinciana, south of Kissimmee. This restoration of a 12,000 acre/4,860ha preserve is a work in progress and allows visitors in for various (well-marked) hiking trails, with a 2-hour buggy tour on Sundays (1.30pm). The preserve's pine and scrubby flatwoods, dry and wet prairies, freshwater marshes and forested wetlands are home to more than 300 wildlife species, including bald eagles, Florida scrub-jays and sandhill cranes, Sherman's fox squirrels, eastern indigo snakes and gopher tortoises, plus more than 50 butterfly species. Come here for a chance to unwind and enjoy the peace and quiet of the Florida countryside. $3 adults, $2 children; buggy tours $7 and $5 extra. Located at the end of Pleasant Hill Road (CR531; follow Hoagland or Poinciana Boulevard south off Highway 192, then turn right on Pleasant Hill), the preserve is open daily 9am–5pm (noon–4 Sun Oct–May). Trails may be closed due to flooding or conservancy work, so call 407 935 0002 in advance or visit **http://nature.org/wherewework/northamerica/states/florida/**

Horse riding

© OCVB

SEMINOLE COUNTY

You may well have arrived in the heart of Seminole County – with its historic town of Sanford – without realising it if you flew into Orlando Sanford International Airport. But it is worth pointing out the possible diversions of a day or so back in this area that will get you well off the beaten track.

Central Florida Zoological Park

This private, non-profit-making organisation puts a pleasant, natural accent on the zoo theme and is set in a wooded 116 acres/47ha of unspoilt Florida countryside with boardwalks and trails around all the attractions. These include more than 100 species of animal, educational programmes, weekend feeding demonstrations, a picnic area, pony rides and a butterfly garden, plus the Zoofari Outpost gift shop. It's good value, too, at $9.95 for adults, $7.95 for seniors (60+) and $5.95 for 3–12s and the park (off exit 104 of I-4) is open daily 9am–5pm (except Thanksgiving Day and Christmas Day). Recent updates have enlarged several exhibits and added new habitats, including an Australian section with emus and kangaroos (www.centralfloridazoo.org).

BRITTIP

Visit Central Florida Zoo at the weekend and you will be offered a series of educational animal encounters (ranging from gators and snakes to hedgehogs).

St John's River Cruise, at Blue Spring State Park, features a family-run, immensely personable 2-hour nature tour of this historic waterway, with interactive narration of the flora, fauna (including manatees in winter) and history. $18 adults, $16 seniors (60+), $12 3–12s. It leaves from Orange City marina several times a day (take Highway 17/92 north from Sanford to French Avenue and head west for 1ml/1.6km). Call 407 330 1612 to check times and book (www.sjrivercruises.com).

For a lower-key approach, the Rivership Romance (daily out of downtown Sanford) is a great choice, especially for the lunch cruises on the wildlife-rich St John's River. The old-fashioned steamer can take up to 200 in comfort and adds a fine meal, live entertainment and a river narration, as well as providing a relaxing alternative to the usual tourist rush. Choose from the 3-hour lunch cruise (11am–2pm Wed, Sat; $38/person), 4–hour lunch cruise (11am–3pm Mon, Tues, Thurs, Fri; $48.50), Sunday Brunch (11am–2pm; $38) or Moonlight Dinner Dance (7.30–11pm Sat; $53.75, all drinks extra). Fridays see the Special Event Show, a themed dinner show that might feature a madcap wedding, a haunted holiday or something equally offbeat to keep you entertained while you eat (7.30–9.30pm; $46.25). To book, call 407 321 5091 or visit www.rivershipromance.com Its dock can be found off exit 101A of I-4, east into Sanford, then left on Palmetto Ave.

One of the most fun and entertaining of the area's airboat rides is to be found at the Black Hammock Fish Camp and Restaurant (off exit 44 on the Central Florida Greeneway, take SR 434 east, turn left on Deleon Street and left on to Black Hammock Road). This quiet backwater on beautiful Lake Jesup is home to Captain Joel Martin, a Frenchman who enjoys his Florida boating, and his 1-hour tour will take you into every nook and cranny of either the east or west lake (and this really is a great lake to explore, positively crammed with gators, including some of the biggest we've seen in the wild). It's an eye-opening adventure, and Captain Martin even keeps his own gators, large and small, back at the Fish Camp. Rides are $35.95 ($29.95 under-10s; 30-min rides $23.95 and $19.95; 45-min private airboat rides $45/person (minimum 4 people, reservations required), 45-min night rides $35.95/person (minimum 4 people). Book in advance on 407 365 1244. Then you can grab lunch or dinner at the **Black Hammock Restaurant** (fine local delicacies, especially the catfish and gator tail, plus other dishes and a kids' menu; 11am–9pm Sun–Thurs, 11am–10pm Fri, Sat; 407 365 2201) or visit the **Lazy Gator Bar** (open from 3pm Mon–Thurs, 2pm Fri, noon Sat and 11am Sun) with nightly drink specials and Happy Hour 3pm–6:30pm. You can rent canoes or fishing boats and enjoy another view of this unspoilt corner (**www.theblackhammock.com**).

Alternatively, **Bill's Airboat Adventures**, on the St John's River east of Sanford, offers 90-min tours in the company of river historian and conservationist Captain Bill Daniel for $40 ($25 under-14s) on his 6-person boat, subject to a $90 minimum (407 977 3214, **www.airboating.com**). **Dana's Fishing and Scenic Tours** can take you out on to Seminole County's lakes and waterways for some brilliant bass fishing or guided scenic tours (by appointment only, call 407 645 5462 or visit **www.fishingincentralflorida.cc**).

Of course, you can just head for one of the splendid **State Parks** and follow the well-marked trails. **Wekiva Springs State Park** offers hiking, bike rentals, canoeing and swimming, plus picnic areas and shelters, and **Little Big Econ** state forest has 5,048 acres/2,045ha of scenic woodlands and wetlands. **Spring Hammock Preserve** offers 1,500 acres/607ha of wilderness to explore, and the **Lake Proctor** wilderness area has 6mls/10km of hiking, biking and equestrian adventures. There are more trails to discover along the Econlockhatchee River at the **Econ River Wilderness Area**, while **Chuluota** has 625 acres/253ha and the **Geneva Wilderness Area** 180 acres/73ha, which includes the **Ed Yarborough Nature Center** (407 665 7352, **www.co.seminole.fl.us/trails**).

Sanford itself is a fascinating city (more of a town by UK standards) on the south shore of Lake Monroe and is a historic centre, full of brick-paved streets, antique shops and an artists' colony at the heart of a major regeneration project. It is very much small-town America, having lost the growth battle with Orlando years ago, but it makes a peaceful diversion with some lovely walks, notably the new **Riverwalk** project and First Street renovations. Head for the **Sanford Museum** (520 East 1st Street) to get an overview of the way the city has grown from its incorporation in 1877, under the patronage of pioneering lawyer and diplomat Henry Sanford, as a hub destination on the St John's River, the 'Nile of America'. The museum (11am–4pm Tue–Fri, 1–4pm Sat; admission free) illustrates the life and times of the city's founder, its growth into the 'celery capital of the world' and its modern history as a US naval base.

From there, head on to **First Street** and check out the turn-of-the-19th-century buildings, stop for a bite at **Morgan's Gourmet Café** and finish up by wandering down to the river. Sanford also has **The Hart Sisters Café, Tea Room and Catering**, a wonderful tea room with a sophisticated Victorian touch. It is one of the prettiest settings for a meal in Florida, serving a mouth-watering array of soups, sandwiches, quiches and soufflés, as well as a fabulous selection of tea trays. This little gem (11am–3pm Tue–Fri, 11am–4pm Sat) can be found on Park Avenue, 13 blocks out of the town centre (407 323

Black Hammock airboat ride

9448, **www.hartsisters.com**). Or you could try the equally stylish and Victorian **Higgins House** (on South Oak Avenue and 5th Street; 407 324 9238, **www.higginshouse.com**).

For more info on Seminole County, visit **www.visitseminole.com** or call in at one of its **Visitor Centers** at Orlando Sanford International Airport (in the Welcome Center as you exit the main building) or at 1230 Douglas Avenue in Longwood (a block west of exit 94 on I-4; 407 665 2900).

> ✠ **BRITTIP**
>
> Need a hotel in Seminole County for a night or two? Look up **www.NorthOrlandoHotels.com** for a great selection of short-term accommodation at good prices.

Further afield

If you enjoy the Seminole County experience and want to travel a little further, head out to the Gulf Coast, just north of Homossasa Springs, and visit the **Crystal River State Park**, which offers another wildlife fiesta. The Crystal River is home to the endangered manatee, and it is possible to go swimming with these wonderful creatures, either on a self-guided or an organised tour. Winter and spring are ideal times for manatee sightings, but the park offers year-round outdoor adventure, with hiking and biking trails, kayaking, canoeing and fishing – or just pack a picnic lunch and enjoy a relaxing afternoon amid the natural beauty.

Lake Louisa State Park is another local gem, situated in Lake County just off Highway 27 (at the west end of Kissimmee's Highway 192). Here you can enjoy some of the most beautiful countryside, with 6 lakes, rolling hills

> ✠ **BRITTIP**
>
> Never touch or disturb a wild manatee. They are protected animals and there are heavy fines, strictly enforced, for harassing them.

(a real Florida rarity!) and scenic landscapes. The park has more than 20mls/32km of hiking trails, a picnic pavilion, swimming in Lake Louisa (with lifeguards on duty end May–beginning September) and offers 20 new cabins (sleeping up to 6), if you fancy staying 'out in the wild'. Lake Louisa is on the **Great Florida Birding Trail** (a 2,000ml/3,200km highway linking 446 major bird-watching sites in the state) and is therefore great territory for a huge variety of birds. Call 352 394 3969 for more info. Entry fee $4/car.

Then there is **Weedon Island Preserve** in St Petersburg, where you can enjoy the rich cultural history of this 3,700 acre/1,500ha seaside nature park. Start at the Natural History Center (the main entrance, confusingly, is at the back!) and learn about the prehistoric and Native American settlements here (plus periodic exhibitions), and go up to the 3rd floor observation deck. There are then several miles of boardwalks and other trails around these tidal wetlands, which are home to a wide variety of plant, bird and animal life, including ospreys, spoonbills, turtles, mangrove crabs, raccoons and gopher tortoises. The more energetic may want to try a paddle round the shallow waters with **Sweetwater Kayaks**, based in the Preserve itself. This wonderfully peaceful close encounter with nature (stingrays, jumping mullet and the occasional manatee) takes 2–3 hours on the self-guided tour (following the markers). $38 for a ½ day single-kayak rental, $54 for double-kayak, or $16 ($23 double) hourly (call 727 570 4844 or visit **www.sweetwaterkayaks.com**).

Weedon Island Preserve

OFF THE BEATEN TRACK

BRITTIP

Insect repellant is essential for any visit to Weedon Island Preserve as it is not sprayed for mosquitoes, and the little pests will feed on tourists!

Dinosaur World

Right on I-4 as you head from Orlando to Tampa (and a nice stopping point) is this notable family-run attraction in Plant City (exit 17) ideal for 3–8s. With more than 150 life-size dinosaurs in a lush, natural setting, plus quiet walking trails, a picnic area, playground and gift shop, it makes a pleasant diversion for an hour or so. There are no rides, audio-animatronics or other gimmicks, just the set-piece dino models, with explanatory signs, plus a cave-themed video theatre, small-scale fossil dig and large 'boneyard' sand pit. The new Skeleton Garden features 6 replica dinosaur skeletons and a palaeontologist-filed work exhibit. It is mildly educational, very laid back and a nice change of pace from the main parks, especially with younger children. There is no food service, but it does have picnic facilities and there are take-away and fast food locations nearby. 9am–6pm daily; $9.75 adult, $8.95 seniors; $7.75 3–12s, under-3s free (813 717 9865, **www.dinoworld.net**).

Day trips and excursions

There is an increasing number of tours and day trips being offered in and around Orlando, visiting as far afield as the Everglades, Miami, Florida Keys and even the Bahamas. And, if you are prepared to put up with a long day out (up to 16 hours), you can see a lot this way. However, if the attraction of a trip to the Everglades is the airboat ride, you are better off going to Boggy Creek Airboats and avoiding the long journey. The 2 principal local tour companies are *Brit's Guide* partners **Florida Dolphin Tours** and **Gator Tours**.

Florida Dolphin Tours should be first on your list to check as it offers an increasingly diverse range of memorable excursions, though it is best known for the swim-with-dolphins tours to the Florida Keys. More importantly, as a British-owned company, it offers our readers a *12½% discount* on all tours (see inside back cover for details). Take your pick from: **Sun, Sand and Scales**, an excellent value all-day trip to Daytona Beach and the beautiful Plaza Resort & Spa for an afternoon of fun in the sun, then a hands-on interactive animal show and an exciting airboat ride in search of gators, followed by a wonderful evening buffet with music and unlimited beer, wine and soft drinks ($109 adults, $79 3–9s; **Kennedy Space Center**, see the future of tomorrow – today! Transportation is included to both the Space Center and Astronaut Hall of Fame. Ask about options such as including an airboat ride, Lunch With An Astronaut, or even the Ultimate Kennedy Experience. It leaves between 7 and 8am (prices from $89 and $79); **Miami Everglades Adventure**, a chance to see the real Florida on an all-day getaway, with an exhilarating airboat ride, gator wrestling, native wildlife exhibits, a visit to Miami's Bayside shopping centre and time to explore the famous South Beach. The tour leaves between 6.15 and 7am but doesn't return until around 11pm ($119 and $99); **Swim With The Manatees**, another all-day adventure (and the No. 1 Florida attraction), this features an all-you-can-eat breakfast buffet and a 2-hour boat trip on the picturesque Crystal River (with snorkel and mask to check out where the manatees swim at close quarters!). There is also a picnic lunch, airboat ride and trip to Homosassa State Wildlife Park, plus an educational briefing on manatees and a chance to see them being fed from the underwater viewing area. It departs between 7.30 and 8.30am ($119 and $89).

Then there are two trademark **Swim With The Dolphins** tours, a 1-day excursion to the beautiful Florida Keys with a 2-hour dolphin programme (and the choice of an organised or unstructured dolphin swim), or the grand 2-day trip, including accommodation, dolphin swim, buffet-style evening meal, Everglades airboat ride, alligator and snake-handling show (interactive!), and a ½ day to see Miami with shopping at Bayside or a boat tour along the inland waterways. The dolphin programme includes a full briefing and then about 30 minutes in the water, with dolphin contact guaranteed. It leaves between 6.15 and 7am, returning around 7.30pm the next day (you must call for rates). Then you can sample the high-energy action of **American Football** with all-day excursions to see the highly fancied Jacksonville Jaguars ($99/person, Aug–Dec); check out the excitement and glamour of **NBA basketball** with the Orlando Magic ($89/person, Nov–Apr); or try its signature **Disney limo trips** – the Grand Floridian character breakfast, Chef Mickey's dinner buffet or Planet Hollywood VIP (from $79). More info on 407 352 5151 or visit **www.florida dolphintours.com**. To enjoy our special discount, just call and say '12½% off with the *Brit's Guide*, please!'

Florida Dolphin Tours also has Skyy, its own **transportation and limo service**, which can provide airport transfers, wedding cars or just a special night out. Cal 407 352 4644 or visit **www.skyylimousine.com** Skyy also offers the *Brit's Guide* discount, so don't forget to ask!

Gator Tours offers yet more possibilities for day trips, with the Kennedy Space Center and Daytona Race Speedway its specialities. The company also features Space Shuttle launches and landings, a wide range of sporting event tours (including golf, Orlando Magic basketball and major motorsport), shopping excursions and even a unique **Orlando City Tour** ($59 adults, $49 2–11s). Its **Kennedy Space Center** trips go out daily and can mix and match with the full range of opportunities there, including Lunch with an Astronaut, the Astronaut Hall of Fame, NASA Up Close Tour and an airboat ride ($87–129 adults, $77–99 2–11s). It offers tickets and round-trip transportation to the Pepsi 400 at world-famous **Daytona Speedway**, while the **Shoppers Paradise** ($39 and $29) excursion visits the Florida Mall and several of the discount outlets in one go. Other notable day tours include transportation to the **Beaches** at Clearwater ($49); an **Everglades and Miami** adventure ($119 and $99); an all-day trip to all the fun of Miami ($69 and $59); and even transport (with or without tickets) to **Gatorland** ($35–49) For full pricing, call 407 522 5911 or visit **www.gatortours.com**

Of course, a great day-trip is just jumping in your hire car and heading to the coast, as Florida has some superb **Beaches** (see Chapter 9, The Twin Centre Option).

SPORT

In addition to virtually every form of entertainment known to man, central Florida is one of the world's biggest sporting playgrounds, with a huge range of opportunities to either watch or play your favourite sport.

Golf

Without doubt, the Number One sport in Florida is golf, with 170 courses within an hour's drive of Orlando. Of course, the weather makes it a popular pastime, but some

The number one sporting activity!

© OCVB

spectacular courses, many designed by famous names like Greg Norman, Tom Watson, Arnold Palmer and Jack Nicklaus, add to the attraction, and there are numerous packages geared to golfers of all abilities. With an 18-hole round, including cart hire and taxes, from as little as $40 (average around $75), it's an attractive proposition and quite different for those used to British courses. If you go in for 36-hole days, it's possible to save up to $30 by replaying the same course, while it is cheaper to play Mon–Thur than Fri–Sun. Sculpted landscapes, manicured fairways and abundant use of water features and white-sand bunkers add up to some memorable golf. Winter is the high season, hence the most expensive, but many courses are busy year-round. Be aware that some courses pair golfers with little thought for age, handicap etc., so, if 2 of you turn up, you may be paired with 2 strangers.

BRITTIP

Golf balls are plentiful and inexpensive in Florida, so there's no need to bring your own. Good-quality clubs are often available for hire, including top brands like Calloway.

Virtually every course will offer a driving range to get you started, plus lockers, changing rooms and showers, while the use of golf carts is universal (many include the amazing GPS system, which gives the yardage for every shot). They all feature comforts like iced water stations and drinks carts that circulate the course (don't forget to tip the trolley drivers). Some have swimming pools, and all offer a decent bar and restaurant for that all-important 19th hole.

Your best starting point is one of the 5 **Edwin Watts** golf shops around Orlando for a free copy of the *Golfer's Guide* or the *Guide To Golf* for a handy introduction to most of the courses available (and perhaps buy some new clubs at the Watts National Clearance

Center just south of Wet 'n Wild on I-Drive; 407 352 2535, **www.edwin watts.com**). **Tee-Times USA** (1888 465 3356) offers excellent advice and a reservation service. Visit Florida publishes an *Official Golf Guide* (850 488 8374, **www.flasports.com**), as does Daytona Beach (1800 881 7065, **www.golfdaytonabeach.com**).

For a unique and personable touch, you can't beat the all-in-one instruction service of **Professional Golf Guides of Orlando**, led by owner/operator and PGA member Phillip Jaffe, who is a mine of golf lore and knowledge, as well as great company. They take up to 3 golfers at a time around some of the finest courses, and can supply transport and clubs if required. The playing lesson is of the highest quality and includes full on-course instruction, course management strategies, game analysis, improvement suggestions, shot-making demos and a wrap-up lesson to leave you with the knowledge and skills to take your game to the next level. It is an eye-opening experience to play alongside Phillip and his staff of PGA professionals and well worth it for the keen golfer who wishes to improve their game in one round. Call 407 227 9869 for rates or visit **www.progolf guides.com**. Alternatively, the **Nick Faldo Golf Institute** on the lower portion of I-Drive (1888 463 2536) is a great place just to hit a few balls.

BRITTIP

An early-morning tee-off in the summer can provide some peaceful and scenic golf.

Walt Disney World has been quick to attract the golf fanatic, with five high-quality courses, including the 7,000yd/6,400m **Palm**, rated by *Golf Digest* in its top 25 (the 18th hole is reputedly one of the toughest in America), plus a 9-hole par-36 course, **Oak Trail**. Fees are $89–$155 for Disney resort guests and $99–165 for visitors, with 50% reductions after 3pm. Call 407 939 4653 for tee-times. Private and group lessons are available under PGA professional guidance, with video analysis and a range of club rentals. The rolling **Osprey Ridge** (up to 7,101yd/6,493m) and the visually intimidating **Eagle Pines** (up to 6,772yd/6,192m – 16 holes with water hazards!) are the newest Disney courses, which were both designed in 1992 by master architects Tom Fazio and Pete Dye respectively.

BRITTIP

Some of the best tee times at the *Walt Disney World Resort in Florida* golf courses are reserved for those staying at a Disney resort.

Another luxury experience is available at the **Hyatt Grand Cypress** on Winter Garden-Vineland Road (407 239 1904; rates $130–170). It has 3 elegant 9-hole courses and a superb 18-hole links-style offering (all designed by golf legend Jack Nicklaus), which present a wonderful challenge. **MetroWest Country Club**, on South Hiawassee Road to the north of Universal Studios (407 299 1099; $89–129), is a 7,051yd/6,447m masterpiece designed by Robert Trent Jones Snr featuring elevated tees and greens, with pleasant rolling fairways and expansive bunkers.

Equally challenging and eye-catching is the **Champions Gate Golf Club** to the south of Disney (exit 58 off I-4), with 2 magnificent Greg Norman-designed courses – the International (a British-style links course) and the National (in more traditional style). The practice facilities, clubhouse, service and coaching (this is the HQ of the renowned David Leadbetter Academy) are world class, and there is a host of special events and stay-and-play packages with the superb Omni Orlando Resort (407 787 4653, **www.championsgategolf.com**).

Also in Seminole, **Magnolia Plantation** is another wonderful

contrast, a heavily wooded and peaceful haven that feels miles from the theme park world and yet is less than ½ hour away up I-4. Woven among the lakes and ponds of the Wekiva River basin, Phillip Jaffe rates it a must-play course (407 833 0818; $40–80). **Falcon's Fire** in Kissimmee is an outstanding course, too, featuring the ProShot digital caddy system and water coolers on all golf carts. Plenty of water around the course assures a testing 18 holes, but it is highly picturesque (407 239 5445; $77–147). **The Orange Lake Country Club** is a huge vacation resort (just 4mls/6km from Disney), with 2 18-hole courses, a 9-hole course and a par-3 floodlit 9. The **Legends at Orange Lake** course (designed by Arnold Palmer) is its top offering (407 239 1050; $57–119). **Kissimmee Oaks** features some majestic moss-draped oaks and local wildlife as well as 18 holes of memorable lakeside golf, all just 3½mls/6km south of Highway 192 in Kissimmee in the Oaks Community off John Young Parkway (407 933 4055; $50–80).

The wonderful **Grande Lakes Orlando** resort complex just off John Young Parkway has a Greg Norman-designed masterpiece, offering 18 holes of Florida nature with a caddie-concierge service (call for rates, 407 206 2400). The rolling and aptly named **Victoria Hills** in DeLand (midway between Orlando and Daytona Beach, exit 116 off I-4) gets a big thumbs up from Phillip Jaffe ('A great track, very challenging!'), with a par-72 course designed by Ron Garl and superb practice facilities (386 738 6000; $39–75). The extravagant **Reunion Resort and Club** (in Davenport, just to the south of Disney, exit 54 off I-4) now has 3 courses – a Watson, Palmer and Nicklaus collaboration, with 18 holes designed by each. Watson's 7,257yd/6,636m Independence Course is possibly the most challenging, with a style not dissimilar to famous Augusta

National (1888 300 2434; $50–85). However, golf here is restricted to those who own property in the resort or are staying here (highly recommended; see page 96). The clubhouse is 5-star in design and facilities and each course is superb just to look at, never mind play.

New courses continue to spring up all the time, notably **Mystic Dunes**, just off the beaten path of Highway 192 near the Disney entrance. This course winds through native oaks and other vegetation and is a real test of golf skills. The clubhouse has a wonderful menu and is stocked with the latest fashions and equipment (407 787 5678; $42–95). **Shingle Creek** is a beauty from great local architect Dave Harman, set in dense oaks and pines along the historic Shingle Creek, the headwater that leads to the Everglades. Located within a mile of the Convention Center, it is a world-class facility with some amazing teaching features, at the heart of this new 5-star convention resort (407 996 9933, **www.shinglecreekgolf.com**; $63–110). The **Legends Golf and Country Club** is just 25 minutes from Disney, on Highway 27 towards Clermont, and offers a pleasant layout with rolling hills unusual for Florida (352 243 1118; $36–45). **Forest Lake Golf Club** has quickly become one of the best in the region, with no houses to be seen, just pure Florida. Just up the Florida Turnpike some 30 minutes from Disney (407 654 4653, **www.forestlakegolf.com**; $43–83). Up in Seminole County, **Rock Springs Ridge Golf Club** (another Jaffe course) offers 27 great holes in a contrasting, natural setting (407 814 7474, **www.forestlakegolf.com**; $30– 55). Not a new course but one that has gained recent prominence as host of the finals of the PGA Tour Qualifying event is **Orange County National**, an awesome 36 holes just to the north of Disney off Highway 545, with a huge driving range and many target greens (407 656 2626, **www.ocngolf.com**; $80–120).

There are dozens of other courses; so this is only a sample. Don't be afraid to ask if green fees are negotiable; they can often be reduced at quiet times of the year or even on a quiet day. There are also often reductions for seniors. When you book, check on the club's dress code, as there are differences from course to course. Typically, you need a collared shirt, Bermuda shorts and no denim.

BRITTIP

Reader John Cartlidge, a keen golfer, advises: 'Take your waterproofs with you. I was looking to buy some in Florida but could only find lightweight slipovers – no use in the UK.'

For those just looking to see golf stars in action, Orlando has several big annual events. The **Arnold Palmer Invitational** at the Bay Hill Club off Apopka-Vineland Road in west Orlando (11–17 Mar 2008) is a major tournament (see Tiger Woods, Vijay Singh *et al.*; 1866 764 4843, **www.bayhillinvitational.com**). The **Funai Classic** is another big PGA date each Oct, held over 2 courses at the *Walt Disney World Resort* (407 835 2525). For the best women's golf, the new **Ginn Open** (every April) offers one of the biggest purses in the game ($2.5m in 2006) and attracts the top players (1877 446 6849, **www.ginnopen.com**).

Mini-golf

Not exactly a sport, but definitely for fun, the many quite extravagant mini-golf centres around Orlando are a big hit with kids and good fun for all the family (if you have the legs left after a day at the parks!). Several attractions and parks offer mini-golf as an extra but, for the best, try out the self-contained centres, of which there are a large variety. Typically, Disney has some terrific courses of its own.

Disney's Fantasia Gardens Miniature Golf Courses, next to the *Swan* hotel just off Buena Vista Drive, is a 2-course challenge over 36 of the most varied holes of mini-golf you will find. Hippos dance, fountains leap and broomsticks march on the 18-hole crazy, golf-themed **Fantasia Gardens** – its style is taken from the classic film *Fantasia*, meaning lots of cartoon fun and a riot of visual gags as well as some diabolically difficult mini-golf. Watch out for *Toccata and Fugue in D Minor*, where good shots are rewarded with musical tones, and *The Nutcracker Suite*, where obstacles include dancing mushrooms! **Fantasia Fairways** is a cunning putting course, complete with rough, water hazards and bunkers to test even the best golfers. The 18 holes range from 40ft/12m to 75ft/23m, and it can take more than an hour to play a full round. Each course costs $10.75 (adult) and $8.50 (child), and they are open daily 10am–11pm.

The 36-hole **Winter-Summerland Mini-Golf Courses** are at the entrance to *Disney's Blizzard Beach* water park. Divided into 2 18-hole courses, these mini works of art feature a 'summer' setting of surf and beach tests (watch out for squirting fish) and a 'winter' variety of snow and ice-crafted holes, all with a welter of visual puns as befits the vacation resort of Santa's elves (yes, that's the theme, and kids love it – you can even see the marks where Santa landed his sleigh!). An adult round is $10.75 (3–9s $8.50), a double round is half price. Open 10am–11pm. *Blizzard Beach* admission is not needed for the mini-golf.

Disney's Winter-Summerland mini-golf

© Disney

Mini-golf is a staple part of the **International Drive** scene, with no fewer than 7 courses in the vicinity, 5 of them recent ones. Check out the 18-hole **Congo River** set-up in front of the Sheraton Studio City hotel and its 36-hole course just south of Wet 'n Wild; $10.45 adults, $8.45 under-10s, both courses for $14.50 and $12.50 – see **www.congoriver.com** for a money-off coupon; 10am–11pm Sun–Thurs, 10am–midnight Fri, Sat); the 36-hole **Tiki Island Golf** behind the Salt Island restaurant north of Sand Lake Road, where a hole-in-one at the last hole sets off the volcano (10am–11.30pm; $10 adults, $9 children, or $13 and $12 for both courses); a **Hawaiian Rumble** 36 holes next to Wonder Works on I-Drive (and on Highway 535 in Lake Buena Vista); 10am–11pm Sun–Thurs, 10am–midnight Fri, Sat; $9.95 adults, $7.95 4–10s for 18 holes and $14.95 and $11.95 for all 36; visit **www.hawaiianrumbleorlando.com** for a discount coupon); the unusual indoor, glow-in-the-dark 18 holes of the **Putting Edge** at Festival Bay, at the top of I-Drive (11am–9pm Mon–Thurs, 10am–10.30pm Fri, 11am–10.30pm Sat, 11am–7.30pm Sun; $8.50 adults, $7.50 7–12s, $6 5–6s, and $4 for a second game); **Pirates Cove**, next to the defunct Mercado, remains the original I-Drive set-up, with caves, waterfalls and rope bridges to test your skills over the 2 18-hole courses (the Captain's Course and the more difficult Blackbeard's Challenge; daily 9am–11.30pm; $9.95 adults, $8.95 children, or $13.95 and $12.50 for all 36 holes). There is a near-identical Pirates Cove set-up at Lake Buena Vista at the back of the Crossroads shopping plaza.

Finally, new in 2007 was the amazingly detailed **Gator Golf and Adventure Park**, just past Carrier Drive, next to Murphy's Arms Pub. Here you can meet Gatorzilla (dubbed 'Florida's fiercest gator!'), watch gator shows and gator wrestling, and sink your teeth into a round of surprisingly challenging mini-golf (10am–11pm

Sun–Thurs, 10am–midnight Fri, Sat; $12 adults, $10 under-12s).

In **Kissimmee**, the wonderfully scenic 36-hole **Congo River Golf & Exploration Co** set-up on Highway 192 (just south of the junction with Highway 535, between mile markers 12 and 13), is arguably the pick of the bunch, open daily 10am–midnight. Then there is the 18-hole **River Adventure** course just north of Medieval Times (markers 14–15; 9am–11pm; $8, second game $4); and the 2 imaginative cowboy-themed courses of **Bonanza Golf** (also on Highway 192 by marker 5) 9am–midnight; $7.95/person. **Pirates Cove** is a 36-hole course next to Old Town (behind the Red Lobster restaurant, between markers 9 and 10; 9am–11.30pm); the 2 courses of **Pirate's Island** (by 192 Flea World and Medieval Times, marker 14; open 9am–11.30pm) and the new **Jungle Golf** (Hwy 192 at mile markers 4 and 5; 9am–11:30pm; $9.95 adults, $8.95 4–12s, all-day play for $11.95).

Freshwater fishing

Freshwater fishing on central Florida's abundant rivers and lakes (St John's River, Kissimmee Chain of Lakes, and Lake Tohopekaliga, for example) attracts enthusiasts worldwide. In addition, many visitors find a quiet day's angling provides an enjoyable and welcome change of pace. The primary draw for most out-of-towners is the opportunity to catch giant Florida bass – which often grow to record sizes in the area's grassy waters – and view some of the wildlife in its natural environment.

To fish in a freshwater lake, river, or stream you need a Florida Freshwater Fishing License, available from the Florida Fish and Wildlife Commission (**http://myfwc.com/license/index.html** to purchase online at a $2.25 surcharge – have your credit card handy). You will be issued a temporary licence number within minutes, enabling you to fish right away. A permanent licence will be mailed to you within 48 hours. The cost of a 7-day licence is $16.50. It is also advisable to book a reservation for a guided trip 2 or more weeks in advance, especially in holiday periods.

AJ's Freelancer Bass Guide Service is the oldest continuously operating guide service in central Florida, specialising in trophy bass fishing on Lake Toho in Kissimmee. Toho is rated the best big bass lake in the USA, and AJ's holds the record for largemouth bass here – 16lb 10oz! Saltwater guide trips are also offered. *The Freelancer* is owned and operated by Captain A James Jackson, one of the top fishing guides in the country, providing a highly personalised service to both regular and novice fishermen. All guides are experienced, full-time professionals and run trips of 4, 6 and 8 hours. Rates start at $250 for ½ day (4-hour) guided trip. For other services, photos, testimonials and fish reports, visit the excellent website **www.orlando bass.com** For reservations call 407 348-8764 or email **capjackson@aol.com** For other Kissimmee fishing opportunities, try **Scenic Lake Tours** (see page 247) or visit the Outdoor Recreation section of **www.floridakiss.com**. Go bass fishing at *Walt Disney World* (from any of 11 of their resort hotels, plus the Marketplace at *Downtown Disney*) and it will cost $125–395 for 2 hours for a boat with up to 5 people. Children's (6–12s) 1- hour fishing tours cost $30.

Seminole County has its share of fishing action, too. Check out **Spotted Tail** for a good range of angling adventures with fly and light tackle (407 977 5207, **www.spottedtail.com**).

Water sports

Florida is mad keen on water sports of all types. So, on any area of water bigger than your average pond, don't be surprised to find the locals water-skiing, jet-skiing, knee-boarding, canoeing, paddling, windsurfing, boating or indulging in any other watery pursuits.

Walt Disney World offers all manner of boats (from catamarans to canoes and pedaloes) and activities (from water-skiing to parasailing) on the main **Bay Lake**, as well as the smaller **Seven Seas Lagoon**, **Crescent Lake** and **Lake Buena Vista**. Parasailing (from *Disney's Contemporary Resort* – see page 67) comes in 2 price categories, a Regular flight, which goes to 450ft/137m for 8–10 minutes, and a Premium flight to 600ft/183m for 10–12 minutes. It costs $95–120 solo or $160–185 tandem, while boat rentals vary from $33/½ hour (21ft pontoon boat) to $125/hour (personal watercraft and wave runners), and can be found at 11 Disney resorts, plus The Marketplace at *Downtown Disney*. To book, call 407 939 0754.

Two other locations worth noting are **Buena Vista Watersports** for jet-skiing ($50/½ hour), water-skiing, wakeboard and tube rides ($70/½-hour) on Little Lake Bryan by the Holiday Inn Sunspree on Highway 535 (**www.bvwatersports.com**) and **Orlando Watersports Complex** just off the Beachline Expressway (528) near Orlando International Airport. This latter is an elaborate teaching facility featuring wakeboarding and water-skiing, by boat and suspended cable, for both novices and experts. It has a huge range of classes and options, for individuals, groups and birthday parties. Call 407 251 3100 or visit **www.orlandowatersports.com**

Horse riding

Orlando is home to one of the foremost equestrian centres in America – the **Grand Cypress Equestrian Center**, which is part of the 1,500 acre/608ha Grand Cypress Resort, and all its rides and facilities are open to non-residents. This stunningly equipped equine haven offers a dazzling array of opportunities for horse enthusiasts of all abilities.

A full range of clinics, lessons and other instructional programmes is available, from ½-hour kids' sessions to all-summer academies, plus a variety of trail rides. Serious horse riders will note that this was the first American equestrian centre to be approved by the British Horse Society, and it operates the BHS test programme. Inevitably, this 5-star facility does not come cheap but it is a worthwhile experience, especially for children. Private lessons are $55/½-hour or $100/hour, while a package of eight 1-hour group lessons is $280. The Western Trail Ride (a 45-minute excursion for novice riders, minimum age 10) is $45 per person. 8.30am–6pm Mon–Fri, 8.30am–5pm Sat, Sun. Take exit 68 on I-4 on to Route 535 north, turn left after ½ml/1km at the traffic lights and then follow the road north for 1ml/1.6km past the Grand Cypress Hotel, and it's on the right (407 239 1938, **www.grand cypress. com/equestrian_center**).

On a smaller scale but none the less charming is the **Horse World Riding Stables** on Poinciana Boulevard, just 12mls/19km south of Highway 192. This gets you further out into the wilds and you can spend anything from an hour to a full day enjoying the rides and lessons on offer. The 3 main rides through 750 acres/304ha of untouched Florida countryside are the Nature Trail ($39 adults, $16.95 5 and under riding double with parent), a walking-only tour of 45–50 minutes for beginners aged 6 and up, the Intermediate Trail (10 and over) for nearly 1 hour ($47), and the Advanced Private Trail, a 75–90 minute trip for advanced riders with a private guide ($69). There is also a picnic area with fishing pond, playing fields, pony rides for under-7s ($7) and farm animals to pet. Riding lessons are $49/hour for group or private lessons. A 3-hour Children's Horse Camp (for 8–14s) is available on Saturdays at 9am (call for prices). There is no charge for just looking, and the stables are open 9am–5pm daily (407 847 4343, **www.horseworldstables.com**).

Spectator events

When it comes to spectator events, Orlando is not quite as well furnished as other big American cities, but there is always something for the sports fan who would like to see a local game. There are no top-flight American football or baseball teams, but there are 2 indoor versions of gridiron (American football), Arena Football and the World Indoor Football League, plus Spring Training (pre-season) for several baseball teams (notably Atlanta in *Disney's Wide World of Sports*™).

However, the main sport is **basketball** with the **Orlando Magic** of the National Basketball Association (NBA). The season runs Nov–May (with exhibition games in Oct), and the only drawback is the 16,000-seat **Amway Arena** where they play (on Amelia Street, exit 83B off I-4, turn left, then left again) is occasionally fully booked. Contact the Center's box office (407 649 3245) to see if there are any tickets left, though you will need to call in person to buy them (from $10 in the upper seats to $240 for the best seats courtside), or try TicketMaster on 407 839 3900 for credit card bookings. **Florida Dolphin Tours** (407 352 5151, **www.florida dolphintours.com**) also offers Magic packages for $89 with transport. More info on **www.nba.com/magic/**

The **Orlando Predators**, one of America's top **Arena Football** teams, is also popular at the same venue (Mar–June, $10–120). Call several days in advance to see one of its lively home games that feature some great entertainment as well as their fast, hard-hitting version of indoor gridiron (407 447 7337, **www.orlando predators.com**). The newest team is the **Osceola Ghost Riders**, playing a

variation on this theme (Apr–Jun, $9–19) with the World Indoor Football League at the **Silver Spurs Arena** in Kissimmee. It is a very much a local product, but they work hard to make all home games entertaining events and it makes for a fun evening (407 210 2383, **www.osceola.lyrehc.com**).

BRITTIP

We rate the local sports experiences very highly if you want to partake in some real Americana. You don't need to understand the details of the game you are watching, just turn up and enjoy the genuine fan-friendly atmosphere and excitement.

For the real thing in American football terms, the nearest teams in the **National Football League** are the **Tampa Bay Buccaneers**, 75mls/120km to the west, the **Miami Dolphins**, some 3–4 hours' drive south, down the Florida Turnpike, or the **Jacksonville Jaguars** way up the east coast past Daytona, a 3-hour drive up I-4 and I-95. Again, TicketMaster can give you ticket prices ($35–95) and availability (Sept–Dec; and the Buccaneers sell out early these days). Once again, *Brit's Guide* partner **Florida Dolphin Tours** (see page 255) runs a limited number of trips to Jacksonville each season, and these are worth seeking out.

A spring training **baseball** opportunity can be seen at Osceola County Stadium in Kissimmee, where the **Houston Astros** take up home each Mar. Being part of the audience here is to experience real local colour. Call 321 697 3201 for more details, or TicketMaster for tickets on 407 839 3900. In truth, the best opportunity is a **Tampa Bay Devil Rays** game in St Petersburg, as tickets are nearly always available and their indoor stadium is superb (see page 271).

Disney's Wide World of Sports™

The best all-round sports facility in the area is inevitably a Disney project, though there is only a handful of genuine spectator events here. *Disney's Wide World of Sports™* is a 220 acre/86ha state-of-the-art complex, featuring 30 sports and just wandering round even when no one is playing is awesome. The complex's main features are a 9,500-seater baseball stadium, a softball quadraplex, an 11-court tennis complex, athletics track, extensive sports field and the **Official All Star Café**® with a massive array of sports memorabilia, multi-screen TVs and themed food.

Top of the crop for a must-see visit is **The Ballpark**, home for Spring Training of baseball's mighty **Atlanta Braves**, where the crowds flock in for pre-season games in late Feb and Mar (highly recommended; tickets $14–25, 407 839 3900). This is a big deal for American sports fans and games do sell out. The complex is also home for a month from mid-July to the NFL's **Tampa Bay Buccaneers** for their pre-season training, and it is an eye-opening experience to watch these amazing athletes in action, even if it is only in practice. Their extensive sports fields cater for soccer, lacrosse, American football, baseball and softball, and you can often see some keen sporting action just with college and high school teams. **Disney's**

Extreme Bulls at Silver Spurs Rodeo

Soccer Showcase in late December is a fine example of this, with some 400 teams competing under the eye of various scouts. The level of skill is sure to surprise you. Kids should watch out for the multi-activity **Sports Experience** centre, where they can try their hand for free at American football, basketball, hockey and other sports and games, plus a play/climbing area for young 'uns. Standard admission is $11 for adults and $8.25 for 3–9s, but it is also an optional extra with all Premium and Ultimate tickets (excluding special events like baseball). *Disney's Wide World of Sports™* is off Osceola Parkway, on Victory Way. Call 407 939 4263 for events and prices or visit **www.disneyworldsports.com**

The **Walt Disney World Marathon** is a major annual event and its 14th running will be on 13 Jan 2008. Some 13,500 runners take part – including some of the world's leading athletes – drawing huge crowds and taking in all 4 Disney theme parks. Be aware that the parks face some serious disruption but, as with the London Marathon, the Disney version is a great spectacle. The annual half-marathon takes place the same weekend.

Rodeo

An all-American pursuit straight out of the Old West, the **Silver Spurs Rodeo** is staged twice a year at the brand new, 8,300-seat Silver Spurs Arena. The biggest event of its kind in the south-east, it is held in early Oct and mid-Feb. However, it sells out fast so book in advance on 407 677 6336 (**www.silverspursrodeo.com**). The event features classic bronco and bull riding and attracts top competitors from as far away as Canada. The new arena is part of the $84m **Osceola Heritage Park**, which includes Osceola County Stadium (for baseball) and the Kissimmee Valley Livestock Show and Fair Pavilion. The **Silver Spurs Arena** is a state-of-the-art facility that can also be used for concerts, and there is not a bad seat in the house. The ease with which it is converted from the rodeo venue and back again, with truckloads of dirt, is quite amazing (sadly, the old family-friendly Friday Night Rodeo in Kissimmee has closed).

Motor sport

For the guaranteed ultimate in high-speed thrills, *Walt Disney World Resort in Florida* has its own speedway oval where the **Richard Petty Driving Experience** is based (in the car park for the *Magic Kingdom*, NOT at the *Wide World of Sports*™). Here you can experience one of its 650-bhp stock cars as either driver or passenger at up to 145mph/233kph, with the programmes devised by top NASCAR driver Richard Petty. Choose from the 3-lap **Ride-Along Experience**; the 3-hour **Rookie Experience** (with tuition and 8 laps of the speedway); the **Kings Experience** (tuition plus 18 laps); and the **Experience of a Lifetime** (an intense 30-lap programme). The Ride-Along Experience will probably appeal to most (16 and over only) – 3 laps of the 1.1ml/1.8km circuit with an experienced driver lasting just 37 seconds a lap but an unbelievable blast all the way. Your start from the pit lane takes you 0–60mph/97kph) in a couple of seconds and you are straight into Turn One with your brain some distance behind – it's a bit like flying at ground level. It's hot and noisy and you must wear sensible clothes (you have to climb in through the window), but it is definitely the real thing in ride terms and a huge thrill.

You don't need to book for the Ride-Along Experience, which is available daily, and there is no admission fee, so you can come along just to watch (8am–1pm). The 3 driving programmes (not Tue or Thurs) all require reservations, while the track is sometimes closed for race testing Oct–Apr. However, wait for the prices: $99 for Ride-Along; $399 for Rookie;

$799 for Kings; and $1,249 for the Lifetime Experience. You must be 18 or over for the last 3 (407 939 0130, **www.1800bepetty.com**).

Race fans will want to visit **Daytona International Speedway** just up the road in Daytona (take I-4 east, then I-95 and Highway 92) for lots more big-league car and motorcycle thrills. It hosts more than a dozen race weekends a year, including stock car, sports car, motorcycle and go-kart, and highlights are the **Rolex 24** (a top 24-hour sports car event, 26–27 Jan 2008), the world famous **Daytona 500** (17 Feb), **Pepsi 400** (5 July) and **Bike Week** (29 Feb–9 Mar). The big events attract almost 250,000 devotees and provide some of the most exciting sport anywhere in the world (386 254 2700, **www.daytonainternational speedway.com**.

And don't forget to visit the fun, interactive **Daytona USA** attraction as well, and the chance to tour the Speedway (see page 270). **The Richard Petty Driving Experience** is available here too (but only for 16s and over) and the $134 fee for 3 laps of the world-famous, steeply banked 2½ml/4km tri-oval includes entrance to Daytona USA as well. There is also a Daytona Highbanks 8 ($525), Daytona Super 16 ($1,249) and grand Daytona Experience ($2,099).

Okay, that's the local area sorted out, now let's take you further afield…

Daytona USA

9 The Twin Centre Option

or To Orlando, And Beyond!

While Orlando and its surroundings continue to get bigger and better year by year, it is equally true that there is a LOT more to see in the rest of Florida and there are some magnificent twin centre options. From St Augustine in the north-east to Key West in the extreme south (the 'Floribbean'!), it is easy to find wonderful resorts, glorious beaches and more family-friendly attractions.

The beaches of the Gulf (west) Coast, the Atlantic Coast from Ormond Beach all the way down to Miami, and the fabulous Florida Keys all feature some of the best and most inviting seaside escapes in the world, while the cities of St Augustine, West Palm Beach, Fort Lauderdale and Miami provide another fascinating facet of the Sunshine State. Two-centre (or fly-drive) options are fairly common with most of the tour operators, but it is also fairly easy to arrange your own excursions from Orlando, be they for

a week, 2 weeks or just a night. A cruise-and-stay holiday is also a great choice these days, with the cruise ports of Tampa, Port Canaveral, Port Everglades (Fort Lauderdale) and Miami all within easy distance of Central Florida.

So, with the idea that you can head out from Orlando in almost any direction in search of a great twin-centre experience. To the east, Cocoa Beach, New Smyrna Beach, Ormond Beach and the famous Daytona Beach all have terrific appeal and are barely an hour's drive. The sea is a degree or so cooler on the Atlantic side of the coast, and the surf and currents are more noticeable, hence this is good surfing territory. North-east you have the historic city of St Augustine about 2 hours away. The west boasts miles of pristine sands from Clearwater Beach all the way south to Naples and lovely Marco Island. This tends to be slightly better for families with younger children, while the Clearwater-St Pete Beach area is a perfect combination with Orlando (about 1½–2 hours' drive). Go south-east and you hit the likes of Vero Beach, West Palm Beach, Fort Lauderdale and incomparable Miami (about a 4-hour drive). Continue south and there's the Keys, a magnificent 110ml/177km chain of islands linked by roads and bridges, culminating in eclectic Key West. So, heading north-east first, here's what you find.

✠ BRITTIP

The Florida Turnpike (toll) is the main route south-east from Orlando, but it is a seriously dull drive. If time is not a factor, try taking the Beachline Expressway (528) east and then I-95 or, better still, Highway 1, south. The journey will be far more rewarding

BRITTIP
To read up more in advance, go to the **Visit Florida** website at http://international.visitflorida.com/uk/

St Augustine

A good 2-hour drive up I-4 and then I-95 brings you to America's oldest city. Founded by Spanish conquistadores in 1565, St Augustine is a genuine historic relic, full of authentic buildings and signs of the original settlement around the imposing Castillo de San Marcos. Much of the original walled city still remains and 'old' is a much-revered term here, as the 18th- and 19th-century Mediterranean influences are seemingly everywhere. Walk the narrow, uneven streets of the **Restoration Area** to discover a host of colonial architectural treasures, now home to gift shops, restaurants, pubs, ice cream parlours, antiques shops, quaint B&Bs and other historic attractions. Golf fans should head for nearby Ponte Vedra, where the **World Golf Hall of Fame** is located.

BRITTIP
Spanish adventurer Ponce de Leon was searching for the Fountain of Youth when he arrived at the site of St Augustine in 1513. The modern day Archaeological Park tells the full story of his arrival and the discovery of the continent of America – and offers the chance to drink the famous waters. Visit **www.fountainofyouthflorida.com**

To see as much of it as possible, you can hop on a horse-drawn carriage, the **St Augustine Sightseeing Train** or the **Old Town Trolley Tours** for a narrated ride around the city. For a spookier experience, try walking the streets at night to experience the 'ghostly' side of the city with **Ghost Tours of St Augustine**, with your guide in period costume. Other tours reveal St Augustine's rich architectural heritage (also the product of British

and colonial American rule). Florida railroad mogul Henry Flagler was another big influence here, building some magnificent hotels for his 'passengers to paradise'. The **Lightner Museum**, formerly Flagler's Hotel Alcazar, is home to his turn-of-the-century treasures, including Tiffany and other glass works of art. Don't miss the hotel's remarkable old indoor swimming pool – considered a wonder in its day. Other attractions around the Old City include modern theatre, opera, art galleries, **Potter's Wax Museum**, **Ripley's Believe It or Not Museum** and a local chocolate factory. Restaurants range from **The Spanish Bakery** that uses heirloom recipes to a modern microbrewery (**A1A Aleworks**), and the famous, family-owned **Columbia Restaurant**, where recipes have also been handed down for more than a century.

BRITTIP
Festivals are an integral part of St Augustine's routine, from monthly art walk nights to annual costumed torchlight re-enactments of British occupation and the City Birthday on 8 September.

Where to stay: the city's premier hotel is the historic **Casa Monica** (904 827 1888, **www.casamonica.com**), but there are also numerous B&Bs, plus chain hotels like Best Western and Hampton Inn. The boutique **St George Inn** (904 827 5740; **www.stgeorge-inn.com**) is a good choice.

More info: Dept of Heritage Tourism, 904 825 1000, **www.historic staugustine.com**

The Space Coast

Further south on the Atlantic seaboard is the area known as the Space Coast, for its proximity to the Kennedy Space Center (see page 211). **Cocoa Beach** is closest to Orlando, barely 50 minutes east (on the Beachline Expressway – 528 – then south on Highway A1A) and offers some good shopping (including the unmissable **Ron Jon's Surf Shop**, a massive neon emporium of all things water related) in addition to the 2 main public beaches. As it's the Atlantic, the sea can be chilly Nov–Mar, but it is developing into a major coastal resort, so the facilities are excellent (**www.cocoabeach.com**). You will also find some absorbing extra attractions. Look out for the **US Space Walk of Fame** in Titusville (a riverwalk with displays of memorabilia, plaques and public art depicting America's history in space), **Merritt Island National Wildlife Refuge** (a 6ml/9km driving tour adjacent to the Kennedy Space Center) and the fascinating and rather moving **American Police Hall of Fame & Museum**, also in Titusville (with all you ever wanted to know about the history of crime and law enforcement, plus a tribute to all the police officers who have died in the line of duty, an indoor shooting centre and helicopter rides; (**www.aphf.org**). Aviation fans may want to check out the **Valiant Air Command Warbird Museum** here, with more than 35 vintage war planes and guided tours through the history of military aviation. Cocoa Beach is also home to the excellent **Astronaut Memorial Planetarium & Observatory**, which holds superb daily shows in its large-screen cinema and world-class planetarium, plus an exhibition hall, art gallery and gift shop, all on Brevard Community College Campus (321 433 7373, **www.brevardcc.edu/planet**).

Some 30mls/48km to the north lies up-and-coming (but still largely undiscovered) **New Smyrna Beach**, with 13mls/20km of pristine white sands, great surfing, shell-collecting and boating at any of the many marinas hereabouts (386 428 1600, **www.nsbfla.com**).

Where to stay: try **Four Points by Sheraton Cocoa Beach** (321 783 8717, **www.starwoodhotels.com**) and **Holiday Inn Oceanfront Resort** (321 783 2271, **www.hicocoabeachhotelsite.com**).

More info: call 321 637 5483 or visit **www.space-coast.com**.

Its more famous neighbour, just to the north, is **Daytona Beach**, which is only an hour from Orlando if you take I-4 all the way east. This area is undergoing something of a transformation from its rather tired old image as a college party town to a more sophisticated seaside resort with all mod cons, including upmarket new hotels and restaurants, but it is still extremely family-friendly (see **www.familybeachbreak.com**). It gets busiest at spring break (the weeks leading up to Easter) but there is something for everyone. The prime attraction is the array of good **beaches** (some of which you can even drive on – for a $5 toll, speed limit 10mph/16kph). From these great open expanses of sands, you can go boating, parasailing, biking, jet-skiing and fishing, while there is also plenty of sight-seeing. Base yourself in the **Oceanfront** area and you are at the heart of things for the beach, with the historic **Bandshell**, the **Pier**, **Boardwalk** (with all the usual seaside fun and games) and the variety of shops and restaurants in the **Ocean Walk Village**.

BRITTIP

Look out for **Speeding Through Time**, a series of memorials and plaques along Daytona's Boardwalk, highlighting the world speed records set on the beaches, including those of Britons Sir Henry Segrave and Sir Malcolm Campbell.

Here you have **RC Theatres' Ocean Walk Movies 10** Cineplex, the fun of the **Mai Tai** bar, seafood emporium **RJ Gator's Florida Sea Grill & Bar**, **Johnny Rockets** diner, **Adobe Gila's Margarita Fajita Cantina** (check out its near-lethal range of cocktails!), **Starbucks** and **Planet Smoothie**, and some unique shopping at the likes of **Maui Nix Surf Shop**, **Candle Gallery**, **Bath Junkie**, and the market-style

Shoppes Bazaar. When you want to eat, our recommendation is the film-themed offerings of **Bubba Gump Shrimp Co** (based on the Tom Hanks movie *Forrest Gump*). With fun decor, a wonderfully casual style and an excellent menu (food that lives up to its surroundings), it is ideal for a quick lunch or a more leisurely dinner.

BRITTIP

Spend the day on Daytona beach, then try some water park fun at Daytona Lagoon after 4pm, when admission is only $9.99.

As if all that isn't enough, you'll also find the new **Daytona Lagoon** here, a combination water park, go-kart track, mini-golf course, arcade and laser tag centre (also with a rock-climbing wall and elaborate ball pool for the young 'uns). The water park consists of a wave pool and lazy river, 10 different flumes and an area purely for toddlers (adults $27.99, juniors (under 4ft/122cm) $19.99). There are 3 9-hole mini-golf courses ($7 for 18 holes), single and double go-karts ($7–9), while the laser tag (must be above 3ft 6in/108cm, $7), rock climbing (3 climbs for $6) and ball play ($5) are also separate items. Find out more on **www.daytonalagoon.com**

The historic **Downtown Daytona Beach** on Beach Street is the heart of the city, with a museum of local history, restaurants, nightclubs, coffee bars and a performing arts theatre, all in a quaint riverside setting. The **Angell & Phelps Chocolate Factory** is another notable curiosity here. Head to the Riverfront in early evening when the street takes on a lively café society style. There are plenty of worthwhile places to eat but, for something different, try the lively style of **Loggerhead Club & Marina** (right on the river at Ballough Road) or the sophisticated **Rain Supper Club** (on Seabreeze Boulevard). Similar upmarket choices are **Chops Restaurant** (on S Ridgewood Avenue)

and **The Cellar** (on Magnolia Avenue).

Other local highlights include a variety of ways to get out and about on the waterways. Cruising the intra-coastal Halifax River to see the sights, including dolphins at play, is highly worthwhile. Check out a **tiny cruise line** (at Halifax Harbor Marina on S Beach Street; 386 226 2343) for 4 different cruises ($12.44–23.24), which include a lovely Sunset/City Lights tour Apr–Oct. Head south from the main beach area along S Atlantic Avenue and you find even more choice for beaches and attractions, including **Sun Splash**, **Frank Rendon Park** and especially **Lighthouse Point Park**, a 52 acre/21ha stretch of nature trails, fishing, observation deck, swimming and picnicking (8am–9pm; $3.50/vehicle). The tide here can retreat by up to 500ft/150m and the beaches, open to the public year-round, tend to be quieter. At the southern end of the beaches is the wonderful **Ponce de Leon Inlet Lighthouse**, with a formidable 203 spiralling steps to the top. This well-preserved national monument is at once a museum and a magnificent recreation of 19th-century Florida maritime life, and the view from the top of the lighthouse – the second tallest in America – is superb. Daily 10am–5pm (9pm Jun–Aug); $5 adults, $1.50 children. It also has a lovely gift shop. Ponce Inlet has some great deep-sea fishing, too – visit **http://inlet harbor.com/fishing.html**

More family-orientated fun can be found at the **Marine Science Center** (just round the corner from the lighthouse), which showcases marine mammal bones, mangrove, manatee and sea turtle exhibits, plus a new seabird sanctuary, along with turtle rehabilitation facilities and a 5,000

BRITTIP

Try **Lighthouse Landing** in Lighthouse Point Park for lunch or dinner for an eclectic piece of Floridian restaurant life.

gallon/22,750 litre artificial reef aquarium, as well as static and interactive educational displays. A boardwalk and nature trail extends throughout the park, which also has a gift shop. 10am–4pm Tues–Sat, noon–4pm Sun (closed Mon); $3 adults, $1 under-13s (**www.echotourism.com/msc**).

Of course, one of the biggest draws is the Daytona racetrack (see page 265), while the accompanying **Daytona USA** attraction is well worth trying even if you're not an out-and-out race fan. This interactive centre offers a series of hands-on exhibits, rides and films to give you a taste of all the high-speed action. Change tyres in a timed pit stop (the fun *Ford 16-Second Pit Stop Challenge*), design and video test a racing car, check out the technology involved, commentate on a race and experience the *Daytona 500* film. Other elements include *Acceleration Alley* (for an additional fee), with full-size NASCAR simulators combining motion, video and sound to capture the thrills of head-to-head racing at more than 200mph/322kph, and *Daytona Dream Laps*, another elaborate motion simulator to put riders inside the Daytona 500 itself. The history and great moments of speedway are well detailed in the Heritage of Daytona and there is a good gift shop. A ½-hour open-sided tram tour of the Speedway stops in Pit Road, giving a real close-up of this amazing arena. The **Pepsi IMAX Theater** features the unique 45-minute *NASCAR 3-D: The IMAX Experience* and 14-minute *Daytona 500: The Movie*. 9am–7pm (not Christmas Day); $24 adults, $19 seniors (60+) and 6–12s (under-6s free with adult), while the Speedway tour on its own is $8.50/person (386 947 6800, **www.daytonausa.com**).

Where to stay: You'll find two of our favourite resorts out here in Daytona. The **Wyndham Ocean Walk Resort** is a huge ultra-modern complex right on the beach at Ocean Walk Village, with versatile accommodation in its luxurious 1-, 2- and 3-bed condos (all with kitchens and fabulous views to each side). With 3 outdoor pools, waterslide and lazy river feature, plus a kids' water play area, 2 indoor pools, 9-hole indoor mini-golf, daily kids' programmes, a spa and an excellent lounge and food court, it is hugely family-friendly (386 323 4800, **www.oceanwalk.com**). Alternatively, the **Shores Resort & Spa** is a real boutique choice on a quieter stretch of the beaches, with an elegant, refined ambience, beautiful rooms (with ultra-comfy beds), charming bar and signature fine-dining Baleen restaurant. It also boasts an excellent pool, kids' pool and fitness centre, plus a heavenly spa with a range of Balinese and Thai treatments (386 767 7350, **www.shoresresort.com**).

More info: call 01737 643 764 in the UK, 1800 854 1234 in US or visit **www.daytonabeach.com**

Immediately to the north is another up-and-coming area, **Ormond Beach**, where you find more smart resorts and great beaches, notably at **Bicentennial Park** (with a nature walk, fishing dock, tennis courts and playground) and **Birthplace of Speed Park** (which commemorates the first automobile race on the beach here in 1903). Just west of Daytona Beach is **DeLand** and St Johns River Country. Located in the western half of the region, this is home to several natural springs and nature preserves (**www.riveroflakesheritagecorridor.com**).

Museum of Fine Arts, St Petersburg

Breakfast with a difference!

Just north of DeLand in DeLeon Springs State Park is the unique **Old Spanish Sugar Mill** grill and griddle house, one of Florida's little restaurant treasures. Famous for its hearty cook-it-yourself breakfasts (daily 9am–4pm, from 8am at weekends), each table has an inset griddle, and you choose your ingredients and get cracking. Pancakes are the speciality (it provides pitchers of batter!), with all manner of fillings, but it also has bacon and eggs, sausage, ham, home-made breads, French toast, sandwiches and salads. You'll struggle to pay more than $8 per person and it is great fun, as well as a local institution. However, as it is inside the State Park, there is a $5/car entry fee (386 985 5644, **www.planetdeland. com/sugarmill**). You can then enjoy the park facilities, which include canoes and kayaks for hire, boat tours and hiking trails (**www.florida stateparks.com**).

Florida's Beach

Head to the west from Orlando and you have the gorgeous **Gulf Coast**, which is a 2-hour drive down I-4 from Orlando and through Tampa on I-275 south to **St Pete Beach** (105mls/ 169km) and **Clearwater Beach** (110mls/177km), while heading further south offers a string of equally beautiful cities and resorts, all of which feature stunning white-sand beaches, great fishing, water sports and far fewer crowds than you would think. The sea is a touch warmer and calmer on this side of Florida so is more suitable for small children.

The huge stretch of beaches and 'cities' from St Pete Beach to Clearwater represents the heart of the Sunshine State seaside experience, hence it is known as 'Florida's Beach' and is also the most popular twin-centre option for British visitors. It has a wonderful array of attractions as well as 35mls/56km of lovely white sands and an average 361 days of sunshine a year. **St Petersburg** itself,

just across the Howard Frankland Bridge from Tampa, is a bright, attractive city, with a range of developments, both recent and historical, which makes a visit worthwhile. Take time here for the **Dali Museum** (9.30am–5.30 Mon–Wed, Fri, Sat, 9.30am–8.30pm Thurs, noon–5.30pm Sun; $15 adults, $13.50 seniors, $4 5–9s), and the **Bay Walk** complex of shops, restaurants and a 20-screen cinema. An additional assortment of museums, notably the elegant **Museum of Fine Arts**, the newly expanded **St Petersburg Museum of History** right on the Pier, the exceedingly child-friendly **International Museum** and the fascinating **Great Explorations Children's Museum** (**www.stpete.org/ art.htm**). Pedestrian-friendly streets and the Pier provide plenty of interest, while fan-friendly Tropicana Field hosts the **Tampa Bay Devil Rays** baseball team (Apr–Sept) for another slice of highly recommended local fun ($8–85; **www.devilrays.com**). Nature lovers should also visit the **Weedon Island Preserve** (see page 254).

Head out to the Beaches themselves and you have a magnificent choice, from the 1,100 acre/445ha **Fort De Soto Park** (voted America's Number One beach in 2005) in the south to stunning **Caladesi Island** in the north. There is plenty to do, too, with the likes of Treasure Island, Sand Key and St Pete Beach all receiving the Blue Wave Award for cleanliness and safety. Fort De Soto Park offers free walking tours of its Spanish-American War era fort, while **John's Pass Village and Boardwalk** is an unusual shopping district full of art galleries and restaurants (and home to the fun Pirate Cruise – a replica sailing ship that offers a 2-hour party cruise daily around the waters of Treasure Island; $30 adults, $20 under-20s, inclusive of beer, wine and soft drinks; 727 423 7824). Parasailing, jet-skiing and fishing are also popular here. One attraction you shouldn't miss is **Dolphin Landings** in St Pete Beach.

Its 8-vessel fleet includes 2 51ft yachts that sail out for 2-hour trips on the calm inland waterway every day (9.30am, noon and 2.15pm) for guaranteed close-up dolphin-watch cruises and sunset sailings ($30 adults, $20 children), plus Shell Island day trips and fishing excursions (727 367 4488, **www.dolphinlandings.com**).

Further north at **Indian Shores** is America's largest wild bird hospital, the **Suncoast Seabird Sanctuary**, usually caring for more than 500 injured birds including birds of prey as well as pelicans, spoonbills and egrets. There is no charge to visit this non-profit-making rehab centre, but it does ask for donations (727 391 6211, **www.seabirdsanctuary.org**).

Clearwater Beach boasts the newly renovated **Marine Aquarium**, a wonderful non-profit organisation that rescues and rehabilitates injured animals, from dolphins to turtles, river otters and more. You can even take a VIP behind-the-scenes tour, which provides access to all the rehab area and a close-up of the dolphins, and try its Sea Safari (especially good for children) that goes out on the intracoastal waterway. 9am–5pm Mon–Sat, 10am–5pm Sun; $9 adults, $6.50 3–12s; add $10/person for the behind-the-scenes tour and $9 for the Sea Safari, or $25 and $20 for both with Aquarium admission (727 441 1790, **www.cmaquarium.org**). **Pier 60** is where the daily sunset celebration (complete with craft stalls and music) is held, and you can also catch **Captain Memo's Pirate Cruise** from the Marina (10am and 2pm daily; $33 adults, $28 seniors and teens, $25

under-13s). Going further north brings you to **Caladesi Island** and another of the world's most picturesque beach spots and a Top 10 American location. Most public beaches will have toilets, changing facilities and picnic tables, but there is usually a parking fee.

BRITTIP

Don't leave Clearwater Beach without visiting the Marine Aquarium's headline attraction, a dolphin called **Winter**, who was rescued from a crab trap as a youngster. Her tail had to be amputated and she was not expected to survive but, happily, she not only lived but learned to swim in a new way.

For those wishing to take it easy rather than drive, the **Suncoast Beach Trolley** is the perfect transport link (daily 5am–10.10pm) both along the beaches and into St Petersburg for $1.50/ride, $3.50 for an all-day pass and $15 for a week pass (727 530 9911, **www.psta.net**). The area also boasts 2,000 restaurants, of which the Key West bistro style of **Frenchy's Rockaway Grill** and **Frenchy's South Beach Café** (both in Clearwater Beach), the **Daiquiri Deck/Oceanside Grill** (Madeira Beach), **Crabby Bill's Seafood** (Indian Rocks, Clearwater Beach and St Pete Beach) and the **Moon Under Water** (St Petersburg) are all well worth visiting.

Where to stay: There's a wide choice of accommodation here. A range of **Superior Small Lodgings** combine beachfront locations with small-scale, personalised service. Check out **Beach Side Palms** as the perfect example – with weekly rates from $725 for a 3-room apartment (727 367 2791, **www.floridassl.com**). There are upmarket hotels, too – witness our family favourite, the superb **Tradewinds Island Resort** on St Pete Beach, an ultra-kid-friendly 774-room complex of 2 resorts with a wide range of facilities, including a huge inflatable beach slide and excellent

Dolphin Landings cruise

restaurant choice, in this blissful location (1800 360 4016, **www.trade windresort.com**) and the huge (and hugely impressive) **Sheraton Sand Key Resort** at Clearwater Beach, a 10-storey edifice with 10 acres/4ha of private beach and facilities including floodlit tennis courts, a fitness centre, children's pool and playground (with supervised programmes in summer), plus the excellent Rusty's Bistro restaurant (727 595 1611, **www.sheratonsandkey.com**).

More info: call 0208 651 4742 in the UK, 727 464 7200 in the US, or visit the excellent **www.floridasbeach.com**.

> ### BRITTIP
> During Easter and the summer months, the beaches are extremely popular with the locals at weekends, so the main stretches tend to get very crowded.

The South-West

Around 2 hours' drive from Orlando is the artsy **Bradenton/Sarasota** area (take I-4 then I-75), which features the superb beachfronts of **Anna Maria Island** (charming and secluded beaches), **Longboat Key** and **Venice** ('the shark tooth capital of the world' and great for fossil hunters). Sarasota is the year-round home to the **Ringling Circus**, and there are many circus-influenced offerings hereabouts, including the Ringling Estates museum, gardens and theatre. There is superb shopping at **St Armand's Circle** in Lido Key, and the **Mote Aquarium** is also worthy of note. In Bradenton, look out for the **Village of Arts**, and the sophisticated **South Florida Museum**, with its manatee mascot. Good seafood is always on the menu here, and you should check out the Spanish/Cuban style of the **Columbia Restaurant** in Sarasota (941 388 3987, **www.columbia restaurant.com**) and lively beachfront **Siesta Key Oyster Bar** (941 346 5443, **www.skob.com**).

Where to stay: Anna Maria Island is full of small-scale B&Bs and cute beachfront inns. The **Hyatt Sarasota** is one of the top resorts in the area (941 953 1234, **www.sarasota.hyatt.com**), while the **Ritz-Carlton** is a Gulf Coast landmark (941 309 2000, **www.ritz carlton.com**).

More info: Sarasota, call 941 957 1877 or visit **www.sarasotafl.com**; Bradenton (and Anna Maria Island), 941 729 9177 or **www.flagulfislands.com**

Go further south (170mls/272km from Orlando) and you have **Charlotte Harbor**, Florida's second-largest bay after Tampa Bay, and home to the lower-key destinations of **Punta Gorda, Port Charlotte, Englewood** and **Boca Grande**. From here, the **Fort Myers/Sanibel** area is only a short drive. This is part of the mini tropical paradise of the **Lee Island Coast**, south of Charlotte Harbor, featuring the history- and nature-rich city of **Fort Myers** and funky **Pine Island**.

> ### BRITTIP
> Don't miss the big local festival, **MangoMania**, in celebration of the local fruit in July each year in Pine Island.

Among the many highlights of the barrier islands are **Fort Myers Beach**, a bustling family-orientated beach town, **Sanibel Island**, centred around its famous shell-strewn beaches, and the bird-watching mecca at the **Darling National Wildlife Refuge**, the quirky jumble of shops and restaurants in **Captiva Island**, and **Bonita Beach**, where the **Great Calusa Blueway** paddling trail heads north for some 90mls/145km. Sanibel is also home to the unique **Bailey-Matthews Shell Museum**, plus a historic village and several wildlife attractions. Canoeing, kayaking and nature tours are all featured here among these truly beautiful beaches.

Where to stay: you will find a good mix of vacation homes and cottages in Fort Myers Beach and Sanibel, while the top hotels are **Lovers Key Resort** (239 765 1040, **www.lovers key.com**) and the **Sanibel Harbor Resort & Spa** (1866 283 3273, **www.sanibel-resort.com**).

More info: call 239 338 3500 or visit **www.fortmyers-sanibel.com**

Continue south for about 230mls/ 368km and you have the magnificent 'Paradise Coast' of **Naples** and **Marco Island**, 2 of Florida's lesser-known seaside treasures. Naples is both a fresh, modern city with plenty of attractions (notably the **Museum of Art**, **Naples Nature Center** and **Corkscrew Swamp Sanctuary**, plus great shopping) and a major beach destination. It's art-tinged ambience is well-evidenced in **Fifth Avenue South**, with boutique stores, sidewalk cafés and art festivals, while **Third Street** and the **Avenues** offer more of this street life and café society atmosphere. **Gallery Row**, the **City Dock**, the **Waterside Shops at Pelican Bay** and **Venetian Village** are other notable shopping districts. The beaches are mere steps away; at the municipal beach, **Naples Pier** juts into placid Gulf waters, while **Lowdermilk Beach** is fully family-friendly, with volleyball and other facilities. Marco Island is the largest of the Ten Thousand Islands, consisting of two main communities: **Marco**,

Tradewinds Island Resort

known for its wide-coved beach and fine resorts, plus a multitude of fishing charters; and **Goodland**, with its eclectic collection of fish house restaurants, plus fishing charters into the Everglades back-waters.

> ### BRITTIP
> The Naples/Marco Island area is the perfect base on Paradise Coast from which to explore the amazing **Florida Everglades** themselves, though you can also reach them from Fort Lauderdale on the east coast.

Where to stay: take your pick from an impressive range of high-quality resorts, including the **Hilton Marco Island Beach Resort** (239 394 5000, **www.marcoisland.hilton.com**), the **Marco Beach Ocean Resort** (239 393 1400, **www.marcobeachoceanresort.com**) and the **Naples Grande Resort & Club** (239 597 3232, **www.naplesgranderesort.com**).

More info: call 1800 688 3600 or visit **www.paradisecoast.com**

Treasure Coast

Returning to the Atlantic Coast, and heading out of Orlando for 2 hours on the Beachline Expressway (528) and Highway 1 brings you to another often-overlooked Florida jewel, **Vero Beach**. Nicknamed the Treasure Coast (for its history of shipwrecks), it boasts the intriguing **McLarty Treasure Museum** and the **Pelican Island National Wildlife Refuge**. Vero Beach itself is located on the barrier island of North Hutchinson but also spreads to the mainland, with an array of art galleries, smart shops, seafood restaurants, small resorts and beach parks, including a boardwalk atop the dunes.

Head south for another hour and you reach **Palm Beach** and the mainland city of **West Palm Beach**, foremost among Florida's most chic communities. A well-established playground of the rich and famous, Henry Flagler's **Whitehall** mansion is a highlight, while the many upscale

Seminole Central

Head west out of Fort Lauderdale and you come to one of the most rewarding parts of the state, the **Ah-Tah-Thi-Ki Museum** and home to the Seminole tribe of Florida. Here you can learn about Native American culture, from its customs to the bitter 19th century Seminole Wars and its modern face as the 'guardians' of the Everglades. See the Living Village and walk the 1ml/1.6km Boardwalk raised over the Cypress Swamp. Then try the nearby **Billie Swamp Safari**, a 2,200 acre/1.6ha Cypress Reservation featuring close-up views of the wildlife (including snakes and gators) via its giant-wheeled buggy, airboat rides and swamp critter shows. You can even stay overnight in its Chickee huts (1800 683 7800 or visit **www.seminoletribe.com**).

restaurants are the places to go celebrity-watching. Also here is the **Lion Country Safari**, with lions, elephants and giraffes among many other animals.

Where to stay: Disney's Vero Beach Resort doesn't always have availability (it is a Disney Vacation Club property first and foremost), but it is 71 acres/24ha of true Disney fantasy and the perfect family resort on this coast (772 234 2000, **www.dvcresorts.com**). In Palm Beach there is really only one place to stay (or visit) – the truly magnificent and opulent **The Breakers**, which is one of America's legendary resort destinations (561 655 6611, **www.thebreakers.com**).

More info: call 561 233 3000 or visit **www.palmbeachfl.com**

Miami and Fort Lauderdale

From Palm Beach, your enjoyable coast drive brings you through increasingly built-up resort territory as you go through Delray Beach, chic Boca Raton, Deerfield Beach and Pompano Beach to **Fort Lauderdale**. This latter has become one of

Florida's most upmarket and enjoyable destinations in recent years, with a great mix of excellent resorts, enticing shopping, engaging attractions and the fabulous beachfront. It also has a canal and waterway network that has seen it dubbed the 'Venice of America', with **water taxis** being more plentiful than the wheeled variety. Top things to see are the **Museum of Discovery & Science** (one of the state's finest), **Bonnet House Museum & Gardens**, **Old Fort Lauderdale Village & Museum** and the unmissable **Las Olas Boulevard** area, full of eye-catching shops and mouth-watering restaurants! Do shop at **Sawgrass Mills**, Florida's largest mall, which has around 350 outlet-style stores with some of the big-name designers, plus the Wanadoo City role-playing park for kids. Fort Lauderdale is also the perfect combination for a few days before or after a cruise, as both Port Everglades and the Port of Miami are only a short distance away.

Where to stay: Look for their **Superior Small Lodgings** or the many high-class resorts now dotting the beachfront, like the **Sheraton Yankee Clipper Hotel** (954 524 5551, **www.star woodhotels.com**) and the 5-star **St Regis Resort** (954 465 2300, **www.starwood hotels.com**).

More info: call 954 765 4466 or visit **www.sunny.org**

If you have taken the full 4-hour drive south from Orlando, you will finally arrive in the state's biggest and most glamorous city, **Miami**. With superb high-rise resort developments, miles of open, accessible beaches, the ultra-chic South Beach area (with its atmospheric **Art Deco District**), fantastic shopping, great sports, scintillating restaurants and nightlife, and an array of outstanding attractions, you could easily spend 2 weeks here and still not see it all. The city is actually separated by 5 miles or more from the Beaches area (a long, sprawling corridor along Collins

Avenue), where you will find most of the resorts and much of the nightlife. High style is almost everywhere, and a narrated **boat tour** (from the **Bayside Marketplace**) will show off many of the mansions of the rich and famous, while you should also tour **Coral Gables** and the older, neater **Coconut Grove** (with its **CocoWalk** shopping district and superbly ornate **Vizcaya Museum**). Other attractions include **Miami Seaquarium** on the island of Key Biscayne, the amazing **Venetian Pool** at Coral Gables, and **Parrot Jungle Island**, especially for children. You are spoiled for choice for shopping, with some of the best at the fashion-conscious **Bal Harbor Shops**, massive **Aventura Mall** and funky **Lincoln Road** in South Beach.

Where to stay: there are boutique hotels and dazzling resorts aplenty; the iconic **Fontainebleau** will be a real star in 2008 after a $1b renovation (305 538 5000, **www.bleaumiami beach.com**); the beautiful **Mandarin Oriental** is about as upmarket as it gets (305 913 8288, **www.mandarin oriental.com/miami**); more modest but still decent is the **Best Western Atlantic Beach Resort** (305 673 3337, **www.bestwstern.com**).

More info: call 305 539 3000 or visit **www.gmcvb.com**

Florida Keys

Leaving Miami behind on Highway 1 brings you into the unique realm of the Keys, a loosely connected archipelago of 1700 islands that arc down into the Caribbean. If you thought mainland Florida was easygoing, wait until you discover the laid-back 'Conch Republic', where shoes and flip-flops are the official uniform and the mix of Floridian and Caribbean influences merge into their own 'Floribbean' culture. Scuba divers are in their element here, with some of the world's best coral reefs in the world, and the renowned **John Pennekamp Coral Reef State Park** is the highlight of the many miles of

National Marine Sanctuary. The first city you encounter is **Key Largo** (made famous by the Humphrey Bogart film), closely followed by **Islamorada**, where you should stop to see **Theater To The Sea**, with its dolphin and sea-lion interaction programmes. If you're looking for fishing, some of the best charters can be found at Islamorada, **Marathon** and **Big Pine Key**.

BRITTIP

Don't miss the opportunity to feed the giant tarpon that hang around the docks by Robbie's boat rentals in Islamorada.

Marathon is the starting point of the amazing **Seven Mile Bridge**, the unofficial eighth wonder of the world, which connects the biggest gap between the islands, while Big Pine Key is home to **Bahia Honda State Park**, one of Florida's finest beaches. Finally, the 375ml/600km drive from Orlando brings you to the southernmost city in the US (just 90mls/145km from Cuba). **Key West** is possibly the most eclectic city in the US, a mixture of the laid-back and outrageous, of street performers and sidewalk artists, cafes and bars (LOTS of bars!), and the former home of **Ernest Hemingway**, whose residence and museum are essential viewing. You should also see the **Key West Aquarium** and unusual **Shipwreck Historeum,** the wonderfully diverse array of shops or just try the many water sports. You must be on the harbour front as the sun goes down though, for the famous daily **Sunset Celebration**, when Key West's party spirit is in full force. The other great feature of Key West is its myriad of ways to get around – you can try the **Conch Tour Train, Old Town Trolley Tours**, pedicabs and bicycles. Just don't expect your stay to be sedate!

Where to stay: guest houses, inns and B&Bs can be found in their greatest number through the Keys, like the **Old**

Miami nice

If you see nothing else in Miami, do spend some time in South Beach (or SoBe as it is known) and the über-cool **Ocean Drive**, full of open-air cafés, art galleries and pulsating nightclubs. Tranquil during the day, non-stop at night, this is where the beautiful people hang out, or just cruise in their Ferraris and Hummers. Here the restored Art Deco gems twinkle at night and will use up plenty of film!

Customs House Inn (305 294 8507, **www.oldcustomshouse.com**) in Key West's Old Town or the utterly charming **Banyan Resort** (305 296 7786, **www.thebanyanresort.com**).

More info: call 1800 352 5397 or visit **www.fla-keys.com**

Cruise-and-Stay

The options for twin-centre holidays don't end just because Florida does. Taking a cruise is fast becoming a popular option with an Orlando stay and, with the introduction of *Disney Cruise Line* in 1998, there's much publicity for these well-priced 3-, 4-, 5- and 7-day sailings out of Port Canaveral, Tampa, Fort Lauderdale's Port Everglades and Miami.

Although a relative newcomer to cruising, Disney has 2 breathtaking ships, the 83,000-ton *Disney Magic* (1998) and *Disney Wonder* (1999), with their own dedicated cruise terminal (plus two more mega-ships for 2011 and 2012). Classic design plus the usual Disney Imagineering have produced these two vessels, which incorporate special features for kids, teenagers AND adults. Both ships are a destination experience in their own right, each having 4 restaurants, a 977-seat theatre, cinema, nightclub complex, choice of bars and a gorgeous spa, while they sail to the Bahamas, the Caribbean and Disney's stunning private island, Castaway Cay (and southern California and Mexico in summer

2008). It's not a cheap option and the 3- and 4-night cruises can feel a bit frenzied, but the 7-night Caribbean cruises – either to St Maarten and St Thomas or Key West, Grand Cayman and Cozumel in Mexico – offer a genuinely relaxing style that is hard to beat. They boast some novel touches with superb on-board entertainment, Disney character interaction and wonderful features like the adults-only champagne brunch. Many tour operators offer *Disney Cruise Line* packages but you can also book cruise-only at great rates with Dreams Unlimited Travel (see page 27) and direct with Disney on 1800 511 9444 or **http://disneycruise.disney.go.com**

The ships are nearly identical in practical terms (both have also updated slightly to enlarge the spa, add a teen lounge, an adults' only coffee bar and provide a huge cinema screen on the funnel to show outdoor films), and the week-long cruises allow you to enjoy fully the wide range of facilities. The impact of the 3-restaurant set-up (where you dine in a different one each night, including the amazing black-and-white *Animator's Palate* that changes colour all around you; a fourth restaurant, Palo, is for adults only), the fabulous entertainment 'district', the vast array of kids' facilities (including Buzz Lightyear's Cyberspace Command Post) and the picturesque beaches of Disney's

The adults-only pool on **Disney Magic**

© Disney

Castaway Cay island is just superb. When you factor in some scintillating theatrical performances, the unique *Pirates of the Caribbean* evening (complete with deck party, on-deck stunts, special effects and fireworks), fabulous food and service, this really is as complete a package as you'll find anywhere at sea.

Other Port Canaveral options (**www.portcanaveral.org**) include the glitzy **Carnival Cruise Lines** (all-modern hardware, party atmosphere; call 1888 2276 4825 in the US or 020 7940 4466 in the UK, **www.carnival cruise.co.uk**) with 3- and 4-day Bahamas voyages on the *Carnival Sensation*, and 7-night cruises alternating to the east and west Caribbean on one of its biggest ships, the *Carnival Glory*. **Royal Caribbean International** (also 2 modern, glamorous ships; call 1866 562 7625 in the US or 0845 165 8414 in the UK, **www.royalcaribbean.co.uk**) has similar 3- and 4-day trips to Nassau and its private island of Coco Cay on *Sovereign of the Seas* and alternating 7-day Caribbean cruises on mega-ship *Mariner of the Seas* (to the Bahamas, St Thomas and St Maarten, or Jamaica, Grand Cayman and Cozumel). There are even 2 casino ships operating daily from Port Canaveral, **Sterling Casino Lines** (1800 765 5711, **www.sterlingcasino lines.com**), and **Suncruz Casinos** (1800 474 3423, **www.suncruzcasino.com**), both operating day cruises (11am–4pm and evening sailings 7pm–midnight Sun–Thurs, and 7pm–1am Fri, Sat) if you feel the need for a stylish flutter. Amazingly, you sail free, and there is only a nominal charge for the buffets aboard, so it can make for a cheap half-day out (provided you don't go mad in the casinos!)

Carnival and Royal Caribbean, plus upmarket **Holland America** (1877 724 5425, **www.hollandamerica.com**) and **Celebrity Cruises** (0845 456 1520, **www.celebritycruises.co.uk**) offer 4–14-day Caribbean cruises from the port

St Pete's Beach

of **Tampa** (**www.tampaport.com**), while there is a huge choice if you venture further south to **Miami** or **Fort Lauderdale**. Rather congested Miami boasts the largest cruise ships in the world (Royal Caribbean's amazing 160,000-ton trio *Freedom*, *Liberty* and *Independence of the Seas*), as well as other cruises from Carnival, Celebrity, **Norwegian Cruise Line** (0845 658 8010, **www.ncl.co.uk**), upmarket **Oceania Cruises** (1800 531 5619, **www.oceaniacruises.com**), the Italian style of **Costa Cruises** (1800 445 8020, **www.costacruises.co.uk**) and 6-star **Crystal Cruises** (1888 722 0021, **www.crystalcruises.com**). Sail from **Fort Lauderdale** (**www.broward.org/port**) and the choice is Carnival, Celebrity, Costa, Holland America, Royal Caribbean, 6-star **Regent Seven Seas Cruises** (023 8068 2280, **www.rssc.co.uk**), **MSC Italian Cruises** (0870 850 4883, **www.msccruises.co.uk**) and glamorous **Princess Cruises** (0845 075 0031, **www.princess cruises.co.uk**).

For more advice, consult another of Simon's publications, *World of Cruising* magazine (0870 429 2686, **www.worldofcruisingmagazine.com**) or specialist UK travel agent, The Cruise Line Ltd (0870 112 1102, **www.cruiseline.co.uk**). In Orlando, try Cruise Planners on 1877 772 7847 or **www.gocruiseplanner.com**

Well, that represents pretty much the full range of holiday choices. Now we need to tell you about how to enjoy all the night-time entertainment…!

Hands up those who still have plenty of energy left – right, this chapter is especially for you. If we can't wear you out at the theme parks and other attractions, we'll just have to resort to a full-frontal assault on your sleep time instead!

For, when it comes to night-time fun and frolics, Orlando has a dazzling collection of possibilities, from its purpose-built entertainment complexes, through its range of dinner shows, to a full array of bars and nightclubs. The choice is suitably widespread and almost always high in quality. Disney raised the bar for the big evening entertainment concept in 1987 when it opened *Pleasure Island*, an imaginative range of clubs, discos and restaurants, and it continues to refine the formula to keep it fresh and appealing with a major rebuild in 2006/7. **Disney's BoardWalk Resort**, which opened its doors in 1996, has added more to its night-time options.

International Drive (I-Drive) caught up with this process in 1997 when **The Pointe Orlando** opened. Although its prime focus is shopping and restaurants, it now has a strong evening entertainment component

with a magnificent array of lively bars, exceptional restaurants and the big Regal Cinemas 20+ IMAX multiplex. Finally, Universal Orlando got with the beat in late 1998 with the opening of **CityWalk**, possibly the most elaborate and sophisticated centre of the lot. They all represent yet another slick opportunity for you to be dazzled and relieved of your cash in the name of holiday fun. However, you should try to experience at least one.

DOWNTOWN DISNEY

The large-scale development of what is now *Downtown Disney* (the old Village Marketplace and *Pleasure Island*) has evolved into a 3-part complex (The Marketplace, *Pleasure Island* and West Side) doubling the size of the old site and providing some world-class entertainment. The recent redevelopment has opened up *Pleasure Island* to a more regular part of the *Downtown Disney* experience

Cinderella's Golden Carousel and Castle

© Disney

rather than just a night-time district, but it is still a different prospect by night than by day. More changes are also in the offing, so be sure to check our website **www.askdaisy.net/orlando** for the latest info.

Pleasure Island

This is still the traditional nightclub zone, which packs in the locals as well as the tourists. You must be 18 or over to enter most clubs (unless accompanied by a parent), and at least 21 to enter 2 of them (see below). *Pleasure Island* (centred between *Downtown Disney* Marketplace and West Side) consists of 7 original club venues and a good range of music types, plus several novel twists. The **Rock 'n Roll Beach Club** is a multi-level live music venue featuring 40 years of classic rock (mainly of the 1980s and 1990s) with a resident cover band and DJs. It also boasts pool tables, arcade games and several bars. Serious clubbers head for **Mannequins Dance Palace** (21 and over), a huge, popular disco, with a revolving dance floor, mirrored walls, dry ice and lasers, plus a pounding sound system and superb lighting. At the **Comedy Warehouse**, the highly talented and quick-witted Improv Co gives periodic shows with guest 'volunteers' (beware of sitting near a phone – you WILL end up in the show!). Queuing can begin up to ½ hour before a performance, which lasts for around 45 minutes and is guaranteed to be different

every time. For a touch of retro groovin', **8Trax** is a homage to 1970s' music, dance and styles (right down to the lava lamps) and usually draws a lively crowd of all ages. The must-see **Adventurers' Club** is our personal favourite, a 2-storey entertainment lounge in 1920s' Gentleman's Club style, which comes to life around you (watch the animal heads and masks) and the stars of the shows mix with the guests. Again an element of improvisation is mixed in with the scripted comedy and, if the cast happens to pick on you, don't try to win a battle of wits – remember that they have the microphone!

The **BET Soundstage Club**™ (21 and over) is a totally modern offering, with an interactive VJ/DJ and featuring the best of R&B, soul and hip-hop sounds. **Motion** (formerly the Wildhorse Saloon) is a cavernous dance club, featuring Top 40 to Alternative music, animated DJs and a giant TV screen. This is another happening club, and is especially popular with the locals at weekends (18 and over only). As well as the clubs, *Pleasure Island* has a big signature Harley-Davidson store and Disney continues to add new shopping opportunities to keep the area fresh. **Raglan Road**, an Irish-themed pub with lively musical entertainment, matching food and a genuine Emerald Isle style, where you really can enjoy the craic, joined the line-up in 2005 (11am–2am). Much of

Raglan Road Irish Pub

the restaurant's interior was shipped over from Ireland (including no fewer than 4 reclaimed 130-year-old bars, with 9 European beers on draft) establishing an authentic backdrop to an original menu created by celebrity master chef Kevin Dundon. Fresh, simple ingredients combined with an imaginative twist make the likes of shepherd's pie, planxty and bread pudding (the best we have tasted!) a real wake-up call for the senses. Live traditional Irish music in its Grand Room is another feature from 9pm each night, plus Irish dancing. Stop in at the gift shop for all your Guinness souvenir needs and be sure to check out Kevin Dundon's *Full On Irish* cookbook to create a taste of Raglan Road at home. Call 407 938 0300 for reservations (**www.raglanroadirish pub.com**). Located to one side of Raglan Road is chippie **Cooke's of Dublin** serving up a taste of home with real chips, beer-battered fish, gourmet battered sausages and 'Do bars' (deep-fried Snickers bars!).

BRITTIP
Raglan Road has established itself as one of Orlando's must-do venues, as much for its genuine pub charm as its fabulous food.

For a full-scale meal, the neighbouring **Portobello Yacht Club** offers excellent northern Italian cuisine in smart, lively surroundings. Of course, you can also visit the many eating outlets elsewhere around *Downtown Disney*, including **Planet Hollywood**® (the largest and busiest of this chain), Brit's Guide favourite **Wolfgang Puck's Café and Dining Room**, **Cap'n Jack's Restaurant** (for great chowder, crabcakes, shrimp or the trademark 'fishbowl' margaritas), and **Fulton's Crab House** (for some of the best seafood in Orlando – see page 317). For **advanced dining reservations** at a Disney restaurant, call 407 939 3463.

The shops and cafés of *Pleasure Island* are open 11am–11pm daily, while the nightclubs kick in from 7pm and close at 2pm. There is an $11.67 charge to enter any of the clubs, or you can buy a 1-Day Pleasure Island Pass for $23.38. A Club Pass is also included as a Plus Pack Option with all Premium tickets and included for the full 2- or 3-week duration with Ultimate tickets. Single club tickets can be bought at *Pleasure Island* itself or at *Downtown Disney* Guest Services.

West Side
This is the most recent element of the 1998 *Downtown Disney* expansion and incorporates the **AMC**® **Pleasure Island 24 Theaters Complex**, with 24 screens and 6,000 seats in state-of-the-art surroundings, as well as an excellent mix of live music, fine dining, unique shopping and *DisneyQuest*, the ultimate in interactive game arcades.

BRITTIP
Save $2 on adult tickets at the AMC® cineplex by visiting before 6pm each weekday.

The cavernous **House of Blues**®, a combination live music venue and restaurant in backwoods Mississippi style, is a must for anyone even vaguely interested in blues, rock 'n' roll, R&B, gospel and jazz – and some top-name bands play here (407 934 2583, **www.hob.com**), while its trademark **Gospel Brunch** on Sundays serves up some fab food with a full gospel show (10.30am and 1pm; $32.50 adults, $16.25 3–9s). 'Praise the Lord and pass the biscuits' is the slogan, and it's a lot of fun. The 500-seat restaurant next door to the concert hall (11am–11pm) also offers some fine fare, including jambalaya, catfish and a host of other delicious Cajun dishes, with more good, footstompin' live music (free) in the **Blues Kitchen** (Thurs–Sat). The inevitable gift shop also stocks some quality merchandise.

Bongos Cuban Café™ (co-owned by Gloria and Emilio Estefan; 11am–2am) brings the sights, sounds and tastes of Old Havana to another imaginative setting, with red-hot Latin music and some excellent Cuban fare. The **Wolfgang Puck® Café** offers a rich experience from the renowned Californian chef, with no fewer than 4 options: the Café, gourmet food in a casual setting; Wolfgang Puck Express, the fast-food version; the Sushi Bar for seafood, pizzas and micro-brew beers; and the Dining Room, an upscale restaurant featuring the best of the group's international cuisine (407 938 9653, **www.wolfgangpuck.com**). It caters for just about every taste (the sushi is to die for) and is very friendly, with excellent kids' menus and games (11.30am–11pm, 6–10.30pm in the Dining Room).

BRITTIP

If you need to escape the *Downtown Disney* hurly-burly, head upstairs to the Virgin™ Megastore, where its coffee/sandwich shop is a relative oasis of (usually queue-free) calm offering a good range of snacks and drinks.

The West Side shopping is also original and engaging, from the basic sweet shop **Candy Cauldron**, which resembles a fairytale dungeon, through the one-off outlets such as **Sosa Family Cigars**, **Sunglass Icon** and the stylish art of **Hoypoloi Gallery**, to the predictable souvenir stores and truly mega **Virgin**™ **Megastore**, the largest music store in Florida, with more than 100 listening stations, a café, hydraulic outdoor stage and a mean sound system!

Wolfgang Puck Café

© OCVB

DisneyQuest

The most unusual element to *Downtown Disney*, *DisneyQuest* is described variously as 'an immersive, interactive entertainment environment', the latest in arcade games, a series of state-of-the-art adventure rides or, as one Cast Member said, 'a theme park in a box'. It houses 11 major adventures, such as *CyberSpace Mountain* (design and ride your own roller-coaster), *Invasion – An Alien Encounter* (a fun virtual-reality rescue mission), *Ride the Comix!* (a virtual-reality battle, this time with super-villains), *Virtual Jungle Cruise* (shooting the rapids, prehistoric style) and *Aladdin's Magic Carpet* (more virtual-reality fun in best cartoon fashion), a host of old-fashioned video games in *Replay Zone*, the latest sports games, a test of imagination in *Animation Academy* and 2 futuristic cafés – Wonderland Café, with computers and internet tables, and Food Quest, straight out of a space-age comic book (both run by the excellent Cheesecake Factory).

BRITTIP

You can buy a combined annual pass for *DisneyQuest* and Disney's water parks at $137.39 for adults and $105.44 for 3–9s that can work out better value for multiple visits.

Two additional highlights are *Radio Disney SongMaker* (a computer-generated professional audio system that creates a CD – starring you!) and *Pirates of the Caribbean: Battle for Buccaneer Gold* (an amazing 3-D immersion in a swashbuckling, cannon-shooting quest for pirate treasure).

You enter *DisneyQuest* via the clever Cybrolator to Ventureport, and you then have 4 main areas to explore: Score Zone (for most of the game-playing), Explore Zone (a mix of role-playing and virtual-reality games), Create Zone (hands-on activities to be your own 'Imagineer')

© Disney

La Nouba at Cirque du Soleil®

and Replay Zone (a 'moonscape' of classic games and rides).

DisneyQuest is open 10.30am–11pm Sun–Thurs, 10.30am–midnight Fri, Sat but, if you want to avoid the queues (the building admits only 1,500), go during the day. A 1-day ticket costs $37.28 ($30.89 3–9s). It's a bit too elaborate for most youngsters but teenagers will absolutely love it.

Cirque du Soleil® – La Nouba

Saving the best for last here, the most eye-catching part of West Side is home to the greatest show on earth (or at least, the greatest we've seen anywhere), the Cirque du Soleil® production *La Nouba*™. Twice a day, 5 times a week, the company's purpose-built, 1,671-seat theatre stages the most stupendous combination of dance, circus, acrobatics, comedy and live music in a 90-minute show that involves more than 60 performers. Anyone familiar with the unique styling, outrageous costumes and captivating sounds of the world-famous Cirque company will have an idea of what to expect, but even they will be left in awe by this stunning multi-dimensional assault on the senses.

The show title comes from the French phrase *faire la nouba*, to party or live it up, and this *La Nouba* does in grand style. It features trampolines, trapezes, balancing acts and even mountain bikes, woven with comedy (watch out for the inspired clowns), innovative dance routines and spellbinding music, all with the most magnificent staging. Some of the stunts are truly jaw-dropping (the final act Power Track/Trampoline alone is worth the entry price), but the overall effect of the constant flow of movement, sublime timing and multitude of different characters (almost to the point where you hardly know where to look at any one time) is a masterpiece of modern theatre.

Words alone do not do it justice – go and see it. It is not cheap, but we believe it is worth every cent and a highlight of any visit to Orlando. Booking is vital and can be done up to 6 months in advance on 407 939 7719. Shows are at 6pm and 9pm Tues–Sat, but try to be early for some excellent pre-show fun. There are 3 pricing groups: Cat. 1 (front centre seats) at $112 for adults and $90 for 3–9s; Cat. 2 at $79 and $63; and Cat. 3 at $63 and $50 (but there is hardly a bad seat in the house). By the way, we've seen it half a dozen times, and still look forward to going again!

Finally, the whole of *Downtown Disney* West Side is characterised at night by some outstanding lighting effects and a vibrant, almost intoxicating atmosphere.

Disney's BoardWalk

Disney's other big evening entertainment offering is part of its impressive Disney's *BoardWalk Resort*, where the waterfront entertainment district contains several notable venues (not counting the excellent micro-brewery and restaurant of the Big River Grille and Brewing Works, the thrilling ESPN Club for sports fans and the 5-star Flying Fish Café). **Jellyrolls** is a variation on the duelling piano bar, with the lively pianists conjuring up a humorous and often raucous evening of audience participation songs (7pm–2am; $5 cover charge; 21 and over only).

The **Atlantic Dance** club features mainly modern dance music (it started life as a classic 1930s dance club and also moved through a Latin phase) with both house and guest DJs, plus occasional live music, all with a huge dance floor and a great bar service and ambience. It's especially popular on Fri and Sat nights, perhaps because there's no longer a cover charge (9pm–2am; closed Sun, Mon). It's strictly 21 and over, so remember your ID (no ID, no entry here). *Disney's Boardwalk Resort* also features some amusing stalls and live entertainers, which add to the carnival atmosphere, while the **ESPN Club** features regular celebrity (American) sports guests.

UNIVERSAL'S CITYWALK

As part of the big Universal Orlando development – and in direct competition with *Downtown Disney* – this 30 acre/12ha spread has just about everything in the world of entertainment. The resort's hub is a busy, bustling expanse of shops, restaurants, snack bars, open-air events and nightclubs. It offers a huge variety of cuisines, from fast food to fine dining, an unusual blend of speciality shops and a truly eclectic nightclub mix, from reggae to rock 'n' roll to salsa to jazz and high-energy

disco, plus the all-new Blue Man Group show. There's a $7 entry fee at the 6 clubs but you can buy a **CityWalk Party Pass** ($11.99) or **Party Pass with Movie** (1 free film at the 20-screen **Universal Cineplex**; $15.40) for entry to all of them, while most multi-day tickets include a Party Pass.

BRITTIP

Park in Universal's multi-storey car park (no charge after 6pm) for all the CityWalk venues. For more info on the complex, call 407 363 8000 or visit **www.citywalkorlando.com**.

The area splits into 3, with the main plaza featuring shopping and restaurants. Among the most original (and amusing) of the 13 shops are **Endangered Species**, with products designed to raise eco-awareness; **Quiet Flight**, for radical surf and beachwear; the retro-American decor of **Fossil** for leather goods, watches and sunglasses; the **Universal Studios Store** for park merchandise; the large **Island Clothing Store** (for Tommy Bahama clothing and other merchandise); and **Cartooniversal**, dedicated to cartoon-based gifts and toys featuring Spider-Man, Scooby-Doo and SpongeBob SquarePants.

CityWalk

Bubba Gump's

For dining, you have the new (in 2006) **Bubba Gump's Shrimp Co**, where the *Forrest Gump* theme permeates from the Southern-inspired menu offerings to the decor and the little flip-sign on your table to tell your server whether you need something (Stop Forrest Stop!) or not (Run Forrest Run!). The menu is predictably heavy on seafood – with prawns done every possible way – but also includes chicken, ribs, sandwiches, salads and more, with catchy names like Bubba's After the Storm 'Bucket of Boat Trash'. The gift shop carries Shrimp beanies, Gump Gear clothing, lots of miscellanea and, of course, A Box of Chocolates. Open 11am–late.

BRITTIP

Mention you are celebrating a birthday at Bubba Gump's and you'll find you quickly become the centre of attention!

NASCAR Sports Grill (formerly NASCAR Café) is a must for motor-racing fans (11am–late), with full-size stock cars and racing memorabilia, tableside plasma screens, videos and interactive games while you dine on burgers, ribs, steaks, pasta and grilled shrimp. The interior has been completely revamped and now has a smart, sophisticated look, with a balcony and patio seating for a taste of the 'Tailgating' experience (that uniquely American 'picnic in the car park' phenomena). **Pastamore** is a

delightful indoor/outdoor Italian diner, with the choice of full-service dining (5pm–midnight) for pizza, pasta, grilled chicken and steaks or the **Marketplace Café** (8am–2am) for panini, pastries and ice-cream. **Emeril's** restaurant is at the 5-star end of the range, a sophisticated and vibrant journey into the cuisine of New Orleans master chef Emeril Lagasse. Fine wines and a cigar bar both add to Emeril's Creole-based gourmet creations, and if you don't try the Louisiana oyster stew here you'll have missed a real treat (lunch 11.30am–2pm; dinner 5.30–10pm Sun–Thurs, 5.30–11pm Fri, Sat). It gets booked up well in advance at weekends, so try weekdays (407 224 2424). **Jimmy Buffet's Margaritaville** (11am–2am) is an island homage to Florida's laid-back musical hero, with 'Floribbean' cuisine (a mixture of Key West and Caribbean), live music and 3 bars, including the Volcano Bar, which 'erupts' margarita mix (!) when the blender needs filling. There is a cover charge ($7) after 10pm when the live band hits the stage.

Across the CityWalk waterway is the **Lagoon Front** location of another huge dining experience, the 2-storey **NBA City**, which is sure to thrill basketball fans with its Cage dining room, interactive playground area and Club lounge where you can watch live and classic games (11am–10.30pm Sun–Thurs; 11am–11.30pm Fri, Sat). Next door is the massive mock-Coliseum architecture of **Hard Rock Live**, a 2,500-seat concert venue with high-tech staging and sound. Big-name bands and performers are on stage several times a week (both Robbie Williams and Oasis have played here) in this slightly retro rock 'n' roll theatre (407 351 LIVE, **www.hardrocklive.com**). And, of course, you can't miss dining at the **Hard Rock Café** here, the world's largest example of this worldwide chain, with its collection of rock 'n' roll memorabilia (including a pink 1959 Cadillac). It remains hugely popular,

Red Coconut Club

so try to get in early for lunch or dinner (11am–2am) to sample its classic diner fare. Collectors of Hard Rock souvenirs will also find prices in the excellent gift shop friendlier here than the UK.

⚓ BRITTIP

CityWalk too crowded? Can't get in any of the restaurants? Jump on one of the boats to the Hard Rock Hotel or Portofino Bay Hotel and you can usually dine without a wait at The Kitchen (Hard Rock), Trattoria del Porto or Mama Della's (Portofino Bay).

Finally, you come to the **Promenade** area, which offers a choice of nightclubs and some more fine dining (notably in the case of Latin Quarter), plus the ubiquitous Starbucks coffee house.

Bob Marley – A Tribute to Freedom is a clever re-creation of Marley's Jamaica home, turned into a courtyard live music venue, restaurant and bars. The bands are excellent, the atmosphere authentic and the place really comes alive at night (4pm–2am, 21 and over after 9pm; cover charge $7 after 8pm). Next up is **Pat O'Brien's**, a faithful reproduction of the famous New Orleans bar and restaurant (4pm–1am), with its Flaming Fountain courtyard, main bar and special duelling piano bar (6pm–2am, with a $7 cover charge; 21 and over only). Excellent Cajun food and world-famous Hurricane cocktails are the order of the day, but don't drink too many and expect to walk back! **CityJazz** is a real contrast, a hip, upmarket centre combining history, education and live music from a series of local and international musicians, with tapas-style food. Visually it is stunning, with good sound quality and, if you're keen on the live music, which varies from swing and R&B to pure jazz, you can easily spend all night here (8pm–1am Sun–Thurs, 7pm–2am Fri, Sat; $7 cover charge). Thurs–Sun, CityJazz becomes **Bonkerz Comedy Club**, with some outstanding stand-up comedy acts at 8pm (18 and over only; $7 cover charge, but still included in the CityWalk PartyPass).

For younger, club-minded visitors, **the groove** is the next generation in disco entertainment, a vivid, pounding, high-energy dance venue designed like a Victorian theatre but with the latest in club music, lighting and special effects (9pm–2am; 21 and over only; cover charge $7). New for a slightly older generation is the **Red Coconut Club**, a retro dance club with a trendy, tropical vibe. With live music, signature cocktails, a cool bar

The Groove

and eclectic South Seas decor, it is a popular CityWalk venue (7pm–2am Sun–Wed; 6pm–2am Thurs–Sat; cover charge $7). Finally, completing the Promenade tour is the **Latin Quarter**, a wonderful venue/restaurant that serves up a genuine slice of Latin American style in its atmosphere, music, dance, decor and cuisine. The food is outstanding – a combination of beef, fresh fish and poultry with tangy fruit sauces, spicy salsas and mouth-watering marinades (don't miss its version of rack of lamb) – the ambience is mesmerising and the sounds are so wonderfully vibrant and alive, you can't help dancing, even in your seat. Drop in for a meal or just check out the music (open 4–10pm). There's even a Latin Quarter Express dining window if you'd like a quick bite on the go.

The newest element of CityWalk is also the most entertaining. **Blue Man Group** descended upon the Sharp AQUOS Theatre (the old Nick Studios building) in 2007 with its unique brand of comedy, music and multimedia theatrics, adding something completely novel to the Universal night time line-up. In its hands (or mouths!) mundane items, like pipes, paintballs and even audience members, become the instruments of wild creativity with sometimes stunning, occasionally somewhat gross but always hilariously gratifying outcomes. The finale is a real corker,

and don't worry if you're seated in the 'poncho section'; the Blue Men will make sure you have adequate protection. It all adds up to an unforgettable evening of family entertainment for just $59–69 adult, $49–59 3–9s. Purchase tickets online at **www.universalorlando.com** or at the theatre box office.

Not breathless yet? Well, there's still the **Universal Cineplex**, a 20-screen cinema complex with a capacity of 5,000 and the latest in film comfort.

THE POINTE ORLANDO

This eye-catching development on I-Drive, almost opposite the Convention Center, is a mix of unique shops, cinemas, restaurants and the **WonderWorks** fun centre (with its magic-themed dinner show). The Pointe is open all day but also has plenty of evening appeal, especially since the completion of a $30m redevelopment, which added 5 new restaurants, including the smooth jazz sounds at **BB King's**, fine dining at **The Capital Grille**, family-style service in **Magianno's Little Italy**, fresh seafood at **The Oceanaire** and the laid-back **Tommy Bahama's Tropical Café and Emporium**.

The big-name stores (10am–11pm) are all upscale and include some imaginative touches to make them stand out from the crowd (see page 325). The restaurants in this collection

Latin Quarter

strive to be different, too. At ground level you have **Johnny Rockets**, an entertaining 1950s-style diner with an indulgent burger-and-milkshake menu (and waiters and waitresses who perform dance routines if the right song comes on the jukebox!). **The Capital Grille** took the place of former landmark FAO Schwartz, adding an elegant dining option with an extensive wine menu (over 400 selections from around the world), dry-aged steaks, chops and seafood, with complimentary valet parking (lunch 11.30am–3pm Mon–Fri, dinner 5–10pm Sun–Thurs, 5–11pm Sat, Sun; bookings advisable on 407 370 4392; **www.capitalgrille.com**).

Similarly upscale is **The Oceanaire Seafood Room**, where you can sip a cocktail in the Lounge before diving into a menu, which is highlighted by daily specials with selections flown in from around the world to ensure the freshest offerings such as Alaskan halibut, Copper River salmon and true Dover sole (**www.theoceanaire.com**).

Maggiannos Little Italy is a journey into family-style Italian dining in a relaxed, friendly atmosphere, with nostalgic touches reminiscent of pre-World War II New York. It's a fun, bustling, bring-the-family kind of place, and a big favourite with the

Maggiano's Little Italy

locals. The menu features fresh pastas, chicken, steaks, veal and chops, plus house specials such as Eggplant, Parmesan and Mushroom Ravioli al Forno. There is also a take-away menu (11am–10pm Sun–Thurs, 11am–11pm Fri, Sat; **www.maggianos. com**). Live music acts make **BB King's** a fine choice for a meal or drinks and a show, while also new to The Pointe is **Tommy Bahama's Tropical Café and Emporium**, with dining in a laid-back, tropical setting. Tommy Bahama's also carries home furnishings, accessories and men's and women's clothing with a casual Island flair (**www.tommybahama.com**).

On the upper level you have **Adobe Gila's**, a fine Mexican *cantina*, home of the 64oz margarita and more than 70 tequilas (!), plus some south-of-the-border dining delicacies – try the signature Gila Wraps. Adobe Gila's is especially popular with locals and is often packed at weekends as it stays open late and features live outdoor music and DJs several days a week. On Fridays and Saturdays the place should be kicking from 6.30pm: on weekdays it's more likely to be 8.30pm (11.30am–2am; 407 903 1477, **www.adobegilas.com**). Another choice is **Hooters** (with its equally famous 'Hooter Girl' waitresses) and their 'soon to be relatively famous' wings, burgers and seafood (11am–11pm; 407 355 7711, **www.hooters.com**).

BRITTIP

Be aware American cinema popcorn is almost invariably of the SALTED variety!

The 21-screen (one of them an IMAX) **Regal** cinema, with its vast and cleverly themed entrance foyer, boasts state-of-the-art stadium seating and sound systems, and you can often see a new film here several months before it gets to the UK. Look for the ticket office on the ground level. For more on The Pointe, call 407 248 2838 or **www.pointeorlandofl.com**

© OCVB

The Capital Grille

DINNER SHOWS

Another source of evening entertainment comes in the many and varied dinner shows that are a major Orlando phenomenon. From murder mysteries to full-scale medieval battles, it's all wonderful imaginative fun, even if the food is usually quite ordinary. As the name suggests, it is live entertainment coupled with dinner and unlimited free wine, beer and soft drinks in a fantasy-type environment, where even the waiters and waitresses are in costume. They always have a strong family appeal and you are usually seated at large tables where you get to know other people, too, but, at $35-50, they are not cheap (especially with taxes and tips). Be aware, too, of the attempts to extract more dollars from you with photos, souvenirs, etc.

Disney shows

Walt Disney World Resort in Florida's offerings here are often overlooked by visitors unless they are staying at one of the hotel resorts. For an excellent night of South Sea entertainment, try **Disney's Spirit of Aloha** (at the Luau Cove at *Disney's Polynesian Resort*). It's a bit expensive at $58.99 for adults (Category 1 seating, including tax and tip) and $29.99 for under-10s;

Category 2 $54.99 and $26.99; Category 3 $50.99 and $25.99. But it is good value all the same as the 2-hour show features some splendid entertainment, varying from the fun to the thrilling (Hawaiian sounds, singers, dancers and other Polynesian acts, including the amazing Samoan fire juggler, all with a strong family story). You need to come to this show hungry as the food is plentiful, with salad, roast chicken, ribs, vegetables and rice, plus a Kilauea Volcano Dessert (or peanut butter and jam sandwiches, chicken fingers, macaroni cheese and hot dogs for the kids). Beer, wine and soft drinks are included, and shows are Tues–Sat at 5.15 and 8pm. You can make reservations up to 180 days in advance, with full payment to be made when booking.

The **Hoop-Dee-Doo Musical Revue** at *Disney's Fort Wilderness Resort & Campground* is an ever-popular nightly dinner show that maintains the resort's impressive cowboy theme, and has great food (all-you-can-eat ribs, fried chicken, corn-on-the-cob, baked beans and strawberry shortcake, plus unlimited beer, wine, sangria and soft drinks). Especially loved by children, it features the amusing song and dance of the Pioneer Hall Players in a merry

American hoedown-style show. Okay, it's corny and a tad embarrassing to find yourself singing along with the hammy action, but it is performed with great gusto – and you're on holiday, remember! The Revue plays nightly at 5, 7.15 and 9.30pm at the Pioneer Hall, Category 1 seating is $58.99 for adults (inclusive of tax and tip), $29.99 for under-10s; Category 2 $54.99 and $26.99; Category 3 $50.00 and $25.99 (under-3s free), and lasts almost 2 hours. Reservations are ALWAYS necessary (can be made up to 180 days in advance; full payment due at the time of booking).

If you can't get enough of the Disney characters, **Mickey's Backyard Barbecue** could be for you. A twice-weekly dinner show, usually Thurs and Sat, Mar–Dec at 6.30pm and 9.30pm, at *Disney's Fort Wilderness* resort, it features Mickey and the gang in a country buffet-style dinner at picnic tables under an open-air pavilion with live music, line dancing, rope tricks and other entertainment, and plenty of character interaction (great for younger children). The all-you-can-eat buffet offers barbecued pork ribs, baked chicken, hot dogs, cheeseburgers and salads with all the trimmings. Like all Disney dining, this is a no-smoking environment, but it could be cancelled if bad weather threatens ($44.99 adults, $26.99 3–9s). To make a reservation for a Disney show, call 407 939 3463.

An alternative is the nightly (and free!) **Electrical Water Pageant** that circles Bay Lake and the Seven Seas Lagoon, passing by each of the *Magic Kingdom Park* resorts in turn. It lasts just 10 minutes so it's easy to miss, but it's almost a waterborne version of the SpectroMagic parade, with thousands of twinkling lights on a floating cavalcade of boats and mock sea creatures. The usual schedule is 9pm at *Disney's Polynesian Resort*, 9.15pm at *Disney's Grand Floridian Resort & Spa* (and you get a grandstand view in Narcoossee's restaurant), 9.35pm at *Disney's*

Arabian Nights

Wilderness Lodge, 9.45pm on the shores of *Disney's Fort Wilderness Resort* and 10.05pm at *Disney's Contemporary Resort*. It can also be seen from the boat jetties outside the *Magic Kingdom Park*.

BRITTIP

Most dinner shows can be quite cool, especially those with animals such as Arabian Nights, Dixie Stampede and Medieval Times, so bring a jacket or sweater to beat the air-conditioning.

Arabian Nights

This lovingly maintained, family-owned attraction is a real large-scale production and one of the most popular with locals as well as tourists. It's a treat for horse lovers but you don't need to be an equestrian expert to appreciate the spectacular stunts, horsemanship and marvellous costumes as some 70 horses, including Arabians, Andalusians, Belgians and Walter Farley's famous black stallion, perform a 20-act show. A brand new storyline features Abra Kadabra, the sultan's genie, acting as mentor to the brash young Hocus Pocus, genie to the princess. The show is staged in the huge arena at the centre of this 1,200-seat 'palace'. Daring gypsy acrobats, magical genies, square-dancing cowboys and a thrilling chariot race all add up to a memorable show that kids, especially, adore. The comical antics of Gaylord Maynard and his Appaloosa stallion Chief Bear Paw, costumes and special effects, including some breathtaking magic, have given Arabian Nights a real boost and helped to keep its appeal fresh. A special **Christmas Holiday Show** takes over for the winter season, and there is also some impressive pre-show entertainment, featuring magician Michael Baron. The food (salad, a choice of New York Strip Steak, grilled chicken breast, Pasta Primavera, chicken tenders or chopped steak, and dessert) is above average, too.

Located just ½ml/1km east of I-4 on Highway 192 (on the left, just to the side of the Parkway shopping plaza, at Marker 8), Arabian Nights runs every evening at 6 or 8.30pm (often both), with occasional matinees. It lasts almost 2 hours, and you can buy tickets ($45.90 adults, $20.33 3–11s; VIP experience $56.60 and $31.03) at the box office 8am–10pm or by credit card on 407 239 9223 (visit **www.arabian-nights.com** for a saving offer or free upgrade). A 'VIP' upgrade adds a souvenir poster, pre-show drink in the VIP area, priority seating (in the first 3 rows) and the chance to meet the stars before the show.

Pirate's Dinner Adventure

This show (which has been revamped several times since it opened in 1997) features one of the most spectacular settings, with the Spanish galleon pirate ship centrepiece being 150ft/46m long, 60ft/18m wide, 70ft/21m tall and 'anchored' in a 300,000 gallon/1,365,000-litre lagoon. It also delivers good value with its pre-show elements, plentiful (if ordinary) food and drink, and the imaginative after-show Buccaneer Bash disco until 10.30pm, plus the Pirate's Maritime Museum, which guests are free to wander around. Coffee is also served at the Buccaneer Bash, and there are

kids' meals (chicken fingers and vegetarian) if the main choice of pork, shrimp and chicken with rice and mixed veg doesn't appeal. The basic premise of the audience being 'hijacked' by the wicked 18th-century pirates is a clever one, even if the actual storyline is occasionally hard to follow. Chaos and mayhem ensue, with the local princess being abducted by the villainous crew of Captain Sebastian (boo! hiss!), and swashbuckling abounds, with sword fights, acrobatics, trapeze artists and boat races. There are plenty of stunts and special effects – plus audience participation, which the kids love ($55.95 adults, $35.95 3–11s; look out for discount coupons).

BRITTIP

When there are 2 or more shows of The Pirate's Dinner Adventure in one night, opt for the last one if you want the disco bash afterwards. A new Pirate's preferred seating upgrade provides front row priority and guaranteed cast interaction for a small extra cost (407 248 0590, **www.orlandopirates.com**).

The show is located on Carrier Drive between I-Drive and Universal Boulevard, and runs daily at 6, 7.30 or 8.30pm (additional shows in peak periods), with appetisers served for 45 minutes until it is time to be seated.

Pirate's Dinner Adventure

© OCVB

Medieval Times

Spain in the 11th century is the entertaining setting for this 2-hour extravaganza of medieval pageantry, sorcery and robust horseback jousts that culminate in furious hand-to-hand combat between 6 knights. It's worth arriving early to appreciate the clever mock castle design and the staff's costumes as you are ushered into the pre-show hall before being taken into the arena itself. The Knights of the Realm show features fast-paced skills tests, loosely centered around a treacherous plot within the king's inner circle. But honour and bravery ultimately prevail, restoring order to the Kingdom, and it is all set to a dramatic musical score played by the Prague Symphony Orchestra. The weapons used are all real and used with skill, and there are some neat lighting and other special effects. You need to be in full audience participation mode as you cheer on your knight and boo the others, but kids (not to mention a few adults) get a huge kick out of it and they'll also love eating without cutlery – don't worry, the soup bowls have handles! The elaborate staging is backed up by an excellent chicken dinner and the serfs and wenches who serve you make it a fun experience. Prices, which include the Medieval Life exhibition (see below), are $54.95 for adults and $34.95 for 3–12s (check its website for discounts). A Royalty

Package upgrade for $10/person includes preferred seating, knight's cheering banner, a commemorative programme and a behind-the-scenes souvenir DVD. Doors open 90 minutes prior to show time. Times vary with the season, so call 1888 935 6877 or visit **www.medievaltimes.com** for more details and reservations. The castle is on Highway 192, 5mls/8km east of the junction with I-4 and has recently undergone a $8m renovation that makes the whole place fresh and inviting.

If you have 45 minutes to spare before the show, the **Medieval Life** exhibition makes an interesting diversion. This mock village portrays the life and times of people living 900 years ago, with artisans demonstrating pottery and tool-making, glassblowing, spinning and weaving, plus a wonderfully gruesome dungeon and torture chamber (definitely not for young children). Stay on after the show (the 2nd show only on busy nights) for **The Knight Club**, with bar service, music, dancing and the chance to meet royalty and knights for autographs and photo opportunities.

Sleuth's Mystery Dinner Shows

This is a real live version of Cluedo acted out before your eyes in hilarious fashion while you enjoy a substantial meal (with a main course choice of honey-glazed Cornish hen,

Medieval Times

Dolly Parton's Dixie Stampede

($28 adults, $16 3–12s, reservations required). Sleuth's is located in the Goodings Plaza on International Drive next to the Mercado, with 3 different theatres, a smart pre-dinner bar area and expanded gift shop.

WonderWorks: Magic Comedy Dinner Show

On a smaller scale but no less fun, this show is at **WonderWorks** on I-Drive (on one corner of The Pointe Orlando). A novel mixture of improvised comedy and clever, close-up magic, the show is accompanied by all-you-can-eat pizza, beer, wine and coke. Set in the intimate Shazam Theater, it features live music, special lighting effects and some slick magic tricks from illusionist Tony Brent and sidekick Danny Devaney. The tricks are all fairly routine, but the show is served up in style and involves plenty of audience participation. There are also a couple of terrific running gags throughout the fast-paced show, but beware of sitting too close to the stage – you WILL end up as part of the act! Performed twice nightly at 6pm and 8pm, it costs a reasonable $21.95 for adults and $14.95 for 4–12s and seniors. Alternatively, a Magic Combo ticket for the show and unlimited access to WonderWorks afterwards (open until midnight, see page 227) is $37.95/$27.95 (407 351 8800, **www.wonderworksonline.com**).

Dolly Parton's Dixie Stampede

The biggest development in Orlando dinner shows for many a year opened in June 2003, when country and western queen Dolly Parton unveiled the fourth venue for her Dixieland extravaganza of music, comedy, horsemanship – and ostrich races! The show features a high-energy cowboy competition (with lots of audience participation) between North and South, with various contests, speciality acts, songs, dance and a huge southern-style feast.

prime rib or lasagne) and unlimited beer, wine and soft drinks. You can choose between 3 theatres and no fewer than 11 different plot settings (several of which have amusing British settings), including *Joshua's Demise*, *Roast 'Em, Toast 'Em* and *Lord Mansfield's Fox Hunt Banquet* (mayhem at an English banquet), that add up to some elaborate murder mysteries. The action takes place all around you and members of the audience can take part in some cameo roles. The quick-witted cast keeps things moving and keep you guessing during the theatrical part of the 2½-hour show, then during the main part of dinner you can think up some questions for interrogation (but be warned, the real murderer is allowed to lie!). If you solve the crime you win a prize, but that is pretty secondary to the overall enjoyment – this is a show we enjoy a lot. Prices are $48.95 adults, $23.95 3–11s and show times vary, so call 407 363 1985 or visit **www.sleuths.com**

Purely for children is **Sleuth's Merry Mystery Dinner Adventure**, with a special kids' dinner, dessert and unlimited soft drinks. Designed primarily for 6–12s (mainly Sat afternoon), it features one of two adventures, *The Faire of the Shire* and *The Magical Journey of Juniper Junior*

Indeed, the food is a major part of the experience – which has been a big hit elsewhere in America – as you chow down on vegetable soup, whole rotisserie chicken, corn on the cob, home-made biscuit (that's a savoury scone to us), barbecue pork loin, jacket potato and apple pastry. Your unlimited drinks are Pepsi, tea and coffee (with some excellent non-alcoholic cocktails available pre-show). Alcohol is limited to 2 glasses of beer or wine per meal.

The high-quality entertainment and the $28m development provide a spectacular venue, with an elaborate musical and comedy pre-show (in the Carriage Room) before the audience moves to the 1,000-seat, 35,000sq ft/ 3,255sq m main arena. Here the headlining abilities of the 32 horses and 30 riders are demonstrated over a series of tests and races, from Roman-style riding to trick riding and fast-paced barrel racing. Spectacular costumes, ostrich races, pig races and a feature buffalo 'stampede', plus a rousing, patriotic finale, American-style, with doves, flags and Dolly's closing anthem, complete the picture. Sadly, Dolly herself does not make an appearance, apart from on screen, but it all adds up to 5-star family fun. A separate **Christmas show** is staged 1 Nov–1 Jan, featuring a live Nativity scene, snow and other seasonal

festivities (the show contest pits North Pole v South Pole!). In many ways this is a more novel and theatrical performance and, if you have seen one, you should definitely see the other.

BRITTIP
You can visit the stars of Dolly Parton's Dixie Stampede – the horses – for free from 10am until show time. You'll find them along the horsewalk outside the venue.

Dixie Stampede operates once or twice a night, depending on the season, at either 5.40pm or 7.40pm (with the main show at 6.30pm or 8.30pm), and lasts almost 2½ hours, including the pre-show, plus browsing time in the inevitable gift shop. It's billed as Orlando's 'most fun place to eat', and it's hard to argue. Located next to Orlando Premium Outlets, just off I-4 at exit 68, or via I-Drive ($48.25 adults, $21.52 4–11s; 407 238 4455, **www.dixiestampede.com**).

THE NIGHTCLUB SCENE
Orlando is blessed with a huge variety of nightlife, from regular discos to elaborate live music clubs and 'duelling piano' bars. The majority are situated in the downtown area, away from the main tourist centres. The *Orlando Sentinel* has a Friday supplement, *Calendar*, which has all the local entertainment listings, while **www.orlandocitybeat.com** details the nightspots, events, happy hours and other essential info. The free *Orlando Weekly* (available from supermarkets and tourist centres) is also a valuable guide, or visit **www.orlandoweekly.com**

Bars and discos come and go at an amazing rate, so don't be surprised if you revisit a nightclub and find it has had a complete change of name and personality. The basic distinctions tend to be **live music clubs**, **mainstream nightclubs**, with the occasional live band, and **bars** with evening entertainment.

There's plenty of nightclub options

Hard Rock Live at Universal Orlando

Live music clubs

The following should give you a representative taste of the most popular venues (in most cases for those aged 21 and over only).

While Hard Rock Live at CityWalk and House of Blues at *Downtown Disney* are the 2 main regular live music venues in town, **The Social** is the next best option in size terms, and offers a far more intimate and 'clubby' atmosphere, along with a great range of local bands, up-and-coming acts and the occasional bigger name (The Killers, Supergrass and Billy Bragg among others) looking for a more offbeat venue. Situated in the heart of the city's downtown area (on North Orange Avenue, right next to Tabu), The Social features the full spectrum of blues, rock, jazz and Latin sounds, with great house and guest DJs in between. The small main auditorium and bar holds up to 400, and the secondary bar provides an excellent hideaway at the back of this well-run club. Its website (**www.thesocial.org**) offers the chance to listen to some of the forthcoming acts and buy tickets in advance, generally $7–20, with free

entry and special price drinks most Tuesdays. Call 407 246 1419 for more info. Check out the local hangout of the **Bar BQ Bar** next to The Social for cheap drinks.

For pure, relaxed jazz and other live music, have a look at the Bosendorfer Lounge at the **Grand Bohemian Hotel** (see page 88), also on South Orange Avenue. Usually 6–10pm every evening (plus Sunday Jazz Brunch 10.30am–2.30pm), the sounds of its $250,000 Bosendorfer piano are well worth travelling to hear.

As a complete alternative to the music scene, **Sak Comedy Lab** (on West Amelia Avenue in the Theater Garage) is like a live version of the TV show *Whose Line Is It Anyway?*. Fast-paced and funny (and with a 'no obscenity' rule for concerned parents), the Sak performers do a mix of competitive ad lib comedy, with every show offering something different and the young performers living on their wits. Consistently voted Florida's best live comedy, see it for yourself Tues–Sat (with 2 different shows Fri and Sat), admission $5–13. Its Lab Rats show (Tues) features Sak's 'students' and is just $2. Booking is advised on Fri and Sat (407 648 0001, **www.sak.com**).

Mainstream nightclubs

In addition to the mainstream DJ dance centres at *Downtown Disney*'s *Pleasure Island* and Universal's CityWalk, **Tabu** (46 North Orange Avenue, just up from Church Street) appeals widely to the young, trendy crowd with regular nightly line-ups, guest DJs and special events, usually of a fairly raucous nature! (Wed–Sun, 21 and over Sat; $7–12; 407 648 8363 **www.tabunightclub.com**).

Cairo on South Magnolia Avenue has quickly become a haunt of the younger set, with 3 rooms featuring dance music, reggae and out-and-out disco – high energy, disco and reggae Fri and Sat, sounds from the 1980s and 1990s on Sun, old school and house every Wed; ladies don't pay the $5–10 cover charge and drink free until 11.30pm on Fri (407 422 3595; **www.cairo-orlando.com**).

The Independent on Orange Avenue on the corner of Washington Street offers alternative and new wave music. Again, it has more of a techno-dance sound, but features various retro-progressive, old wave, goth and indie college rock. The club has 3 contrasting levels, including an area with pool tables. Doors open at 10pm; cover charge $5 (407 839 0457; **www.independentbar.net**).

The Club at Firestone is also hard to categorise but scores well with the alternative/progressive crowd. It ranges from mainstream disco to acid jazz lounge, with something different each Fri, Sat and Sun. Separate rooms inside the club feature Regaton salsa, house, electronic and hip-hop, with its Latin Ladies Night on Fri, and special guest DJs on Sat. North of Church Street on the corner of Orange Avenue and Concord Street. Cover charge $5 (407 872 0066; **www.clubatfirestone.com**).

The **Blue Room** (West Pine Street) is another lively offering, though more

Club Firestone

intimate, drawing a more diverse crowd with its mixture of art, music and style. Completely remodelled in 2004, it features live DJs and drink specials Wed–Fri (9pm–3am) and each Sat combines hip-hop, dance and R&B in a highly successful style, with the special mixing of DJ Gerry LeBorge. A smart, stylish 2-level venue, this should please even the most particular of clubbers. Cover charge usually $10 (407 843 2583, **www.blueroomorlando.com**).

For the gay scene, **Parliament House** (on North Orange Avenue) and **Southern Nights** (Bumby Avenue and Anderson Street) remain the most happening venues in the area, while the **Cactus Club** (on North Mills Avenue), **Studz Bar** (both on Edgewater Drive) and **Wylde's** (on South Orange Avenue) are also popular.

Bars

With live entertainment, extrovert barmen, sports-themed bars and raw bars (offering seafood, often by the bucket!), the choice is, as ever, wide-ranging. Bars of all types simply abound in Orlando. The area around Church Street is the core of this development (even since much of

Church Street Station closed), with a terrific range of restaurants and bars. Look out in particular for the raucous **Mako's** and **Antigua** (DJ house music). Easy to overlook next to Antigua is the highly recommended **Big Belly Brewery**, with a micro-brewery and an impressive range of other beers (as well as an outrageous collection of wall art), and above that is roof-top bar **Latitudes**. New in 2007 was **The Orlando Brewing Co**, creators of hand-crafted organic beer, with 21 beers on tap, 6 of which are its own, brewed on site and served by the pint in a 100-seat tasting room. Brewery tours are available, as is Wi-Fi access, live entertainment and a gift shop, 3–10pm Mon–Thurs, noon–late Fri, Sat, noon–9pm Sun. Find it at 1301 Atlantic Ave (next to the Amtrak train station) or visit **www.orlandobrewing.com**.

Travel out past Church Street into Orange Avenue and Pine Street and you are into real locals' territory with the likes of **One-Eyed Jack's**, which has a party pop atmosphere and live music singalongs, and is connected to the **Loaded Hog** and **Wall Street Cantina** (packed at weekends – there's often a queue to get in but, once in, you can roam between all 3). Watch out for **Alpha Bar** (with an old school club vibe), **Eye Spy** (a high-tech bar with inside and outside seating), **Sky 60** (Miami-style rooftop bar), **Room 39** (a cool lounge that likes to groove) and **Lizzy McCormack's** (just one of downtown's Irish pubs). Turn left on to West Central Boulevard and you find **Kate O'Brien's Irish Pub** for more lively bar entertainment (and a great beer garden); the similarly Irish-themed **Scruffy Murphy's** is a block further north on Washington Street. There is no cover charge and it has a real good-time atmosphere. South on Orange, on Fri and Sat the underground **Tanqueray's Bar and Grille** offers live music.

On Pine Street you have the **Pine Street Bar and Grill** (11am–2am Mon–Fri, 8pm–2am Sat, Sun) for one of the best bar-restaurants in the area, ideal for a late-night snack, with pool and billiards, and **The Clubhouse** sports bar (formerly Maui Jack's Draft House and Raw Bar). The **AKA Lounge** is where Orlando's hottest DJs come to spin, while **Back Booth** is a top bar for live music and imported beers. The eclectic duo of **Slingapour's** and **The Globe** (the latter an off-the-wall diner) are also worth seeking out for a lively drink or three on Wall Street, just off Orange, boasting a range of bars, a pool hall and live music, as well as The Globe's fun eating style. More new style can be found here at the handy **Monkey Bar** (a Martini lounge with food) and the **Waitiki Retro Tiki Lounge** (nightlife with a Polynesian flavour).

House of Blues

© OCVB

Other new bars to watch out for are **Rhythm & Flow** (an upscale lounge bar with high-end cocktails), **Matador** (a Spanish-styled bar) and **Cleo's** (a lounge with live music).

Sports bars

Finally, with the multitude of sports bars that are another particularly American speciality, **Friday's Front Row Sports Grill** on I-Drive (just south of the Sand Lake Road junction) is a major landmark that even the locals enjoy. Here you can catch all the action on 84 TV screens, plus enjoy some 100 beers from around the world (the bar features $1.99 domestic 12oz drafts and half-price on select appetisers during Ecstatic Happy Hour!) as well as try out its basketball nets, pool tables and shuffleboard, and rub shoulders with local sports stars from time to time. The food is the regular TGI Fridays menu but there is plenty to keep the kids amused too (paper tablecloths to colour, and video games). The atmosphere varies according to the time of day and which sports event it is (pretty rowdy for Orlando Magic basketball games), so call 407 363

Best of British

1414 for up-to-the-minute info (daily 11am–2am; **www.frontroworlando. myfridays.com**).

In Kissimmee, head for the **Oasis Sports Bar and Grill** next to Old Town on Highway 192, which is exceedingly Brit-friendly and shows all UK soccer (407 396 0090, **www.oasis192.com**). Our favourite is the **Orlando Ale House** group, with a fine example on Kirkman Road, opposite Universal Studios (407 248 0000). It has more than 30 TVs, a raw bar and good seafood, and also an above-average range of beers (**www.alehouseinc.com**). A new chain worth noting is **Buffalo Wild Wings Grill & Bar**, with 3 Orlando locations (notably on International Drive just south of Wet 'n Wild, 11am–1am Mon–Thur, 11am–2am Fri, Sat, noon–midnight Sun; 407 351 6200), where masses of chicken-orientated dishes (including signature Buffalo wings with 14 different sauces; watch out for the Blazin' – it's seriously hot!) are served up in a casual, lively atmosphere, highlighted by its Buzztime Trivia System at each table and multiple big-screen TVs (**www.buffalowildwings.com**).

Walt Disney World Resort in Florida can boast the excellent **ESPN Club** at *Disney's BoardWalk Resort*, a full-service restaurant with sports broadcast facilities, video games, more than 70 TV monitors, giant scoreboards and even a Little League menu for kids. No sports fan should miss it. Equally, **NBA City** (for basketball fans) at Universal's CityWalk, and the **Cricketers' Arms** and **Orlando George & Dragon** (for British sport) in Festival Bay and next to Wet 'n Wild should not be overlooked, especially for TV addicts (**www.cricketersarmspub.com** and **www.britanniapubs.com**). There is also the recent **Best of British Soccer World** on I-Drive (see page 310).

Now you'll want to know a lot more about where, when and how to tackle that other holiday dilemma – where to eat. Read on…

11

Dining Out

or Man, These Portions are HUGE!

Eating is a Big Deal in America. Consequently, dining out is an essential component of its entertainment business. Whether it's breakfast, lunch or dinner, the experience needs to be well-organised, filling and good value. The options for dining out are seemingly omnipresent and large scale.

However, this is all good news for us Joe Tourists because it means it's impossible to go hungry and easy to feed the family without breaking the bank (though you will find some restaurants tend to rush through meals – they are not the focal point they usually are in Europe).

Variety

The variety, quantity and quality of restaurants, cafés, fast-food chains and snack bars is in keeping with the local tradition of eating as much and as often as possible. At first glance, the choice is overwhelming. Cruising along I-Drive or Highway 192 will reveal a bewildering array of eateries.

As a general rule, food is plentiful, relatively cheap, available 24 hours a day and nearly always appetising and filling. You will encounter an increasing number of fine-dining possibilities, but the basic premise remains that you will get good value for money and are unlikely to need more than 2 meals a day. Put simply, portions tend to be large! Service is

also efficient and friendly, and it's usually hard to come by a bad meal. The one real exception is if you like fresh veg. The US diet often seems to overlook this staple, but if you look up the vegetarian options we give you or visit buffet outlets such as **Sweet Tomatoes**, you will find a more balanced choice.

Exceptional deals

In keeping with the climate, most restaurants tend towards the informal (T-shirts and shorts are usually acceptable) and cater readily for families. This also leads to 2 exceptional deals for budget-conscious tourists, especially those with a large tribe. Many hotels and restaurants offer 'kids eat free' deals, provided they eat with their parents. The age limits can vary from under-10 to under-14, but it obviously represents good value. The all-you-can-eat buffet is another common

There are opportunities from formal to casual

© OCVB

chain-restaurant feature. This means you can probably eat enough at breakfast to keep you going until the evening! A few establishments also offer early-bird specials – a discount if you dine before 6pm. Be aware that 5.30–7.30pm is rush hour for many restaurants and you may have to wait for a table. Try to arrive by 5pm or after 8.30pm.

BRITTIP

As portions are so large, you can save money by sharing a main course. Your waiter or waitress will be happy to oblige (provided you keep their tip up to the full rate).

Don't be afraid to ask for a doggy bag if you have leftovers (even if you haven't brought the dog!). The locals do it all the time and, again, it is highly wallet-friendly. Just ask for the leftovers 'to go'. And don't hesitate to tell your waiter or waitress if something isn't right. Americans will readily complain if they are not happy, so restaurants are keen to make sure everything is to their diners' satisfaction.

And, please, don't forget to tip. The basic wage for waiters and waitresses is low, so they rely heavily on tips as part of their income – and they are taxed on tips whether they receive them or not. Unless service really is shoddy, in which case you should mention it, the usual rate for tips is 10% of your bill at buffet-style restaurants and 15% at full-service restaurants. It is worth checking to see if service is already added to your bill, though this is not as common in the US as it is in the UK.

With Orlando being the world's favourite holiday destination, and with the city springing up from eclectic roots, you will encounter a

BRITTIP

Don't worry about eating 'dolphin', it's a different species called dolphin-fish or mahi-mahi.

Open-air dining

© OCVB

huge array of food types. Florida is renowned for its seafood, which comes much cheaper than in the Mediterranean. Crab, lobster, shrimp (what we know as king prawns), clams and oysters can all be had at decent prices, as well as several dozen varieties of fish, many of which you won't have come across before. Latin-influenced cuisines (notably Cuban and Mexican) are common, but there is also plenty of Asian fare, from Chinese and Indian to Japanese, Thai and Vietnamese. The big shopping malls offer a good choice in their food courts, which are often particularly good value. 'Cracker' cooking is original Floridian fare, and the more adventurous will want to try a local speciality – alligator – either stewed, barbecued, smoked, sautéed or braised. Fried gator tail 'nuggets' are a local favourite. And you must try Key Lime Pie – a truly wonderful dessert.

How to order

Ordering food can be an adventure in itself. The choice for each item is often the cue for an inquisition! You can never order just 'toast' – it has to be white, brown, wholewheat, rye, muffin or bagel; eggs come in a baffling variety of ways (order them 'sunny side up' for a traditional British fried egg; 'over easy' is fried both sides but still soft); an order of tea or coffee usually brings the response 'Regular or decaf? Iced, lemon, green, herbal or English?' and salads have more dressings than the NHS. Ask to see a menu if it isn't displayed. It is no big deal to Americans and they won't feel insulted if you decide to look somewhere else.

Vegetarian options

In a country where beef is culinary king, vegetarians often find themselves hard done by. However, there are a couple of bright spots, plus a handy hint when all seems lost. Firstly, there are 2 notable vegetarian restaurants in Orlando, the Indian cuisine of **Woodlands** on the South Orange Blossom Trail (407 854 3330) and the **Chinese Garden Café** on West Colonial Drive downtown (407 999 9799), while the tapas-style **Café Tu Tu Tango** on I-Drive serves a good variety of veggie dishes. However, most of the upscale restaurants should be able to offer a vegetarian option and will be happy for you to ask in advance. *Walt Disney World Resort in Florida* is slightly more enlightened in that the **California Grill** (in *Disney's Contemporary Resort*), **Citricos** (*Grand Floridian Resort & Spa*), **Le Cellier** (Canada pavilion in *Epcot*) and **Spoodles** (*Disney's BoardWalk*) feature good vegetarian choices, while the seafood-orientated **Flying Fish** (*Disney's Boardwalk*) and **'Ohana** (*Disney's Polynesian Resort*) can also serve up decent veggie fare if asked. Most full-service restaurants (notably **Bongos Cuban Café™** and **Wolfgang Puck's® Café** in *Downtown Disney*) and even some of the counter-service ones can usually cater for non-menu requests. It's always worth asking.

However, **Sweet Tomatoes** (on I-Drive by the Kirkman Road junction) is notably the most vegetarian-friendly outlet in Orlando and consistently

gets great reader feedback. A salad buffet restaurant with some of the best meal deals in Florida, it has an all-you-can-eat choice for $7.29 at lunch ($8.99 at dinner, after 4pm) that includes a vast salad spread, a choice of soups, pizza, pasta, bread and pastries, plus fruit and frozen yoghurt. Drinks are $1.89 (with free refills) and kids' meals are $1.99 for 3–5s and $4.99 for 6–12s, free for under-3s. Open 10.30am–9pm Mon–Thurs, 11.30am–10pm Fri, Sat, 9am–9pm Sun (**www.soupplantation. com**). **Chamberlin's Market and Café** (with 8 Orlando locations) is another more enlightened choice, with home-made soups, vegetarian chilli, salads, sandwiches and blissful fresh fruit smoothies (**www.chamber lins.com**). The **Panera Bread** chain also offers some decent veggie options (plus free wireless internet).

BRITTIP

American bacon is always streaky and crisp-fried and sausages are chipolata-like and slightly spicy.

Eating 24/7

It's not unusual to find restaurants that never close – you can eat around the clock, or '24/7' as the Americans say. So, especially for those who can't sleep on their first night in the USA (plus those who just like to eat!), here is a guide to where you can go for a snack or even a full-scale meal at 4 in the morning:

Chain restaurants: Denny's, Waffle House, Steak & Shake, some McDonald's. **Individuals:** B-Line Diner (Peabody Hotel, I-Drive), Planet

BRITTIP

An excellent section of Deb Wills' unofficial Disney website lists places that cater for special dietary needs, including veggie, at **www.allears net.com/din/ special.htm**.

The Samba Room

© OCVB

Java (Gaylord Palms Resort), Crumpets (Grosvenor Resort), Mainstreet Market (Hilton at *Walt Disney World Resort*) and the Village Inn (in St Cloud).

 BRITTIP

If there are several of you drinking beer, ordering a pitcher will work out cheaper than buying it by the glass.

Drinking

The biggest complaint from Brits on holiday in the USA is about the beer. With the exception of a handful of English-style pubs (see pages 310–11), American beer is always lager, either bottled or on draught, and ice cold. It goes down great when the weather's hot, but it is generally weaker and fizzier than we're used to. Of course, there are exceptions and they are worth seeking out (try Killian's Red, Michelob's Amber Bock, Budweiser brew Bare Knuckle Stout or Sam Adams beers for a fuller flavour), but if you are expecting a good, old-fashioned British pint, forget it (though the **Cricketers Arms** at Festival Bay has introduced a new chilling process for some of its ales, which serves them closer to the proper temperature). You should also look out for **The Big River Grille** at *Disney's Boardwalk Resort*, **Big Belly**

Brewery in downtown Orlando or any of the excellent **Hops Bar & Grill** chain, which are all micro-breweries. Spirits (always called 'liquor' by Americans) come in a typically large variety, but beware ordering just 'whisky' as you'll get bourbon. Specify if you want Scotch or Irish whiskey and demand it 'straight up' if you don't want it with a mountain of ice. Also, when you order a Coke or similar from a counter-service outlet at the parks, ask for 'no ice' or 'light ice' unless you want a drink that is 50% ice.

 BRITTIP

Most Orlando supermarkets don't sell spirits, just beer and wine (and some liqueurs, like Kahlua). If you want whisky, gin etc., you need to seek out a 'liquor store' like the ABC chain.

If you fancy a cocktail, there is a massive choice and most bars and restaurants have lengthy happy hours with good prices. Good-quality Californian wines are better value than European. If you are sticking to soft drinks ('sodas') or coffee, most bars and restaurants give free refills. You can also run a tab in the majority of bars and pay when you leave. But please note that Florida licensing laws are stricter than ours and **you must**

bluezoo

© OCVB

There are more than 5,000 restaurants in Orlando

be 21 or over to enjoy an alcoholic drink in a bar or lounge or to sit at a bar. You will often be asked for proof of age before you are served (or allowed into a club), and this means your passport or photo driving licence. Don't bother to argue – no photo ID, no beer!

BRITTIP

Tourist brochures often include money-off coupons for certain restaurants, and you can make useful savings here.

That gives you the inside track on HOW to eat and drink like the locals. Now you will want to know WHERE to do it, so here's a guide to that profusion of variety. At the last count there were 4,000-plus restaurants in greater Orlando, so it would be a tall order to list every one; however, the following selection covers the main areas. We group them into: *Fast and Furious, Family Favourites, A Novel Touch* and *Deluxe Dining*. As a general rule, the price increases through all 4, from budget (typically under $10/person a meal) to modest ($10–20), above average ($20–30) and deluxe (more than $30 a head). The first thing you need to do is make sense of the **chain restaurants** here.

Knowing your Perkins from your Chevys is vital tourist info, while outlets like Macaroni Grill and Bahama Breeze are well worth knowing about. Of course, you will also find all the main American brands we have in the UK.

Fast and furious

This section is reserved primarily for all the counter-service fast food outlets, and the array of quick, friendly outlets that can provide service on a sit-down basis. If you are a fan of **McDonald's**, there are around 70 outlets in the area, from small drive-in types to a mega, 24-hour establishment on Sand Lake Road (near the junction with I-Drive), that also has the biggest Play Place for kids of any McDonald's in the world. **Burger King** is well represented, with 45 outlets, as is another familiar US franchise, **Wendy's**, which has 25 restaurants. **KFC** has 25 branches in the area, and you will also find **Pizza Hut** and **Domino's Pizza**, both of which deliver locally – and even to hotel rooms.

For other local variations on the fast-food theme, check out **Checkers** or **Hardees** for burgers, **Popeye's Famous Fried Chicken & Biscuits** or **Chick-fil-A** as a KFC alternative, **Taco Bell**, if you'd like the cheap and cheerful Mexican option, or **Arby's** for a range of hot roast beef sandwiches that make a nice change from burgers. **Dairy Queen** offers a mix of burgers, hot dogs, pork sandwiches and ice-cream dishes, while **Papa John's**, **Little Caesar's** and **Hungry Howie's** make a decent alternative to Pizza Hut.

A particularly American form of take-away is the 'sub', or torpedo-roll sandwich. This is what you will find at any branch of **Subway**, **Sobik's**, **Quiznos** or **Miami Subs**. An even better bet is the health-conscious **Tijuana Flats** chain, which started in central Florida and now has 13 local outlets, most notably on E Central

BRITTIP

Tijuana Flats promises: 'No microwaves – no lard – no plutonium – no anti-matter – no dragon meat – no stinking badges – no dirt – no plastic parts – no running with scissors.' And we think that's a good thing!

Boulevard in downtown Orlando near Lake Eola. Its Tex-Mex style is geared around fresh, hand-made products in a lively, convivial atmosphere. Check out its burritos, quesadillas, enchiladas, tacos and salads, and you'll struggle to spend more than $10/person (**www.tijuanaflats.com**).

Many of these establishments will also have a drive-through window, which is fun to try at least once. Simply drive around the side of the building where indicated and you will find a take-away menu and a voice box to take your order. Carry on around the building (don't wait by the voice box!) and you pay and receive your food at a side window. You will probably find your car has a slide-out tray from the dashboard area that will take a cup.

Another variation on this theme is **Sonic**, a modern version of the old American drive-in diner, where you stay in your car and the 'carhop' waiter or waitress comes to your window, takes the order and delivers it while you sit behind the wheel. The fare – burgers, hot-dogs, wraps, salads and sandwiches – won't win any

awards, but the style is fun. Check out its location on I-Drive just north of Kirkman Road (7am–11pm; **www.sonicdrivein.com**). And, if you are hooked on burgers and similar fare, we suggest you try the **Steak 'n Shake** chain. This classic diner-style option is open 24/7 and cooks everything to order, with counter, table service and a drive-through. They also serve proper hand-dipped milkshakes and malts that are worth going in for on their own!

After all the fast food choices, there is then a range of restaurants that specialise in more regular fare, still with a predominantly American theme but with greater variety. None of them is licensed (so no alcoholic drinks), but they all offer some of the best breakfast fare at wallet-friendly prices. Here you will also find many of the famous all-you-can-eat buffets.

BRITTIP

A buffet breakfast at Ponderosa or a similar establishment should keep you going until tea-time and is a good way to start a theme-park day.

The most popular are the **Ponderosa Steakhouse** and **Sizzler** restaurants. Whether it's breakfast, lunch or dinner, you'll find consistent if unspectacular food (we have had a few reports of poor quality in recent years, but by and large they turn out great quantity and, therefore, value for money). You order and pay for your meal as you enter and are then seated, before being unleashed on some huge buffet and salad bars. Ponderosa has the rather flashier style (and the better reputation in town) but you'd be hard pushed to tell whose food was whose. Expect to pay $5–7 for the breakfast buffets and $8–11 for lunch and dinner (there IS a difference in price depending on location, with I-Drive tending to be a dollar or two dearer). Standard dinner fare includes chicken wings, meatballs, chilli, ribs, steaks (for a

The Ponderosa

It's McDonald's, Jim, but not as we know it!

McDonald's is not renowned for its healthy options – until you come to Orlando and find the restaurants owned and operated by Oerther Foods, who pioneered the chain's Bistro Gourmet menus. Oerther has 19 McDonald's outlets, all of which are themed, while 12 are open 24 hours and 7 feature the new bistro offerings, which are an amazing deviation from the fast-food norm. As well as the usual Big Mac and fries, they feature fresh pasta selections, hand-made pizza, gourmet sandwiches, veggie wraps, mountainous salads, gourmet coffees and eye-catching desserts. You order in the normal way, then watch your meal being created for you at the deli counter. Portions are generous, freshly made and quite delicious. Bistro breakfast selections (7am–10.30pm) include Eggs Benedict, Belgian Waffles and French Toast. The 19 themed locations vary from 1950s (at 5890 S Orange Blossom Trail) to Motorbikes (5400 S Kirkman Road) and an African Safari (2944 S Kirkman Road). The finest examples, though, are the Sand Lake Road duo – The World's Largest Entertainment McDonald's & PlayPlace (6875 Sand Lake Road) and Sand Lake Too (7344 Sand Lake Road), an ultra-modern venue. The former features a huge games arcade and vivid themed areas, plus a remodelled Kids' Club and toddler area, with animatronics and other fun features (bistro hours 7am–11pm Mon–Thurs, to 3am Fri–Sun; regular McDonald's menu available 24 hours). Look up more at **www.mcfun.com**

small extra supplement) and seafood, while their immense salad bars are also a big draw. Both are open 7am– late evening and you will find them in all the main tourist spots. Visit **www.ponderosasteakhouses.com** and **www.sizzler.com**

However, the breakfast buffet theme is served rather better by 3 other local chains, **Golden Corral**, **Black Angus** and **Shoney's**, where you may pay a bit more but the extra quality is undeniable. Golden Corral especially impresses for its fresh style (7.30am– 10pm; **www.goldencorral.com**) and delicious Carver's Choice of roast meats plus the usual buffet deals, an excellent vegetable selection and a terrific dessert bar (usually at least 20 choices, plus ice-cream and toppings!). There is also a weekend supplement at some Golden Corral outlets as they add steak to the main choice. Shoney's (7am–11pm; **www.shoneys.com**) has an extensive à la carte menu as well as its excellent buffets, all with a Southern-tinged accent. Black Angus (7am–11.30pm) is the odd-one-out in that it becomes a full-service (i.e. with a bar) steakhouse after breakfast (**www.black angusorlando.com**). You can also check out **CiCi's Pizza** (our favourite), which

features a pizza (up to 16 types), salad and dessert buffet all for a bargain $5 (under-3s eat free; 11am–10pm; **www.cicispizza.com**). You'll be hard-pushed to get better value than **Fazoli's**. Its fresh Italian market style is served up with a menu that features 20 main course items at $6 or less, either dine in or drive-through, plus unlimited breadsticks and drinks when you dine in. It's a great alternative to fast food (10.30am– 10pm Sun–Thurs, 11pm Fri, Sat; **www.fazolis.com**).

If you want the true American touch (especially for breakfast), you should also consider the following, which all have a more homely feel but are equally good value for money. For a

Café Tu Tu Tango

hearty breakfast at any time of day, **International House of Pancakes** (or IHOP) and the **Waffle House** are both a good bet. You'll struggle to spend more than $7 on a full meal, whether it be one of their huge breakfast platters or a hot sandwich with fries. Waffle Houses are open 24 hours a day (**www.wafflehouse.com**) and IHOPs 6am–midnight (**www.ihop.com**). Another traditional 24-hour family restaurant is **Denny's Diner**, the nearest thing to our Little Chef. Again, their wide selection makes a traditional bacon-and-egg breakfast seem ordinary, and they do an excellent range of toasted sandwiches and imaginative dinner meals, like grilled catfish, as well as a Senior Selections menu, featuring smaller portions at reduced prices for over 55s (**www.dennys.com**). **Perkins Family Restaurant** has a lookalike menu (some branches open around the clock; **www.perkinsrestaurants.com**). For a really hearty breakfast try Perkins Eggs Benedict (2 eggs and bacon on a toasted muffin with hash browns and fresh fruit), while its bread-bowl salads are equally satisfying. The **Friendlys** chain is another cheerful diner, with a typical array of American fare, plus delicious ice-cream-based desserts (**www.friendlys.com**). Two others worthy of note (especially for breakfast) are the chains of **Panera Bread** (wonderful pastries and fresh breads, sandwiches, soups and salads, plus good vegetarian options; 7am–10pm; **www.panerabread.com**) and **First Watch**, specialising in breakfast and lunch only (all manner of egg dishes, gluten-free and low-carb choices, plus great coffee and pastries, all served double-quick; 7am–2.30pm; **www.firstwatch.com**). Panera's also offers something of a rarity in the US – decent bread. American bread tends to be stodgy and sweet (corn bread in particular is more like cake), but Panera's specialises in a range of crusty, fresh-baked loaves that appeal more to European palates.

Cracker Barrel

Brit's Guide recommendations in this category, though, go to **Cracker Barrel** and **Bob Evans**. If you are travelling on the major highways of Florida and you see one of the 50 branches of Cracker Barrel, check out its delightful Old Country Store style, with mountainous breakfasts, well-balanced lunch and dinner menus, Kid's Stuff choices and an old-fashioned charm that is a nice change from the usual tourist frenzy (6am–10pm Sun–Thurs, 6am–11pm Fri, Sat; **www.crackerbarrel.com**). The **Bob Evans** chain is also notable for its friendly, country-style, hearty menus (plus low-carb options) and delicious desserts (6 or 7am–10pm; **www.bobevans.com**). It also offers a good take-away and country store selection. And don't forget the great **Sweet Tomatoes** (see page 301) for the best all-round buffet in town.

Family favourites

Moving up into the next price category (and with a greater range of facilities), we have the following selection. For full-service American restaurants, Orlando is blessed with about every type you can imagine, while some chains have gone on from here to national fame (like the Olive Garden restaurants). Nearly all feature a bar if you just prefer a drink and many have multiple TVs. Children are well catered for with their own menus and activity packs in many cases. Unless specified, they are in multiple locations in Florida.

Boston Market restaurants (11am–10pm; **www.bostonmarket.com**) set their store by typical home cooking, buffet style (though they don't serve breakfast). They specialise in freshly carved meats, rotisserie chicken, decent vegetables (praise be!) and excellent value if you have a hungry brood to feed.

Steak and Ale is a popular, basic diner (11.30am–10pm Mon–Thurs, 11.30am–11pm Fri, noon–11.30pm Sat, noon–10pm Sun; **www.steak andale.com**). It does some good steaks and ribs, plus tempting seafood and chicken dishes, with early bird specials of a 3-course set meal 4–7pm (4–6pm Nov–Mar), and 2-for-1 drink specials. The **Bennigan's** chain (11am–2am; **www.bennigans.com**) is a *Brit's Guide* favourite for its friendly, efficient service, smart decor and tempting menu, especially at lunchtime. It has a bar atmosphere straight out of the TV programme *Cheers*, and its Irish flavour comes into its own on St Patrick's Day (17 Mar). Happy Hour(s!) are 2–7pm and 11pm–midnight. Similarly, **Houlihan's** is a classic bar-restaurant with plenty

of style, cheerful service, an extensive and appetising menu (look out for its Down Home Pot Roast) – and seriously large portions (but also a mini-dessert option; 11am–1am; **www.houlihans.com**).

Anyone familiar with the **TGI Fridays** chain will know what to expect from this group, and Orlando boasts several of the newest design (notably on I-Drive just north of The Pointe Orlando), which refines its loud, eclectic style a little. The drinks menu is the size of a book (with more specials than you can shake a cocktail stick at) and the main menu is heavy on wings, ribs, burgers and steaks (11am–2am; **www.tgifridays.com**). Equally lively, **Hooters** makes no bones about its style. 'Delightfully tacky yet unrefined,' they say, and this is a relatively simple establishment, especially popular with the younger, beach-party crowd – and for the famous Hooter Girl waitresses (11am–midnight Mon–Thurs, 11am–1am Fri, Sat, noon–11pm Sun; **www.hooters. com**). The entertaining menu features seafood, salads and burgers, plus Hooters Nearly World Famous Chicken Wings in 8 strengths (beware the Samurai!).

Uno Chicago Grill is the place to go if you're bored with Pizza Hut, as it specialises in deep-dish pizzas plus pastas, chicken dishes, steaks and salads, (11am–midnight; **www.unos. com**), while **Applebee's** calls itself the

Sizzling Chicken and Shrimp at TGIs

© Disney

Victoria & Albert's at Disney's Grand Floridian

'Neighbourhood bar and grill', and offers a rather more health-conscious menu with good salads and weight watchers' choices as well as a tempting array of steaks and chicken dishes (11am–midnight; **www.apple bees.com**). **Hops** puts the accent on its in-restaurant breweries, with 4 standard 'house' beers (all of which are well worth trying) and seasonal specials, while it serves a good selection of casual dining menu items (steaks, chicken, pastas and seafood in its own signature sauces and marinades) in a pleasant, airy restaurant (11am–11pm; **www.hops restaurants.com**). A local speciality is the **Orlando Ale House** chain, one of the most pub-like of the local bar-restaurants, with pool tables and a host of TV screens for the latest (American) sports. With a friendly, efficient style and a surprisingly varied menu for a basic diner-type establishment, this is a great place to hang out with friends, bring the family or just pop in for a drink (11am–2am; **www.alehouseinc.com**).

Cowboy style

Sonny's Real Pit Bar-B-Q is a national chain with no great pretensions, just masses of food of the barbecue persuasion served up in friendly, let's-get-messy style. The good kids' menu makes it ideal for families, and try the ribs and the own-recipe coleslaw (11am–10pm; **www.sonnysbbq.com**). In a similar mould, **JT's Prime Time** (just past Orange Lake Country Club on West Highway 192) has another heavily barbecue-orientated menu, good kids' choice (plus a games room), and a slice of old pioneer style. It is also popular at weekends (noon–11pm). The **Lone Star Steakhouse** takes you to Texas for its mesquite-grilled steaks, ribs, chicken and fish, with a friendly Lone Star state welcome and roadhouse ambience (plus large portions!). Kids eat free with parents on Tues (11am–11pm; **www.lonestarsteakhouse.com**). **Chili's** restaurants take you into Tex-Mex territory, an Americanised version of Mexican cuisine that originated in Texas, but places the emphasis more on steak and ribs and less on tortillas and spices. Service is frighteningly efficient and, if you are looking for a quick meal, you'll be hard-pushed to find a speedier turnaround than here (11am–1am Mon–Sat, 11am–11pm Sun; **www.chilis.com**). **Chevy's** offers a similar slice of Mexicana, while still providing reassuring American selections. Its salsa is freshly made every hour, and the tortilla chips, guacamole and tortillas are equally appetising (4–11pm Mon–Thurs, 4pm–midnight Fri, 11am–midnight Sat, 11am–11pm Sun; **www.chevys.com**). A more elaborate Mexican offering is **Don Pablo's**. Clever theming, a lively atmosphere (especially round the Cantina bar) and classic, well-explained menus make for a fun experience (11.30am–

N-ice one, Maggie!

Orlando boasts a number of mouth-watering ice-cream parlours, many of which offer some truly heavenly concoctions. Check out **Cold Stone Creamery**, **Carvel**, **Baskin Robbins** and **Marble Slab Creamery** for examples of these dreamy delights. However, our award for the crème de la crème in this area goes to **Maggie Moo's**, which has a new outlet at The Pointe Orlando. Its award-winning ice-cream can be combined with a myriad of wonderful ingredients and mixed into cups and cones that are utterly Moo-velous! It also mixes some of Simon's favourite milkshakes. More info at **www.maggiemoos.com**

10pm Sun–Thurs, 11.30am–11pm Fri–Sat; **www.donpablos.com**).

The **Olive Garden** restaurants are one of America's big successes as they have brought Italian food into budget, mass-market range, and its first outlet was right here on I-Drive. The light, airy dining rooms create a relaxing environment and, while it doesn't offer a huge choice, what it does, it does well and in generous portions. Pastas is the speciality, but it also offers chicken, veal, steak, seafood and great salads, plus unlimited refills of salad, garlic breadsticks and non-alcoholic drinks (11am–10pm Sun–Thurs, 11am–11pm Fri, Sat; **www.olivegarden.com**).

International flavours

Your restaurant choice extends beyond the obvious to an array of international cuisines, notably **Chinese** and **Indian** (though many outlets are pretty uninspired, not to mention downright insipid). **Bill Wong's Famous Super Buffet** (yes, they really do call it that) on I-Drive offers a cross between Chinese and diner-type fare. The all-you-can-eat 100-item buffet features jumbo shrimp (and that means JUMBO!), as well as crab, prime rib, fresh fruit and salad. Think cheap and cheerful and that's Bill Wong's (11am–10pm).

Similarly, the **Sizzling Wok**, on Sand Lake Road just across from the Florida Mall, offers an opportunity to get stuck into a massive Chinese buffet at a very reasonable price (11am–10pm Sun–Thurs, 11am–10.30pm Fri, Sat). The **China Café** on I-Drive (at the corner of Kirkman Road) is also above average, with a lunch buffet 11am–3pm and a well-presented array of dishes (the crispy duck is outstanding). Daily specials also feature (11am–11pm). Tucked away in a plaza off Apopka-Vineland Road, just past the Crossroads shops near *Downtown Disney*, is the **Dragon Court Buffet** (look for it behind the IHOP). This locals' favourite serves a magnificent spread of fresh, appetising dishes at a terrific lunch price. With more than 50 items on offer, including a sushi selection, this is well worth trying (11am–midnight; 407 238 9996).

If you have come all this way and still fancy a curry, you can also get a decent chicken tikka masala and naan bread (though it tends to be more expensive than in your local high street unless you opt for the buffet choices). In fact, there are more than a dozen Indian restaurants in the Orlando area, but some are distinctly better than others. Possibly the best is **Flavours of India** on S Kirkman Road, just south of I-Drive, with smart decor, attentive service and a good range of dishes (11.30am–10.30pm; 407 264 2877). Others worth trying are

Olive Garden

Aashirwad on the junction of Kirkman Road and I-Drive), with an excellent lunch buffet and some seriously spicy Mughlai dishes (11am–10.30pm; 407 370 9830); down on Highway 27 in Davenport (close to the Highlands Reserve community) is the highly regarded **Spice of Life**, with an excellent lunch buffet in addition to its à la carte menu (11.30am–10.30pm; 863 424 6199); and **India Palace**, our 'local' at 8530 Palm Parkway, Lake Buena Vista, into an unassuming location tucked in a small shopping plaza but serving up excellent food in large amounts and with a good, friendly service (11.30am–11pm Tues–Sun, 5–11pm Mon; 407 238 2322).

Home from home

Having extolled the virtues of the American-style diners and others, it is appropriate to note the handful of British pubs appealing to UK visitors. All offer a predictable array of pub grub and imported British beers. You'll find the odd Brit or two working behind the bar and you can happily take the kids into them, providing they don't sit at the bar. First among them is the **Cricketers Arms** (9am–1am), which has moved from The Mercado to Festival Bay at the top of I-Drive and is a favourite haunt of British visitors. This is due to the large selection of beers (up to 17, including real ales), a Happy Hour, appetising food, live evening entertainment, comfortable indoor and outdoor seating and (soccer fans take note) live Premiership and other domestic matches. It gets busy in the evenings, its live music is usually good, and many of the staff are Chelsea fans – but we don't hold that against them! NB: There is sometimes a cover charge for footy (see **www.cricketers armspub.com**). Also on I-Drive (in a small plaza immediately south of Wet 'n Wild) is the **Orlando George & Dragon**, another all-British operation that serves a hearty traditional breakfast as well as typical pub fare

© OCVB

There's casual dining in many hotels and bars

for lunch and dinner. Open 9am–2am; kitchen until 11pm (407 351 3578), it stocks Guinness, Boddingtons, Stella, Fosters, Newcastle Brown, Bass and Carlsberg (among others), and also features darts, pool, karaoke, Sky Sports and live entertainment on its outdoor patio. This is *the* place to come for a traditional Christmas turkey dinner, while St George's Day (23 April) is celebrated in style, too. A more recent I-Drive arrival is **Best of British Soccer World** (opposite Ripley's Believe It Or Not). Formerly in the Food Court at The Mercado, the owners have gone for a much larger-scale experience, with 12 flat-screen TVs, plus a giant theatre-style screen for all the big games. It boasts 8 British beers on tap, plus a video arcade, pool and darts, Curry Nights, a traditional roast on Sundays, karaoke and even 2 internet terminals. Typical menu items include shepherd's pie, fish 'n' chips, ploughman's, burgers, steaks and kids' specials, while its full breakfast really is the Best of British (8am–midnight; 407 264 9189, **www.bobssoccerworld.com**).

Highway 192 in Kissimmee sports a few fairly derivative pubs, all keen to appeal to the home market. The best are the well-kept **Stage Door**, 6mls/10km west of the junction with

I-4 and west of marker 4, just past Lindfields Boulevard (863 424 8056) and the great family choice of **The Pub**, out on Highway 27 in Davenport (just at the junction with I-4, exit 55). It has a great range of beers, excellent food (from a wonderful US-UK crossover menu), multiple TVs and a genuine family-friendly touch (11am–1.30am Mon–Sat, 11am–midnight Sun; 863 424 4242, **www.thepubb.net**).

A novel touch

When it comes to restaurants with that 'something different' factor, Orlando has them by the barrow-load. From the Wild West to Little Italy and High Speed to High Style, there are plenty of choices to make your meal go with a themed swing (though you will find the price going up to match the surroundings).

Cattleman's Steak House goes for the cowboy approach, with a neat saloon bar, early bird specials (4–6pm) and the Little Rustlers' Round-up menu for the kids. Steaks are the order of the day, but you can also try chicken, seafood and pork (5pm–10pm Mon–Fri, 12:30–10pm Sat, 12:30–9pm Sun, lounge open 30 minutes earlier). Perhaps more fun is **Logan's Roadhouse** where the rustic atmosphere features masses of peanuts in their shells, which end up all over the wooden floor. Burgers, chicken, steaks and ribs are its stock-in-trade, while it also offers an express lunch selection (11am–10pm Sun–Thurs, 11am–11pm Fri, Sat; **www.logansroadhouse.com**). The popular **Outback Steakhouse** has an Australian slant on its theme, and with some of the best fare (and biggest portions). Its thick, juicy, well-seasoned steaks, ribs and seafood selections are all above average, while its trademark is the Bloomin' Onion, a large fried onion with a special dipping sauce. It also features a good kids' menu (4–10.30pm Mon–Thurs, 4–11.30pm Fri, 3.30pm–11.30pm Sat, 3.30–10.30pm Sun; **www.outback.com**).

BRITTIP

At the Outback Steakhouse, don't miss the Bloomin' Onion, Roasted Garlic Mashed Potatoes and Chocolate Thunder from Down Under for dessert!

For barbecue with style, try **Wild Jack's** (on I-Drive, just north of Sand Lake Road), where the magnificent wood-smoked aroma hits you as you walk in the door. The huge interior features a big open-pit barbecue where you watch your food being cooked. Steaks, ribs, chicken and turkey represent the main choices and they are all served with panache. Happy Hour is 4–7pm and kids eat free with a full-paying adult (11.30am–11pm; 407 352 4403).

Another good choice is the atmospheric **Key W Kool's Open Pit Grill** on Highway 192 (by marker 4) with mouth-watering steaks, daily specials and a succulent, inviting aroma (4–11pm; 407 396 1166). We also recommend **Tony Roma's**, which rightly pronounces itself 'famous for ribs'. The airy decor and ambience, clever kids' menu (the Roma Rangers Round-up, full of puzzles and games), junior meals, and melt-in-the-mouth ribs are a winning combo. You can still get chicken, burgers and steaks, but why ignore a dish that's done this well? (11am–midnight Sun–Thurs, 11am–1am Fri, Sat; **www.tonyromas. com**). **Smokey Bones** goes for the rustic, log-cabin touch, and some of

Citrico's

DINING OUT

© OCVB

the most succulent, deep-smoked barbecue in town. It serves up fish, chicken, burgers and salads, but we recommend the barbecue platters. Sports fans are well served with a huge array of TVs throughout the bar and restaurant (11am–11pm; **www. smokeybones.com**). NB: This chain restaurant is closing nationally, but should remain in Orlando.

The Italian job

Good Italian family-style dining has some excellent chains here, too. The **Macaroni Grill** offers a wonderful slice of Little Italy as its spacious restaurants are stylish, comfortable and well served, with excellent à la carte and family-style menus (serving 8–10). The pasta and wood-oven pizzas are first class and the wine list is impressive (11.30am–10pm Sun–Thurs, 11.30am–11pm Fri, Sat; **www.macaronigrill.com**). **Carrabba's** comes direct from Sicily, with casual-but-elegant dining in a warm, festive atmosphere. House specialities include crispy calamari, chicken marsala, tender fillet, interesting pasta dishes and hand-made pizzas in a wood-burning oven. The children's menu is one of the best and the style is very child-friendly (4–10pm Sun–Thurs, 3–11pm Fri, Sat; **www.carrabbas.com**). Equally stylish is **Brio Tuscan Grille**, a real slice of la dolce vita with some superb taste sensations. The menu emphasis is on prime steaks and chops, pasta specialities and flatbreads prepared in an authentic Italian wood-burning oven. The interior decor is also well above average, but it is also on the

Ming Court

© OCVB

pricier side (11am–10pm Sun–Thurs, 11am–11pm Fri, Sat; **www.brio italian.com**). **Antonio's** (an impressive local chain), goes more upmarket, with 3 restaurants (including one with a café, deli and superb wine shop) that all feature an individual, exclusive style as well as outstanding cuisine – sensational risottos are a signature dish, while veal and New York strip steak are an equally wise choice (5–10pm Mon–Sat; **www.antonios online.com**).

Seafood specials

The choice of seafood eateries is equally wide, with some fun chains and excellent individuals. **The Crab House** is self-explanatory: garlic crabs, steamed crabs, snow crabs, Alaskan king crabs… You could try its prime rib, pasta or other seafood, but it would be a shame to ignore the house speciality (11.30am–11pm Mon–Sat, noon–11pm Sun; **www. crabhouseseafood.com**). Part of the same chain is **Joe's Crab Shack**, more fun and inventive but less seafood-based (despite the name). Distinctly family-friendly with its Sand Lot play area, this is ideal if you don't want to go the whole shellfish hog (11am–10pm Sun–Thurs, 11am–11pm Fri, Sat; **www.joescrabshack.com**). **Landry's Seafood** is from the same company, but with a more elegant touch. There is a fresh catch of the day, seafood platters and an excellent salad bowl with each dish, and the staff really know the menu (11am–10pm Sun–Thurs, 11am–11pm Fri, Sat; **www. landryseafoodhouse.com**).

Red Lobster is part of the Olive Garden chain and is for the family market, with a varied menu, lively atmosphere and one of the best kids' menu/activity books. While lobster is the speciality, the steaks, chicken, salads and other seafood are equally appetising, and it does a variety of combination platters (11am–10pm Sun–Thurs, 11am–11pm Fri, Sat; **www.redlobster.com**). **Boston Lobster Feast** is the place for a real blowout,

Get the Pointe!

Maggiano's Little Italy heads a new line-up of restaurants at The Pointe Orlando on I-Drive that have huge tourist appeal. From the fun **Johnny Rockets** diner to the sophisticated (and expensive!) **Capital City Grille**, there is an enormous range of choice, plus several novel options with terrific family appeal. **Maggiano's** is top of our list (especially if you have a hungry brood to feed) as its chic 1940s style disguises the fact it serves up huge amounts of food at very reasonable prices (especially its Family Style platters). Everything has a rich, appetising flavour, served up with panache, and their cannelloni and other pasta dishes are beyond delicious (**www.maggianos.com**). Equally, **Tommy Bahama's Café** is a refreshing option with its 'Floribbean' ambience and menu. The starters are meals in themselves while the array of salads, seafood, sandwiches, steaks and chicken is among the best hereabouts. There is even a Small Salad selection for those who can't handle the larger portions (like us!). The Bungalow Bar also serves some impressive cocktails and Tommy's own brews (**www.tommybahama.com**).

with an unlimited lobster and seafood buffet. There are excellent-value early-bird specials (4.30–6pm Mon–Fri, 2–4.30pm Sat, Sun), and, while it is not gourmet fare, its 40-item Lobster Feasts are guaranteed to stretch the stomach (4.30–10pm Mon–Fri, 2–10pm Sat, Sun; **www. bostonlobsterfeast.com**).

McCormick and Schmick's is easily the most quality-conscious of the seafood chains, but there is nothing mass-produced about it. The chef creates a daily menu based on product, price and availability (with a prominent list of what's fresh). Oysters are a speciality, along with soups and salads, and you will be hard-pushed to find better prawns, scallops and salmon (11am–11pm Mon–Thurs, 11am–midnight Fri, Sat, 11am–10pm Sun; **www.mccormickand schmicks.com**).

Themed cuisine

Next, we come to a series of restaurants where a lively menu is matched by equally upbeat decor and service. Step forward the **Bahama Breeze** restaurants, appealing for their striking Caribbean styling (which includes an outdoor patio bar with live music) and food that puts most diner fare to shame. Try West Indies Patties, Fresh Ahi Tuna or the Jerk Chicken Pasta. Service is in keeping with its personable style and there is a pleasing individual touch.

We'd say you will struggle to get better food from any other themed restaurant in Orlando. Of its 2 locations, Lake Buena Vista is slightly easier to get into as the I-Drive outlet always draws a crowd. The decor is refreshing and entertaining, and it's worth just popping in for a drink (4pm–2am Mon–Sat, 4pm–midnight Sun; **www.bahamabreeze.com**). Also noteworthy is the **Cheesecake Factory**; while its feature is desserts (over 30 cheesecakes), the rest of the huge menu is impressive in an eclectic, high-tech setting. Mexican dishes jostle with pizza, pasta, seafood, burgers, steaks and salads, plus it offers a great brunch selection – come here hungry (11am– 11pm; **www.thecheesecakefactory.com**).

BRITTIP

Bahama Breeze restaurants do not take reservations and are often busy, so there can be quite a wait 6–8pm. 'It's that popular but well worth the wait,' says reader Chris Beckett.

Another restaurant high on style and quality is **Café Tu Tu Tango**. The accent is artist-colony Spanish, with a really original tapas-style menu, live entertainment and artwork all over the walls that changes daily. Vegetarians are well catered for, and you can try some succulent pizzas, seafood, salads and paella. Mexican and Chinese dishes are also on offer, along with a well-thought-out kids' menu. The fun atmosphere complements the rich array of dishes perfectly (11.30am–midnight; **www.cafetututango.com**). The **B-Line Diner**, inside the Orlando Peabody Hotel on I-Drive, is a fab art deco homage to the traditional 1950s-style diner, faithful in every detail. You sit at a long counter or in one of several booths, with a good view of the chefs at work and with a rolling menu that changes 4 times a day. The food is way above usual diner standards, but the prices aren't. Desserts are displayed in a huge glass counter and we challenge you to ignore them (open 24 hours; 407 352 4000).

Planet Hollywood can also be found here (next door to *Downtown Disney Pleasure Island*) and is pure fun. The food is fairly predictable, though it is served with pizzazz and the cavernous interior provides a party atmosphere, complete with film clips and movie memorabilia. Some great cocktails, too, but visit mid-morning or mid-afternoon to avoid the queues (11am–2am; **www.planethollywood. com**). Disney also has 2 versions of the eco-aware **Rainforest Café** chain (outside the *Animal Kingdom* and in *Downtown Disney*), one with a huge waterfall exterior and the other topped by a 'volcano', and they have to be seen to be believed. You don't dine, you go 'on safari' in a rainforest setting amid audio-animatronic animals (including elephants and gorillas), thunderstorms, tropical birds, waterfalls and aquariums. It's

great for kids and the food is above average. Unless you arrive before midday, you'll have a wait, but that's no hardship given their locations. Beware the huge gift shop! (11am–11pm; **www.rainforestcafe.com**).

Hard Rock Café is a worldwide chain but its Orlando outlet (at Universal's CityWalk) is a bit special. With tall, statuesque pillars, it stands like a coliseum of rock and boasts more music memorabilia than any other location. If you have never tried the loud, lively style, this would be worth a visit. The food – salads, burgers, steaks, ribs, chicken and sandwiches, including the trademark pulled pork speciality – won't win any awards, but it is consistent and hearty (and plentiful!), though it doesn't cater quite so well for youngsters (11am–midnight; **www.hardrock.com**).

There are plenty of Irish-themed pubs in town, but none comes close to matching **Raglan Road** at *Downtown Disney* for style, authenticity – and wonderful food. From the superb interior decor – much of it imported from Ireland by the Dublin-based owners – to the eye-catching bars and fabulous range of beers and whiskeys, this is a real taste of the Emerald Isle in every way (even its beer pumps have been specially brought over to ensure sublime supping!). Live music from 8 each evening adds to the atmosphere, and there are 3 separate, spacious bar areas, 2 outdoor terraces and even a neighbouring chippie (Cooke's of Dublin), plus the inevitable gift shop, to provide a well-rounded experience. You could treat it just like a pub and enjoy a drink at the bar, but we recommend finding a table and sampling the superb modern-Irish cuisine of master chef Kevin Dundon. For starters, try the Drunk Chicken (a whiskey-glazed kebab) or Dalkey Duo (battered sausages), while the rack of lamb, planxty, Kevin's Kudos (his signature dish – oven-roasted loin of bacon) and It's Not Bleedin' Chowder (!) are

Ming Court

© OCVB

Our Top 10

Here's our current Top 10 from the ever-changing diner restaurant scene:

1 **Maggiano's Little Italy** – superb food in a chic atmosphere.

2 **Raglan Road** – a truly original and authentic Irish pub experience.

3 **Café Tu Tu Tango** – an ideal combo of entertainment and great tastes.

4 **Bahama Breeze** – just gotta love that eclectic Caribbean style.

5 **Tommy Bahama Café** – a truly refreshing choice.

6 **Macaroni Grill** – one of our 'locals,' consistent and friendly.

7 **Outback Steakhouse** – great value and hard to fault, with some neat twists.

8 **Orlando Ale House** – another of our regular haunts; lively and fun.

9 **Sweet Tomatoes** – simply the best of the buffets; no argument.

10 **Steak 'n Shake** – good fun for a quick burger and fab milkshake.

all first class. If nothing else, try Kevin's version of bread pudding and you will be in holiday heaven for the rest of the evening (11.30am–2am; **www.raglanroadirishpub.com**).

Asian extravaganza

While there are plenty of Chinese outlets, the Rolls-Royce version is the beautiful **Ming Court** on I-Drive, opposite The Pointe Orlando. With a magnificent setting and live entertainment most evenings, you can easily convince yourself you have been transported to China itself! The menu is extensive and beautifully presented by friendly servers, who make you feel at home the moment you walk in. Many dishes can be had as a side order rather than a full main course to give you the chance to try more, while the basil chicken is one of our true favourites (11am–2.30pm, 4.30pm–midnight; **www.ming-**

court.com). Similarly (though less distinctively), **PF Chang's China Bistro** mixes classic Chinese fare with an American bistro style that makes fans of virtually all who sample it. Try the spicy ground chicken and eggplant, the Cantonese roasted duck or Oolong marinated sea bass for dishes with real distinction. There is also a good veggie selection (5–11pm; **www.pfchangs.com**).

Apart from the superb Teppenyaki Rooms at Disney's *Epcot* park, you can find other excellent Japanese-themed restaurants. **Shogun Steakhouse** is a national chain ideal for those a little unsure whether to go for the full Japanese experience. The service is Teppanyaki-style, at long, bench-like tables with the chef cooking in front of you, but you can still order a no-nonsense steak or chicken (6–10pm Mon–Thurs, 6–10.30pm Fri–Sun; 407 977 3988). **Kobe** also brings a touch of Americana to its dining. It goes for the mass market but still achieves individuality with the chef preparing the food at your table (11.30am–11pm; **www.kobe steakhouse.com**). **Ran-Getsu**, on I-Drive opposite The Mercado, does for Japanese cuisine what the Ming Court does for Chinese – it's stylish, authentic, as much an experience as a meal, and reasonably priced (5pm–midnight; **www.rangetsu.com**). Possibly the best, though, is **Seito Sushi** in the Winter Park Village, with a formal Japanese-style sushi bar and a more inviting, small-scale approach (11.30am–2.30pm, 5–10pm; 407 644 5050; **www.seitosushi.com**).

The **Red Bamboo** (on S Kirkman Road just north of I-Drive) is a wonderful mix of authentic Thai flavours and clean, contemporary decor. Its soups and curries are to die for, while the house speciality Smokey Pot is a stew of marinated prawns, vegetables and glass noodles in chilli sent from heaven (11am–2.30pm Tues–Fri, 5–10pm Sat, noon–10pm Sun, closed Mon; 407 226 8997).

Steaks and more steaks

Just about every restaurant you visit will feature steak on the menu, but there are a handful that make it their speciality (though price-wise they are more in deluxe territory). **Charley's Steak Houses** cook over a specially built wood-fire pit and consistently earn high marks from meat-lovers throughout the US. All the meat is specially aged, hand-cut and seasoned, making for a superb array of steaks and chops and, while they also offer fine seafood, you'd be foolish to overlook their stock-in-trade (5–11pm; **www.charleyssteak house.com**). Equally imaginative is **Vito's Chop House** (in front of the Castle Hotel on I-Drive). Its choice beef cuts – check out the Tuscan T-Bone – are aged for 4–6 weeks and cooked over wood fires. Pork chops, seafood and pasta are also available, as well as an extensive wine list (5–10.30pm Sun–Thurs, 5–11pm Fri–Sat; **www.vitoschophouse.com**).

Ruth's Chris Steak House, another major chain, also offers prime beef in a mouth-watering variety of choices. It isn't cheap, but you'll be hard-pushed to get a better steak. Simply seared, seasoned and served, they are the reason it has more than 80 locations worldwide (5–11pm Mon–Sat, 5–10pm Sun; **www.ruthschris.com**). **Morton's of Chicago** has a more upmarket (sometimes pretty smoky) style, with a lively ambience that adds to the enjoyment of its trademark steaks, which are cooked on an open range. It doesn't come cheap, especially as vegetables are extra, but

eating here is always memorable (5pm–midnight Mon–Sat, 5–11pm Sun; **www.mortons.com**). Similarly, **Shula's Steak Houses** are both expansive (on your waistline) and expensive. The porterhouse and prime rib steaks are outstanding, and this chain (owned by famous ex-American football coach Don Shula) is highly popular with locals at the *Walt Disney World Dolphin Hotel* (5–11pm; **www.donshula.com**).

Locals consistently rate **Del Frisco's** (on Lee Road in north Orlando) their favourite steakhouse and the more formal dining experience is enhanced by prime steaks and lobster, beautifully cooked and presented (407 645 4443; **www.delfriscos orlando.com**). Recent discovery **Porterhouse** is another hidden gem, at the Orlando Airport Marriott just off Semoran Boulevard. Under British chef Tony Hull, it has a relaxed, intimate ambience that perfectly sets off its prime cuts of beef, chops and grilled seafood, plus a good wine list and dreamy desserts (407 816 4055).

And, if you'd like the best Cuban experience, the **Samba Room** on West Sand Lake Road is an elegant lakefront restaurant full of Latin ambience. The menu exhibits a wonderfully exotic touch, with the likes of Mango-barbecued Ribs, Cachaca-smoked Boneless Chicken and Sugar Cane Beef Tenderloin, and its range of cocktails is suitably Cuban-laced. Extremely popular, so reservations are advised, and a touch pricier than the rest (11am–midnight Mon–Sat, noon–10pm Sun: 407 266 0550; **www.sambaroom.net**).

Deluxe dining

Finally, if you fancy really splashing out, here are some notable suggestions where both the food and ambience are way above average, albeit with prices to match. Fine dining is on the increase in Orlando, most notably in the area of Sand Lake Road immediately to the west of I-4

Hard Rock Café

Flying Fish

© Disney

(the Fountains and Venezia Plazas). These top restaurants are so popular it's advisable to book well in advance. If you're looking for a romantic evening out, you can't go wrong with any of these.

Trendy **Seasons 52** is the most upmarket offering of the Darden group (Bahama Breeze, Olive Garden, Smokey Bones, Red Lobster). The restaurant's name refers to the fact that different fresh products come into season each week, and this is reflected in the menu. New items therefore feature weekly, with some seriously creative cuisine choices. It's also designed to be totally health-conscious, with a balanced approach to carbohydrate and fat content. All appetisers, salads and soups range from 100–250 calories, the majority being either grilled or oven-roasted, and all entrées are in the 300–475 calorie range. Your server will be able to offer bags of advice – not least with an extensive wine list (4.30–11pm, Plaza Venezia; 407 354 5212, **www. seasons52.com**).

Another great place for seafood (in the Fountains Plaza on West Sand Lake Road) is the splashy **Moonfish**, a true individual in both decor and menu terms. You could make a feast of its appetisers alone, while its sushi and sashimi are inspired and it has a superb raw bar. Many restaurants that go for the avant-garde look often fail to deliver the goods, but Moonfish does not fall into that trap. It also makes a good romantic choice (but

not at the tables nearest the bar; 11.30am–10pm; 407 363 7262, **www.fishfusion.com**).

A third notable restaurant in this vicinity (the Plaza Venezia) is **Timpano Italian Chophouse**, a richly decorated upscale classic diner, with cuisine and service to match. The dark, elegant interior is bustling and convivial and the 1950s' New York Italian accent is carried through with great style. And, from its trademark Martini Bar to the tiramisu dessert, everything is served up with style and taste. Menu highlights include filet mignon, pork chops and Maine lobster, plus linguini, baked ziti and its home-made focaccia bread. (11am–10pm Mon–Fri, noon–11pm Sat, noon–10pm Sun; 407 248 0429, **www.timpanochophouse.com**).

Good seafood is not hard to come by, but great seafood is the preserve of a handful – like **Fulton's Crab House** in *Downtown Disney*'s Marketplace. This mock riverboat has 6 different dining rooms (albeit each with the same menu), plus the Stone Crab Lounge, which features a busy raw bar. The interior is filled with nautical props, photos and lithographs, giving it a wonderfully eclectic, period atmosphere, but the real attraction is the food – some of the freshest and most tempting fish, crab and lobster dishes in Florida. The Alaskan king crab is a rare treat, the snow crab claws and the tuna filet mignon are as succulent as they come, but there are fresh specials every day (the air shipping bills for which are posted in the main hall), as well as a children's menu. The Stone Crab Lounge serves lunch and dinner 11.30am–11pm, while the restaurant is open for dinner only (4–11pm; 407 394 2628, **www.levyrestaurants.com**).

The **Flying Fish**, at *Disney's Boardwalk Resort*, is also a 5-star seafood experience. The menu is not overburdened with choice, but what it does is wonderfully presented. Its 'Peeky Toe' Crab Cake starter melts in the mouth, while the Potato-wrapped Red Snapper and Pan-seared Yellowfin Tuna are outstanding. Steak and duck, plus a vegetarian option, are also available (4–11pm Mon–Sat, 4–10pm Sun; 407 939 3463).

Sticking with the Disney theme and returning to *Downtown Disney*, next to Fulton's Crab House is another of our favourites, the **Portobello Yacht Club**. It's easy to miss in its tucked-away location but don't, for this is an Italian experience of great richness and taste sensations. From the complimentary glass of Italian sangria and fresh bread with oven-baked garlic to the classically elegant menu and full wine list, this is a restaurant to be savoured in relaxed style. You can choose from something as simple as pizza or a classic Caesar salad to proscuitto and sage-wrapped yellowfin tuna, with fine steaks, rack of lamb, veal and great pastas. It all adds up to one of the most enjoyable dining options anywhere in *Walt Disney World*, and reservations are not always necessary (11.30am–midnight; 407 934 8888, **www.levy restaurants.com**).

The opening of Universal's Hard Rock Hotel brought with it the **Palm Restaurant**, the latest in an upscale nationwide chain that has a big celebrity following. Founded in New York in 1926, it is famous for prime-aged steaks and jumbo lobsters, served in spacious, elegant surroundings and with personable,

knowledgeable service. The house speciality, Jumbo Nova Scotia Lobster, is spectacular. Its steaks are special, too, plus you can choose swordfish, crab, salmon, pork, veal and pasta. All this is reflected in the prices, and vegetables are extra, but the lunch menu is more modest, while maintaining the quality (11am–11pm Mon–Sat, noon–10pm Sun; 407 503 7256, **www.thepalm.com**).

Find a fine hotel and you will find a fine restaurant these days, and that is true of the Omni Orlando resort at Champions Gate, where **Zen** is a wonderful Asian-themed restaurant with a tempting menu. With a sake bar, sushi bar and its beautifully elegant main restaurant, this is an oasis of Oriental charm and style, with food to match. Highlights are the mouth-watering Beijing Spare Ribs and Sautéed Shrimp with Chile Pepper Sauce and Glazed Walnuts, or just opt for the Zen Experience, a multi-course sampler (6–10pm Tues–Sun; 407 390 6664, **www.omni hotels.com**).

Salt Island Chophouse and Fish Market is not only an unusual name on International Drive (just north of Sand Lake Road), it is also an unusual place to find a truly fine dining establishment. It's a complete original too, from its tiki-torch outdoor terrace and complimentary valet parking to the unusual aquatic interior decor (complete with large aquariums) and live jazz lounge. The comprehensive wine list superbly offsets the heavily steak and seafood dominated menu, while service is suitably refined. All the dishes are well explained and even demonstrated, and you'll find it hard to choose between the likes of its oak-grilled steaks, trademark blackened grouper and daily seafood specials. For a romantic occasion, try to get a table in the Waterfall dining room (5–11pm; 407 996 7258, **www.salt islandrestaurant.com**).

A great favourite of ours is the lovely **Jiko** at *Disney's Animal Kingdom*

The Venetian Room

© OCVB

Buffet at Universal's Royal Pacific

Lodge, possibly its most imaginative and impressive culinary offering to date. Maintaining the hotel's African theming with its decor and lighting, Jiko ('the cooking place') features twin wood-burning ovens, a masterful menu and an exclusive selection of South African wines. The menu has Indian, Asian and African influences, with dishes like Banana-leaf Steamed Sea Bass, Whole Roast Papaya Stuffed with Spicy Minced Beef and Oven-baked Garlic Chicken Tagine. The personal service and ethnic ambience underline the adventure of eating here and make it a real highlight, while it is perfect for a romantic meal (5–11pm; 407 939 3463).

Old Hickory Steakhouse is another hotel-based offering in the Gaylord Palms on I-Drive South. The elaborate Everglades theme gives it an extra dimension, but the steak needs few gimmicks as the house speciality of certified Black Angus beef is aged for 21–35 days and cooked to perfection. Side dishes are extra, but the attentive service and alternatives such as oven-roasted swordfish and Maine lobster provide a memorable experience. Watch out, too, for its artisanal cheese course, imported by trendy New York chef Terrance Brennan (5–10.30pm Mon–Fri, 5–11pm Sat, 5–10pm Sun; **www.gaylordhotels.com**).

Returning to Disney (as everyone does), **Wolfgang Puck's** is an unusual mix of styles and restaurants (4 of them) under one roof, but it represents some of the best family dining in *Downtown Disney*, with a great couples' option in the **Dining Room**. The main Café is smart enough, but head upstairs to the gourmet restaurant and you are in seriously romantic territory, with a great view of *Pleasure Island* and service to match. The contrast with the fun hubbub below is striking, while the menu is well thought out and varied – try the Braised Duck Papardelle or Pan-roasted Florida Grouper for a different taste sensation (6–10.30pm; 407 938 9653; **www. wolfgangpuck.com**).

When it comes to one of the hippest places in town, **bluezoo** (at the *Walt Disney World Dolphin Hotel*) not only looks the part, it also serves up some of the finest food in the Disney realm. Celebrity chef Todd English has made a name for himself by creating individual and contrasting restaurant experiences in places as diverse as Seattle and the liner *Queen Mary II* – and bluezoo is another gem. With an under-the-sea-themed decor that benefits from superb lighting (dine here later rather than earlier for the full effect), it has a wonderfully soothing effect, whether you are just at the bar or in one of the 3 main areas of the restaurant. Both the service and the waiting staff's knowledge of the cuisine and extensive wine list are impeccable, so feel free to let them steer you around a mouth-watering menu. Fish is the signature ingredient (though rotisserie chicken, beef filet and slow-roasted pork chop are also on offer) and seafood lovers will struggle to narrow down the choice here: Miso-glazed Chilean Sea Bass, Roasted Swordfish Paella, Seared Nori-wrapped Tuna, Cantonese Lobster and more, or you could just opt for

BRITTIP

For a special occasion, particularly a romantic one, bluezoo, Jiko, Capital City Grille and Tchoup Chop are the pick of a rich crop.

bluezoo's Dancing Fish – your choice of freshly caught fish, whole-roasted over its special rotisserie (3.30–11pm daily; 407 934 1111; **www.theblue zoo.com**).

Finally, we have saved the best for last with what we consider the most amazing restaurant experience in central Florida. **Tchoup Chop** (pronounced 'chop chop'), at Universal's Royal Pacific Resort, is from the gourmet stable of New Orleans master chef Emeril Lagasse, and it offers Asian-Pacific fusion cuisine in the most eye-catching setting. Service is a team effort at each table (which can be off-putting), but the superb menu is well presented and explained. And oh, that menu! Taking some of the most aromatic and flavoursome elements of Thai, Chinese, Japanese, South Seas and other Pacific Rim cultures, Lagasse has conjured up a delectable array of dishes. Start with Homemade Dumpling Box (with a fresh port and ginger filling, hand-rolled, steamed and served with sake soy dipping sauce) or Polynesian Crabcake (with ginger, scallion, aioli and papaya salsa), then graduate to Macadamia-nut Crusted Atlantic Salmon (with ginger soy butter sauce, steamed rice and stir-fried vegetables), Tchoup Chop's Clay Pot of the Day (served with steamed rice and seasonal

Tchoup Chop

vegetables) or the Hawaiian Dinner Plate including smoked ribs, kahlua pork, teriyaki-grilled chicken, chorizo potato hash and baked macaroni. Dinner here is exceptionally busy, so try lunch if it can't squeeze you in (11.30am–2pm; 5.30–10pm Sun–Thurs, 5.30–11pm Fri, Sat; 407 503 2467, **www.emerils.com**).

Best of the rest

There are at least another dozen worthy of a passing mention here: **Everglades**, the smart steak and seafood-orientated dining room inside the Omni Rosen Center hotel on I-Drive; **Sunset Sam's**, the Gaylord Palms' Key West-style restaurant inside its magnificent resort; **Roy's**, a hugely upscale Hawaiian-themed choice in the Plaza Venezia on West Sand Lake Road; **Doc's**, a wonderfully stylish choice downtown, with a Martini lounge, great lunches and superb dinner menu, featuring fine seafood, sushi and sashimi, as well as great steaks; the **Stonewood Grill**, a real locals' choice on Dr Phillips Boulevard, with a style light years away from usual tourist fare; the **Venetian Room**, the surprising upscale dining venue at the Caribe Royale Resort on World Center Drive; **Boheme Restaurant**, a quite magnificent menu from this tucked-away gem at the Grand Bohemian hotel in downtown Orlando; **Le Jardin du Castillons**, a small but eye-catching French restaurant just off Park Avenue in Winter Park; **Norman's**, the feature restaurant of celebrity chef Norman Van Aken at the Grand Lakes Resort; **Capital City Grille**, one of the additions to The Pointe Orlando, with sumptuous decor and cuisine to match, featuring caviare, oysters and signature steaks; **Texas de Brasil**, an unusual but delicious Brazilian-style steakhouse with a wonderfully upscale touch; and **Citrico's**, the most chic of *Disney's Grand Floridian Resort* restaurants.

Now on to another of our favourite topics – shopping…

12

Shopping

or How to Send Your Credit Card into Meltdown

As well as being a theme park wonderland, this vast area of Central Florida is a shopper's paradise, with a dazzling array of specialist outlets, malls, flea markets and discount retailers. New centres are also springing up all the time, from smart malls to cheap gift shops – and you can hardly go a few paces in the main tourist areas without a shop insisting it has the 'best bargains' of one sort or another.

With the exchange rate in recent years being so favourable for UK visitors, shopping has become as much of an attraction as the theme parks. The only danger is seriously exceeding your baggage allowance for the flight home – or your Duty Free allowance.

Your limit in the catch-all duty category of 'gifts and souvenirs' is still only £145 per person, and it is easy to go way beyond that. Although paying the duty and VAT can still be cheaper than buying the same items at home, you should remember to keep your receipts and go through the 'goods to declare' channel.

You pay duty (which varies depending on the item) on the total purchase price (i.e. inclusive of Florida sales tax) once you have exceeded £145, plus VAT at 17.5%. You CANNOT pool your allowances to cover one item that exceeds a single allowance. Hence, if you buy a camera that costs £200, you have to pay the duty on the full £200, taking the total to £213.20, and then VAT on that figure. However, if you have several items that add up

The Florida Mall

© OCVB

to £145, and then another that exceeds that, you pay the duty and VAT only on the excess item (and customs officers usually give you the benefit of the lowest rate on what you pay for). Duty rates are updated regularly and vary from 2.7% (e.g. golf clubs) to 15% (e.g. mountain bikes). For more info, contact the Customs and Excise National Advice Service on 0845 010 9000 or visit **www.hmce. gov.uk**.

Your ordinary duty-free allowances from America include 200 cigarettes and 1 litre of spirits or 2 litres of sparkling wine and 2 litres of still wine. Alligator products, which constitute those of an endangered species (to UK authorities), require an import licence, and you should consult the Department of the Environment for more info.

BRITTIP

Pick up the *Orlando Sentinel* newspaper on a Sunday and you will get the full local lowdown on all the great sales for the coming week.

When it comes to the fun part of shopping (and American stores are genuinely fun to just browse, let alone splash out in), you can expect to pay the same number of dollars as you do pounds for items like clothes, books and CDs, and real bargains are to be had in jeans, trainers, shoes, sports equipment and cosmetics. Virtually everywhere offers free, convenient

Shopping at Disney

© Disney

parking, while American shop assistants couldn't be more polite and helpful. Be aware, though, of the hidden extras of shopping costs. Unlike our VAT, Florida sales tax is NOT part of the displayed purchase price, so you must add on 6 or 7% (depending on the county) for the final price. Also, some shops will ask for photo ID with credit card purchases, so if you have a new UK card driving licence it is useful to have it with you.

That's the mechanics of shopping; here's a rundown of the main attractions and the fun to be had.

Downtown Disney

The heart of *Walt Disney World* in many ways is its *Downtown Disney* district, split into 3 linked sections: *Disney Marketplace, Pleasure Island* and *West Side*. This is typical Disney, a beautiful location, imaginative architecture and a host of one-off elements that make shopping a pleasure, with no fewer than 48 shops and dining opportunities. A water-taxi links the 3 main elements of this 120 acre/48.5ha plaza, making for easy movement around the whole area.

BRITTIP

Don't buy electrical goods in the US – they won't work in the UK without an adapter. Some games systems (notably the Nintendo Gamecube) are NOT compatible with UK players. Hand-held games are fine, though.

In the *Marketplace* (9.30am–11pm), don't miss the **World of Disney** store, the largest of its kind, which now includes **Bibbidi Bobbidi Boutique** (where young girls can have hair, make-up and nails done in true Princess style), the **Lego Imagination Center** (an interactive playground and shop), the amazing **Art of Disney** and **Team Mickey's Athletic Club**. **Once Upon A Toy** is a gigantic toy emporium complete with a host of classic games, many with a Disney

Orlando's Shopping Centres

A Downtown Disney
B Oviedo Marketplace
C The Pointe Orlando
D Old Town
E Festival Bay
F Prime Outlets International
G Wal-Mart SuperCenter
H West Oaks Mall
I The Loop

J Lake Buena Vista Factory Stores
K Orlando Premium Outlets
L Flea World
M Osceola Flea and Farmers' Market
N Florida Mall
O Shops of Celebration
P Altamonte Mall
Q Seminole Towne Center
R 192 Flea Market

S Plaza Venezia
T Mall at Millenia
U Park Avenue
V Winter Park Village
W Kissimmee Historic District/Farmers' Market
X Goodings International Plaza
Y Crossroads Plaza
Z Fountains Plaza

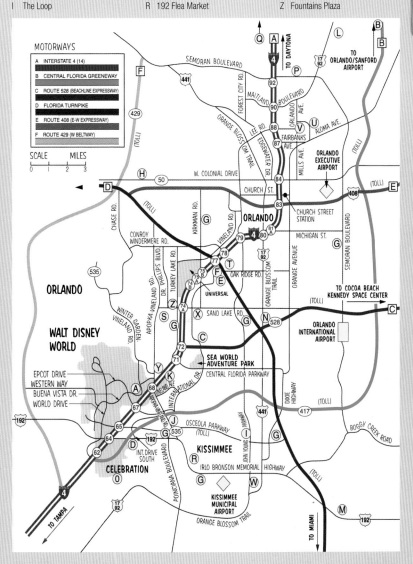

theme, for kids to try. Other worthwhile one-offs are the blissful **Basin** (for hand-carved soaps, bubble baths and shampoo bars) and **Disney's Wonderful World of Memories** (for all scrapbook fans, plus the only place to get a Disney postmark for your postcards home!). **Arribas Brothers** is another big, attractive store of gifts (including hand-blown glass) and collectibles. Those keen on the Disney hobby of pin trading should check out **Pin Traders**, while **Summer Sands** offers excellent swimwear and casual clothing. For bargain-hunters, the aisle next to **World of Disney Kids** and **Disney Tails** offers **Mickey's Mart** – everything for $10 or less.

Dancing fountains and squirt pools (where kids tend to get seriously wet), the lakeside setting and boating opportunities all add to the appeal here. Restaurants include the superbly themed **Rainforest Café**, **McDonald's**, **Wolfgang Puck Express** and the casual waterfront setting of **Cap'n Jack's Restaurant**, while ice-cream and chocolate fans should check out **Ghirardelli's** for cool sundaes and super shakes. For a British touch, opt for one of the range of speciality hot sandwiches and salads at the **Earl of Sandwich**, which start at $5.75 (some will feed 2!), making them some of the best-priced fare in *Downtown Disney*. For an upmarket touch, we rate **Fulton's Crab House** and **Portobello Yacht Club** (see Chapter 11, Dining Out). The new **T-Rex: A Prehistoric Family Adventure** is due to open here in early 2008, another innovative restaurant from the people who run the Rainforest Café, so expect dining with dinosaurs and plenty of

BRITTIP

Parents beware! The Bibbidi Bobbidi Boutique hair and make-up shop is hideously expensive. Packages range from $35–175, so you may want to steer your Princesses gently away!

© OCVB

Prime Outlets is reopening after renovation

interactive features! There will be a Build-A-Dino workshop in its giftshop, and an extensive menu featuring soups, salads, pizza, pasta, sandwiches, burgers, chicken, steak and seafood.

The shops of *Pleasure Island* were completely revamped in 2006, with several familiar outlets closing; a new and enlarged **Harley-Davidson** store is now the cornerstone here. An open-air café is due to open in late 2007, but the one unmissable element is wonderful **Raglan Road**, an Irish-themed pub and restaurant, with live music every evening (see pages 280 and 314). This whole area was opened up in 2006 to make it a more continuous part of *Downtown Disney*, with a large bridge to the West Side, wider walkways and a water-taxi dock.

Continuing into *West Side* (10.30am–11pm) gives you the superb **AMC 24** cinema complex and the world's largest **Virgin Megastore**, plus another 18 retail and dining outlets. The **Hoypoloi Gallery** is one of our favourites for an eclectic range of artwork from metal to glass, while **Magic Masters** (all kinds of tricks and souvenirs, with demonstrations), **Celebrity Eyeworks Studio**, **Pop Gallery** and **Starabilias** are all highly original. The dining choice is superb, with **Planet Hollywood**, **House of Blues**, **Bongo's Cuban Café** and our favourite, **Wolfgang Puck** – an ultra-versatile family-friendly restaurant.

Downtown Disney can be found off exits 67 and 68 of I-4 and is well signposted (exit 68 can be congested at peak periods, though).

International Drive

This core tourist area is simply awash with shopping of all kinds, from the cheapest and tackiest plazas, full of tourist gift shops, to clever, purpose-built centres. Some of the shops just north of the Sand Lake Road junction are best avoided, while the northern end of I-Drive is undergoing a major redevelopment.

This area has been renowned for discount outlet shopping – a local speciality, offering name brands at heavily reduced prices to clear. There has been a lot of change in recent years, though, with the iconic Mercado closed and awaiting reconstruction, the Pointe Orlando completely rebuilt and the former Belz Discount Outlet World sold and reborn as **Prime Outlets International**.

This latter, at the very top of I-Drive, is reopening in two stages following extensive demolition of most of the old Belz units, re-emerging as a vibrant and attractive 100-shop

centre after a $250m makeover. The new design is far more coherent, European village style, with a beautiful canal through the centre, outdoor seating, a Market Place Pavilion and a free-standing Guest Services centre. The first phase opened in summer 2007, with a host of major brands, many of them new to Orlando. The **Neiman Marcus Last Call Clearance Center** will certainly attract the fashion-conscious, as will the **Hugo Boss Factory Store**, **White House/Black Market**, **Esprit** and **Jones New York Outlet**. Other familiar names include **Nike Super Store**, **Tommy Hilfiger**, **Crabtree & Evelyn** and **Starbucks**. Phase 2 opens in spring 2008, adding more international brands such as **Banana Republic**, **BCBG/MaxAzria**, **Bath & Body Works** and **Brooks Brothers**, while you should also look for designer stores from **Michael Kors**, **J Crew** and menswear specialist **Hickey Freeman**. Add in an attractive **food court**, and you will have one of the brightest shopping centres in the area. Open 10am–10pm (9pm Sun) in summer, and 10am–9pm (7pm Sun). For more info, call 407 352 9600 or visit **www.primeotlets.com** for more info.

Another major I-Drive complex has also undergone a change, with **The Pointe Orlando** completing a massive

The Pointe

© OCVB

redevelopment in 2007. The dramatic rebuild has opened a new entrance plaza directly from I-Drive, as well as adding a wealth of new shops and especially restaurants, making this a great choice for an evening out as well as retail therapy. The upscale **Capital Grille**, featuring dry-aged steaks, seafood and tantalising desserts, is new in central Florida, along with **The Oceanaire**, whose menu changes daily to highlight seafood flown in from around the world to ensure the freshest selections. **Magiannos Little Italy** serves exceptional family-style Italian dining in a relaxed, friendly atmosphere with vintage 1940s Chicago decor, while nightly entertainment by local, regional and national acts make **BB King's** restaurant and bar a spirited choice for a meal or drinks and a show.

BRITTIP

At Maggiano's, portions are huge, even by Orlando standards! The Bombalina appetiser platter will easily feed a family of four, while its Family Style meals feature all-you-can-eat refills, which ensures no one leaves hungry. Great value.

Also new to The Pointe is **Tommy Bahama's Tropical Café and Emporium**, with dining in a laid-back, tropical setting. Tommy

Tommy Bahama's

Bahama's also carries home furnishings, accessories and men's and women's clothing with a casual Island flair. The menu is tropical and refreshing, too, great for lunch or dinner, with highlights being their Loki Loki Tuna appetiser and mouth-watering shrimp entrees (plus sandwiches, chicken, fresh fish and fabulous salads). Ultra-chic wine bar **The Grape** is another neat addition, with a tempting range of easy-drinking wines and a unique classification for even non-wine-buffs to understand. It also offers wines by the bottle (and case!), with a try-before-you-buy policy from its retail store, plus live jazz on Friday and Saturday evenings (**www.yourgrape.com**). Other dining choices include the upmarket Greek style of **Taverna Opa**, the lively **Johnny Rockets** American diner, **Pizzeria Valdiano**, **Starbucks**, **Hooters** (wings, ribs, chicken and the famous Hooters girls) and **Adobe Gila's** (Mexican style, with a killer range of margaritas!).

Among some 30 smart stores, you can indulge your passion for fashion at **Victoria's Secret**, **Armani Exchange**, **Image Leather**, **Chico's**, **Gray Fifth Avenue** and the **Everything But Water** swimwear store, or stock up on gifts and souvenirs at **Bath & Body Works**, **Yankee Candle**, **Sunglass Hut** and the excellent **Tharoo & Co** jewellery. **Players Golf** is a keen draw for golf fans, while **Footlocker**, **Bimini Shoes** and the **Discovery Channel Store** all offer more options.

The revamped **Regal Cinemas Stadium 20 + IMAX** cineplex shows first-run movies in large screen format, often debuting films a month in advance of UK release. Parking is at The Pointe's multi-storey car park, but several stores and restaurants will redeem your parking ticket if you shop there. It is open 10am–10pm daily (11am–9pm Sun), but later at the bars and restaurants (407 248 2838, **www.pointeorlando.com**).

© OCVB

Festival Bay

Another bright centre is **Festival Bay**, again at the top of I-Drive. Its mix of shops and entertainment is quite unusual, and many of the stores will be unfamiliar to Brits, but don't let that put you off as there is much to discover here. The emphasis is as much on entertainment as shopping, and the village street style is aimed at the casual wanderer. The main entrance is graced by a huge fountain and multi-coloured tiling, while it also features **Ron Jon's Surf Shop** battling for prominence with **Fuddruckers** diner (superb burgers), the fun **Dixie Crossroads** seafood restaurant and **Bergamo's** Italian restaurant (formerly at The Mercado). Pub fans will also want to know the popular **Cricketers Arms** has relocated here from The Mercado next to Fuddruckers.

Step inside the mall doors (for it is mainly an enclosed centre) and you discover a huge water feature and another 58 stores and restaurants, plus **Vans Skate Park**, the superb **Cinemark 20-screen Movie Complex**, and (in summer 2008 – they hope!) the unique **Ron Jon's Surf Park**. The massive **Bass Pro Shops Outdoor World** is worth checking out for its range of outdoor clothing and equipment (fishing, boating, hunting, hiking) as well as the amazing themed decor, while **Shepler's Western Wear**'s range of apparel, boots and other footwear has to be seen to be believed (all at great prices, too).

Steve & Barry's University Sportswear is another unusual clothing store (especially for the value-conscious – there are some serious bargains to be had here), while the **Universal Orlando Store** was new in 2007 (good for discounted merchandise). Other standouts are **Kasper** (women's attire), **Nine West** (women's shoes and accessories) and **Jones New York**, **Charlotte Russe**

(trendy women's clothing), **Zirbes Emporium** (an eclectic gift-and-furniture store) and **Swim Smart**, plus a unique, glow-in-the-dark mini-golf course, the **Putting Edge**, which is a great place to occupy the kids for a while. The huge **Monkey Joe's** play centre is another ideal opportunity to let the youngsters (3–8s) run free (with a Parent Area including TVs and relaxing seating), while there is also the **Fantasy Arcade** for video games.

Vans Skate Park is perfect for anyone with a skateboard or roller-blade obsession (visit **www.vans.com**, then Skateparks, then Orlando), offering 6 2-hour sessions a day (10am–midnight) as well as a full range of safety equipment and board rentals, plus a chill-out lounge.

BRITTIP

International visitors can go to the Guest Services booth, with photo ID, and pick up a free advantage card offering $200 in savings throughout Festival Bay.

There is no food court, but there are small dining outlets dotted around, notably **New York Deli**, **Asian Café**, **Auntie Anne's**, **Sandella's Café**, **Cold Stone Creamery** (superb ice-cream), **Smoothy Bee** and **Villa Pizza**

BRITTIP

The new-look Cricketers Arms features one of the biggest ranges of beers in Florida, with 17 on tap, including 4 hand-drawn ales. It even has a special Sampler Platter on its own 'cricket bat' server!

Cuccina. The 3 feature restaurants are all great choices for a meal or just a post-shopping snack. **Fuddruckers** is a highly tempting counter-service diner offering all manner of burgers (including ostrich, turkey, salmon and vegetarian options), salads, soups and desserts, and **Dixie Crossroads** is a casual seafood emporium specialising in rock shrimp, Maine lobster, snow crab and scallops. **Bergamo's** has long offered good-quality Italian dining (pasta, seafood, veal and prime Angus steaks), plus its signature singing waiters, who range from Grand Opera to folk songs. **The Cricketers Arms** also offers typical pub grub, plus a terrific range of local and imported beers, as well as live entertainment and the all-important footy on the TV! It even has a private function/dining room (see also page 310). Festival Bay is open daily (10am–9pm, 11am–7pm Sun; 407 351 7718, **www.shopfestivalbaymall.com**).

Shopping at Baywalk, St Pete's

Inside the Mall at Millenia

Kissimmee

Kissimmee's version of the purpose-built tourist shopping centre is **Old Town**, an antique-style offering in the heart of Highway 192, with a tourist-friendly mix of shops, restaurants, bars and fairground attractions, all set out along brick-built streets. The 50 shops range from standard souvenirs, novel T-shirt outlets and Disney merchandise to sportswear, motorbike fashions and other collectables (check out the **Old Town General Store** for a step back in time, or the **Old Town Portrait Gallery** for period style photographs). The individual style of **Out Of This World Embroidery** offers a 'you name it, we'll stitch it,' service, while **Black Market Minerals**, **Kandlestix**, **Andean Manna** and **Magic Max** are also great for novel gift ideas.

There are 8 restaurants or snack bars and some amusing diversions, like the 2-storey **Haunted House of Old Town** and the **Hollywood Wax Museum and Tower of London Experience**. Those in need of some pampering or a massage should head for the **Time For Pleasure Day Spa** (daily 10am–10pm). **Fred Marion's Sports Grill** restaurant is an excellent dining choice, with great ribs, burgers and salads (plus sports on its big-screen TVs) but the **Blue Max Tavern** is a fun alternative. New additions

Jam Rock Caribbean Café and **Old Town Chippy** (British-style fish 'n' chips) are also worth trying, while there are other snack outlets, with offerings from popcorn to candy.

Allow up to 4 hours here and try to take in the weekly **Saturday Nite Cruise** at 8.30pm, a drive-past of 300-plus vintage and collector cars (the biggest in America) that has become a real trademark here. A **Friday Nite Cruise** features cars built between 1973 and 1987, plus live music and prizes. Every Thursday is **Motorcycle Nite** from 6pm, and the place can get fairly raucous later on, with plenty of alcoholic libations (witness the **Sun on the Beach** bar). Parking is free and Old Town is open 10am–11pm daily (rides open noon–11pm; 407 396 4888, **www.old-town.com**).

Kissimmee is short of quality shopping otherwise, as the Kissimmee Manufacturers' Outlet Mall and Osceola Square Mall are in urgent need of refurbishment. However, a new (in 2005) 44 acre/18ha development **The Loop** helps redress the balance. This open-air plaza (at the junction of Osceola Parkway and John Young Parkway) offers a unique mix of shops and restaurants, plus a 16-screen **Regal Cinema**, in a pedestrian-friendly setting, with the shops grouped around the large car park. Many of the shops may not mean much to UK

Historic Sanford is a good place for antiques

© OCVB

Lake Buena Vista Factory Stores

visitors but are well worth visiting, notably **Ross** (a huge discount warehouse of clothes, shoes, linens, cosmetics and more), **Kohl's** (a well-priced department store), **Bed, Bath & Beyond** (an amazing range of household wares), **Pacific Sunwear** (beach and casual wear), **Old Navy** (clothing), **Michaels** (arts and crafts), **Sports Authority** and **Famous Footwear** (discounted shoes and trainers). In addition, there is a hairdresser, nail salon, chemist (**CVS**) and a superb line-up of 10 restaurants and cafés. Look out in particular for **Johnny Rockets**, the excellent Italian style of **Macaroni Grill**, **Red Brick Pizza**, the gourmet Mexican of **Chipotle Mexican Grill**, **Shane's Rib Shack** and the hearty fare of **Panera Bread** (great soups, salads and sandwiches). In all, The Loop boasts more than 40 stores and cafés; daily 10am–9.30pm (11am–6pm Sun), later at the restaurants and cinemas (407 343 9223, **www.attheloop.com**). A second centre, **Loop West**, will begin to open (with **JC Penney**) in late 2007. Another new outlet will be the upmarket department store **Belk** (2008), along with another 30 shops and restaurants.

Lake Buena Vista

The Lake Buena Vista area has 2 of the best discount outlet centres, with a range of goods to make even the most jaded shopper salivate – and prices to match! High on your list of 'must visit' shops should be **Orlando Premium Outlets**, which is a huge hit with UK visitors. With a fresh look and style, and a legion of big-name designers (from Nike, Adidas and Gap to Polo Ralph Lauren, Dior, Hugo Boss, Ferragamo and Zegna), it can be found on Vineland Avenue between I-Drive and I-4 (just south of SeaWorld; or exit 68 off I-4). In all, it offers 115 stores of well-known brand names (like Timberland, Reebok, Diesel, Fossil, Banana Republic, French Connection and Calvin Klein) in a semi-covered pedestrian plaza, with easy free parking and the added convenience of being at the south end of the I-Ride Trolley (main line). Other significant signature shops are **Samsonite Company Store**, **Ecko** (upscale T-shirts, jeans and sportswear), **Fendi** (stylish women's clothing and signature handbags), **Little Me** (baby/toddler clothes), **Mikasa** (household items), **Factory**

Brand Shoes (a mini-warehouse of footwear fashion) and **KB Toys** (a huge discount choice for kids of all ages). Watch out also for big Disney bargains at the **Character Premiere**.

BRITTIP

Brit's Guide **Personalised Itinerary Planner** clients will receive Orlando Premium Outlets' special Premier Platinum VIP Discount voucher, for significant extra savings at many shops. See page 49.

The food court is quite tempting, too, with 11 outlets from **JR's Steakery** and **Max Orient** to **Starbucks** and **Subway**. Daily 10am–11pm (9pm Sun; 407 238 7787, **www.premium outlets.com**).

For those without a car, there is a daily free shuttle service from hotels in the Lake Buena Vista area (advance reservations are required) but it costs $10/person from Highway 192 in Kissimmee. Call 407 390 0000 for reservations. The **Lynx** bus service also stops here (407 841 2279) or you can try **Star Taxi** (407 857 9999).

BRITTIP

After shopping at Orlando Premium Outlets, look to grab afternoon tea, with home-made scones, or a glass of wine or speciality beer at the new **Sherlock's** tea-room and wine bar, all with a proper British touch (near the Outback Steakhouse).

Lake Buena Vista Factory Stores offers another range of big-name products at discount prices, from Fossil, Sony, Reebok and Liz Claiborne and London Fog to a budget-priced **Disney Character Outlet**, **OshKosh B'Gosh** superstore and (the better priced) **Carter's For Kids**. It is another open-air plaza, with almost 50 stores spread over 6 acres/2.5ha and with plentiful, convenient parking. It's slightly off the beaten track and therefore not quite

as busy as some of the others. New shops are opening all the time, and recent additions include stylish **Tommy Hilfiger**, funky **Aeropostale**, **Bass Shoes**, **Hard Rock Outlet Store**, **Converse** and **Rawlings Factory Store** for sporting goods. There is also a decent food court (now serving beer in deference to British requests!) and a kids' playground. Some of the stores and brand names may not be well known to us, but the likes of **Old Navy** (excellent value casual clothing), **Perfume Smart** (heavily discounted fragrances and other cosmetics), **SAS Shoemakers** (think Hush Puppies, only cheaper!) and **Rack Room Shoes** (big names at serious savings) are worth discovering. **Borders Books Outlet** offers great bargain books, **Camera Outlet** carries a large selection of European Pal systems, and **World of Coffee** is both an internet café and one of the most pleasant places you could find to sip a latte and enjoy a cake or pastry, with its outdoor terrace and bird cages.

BRITTIP

If you are into scrapbooking or other arts and crafts, you should seek out one of Orlando's 8 **Michaels** stores, which are a scrapbooking heaven!

Other services include the welcome lounge and off-site airline check-in for **Travel City Direct**. The Factory Stores are on SR 535 (2mls/3km south off exit 68 on I-4) and are open daily 10am–9pm (6pm Sun). Their shuttle service picks up at hotels and condo units in a 10ml/16km radius (407 238 9301, **www.lbvfs.com**).

Sak's Fifth Avenue

© OCVB

⚜ BRITTIP

Go to **www.lbvfs.com** for up to $400 in discount coupons.

Malls

If the discount outlets often represent the best value, the choice and style of the area's malls are unarguable and well worth adding to your holiday agenda. They contain a huge range of shops and, if you can take advantage of their periodic sales, you will be firmly on the bargain trail. The top 2 locally are the Florida Mall and the Mall at Millenia, and both offer a contrasting shopping experience.

⚜ BRITTIP

Need a good book? Make a beeline for **Barnes & Noble**, on West Sand Lake Road in the Venezia Plaza or on the South Orange Blossom Trail opposite the Florida Mall. There's a great coffee shop there, too.

The **Florida Mall** is the largest in central Florida and features over 250 shops, with 7 large department stores and an excellent food court with a choice of 16 outlets and a children's play area, plus the lively bar-restaurant **Ruby Tuesday**, the smart Mexican-influenced **Salsa Taqueria and Tequilla Bar**, **California Pizza Kitchen** and hearty **Buca di Beppo**. Located on the South Orange Blossom Trail, on the corner of Sand Lake Road, this spacious and

The Mall at Millenia

© OCVB

extremely smart mall is open daily 10am–9pm (12pm–6pm Sun). Highlights are the department stores, led by the upmarket (but expensive) **Saks Fifth Avenue** and **Macy's** (formerly Burdines), plus **JC Penney**, **Nordstrom** (which also has a sit-down café), **Sears** and **Dillard's**. Other shops worth looking out for are **Bath & Body Works**, **Williams-Sonoma** ('the place for cooks' – and how!), **PacSun** (beachwear and more) and (for kids) **Build-a-Bear Workshop**, **KB Toys**, **EB Games** and one of only 2 **M&M World** stores in the country! The new **Adrenalina The Extreme** store features a huge range of extreme sports gear and apparel. You can also benefit here from a discount coupon packet (from Guest Services) that includes a handy international size chart to help deal with American sizing. Extra services include free wheelchair use, pushchair rental and foreign currency exchange. There are even spa and beauty treatments in the Lancôme Institut de Beauté in Dillard's, the JC Penney styling salon and day spa, and the Elizabeth Arden salon at Saks Fifth Avenue (407 851 6255, **www.simon.com**). The Mall also benefits from the integral **Florida Hotel & Conference Center**, with a lovely bar area and new restaurant.

⚜ BRITTIP

Kids – let your parents take you to the Florida Mall, then insist on visiting the huge Toys R Us store at the front and then M&M World inside the mall!

If the Florida Mall is the biggest shopping venue in town, the **Mall at Millenia** (which opened in October 2002) is the smartest. Located just off I-4 to the north of Universal Orlando (exit 78), it is the most upmarket, dramatic and technologically advanced shopping complex in Florida, with New York's most famous department stores – Bloomingdale's, Neiman Marcus and Macy's – among a select number of other top-name

Blue Martini

© OCVB

boutiques such as Tiffany & Co and Louis Vuitton. The entrance features a 60ft/18m glass rotunda with a flowing water garden theme and a helpful concierge desk (valet parking is also available). Then you can head out in one of four directions over the marble and terrazzo floors or go upstairs to the refreshing, high-quality 13-outlet food court, the Orangerie Cafés, where the only difficulty is deciding which of the tempting (and health-conscious) eateries to choose. Look out for **Bistro Sensations** (wonderful salads, pastas, pittas and wraps), the authentic Mandarin-style of **Chinatown**, the fresh **Nori Japanese Grill** (beef and chicken teriyaki and excellent sushi, all prepared on the spot) and the **Southwest Grill** (succulent chicken, barbecue beef and salads), plus **Tony's & Bruno's** for Italian specialities (pasta, pizza, salads, cheesecake).

BRITTIP

Visit the concierge office at Mall at Millenia, fill out its marketing questionnaire and receive a free gift.

The grand architecture is also focused on 5 separate courts along a flattened, serpentine S-shape, topped by a flowing, arched glass roof like some gigantic conservatory. On 2 airy levels (3 in Bloomingdale's and Macy's) and with 8 Juliet balconies connecting the 2 sides, the mall consists of a colossal amount of glass, plus a stunning Grand Court, featuring a dozen

20ft/6m columns capped by curved plasma video screens. And, while around 20% of the 150 outlets are upscale and exclusive (Cartier, Chanel, Lacoste, Jimmy Choo, Dior, Coach etc., plus the luxury of Neiman Marcus for brands like Gucci and Prada), the other 80% comprise more mainstream shops like Gap, Banana Republic and Victoria's Secret. Several outlets provide a distinctive experience – **Metropolitan Museum of Art**, **Z Gallerie**, **Kirkland's** and **Rocks Fine Jewellery** – without the price tag to go with it.

The 4 main restaurants are also first class: heavenly **Cheesecake Factory**, gourmet seafood **McCormick & Schmick**, **PF Chang's China Bistro** and **Brio Tuscan Grille**. On top of that (AND the **Orangerie Cafés**), you have the excellent fresh sandwich style of **Panera Bread**, the **California Pizza Kitchen** and a **Johnny Rockets** diner. This is also the only mall with a US post office inside (NB: standard postcards back to the UK cost 81c; 90c for large ones). A currency exchange is available, as are international phone cards. The **first Friday** of each month also sees a free concert in the Main Entrance (5.30–8.30pm), featuring some outstanding performers, from jazz and blues to rock and soul. The chic **Blue Martini**, a speciality martini bar, sushi-tapas restaurant and live music venue, is well worth trying for something a bit special. With more than 29 unique martinis, plus an extensive wine list, premium cigars and a tapas-style menu, this is the current trendy hangout, with an outdoor terrace and indoor stage room. There is live music – jazz and R&B – 7.30–11.30pm, then dance music with the house DJ. Hours are 4pm–2am Mon–Fri and 1pm–2am Sat, Sun, Happy Hour 4–7pm Mon–Fri (**www.bluemartini lounge.com**). All in all, this takes the shopping experience in Florida to a new level; open 10am–9pm Mon–Sat, 12am–7pm Sun (407 363 3555, **www.mallatmillenia.com**).

Festival Bay Mall

There are 4 alternatives to these popular (and busy – especially at weekends) malls: the **Altamonte Mall**, on Altamonte Avenue in the suburb of Altamonte Springs (take exit 92 off I-4 and head east for ½ml/800m on Route 436, then turn left); **Seminole Towne Center**, just off I-4 to the north of Orlando on the outskirts of Sanford (exit 101C off I-4); **Oviedo Marketplace**, to the east of Orlando (right off exit 41 on the Central Florida Greeneway, 417); and **West Oaks Mall**, on West Colonial Drive (SR50), in the suburb of Ocoee, west of downtown Orlando (take the Florida Turnpike to exit 267A with SR50, and go back east on 50 for 1½mls/2.5km). The Altamonte Mall is the best of the bunch and well off the beaten tourist track, featuring 160 speciality shops, 4 major department stores – Macy's, Dillard's, JC Penney and Sears – 15 restaurants, including **Bahama Breeze**, **Seasons 52** and the **Orlando Ale House**. An 18-screen cinema, food court and children's soft-play area round out the offerings. Open daily 10am–9pm Mon–Thurs, 10am–10pm Fri, Sat, 11am–6pm Sun, it offers a VIP savings book to visitors at the Customer Service Center (**www.altamontemall.com**). Shop during the week and you'll feel as if you have the place to yourself!

Flea markets

The locals also have a passion for flea markets, highlighted by **Flea World**, America's largest covered market, with 1,700 stalls spread over 104 acres/42ha, including 3 massive (air-conditioned), themed buildings and a 7 acre/2.8ha amusement park, **Fun World** (rides are about $2 each). Flea World is open 9am–6pm Fri, Sat and Sun (Fun World 9am–6pm Sat and Sun only), and can be found a 30-minute drive away on Highway 17/92 (best picked up from exit 90 on I-4) between Orlando and Sanford (to the north). The stalls include all manner of market goods (nearly all new or slight seconds), from fresh produce to antiques and jewellery, while there is a full-scale food court and a 300-seat pizza and burger eatery, the **Carousel Restaurant**, plus free entertainment on the Fun World Pavilion stage. 407 330 1792 or visit **www.fleaworld.com**

On a smaller scale is **the Osceola Flea and Farmers' Market** at the east end of Highway 192 in Kissimmee (8am–5pm Fri–Sun), offering food, clothing, household and kitchen supplies, electronics, sporting goods, collectables and handicrafts (407 846 2811). In downtown Kissimmee, Toho Square is home to a small **Farmers' Market** each Thurs (7am–1pm), with everything from fresh produce to jewellery and candles. Nearby, **Susan's Courtside Café** offers delicious sandwiches, pizzas, salads, smoothies and coffees (7am–8pm Mon–Fri). The **192 Flea Market**, in the heart of Highway 192 just past Medieval Times (marker 15) and the Wal-Mart Supercenter, is more convenient for the main tourist area and is open 7 days a week (9am–6pm), with 400 booths from apples to timeshares, plus as many cheap Disney T-shirts as you can carry!

Traditional shopping

The attractions and possibilities of Winter Park's **Park Avenue** have been detailed in Chapter 8 (see page 241), but the area also has **Winter Park Village**, a small, upscale, open-plan development of boutiques, larger speciality stores like Borders Books, and some fine restaurants. The Village is on North Orlando Avenue – exit 87 off I-4, head east on Fairbanks Avenue, then north on Highway 17/92, North Orange Avenue, for 2mls/3km, and it is on the right. It offers a nice change from the usual malls and plazas – as well as some excellent dining at **PF Chang's China Bistro** (try its spicy Szechuan chicken), **Brio Tuscan Grille** (fine Italian fare), the superb **Seito Sushi** and gorgeous **Cheesecake Factory**.

More traditional shopping can also be found in the revamped **Historic District of Kissimmee** on Broadway, 2 blocks south of Highway 192 on Route 17/92, along Main Street and Broadway. These are a number of restored turn-of-the-century buildings featuring craft and gift shops, a children's boutique, a country store and 7 restaurants (including **Azteca's** for fine Mexican fare – lunch specials $3.99 Mon–Fri), plus antiques, Western wear and

sportswear. The shops are open 9am– 5.30pm weekdays (when they are busiest) and 9am–3pm Sat.

Supermarkets

Apart from the big chemist chain stores, **CVS** and **Walgreens**, which both sell a huge range of goods (including medical, personal and health care essentials, baby and child care needs, cosmetics, household wares, limited sportswear, photo processing, gifts and speciality items), there are any number of supermarkets in Orlando. High on many people's lists is **Wal-Mart**, the warehouse-like American supermarket that sells just about everything. There are no fewer than 21 Wal-Marts in central Florida, 16 of which are the open-24-hour Supercenter kind. The main tourist area stores are on Highway 27 (just north of 192), Highway 192 by Medieval Times (between markers 14 and 15), Osceola Parkway (at Buenaventura Lakes), John Young Parkway (at Sand Lake Road), on Kirkman Road (north of Universal Boulevard), by Highway 535 and Osceola Parkway and a brand new store on Turkey Lake Road.

BRITTIP

Wal-Mart offers 1-hour photo processing at great savings on UK prices, as do branches of Walgreens.

There is plenty of supermarket choice, though, and you will find better-quality produce at the likes of **Publix** (throughout the main tourist areas, notably on Highway 192 and 27); **Goodings** (on I-Drive and the Crossroads plaza near *Downtown Disney*); **Winn-Dixie** (a major south-east US chain) and **Albertson's** (mainly Orlando and to the north – the store at Dr Phillips Boulevard is close to I-Drive). The real Rolls-Royce of food stores will open a new Orlando branch on Turkey Lake Road in 2008 – **Whole Foods Market** is a superb fresh produce emporium, with plenty of chances to sample as you go, plus a hot-food counter to grab a meal at the end (**www. wholefoodsmarket.com**). For clothes, DIY, home furnishings, gifts, toys, electrical goods, household items and groceries, visit **Target** (its new superstores on Highway 192 just west of Highway 535 and near Mall at Millenia are fine examples).

Specialist shops

Keen shoppers will want to check out other individual outlets that might not mean much at first glance. **Ross** (10 in Orlando, see **www.rossstores. com**) carries a huge range of discounted brand name clothes,

shoes, linens, towels and other goods (9.30am–9.30pm Mon–Sat, 11am–7pm Sun), and **Marshalls** (5 in Orlando, **www.marshallsonline.com**) and **TJ Maxx** (also 5, **www.tjmaxx.com**) are similar. For jeans and more, **World of Denim** (and **Denim Place**) has 6 shops in the main tourist areas (good for Tommy Hilfiger, DKNY, Calvin Klein, Polo, Lee and more), while **The Sports Authority** and **Sports Dominator** offer all manner of sporting goods and apparel. Golfers should visit the **Edwin Watts Golf** shops (including the I-Drive clearance centre, **www.edwinwatts. com**), or any of the **Special Tee Golf & Tennis** shops. You can pick up some great deals on golf clubs in particular. By the same token, anglers can stock up on the latest gear at bargain prices at **Bass Pro Shops Outdoor World** (Festival Bay).

Now that the shopping is done, it's time to think about the journey home…

Bass Pro Shops Outdoor World at the Festival Bay Mall

Going Home

or Where Did The Last Two Weeks Go?

And so, dog-tired, lighter in the wallet but (hopefully) blissfully happy and with enough memories to last a lifetime, it is time to deal with that bane of all holidays – the journey home.

If you have come through the last 2 weeks relatively unscathed, here's how to avoid any last-minute pitfalls.

The car

Returning the hire car can take time if you had to use an off-airport car depot, so allow ½ hour. The process is much slicker with the firms that operate directly from the airports. Most airlines require you to arrive 3 hours before an international flight, so don't be tempted to leave your check-in until the last minute. Virgin and Travel City Direct's morning check-in facilities at their *Downtown Disney* and Lake Buena Vista Factory Stores facilities are a major bonus in making this aspect smoother for their passengers.

Now you'll have time to kill, so here is a guide to the 2 main airports.

Orlando International Airport

Orlando International is 46mls/74km from Cocoa Beach and 54mls/87km from Daytona Beach on the east coast, 84mls/135km from Tampa and 110mls/177km from Clearwater and St Petersburg to the west, 25mls/40km from *Walt Disney World* and 10mls/16km from Universal Orlando; so always allow enough time for the return journey plus check-in. The Beachline Expressway (528) can get quite congested in the afternoon, for example, and the Central Florida Greeneway (417) is often a better bet.

This modern airport is the third largest in size in the USA, the 14th for number of passengers (No. 1 in Florida) – and the top rated for passenger satisfaction. It hit a record 34.7 million passengers in 2006 (more than 90,000 a day), above Gatwick and San Francisco. It can get busy at peak times, but its 854 acre/345ha terminal complex usually handles crowds with ease, and this is one of the most comfortable airports you could ever hope to find. It boasts great facilities, and its wide, airy concourses make it feel more like an elegant hotel (one end is actually the airport-owned Hyatt Hotel).

The Great Hall at Orlando International Airport

Ramps, restrooms, wide lifts and large open areas ensure easy wheelchair access, and there are features like TDD and amplified telephones, wheelchair-height drinking fountains, Braille lift controls and companion-care restrooms to assist any travellers with disabilities.

In keeping with the area, the international airport is always engaged in staying a step ahead, with a major food court, extra restaurant options and some superb shops. Should you have more than 3 hours to spare, it is worth taking the 15-minute taxi ride to the Florida Mall, or checking in early, keeping the car and visiting Gatorland about 20 minutes away (see page 221).

BRITTIP

You are advised to leave all luggage unlocked (no combination locks or padlocks) when you check in for your return flight as the TSA security opens a LOT of bags during its screening process and have the right to access any case, locked or unlocked.

Landside

As with all international airports, you have a division between LANDSIDE (for visitors) and AIRSIDE (where you need to have a ticket).

Orlando's Landside has 3 levels: **One** is for ground transportation, tour operator desks, parking, buses and car rental agencies; **Two** is for Baggage Claim (which you negotiated on your arrival) and private vehicles meeting passengers; **Three** is where you enter on your return journey as it holds the check-in desks, shops and restaurants.

Level 3 divides into 5 inter-connected sections: **Landside A** is the check-in for **Gates 1–29** and **100–129**. Here you will find American Airlines, Air Canada, Continental, Aer Lingus, Southwest and JetBlue. **Landside B** has check-in desks for **Gates 30–99** and the likes of Air France, BA, Delta,

Northwest, United, Spirit, US Airways, AirTran and Virgin. Once you have checked in, you can explore both the **East** and **West** sections of the main concourse on Level 3. These house a good mix of shops and restaurants, plus currency exchange, information desks and ATM machines, while the Hyatt Hotel is also in the East Hall. The East and West Halls are then linked by the shops, restaurants and services of the **North** and **South Walks**. In all, there are 40 places to shop and eat, plus a handy food court, and it is almost like being in a smart shopping mall.

There is a games arcade, a Suntrust bank, post office and even the relaxing **D-parture Spa and Salon** (have a massage before you fly!). Many shops feature outstanding design and even photo opportunities: see the 2 **Disney** stores, **Harley-Davidson**, **Universal**, **SeaWorld/Busch Gardens** and **Kennedy Space Center**. Other notable shops are the blissful bath products of **Lush**, the natural cosmetics of **L'Occitane**, the unique apparel of **Del Sol**, **Borders Books** (with its **Seattle's Best** coffee bar), **Perfumania**, **Ron Jon Surf Shop**, **Florida Market**, fashion accessories of **Bijoux Terner** and **Hudson News**.

Dining here is also a pleasure. The 8-counter food court features **McDonalds**, **Sbarro**, **Carvel** ice-cream, **Krispy Crème** and **Nathan's Hot Dogs**, as well as the healthier options of **Zyng's Asian Noodlery**, **Fresh Attractions Deli** and **Chick-Fil-A**. **Macaroni Grill** is a tasty Italian option, while **Fox Sports Sky Box** adds a multi-screen TV set-up plus counter and table service; and upstairs at the West Hall is **Chili's Too**, a cheerful, quick-service Tex-Mex bar-diner. The **East Hall** tends to be quieter and more picturesque as it is dominated by the 8-storey Hyatt Hotel atrium. Up the escalator is the main entrance, and to see out your visit in style, **McCoy's Bar and Grill** (up and turn right) is a smart bar-

Take to the AirTran

To really make the most of your American adventure, the *Brit's Guide* can thoroughly recommend exploring some other key cities direct from Orlando with **AirTran Airways**, who we fly with regularly and which is one of the most reliable operators in the US. It offers low fares – especially if you book well in advance (sign up for its email sale alerts and special offers) – and a route network that includes San Diego (southern California's hidden secret), New York, Washington and Buffalo/Niagara, all non-stop from Orlando. In all, it covers 55 US destinations, also using a major hub at Atlanta to cities like Las Vegas, Los Angeles and San Francisco, plus the Bahamas, with a modern fleet of Boeing 717 and 737 aircraft (including live XM satellite radio). Other major US gateways include Detroit, Philadelphia, Raleigh-Durham, Boston, Chicago and Dallas, which all provide connecting flights to the UK for alternative transatlantic routes. For a low-cost carrier it is rare in offering a business upgrade at less than business-class prices; in fact, it puts many scheduled services to shame. Book online (**www.airtran.com**) for the best bargains, or call 1800 247 8726 in the US/001 678 254 7999 from the UK. If you are staying on the Florida coast, AirTran also flies from Tampa, Miami, Sarasota/Bradenton, Fort Myers, Fort Lauderdale, West Palm Beach, Daytona Beach and Jacksonville, making it one of the Sunshine State's most user-friendly airlines.

restaurant with a grandstand view of the runways. To go really upmarket, take the lift to the 9th-floor **Hemispheres** (breakfast and dinner only). You'll have an even more impressive view, and its superb Continental cuisine and wine-tasting evenings offer some of the best fare in the city. It's pricey, but the service and food are 5-star.

BRITTIP

Save some film (or card space) for the excellent photo opportunities at the airport: outside the Disney stores, the 2 Harley-Davidson shops and the Kennedy Space Center outlets.

Airside

Once it is time to move on to your departure gate, be aware of the 4 satellite arms that make up the airport's Airside. This is where you will probably need to queue as the security screening takes time, and you should allow AT LEAST 30 minutes. The 'arms' are divided into **Gates 1–29** and **30–59** at the west end, and **60–99** and **100–129** (all American domestic flights) at the east. All the departure gates are here, plus duty-free shops and more restaurants.

The 4 satellites are each connected to the main building by an automated tram, so you need to be alert when it comes to finding your departure gate. There are no tannoy announcements for flights, so you should check your departure gate and time when you check in. However, there are large monitors in the terminal with all the departure information. The usual gates are:

- **Aer Lingus, American and Continental:** 1–29
- **Air Canada, Northwest, Spirit, United and US Airways:** 30–59
- **AirTran, British Airways, Delta and Virgin:** 60–99
- **JetBlue and Southwest:** 100–129

AirTran

ORLANDO INTERNATIONAL AIRPORT

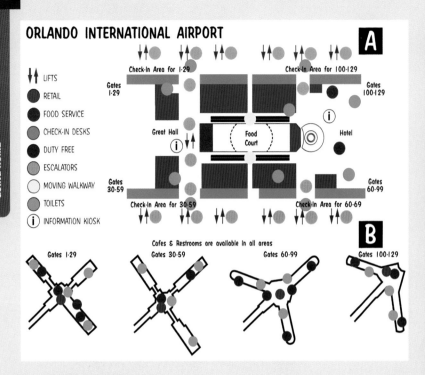

A

LIFTS
RETAIL
FOOD SERVICE
CHECK-IN DESKS
DUTY FREE
ESCALATORS
MOVING WALKWAY
TOILETS
(i) INFORMATION KIOSK

Check-In Area for 1-29
Check-In Area for 100-129
Gates 1-29
Gates 100-129
Great Hall
Food Court
Hotel
Gates 30-59
Gates 60-99
Check-In Area for 30-59
Check-In Area for 60-69

B

Cafes & Restrooms are available in all areas

Gates 1-29
Gates 30-59
Gates 60-99
Gates 100-129

ORLANDO SANFORD INTERNATIONAL AIRPORT

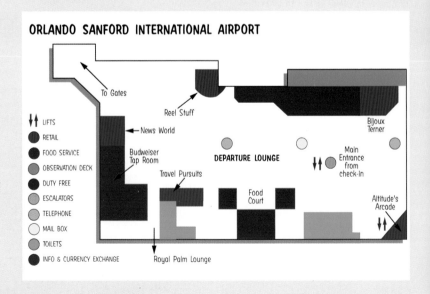

LIFTS
RETAIL
FOOD SERVICE
OBSERVATION DECK
DUTY FREE
ESCALATORS
TELEPHONE
MAIL BOX
TOILETS
INFO & CURRENCY EXCHANGE

To Gates
Reel Stuff
Bijoux Terner
News World
Budweiser Tap Room
DEPARTURE LOUNGE
Main Entrance from check-in
Travel Pursuits
Food Court
Altitude's Arcade
Royal Palm Lounge

Although there isn't as much choice as at the main terminal, you should find the Airside areas just as clean and efficient, with the bonus of 2 duty-free shops (your purchases are delivered to the departure gate for you to collect as you board). Both stores were significantly upgraded in 2006, with merchandise expanded to include designer sunglasses, jewellery, handbags, fashion watches, new perfumes and a selection of travel retail exclusives.

At **Gates 1–29**, you will find the first duty-free shop, a newsagents (the Keys Gift Shop), 2 **Café Azalea** lounge bars, **Pepito's Cuban Café**, and a mini food court featuring **Starbucks**, **Burger King**, **Cinnabon** and **TCBY** ('The Country's Best Yogurt').

Gates 30–59 have **Café Azalea**, **Pepito's Cuban Café**, **the Floribbean Court** (with **Miami Subs**, **Villa Pizza**, **Freshens Yogurt** and the **Manatee** bar/lounge) and **Hudson News**.

Gates 60–99 (the main satellite for UK flights) offer another good duty-free shop, a currency exchange, **Stellar News & Gifts**, the speciality **Mindworks** shop, **The Grove** snacks and candy and a mini play area. A food court contains **Burger King**, **Nathan's Hot Dogs**, **Carvel**, **Starbucks** and **Fresh Attractions** deli, plus the excellent table service of the **Outback Steakhouse Outpost** and bar.

Gates 100–129 offer 2 **Johnny Rivers Smokehouse Express** outlets, a food court with **Freshens Treats**, **McDonald's** and **Sbarro Pizza**, plus **Seattle's Best Coffee**, **Au Bon Pain** café, **Kafe Kalik** bar/lounge and 4 shops. For more details, visit **www.orlandoairports.net**, which features live departure and arrival info.

Orlando Sanford International Airport

Returning to what is now the main Orlando gateway for British charter flights should be a relatively simple experience, providing you retrace your route on the Central Florida Greeneway (following signs for Orlando *Sanford* airport, NOT Orlando International) and come off at exit 49. Turn first right at the lights, then first right again on to Lake Mary Boulevard and follow it to the airport. The efficiency of Alamo and Dollar's car return adds to the simplicity. NB: the airport turn-off sign is immediately after the toll plaza before exit 49 and is easy to miss, so be aware once you go through that toll plaza that you need the very next turn-off.

Orlando Sanford was created as a full international airport in 1996, as an initiative between the airport authorities and several British tour operators. And so MyTravel (Airtours), Thomson (Thomsonfly), Monarch,

Airside 4 at Orlando International Airport

Thomas Cook, XL Airways, the burgeoning Travel City Direct and First Choice (First Choice Airlines), plus the new Sanford operations of Icelandair and Scotland's flyglobespan, all now go for this simpler option. Of course, you are further north, so your journey time is 45 minutes longer and you have to pay an extra $3 in tolls compared with the journey to and from Orlando International but, providing you follow the simple directions, you should have no problem retracing your steps here.

And, while this charter gateway is smaller than Orlando International, it boasts a spacious check-in area and works hard to make the departure as painless as the arrival, especially with its Royal Palm Lounge (formerly the Guest House) facility. Monarch, Thomas Cook, Icelandair and flyglobespan usually use **Terminal B** for check-in: the other UK airlines check in at **Terminal A**. But all passengers use the same international departure lounge in Terminal A. It continues to grow with both domestic and international traffic, and has recently finished a major facility upgrade, notably in Terminal B and Royal Palm Lounge.

There are no food or beverage outlets at the check-in level at Terminal A, but you can walk across to Terminal B where there is a new **Ritazza Café** and food court. Once checked in, you need to pass through security (again, allow a minimum of 30 minutes) to reach the International Departure Lounge. Here you have the new **Budweiser Tap Room**, which serves a decent selection of international beers, and the handy **Food Court**. The 4-part outlet offers American Grill (burgers and fries), Daily Specials (shepherd's pie, chicken pot pie, lasagne and more), Sweet Endings (baked goods and pastries) and the aptly named Grab-N-Go (soft drinks, snacks and bottled water). There is then an extensive **Duty Free** store (also with an increased range of merchandise), a new **Bijoux Terner** shop (fashion accessories – everything $10!), **Reel Stuff** character gifts from the likes of Disney, TV and film, and entertainment shop **Travel Pursuits**, featuring travel games, electronic toys, soft toys, Lego and K'Nex sets and novelty sweets, as well as **News World** for souvenirs, confectionery, books and magazines (including UK newspapers). **Altitudes Arcade** (neatly located in one corner) is guaranteed to appeal to the kids, while there is also an **Information and Currency Exchange** kiosk. Smoking is not allowed inside the Lounge, but there is an extensive outdoor deck for smokers.

The big extra here, though, is the **Royal Palm Lounge**, a premium lounge available to all passengers for a modest fee. It's in a separate annexe from the main lounge and is an oasis of comfort and quiet, more reminiscent of a hotel. Split into 2 distinct halves, it boasts a pleasant café bar, where you can enjoy unlimited tea, coffee, soft drinks and snacks (plus 2 glasses of beer or wine per over-21). It also provides 2 home theatre lounges, with widescreen TV and surround-sound, for recently released films; 2 quiet reading rooms; 11 computer terminals for internet access and email; a youth entertainment centre, with 14 Sony PlayStation 2 consoles; a separate toddlers' playroom with soft toys and

Duty-free delight

For those who can't resist a bargain, it is worth saving some shopping time for the airport duty-free stores. Prices are up to 60% cheaper than in the UK, better even than the local malls. Here is a guide to some of the savings:

Perfumes –	Calvin Klein 45%, Chanel 25%
Cosmetics –	Clinique 40%
Alcohol –	45%
Tobacco –	60%
Watches –	Gucci 25%, Tag Heuer 35%

GOING HOME

Your chance to give something back

After hopefully having the holiday of a lifetime, you might like to know about 2 charities helping children with serious illnesses to have a memorable time here. **Give Kids the World Village** is an amazing organisation in Kissimmee, providing a week's holiday in central Florida for children with life-threatening illnesses. GKTW works with over 250 wish-granting foundations worldwide to provide an unforgettable Wish Vacation for children and their families. It is set up as a resort and includes meals, accommodation, transportation, whimsical venues, donated theme park tickets and many other thoughtful touches in a magical setting. It's a charity I am happy to support myself, and I hope you will too. You can make a donation through its website – **www.gktw.org** – or send to: Give Kids The World, 210 South Bass Road, Kissimmee, Florida 34746, USA.

Equally, **Dreamflight** is a registered UK charity taking seriously ill children (aged 8–14) to Florida annually, often with the help of British Airways. It costs around £1,400 per child and, while many people generously donate their time to help, cash donations are essential. You can contribute by post: Dreamflight, 7C Hill Avenue, Amersham, Bucks HP6 5BD (01494 722733), online at **www.just giving.com**, or by email to **office@dream flight.org**. Look up more on **www.dreamflight.org**. Thanks for any contributions to these worthwhile organisations.

games; a smoking lounge; and a left-luggage area. The Royal Palm Lounge is billed as an airport lounge with the comforts of home and it is well worth the $25 each extra ($20 for children) to while away the last few hours on US soil. Most tour operators offer it in advance at a discount, or you can book on arrival or through your reps at the resort. With its increased capacity and facilities, this is a very satisfying way to conclude a holiday. See the Royal Palm Lounge (and more info on airport facilities) on **www.OrlandoSanfordAirport.com**

Whether you are using Orlando International or Orlando Sanford, you can also expect the return flight to be about an hour shorter than the journey out thanks to the Atlantic jetstreams that provide tail-winds to high-level flights. Nevertheless, you will land back at Gatwick, Manchester, Glasgow or wherever rather more jet-lagged than on the trip out because the time difference is more noticeable on eastward flights, and it may take a day or so to get your body clock back on local time. It is very important not to indulge in alcohol on the flight if you will be driving when you land.

And, much as it may seem like a good idea, the best way to beat Florida jet-lag is NOT to go straight out and book another holiday to Orlando!

But, believe us, it is almost impossible to resist the lure of this theme park wonderland once sampled – you WILL be back!

Orlando Sanford International Airport

© OCVB

Your Holiday Planner

Example: 2 weeks with Disney's 5-Day Premium Ticket and Orlando FlexTicket

(Disney's 5-Day Premium Ticket gives 5 days at their 4 main theme parks, plus 4 visits to *Blizzard Beach, Typhoon Lagoon, Pleasure Island, DisneyQuest* and/or *Disney's Wide World Of Sports*™, valid for 14 days from first use. The Orlando FlexTicket is valid for Universal Orlando's 2 parks, SeaWorld, Aquatica, Wet 'n Wild and CityWalk for 14 days from first use.)

Day	Our Example	Your Planner
ONE (Sun)	Arrive 2.40am local time, Orlando Sanford airport; transfer to resort – check out local shops and restaurants	
TWO (Mon)	Attend tour operator Welcome Meeting; rest of day at UNIVERSAL STUDIOS	
THREE (Tues)	Chill-out day at *Disney's Blizzard Beach* water park	
FOUR (Wed)	All day at MAGIC KINGDOM PARK (Wishes fireworks at 9pm)	
FIVE (Thurs)	All day at DISNEY-MGM STUDIOS (Fantasmic! show at 8.30pm)	
SIX (Fri)	All day at EPCOT Park (IllumiNations at 9pm)	
SEVEN (Sat)	Have a lie-in, then try some shopping at Orlando Premium Outlets and Lake Buena Vista Factory Shops	
EIGHT (Sun)	DISNEY'S ANIMAL KINGDOM PARK Eve: Medieval Times Dinner Show (8pm)	
NINE (Mon)	ISLANDS OF ADVENTURE Eve: CityWalk and dinner at Hard Rock	
TEN (Tues)	Kennedy Space Center Eve: International Drive	
ELEVEN (Wed)	All day at SEAWORLD ADVENTURE PARK (Mistify at 10pm)	

Day	Our Example	Your Planner
TWELVE (Thurs)	Have a chill-out day; head for *Disney's Typhoon Lagoon* water park	
THIRTEEN (Fri)	UNIVERSAL STUDIOS Eve: Dolly Parton's Dixie Stampede dinner show	
FOURTEEN (Sat)	Have a lie-in, then head for MAGIC KINGDOM PARK (Wishes fireworks at 9pm)	
FIFTEEN (Sun)	Gatorland/Back to airport; return flight at 5.30pm	

Busy Day Guide

NB: These days can change on a month-by-month basis; for the most up-to-date info, please check our website, **www.askdaisy.net/orlando**

Day	Busiest	Average	Lightest
Mon	*Magic Kingdom; Disney's Animal Kingdom*	*Disney-MGM Studios*	*Epcot;* Universal Studios; Islands of Adventure; Busch Gardens; Kennedy Space Center; SeaWorld; water parks
Tues	*Epcot; Magic Kingdom*	*Disney's Animal Kingdom;* Universal Studios	*Disney-MGM Studios;* Busch Gardens; IoA; Kennedy Space Center; SeaWorld; water parks
Wed	*Disney-MGM Studios* (high season)	*Disney's Animal Kingdom;* Islands of Adventure; SeaWorld; water parks	*Magic Kingdom; Epcot;* Busch Gardens; Kennedy Space Center; Universal Studios
Thurs	*Magic Kingdom;* Universal Studios	*Epcot;* Busch Gardens; SeaWorld; water parks	*Disney-MGM Studios; Disney's Animal Kingdom;* IoA; Kennedy Space Center
Fri	*Disney-MGM Studios;* (high season) SeaWorld; Water Parks	*Disney's Animal Kingdom;* IoA; Busch Gardens; Kennedy Space Center	*Magic Kingdom; Epcot;* Universal Studios
Sat	*Disney's Animal Kingdom;* Busch Gardens; IoA; Kennedy Space Center; SeaWorld; Universal Studios; water parks	*Magic Kingdom; Epcot*	*Disney-MGM Studios* (high season)
Sun	*Epcot; Magic Kingdom;* IoA; Kennedy Space Center; SeaWorld; water parks	*Disney-MGM Studios;* Busch Gardens; Universal Studios	*Disney's Animal Kingdom*

Index

Copyright notices

The author and publisher gratefully acknowledge the provision of the following photographs.

Cover: Disney's Magic Kingdom © Disney.

AirTran 339; Arabian Nights 290; Astronaut Hall of Fame 215; Best of British Sports Bar 298; Black Hammock 253; Blue Heron Cruises 243; Best Western Lake Buena Vista 73; Blue Heron Beach Resort (92 bottom); Boggy Creek Airboat Rides 25; Bubba Gump's Shrimp Co. 5, 285; Busch Gardens 13, 33 (bottom), 200, 201, 202, 203, 204, 206, 207, 208; Café Tu Tu Tango 305; Chalet Suzanne 219; Club Firestone 296; Cracker Barrel 306; Daytona Beach 48 (bottom), 60, 264, 265; Dinosaur World 46; Doubletree Castle Hotel 78; Festival Bay Mall 334; Floridays Resort 95; Gatorland 223; Historic Bok Sanctuary 28; Holy Land Experience 230; I-Ride 53; Kennedy Space Center 209, 212; Lastminutevillas.com 99; Leonardo.com 91; Mears Transportation 55; Medieval Times 292; Meridian Palms 79; Ming Court 314; Mount Dora 42, 98; Nickelodeon Family Suites 74; Olive Garden 309; Orange Lake Resort 93 (bottom); Orlando Airports 337, 341; Orlando Fire Museum 47; Orlando Vista Hotel 82; Orlando/Orange County Convention and Visitors Bureau, Inc. 18, 27, 32, 50, 56, 57, 61, 62, 87, 88, 89, 100, 101, 102, 216, 217, 218, 226, 227, 231, 232, 234, 242, 249, 253, 256, 282, 288, 289, 291, 293, 294, 297, 299, 300, 301, 302, 303, 310, 311, 312, 318, 319, 321, 324, 325, 327, 329 (top and bottom), 330, 331, 332, 333, 334, 336, 343; Ponderosa 304; Portofino Bay Hotel 84; Raglan Road Irish Pub 280; Reunion Resort 96; Ritz-Carlton Orlando 90; Ron Jon's Rrestaurant 229; Royal Pacific Resort 83; St Pete's and Clearwater Tourist Office 21, 22, 270, 272, 278, 328; SeaWorld and Discovery Cove 37, 104, 185, 186, 187, 188, 189, 190, 191, 192, 193, 194, 195, 196, 197, 240; Sheraton Studio City 80; Sherlock's 246; Shingle Creek 85; Silver Springs 221; TGI Friday's 307; The Simpsons™ Twentieth Century Fox Film Corporation 168; Tommy Bahama's 326; Tradewinds Resort 274; Universal Orlando/Islands of Adventure 7, 16, 17, 23, 34, 38, 160 (top), 94, 161, 162, 165, 166, 167, 169, 170, 172, 175, 176, 177, 178, 179, 180, 181, 182, 284, 286, 287 (top and bottom), 295, 316, 320; Waldo Wright's Flying Service 224; Weeden Island Preserve 254; Wet 'n Wild 237, 238, 239

Page 15 Mariachi Cobre at Epcot © Disney
Page 24 The Tree of Life at Disney's Animal Kingdom © Disney
Page 26 Disney's Cruise Line © Disney
Page 30 Sleeping Beauty signing autographs © Disney
Page 33 (top) Disney's Port Orleans Resort © Disney
Page 36 Rock 'n' Roller Coaster Starring Aerosmith
Page 40 Boating at Disney's Boardwalk Resort © Disney
Page 41 Downtown Disney © Disney
Page 43 Cinderella wedding at Walt Disney World Resort © Disney
Page 44 Downtown Disney West Side © Disney
Page 45 TriceraTOP Spin at Disney's Animal Kingdom © Disney
Page 63 Disney's Boardwalk Resort © Disney
Page 64 Woody at Disney's All-Star Movie Resort © Disney
Page 65 Disney's Beach Club Resort © Disney
Page 67 Disney's Port Orleans Resort © Disney
Page 69 Disney's Grand Floridian Resort and Spa © Disney
Page 70 Wilderness Lodge © Disney
Page 92 (top) Disney's Boardwalk Inn © Disney
Page 93 (top) Fort Wilderness cabin © Disney
Page 105 Mickey's PhilharMagic © Disney
Page 106 Guests at the Magic Kingdom © Disney
Page 108 Liberty Belle Riverboat © Disney
Page 109 Primeval Whirl at Disney's Animal Kingdom © Disney
Page 111 Guests at the Magic Kingdom © Disney
Page 113 Main Street USA with Cinderella's Castle © Disney
Page 114 The Jungle Cruise © Disney
Page 115 Magic Carpets of Aladdin © Disney
Page 116 Big Thunder Mountain Railroad © Disney
Page 118 It's a Small World © Disney
Page 119 Mad Tea Party © Disney
Page 120 Space Mountain © Disney
Page 121 Buzz Lightyear's Space Ranger Spin
Page 122 Wishes Firework Show © Disney
Page 123 Cinderella Castle at the Magic Kingdom © Disney
Page 124 Fireworks at the Magic Kingdom © Disney
Page 127 Soarin'™ at Epcot © Disney

Page 125 Epcot monorail © Disney
Page 129 Test Track © Disney
Page 130 'Honey, I Shrunk the Audience' © Disney
Page 131 The Seas with Nemo and Friends
Page 132 Spaceship Earth © Disney
Page 134 Italy Pavilion © Disney
Page 135 Morocco Pavilion © Disney
Page 137 International Food and Wine Festival © Disney
Page 138 The Living Seas © Disney
Page 141 Catastrophe Canyon © Disney
Page 142 Hollywood Tower of Terror © Disney
Page 143 Lights, Motors, Action! Extreme Stunt Show © Disney
Page 144 Toy Story Mania © Disney
Page 145 Journey into Narnia © Disney
Page 146 Playhouse Disney Live on Stage! © Disney
Page 147 The Hollywood Brown Derby restaurant © Disney
Page 148 Mickey's Very Merry Christmas Parade © Disney
Page 149 Jedi Training Academy © Disney
Page 152 Finding Nemo – the Musical © Disney
Page 153 It's Tough to Be a Bug © Disney
Page 154 Kilimanjaro Safaris © Disney
Page 155 The Boneyard at Disney's Animal Kingdom © Disney
Page 156 Primeval Whirl © Disney
Page 158 Kali River Rapids © Disney
Page 159 Expedition Everest © Disney
Page 160 Mickey's Jammin' Jungle Parade © Disney
Page 235 Disney's Typhoon lagoon Crush 'n' Disney Gusher © Disney
Page 236 Disney's Blizzard Beach © Disney
Page 260 Disney's Winter-Summerland Mini-golf © Disney
Page 277 Adults-only pool on Disney Magic © Disney
Page 279 Cinderella's Golden Carrousel and Castle © Disney
Page 283 La Nouba at Cirque du Soliel© © Disney
Page 308 Victoria and Albert's Restaurant © Disney
Page 317 Flying Fish Café at Disney's Boardwalk Resort © Disney
Page 322 World of Disney© merchandise store © Disney

Acknowledgements

The authors wish to acknowledge the help of the following in the production of this book: The Orlando/Orange County Convention and Visitors' Bureau, Travel Industry Association, Visit Florida, The Kissimmee/St Cloud Convention & Visitors' Bureau, St Petersburg/Clearwater Area Convention and Visitors' Bureau, Daytona Beach Area Convention & Visitors' Bureau, Seminole County Convention & Visitors' Bureau, Mount Dora Chamber of Commerce, Walt Disney Attractions Inc., Universal Orlando, The Busch Entertainment Corporation, The British-American Chamber of Commerce, The Greater Orlando Aviation Authority, Orlando-Sanford International Airport and Alamo Rent A Car.

In person: Danielle Courtenay, Alyson Gernert (Orlando CVB), Larry White, Chris Aguilar (Kissimmee CVB), Patsy Heffner (Osceola County Tax Collector), Mary Haban, James Raulerson (St Petersburg/ Clearwater CBV), Tangela Boyd, Georgia Turner (Daytona Beach CVB), Tom Bartosek (Florida's Space Coast), Betsy Couch (Visit Florida), Andrea Farmer (Kennedy Space Center), Cathy Hoechst(Mount Dora Chamber of Commerce), Louisa Williams, Jason Lasecki, Geoff Pointon, Nikki Palmas, Alix Vonk (Walt Disney), David McKee, Rhonda Murphy (Universal), Carolyn Fennell (Orlando Aviation Authority), Lorraine Ellis (Get Married In Florida), Andy James, James Brown (Florida Dolphin Tours), Susan Flower (Discovery Cove), Oliver Brendon, Sarah Rathbone (Attraction Tickets Direct), Jacquelyn Wallace (SeaWorld), Aimee Jeansonne-Becka, Janeche Petrou (Busch Gardens), Laura Richeson (Bennett & Company),Michael Caires, Greg Dull (Orlando Sanford International Airport), Allan Oakley (Alexander Homes & Associates), Nigel Worrall (Florida Leisure), Bob Mandell (Greater Homes), Bill Cowie (BACC), Wrenda Goodwyn (International Drive), Trevor Thompson (SkyVenture), Jeff Stanford (Orlando Science Center),Michelle Harris (Gatorland), Terry Lynn Morris (Lake Buena Vista Factory Stores), John Stine (Fantasy of Flight),Mariela Rubio (Medieval Times), Billy Seay (Arabian Nights), Donna Connelly, Lance Lancaster (Sleuths), Lauren Skowyra (Reunion Resort), Phillip Jaffe (Pro Golf Guides of Orlando), Karen Pitcherello (Mears Transportation), Tori Sullivan (Gator Tours), Mary Deatrick (Deatrick PR for Shingle Creek Resort),Maurice Arbelaez (Floridays Orlando Resort), Jackie Young (Prime Retail), Sarah Wilson (Waldo Wright's Flying Service), Sally March (Mall at Millenia), Leigh Jones (Orlando Premium Outlets), Shannon Clayton (The Pointe Orlando), Margie Long, Michele Peters (Boggy Creek Airboats), John Cooke (Raglan Road), Elaine Cavanaugh (Bubba Gump Shrimp Co), Phil Coppen (Cricketers Arms), Wayne Gray (FRO Group), Jennie and Paul Skingley (Best of British Soccer World), Mark and Penny Thornhill (Sherlock's) and Lori Babb.

Special thanks to Pete Werner and all at the DIS – you know who you are!

Got a red-hot Brit Tip to pass on? The latest info on how to beat the queues or the best new restaurant in town? We want to hear from YOU to keep improving the guide each year. Drop us a line at: Brit's Guide (Orlando), W. Foulsham & Co. Ltd, The Publishing House, Bennetts Close, Cippenham, Slough, Berkshire SL1 5AP. Or e-mail **britsguide@yahoo.com**